T0304303

Resources, Production and Structural Dynamics

Economists since the First Industrial Revolution have been interested in the links between economic growth and resources, often pointing to resource scarcities as a hindrance to growth. Offering a counter perspective, this volume highlights the positive role that scarcities can play in inducing technical progress and economic growth. It outlines a structural framework for the political economy of scarcity and rents, and offers a novel way of organizing the evidence concerning the role of resources in industrial growth. This book proposes a major shift in the treatment of scarcity issues by focusing on bottlenecks and opportunities arising within the production system, and will appeal to economists and policy makers interested in the role of resources as triggers of structural change.

MAURO L. BARANZINI is Professor of Economics at the University of Lugano, Switzerland. He is also a Fellow of the National Lincei Academy, Rome, which in 2009 awarded him, jointly with Andreu Mas-Colell, a prize for his contribution to economic theory. He has contributed widely to the theory of income and wealth distribution, and to the theory of accumulation under different saving assumptions.

CLAUDIA ROTONDI is Professor of Development Economics at the Catholic University of Milan. Her research interests focus mainly on the economics of institutions, taking into account the history of economic thought, and analyzing the role of liberalism in economic policy, social market economy, and the origin and diffusion of economic ideas.

ROBERTO SCAZZIERI is Professor of Economic Analysis at the University of Bologna. He is a Fellow of the National Lincei Academy, Rome, which in 2004 awarded him the Linceo Prize for research in structural economic analysis. He is also a Senior Member of Gonville and Caius College and Life Member of Clare Hall, Cambridge. He has contributed widely to the theory of production and economic dynamics, as well as to the political economy of institutions and the history and epistemology of economic analysis.

Resources, Production and Structural Dynamics

Edited by

Mauro L. Baranzini, Claudia Rotondi and Roberto Scazzieri

CAMBRIDGE
UNIVERSITY PRESS

University Printing House, Cambridge CB2 8BS, United Kingdom

Cambridge University Press is part of the University of Cambridge.

It furthers the University's mission by disseminating knowledge in the pursuit of education, learning and research at the highest international levels of excellence.

www.cambridge.org
Information on this title: www.cambridge.org/9781107079090

© Cambridge University Press 2015

First published 2015

A catalogue record for this publication is available from the British Library

Library of Congress Cataloguing in Publication data

ISBN 978-1-107-07909-0 Hardback

Cambridge University Press has no responsibility for the persistence or accuracy of URLs for external or third-party internet websites referred to in this publication, and does not guarantee that any content on such websites is, or will remain, accurate or appropriate.

To Alberto Quadrio Curzio in recognition of his contribution to economic scholarship

Contents

Figures

Tables

Contributors

ANTONIO ANDREONI, Lecturer in Economics, Department of Economics at SOAS, University of London, and Research Fellow at the Centre for Science, Technology and Innovation Policy (CSTI), Institute for Manufacturing, University of Cambridge.

MAURO L. BARANZINI, Professor of Economics, University of Lugano, Switzerland; Fellow of the National Lincei Academy, Rome.

HEINRICH BORTIS, Professor of Economics, University of Fribourg, Switzerland.

IVANO CARDINALE, Research Fellow and Lecturer in Economics, Emmanuel College, Cambridge.

D'MARIS DALTON COFFMAN, Senior Lecturer in Economics, The Bartlett School, University College London, and Fellow of the Cambridge Endowment for Research in Finance.

LILIA COSTABILE, Professor of Economics, University of Naples 'Federico II'; Life Member of Clare Hall, Cambridge.

CARLO D'ADDA, Fellow of the National Lincei Academy, Rome; former Professor of Economics, University of Bologna.

CONSTANZE DOBLER, Executive Board Assistant, Hugo Brennenstuhl GmbH & Co. KG; former Research Assistant, Chair of Economic Theory, University of Hohenheim, Stuttgart.

FAYE DUCHIN, Professor of Economics, Rensselaer Polytechnic Institute, Troy, New York; former Director of the Institute for Economic Analysis, New York University.

MARCO FORTIS, Professor of Industrial Economics and Foreign Trade, Catholic University of Milan; Director of the Edison Foundation, Milan.

ANDREA GOLDSTEIN, Senior Economic Affairs Officer, ESCAP, Seoul.

HARALD HAGEMANN, Professor Emeritus University Hohenheim, Stuttgart; Life Member of Clare Hall, Cambridge.

HEINZ D. KURZ, Professor of Economics, University of Graz.

MICHAEL A. LANDESMANN, Professor of Economics, University of Linz and Research Director, Vienna Institute for International Economic Studies; former Lecturer, Fellow of Jesus College, and Senior Research Officer, University of Cambridge.

KEUN LEE, Professor of Economics, Seoul National University.

PIER CARLO NICOLA, Fellow of the National Lincei Academy, Rome; former Professor of Mathematical Economics, State University of Milan.

LUIGI L. PASINETTI, Fellow of the National Lincei Academy, Rome; former Professor of Economics, Catholic University of Milan and Reader in Economics, University of Cambridge and Fellow of King's College; Honorary Fellow of Gonville and Caius College, Cambridge.

PIER LUIGI PORTA, Professor of Economics, University of Milano Bicocca; Visiting Fellow, Wolfson College, Cambridge.

ALESSANDRO RONCAGLIA, Professor of Economics, University 'La Sapienza', Rome; Fellow of the National Lincei Academy, Rome.

CLAUDIA ROTONDI, Professor of Development Economics, Catholic University of Milan.

NERI SALVADORI, Professor of Economics, University of Pisa.

ROBERTO SCAZZIERI, Professor of Economic Analysis, University of Bologna and Fellow of the National Lincei Academy, Rome; Senior Member of Gonville and Caius College and Life Member of Clare Hall, Cambridge.

SUNANDA SEN, National Fellow of the Indian Council of Social Science Research and Visiting Professor, Institute for Studies in Industrial Development, Delhi; former Professor of Economics, Jawaharlal Nehru University, Delhi; Life Member of Clare Hall, Cambridge.

ALBERT E. STEENGE, Professor of Economics, University of Groningen, The Netherlands.

MOSHE SYRQUIN, Professor of Economics, University of Miami; Research Fellow, International Centre for Economic Research (ICER), Turin.

KUMARASWAMY VELA VELUPILLAI, Professor of Economics, New School of Social Research, New York; former Fellow in Economics, Girton

College, Cambridge; Professor of Economics, University of Lund and Professor of Economics, University of Trento.

STEFANO ZAMAGNI, Professor of Economics, The Johns Hopkins University (Bologna Centre); former Professor of Economics, University of Bologna.

Preface

Non-produced natural resources and primary commodities (such as land and mines, agricultural products, minerals and energy sources) are *structurally scarce* within any given production system with given technology, and play a fundamental role in the structural dynamics of economic systems. At least since the first Industrial Revolution, a central feature in the evolution of modern economies has been the critical relevance of the linkage between technical progress and patterns of natural resources utilization, and the influence of that linkage upon the timing and character of growth processes. Technical progress has often reduced the structural scarcity of natural resources and primary commodities, in the sense of reducing their 'non-producibility' through switches from one natural resource base to another, thus bypassing bottlenecks and enhancing production opportunities. A classic example is the substitution of coal for wood as a resource for iron production in mid-eighteenth-century England. Instances like this call attention to the relationship between scarcity and producibility in the long-term dynamics of economic systems. As Alberto Quadrio Curzio has pointed out, the 'antagonism-coexistence' between the scarcity of natural resources and primary commodities on the one hand and the producibility of commodities and means of production on the other hand has perhaps been the most important feature of economic dynamics in the last few centuries. This antagonism-coexistence is often overlooked by analyses that exclusively focus on technical progress and sustained growth in the industrial economies.

This point of view stresses the central role of production interdependencies between different components of the economic system, their impact on the pattern of resource utilization, and their dependence on the resources that come to be dominant at any given time. This web of interconnections has far-reaching implications beyond the internal structure of the production system. For resource bottlenecks may have effects on income distribution as well as shift capital accumulation from one path to another. As productive interdependencies may be associated with a given social structure, changes in interdependence triggered by switches to different resource bases may in turn entail significant variations in the relative position of social groups. This approach also suggests a major shift in the treatment of sustainability issues, since emphasis is placed on bottlenecks and opportunities arising from within the production system, and not primarily on the identification of trajectories of optimal paths of allocation of given resources among alternative uses.

This research programme, started in the mid-1960s by Alberto Quadrio Curzio, has provided a seminal analytical framework for the structural investigation of resource-based economic dynamics. His contribution has revived the analysis of production, resources and rents along the classical (mainly Ricardian) line of inquiry. The aim of this volume is to build on this research programme and to provide the foundations of a political economy of resource-based dynamics.

MAURO L. BARANZINI
CLAUDIA ROTONDI
ROBERTO SCAZZIERI

Acknowledgements

The preparation of this volume has been made possible by a number of institutions and scholars who have supported our research in manifold ways. First of all thanks are due to our present academic institutions, respectively the University of Lugano, Switzerland; the Catholic University of Milan; the University of Bologna; and Gonville and Caius College and Clare Hall, Cambridge. We also thank the following institutions for providing, at various stages, research facilities and an intellectual environment that has stimulated our work in a fundamental way. In Italy, we thank the National Lincei Academy, Rome, its Interdisciplinary Research Centre 'Beniamino Segre', and the Edison Foundation, Milan. In Cambridge, we thank the Research Seminar in Political Economy at Emmanuel College; the Centre for Financial History, Newnham College; the Cambridge Seminar in the History of Economic Analysis (CAMHIST), Clare Hall; and the Centre for Research in the Arts, Social Sciences and Humanities (CRASSH). Furthermore we thank the Centre for Research on Economic Analysis and International Economic Development (CRANEC), Catholic University of Milan; the Centre for Banking Studies, Villa Negroni, Vezia, Switzerland; the Institute of Advanced Study, University of Bologna; and the Swiss National Science Foundation, Berne. We are also grateful to the colleagues and friends who accepted our invitation to take part in this project, and have contributed to the 'invisible college' of which this volume is a product.

MAURO L. BARANZINI
CLAUDIA ROTONDI
ROBERTO SCAZZIERI

1 Resources, producibility and economic dynamics: a framework

Mauro L. Baranzini, Claudia Rotondi and Roberto Scazzieri

1. Introduction

1.1 Resources in political economy

The evolving relationship between the ownership and utilization of non-produced resources, the distribution of national income and wealth, and the formation and investment of capital funds within and across countries is a central feature in the structural dynamics of the world economy. Important features of that relationship have been a central focus of the theory of economic dynamics since Thomas Robert Malthus's (1815a, 1815b), Edward West's (1815) and David Ricardo's (1817) analysis of *decreasing returns* due to the emergence of scarcities and complementarities between productive inputs (which implies that the utilization of any given technique requires the maintenance of given proportions between those inputs). In Malthus's, West's and Ricardo's pioneering work, decreasing returns at the level of production units (such as the single productive establishment or the aggregate of production processes using a given non-produced resource) are associated with system-wide effects due to the interplay of (i) constraints due to the limited availability of non-produced and appropriable resources; (ii) the saving and accumulation behaviour of individuals and socio-economic groups; and (iii) income distribution between types of income (such as wages, profits and rents) as well as between socio-economic groups (such as workers, capitalists and rentiers).

Subsequent contributions took up and developed the classical economists' insights into those issues by exploring (i) the manifold dimensions of non-producibility and scarcity in a dynamic setting (Jevons, 1865; Quadrio Curzio, 1975; Leontief, Carter and Petri, 1977; Duchin and Lange, 1994); (ii) the opportunities generated by the discovery and utilization of new resource bases (Rosenberg, 1982; Wrigley, 1962, 1988, 2010); (iii) the determination of prices, income distribution and rents in the case of production systems constrained by non-produced resources (Sraffa, 1960; Quadrio Curzio, 1967); and (iv) the accumulation behaviour of socio-economic groups in economic systems subject to manifold types of resource constraints

1

and corresponding structural dynamics (Pasinetti, 1960; Baranzini, 1991; Baranzini and Scazzieri, 1990, 1997; Landesmann and Scazzieri, 2009).

The above interplay of constraints, opportunities and saving-accumulation behaviour may sometime trigger a tendency towards *decreasing returns*, and sometime reverse this tendency and lead to *increasing returns*.

Production linkages between sectors dependent on different resource bases are essential in determining to what extent technical progress will be effective; that is, in determining the actual influence of technical innovation at the level of individual establishments or industries on the growth and employment performance of the whole economic system. In particular, technical innovation at the level of single establishments, establishment networks or industries could be associated with technological retardation at the level of the economic system as a whole (due to mismatches between different production activities, or between sets of production activities). On the other hand, changes in the relative weight of given processes could be associated with technological improvement even in the absence of technical innovation (due to changes of proportions between production processes allowing a better coordination of production activities). This may lead to decreasing or increasing returns depending on the efficiency order or on the 'rentability order' of processes that use non-produced resources. The latter case (increasing returns) may arise from the utilization of 'residual' means of production that had previously gone out of use due to a change in production technology and/or in the rentability order of processes using a scarce resource (Quadrio Curzio, 1967, 1975, 1980, 1986, 1987, 1990; Quadrio Curzio and Pellizzari, 1999; Scazzieri, 2014; see also Section 5 in this chapter).

The structural theory of non-produced resources calls attention to the existence of long-term constraints that are at work underneath the surface of markets and ultimately shape the global and long-term patterns of growth, distribution and accumulation. This theory thus alerts us about critical features of economic dynamics that would otherwise go unnoticed. This research tradition is rich both in terms of analytical modelling and in terms of empirical and historical investigations. Building on classical contributions (Malthus, Ricardo and Jevons), this line of investigation has addressed the role of resource constraints in an interindustry framework and has more recently emphasized the importance of resource pooling and resource bottlenecks in stimulating technical change, and also in inducing processes of *selective* saving formation across the world economy, as shown by the recent emergence of sovereign funds.

A central feature of the structural tradition in the study of resource-induced economic dynamics is the attention to the influence of changing resource constraints on the compositional dynamics of the economic system, quite independently of the behavioural propensities of individual agents or groups.

In short, the structural approach emphasizes the *direct* influence of resource constraints on the structure and long-term dynamics of the economic system, mainly through the elimination of technological alternatives from the set of feasible production possibilities (*technology contraction*), and the generation of new opportunities through technological interrelatedness associated with the switch to a new resource base (*technology expansion*) as pointed out by Scazzieri (1982, 1993). In either case, resource availability and resource dynamics work *directly* on the structural and material side of the production system, rather than indirectly through their influence on agents' choices and prices (see also Baranzini and Scazzieri, 1986; Scazzieri, 1993; Landesmann and Scazzieri, 2009; as well as Silva and Teixeira, 2008).

This argument calls attention to the existence of critical, if seldom acknowledged, thresholds along the dynamic path of any given economic system, due to both the utilization of non-produced resources and changes in which resources are used across different time periods. The existence of those thresholds may thwart the economic system from one dynamic path to another. This possibility highlights the important role of economic (structural) policy in stimulating or slowing down the pace of resource-induced structural transformation (that is, structural transformation induced by constraints on resource availability and by the switch from one resource base to another).

1.2   Aim of the volume

The aim of this volume is to present a comprehensive assessment of the structural economic analysis of non-produced and appropriable resources from the point of view of long-term dynamics and within a political economy framework.

The multi-sectoral approach to production and structural dynamics provides the analytical framework for most contributions in the volume. However, a feature that distinguishes this volume from the greatest part of the multi-sectoral modelling literature (as discussed, for instance, in Leontief, 1941, 1951; Pasinetti, 1965, 1977, 1981) is the central role assigned to a multi-sectoral, resource-constrained economy, in which inter-sectoral relationships are characterized by complementarity or limited substitutability. In this economy, material bottlenecks and technological linkages are central factors explaining the course of economic dynamics and the structural transformations associated with it. The utilization of non-produced resources under technological or organizational complementarity (or limited substitutability) brings about the possibility of decreasing returns as the economic system hits scarcities of different types. In particular, the resource-based theory of structural dynamics highlights the conditions under which decreasing returns of the intensive or extensive type may occur. In either case, the production structure of the economic system consists of a set of interdependent processes in which processes using non-produced resources make use of different 'types' of the same resource, or of different techniques with the same resource type.

The overall production structure may be represented either by a single *global technology* or by many *combined technologies*. The former approach unifies the techniques using non-produced resources and gives a synthetic view of production interdependencies within the single period, while the latter approach keeps those techniques distinct even if it keeps track of their interconnection across different periods. With a global technology the one-to-one correspondence between commodities and processes is dropped and special technical coefficients ('splitting coefficients') are introduced to allow for the delivery of the same commodity by different processes (Quadrio Curzio, 1987, 1990; Quadrio Curzio and Pelizzari, 1999). Under binding resource constraints, a global technology allows identification of the conditions under which technical complementarities bring about decreasing returns as the scale of the overall process is increased. On the other hand, the consideration of combined technologies emphasizes the dynamic complementarities leading to increasing returns when technical change allows a better utilization of residuals (see above) (Quadrio Curzio, 1975, 1986, 1990; Quadrio Curzio and Pellizzari, 1999; see also Quadrio Curzio, 1987). Whenever this is the case, it is possible to explain structural change as a response of the economic system to the existence of triggers (such as population dynamics or institutional transformation) working their way through technological or organizational complementarities and bottlenecks.

Decreasing returns lead to the successive activation of inferior techniques, and thus to the utilization of a global technology at any given time (say, multiple qualities of mineral ore, multiple types of agricultural land, etc.). Similarly, increasing returns are associated with the activation of combined technologies allowing a better utilization of the complementarities between those very techniques. In either case, paths of uneven dynamics of a purely structural character are generated. Four features of those paths are especially important[1]:

1. *complementarities and bottlenecks* work underneath the surface of markets and become primarily visible *in the long run*;
2. *technological interrelatedness* is central in generating patterns of uneven evolution and structural change;
3. *alternative time horizons* may be associated with different criteria for the ranking of the technical opportunities available at any given time

---

[1] See Quadrio Curzio (1975, 1986, 1990, 1996), Quadrio Curzio and Pellizzari (1999), Scazzieri (1982, 1993, 2014), Marengo and Scazzieri (2014).

(so that alternative paths of structural change may be highlighted depending on which time horizon is adopted);

4. *technological distribution* (with the formation of structural rents) becomes visible independently of the functional, social and personal distributions of income. This type of distribution may affect the choice of techniques and be in turn affected by the course of structural dynamics.

2.   Resources, producibility and scarcity

Since the late 1950s, discussions among academic economists have focused on topics that, in spite of their apparent technical nature, are controversial above all because of their being rooted in different ways of looking at the 'scope and method of economics science'.[2] This is particularly true for the three phases of the 'Cambridge controversies' (Cambridge being both Cambridge, England, and Cambridge, Mass., United States) that flared up in the second half of the twentieth century: the first concerning the measure of the productivity increases (Luigi L. Pasinetti and Nicholas Kaldor *versus* Robert Solow and colleagues); the second on the distribution of income and rate of profits determination (Nicholas Kaldor, Luigi L. Pasinetti, Joan Robinson, Pierangelo Garegnani, John Eatwell, Richard F. Kahn and Geoffrey Harcourt *versus* Paul A. Samuelson, Franco Modigliani, James E. Meade and Christopher J. Bliss); the third on capital theory, i.e. capital reversing and reswitching (Pierangelo Garegnani, Luigi L. Pasinetti, Piero Sraffa, Joan Robinson *versus* Paul A. - Samuelson and David Levhari). To this we may add the controversy of the life-cycle *versus* intergenerational capital stock (Franco Modigliani and his pupils *versus* Laurence Kotlikoff, Larry Summers, Mauro Baranzini and others). Partly because of the debates caused by these and still other controversies, but also as the result of the publication of *Production of Commodities by Means of Commodities* by Piero Sraffa (1960), as well as Arrow and Debreu's 'Existence of an Equilibrium for a Competitive Economy', *Econometrica* (1954), Christopher C. Bliss's *Capital Theory and the Distribution of Income* (1975), and a few other milestones of economic theory, there has been a revival of interest in the object and method of economics, such as our science had not seen since the publication of *The Nature and Significance of Economic*

---

[2] This argument refers to a dichotomy initially put forward by Sir John Hicks and Luigi L. Pasinetti; see the later argument in this section. See also the reviews by Baranzini (1979) and Lutfalla (1983). In his contribution to the *Essays in Honour of Luigi Pasinetti*, Quadrio Curzio (1993, p. 247) discusses the 'object and method of economics' and maintains that the most specific elements of economic reality, in particular, production and exchange, represent 'the archetypes of any economic reality'.

Science by Lord Robbins (1932) and *The Political Element in the Development of Economic Theory* by Gunnar Myrdal (1953).[3]

A new way of looking at the evolution of economic ideas slowly emerged in the 1970s, mainly based on statements of Sir John Hicks and Luigi Pasinetti. Alberto Quadrio Curzio and Roberto Scazzieri[4] were the first to study the implications of such a proposal and its application to the documentation of a particular period in the history of economic analysis and economic history, especially in their Introduction to the four volumes on the leading economists since David Ricardo (Quadrio Curzio and Scazzieri, 1977–1982). Hicks and Pasinetti had in fact suggested that is no longer possible to see the development of economic theory as a linear evolutionary process from the Mercantilists to contemporary economics. A number of alternative 'paradigms' characterize the past and present situation of our science, and both John Hicks (1976) and Luigi Pasinetti (1964/5) seem to agree on a fundamental distinction between the theories centred on the analysis of the production phenomena and the theories centred on the analysis of exchange. Hicks, in order to emphasize the distinction, labels 'political economy' as the first group of theories, and 'catallactics' the second. This is how Quadrio Curzio and Scazzieri (1986, p. 378) discuss the exchange paradigm:

The fundamental idea of exchange was the first to be developed systematically. It was present in the studies of money and value between the sixteenth and the seventeenth centuries, and it dominated the minds of the Mercantilists, who applied it to the study of trade relations between states. The principle of the maximization of national wealth constitutes an early expression of such an idea. With the early Marginalists, the fundamental idea of exchange was applied to individual behaviour for the maximization of utility; in later marginalism, it was applied to the behaviour of producers and consumers for the maximization of profit and utility. Finally, this fundamental idea was used for the determination of the 'welfare' of society as a whole. Step by step, the fundamental idea of exchange gains precision and articulation, with the concepts of 'scarcity' of resources with respect to ends, of 'efficiency' in the use of given resources, of 'one-wayness' of production from 'primitive' factors of production to products. This fundamental idea is finally crystallized in the principle that every economic problem can be reduced to the mathematical problem of maximizing an objective function subject to scarcity constraints.

On the production paradigm they write:

The history of the fundamental idea of production is no less complex. Already with English political arithmetic (William Petty and others), with Quesnay and other Physiocrats, the central problem of political economy had been identified in the process

---

[3] Myrdal's book was first published in Swedish in 1930 and translated into German two years later.

[4] In particular we may mention the five volumes of *Protagonisti del pensiero economico* (Quadrio Curzio and Scazzieri, 1977–1982, 1983), 'The Exchange Production Duality and the Dynamics of Economic Knowledge' (Quadrio Curzio and Scazzieri, 1986) and 'On Economic Science, Its Tools and Economic Reality' (Quadrio Curzio, 1993).

of the production (and reproduction) of an economic system. And soon appeared the concepts of the 'circular flow' of production (that is to say, of the production of commodities by means of commodities), of 'interdependence' between sectors of the economy, of 'net product' or 'surplus' (the excess of social product over aggregate means of production). These concepts were elaborated in various ways and not only in the same direction by later authors. Classical English and Scottish economists like Smith, Malthus and Ricardo examined the relations between net product and accumulation, the problem of the distribution of the social product between different classes in society and between wages, profits and rents, and the question of effective demand. . . . After a period of relative inactivity (during which, however, important contributions to the theory of value and the theory of structural dynamics can be found), the fundamental idea of production became once again of primary significance, with Kalecki, Keynes, von Neumann, Leontief, Sraffa and others. In contrast with the fundamental idea of exchange, one can say that the core of the fundamental idea of production is that the 'wealth' of an economic system depends on its capacity to create a net product or surplus, on the distribution of the latter between the recipients of wages, profits and rents, and on the distribution of the surplus between consumption and investment (the growth of wealth through time is made to depend on this latter variable). (Quadrio Curzio and Scazzieri, 1986, pp. 378–9)

Quadrio Curzio and Scazzieri (1977–1982, 1983, 1986) were the first to systematically examine the implications of the production/exchange duality in the analysis of specific historical configurations of the economic system. Baranzini and Scazzieri (1986) further pursued the investigation of the duality by examining the parallel developments and mutual influences between the two corresponding lines of research.

3. Structural economic dynamics and the distribution of income: the macro-social approach and the structural approach

Structural economic dynamics investigates the way in which economic expansion is associated with changes in the sectoral composition of the economic system (Perroux, 1939; Furtado, 1967; Leontief, Chenery *et al.*, 1953; Pasinetti and Scazzieri, 1987b). Different types of income distribution have been examined in connection with research on structural dynamics. In particular, two main approaches can be distinguished: one is the macro-social theory of the classical or post-Keynesian type, the other is the structural and technological theory of the multi-sectoral type. These two approaches have a common conceptual background associated with the theory of income distribution originally formulated by David Ricardo (1817). Such a background may be summarized as follows:

1. Production (Y), initially measured in terms of corn, is distributed among wages (W), profits (P), and rents (R). Wages, profits and rents are

determined by the interaction of demographic, technical and economic factors. Total wages are equal to the unit wage (w) times the number of workers employed (L).

2. Ricardo relates the level of wages to the physiological necessity of workers to live and reproduce themselves, i.e. the so-called *natural wage rate*. More precisely, David Ricardo 'is convinced that in any particular type of society there exists a *real* wage-rate (so to speak, a certain *basket of goods*) which can be considered as the "natural price of labour". It needs not necessarily be at a strict *subsistence level* (the minimum physiological necessities of life); but at that level which in a given country and in a given state of society, besides allowing workers to live, induces them to perpetuate themselves "without either increase or diminution"' (Pasinetti, 1960a, p. 80).

3. The market wage unit depends on supply and demand of labour. According to Pasinetti, always '[w]hen capitalists accumulate capital, demand for labour increases and the market wage-rate rises above its natural level. However, Ricardo believes that such a situation cannot be other than a temporary one because, as the conditions of workers become "flourishing and happy", they "rear a healthy and numerous family" and the growth of population again brings back the real wage-rate to its *natural* level' (Pasinetti, 1960a, p. 80). The operating of this mechanism takes at least one generation, even if Ricardo's analysis is carried out as though this mechanism would operate almost immediately. Conversely, if the wage unit falls below the *natural wage rate*, the workers' families will have fewer children until the natural level is reached again.

4. What remains after having paid wages is a residual that will be distributed between rents and profits. Rents are determined by the difference between total production and the quantity of production obtained by multiplying all labour force by the product of the marginal land put into cultivation (this is the land that comes 'last' in the given order of fertility). The share of product exceeding the productivity of the least fertile land goes to the benefit of the landlords in terms of rent. What remains of total production, after payment of wages and rents, is retained, in the form of profits, by the capitalists, who are the real organizers of the production process.

Current research has developed this conceptual framework along two principal lines of investigation. On the one hand, income distribution has been investigated under the hypothesis that income shares (such as the wage share or the profit share in national income) are associated with the relative bargaining power of social classes or groups (social theories of income distribution of the classical, Ricardian or Marxian types), *or* with the condition for investment under the steady growth assumption (social theories of income distribution of the post-Keynesian type). On the other hand, income distribution has been associated with the structural analysis of the technological conditions that may determine the formation of specific types of income (such as structural rents due to utilization of non-produced resources) independently of which individuals or social groups might be their final beneficiaries (see, in particular, Quadrio Curzio, 1967, 1975, 1980, 1990; Quadrio Curzio and Pellizzari, 1999).

The macro-social income distribution and wealth distribution and accumulation have been in the foreground of the classical, post-Keynesian and structural lines of research. The so-called Cambridge controversy on profit determination and growth rate determination has been a classical instance of the mutual influences between these analytical traditions (Harcourt, 2012). The following main points may be recalled. A number of these research students, research fellows and young lecturers were in England and particularly in Cambridge and Oxford in the early 1960s, when the 'Cambridge controversy' on profit determination and income distribution was taking off, following the publication of Nicholas Kaldor's (1956) seminal paper 'Alternative Theories of Distribution' and the long gestation and publication of Luigi L. Pasinetti's (1962a) generalization of the *Cambridge Theorem* ('The Rate of Profit and Income Distribution in Relation to the Rate of Economic Growth'). It is also important to mention in this connection the contribution of John Hicks in *Capital of Growth* (Hicks, 1965). In fact, in those years, three Cambridge scholars, Luigi L. Pasinetti, Nicholas Kaldor and Joan Robinson, were preparing their papers on the *Cambridge Theorem* that would be published in the 1966 special issue of the *Review of Economic Studies*, along with the long and provocative double paper of Paul A. Samuelson and Franco Modigliani with the title 'The Pasinetti Paradox in Neo-Classical and More General Models'. These issues were discussed in seminars as well as in lectures held in Cambridge and Oxford during those years (Mari, 2010). Luigi Pasinetti contributed to this line of research also with his Cambridge Ph. D. thesis on a new disaggregated model of economic dynamics in which technical progress and changes in the composition of consumers' expenditure bring about the need of changes in the relative proportions of sectors (Pasinetti, 1962b, 1965).

The structural and multi-sectoral theory of income distribution is to a large extent derived from the analytical framework presented in Piero Sraffa's *Production of Commodities by Means of Commodities* (Sraffa, 1960). This work outlined a theory of production, prices and income distribution in a stationary or single-period system. On this basis, Quadrio Curzio addressed the role of non-produced resources within the analytical framework of multi-sectoral analysis (see earlier). Sraffa had mainly investigated income distribution between wages and profits within a multi-sectoral framework

in which rent formation was also considered. However, neither rent formation nor natural resources belonged to the core of his theory (Sraffa, 1960,
Ch. XI). Quadrio Curzio emphasized non-produced resources and examined
their influence upon income distribution, accumulation, growth and structural change.

The structural analysis of non-produced resources identifies the possibility
of intertwined trajectories of decreasing and increasing returns due to sectoral
interdependencies and presents an overall picture of the dynamics of rents (of
the structural type) that must be distinguished from the analysis of rents in the
macroeconomic (Keynesian) theories of income and wealth. For in the former
case there is a concentration of attention upon the technological determinants
of rents (as 'differential rents'), whereas in the latter case attention shifts to
'absolute rents' and to the entitlements of certain individuals or social groups
(see Section 2 of the final chapter of this volume).

4.   The rationale and structure of the volume

The relationship between non-produced resources and production interdependencies is central to economic systems whose long-run dynamics is determined
by the interplay of resource bottlenecks and technical opportunities arising
within the production structure. As we have seen, those dynamics are characterized by the emergence of scarcities at various points of the production
system, and by the adoption of individual techniques and/or production technologies that allow the overcoming of scarcities by an increase in the degree of
producibility of means of production. The long-term relationship between
scarcity and producibility, and the different paths followed by attempts to
overcome scarcities, reflect the structural interdependence between sectors
and between techniques, and the socio-institutional constraints determining
the relative positions of individuals and groups within the social structure. The
interplay between structural constraints and socio-institutional conditions also
determines the effectiveness of any given society in pursuing long-term policies consistent with the transformation of scarcities into producibilities.

This conceptual scheme has suggested the organization of this volume into
five parts: Part I focuses upon 'Resources and Distribution in a Structural
Perspective'; Part II assesses 'Structural Dynamics: Resources and Multi-
Sectoral Linkages'; Part III considers 'Resources, Institutions and Social
Structures'; Part IV focuses on the themes of 'Resources, Industrial Change
and the Structure of the World Economy'; Part V discusses ways to examine
the 'Political Economy of Resources and Structural Change' and brings the
volume to a close with a chapter by the editors on 'Resources, Scarcities and
Rents: Technological Interdependence and the Dynamics of Socio-Economic
Structures'.

The contributions in Part I examine the role of non-produced resources from the point of view of a set of relatively persistent positions of individuals and groups within the social structure. Here, the ownership and utilization of resources give entitlement to certain income shares and these in turn may slowly reinforce or modify the relative positions of individuals or groups within the social structure. In other words, it is assumed that the existence of non-produced resources influences income distribution from the point of view of a given ownership structure and a given distribution of wealth. The contributions in this part call attention to the distributional asymmetries that may be identified in a private ownership economy in which income flows presuppose a specific allocation of property entitlements. These asymmetries are investigated by contrasting rent formation arising from productive interdependencies with rent formation in allocation models of the neoclassical type.

The contributions in Part II examine features of the long-term structural dynamics of economic systems associated with changes in the pattern of utilization of non-produced resources (natural scarcities), and/or in the uneven distribution of technical progress among firms or sectors (technological scarcities). The principal focus of this part is the effect of technological, social and financial interdependencies on the dynamic path followed by an economic system subject to upper bounds on the availability of essential and non-produced resources, or on the availability of limited technological opportunities. Complementarities bring about bottlenecks and make material and financial linkages a principal factor in determining uneven dynamic paths characterized by non-proportionality of expansion across different sectors. The contributions in this part highlight the role of natural and technological scarcities in making the economic system move along one or another direction, as well as the relationship between scarcities, structural sustainability requirements, and policy decisions in determining which paths an economy system can and/or is likely to follow. The dynamic path of an economic system subject to the interplay of scarcity and structural constraints is inherently open-ended.

The contributions in Part III assess the implications of the degrees of freedom associated with the structural constraints upon distribution and non-proportional growth in a resource-constrained economy. The contributions in this part of the volume draw attention to the role of institutions in the structural evolution of an economic system at different periods of its history. Structural change before industrialization is subject to conditions different from those constraining structural change after the industrial take-off. In this connection, also the interdependence between scarcity and producibility, and the way in which scarcity may be overcome in each particular case, take a different character in a pre-industrial versus an industrial economy. For example in a pre-industrial economy long-term credit expansion may take place independently of liquidity needs arising from interdependence among productive sectors; while an industrial economy requires liquidity provision at specific times and particular inter-sectoral junctures associated with the development of its production core. Production interdependencies do not entirely determine the path any given economy follows in historical time. Institutional arrangements, legal traditions, and historical contingency may be of critical importance in determining which social and political triggers would be effective in shifting the economy to a high-growth scenario, and or in maintaining the economy on a low-growth path. Pre-industrial economies, developing economies, and economies in transition from planned to market institutions face different problems of structural and institutional adjustments to constraints due to limited resource availability. These constraints take a different form depending on the configuration of the relationships between socio-economic groups. The economic system is thus open to a plurality of alternative dynamic paths depending on social context.

The contributions in Part IV focus on the relationship between transformations of industrial structures, changes in the resource utilization pattern associated with such transformations, and the corresponding variations in the institutional and organizations features of economic systems. Industrial revolutions have been associated with the emergence of bottlenecks and opportunities in the field of primary resources utilization. At the same time, such changes have often entailed deep transformations of institutional forms and corresponding public policies meant to steer the economic system along given trajectories of industrial change. This part of the volume draws attention to the existence of contradictory and/or compatible interests of socio-economic groups, and to the ensuing policy decisions. In fact different constellations of interests may shift the economy from one dynamic path to another under given resource bottlenecks and given technological or organizational interdependencies. Any given stage of industrial transformation is characterized by different opportunities and/or constraints due to the given pattern of resource use. In particular, this pattern may be a critical factor in influencing the relative positions of social groups within any given economic system as well as the relative positions of different economic systems at the level of the international economy.

Part V provides a critical assessment of the research programme pursued in the volume by focusing on the relationships between resources, structural rents and structural dynamics. This is done by addressing the specific character of rent formation when the production system has to use a plurality of methods of production with different degrees of efficiency. In this frame, rents take a technological character ('technological rents') and closely reflect the interdependencies among production sectors or processes rather than the relative scarcities of different resources. In particular, scarcities of the technological type are different from natural scarcities and may become the source of uneven dynamics grounded in complementarities among production processes. There exists a close connection between the productive interdependencies and the social interdependencies generated by the functional distribution of income and wealth, *via* the accumulation process, in a social structure where groups have different saving propensities. This part emphasizes the changing relationships between natural and technological scarcities in economic history, also underlining the relationship between 'producibility' and 'scarcity' as the critical indicator showing the specific position of non-produced resources at any given stage of structural economic dynamics.

Taken in their unity the contributions in this volume suggest a comprehensive framework for the structural analysis of a resource-based economic dynamics. This research programme, which Alberto Quadrio Curzio started in the mid-1960s, has been developed by him and others along a plurality of distinct but interconnected lines of research, which range from the theories of production, prices-distribution, and structural dynamics to the analysis of resource utilization patterns, institutions and policies. This volume builds on this research programme and highlights the central role of non-produced resources in the political economy of industrialization, development and structural change.

5.   The contributions

Part I ('Resources and Distribution in a Structural Perspective') begins with a chapter by Luigi L. Pasinetti: 'On the Origin of the Theory of Rent in Economics'. His analysis confirms the fact that economists sometimes tend to examine a large domain of economic phenomena by adapting theoretical concepts that had originally been devised for a much narrower range of special or different issues. According to Pasinetti the year 1815 has become significant to historians of economic thought for the publication of five well-known pamphlets, whose impact on economic theory went far beyond their aims. Following Piero Sraffa's reconstruction, they appeared in a short time period of three weeks: first, on 3 February 1815, Robert Malthus's *Inquiry on Rent*; on 10 February, Thomas Robert Malthus's *Grounds for an Opinion*; on 13 February, Edward West's *Essay on the Application of Capital to Land*; and finally on 24 February, Robert Torrens's *Essay on the External Corn Trade* and David Ricardo's *Essay on Profit*. The concurrent publication of these five essays is often cited as a major example of simultaneous discovery in economic theory. They all share the differential theory of *rent* – both in its extensive and (with the exception of Torrens) in its intensive version – and the so-called 'Law of diminishing returns' to land cultivation. The former has been taken as the source of the 'marginal principle' in the theory of production and income distribution, as applied to *all* factors of production, and not only to land. The latter is one of those controversial ideas that has influenced economic theory ever since. Yet, in spite of criticism and opposition, the 'Law of diminishing returns' immediately became one of the cornerstones of nineteenth-century mainstream political economy. James Mill, in his *Elements of Political Economy*, immediately expounded the 'Law of diminishing returns' as a general rule. And when his son, John Stuart Mill, wrote his *Principles of Political Economy* in 1848, he presented the 'Law' in a chapter headed 'Of the Law of the Increase of Production from Land', adding that 'This general law of agricultural industry is the most important proposition in political economy. Were the law different, nearly all the phenomena of the production and distribution of wealth would be other than they are' (Mill, 1848, 1st edn, vol. I, p. 212). This allows Pasinetti to conclude that:

The consequences of this diversion from classical economics were of paramount importance. As the process of industrialization, in the second part of the nineteenth century, began to spread from England to Western Europe and to the United States, the emphasis of economic theory was bound to shift from agricultural production to industrial production. Capital accumulation, rather than extension of land cultivation, became the central subject of economic investigation. It should have needed specifically invented tools of analysis, suited for its particular characteristics; it underwent instead an extension of analytical tools that had been invented for land cultivation. (Pasinetti, this volume)

The second chapter of this part is by D'Maris Dalton Coffman on 'The Political Economy of Corn Markets'. This chapter examines corn markets in England and Wales during the first 150 years of administration of the Corn Laws and compares them with corn markets in the United States in the nineteenth and twentieth centuries. The aim of this contribution is to assess the formative role of context-specific social constructions (such as markets) upon the development of political economy. This is done against the background of economic theories contemporary to the historical developments being considered (Malthus's, West's and Ricardo's theory of differential rents in nineteenth-century England and Wales; the efficient markets hypothesis in twentieth-century United States). Coffman highlights the critical role of market structures in influencing the focus of corresponding developments in economic theory. Thus the Corn Laws debates in nineteenth-century England and Wales reflect conditions of existing or potential land scarcity and call attention to the role of material constraints in shaping interdependencies between productive sectors and/or social groups. On the other hand, corn markets in twentieth-century United States induced 'a different set of preoccupations', as reduction of price volatility, protection of stakeholders, and prevention of market abuse dominated debates mostly concerned with the dynamics of trading in grain futures. The cleavage between the two sets of conditions, however, should not obscure the fact that in either case markets were 'internally structured' and were the domain of multiple interdependencies. Conditions of binding scarcities (England and Wales) had been at the origin of the classical theory of differential rents, while conditions of seemingly unbounded producibility (United States) had drifted attention away from material constraints inducing a focus on the effectiveness and 'fairness' of markets. In either case, corn markets data provide an invaluable empirical base for the disentangling of the complex relationship between producibility and scarcity, and for the assessment of the way in which this relationship shapes the interdependencies between productive sectors and between social groups.

In the following chapter ('The Classical Theory of Rent'), Heinz D. Kurz and Neri Salvadori tackle in simple terms the principles of extensive and intensive diminishing returns, and thus extensive and intensive rent. Although the chosen framework is reduced to essential features – corn is produced by means of labour and land(s) only – some of the results come as a surprise. The authors show, in particular, that in the conditions given, an aggregate production function for corn can be constructed both in the case of extensive and in the case of intensive diminishing returns and a fortiori also in the more general case that combines both kinds of returns. This latter result was disputed by Morishima (1989) in a criticism of Luigi Pasinetti's paper on Ricardo's theory of profits and differential rent (Pasinetti 1960a). In addition, the authors show that other than in extremely special cases there is no presumption that the order of fertility will coincide with the order of rentability, a view advocated by authors such as Ricardo, von Thünen and Marx. Finally the authors conclude that no production function can generally be constructed as soon as there are produced means of production, or capital goods, employed in the production of corn. Even the case in which there is only seed corn allowed for can be shown to typically create difficulties in the regard under consideration. Hence the reader must not consider such argument as supportive of the use of aggregate production functions.

In the fourth chapter ('Profit, Productive Rent, and Parasitic Rent') of Part I, PierCarlo Nicola maintains that economic categories of wage, profit and rent have always been the bases on which to build the theory of the distribution of income and accumulation of wealth. The term 'rent' (in Ricardo's terminology) is the payment to the landlord for the use of land to produce commodities, while 'wage' is paid to workers for their productive services, and 'profit' is the reward for the use of production means different from land and labour. Nicola maintains that in all economic systems, whether capitalistic or centralized, there is also a second type of 'rent', which may be defined 'unproductive' or 'parasitic', received by those individuals who do not contribute in an active way to the production of national income. This type of rent, however, is spent by their recipients in order to purchase a quota of the national income. Hence, in Nicola's chapter, land is convened with all other production factors and the corresponding payment is included in the category of profit, while the term 'rent' is understood in a totally unproductive meaning. It seems useful to state that Nicola's chapter may be placed inside the sphere of the marginal theory of income distribution; 'rent' is here assimilated to 'profit', by considering land on a par with every other material input. From a social or 'normative' viewpoint, wages are the quota of national income that does not raise particular questions. Socially speaking, profits are somewhat more difficult to explain, at least according to an ethical viewpoint; they are however the main source of investment. Rents are, however, often considered as negative from a social viewpoint, as they subtract a share of national product from profits and wages, with the consequence of reducing the potential rate of growth of the economy in a framework where savings become automatically investment. We may for instance consider on the one hand the treasury bonds inherited by a consumer with no role in economic activity and its interests wholly consumed by him. At the other extreme we may consider pension payments, received by retired workers for their past contribution to the productive process, a sort of delayed wage payment. The 'rent' considered here by Nicola is of the first type; hence it may be named 'unproductive' or 'parasitic', and every person perceiving such an income is called *rentier*. Nicola's chapter modifies to an important extent the traditional framework of macroeconomic models, by introducing the category of those who receive unproductive rents (whom he calls *rentiers*): they are individuals who spend their incomes without taking part in the production of the goods and services. Of course, as we have pointed out at the beginning, in the real world there are also individuals receiving *Ricardian* rents, as landlords who own and provide an important factor of production, i.e. land. In the model here developed, they are considered on a *par* with capitalists, and their incomes are included in the category of profit. This leads the author to state that:

Many of us think that socially speaking profits are not to be valued more than rents, be they productive or parasitic. The model put forward here goes against this viewpoint and shows how in every decentralized economy profits are important as wages are, differently from unproductive rents. Thus, the category of profit has an ethical valence, more or less like wages, while unproductive rents cannot deserve such a positive opinion. Once more, it seems useful to underline that, thanks to the constrained maximization of GDP ... , the class contest between workers and capitalists may be resolved by means of the mathematical calculus, which objectively states the optimal distribution of production between wages and profits. (Nicola, this volume)

Part II ('Structural Dynamics: Resources and Multi-Sectoral Linkages') has a first chapter by Albert Steenge. In his chapter on 'Limits, Resources, and Distributional Trade-offs: Structural Constraints and Opportunities', he discusses the structure of input–output models in terms of relations between the input coefficients and several other types of coefficients and parameters. The author focuses on interconnections that must exist in an economy that is able to reproduce itself, i.e. that produces just as much in terms of output as it needs in terms of inputs. Further he introduces the notions of 'internal structure' and 'scale', represented by an augmented input coefficients matrix with dominant eigenvalue equal to 1 and the corresponding eigenvector, which has a double function, standing both for the vector of total outputs and the vector of total inputs. The system put forward by the author may be used to model the effects of many types of scarcities, particularly those involving resources being in short supply. Scarcities of the type lead to the necessity of trade-offs between commodity allocations: higher consumption demand will mean that fewer resources are available for industrial production activities. To obtain the actual trade-off curves, the author considers a system determinant that is a function of all model coefficients or parameters, and which must be 0 in equilibrium. By fixing certain parameter or coefficients, the so-called trade-off functions between the remaining ones can be obtained. The graphs of a number of cases are provided. The author points finally out that the methods suggested require further investigation.

In the following chapter on 'Producible Resources and Producibility Prices in a Dynamic Leontief-Type Model', Carlo D'Adda draws attention to the dynamic feasibility constraints associated with the use of produced inputs. In fact, as D'Adda argues, it is in the nature of a Leontief-type economy 'to represent the relative size of the productive sectors of an economic system and at the same time to determine the prices of sectoral products' (D'Adda, this volume). Leontief's prices express the conditions to be met by the accumulation of physical capital goods if the economic system is set to follow a given path of expansion. Such prices must be consistent with the physical requirements due to the technology in use, and *may or may not* coincide with the prices at which productive sectors exchange intermediate commodities with one another. This frame highlights the relationships between conditions for physical capital accumulation in the different sectors and the price ratios at which intra-industry trade takes place. In fact, Leontief prices may be considered as '*producibility prices* that include cost of current inputs, cost of the period sectoral capital additions and cost of labour' (D'Adda, this volume). Resources for growth are necessary and partly consist of intermediate products delivered from within the system, but they must be produced (in a closed economy) according to relative proportions expressed by the aforementioned price ratios. Producibility prices may or may not coincide with actual prices and different criteria of price determination (such as market prices under alternative market forms, or 'administered' prices) may be the most effective ones in satisfying sustainability conditions in different historical and social contexts. The difference between the vector of actual prices and the vector of producibility prices points to different degrees of 'exploitation' (positive or negative) achieved in the different sectors, which are shown by comparing one by one the different components of the two vectors. The chapter concludes by emphasizing the role of economic policy in shifting producible resources for growth from one sector to another, and in making a sustainable accumulation path possible.

The third chapter of Part II on 'The Transformative Potential of Input–Output Economics for Addressing Critical Resource Challenges of the Twenty-First Century' is by Faye Duchin, a scholar who has been one of the closest pupils and collaborators of Wassily Leontief. The author starts from the assumption that the critical economic challenges of our times revolve around the large and growing volume of global economic activities relative to the environmental base and the rapid transmission of economic problems among geographic macro-regions. In fact she argues that input–output economics is uniquely suited to understanding and analysing these kinds of challenges, and to itemizing its characteristic strengths, something which surprisingly has not before been systematically undertaken. She then identifies both the most pressing needs for further development of the field and the obstacles it faces. This requires, according to Duchin, a new approach, in particular an input–output theory of resources and resource rents. Describing the distinctive features of existing theory and developing new theory have lagged well behind data compilation and empirical analysis. This is explained by both self-imposed priorities and the difficulty of successfully challenging the dominant assumptions and building blocks of mainstream economic theory. Using the prospects for extensive recycling of materials on a global scale to illustrate her arguments, the author formulates an inquiry into emerging resource problems as a critical experiment for input–output economics. She comes to the conclusion that the realization of the 'transformative' potential of the field hinges on the development of a body of new theories that start, not from abstraction, but from the problems to be addressed, and from existing input–output models and databases, with the objectives of refining them, integrating them and extending their conceptual reach. The approach is problem-driven, empirically rich, and may benefit from a long history of economic theorizing about resources.

In the fourth chapter of Part II ('Capital Mobility and Natural Resources Dynamics: A Classical-Keynesian Perspective') Heinrich Bortis addresses the relationship between financialization and capital mobility on the one hand, and structural change and the management of non-produced natural resources on the other hand. Within this framework the interrelated phenomena of income distribution and employment level play a crucial role. The author in particular considers the functioning of the entire socio-economic system. Classical-Keynesian political economy, grounded on the surplus principle of income distribution and on the Keynesian principle of effective demand, seems to the author the most appropriate framework of analysis. In any case, according to Bortis, it is more promising, in the analysis of the financialisation process and capital mobility in relation to structural change and natural resources utilization, than the standard neoclassical model of rational choice. Bortis maintains that the neoclassical vision is based on Say's Law, implying that savings are always invested. In this view, financialization reflects an abundance of saving, and capital mobility implies that savings are invested in an efficient way in large areas. Higher growth in all countries and regions would result. Economic structures basically result from market processes where non-produced natural resources are managed through a framework of intertemporal markets. On the other hand, in the classical-Keynesian view the close link between saving and investment is cut, and the paradox of thrift implies that, in principle, higher saving/income ratios are associated to lower investment volumes; this is valid in the short run, but, much more importantly, in the long run, too, as emerges from considering the long-period output and employment trend pictured by the supermultiplier. On this basis one may attempt to unveil the mechanism through which financialization and capital mobility lead to increasing inequalities in income distribution and higher levels of involuntary unemployment. The principle of effective demand, the surplus principle of distribution and the principle of increasing returns to scale all play a fundamental role in pushing the long-period output and employment trend downwards. This downward movement will be accompanied by structural change. Financialization and capital mobility associated with growing inequalities in income distribution affect, in their turn, the management of non-reproducible resources. In medium- and long-term cyclical movements saving and investment are, in a post-Keynesian vein, positively related. This gives rise to instabilities reflected in movements of output and employment around the long-term trend. Increasing financialization accompanied by higher capital mobility may enhance instability and negatively affect the proper functioning of structures, and may influence the extraction and pricing of non-exhaustible resources in an inappropriate way, mainly because of the predominance of particular interests and of speculation. The complex problems dealt with in this chapter cannot be tackled through the regulation of behaviour. A new economic and financial world order, along Keynes's 1944 Bretton Woods proposals, is indeed required, such that financialization may be reduced and capital mobility restrained. Long-period incomes and employment policies along Keynes/Beveridge lines should bring about more harmonious socio-economic structures. According to Bortis, a global utilization strategy for natural resources would require a World Resources Agency, acting in the interest of present and future generations by preserving the natural environment.

The fifth chapter of Part II is by Kumaraswamy Vela Velupillai on 'The Chimera of a Complete Analysis of Economic Dynamics'. Velupillai argues that obsession with the desire for a complete analysis of economic dynamics is analogous to the classic – but forlorn – search for a qualitative determination of all possible types of motions. It is possible, perhaps even desirable, to separate the notion of complete analysis of any problem – not only in economics – and the idea of a complete economic dynamics, independent (at least in the latter case) of the feasibility of its complete analysis. The earliest attempt to seek a formalization of a notion of complete economic dynamics was in a classic contribution by Kuznets at the dawn of the era that sought to integrate equilibrium theory with dynamics (Kuznets, 1930). On the other hand, all attempts, in every kind of economic theory, at formulating 'General Theories' – be it The General Theory of Employment, Interest and Money or General Equilibrium Theory – always are attempts at building complete theories and choosing a select set of tools and methods for its analysis, from which special theories are derived. The author maintains that there can be no 'complete analysis' of economic dynamics, not even a 'complete' formalization of this tortuous notion. However, algorithmic dynamics is replete with undecidabilities and incompleteness, in the strict meta-mathematical senses; it is also richly endowed with uncomputabilities in recursion theoretic senses. Carrying the suggested equivalences a little further, it would be natural to ask what kind of problems can be posed to such a 'machine' (or to the economic system) and ask whether we can classify the admissible problems on a sliding scale, first separating the decidable problems from the undecidable ones. Such questions lead immediately to structuring the data, which is the bridge between theory and empirical implementation, in terms of sets of numbers that are recursive, recursively enumerable and recursively enumerable but not recursive.

The following contribution by Michael A. Landesmann ('Ricardian and Schumpeterian Rents: Fundamental Ingredients for Structural Economic Dynamics') addresses the issue of technological differentiation and technological dynamics as an important feature in the structural dynamics of economic systems. In particular, Landesmann makes use of the Ricardian differential rent framework in order to explore the implications of scarcities deriving not from limited availability of a non-produced resource (such as land or mineral ore) but from limited access to technology. This chapter outlines a conceptual framework for the analysis of the relationship between technological and distributional dynamics in a single-sector and then in a multi-sectoral framework. The chapter starts with the acknowledgement that technical innovation is often associated with the emergence of rents (according to a tradition followed by Schumpeter but going back at least to Hans von Mangoldt). Technological rents due to temporary technological monopoly within particular productive sectors may exert an influence that goes much beyond the confines of the originating sector. For rents may be transferred, through direct investment or through the intermediation of the financial system, from one productive sector to another, thereby generating a cumulative process at the scale of the overall economic system. This dynamics of rent transfers may either stimulate or dampen overall economic growth. For rents may either be invested in technologically progressive activities or in activities that may deliver significant returns independently of technical progress. Landesmann explores the 'growth retarding and growth enhancing features' associated with the formation and distribution of rents across productive sectors, and points to the role of social structures and institutional factors in determining what the ultimate impact of rent formation upon structural economic dynamics will be.

The final chapter of Part II is by Ivano Cardinale on 'Towards a Structural Political Economy of Resources' and draws attention to the relationships between the technological and the sociopolitical dimensions of structural dynamics in general, and of shifts from one resource base to another in particular. He considers the economic and political-economic conditions that make possible and activate specific paths of structural change. The analysis is carried out in terms of the analytical framework provided by the study of sectoral interdependencies first outlined in Quesnay's *Tableau Economique* and refined by the contributions of von Neumann, Sraffa, Leontief, Pasinetti and Quadrio Curzio. This representation visualizes the sectors that make up the macro-economy as well as the interdependencies among those sectors. Cardinale suggests using those representations to study not only technical relationships between industrial sectors, but also sociopolitical relationships between the political interests of those sectors. He proposes a framework based on two sets of conditions for the transition between resource bases. The first set concerns the feasibility of the 'final state', which is characterized by changes in production coefficients across sectors, and reflects the emergence of new production processes as well as changes in the proportion between old and new processes. Second, the traverse towards such a final state must be consistent with the technical as well as socio-economic structure of a given economy. Either set of conditions has both economic and political-economic prerequisites. In particular, the latter set of prerequisites provides a heuristic in the coalitions of interests compatible with the achievement of the aforementioned final state, and can help explain which path of structural change is realized among the many that are possible for a given economy.

Part III ('Resources, Institutions and Social Structures') starts with the contribution by Lilia Costabile on 'Monetary Analysis, Financial Innovation and Institutions before the Industrial Revolution: a Paradigm Case'. According to the author, structural economic dynamics includes, indeed requires, the analysis of how different sectors interact in shaping the evolution of whole economic systems. The financial/monetary sector has been an integral, important part of the economy since the Middle Ages, and up to its phenomenal growth in the last few decades. The introduction of paper money thus provides a paradigmatic example of the principle of antagonism and/or synergy between scarcity and reproducibility: antagonism can be turned into synergy by appropriate institutional development. A 'paper economy', and the financial institutions which support it, can facilitate economic linkages and transactions seeing as liquidity is necessary to economic activity. Nevertheless, when the virtuous circle between monetary/financial institutions and the real economy is disrupted, the stage is set for economic disorder, with consequences that may go beyond the strictly economic realm and impact on the political and social domains. The first aim of this chapter is to elucidate the causes and consequences of a 'scarcity of money', or, in modern parlance, of liquidity constraints. This will be done by taking a historical approach and considering the monetary vicissitudes of the Kingdom of Naples between the second half of the sixteenth century and the first decades of the seventeenth century. The second, related, aim of this chapter is to inquire into the ingenious remedies devised by economic agents in order to transform monetary scarcity into 'abundance', thus 'escaping golden and silver fetters', to borrow Barry Eichengreen's (1995) well-known analogy. The solution found in the historical example discussed here was to invent institutions capable of undertaking liquidity creation: the 'public banks of Naples', which, perhaps for the first time in the Western world, initiated the circulation of fiduciary money in the form of paper notes. At that time in history, however, discipline was imposed on debtors by the national boundaries within which the circulation of paper money was restricted. As the quotation from Galiani in the epigraph clearly indicates, paper money was not accepted in international circulation, particularly because the Kingdom of Naples was a peripheral state liable to invasion by hostile neighbours – which, in fact, often happened in its history. But the seeds had been sown for more serious convertibility problems in the future.

The second chapter of Part III is by Constanze Dobler and Harald Hagemann on 'Institutions, Resources and Economic Growth in Transition Processes: the Case of Russia'. The aim of their chapter is to examine the transition process from a centrally planned to a market economy. It focuses on a number of issues at the centre of this part of the volume. Dobler and Hagemann's chapter examines the transition in Russia from a planned to a more liberalized economy, focusing on the role institutions played before and during the process. It broadly describes the developments of the last twenty years. In Russia, first a 'Big Bang approach' was applied. That is to say, transition was conducted all of a sudden, omitting important underlying reforms. This practice should function as a shock therapy. Hence, the approach should leave no other chance than an abrupt adaption to the new free-market rules. These rules would then lead to fast economic growth and development, as they did in other places. However, since Russian GDP per capita and thereby living standards deteriorated dramatically in the years after the collapse of the Soviet Union in December 1991, the plan did not work. At any rate, Russian economic indicators have recovered since then and partly achieved their pre-1991 levels at the end of the last decade. The last part of the chapter is dedicated to an examination of the conditions, difficulties and results of the decision by the Russian authorities to make their way to a path of sustained growth. This chapter brings to the fore, the central role played by resources and multi-sectoral linkages on the structural dynamics associated with this process of economic transition.

The following chapter is by Alessandro Roncaglia on 'Institutions, Resources and the Common Weal'. This chapter examines the definition of wealth according to the institutional and socio-economic setting of the society considered. Hence the structural dynamics of wealth is brought to the fore. Roncaglia starts by stating that it is quite difficult to point to a specific time as marking the birth of political economy as a social science. There are good reasons to invoke the name of William Petty (1623–1687) in this respect, and his Political arithmetic; however, some important notions were already present in previous writings. Often, such notions first appeared with a somewhat vague meaning, and were increasingly closely specified at a later stage, especially when embodied in formal models of the economy. Scientific progress in economic analysis is connected to increasing precision in the definition of the concepts utilized in the analysis. Following Roncaglia, a basic concept in economic analysis, whose evolution provides a test ground for the methodological issues mentioned here, is the notion of the common weal. Its original content reappears, and has continually been reappearing in the history of economic thought, within other concepts and within different contexts. Roncaglia first recalls an early instance of the use of this notion, the *Discourse on the Common weal of This Realm of England*. Written in 1549 but first published only in 1581, it is a dialogue between a doctor, a knight, a merchant, an artisan (a capper) and a husbandman – representing the different classes of society and their different interests and points of view – dealing with the economic and social situation of England at the time. Long attributed to John Hales, it has also been ascribed to Thomas Smith or to William Stafford. Roncaglia then goes on to consider the different aspects of its substantive content, from the material idea of the common weal identified with the wealth of nations to the contemporary notion of happiness as the true aim of human behaviour. Subsequently Roncaglia considers Adam Smith's notion of the wealth of nations, focused on the material aspect of production, and his notion of self-interest, where the pursuit of material welfare is balanced with the ethical element of care for others. This is followed by a discussion of Bentham's reduction of the common weal to a mono-dimensional magnitude with his utilitarianism, and by John Stuart Mill's criticisms, which in a sense bring us back to Smith's views. The author goes on to consider the marginalist-neoclassical individualism, with a cursory consideration of Pareto's notion of optimality. Finally the author introduces some contemporary theories concerning aspects of the notion of 'common weal', such as the growing use of social capital or civil economy, as well as Amartya Sen's notion of development of capabilities. Roncaglia maintains that the sixteenth-century notion of 'common weal' embodies an essential element, which has been re-evaluated in present-day debates, namely its 'multidimensional' nature. The common weal notion appears as a criterion for evaluation whenever we look for a 'good' situation for society as a whole. Thus economic well-being matters, but also its sufficiently egalitarian distribution, as well as other elements such as personal security, environment, political freedoms, culture, solidarity and so on. This leads Roncaglia to conclude that:

The monodimensional specifications that the notion of common weal received, such as the Smithian notion of the wealth of nations, are useful – even very useful – if we recognize their limits and utilize them – as Smith did – in a context open to taking other relevant elements into account. However, we must retain a distinction between subjective and objective notions: the former (from the maximum utility principle to the notion of happiness) are connected to marginalist/neoclassical economics, while the latter are derived from the objective Smithian notion of the wealth of nations. Failure to perceive this distinction is a drawback in the debate: when dealing with a multidimensional notion, interpreting its dimensions entails clear specification of the underlying vision of the economy and the society. (Roncaglia, this volume)

Stefano Zamagni, in his chapter on 'Development, Capabilities and Institutions', discusses the relationship between legal frameworks, institutional arrangements, and the realization of human capabilities. According to the author, when legal norms – whose enforcement depends on coactive sanctions – run against social and moral norms – whose enforcement is based on shame and guilt, respectively – they fail to achieve their expressive effects. The chapter shows that inexpressive laws can not only be ineffective, but can push the values of society away from those expressed by the law. Just like expressive laws can foster consensus in heterogeneous groups, inexpressive laws can decumulate social capital by creating a social divide and in so doing can jeopardize the prospects of future development of the economy. Irreversible structural change presupposes an institutional framework compatible with the change that is envisaged, and changes feasible under certain institutional conditions may be unfeasible if other institutional conditions are in place. This chapter highlights the interdependence between institutional change and structural economic dynamics, and calls attention to the fact that the institutional framework of structural change is itself a complex bundle of formal norms and informal dispositions. Zamagni addresses the internal hierarchy of any given institutional set up, and points to the possibility of mismatches between its formal and informal components. The consequences for dynamic analysis are far-reaching in so far as an institutional framework in which formal and informal norms are not mutually congruent is unlikely to generate a self-sustained and irreversible process of structural change. This chapter concludes with a discussion of the relationship between economic development as structural change and political development, and compares the 'elitist-competitive' and 'deliberative' models of democracy. This comparison leads the author to emphasize the advantages of the deliberative vision of politics in so far as it is conducive to a better integration between the formal and informal aspects of institutions, and is thus more effective in enhancing the formation and realization of capabilities.

The final chapter of Part III is by Pier Luigi Porta on 'Conquering Scarcity: Institutions, Learning and Creativity in the History of Economic Ideas'. The aim of this chapter is to emphasize the relationship between 'scarcity' and 'creativity' as an important thread in the evolution of economic ideas. This is done by exploring the manifold routes suggested to conquer scarcity through institutional changes. Such an approach leads Porta to address particular historical episodes – the Scottish and Italian Enlightenments, the civil economy tradition, and the twentieth-century Cambridge revival of classical political economy. He looks into the way in which these different episodes address institutional change as a possible route to overcome scarcity bottlenecks on a dynamic path. The Enlightenment episodes are characterized by emphasis on wealth as a flow of products rather than as a stock or fund of resources, and by the consideration of open social orders as prerequisites for economic development (Smith, Beccaria, Genovesi, Verri). The relevance of the institutional frame for development re-emerges with the civil economy tradition, and with the contribution of the Cambridge School to the analysis of the interrelation between technical conditions and institutional arrangements. A final theme of this chapter is an appraisal of Luigi Pasinetti's 'separation theorem' as a contribution to the investigation of the linkage between the structural ('natural') and the institutional levels of economic analysis.

Part IV ('Resources, Industrial Change and the Structure of the World Economy') starts with Moshe Syrquin's chapter 'Resources, Industrial Transformation and the Structure of the World Economy'. Syrquin stresses that in a neglected work of 1964, Kuznets summarized some of the results emerging from his work on *Modern Economic Growth* (MEG), and used them to speculate on diversity, interdependence, war, conflict, and cooperation among nations. It was an unusual Kuznets: speculative rather than precise and quantitative. The content and the approach clearly reflect the deep impact on Kuznets that must have been left by the horrors of World War II and the palpable threats of oppression and aggression of authoritarian regimes. No one was more appreciative than Kuznets of the benefits brought about by MEG, but he was also keenly aware of its potential for destruction. In Syrquin's view, Kuznets is cautiously pessimistic in reflecting on the threat to world peace from authoritarian regimes and on the limited spread of the process of *Modern Economic Growth*, with the resulting increased divide among rich and poor nations. Syrquin's chapter discusses some of Kuznets's arguments in his 1964 lectures, by highlighting the political and economic environment at the time he was writing and how it had evolved. It is noteworthy that, in discussing prospects and limitations of the diffusion process, both Kuznets and Syrquin highlight the role of unevenness across regions and productive sectors due to the uneven distribution of natural and human resources. Against this background, Syrquin updates Kuznets's analysis by taking into account the changes in the geopolitical environment over the past fifty years, primarily the end of the Cold War, the spread of globalization, and the rise of China and other Asian economies. Finally the chapter reviews various projections of expected changes in the global economy to the year 2050 and the main challenges that such changes imply for conflict and cooperation.

The issue of structural changes in the world economy is also taken up by Marco Fortis in Part IV's second chapter, 'Transformation and Resources in the "New" Geo-economy'. The author addresses the recent evolution and projections of the gross domestic products of the major world economies and concentrates on the changing proportions of the world manufacturing output across those economies. The data structuring problem is also central in this contribution, which adopts the methodology initially proposed by Nikolaj Ivanovich Tugan Baranovsky ([1894, 1900] 1913), and followed by Arthur Spiethoff (1903, 1925), by taking consumption data of raw materials and industrial materials as key statistical indicators in the study of growth and economic fluctuations. In Fortis's analysis, the consumption of basic means of production calls attention to important features of economic structure due to the pervasive character of their utilization (they enter as essential inputs in a large variety of industrial processes). For this reason, the consumption of raw and industrial materials is taken to measure the 'depth' of any given growth process (the degree to which growth results from interdependencies between industrial sectors), and the corresponding role of different non-produced resources in different stages of economic and technological dynamics. In Fortis's view, raw material consumption data unmistakably show that the distribution of world manufacturing output has radically changed over the past ten to fifteen years, with the rising of new leaders such as China, South Korea, India and Brazil beside the traditional developed countries, and with new outsiders such as Mexico and Turkey taking higher positions in industrial raw materials consumption. As this analysis shows, the changing distribution of manufacturing output across countries is associated with a changing distribution of industrial raw materials consumption, even if it is acknowledged that industrial consumption data for basic products may underestimate advanced countries' manufacturing output values. This chapter shows that changing patterns of consumption for raw materials and industrial materials reflect changes in the relative position of industrial nations across the different stages of manufacturing production in the world economy.

The third chapter of Part IV is by Sunanda Sen on 'Developmental State and Structural Economic Dynamics: Necessity of Industrial Structure'. This chapter examines the changes in the institutional framework of developing policies over the past three decades and assesses in that light the changing positions of social groups relative to incomes derived from ownership of non-produced assets. She highlights in particular the way in which national configurations of economic and political interests have shifted from social coalitions supporting economic development in terms of the expansion of a national industrial base to social coalitions supporting economic growth via international capital flows and financial development. The demise of the developmental state led to a stop of policy interventions aimed at achieving self-sufficiency in strategic sectors such as the production of steel, cement and pharmaceutical products. An important feature of the social and political transformations that Sunanda Sen examines is the disappearance, or at least the severely diminished importance, of the national elites setting national development as their primary objective (national bourgeoisie) and the growing importance of social groups whose income is primarily derived as rentier income from the holding of 'stocks of equities, real estates and even commodities' (Sunanda Sen). This sociopolitical transformation is seen to be central to the explanation of ongoing developments in countries such as India, in which the national elites who were previously supporting 'industrialization in protected home markets' have more recently shifted to a different policy agenda characterized by the opening up to linkages with international financial markets. In Sunanda Sen's analysis, processes taking place in developed and developing countries mirror one another and point to a fundamental change in the relationship between credit arrangements and productive activities. Both in developed and developing economies the share of rentiers income has considerably increased, and the question may be raised as to what extent this institutional transformation affects the growth and employment prospects of the economic systems under consideration.

The fourth chapter of Part IV is by Andrea Goldstein and Keun Lee on 'Resources, Institutional Forms and Structural Transformation in the BRICKs: the "Hybrid Model of Late Capitalism"'. This chapter examines policy issues associated with the governance of long-term structural changes. In particular, it focuses on the ongoing restructuring of the global economy in terms of the changing scope and configuration of large multinational companies.

Evidence discussed by the authors show that the 'economic periphery' accounts for a rising share of the world largest companies. An important feature of this rising trend is that large firms in the BRICK economies of Brazil, Russia, India, China and Korea show little convergence towards the Western model or firms' organization. This is because public companies with dispersed ownership are largely absent in those economies. This scenario is interpreted in terms of a hybrid model of late capitalism that differs from both (i) the dependency-theory approach emphasizing the ancillary role of local firms and state owned enterprises, and (ii) the new-liberal approach based on the convergence to the paradigm of the widespread ownership company with little or no state involvement. This contribution challenges the deterministic view that would confine large corporations in the periphery to secondary positions, while underlining that their success has substantially modified the geography of the world economy. This contribution highlights the central role of direct state intervention in fostering the growth of large national companies at the early stages of industrial and economic development.

The final chapter of Part IV is by Antonio Andreoni on 'On Manufacturing Development under Resources Constraints'. The approach of this chapter takes up the theoretical framework of the structural analysis of resources and links it with empirical evidence on trajectories of manufacturing development at different stages of economic growth. This is done by underlining the relationship between stages of growth and patterns of resource utilization. In this connection, Andreoni emphasizes that resources constraints are sector-specific and affect production tasks differently depending on (i) the level of aggregation considered, and (ii) the specific production units at each level of aggregation. As a result, resources opportunities and bottlenecks affect economic dynamics in a different way depending upon the character of structural transformation and the pattern of production specialization. This chapter shows the relevance of resource-based multi-sectoral models of production in disentangling the structural complexity of dynamic processes and in identifying feedback mechanisms at the origin of cumulative causation paths. Economic development taking place through manufacturing structural change is inherently associated with the transformation of the role of scarcities in reflecting production interdependencies along a dynamic trajectory. In this connection, Andreoni emphasizes the importance of global resource bottlenecks and the associated identification of a number of 'resource-related global risks'. The utilization of a structural heuristic capable of detecting resource-sensitive points within the scheme of production interdependencies within and across economic systems is a necessary condition for the design of effective manufacturing development policies under actual or potential resource bottlenecks. This approach would detect alternative possibilities for the political economy of resources and would identify alternative strategies by which the economic system may be able to overcome technological scarcities through technological and organizational change.

Part V ('Towards a Political Economy of Resources and Structural Change') brings the volume to a close and emphasizes the relationship between resources, rents and structural dynamics as the unifying theme of this work. This Part includes a single chapter by Roberto Scazzieri, Mauro Baranzini and Claudia Rotondi ('Resources, Scarcities and Rents: Technological Interdependence and the Dynamics of Socio-Economic Structures') in which the three editors take stock of the research programme behind the conception of the volume and propose ways in which the structural analysis of resources can be developed into a political economy of technological complementarities and structural change. The chapter argues that this research programme has led to a reassessment of the concept of economic scarcity: first, by emphasizing its dual character between 'natural scarcity' and 'technological scarcity'; and second, by drawing attention to the changing relationships between natural and technological scarcities in economic dynamics. We maintain that this view of scarcities has far-reaching implications for the political economy of growth and development and explore ways in which the structural profile of technological interdependence leads to a new approach to the analysis and policy of structural change in a resource-constrained economy.

REFERENCES

Arrow, K. J., and Debreu, G. (1954) 'Existence of an Equilibrium for a Competitive Economy', *Econometrica*, 22.3, pp. 265–90.

Baranzini, M. (1979) 'Review of *Protagonisti del pensiero economico*, Vol. I: *Nascita e affermazione del marginalismo* (1871–1890); Vol. II: *Tradizione e rivoluzione in economia politica* (1890–1936)', ed. by A. Quadrio Curzio and R. Scazzieri, *The Economic Journal*, 89.3, pp. 480–2.

(1991) *A Theory of Wealth Distribution and Accumulation*, Oxford: Clarendon Press.

Baranzini, M., and Harcourt, G. C. (eds.) (1993) *The Dynamics of the Wealth of Nations: Growth, Distribution and Structural Change: Essays in Honour of Luigi L. Pasinetti*, Basingstoke: Macmillan; New York: St. Martin's Press.

Baranzini, M., and Scazzieri, R. (eds.) (1986) *Foundations of Economics. Structures of Inquiry and Economic Theory*, Oxford and New York: B. Blackwell; in particular 'Knowledge in Economics: A Framework', pp. 1–87.

(1990) *The Economic Theory of Structure and Change*, Cambridge: Cambridge University Press; in particular 'Introduction', pp. 1–20; and 'Economic Structure. Analytical Perspectives', pp. 227–333.

Bliss, C. J. (1975) *Capital Theory and the Distribution of Income*, Amsterdam and Oxford: North-Holland.

Duchin, F., and Lange, G.-M. (1994) *The Future of the Environment. Ecological Economics and Technological Change*, Oxford and New York: Oxford University Press.

Furtado, C. (1967) *Teoria e politica do desenvolvimento económico*, São Paulo: Companhia Editora Nacional.

Harcourt, G. C. (2012) 'Luigi Pasinetti: the Senior Living Heir of the Cambridge School of Economics and the Last of the Great System-Builders', in R. Arena and P. L. Porta (eds.) *Structural Dynamics and Economic Growth*, Cambridge: Cambridge University Press, pp. 137–44.

Hicks, J. R. (1965) *Capital and Growth*, Oxford: Clarendon Press.

(1976)'"Revolutions" in Economics', in S. J. Latsis (ed.) *Method and Appraisal in Economics*, Cambridge: Cambridge University Press, pp. 207–18.

Jevons W. S. (1865) *The Coal Question: An Inquiry Concerning the Progress of the Nation, and the Probable Exhaustion of Our Coal-Mines*, London: Macmillan.

Kaldor, N. (1956) 'Alternative Theories of Distribution', *Review of Economic Studies*, 23.2, pp. 83–100.

Kuznets, S. (1930) *Secular Movements in Production and Prices*, Boston and New York: Houghton Mifflin Company.

Landesmann, M. A., and Scazzieri, R. (eds.) (2009) *Production and Economic Dynamics*, Cambridge: Cambridge University Press (1st edn 1996).

Leontief, W. W., Carter, A. P., and Petri, P. A. (1977) *The Future of the World Economy. A United Nations Study*, New York: Oxford University Press.

Leontief, W. W., Chenery, H. B. *et al.* (1953) *Studies in the Structure of the American Economy: Theoretical and Empirical Explorations in Input-Output Analysis*, White Plains, NY: International Arts and Sciences Press.

Lutfalla, M. (1983) Review of Quadrio Curzio, A. and Scazzieri, R. (eds.) *Protagonisti del pensiero economico*, t. 3, *Rivoluzione industriale e economia politica (1817–1848)* and t. 4, *Struttura produttiva, scambio e mercati (1848–1872)*, Bologna: Il Mulino (1982), *Revue d'économie politique*, 93.4, pp. 610–11.

Malthus, T. R. (1815a) *The Grounds of an Opinion on the Policy of Restricting the Importation of Foreign Corn*, London: John Murray.

(1815b) *An Inquiry into the Nature and Progress of Rent and the Principles by Which it is Regulated*, London: Murray.

Marengo, L., and Scazzieri, R. (2014) 'Embedding Production: Structural Dynamics and Organizational Change', *Structural Change and Economic Dynamics*, 29.1, pp. 1–4.

Mari, C. (2010) *Kaldor, Cambridge and the Keynesian Theory of Income Distribution*, PhD thesis, Lugano, Switzerland: USI.

Mill, J. S. (1848) *Principles of Political Economy with Some of their Application to Social Philosophy*, London: J. W. Parker.

Morishima, M. (1989) *Ricardo's Economics*, Cambridge: Cambridge University Press.

Myrdal, G. (1953) *The Political Element in the Development of Economic Theory*, London: Routledge and Kegan Paul (1st edn 1930).

Pasinetti, L. L. (1960a) 'A Mathematical Formulation of the Ricardian System', *Review of Economic Studies*, 27.2, pp. 78–98.

(1960b) 'Cyclical Fluctuations and Economic Growth', *Oxford Economic Papers*, 12.2, pp. 215–41.

(1962a) 'Rate of Profit and Income Distribution in Relation to the Rate of Economic Growth', *Review of Economic Studies*, 29.4, pp. 267–79.

(1962b) 'A Multi-Sector Model of Economic Growth', a Ph.D. dissertation submitted to the Faculty of Economics and Politics of the University of Cambridge.

(1964/5) 'Causalità e interdipendenza nell'analisi econometrica e nella teoria economica', in *Annali dell'Università Cattolica del Sacro Cuore 1964–65*, Milan: Vita e Pensiero, pp. 231–50.

(1965) *A New Theoretical Approach to the Problems of Economic Growth*, Vatican City: Pontificiae Academiae Scientiarum Scripta Varia.

Pasinetti, L. L., and Scazzieri, R. (1987a; 2008) 'Capital Theory: Paradoxes', in J. Eatwell, M. Milgate and P. Newman (eds.) *The New Palgrave Dictionary of Economics*, vol. I, London: Macmillan, pp. 363–8.

(1987b) 'Structural Economic Dynamics', in J. Eatwell, M. Milgate and P. Newman (eds.) *The New Palgrave Dictionary of Economics*, vol. IV, London: Macmillan, pp. 525–8.

Perroux, F. (1939) *Cours d'économie politique*, 2nd edn, Paris: Domat Montchrétien.

Quadrio Curzio, A. (1967) *Rendita e distribuzione in un modello economico plurisettoriale* [Rent and Distribution in a Multi-sectoral Economic Model], Milan: Giuffrè.

(1975) *Accumulazione del capitale e rendita* [Accumulation of Capital and Rent], Bologna: Il Mulino.

(1980) 'Rent, Income Distribution and Orders of Efficiency and Rentability', in L. L. Pasinetti (ed.) *Essays on the Theory of Joint Production*, London: Macmillan, pp. 219–40. Reprinted in H. D. Kurz and N. Salvadori (eds.) (2003) *The Legacy of Piero Sraffa*, Cheltenham: E. Elgar, vol. II, pp. 311–41.

(1986) 'Technological Scarcity: An Essay on Production and Structural Change', in M. Baranzini and R. Scazzieri (eds.) *Foundations of Economics, op. cit.*, pp. 311–38.

(1987) 'Land Rent', in J. Eatwell, M. Milgate and P. Newman (eds.) *The New Palgrave. A Dictionary of Economics*, London: Macmillan, vol. III, pp. 118–21.

(1990) 'Rent, Distribution and Economic Structure: A Collection of Essays', *Quaderni IDSE*, 1, Milan: CNR.

(1993) 'On Economic Science, Its Tools and Economic Reality', in M. Baranzini and G. C. Harcourt (eds.) *The Dynamics of the Wealth of Nations: Growth, Distribution and Structural Change. Essays in Honour of Luigi L. Pasinetti, op. cit.*, pp. 246–71.

(1996) 'Production and Efficiency with Global Technologies', in M. A. Landesmann and R. Scazzieri (eds.) *Production and Economic Dynamics*, Cambridge: Cambridge University Press, pp. 105–26.

Quadrio Curzio, A., and Miceli, V. (2010) *Sovereign Wealth Funds. A Complete Guide to State-Owned Investment Funds*, Petersfield, Hampshire: Harriman House.

Quadrio Curzio, A., and Pellizzari, F. (1999) *Rent, Resources, Technologies*, Berlin: Springer.

Quadrio Curzio, A., and Scazzieri, R. (eds.) (1977–1982) *Protagonisti del pensiero economico*, 4 vols., Bologna: Il Mulino.

(1983) *Sui momenti costitutivi dell'economia politica,* vol. V of *Protagonisti del pensiero economico*, Bologna: Il Mulino.

(1986) 'The Exchange-Production Duality and the Dynamics of Economic Knowledge', in M. Baranzini and R. Scazzieri (eds.) *Foundations of Economics, op. cit.* pp. 377–407.

Ricardo, D. (1817) *On the Principles of Political Economy and Taxation*, London: John Murray.

Robbins, L. (1932) *An Essay on the Nature and Significance of Economic Science*, London: Macmillan.

Rosenberg, N. (1982) *Inside the Black Box: Technology and Economics*, Cambridge: Cambridge University Press.

Samuelson, P. A., and Modigliani, F. (1966a) 'The Pasinetti Paradox in Neoclassical and More General Models', *Review of Economic Studies*, 33.4, pp. 269–301.

(1966b) 'Reply to Pasinetti and Robinson', *Review of Economic Studies*, 33.4, pp. 321–30.

Scazzieri, R. (1982) 'Scale and Efficiency in Models of Production', in M. Baranzini (ed.) *Advances in Economic Theory*, Oxford: B. Blackwell, pp.19–42.

(1993) *A Theory of Production: Tasks, Processes and Technical Practices*, Oxford: Clarendon Press.

(2014) 'A Structural Theory of Increasing Returns', *Structural Change and Economic Dynamics*, 29.2, pp. 75–88.

Silva, E. G. and Teixeira, A. A. C. (2008) 'Surveying Structural Change: Seminal Contributions and a Bibliometric Account', *Structural Change and Economic Dynamics*, 19.4, pp. 273–300.

Spiethoff, A. (1903) 'Die Krisentheorien von M. v. Tugan Baranovsky und L. Pohle', *Jahrbuch für Gesetzgebung, Verwaltung und Volkswirtschaft*, 27, pp. 331–60.

(1925) 'Krisen', in *Handwöterbuch der Sozialwissenschaften*, Jena, G. Fischer, vol. 6, pp. 8–91.

Sraffa, P. (1960) *Production of Commodities by Means of Commodities. Prelude to a Critique of Economic Theory*, Cambridge: Cambridge University Press.

Tugan Baranovsky, M. I. ([1894, 1900], 1913) Les crises industrielles en Angleterre, translated from the second Russian edition by J. Schapiro, Paris: M. Giard et E. Brière.

West, E. (1815) *Essay on the Application of Capital to Land, with Observations Shewing the Impolicy of any Great Restriction of the Importation of Corn*, London: T. Underwood.

Wrigley, E. A. (1962) 'The Supply of Raw Materials in the Industrial Revolution', *Economic History Review*, 15.1, pp. 1–16.

(1988) *Continuity, Chance and Change: the Character of the Industrial Revolution in England*, Cambridge: Cambridge University Press.

(2010) *Energy and the English Industrial Revolution*, Cambridge: Cambridge University Press.

Part I

Resources and distribution in a structural perspective

2   On the origin of the theory of rent in economics

Luigi L. Pasinetti

A Preliminary Note:

This chapter was originally written in English, in the early 1990s, at the invitation of Professor Bertram Schefold, who at the time was, in Germany, the Chief Editor of a series of volumes on the *Klassiker der Nationalökonomie*. In such a series (of *Classics in economics*) the texts were reproduced from the original in facsimile. Each volume was then accompanied by a specific Vademecum book in German (i.e. a companion) with appropriate comments.

The present chapter was therefore translated in German and published as the leading comment (with the title *Das Vermächtnis der politisch-ökonomischen Pamphlete von 1815*, see Pasinetti, 1996) in the companion to the volume in the series reproducing the five famous pamphlets – all published in London in February, 1815 – that have traditionally been considered as the origin of the theory of rent.

The original English text was never published. It is published here for the first time, with only a few minor re-arrangements, especially at the beginning, made necessary to render it independent of the other contributions to the *Klassiker der Nationalökonomie* series.

I should like also to mention that the impact of the historical events described in the present chapter have been relevant in other directions as well, independently of the theory of rent. I resumed them, in fact considerably expanded, on two other occasions: i) in my severe critique of the so-called Law of diminishing returns, in a Lecture delivered at the Annual Meeting of the Royal Economic Society in Nottingham, March 1999 (see Pasinetti 1999); and ii) in an equally strong 'critique of the Neoclassical theory of growth and income distribution' conceived as a twin paper (the opposing side being taken by R.M. Solow) as prospective Encyclopedia items for the *Istituto della Enciclopedia Treccani*, then published in the *BNL Quarterly Review* (see Solow, 2000; Pasinetti, 2000).

I am glad to dedicate this paper to Alberto Quadrio Curzio, who made of Rent (framed within Piero Sraffa's theoretical framework) the starting point of his research activity, and then never abandoned the subject of non-reproducible resources in his subsequent contributions, even when dealing with problems of economic growth, development, and international relations.

1.   Five famous essays

The year 1815 – besides marking long-lasting changes in the history of the Western world – has also become noteworthy to historians of economic thought for the publication of five famous pamphlets whose impact on economic theory has gone far beyond their original aims. They appeared in the remarkably short time of 3 weeks: from 3 February (date of publication of Malthus's *Inquiry on Rent*) to 24 February (date of publication of Ricardo's *Essay on Profit*); the intermediate dates being, according to Piero Sraffa's accurate recontstruction (1954, p. 5): 10 February (Malthus's *Grounds for an Opinion*), 13 February (West's *Essay on the Application of Capital to Land*) and 24 February (Torrens's *Essay on the External Corn Trade*).

The concurrent publication of these five essays is often cited as a major example of simultaneous discovery in economic theory. They all share the differential (sometimes also, improperly, called 'Ricardian') theory of rent – both in its extensive and (with the exception of Torrens) in its intensive version – and the so-called Law of diminishing returns to land cultivation. The former has been taken as the source of the 'marginal principle' in the theory of production and income distribution, as applied to *all* factors of production, and not only to land. The latter is one of those (controversial) ideas that have influenced economic theory ever since.

2.   No coincidence

In spite of first appearance, it is not difficult to realize that the publication of these five essays in those three weeks was not due to chance. As all Authors explicitly say, their pamphlets were published in anticipation of, and as a contribution to, the discussion on the Corn Bill, which was before the House of Commons. The Parliamentary debate was tabled to begin on 17 February 17; the new Corn Law was actually passed on 15 March 15.

There can be few doubts on the crucial relevance of the trade of corn – a major item in food consumption of the working class – in the second decade of the eighteenth century, in a country such as Great Britain, where the Industrial Revolution was under way and population was increasing at an unprecedented rate.

The price of corn, over the previous few decades, had increased enormously (and so had rents), though with substantial fluctuations. To give an idea of the order of magnitude, the *average* price of corn, which was 45s. *per* Winchester quarter in the 1770s, rose to 82s. in the 1800–9 decade; it peaked to the range of 150s. in 1812! But in 1813, owing to a huge harvest, it fell dramatically to the range of 70s.; it continued to fall in 1814, owing to expectations of the consequences of the end of the war[1]. Quite understandably the landlords were alarmed, and they were crying out for import protection.

In the previous years, the high price of corn (and the increased rents) had rendered the landlords an unpopular class. Both the House of Commons and the House of Lords had appointed Select Committees to investigate on the problem of the high price of corn. Their Reports were before Parliament and had become the subject of heated discussions.

All five of the essays mentioned here were part of that debate. Their authors admitted great haste and apologized for imperfections of exposition, due to the necessity of quick publication. Malthus even added a preliminary advertise-ment (to his first pamphlet) warning the readers that events 'have induced me to hasten its appearance. It is the duty of those who have any means of contributing to the public stock of knowledge not only to do so, but to do it at the time when it is most likely to be useful' (Malthus, 1815a, p. i). Even Torrens, who was publishing a book of 350 pages, which must have been in progress for some time, expressed in his preface 'the hope of contributing something to the right decision of a question ... which has come before the legislature'; adding that 'the vital interest of the whole community, rendered him not unwilling to depart from ... his original design and to conjoin controversial detail with general disquisition' (Torrens, 1815, p. XV).

West began by saying that he had been 'reading lately the reports of the corn committees', and that 'a correct understanding ... of the corn question ha[s] induced [him] to hazard this publication before the meeting of Parliament' (West, 1815, p.1). We know that Ricardo, on his part, made a great effort, given his confessed strong difficulties in expressing himself in writing, to bring out his essay in time. He wrote it as a reply to, and in open polemics with, Malthus, hoping to bring support to the cause of unconditional free trade (in opposition to Malthus's qualified recommendation for protection).

There was therefore no coincidental discovery, but a determined effort on the part of all the authors to partake in the ongoing discussions, with the aim at influencing a Parliamentary decision reputed to be of great importance to the nation.

3.   The beginning of Ricardian economics

Imminence of an important Parliamentary debate thus explains publication of those five essays in February 1815. Simultaneous *publication*, however, does *not* necessarily imply any sudden discovery. Their authors had been

---

[1] These data are taken from Cannan (1903, pp. 148–50). A more recent reconstruction by Mitchell (1962) differs in details, but shows the same sort of huge fluctuations. Mitchell gives the Winchester peak price at 148.50s. *per* Winchester quarter in the year 1800 (Mitchell, 1962, p. 487).

thinking about the problems under discussion for some time – perhaps for many years. Malthus – certainly a most authoritative writer – thought it expedient to convey his arguments in two separate pamphlets. The first one (*Inquiry on Rent*) is a typically academic essay – all centred on presenting a *theory* of rent. He says explicitly that he is using notes that had been the basis of his lectures at East India College. In the essay, the theory of rent is the central subject, while the idea of diminishing returns enters as a consequence of a dynamic application of the theory of rent to a situation in which land is given and population is growing. The second pamphlet, on the other hand, is an open statement of policy. Malthus resumes arguments given in a previous pamphlet of his, published in spring 1814 ('Observations on the Effects of the Corn Laws ... '), and states openly where he stands, giving his 'grounds of an opinion' in favour of a partial restriction on the import-ation of corn.

By contrast, West's pamphlet is all centred on the *Law of diminishing returns*: 'a principle of political economy ... which occurred to me some years ago', and which he found 'confirmed by many of the witnesses ... on reading lately the reports of the corn committees' (West, 1815, p. 1). In a fifty-five-page essay, the differential theory of rent only comes in the last seven pages. The exposition of the theory of rent is clear, but the focus of the essay is on diminishing returns. Sraffa (1954, p. 6) states that West's presentation of the theory of rent was independent of Malthus's. Yet, it does not seem inconceiv-able to me – West's essay being published ten days after Malthus's widely publicized *Inquiry on Rent* – that the last seven pages on rent might have been added at the last moment, after reading Malthus's essay, at the end of an almost-ready pamphlet basically devoted to diminishing returns.

It is also conceivable that something similar might have happened with Torrens's essay, where a differential theory of rent, in the extensive version only (as he considers, in succession, first-rate quality land, second-rate quality land, third-rate quality land, etc.) only appears in the last chapter (pp. 315–25 of Torrens, 1815).

The case of Ricardo' paper is less uncertain. He was, in a sense, a novice to economic theory discussions; he had mainly been a businessman. Up to 1813, his letters and writing had been concerned with currency questions. But in 1813 and 1814 he had passionately begun to apply his mind to the relation between the growth of capital and the rate of profits. It is in this connection, i.e. with reference, and *only* with reference, to profits that he had been applying the principle of diminishing returns to land cultivation. Sraffa (1954, p. 7) is convinced that, in this form, he had applied the principle as early as 1810 or 1811 (in his *Notes on Bentham*). Rent, however, had not entered his elabor-ations before February 1815. Quite clearly, when he read Malthus's *Inquiry on Rent*, he must have been, so to speak, struck by light. He read both Malthus's essays voraciously – according to Sraffa's reconstruction (Sraffa, 1954, p. 5), by 6 February and 13 February respectively. One can imagine how Ricardo could see all parts of his work over the previous years at last coming into place. The differential theory of rent must have appeared to him as the final missing piece that he needed to complete his mental model.

He read the other papers too, but *after* the publication of his essay (West's by 9 March and Torrens's by 14 March, according to Sraffa's reconstruction; see Sraffa, 1954, p. 5). In them he found only confirmation of his ideas. As the whole picture had, so to speak, clicked together in his mind, he openly acknowledged Malthus's contribution on rent. (When, later, he read West's, he also added West to Malthus as deserving recognition of priority on the theory of rent – see the preface to his *Principles*; Ricardo, 1817.)[2]

Reading all these essays at a distance of almost two centuries, it strikes me as remarkable how Ricardo's essay is decisively towering over all the others. Malthus's essays are very ably laid out and finely argued, but they are concentrated on rent. West's and Torrens's essays are competent arguments on the issues at stake; yet in their concern on diminishing returns and on the corn trade they are clearly dated. Ricardo's essay is quite different. It really is remarkable for the completeness of the theoretical framework on the basis of which he carries out his arguments. Ricardo begins with rent straightaway and links it up with profits; he continues with growth of population and capital, and links them up with diminishing returns. He really is able to bring together all the pieces one by one, in a remarkably complete, logically consistent theoretical scheme, in which the various elements appear as coherent parts of a whole scheme of a working economy. Though the details were to become much clearer only two years later in his *Principles* (Ricardo, 1817), one can see here already a theory of production, a theory of income distribution, a theory of relative prices (agriculture versus manufactures) and most of all a dynamic theory concerning the movement through time of a capitalist economy.[3]

It is this remarkably complete model that leads him to the sad conviction of a tendency towards a stationary state. And it is this eventuality that leads him to argue very powerfully and passionately for free external trade of corn, as the way to avoid an otherwise gloomy course of events in which growth of

---

[2] This was not enough to satisfy West, who – after Ricardo's death – made strong claims for himself, mainly with reference to the law of diminishing returns (see his 'Introduction' in West, 1826). 'His evident resentment against Ricardo was probably unjustified', Schumpeter writes (1954, p. 476). Cannan is even severer with West's complaint, which he considers 'quite unfounded' (Cannan, 1903, p. 280).

[3] The richness of Ricardo's framework is so remarkable as to have stimulated many modern economists to shape it in the form of a rigorous mathematical model. I myself gave a formulation of it in my *Mathematical Formulation of the Ricardian System* (Pasinetti, 1960). The reader may look at this mathematical formulation, a simplified two-commodity version, as an aid to interpret Ricardo's 1815 essay.

population, increase of rent, fall of the rate profits, and compression of wages towards subsistence would only lead, in the long run, to the misery of a stationary state.

The importance of Ricardo's essay is unquestionable. It was the beginning of an intense correspondence with contemporary economists who urged him to be more exhaustive; he responded by putting to task all the energies he had available. From the intention of writing a second edition of this essay sprang his major work, the *Principles of Political Economy and Taxation* (Ricardo, 1817).

That 1815 essay was the beginning of Ricardian economics.

4.   Impact on economic theory

But quite apart from the beginning of Ricardian economics, which was an event on its own, there can be no doubt that the impact of those five essays on the development of political economy was enormous.

Ever since, the differential theory of rent has remained a milestone in the history of economic analysis. Adam Smith had been confused, and even contradictory, on the subject of rent. By 1815, all influential scholars became convinced that political economy had at last been enriched by a solid theory of rent. No longer did rent appear as a sort of 'monopoly price', as Adam Smith had called it, but a necessary technological consequence of the fact that high-quality land is scarce, and in general that the given natural resources, for sheer technological reasons, yield different productivities and thus differential gains.

It must be pointed out, however, that this theory of rent was not original. James Anderson, in his work *Enquiry into the nature of the Corn Laws with a view to the new Corn Bill proposed for Scotland*, published in 1777, had anticipated it, and very clearly so.

His famous passages have been reprinted in many places: for example, in McCulloch's edition of the *Wealth of Nation* (McCulloch, 1828, p. 45) and in Cannan (1903, pp. 371–2). They are too long to be reproduced here; of interest to readers, however, may be yet another passage of his on rent, from another of his work: *Observations on the means of exciting a spirit of National Industry*, also published in 1777:

In every country there are various soils, which are endued with different degrees of fertility; and hence it must happen that the farmer who cultivates the most fertile of these can afford to bring his corn to market at a much lower price than others who cultivate poorer fields. But if the corn that grows on these fertile spots is not sufficient fully to supply the market alone, the price will naturally be raised in that market to such a height as to indemnify others for the expense of cultivating poorer soils. The farmer, however, who cultivates the rich spots will be able to sell his corn at the same rate in the market with those who occupy poorer fields; he will, therefore, receive much more than the *intrinsic* value for the corn he rears. Many persons will, therefore, be desirous of obtaining possession of these fertile fields, and will be content to give a certain premium for an exclusive privilege to cultivate them; which will be greater or smaller according to the more or less fertility of the soil. It is this premium which constitutes what we now call *rent*, a medium by means of which the expense of cultivating soils of very different degrees of fertility may be reduced to a perfect equality. (Anderson, 1777a, p. 376)

It is interesting to note that this passage was part of a criticism in which Anderson implicated Adam Smith. Yet he did not explicitly point out that Smith was incorrect, and Smith (who must have seen Anderson's criticism, as Cannan points out – see Cannan, 1903 p. 221) did not correct his theory. James Anderson's remarkable theory was thus simply (and sadly) missed.

The differential theory of rent remained dormant, only to be re-discovered and hailed as a great contribution in 1815, when it was presented in conjunction with the Law of diminishing returns.

An important point to stress is that James Anderson had always been a strong opponent of the idea of diminishing returns to cultivation of land. His opposition was not based on any abstract reasoning; it came from personal experience: he was a farmer and an experienced agriculturist. As all farmers, he was in favour of protection, but on the basis of an unusual argument. He thought that protection would indeed force inferior lands into cultivation, but these inferior lands would eventually be made as productive as the other (originally more fertile) lands. He was a strong believer in agricultural progress and indefinite increasing returns. The point is worth mentioning as it shows, incidentally, that the differential theory of rent and the Law of diminishing returns are quite separate theories and do not imply each other.

When Malthus published his *Essay on the Principle of Population* (1798), James Anderson was among his strongest critics (see Anderson, 1801). Malthus had presented his *Principle of Population* on the rather weak theoretical ground that there is an inconsistency between a natural 'geometric' progression of population growth and a factual 'arithmetical' progression of the means of subsistence. It was precisely in replying to Anderson's criticisms, in the 2nd edition of his *Principle of Population* (1803) as Edwin Cannan (1903, p. 146) points out, that Malthus developed, in a rather casual way, an argument that implied the principle of diminishing returns, but applied in reverse.[4] It took some time before the idea dawned clearly in his mind.

The same must have happened to West, Torrens and Ricardo, though at various stages, before 1815.

---

[4] See Malthus (1803, 2nd ed., p. 472). Malthus considers the case of an accidental de-population, quite logically remarking that, in such an event, cultivation would be abandoned on the least fertile lands.

In any case, it is only with the publication of the five essays in February 1815 that the Law of diminishing returns to land cultivation becomes a clear, explicitly stated principle of political economy.

Again we might ask: why in February 1815?

It was stated earlier that the five pamphlets were all published in February 1815 in order to contribute to, and to influence, a decision that was about to be taken by the House of Commons. Now we can look at the other side of the coin. All authors had read, very carefully, the Reports of the Committees of Inquiry on the corn question. From these Reports, one can see very clearly what had happened in England in the previous decades. The Industrial Revolution had been associated with an unprecedented growth of population (in fact, *more* than in 'geometric' progression). This, coupled with the Napoleonic wars and the inevitable difficulties of importation of corn, had caused a rapid increase of demand for food, which had led to expansion of agricultural production, through the passing of a succession of 'enclosure acts', in order to extend cultivation to formerly uncultivated lands. The obvious consequences had been a higher price of corn and higher rents.

To see 'diminishing' returns in this process was simply a rationalization of factual historical events: actually of a historical circumstance, which was characteristically typical of a specific country (England) and of a specific period of time (late eighteenth and early nineteenth centuries).

Incidentally, but very significantly, it must also be noticed that, from a purely analytical point of view, the principle of diminishing returns suited Malthus's theory of population very nicely.

In the place of the earlier weaker arguments on 'geometric' versus 'arithmetic' progressions, a scientific principle could be presented, which allowed Malthus to assert that, as the number of people increase, it is true that 'a pair of hands comes with every mouth', but while the new mouths require as much food as the old, the new hands produce less and less. Ricardo, on his part, turned this into a powerful argument against protection. Free trade of corn would stop extension of cultivation to less productive lands and hence divert production potential to manufactures, where all agreed that diminishing returns would not apply.

Factual historical evidence and analytical convenience seemed to go hand in hand.

The differential theory of rent – which had been ignored as long as it had been proposed (by James Anderson) within a static framework – became a powerful analytical tool when it was applied in a dynamic scheme, in which extension of cultivation of land is coupled with diminishing returns to scale. For the emerging science of political economy this marked a turning point.

5.   The 'Law' (or pseudo-Law?) of diminishing returns

But how accurate, or how reliable, or how meaningful is a 'Law' of diminishing returns?

One has a pretty good idea of what is meant by a 'law' in physics. The 'law of gravitation', for example, is a universal law expressed by a formula that describes how bodies fall in ideal conditions of no attrition. On the 'Law of diminishing returns', however, no one would say that it expresses in any way any 'ideal' condition. It rather expresses how an economy moves in *hypothetical* conditions. The hypothesis is that technology does not change, or changes at a speed that is insufficient to prevent a fall of productivity as production is expanded.

In fact, not one of the authors we are considering asserts that diminishing returns represent a universal principle. To begin with, they present it *only* for agricultural production. This is an important point. They all imply that, in manufacturing production, the opposite is the case, namely that productivity is increasing. Moreover, they admit that technical progress goes on in agriculture as well, but not at a sufficient speed.

Ricardo, in his essay, is the most logically consistent of all. He is always very careful in *not* denying that 'improvements might take place in agriculture' (1815, p. 11); however, at the same time he is convinced that they would not proceed at a sufficiently speedy pace. Therefore (quite remarkably from an analytical point of view), he explicitly says that, for clarity, he leaves them aside. He cuts short all hesitations: 'We will, however, suppose that no improvements take place in agriculture, and that capital and population advance in the proper proportion' (1815, p. 6). In this way, absence of technical progress in agriculture becomes an explicit *assumption*. Once this assumption is granted, even the simple two-commodity version of Ricardo's model (with an agricultural good and a manufactured good) is by itself sufficient[5] to show how all of Ricardo's conclusions logically follow, as 'capital and population advance in the proper proportions'. He obtains in logical succession: lower-fertility lands brought into cultivation, higher rents, lower rate of profits, higher price of corn, movement towards the gloomy conditions of a stationary state, with wages compressed at subsistence, profits at their minimum, rents at their highest. And he concludes:

It follows then, that the interest of the landlord is always opposed to the interest of every other class of the community ... High rents and low profits, for they invariably accompany each other, ought never to be the subject of complaint, if they are the effect of the natural course of things. (Ricardo, 1815, p. 20)

---

[5] This can be seen clearly in Pasinetti (1960).

The relevant point to note is that technical progress in manufactures, *however pronounced it may be*, does not make the slightest difference to Ricardo's conclusions. For, it is the process of production of the agricultural good that acts as a bottleneck.

The way out, for Ricardo, is free external trade. If corn is imported, the country will specialize in manufactures, and the process of diminishing returns (as it only affects agriculture) will be brought to a halt!

The argument is incontrovertible; but it stands on the crucial *hypothesis* of no (or in any case insufficient) technical progress in agriculture.

This can hardly be said to be a 'universal law'. In spite of what some interested witnesses might have said in their testimonials at the Corn Committees, many – and James Anderson was one of them – would claim that it was not even the case in England at that time. Cannan (1903, p. 152) remarks that diminishing returns can be seen as denied even in statements of the Chairman of the Committee (Sir Henry Parnell).

Unlike the theory of rent, the Law of diminishing returns in agriculture did not meet general acceptance, even at the time it was presented.

Notable examples of strong critique are those by Thomas Chalmers, in England, and by H. C. Carey (1837), in the United States. Chalmers, in his *Political Economy*, argued at length that 'The doctrine or discovery ... promulgated by Sir Edward West and Mr. Malthus ... that the land of greatest fertility was first occupied ... is not accordant with historical truth' (Chalmers, 1832, chap. I, 2–6). Carey on his turn, in his *Political Economy* (1837), insisted on pointing out that *precisely* the way in which the Law of diminishing returns was illustrated by both West and Ricardo, namely by the process of starting cultivation on the most fertile land in a newly settled country, was contradicted by historical facts. Certainly that was *not* the way in which things happened in the United States.

Yet, in spite of criticism and opposition, the Law of diminishing returns immediately became one of the cornerstones of nineteenth century mainstream political economy. James Mill, in his *Elements of Political Economy* (1821) immediately expounds the Law of diminishing returns as a general rule, without even mentioning the possibility of new discoveries or improvements. And when his son, John Stuart Mill, wrote what came to be considered the synthesis of classical theory – his *Principles of Political Economy* (1848) – he presented the 'Law' in a chapter headed 'Of the Law of the Increase of Production from Land', warning that 'This general law of agricultural industry is the most important proposition in political economy. Were the law different, nearly all the phenomena of the production and distribution of wealth would be other than they are' (Mill, 1848, 1st edn, vol. I, p. 212). But John Stuart Mill must have felt uneasy, and not at all on solid ground, as is proved by the fact that he kept on modifying his presentation of the 'Law' in the successive editions of his *Principles*. In examining the succession of John Stuart Mill's many qualifications, Edwin Cannan points out that Mill ends up by admitting a surprisingly high number of exceptions. Cannan concludes:

we should be at a loss to conceive why Mill should be at the trouble of developing a law which: 1) does not operate in the very early date of the history of society; 2) is liable to temporary supersessions; 3) has been made head against by an antagonizing principle, namely the progress of civilization, throughout the whole known history of England (Cannan, 1903, p. 177).

But what kind of 'Law' can this be? No wonder Cannan ends up by calling it 'The pseudo-scientific law of diminishing returns' (p. 181), pointing out that it is based on 'pseudo-historical characteristics' (Cannan, 1903 p. 175).

Yet it became generally accepted. The effect of it all was to generate unjustified pessimism on the future of industrial economies.

Interestingly enough, this unjustified pessimism, which characterized the political economy that came out of the Malthus–West–Torrens–Ricardo essays, was perhaps better perceived by external observers rather than by the internal practitioners of the new science.[6] Thomas Carlyle, the Scottish poet and writer, was quick in noticing a contrast between the actual possibilities of progress and the gloomy conclusions of the economists. His epithet, defining political economy as the 'dismal science', has become famous.

6. Extensions of the theory of rent and their crucial consequences

The idea that technical improvements would not be strong enough to win the terrible curse of the scarcity of natural resources, and in particular of land, shaped the minds of economists for the whole of the nineteenth century.

Even Marx, the theorist of historical change, was not able to escape from such an idea. Unlike all classical economists, he (unconvincingly) rejected the differential theory of rent, mixing up rent and profits, and considering them all as being parts of surplus value and exploitation. In so doing, however, he fell into the trap of applying diminishing returns to capitalistic accumulation in general, and not only – as the classical economists had done – as a consequence of extension of cultivation of land. The Law of diminishing returns was thus transformed into a 'law of the falling rate or profits' *tout court*, which turned out to be one of his major blunders.

One might say that, most significantly in this respect, the marginalist economists, at the end of the nineteenth century, ended up falling exactly into

---

[6] Later on, among historians of economic thought, Schumpeter was perhaps the most perspicacious of all in pointing it out, though in the middle of many other hints in various directions (Schumpeter, 1954, pp. 570–4).

the same trap. They converted the 'marginal principle', *which the classical economists had applied to land only*, into a *general principle*, to be applied to *all* factors of production.

This is something that the classical economists would never have done. In their elaborations – as is evinced most clearly by Ricardo's scheme – the differential theory of rent served the purpose of *separating* the effects of extension of production on land (where diminishing returns were supposed to prevail) from those of extension of production in manufactures (where constant or increasing returns were taken for granted). By extending the marginal principle outside the processes of land cultivation, the marginalist economists automatically and imperceptively carried *beyond* such processes precisely those characteristics that the classical economists had carefully confined to land.

The consequences of this diversion from classical economics were of paramount importance. As the process of industrialization, in the second part of the nineteenth century, began to spread from England to Western Europe and to the United States, the emphasis of economic theory was bound to shift from agricultural production to industrial production. Capital accumulation, rather than extension of land cultivation, became the central subject of economic investigation. It should have needed specifically invented tools of analysis, suited for its particular characteristics; it underwent instead an extension of analytical tools that had been invented for land cultivation.

Böhm-Bawerk, the principal mainstream theorist of capital, conceived capital accumulation as an increase in the 'roundabout methods' of production, which he tried to express in terms of an increase of the 'average period' of production. It should be noted that, in this version, the marginal principle and the principle of diminishing returns became undistinguishable parts of the same conception.

This put into motion a series of *analytical* adaptations, which proceeded from two opposite sides. On the one side, the principle of marginal land had to be shaped in such a way as to suit the characteristics of all other factors of production, which led to the application of the marginal principle *only* in its intensive version. The principle of diminishing returns was thereby shaped in the form of diminishing returns to changing proportions, associated with variations in the opposite direction, of the factor prices (the growth of capital with respect to labour causing a fall of the rate of profits). This was interpreted as the process of *substitution* of capital for labour – indeed an important process but very peculiarly presented at a *constant* state of technical knowledge. On the other side, a series of *assumptions* were introduced in order to assimilate the characteristics of all factors of production (and, most of all, of capital) to the characteristics of land.

Knut Wicksell, adding rigour to Böhm-Bawerk's theory of capital, enshrined the relation among the factors of production in what later became known as the 'neoclassical production function', in which all factors enter production on exactly the same footing. This conception of production, which has dominated economic theory up to our own days, required an *analytical* (not a factual) distinction between two types of changes of returns: i) changes due to variation of the *scale* of production, at constant factor proportions; and ii) changes due to variations of the *proportions* among the factors of production (supposed to represent the process of substitution of capital for labour).

In theory, the first process of variations might yield constant, decreasing or increasing returns, but in general increasing returns have been excluded, by *assumption*. The second process of variations had to be conceived as going opposite to changes in factor prices, again, by assumption, as convexity of the production function is – *not* an observed fact – but a necessity of the theory.

The theory of income distribution was associated – without any explicit justification – *only* with the second process of variations (i.e. with the variations of the factor proportions).

It sounds in fact extraordinary that the theory of production should have proceeded on such important questions simply by an analytical process of, bit by bit, extension, and of assumptions, introduced on the basis of convenience, *not* on the basis of observation or logic!

This analytical process has proceeded a long way indeed, in spite of it going, quite clearly, against what Malthus, West, Torrens and Ricardo intended at the beginning. It was no doubt strongly favoured and propitiated by the parallel development of the notion of marginal utility in the theory of consumption.[7]

Now and then, there have indeed been oppositions to such extensions, but they have not been successful within the profession of economists. In the 1960s, a controversy on capital theory flared up, at the end of which everybody had to agree that the assumption of diminishing returns to changing proportions, when applied to capital and labour, has no logical foundation. In general, there exists no monotonic association between variations of the *proportions* of capital to labour (or of capital to land or to any non-produced factor of production) and the rate of profits. The implication is that the *extension* of the marginal principle of income distribution to *capital* and labour (or to capital and land) has no logical foundation. More in general, and more specifically, the assumption of a general 'well-behaved' (as it has been called) production function is totally unwarranted. (See Pasinetti *et al.*, 1966.)

---

[7] It may well remain an open question whether the generalization of the marginal principle was mainly due to extension of the theory of rent in production theory or to the development of the notion of marginal utility in the theory of consumption. There is in any case no doubt that the two developments reinforced each other.

What is indeed surprising is that uncritical acceptance of diminishing returns to changing proportions as applied to capital remains very widespread. The results of the 1966 discussions on capital theory are generally ignored. In most of the economics textbooks and in most of the papers appearing in what are today's reputed and prestigious economic journals, mainstream economists are freely using production functions involving Labour and Capital with decreasing returns to changing proportions, apparently without the slightest doubt as to their appropriateness, and most of the time even without giving the slightest warning or information on previous criticisms and discussions.

Of all this – it must be stressed – the authors of the five 1815 essays in political economy are entirely innocent.

7.   Technical progress versus limited natural resources

Ricardo could never have imagined that an innocent *assumption* ('We will, however, suppose that no improvements take place in agriculture . . .', Ricardo, 1815, p. 6), that so well served him in the analytical purpose of isolating the field of diminishing returns (agriculture) from that of constant or increasing returns (manufacturing), would generate such long-term effects. His assumption was meant to be confined to production on land. Obviously he could not anticipate, even less prevent, the use that later economists would make of it.

Once the assumption of no technical progress was extended to production in general, the effect was that, with the exception of a few isolated cases, technical change disappeared from economic analysis for more than a century.

Only in the post–World War II period have economists rediscovered the relevance of technical progress and have begun to reintroduce it, at first timidly then with force, into economic investigations. But re-introducing technical change, after a century and a half of economic analysis based on the assumption of a stationary technology, has not proved to be easy at all.

The re-discovery of technical progress effectively began with Roy Harrod's (1948) very simple device of considering a rate of productivity growth, side by side to the rate of population growth, in his macro-economic model. But Harrod's simple device could not be taken as proposed. When empirical research created a shock by revealing that almost all the growth of production per man that had taken place in the first half of the twentieth century was due to a 'residual', i.e. to something that had not been considered and which could not be but technical change, the response was *not* an adaptation of economic analysis to such newly discovered and astonishing evidence, but further *assumptions* about how the facts would have to be in order to fit them into the pre-conceived theoretical scheme. The conception of capital accumulation, based on the distinction between changes of scale at constant returns and changes of factor proportions, was not modified. Instead, a *third* element of change was superimposed on the others, in the form of a 'shift' through time of the production function.[8] The arbitrary nature of the resulting tripartition was never put into question, in spite of it not even being exhaustive; so much so that, in the latest versions of neoclassical 'new growth models', also increasing returns are introduced, with the consequence of having to appeal to imperfect competition in order to make the model logically consistent.

Nevertheless, one must acknowledge that, at last, an enormous outburst of economic research concerning technical progress (in many of its aspects: inventions, innovations, diffusion of knowledge, etc.) has taken shape in the last few decades. Economists seem at last to have woken up to the necessity and importance of investigating the effects of technical change – under an impulse that has mainly come from outside, and most of the time against, mainstream economics.

The situation is quite puzzling. According to logic, one should expect that the investigation of the economic consequences of technical progress be carried out with reference to the characteristics and specificities of the phenomenon to be investigated, namely *technical change*, without of course precluding the possibility of resuming, at the appropriate place, the other sources of production and of growth. In practice, within the framework of mainstream economics, this has been revealed to be something very difficult to achieve.

Is there, perhaps, something else, or further, that may be learnt from the authors of the 1815 pamphlets?

Let me note that they clearly perceived two important features of the problem they faced. First of all, they realized that, with a growing population, the economic future of humankind would be decided by the prevalence of one of two opposing trends: the improvements of technology and the increasing limitations and constraints of Nature. Secondly, they perceived (an aspect that can be seen extraordinarily well in Ricardo) that, for analytical reasons, they had to make a choice and concentrate on one of the two trends, hopefully the most important one.

By dramatic under-estimation, they made the wrong choice.

---

[8] The standard reference is Solow (1957), who estimated that the change of productivity in the US economy, 1909–49, was due 87.5% to the 'residual', re-interpreted as a 'shift' of the production function, and 12.5% to increased proportion of capital to labour (i.e., increased capital intensity). I was the first to criticize strongly these results (Pasinetti, 1959), pointing out how arbitrary the assumptions were behind the various distinctions. More specifically and very simply, I pointed out that, by using the same data used by Solow, from 1909 to 1949, the capital-output ratio in the US economy decreased from 2.75 to 2.20. Hence, in that period, capital intensity *decreased*, not increased as Solow's model implied.

Yet, the following economists did not correct them; on the contrary they exasperated the effects of that choice, effectively ending up with changing the original content of economics itself. From a science that inquires into the nature and causes of the wealth of nations, as it was intended by the Classics, they made it (as Lionel Robbins, 1932, could conclude a century later) a science that deals with the use of scarce means to achieve given ends.

Nobody can obviously deny that, in taking advantage of our increasing technological knowledge for the production of the wealth in our time, we face today, as no less than two centuries ago, the task of how to allocate with efficiency and judiciousness and according to our choices (individual and social), the natural resources that we have inherited, at the same time preserving the environment that our marvelous planet is endowed with. But *increasing* technical knowledge implies that – even with given natural resources – the *constraints and limitations are not given*: they are moving all the time!

A kind of contrast and opposition seem to have emerged. Super-imposing now an economics that deals with an evolving technology, on top of a solidly pre-established, pre-developed economics that deals with the characteristics of an efficient management of scarce resources at a given technology, seems to reveal a sort of profound difficulty. Assumptions become necessary more in order to eliminate contradictions than in order to facilitate investigation.

In such a situation, the 1815 essays in political economy prompt a challenging thought.

Why not go back to where Malthus, West, Torrens, and Ricardo began, and radically change their starting hypothesis? If history has revealed that their original choice was mistaken, the obvious course to take would seem to be to reverse that choice. Granted that *analytical* reasons impose, as they realized, that we should focus, *at least at the beginning*, on only one of the two trends, we may well begin by developing a political economy based on progress of technical knowledge alone,[9] rather than, as has happened, on scarcity of given resources alone.

Once the most important factor (technical change) behind the wealth of nations has been appropriately investigated as such, without the risk of stifling the efforts with possibly contradictory features imposed by other, pre-shaped, frameworks of analysis, it may well turn out to be easier, at a later stage of investigation, to introduce the integrations and complications connected with the limitations of Nature, rather than insisting on a course of analysis that has done the opposite so far – with many complications and little reward.

---

[9] This proposal is not made in the abstract. To provide a complete model in which the increases of production are entirely due to growth of labour productivity and the variations in output proportions are due to individuals' and social choices in consumption patterns is indeed possible. I showed it myself at the time I was writing the present chapter (see Pasinetti, 1993).

REFERENCES

The five pamphlets at the origin of the theory of rent:

Malthus, T. R. (1815a) *An Inquiry into The Nature and Progress of Rent and the Principles by Which it is Regulated*, London: John Murray.
  (1815b) *The Grounds of an Opinion on the Policy of Restricting the Importation of Foreign Corn*, London: John Murray.
Ricardo, D. (1815) *An Essay on The Influence of a Low Price of Corn on the Profits of Stock*, London: John Murray.
Torrens, R. (1815) *An Essay on the External Corn Trade*; London: J. Hatchard.
West, E. (1815) *Essay on the Application of Capital to Land*, *London*: T. Underwood.

Other References

Anderson, J. (1777a) *Observations on the Means of Exciting a Spirit of National Industry; Chiefly Intended to Promote the Agriculture, Commerce, Manufactures and Fisheries of Scotland*, Edinburgh: T. Cadell-C.Elliot.
  (1777b) *An Enquiry into the Nature of the Corn Laws, with a View to the New Corn Bill Proposed for Scotland*, Edinburgh: Mundell.
  (1801) *A Calm Investigation of the Circumstances That Have Led to the Present Scarcity of Grain in Britain, Suggesting the Means of Alleviating the Evil and of Preventing the Recurrence of Such a Calamity in the Future*, London: John Cumming.
Cannan, E. (1903) *A History of the Theories of Production and Distribution in English Political Economy from 1776 to 1848*, 2nd edn, London: P. S. King & Son.
Carey, H. C. (1837–1840) *Principles of Political Economy*, 3 vols., Philadelphia: Carey.
Chalmers, T. (1832) *On Political Economy in Connexion with the Moral State and Moral Prospects of Society*, Glasgow: William Collins.
Harrod, R. F. (1948) *Towards a Dynamic Economics*, London: Macmillan.
Malthus, T. R. (1798) *An Essay on the Principle of Population*, London: J. Johnson (2nd edn 1803).
  (1814) *Observation on the Effects of the Corn Laws, and of a Rise or Fall in the Price of Corn on the Agriculture and General Wealth of the Country*, London: J. Johnson and Co.
McCulloch, J. R. (1828) as editor, of A. Smith, *An Inquiry into the Nature and Causes of the Wealth of Nations*, 4 vols., London-Edinburg: Adam Black.
Mill, J. S. (1821) *Elements of Political Economy*, London: Baldwin.
  (1848) *Principles of Political Economy, with Some of Their Applications to Social Philosophy*, London: John W. Parker.
Mitchell, B. R. (1962) with the collaboration of Phyllis Deane, *Abstract of British Historical Statistics*, Cambridge: Cambridge University Press.
Pasinetti, L. L. (1959) 'On Concepts and Measures of Changes in Productivity', *The Review of Economics and Statistics*, 41.3, pp. 270–82.
  (1960) 'A Mathematical Formulation of the Ricardian System', *The Review of Economic Studies*, 27.2, pp. 78–98.
  (1993) *Structural Economic Dynamics: A Theory of the Economic Consequences of Human Learning*, Cambridge: Cambridge University Press.

(1996) 'Das Vermächtnis der politisch ökonomischen Pamphlete von 1815' in
  B. Schefold (ed.) *Vademecum zu den Klassikern der Differentialrenten Theorie –
  Die «Corn-Law Pamphlets» von 1815*, Düsseldorf: Verlag Wirtschaft und
  Finanzen GMBH ein Unternehmen der Verlagsgruppe Handelsblatt, pp. 41–62.

(1999) 'Economic Theory and Technical Progress' (given as the *Economic Issues*
  Lecture to the Royal Economic Society Annual Conference, Nottingham, England,
  31 March 1999), *Economic Issues*, 4.2, pp. 1–18.

(2000) 'Critique of the Neoclassical Theory of Growth and Distribution', *B.N.L.
  Quarterly Review*, 53.215, pp. 383–431.

Pasinetti, L. L. *et al.* (1966) 'Paradoxes in Capital Theory: A Symposium', ed. by P.A.
  Samuelson, *The Quarterly Journal of Economics*, 80.4, pp. 503–17.

Ricardo, D. (1817) *On the Principles of Political Economy and Taxation*, London: John
  Murray.

Robbins, L. (1932) *An Essay on the Nature and Significance of Economic Science*,
  London: Macmillan.

Schumpeter, J. A. (1954) *History of Economic Analysis*, New York: Oxford University
  Press.

Solow, R. M. (1957) 'Technical Change and the Aggregate Production Function',
  Review of Economics and Statistics, 39.3, pp. 312–20.

(2000) 'The Neoclassical Theory of Growth and Distribution', *B.N.L. Quarterly
  Review*, 53.215, pp. 349–81.

Sraffa, P. (1954) 'Note on "Essay on Profits"', in *The Works Correspondence of David
  Ricardo'*; ed. by P. Sraffa with the collaboration of M.H. Dobb, vol. IV, *Pamphlets
  and Papers 1815–1823*, Cambridge: Cambridge University Press, pp. 3–8.

West, E. (1826) *Price of Corn and Wages of Labour, with Observations upon
  Mr. Smith's, Mr. Ricardo's and Mr. Malthus's Doctrines*, London: J. Hatchard
  and Son.

3   The political economy of corn markets

D'Maris Dalton Coffman

1.   Introduction

Despite the efforts of organizations such as the Institute for Fiscal Studies, many current public debates about taxation are conducted without a sufficient empirical base. The participants are, rather, motivated by ideology – reasoning from theoretical principles – while advancing claims about the presumptive distributional effects of a particular tax. By contrast, eighteenth-century moral philosophy and nineteenth-century political economy self-consciously developed against the backdrop of the British state's growing statistical capacities. Debates about the Corn Laws, for instance, were mediated by a wealth of data generated from the English Corn Returns, which in turn produced improvements in the way the data was handled (Adrian, 1977; Fairlie, 1969; Barnes, 1930; Fay, 1932).

As early as 1685, the British parliament appointed independent inspectors to report at quarter sessions the market prices of 'corn' (which in the English context meant 'grain' in a general sense, including wheat, barley, malt, rye, oats and peas/beans) in the English maritime districts with an eye to adjusting and enforcing the custom duties and bounties on imported foreign grains (Coffman and Ormrod, 2014). From 1770, inspectors were required to report weekly quantities and prices for specified coastal and inland market towns to the official corn commissioners. The prices were, in turn, published in the *London Gazette*. After 1820, the *Gazette* printed quantities as well as prices for up to 290 markets. Eighteenth-century moral philosophers and nineteenth-century political

The author would like to thank the Leverhulme Trust, the Newton Trust, the Centre for Financial History, Newnham College and the History Faculty, University of Cambridge. The Corn Returns Online website was financed by the Institute for New Economic Thinking Grant INO11-00055. The author would like to thank the audience, and especially Professor David Ormrod, Dr Lucy Adrian, Dr Louise Pryor, and Dr Ivano Cardinale, of the workshop, 'The English Corn Returns and the State, 1685–1865', held at Newnham College on 16 March 2013. Some of the factual information about the provenance of the Corn Returns was first published by the author in D'Maris Coffman and David Ormrod, 'Corn Prices, Corn Models and Corn Rents: What can we learn from the English Corn Returns?' in *Money, Prices and Wages: Essays in Honour of Nicholas Mayhew* (co-ed. by Martin Allen and D'Maris Coffman) (Palgrave Macmillan, Palgrave Studies in the History of Finance, 2014). The author would like to thank Palgrave Macmillan for their permission to incorporate this material, where cited, into this chapter, as this is a very different audience.

economists including Adam Smith, Thomas Robert Malthus and David Ricardo used this data to debate with each other about the distributional effects of the corn bounties and Corn Laws (Coffman and Omrod, 2014).

This chapter explores the seminal role of grain markets in economic theory, before examining the structure of English and North American grain markets, the origins and evolution of the Corn Returns, and the use of the Corn Returns in the first 150 years of administration of the Corn Laws; the chapter ends with a consideration of the empiricist impulse within early political economy and with it how certain modes of analysis were brought to bear on contemporary policy debates. In so doing, the chapter simultaneously explores both the purposes to which contemporaries put this data and considers how the Corn Returns might be used by practicing economic historians to answer fundamental questions about the agricultural revolution, the structure of agrarian capitalism, the volatility of English corn prices and harvests, and most importantly about the trade-off between manufacturing and agricultural sectors in the late eighteenth and early nineteenth centuries.

Most twentieth-century price histories, including those produced by William Lord Beveridge for the International Price History Commission, ignored the Corn Returns in favour of institutional records of corn purchases (Beveridge, 1939; Coffman and Omrod, 2014). The author became interested in this material during a short-lived attempt in 2011 to establish a Second International Price History Commission, during which she laterally acquired a grant from the Institute for New Economic Thinking to digitize this material and to make it publicly available in usable form through the *Corn Returns Online*[1]; she was subsequently awarded a Leverhulme/Newton Trust Early Career Fellowship with the aim of exploring the intellectual origins of the agricultural revolution in Britain.

In framing such an analysis, the author is heavily indebted to Alberto Quadrio Curzio's treatment of Ricardian structural dynamics, which nearly thirty years ago he first posited as 'based on the relative scarcity of natural resources on which, nevertheless, technical progress was able to operate' (Quadrio Curzio, 1986, p. 312). The British experience remains the cardinal case of a nation's successful 'adoption of technological innovation that removed or shifted upwards the original constraint,' thereby overcoming severe economic scarcities (Quadrio Curzio and Pellizzari, 1999, p. 4), so much so that it is Britain's example that developing countries consciously attempted to emulate in the twentieth century (Rostow, 1960; Gerschenkron, 1962). How far the primary sector, agriculture, in eighteenth-century Britain can be said to exemplify the 'law of diminishing returns' is essentially an empirical question, which data from the *Corn Returns* can help to answer.

---

[1] See Corn Returns Online (www.cornreturnsonline.org).

In pursuing such a research agenda, the author is collaborating with the Cambridge Group for the History of Population and Social Structure's 'Occupational Structure of Britain 1379–1911' project and especially researchers on their Leverhulme-funded project on 'Transport, Urbanization and Economic Development c.1670–1911,' which maps the growth of canals and railways in England in Wales. Further efforts by Alex Trew at the University of St Andrews to digitize the locations of English country banks and post offices should further enrich the modelling by affording a role for finance.

Without a doubt, the recent revolution in information computing technology (ICT) these last forty years has fundamentally enriched the methodological tools available to quantitative economic and social historians. Freed from the formal modelling assumptions of dynamic stochastic general equilibrium which underpin much of cliometrics or 'New Economic History,' the next generation of quantitative economic and social historical scholarship will be guided by the machine-learning tools that we now associate with 'Big Data' (Coffman and Ormrod, 2014). This is an exciting time to be working in the field, in that it is reminiscent of the late seventeenth-century and early eighteenth-century moment in which the relatively theory-free enquiries of the early 'political arithmeticians' set the stage for 'classic political economy' of the nineteenth century, or of the way in which the self-consciously empirical approaches of early twentieth-century econometrics bequeathed characterizations of market efficiency that came to underpin much of modern mainstream economics. If, in retrospect, the former approach seems more promising than the latter, then it can be hoped that more sophisticated modelling (whether agent-based or sectoral-based) will offer a salutary corrective. Whether or not these approaches live up to their promise, they still have to contend with the structural approach advocated by Alberto Quadrio Curzio's research programme, which highlights the importance of both vertical hierarchies and horizontal interdependencies within domains of consumption and production that remain constrained by the relative scarcity of natural resources (Quadrio Curzio, 1990, 2011).

2.   Grain markets in economics

Productive agricultural land is perhaps the emblematic 'natural endowment' of an economy, a stylized fact accepted as a truism in early modern Europe by those who thought in terms of a medieval demesne state where the Crown and noble lords alike financed their households through rents from their lands (Coffman, 2013, pp. 6–7). In his suggested reforms of the fiscal system, this formulation was promoted by the political arithmetician and early tax theorist William Petty (1662), who had, after all, conducted the Down Survey of Ireland, and who wanted an 'accumulative excise' on the houses of land-owners/tenants and merchants/manufacturers alike. In the French context, the importance of land was elaborated by the physiocrat François Quesnay (1758) in his *Tableau économique*. In Quesnay's model, the land was the source of all 'net product', not because manufacturing did not have a vital economic role, but rather because manufacturers were posited to perform the function of transforming the produce of the land into merchandise for consumption. Such a framework was axiomatic rather than normative, insofar as Quesnay defined 'net product' as the difference between the quantity of corn produced in an economy and the quantity of corn consumed. Quesnay's two-sector model presupposed a stationary economy, as there was no place afforded for accumulation, innovation or growth; Adam Smith, building on Petty, was in an English tradition of economic writers who became interested in questions of accumulation, distribution and dynamics (Quadrio Curzio and Pellizzari, 1999, p. 8; Quadrio Curzio, 2011, pp. 21-22).

With the monetization and commercialization of society in the late medieval and early modern period, the Smithian 'market' became the domain in which these processes occurred (Coffman and Ormrod, 2014). Smith's quasi-historical account of the institutional development of grain markets in his 'Digression Concerning the Corn Trade and Corn Laws' (Smith, [1778] 1976, book iv, ch. v, pp. 524–43) has influenced the views of historians and economists alike (Coffman and Ormrod, 2014). Coffman and Ormrod (2014) argue: 'less attention has been paid to Smith's cogent description of what he regarded as "the ancient policy of Europe" towards the different regulations governing the marketing of the produce of the primary and secondary sectors, which were in the primary sector designed to discourage speculation, while in the secondary one protecting the interests of shopkeepers in towns' (pp. 203–4):

What the manufacturer was prohibited to do [retail his own merchandise], the farmer was in some measure enjoined to do; to divide his capital between two different employments; to keep one part of it in his granaries and stack yard, for supplying the occasional demands of the market; and to employ the other in the cultivation of his land. But as he could not afford to employ the latter for less than the ordinary profits of farming stock, so he could as little afford to employ the former for less than the ordinary profits of mercantile stock. Whether the stock which really carried on the business of the corn merchant belonged to the person who was called a farmer, or to the person who was called a corn merchant, an equal profit was in both cases requisite in order to indemnify its owner for employing it in this manner; in order to put his business upon a level with other trades, and in order to hinder him from having an interest to change it as soon as possible for some other. The farmer, therefore, who was thus forced to exercise the trade of a corn merchant, could not afford to sell his corn cheaper than any other corn merchant would have been obliged to do in the case of a free competition. (Smith [1778] 1976, book iv, ch. v, pp. 529–30; quoted in Coffman and Ormrod, 2014)

In 1776, Adam Smith depicted markets as institutional spaces, but that insight has often been obscured in subsequent accounts of economic development, especially those associated with the Washington Consensus or with modern neoclassical economics. As one recent commentator on the political economy of market regulation in the early twentieth-century America observed, 'conventional explanations of industrialization have begun with an assumption that an unregulated national market existed in the United States, almost as a birthright of national existence. Unregulated national markets, however, are not like iron ore deposits or other natural endowments; they are politically constructed social realities' (Bensel, 2000, p. xxi)[2]. Early nineteenth-century debates about repeal of the Corn Laws, which rested in large part on analysis of data furnished by the Corn Returns, supplied the categories of analysis that made construction of such social realities possible.

By the same token, grain futures by total value of contracts outstanding and total turnover represent a very small fraction of today's global futures trading, nevertheless the 'wheat future' is the paradigmatic contract. Although most economic historians are familiar with the evidence for organized futures trading in Baltic grain in Amsterdam as early as the sixteenth century (van Tielhof, 2002) and with trading in rice futures in Dojima Japan in the seventeenth and eighteenth centuries (Wakita, 2001), economists working on historical commodities markets usually rely on price data from the Chicago Board of Trade because of the high volume and continuous nature of the trading and price registration from the 1850s onwards. Despite the existence of well-organized corn markets in Britain, organized futures trading never developed, but rather hedging was limited to 'curb trading' of informal contracts-for-difference outside corn exchanges or in customized forward contracts between corn merchants (Baker, 1970; Thirsk, 1985).

By the early twentieth century, North American commodities markets were highly developed and integrated across national borders. The Council of North American Grain Exchanges provided supervision of all 'contract markets', of which the Chicago Board of Trade, the Minneapolis Chamber of Commerce (which also marketed Canadian wheat), the Board of Trade of Kansas City, the Duluth Board of Trade, the Merchants' Exchange of St Louis, and the Milwaukee Chamber of Commerce were the most important, representing over 99.9 per cent of the volume traded. In the 1920s, the US federal government undertook to monitor these markets in order to design better incentive systems, to guard against institutional failure, to formulate effective public policies to curb 'excessive' speculation and to mitigate the effects of recurring agricultural crises in the interwar period.

---

[2] I am grateful to one of my doctoral students, Mr Rasheed Saleuddin, for pointing me towards Bensel (2000), as the literature on the political economy of regulation in North America in the twentieth century is ironically better developed than that of nineteenth-century Britain.

The individual exchanges competed with one another to attract business, published elaborate annual reports (which included daily, weekly and monthly price data and occasional volumes traded), promoted best practice and cooperated (to varying degrees) with the Grain Futures Administration to monitor the positions of the biggest players in the market. There was a high degree of convergence in market microstructure: standardization of contracts, regularization of clearing rules, continuous price registration, clearing of information, consistency in margin requirements, and reliability of disciplinary and enforcement mechanisms. Hedging, speculation and arbitrage were widespread, and well understood. Although most defenders of futures markets relied upon Alfred Marshall's defence of futures markets as a form of 'price insurance', sophisticated contemporary commentators also argued that speculators provided the liquidity and 'heterogeneity of belief' needed for a continuous market (Hoffman, 1937). The operation of a continuous market, in turn, supplied middlemen with access to easy credit, as pyramids of commercial loans could be secured by 'grain paper'. Practices such as 'inter-market hedging' and 'cash-and-carry arbitrage' connected the liquidity pools while supplying insurance against price fluctuations (Hoffman, 1937).

The voluminous data collected by the individual exchanges, the Grain Futures Administration, and the Department of Agriculture more broadly, functioned much as the English Corn Returns had done a century earlier in furnishing a generation of contemporary researchers with unparalleled insight into the dynamics of these markets (Hoffman, 1941). It was in this context that Holbrook Working of the Stanford Food Research Institute formulated the weak form 'efficient markets hypothesis' discussed later in this chapter (Working, 1942; Working, 1960). Working, who was arguably the founder of modern econometrics, mobilized this data in his thorough investigations of market microstructure. His 'Working Curve', which explains a stylized fact in commodities markets (Carter and Giha, 2007), represented a rebuttal of Keynes's own account of backwardation.

2.1   Early political economy and the corn model

Although Smith denounced William Petty, Josiah Child and other seventeenth-century writers as mercantilists, he was heavily indebted to them for their characterizations of the potential of the secondary sector, manufacturing, which in Smith's own lifetime had transformed the economic and social lives of his countrymen. The British Isles, which in 1650 had been the object of ridicule by the Dutch for the comparative poverty of the king and his kingdom, by 1750 was the envy of European visitors (Scott, 2003; Coffman and Ormrod, 2014). As Coffman and Ormrod (2014) have argued, 'the "corn model" is simply a heuristic for measuring and comparing value, i.e. for distinguishing between nominal and real values (McNally, 1988, p. 245), as "the money price of corn regulates that of all other commodities" (Smith, [1776] 1976, book iv, ch. v, p.509)'. Smith used William Fleetwood's long-range price index in *Chronicon Preciosum: or An Account of English Money, the Price of Corn and Other Commodities, for the Last 600 Years* (1707) in his 'Digression on Silver' to demonstrate empirically 'what he derived stated axiomatically in Book IV, Chapter 5, namely that "the money price of labour, and of everything that is the produce either of land or labour, must necessarily either rise or fall in proportion to the money price of corn" (Smith [1776] 1976, book iv, ch.v, p.510)' (Coffman and Ormrod, 2014, pp. 202–3).

Smith's heuristic was not what Malthus, Ricardo and the Ricardian socialists meant when they variously used a 'corn model', or even 'corn models', to frame their theoretical discussions of rents, gluts and surplus value (Glyn 2006; Coffman and Ormrod, 2014). As Quadrio Curzio and Pellizzari noted, Malthus remained pre-occupied with demographic crisis and wished to ascertain the extent to which 'the demographic regime was in danger of collapse due to the absolute scarcity of natural resources, whereas Ricardo develops what they categorize as theory of "relative dynamic scarcity" which is amenable, over some time horizons, to technological progress but ultimately constrained by his formulation of a principle of diminishing returns' (Quadrio Curzio and Pellizzari, 1999, p. 9; see also Quadrio Curzio, 1990; Coffman and Ormrod, 2014). As Coffman and Ormrod (2014) explain, 'Ricardo's theory of differential rents accounts for both the existence of differently productive types of agricultural land and for the possibility of capital improvement of marginal lands. National markets for agricultural produce thus have the effect of 'equalizing' rents, such that tenants on fertile lands pay more than those who must work harder to generate agricultural produce from less fertile estates.'

David Ormrod and his colleagues at the University of Kent have recently called some aspects of Ricardo's account into question while confirming other elements of his story (Ormrod, Gibson and Lyne, 2011; Coffman and Ormrod, 2014). In their analysis of the rent rolls of the Rochester Bridge Trust, a major institutional landowner in Kent and London, they discovered that the practice of offering 'beneficial rents' (which were far below market value) continued well into the nineteenth century. The time lag for rent adjustment after capital improvement could be significant, and often did not occur until subdivision of the lease reflected changes in land use. The Kent group's 'estate reconstitution' method carefully traces the changing composition of estates over time. Analysis of the wardens' accounts shows that rent was adjusted most frequently at the rural-urban fringe, where depleted low-rent farmland and wastelands were reclaimed and reused for industrial purposes, as they were in Dartford and the Frindsbury Peninsula to accommodate a local paper industry (Coffman and Ormrod, 2014). In general, leases were sub-divided and adjusted as a result of changing land use rather than in response to incremental improvements in agricultural yields. On the other hand, this was what Ricardo argued would happen if the free importation of foreign corn made farming marginal lands uneconomic, thus making them available for conversion to industrial use (Coffman and Ormrod, 2014). As Coffman and Ormrod (2014) acknowledge, more work must be done to extend this analysis to non-institutional landowners, particularly yeoman farmers, though doing so is more difficult because of the problem of identifying suitable archival sources. Yet they believe that pattern is likely to prove the dominant one, especially in the south. In England and Wales, rental markets were never as frictionless as Ricardo's corn model required. Nevertheless, Ricardo's formulation of differential rents represented a major theoretical innovation and raised the possibility of inter-sectoral shifts in land use, which might even be driven by policy, intentionally or deliberately (Coffman and Ormrod, 2014). This, in turn, recalls Quadrio Curzio's formulation of the distinction between differential rents and scarcity rents (Quadrio Curzio and Pellizzari, 1999, p. 14; Quadrio Curzio, 1990).

2.2   *Holbrook Working and the efficient markets hypothesis*

A century later, those interested in grain markets had a different set of preoccupations. From the inception of trading in grain futures in Chicago in the 1850s, North American grain contract markets had been notoriously volatile, fuelling attempts in the Progressive Era to ban futures trading entirely. Significant grain price increases through World War I gave way to unprecedented commodity deflation beginning in 1919. In order to reduce volatility, protect stakeholders and prevent market abuse, the US federal government attempted first to regulate grain contract markets with the establishment of the Grain Futures Act of 1922, followed by the Commodity Exchange Act of 1936 (which required all commodity futures and options to be traded on exchange), and later supplemented this strategy with direct intervention in the wider agricultural economy with the Agricultural Adjustment Acts (1933, 1938). The Canadian government, by contrast, preferred to implement price controls and production quotas through agricultural marketing boards.

The interwar period in the United States saw the development of a significant federal bureaucracy to supervise the agricultural sector, including grain contract markets, and made substantial funds available to academic researchers to explore their dynamics. The two most influential recipients of this funding were the Food Research Institute at Stanford University and the Insurance Department of the Wharton School of Commerce and Finance at the University of Pennsylvania. The Wharton group was firmly committed to Marshall's view of futures trading as 'price insurance', whereas the Stanford group was run by agricultural economists who called themselves 'methodological statisticians' rather than economists. They fundamentally disagreed with both Keynes and their colleagues at Wharton, as they saw 'hedging' not in terms of price insurance, but rather as vehicle for speculating on future changes in the spread between spot and futures prices.

Perhaps the most famous of these researchers was Holbrook Working, who was a fellow of the American Statistical Association, a fellow of the Econometric Society, a member of the Cowles Commission (where he worked on securities prices), and a co-founder of *Econometrica*. It is no exaggeration to say that the Stanford Food Research Institute 'led the world in the creation and application of what are now known as econometric techniques' (Fox 1986). After long experience in analysis of the Chicago wheat futures market, Working (1934) developed an econometric test for whether or not a given time series of commodity or securities prices could be generated by aggregating series of statistically generated, randomly fluctuating time series – or what today is known as the 'random walk' and is a test for informational efficiency (Sewell, 2011). Yet unlike his successors, Working also believed it was possible to discern structure in these apparently random fluctuations (McKenzie, 2006, p. 95; Working, 1958).

2.3 Grain Markets and sectoral interdependencies

Debates about the Corn Laws were in essence a dispute over the inter-sectoral distribution effects of the price impact of imported corn. Landowners and their tenants, who had brought marginal lands into production during the Continental Blockade (1806–14), were threatened by the spectre of renewed competition from foreign grains. Manufacturers, on the other hand, apprehended that relatively higher English food prices would be expressed in wages, rendering them less competitive than they otherwise would be. Although there were some exceptions, attitudes towards repeal of the Corn Laws generally broke down along sectoral lines. Reconstructions using the Corn Returns data set make it possible to speak directly to contemporary concerns about the price impact of imported corn in the context of debates about the Corn Laws. When Jeffrey Williamson (1990) first explored this question twenty-five years ago, he concluded that more rigorous empirical work was needed, as his results turned on differing estimates of 'trade elasticities'. These depended upon whether or not Britain was a 'price-taker' in agricultural markets with results that range from an effective tax on manufacturing profits as high as 22 per cent to almost negligible (Coffman and Ormrod, 2014).

It is crucial to point out that the Corn Laws were not, as some imagine, first imposed during the Napoleonic Wars, but rather were part of a more general system of regulation of corn imports and exports that dated from the twelfth century (Barnes 1930). They had periodically been a source of inter-sectoral disputes, with a recent ban on distilling of grain in 1760 a response to high grain prices and fears of famine. For most of the eighteenth-century, the Corn Laws functioned not to protect domestic producers against foreign competition, but to incentivize them to export grain through the system of grain bounties so despised by Smith (Ormrod, 1985, pp. 14–16, 81–3). Although the system was meant to reduce price volatility, the corn bounties favoured farmers in that they ensured a floor on grain prices, encouraging exports overseas in good years while depleting stock levels available for years of poor harvest. Thus one empirical question that can be answered with the earlier data is how far these corn bounties contributed to price volatility in affected grains versus controls.

The data set (1770–1865) spans the advent and end of the Continental Blockade (1806–14), which was thought responsible for the expansion of British agriculture into marginal lands during the Napoleonic Wars, the nineteenth-century Corn Laws (1815–46) that followed in the aftermath of fears of agrarian crisis, and also and the rise of North American agriculture in the decade after 1850. The data includes all of the coastal ports into which corn was imported. In conjunction with data on corn imports, it should now be possible to estimate accurately the trade elasticities for agricultural commodities (Williamson, 1990, p. 145; Coffman and Ormrod, 2014).

As Coffman and Ormrod (2014) observe, the Corn Returns are suited to this purpose because the six commodities (wheat, rye, barley, oats, peas and beans) represent the range of substitute goods (rye and oats being purchased when wheat is too expensive, especially during the French Revolutionary and Napoleonic Wars) available to the consumer and the brewers. Unlike comparable continental European sources, the Corn Returns report actual quantities sold and prices at sale rather than crop yields and assize prices (Coffman and Ormrod, 2014). Coffman and Ormrod (2014) hope to revisit and finally settle the question of how far the Corn Laws enriched agrarian interests at the expense of the burgeoning manufacturing sector or of urban labourers, and how far their repeal provided a boost to British manufacturing. In doing so, it will be possible for the first time to mediate between claims in the contemporary polemical literature about the economic incidence of the Corn Laws and inter-sectoral distribution effects.

In a similar vein, the contribution of the agricultural sector to the Great Depression remains a subject of heated debate. Traditionally the proponents of direct causation fell into two camps: those who argue for persistent overproduction amidst falling prices and declining international demand, and those who see linkages between a crisis in the rural banking sector and the general banking crisis of 1930. Although recent work by Giovanni Federico rejects both hypotheses in their strong forms, he remains convinced that low 'elasticity of supply' persisted in the agricultural sector (in contrast with manufacturing where output fell), especially as the opportunity costs of farmers' labour remained low (2005, p. 972). Such behaviour was presumably encouraged by what James Hamilton characterized as the persistent inability of grain futures markets to anticipate deflation, thereby signalling to producers the viability of their strategy (Hamilton, 1992; Cecchetti, 1992).

Holbrook Working's characterizations of relevant market microstructures and evaluation of their efficiencies is particularly helpful in mediating these claims. In a recent working paper, the author and a colleague argue that Hamilton ignores the well-established concept of the cost-of-carry in commodity markets, and therefore makes erroneous conclusions that are used to defend certain assertions that deflation during the Great Depression was unexpected (Saleuddin and Coffman, 2014). As with the Corn Returns, the data supplied by the grain exchanges makes this kind of investigation possible nearly a century later, when we have the computing technologies available to run more realistic simulations. While the survival of this material in the American case was ensured by the creation of the Grain Futures Administration, the institutional story in Britain was rather more contingent.

3.   The origins and applications of the Corn Returns

The requirement of collecting and certifying market prices of 'corn' was established by statute in 1685.[3] After 1770, however, they were printed in the *London Gazette*. Although extraction of this data was cumbersome, doing so permitted the construction of a weekly series from 1770–1820 for 25 coastal markets and 23 inland markets as well as North and South Wales and the London Corn Exchange. From 1820–64, data for the 139 markets in maritime districts included quantities as well as prices. After 1828, quantities are published for an additional 79 inland market towns. By 1842, the returns were extended to include quantity and price data for a total of 290 market towns (Coffman and Ormrod, 2014).

Monthly selections of weekly returns from 1748–70 were printed in *The Universal Magazine of Knowledge and Pleasure* (London, 1747–1803). Consistencies in the frequency of returns (weekly) and the commodities listed in the *Universal Magazine*, when compared with those published by John Houghton in *A Collection of Letters for the Improvement of Husbandry and Trade* (1692–1702), have led Lucy Adrian, John Chartres (1975) – after his work on the Houghton data in *An Agrarian History of England and*

---

[3] See 'James the Second, 1685: An Additionall Act for the Improvement of Tillage' [Chapter XIX. Rot. Parl. nu. 19.], *Statutes of the Realm: volume 6: 1685–94* (1819), pp. 21–3. After 1770, malt was returned separately. See 10 Geo III c 39 in *The Statutes at Large, from Magna Charta, to the Twenty-fifth Year of the Reign of King George the Third, Inclusive: volume 8* (1786), pp. 119–20.

Wales – and this author to suspect that Houghton's data was supplied not, as Houghton occasionally claimed, from his correspondents, but rather from the official Corn Returns (Coffman and Ormrod, 2014).[4]

As Coffman and Ormrod (2014) observe, contemporary authors did not readily accept the value or reliability of the Corn Returns, but rather fiercely debated both the practices of inspectors and the statistical methods used to calculate averages. This high level of interest stemmed not from problems with the sources themselves, as some have assumed (Brunt and Cannon, 2013; Vamplew, 1978) but rather from the significance of the uses to which they were put in public policy debates about Repeal of the Corn Laws, the belated abolition of the assizes of bread in 1863 (as those on beer had been abandoned in 1672), and the commutation of tithes in 1836. Local newspapers often reprinted the prices reported in the *London Gazette*, thereby increasing the dissemination and the scrutiny of the system (Adrian, 1977, pp. 219–20). Following Adrian (1978), Coffman and Ormrod (2014) argue that this produced continual improvements in oversight and the extension of the system to a successively larger number of inland market towns. Although there are scattered errors and inconsistencies (most often introduced by the printers), Coffman and Ormrod (2014) argue that there is little reason to believe the data is any more or less reliable than that collected by the modern state. As they observe, at least one leading historian of the early Industrial Revolution thought that the eighteenth- and nineteenth-century statistics were more reliable than those produced by the twentieth-century British state (Deane, 1979, pp. 62–4; Coffman and Ormrod, 2014). Moreover, rigorous statistical tests on a sample of the data in the 1970s confirmed the internal consistency of the records (Adrian, 1977).[5] As Coffman and Ormrod (2014) have noticed, 'this unrivalled, if neglected, source on the operation of eighteenth- and nineteenth-century English agricultural markets consists of over six million data points'.

The *Corn Returns Online* is a public resource that should assist historical geographers and economic historians wishing to construct long-term, regionally and locally granulated price and wage histories for the United Kingdom; more immediately, it assists those economic and financial historians wanting to put agricultural markets within the wider context of the rapidly industrializing English economy (Coffman and Ormrod, 2014). Because quantity and price

---

[4] The author is also working on an intellectual biography of John Houghton, which brings together his careers as an excise officer, newspaperman, exotic grocer, grain speculator, and member of the Georgical Committee and fellow of the Royal Society. Houghton did report other price data, including stocks, exchange rates and local prices of retail goods, which his correspondents supplied him in exchange for free subscriptions. The agricultural price data, however, is far more robust, complete and systematic than the data that Houghton obtained in that fashion.

[5] Debate on this subject was continued between Wray Vamplew and Lucy Adrian in *Journal of Historical Geography*, 4.3 (1978) pp. 291–3.

data together allow for sophisticated analysis of agricultural marketing, corn-hog cycles, cross-elasticities of demand, and seasonal fluctuations in supply and demand of chief agricultural commodities, this data set offers unparalleled insight into what Lucy Adrian, in accord with Adam Smith, once called 'the integrated nature of farming as a financial enterprise' (Adrian, 1977, p. 236; Coffman and Ormrod, 2014).

4. The use of the Corn Returns in administration: 150 years of the Corn Laws

The creation and publication of the Corn Returns in the *London Gazette* was an expensive undertaking, pursued over the course of almost a century. How did contemporaries use this data? A recent attempt to tackle this question can be found in Brunt and Cannon (2013). In their account, the main goal of the earlier corn bounties (which they do not call Corn Laws) of 1672 and 1688 was to provide an incentive for capital improvement to agricultural lands. Their main evidence for this comes from the views expressed by authors of early twentieth-century treatments of corn legislation (Brunt and Cannon, 2013, p. 3; Fay, 1932, pp. 20–1). As noted in Coffman and Ormrod (2014), whatever the rationale, this legislation had the effect of ensuring farmers a minimum price for their grains by offering an export bounty in good years, coupled with a protective tariff, which was not in effect in years of bad harvests.

In their account, Brunt and Cannon (2013, pp. 3–4) argue that the most immediate source of the requirement to report corn prices was to prevent abuses in the system of oaths whereby captains of outbound vessels were allowed to swear to the market prices in port (Coffman and Ormrod, 2014). The frauds and perjuries were such that the Treasury soon ran a deficit, having paid out far more in corn bounties than it collected in tariff revenue (Ormrod, 1985). Although this was true for most of the eighteenth century, Brunt and Cannon (2013) seem unaware of the requirement to report prices from 1685 onwards, despite their commitment to the view that the legislation was motivated by encouraging improvement of the land. That was certainly John Houghton's project in *Collections for the Improvement of Husbandry and Trade* (1692–1703), in which he chose to publish the Corn Returns from the 1690s, but there is little evidence for this in the preambles of the relevant acts (Coffman and Ormrod, 2014).

Coffman and Ormrod (2014, p. 200) instead emphasize that 'the 1770 legislation may have been meant to improve the mechanics of reporting, but the most important consequence was to make the Corn Returns public for the first time through their publication in the *London Gazette*). An equally important use of the Corn Returns for much of the eighteenth century was to monitor the domestic grain trade, so that bans on distilling of grains could be imposed in times of dearth (Coffman and Gao, 2011). This data, in conjunction with that collected by the Excise Office, was also useful in resolving discussions about the optimal mix of taxes on beer and ale, malt and hops, by offering contemporaries a means to assess competing claims about who bore the economic incidence of these taxes (Cardinale and Coffman, 2014). As Adrian (1977) reported when she found flysheets from these periodicals amongst the account books of East Anglian farmers, landowners and their tenants both read the *Universal Magazine*, *Gentleman's Magazine* and *London Gazette* in order to decide where to market their grain, though in her view they were also as often interested in the price of coals, seeds and other agricultural inputs in the markets as they were in the prices their own grains would command (Coffman and Ormrod, 2014). The landowning gentry and their tenants 'followed the Corn Returns as eagerly as people follow stock markets today' (Coffman and Ormrod, 2014, p. 200).

5.   Reassessing the empiricist impulse in early political economy

Hopefully this overview of the political economy of grain markets has made readers question some of the stylized facts about the repeal of the Corn Laws. While the dispute was, indeed, a product of competition between the primary and secondary sectors for perceived economic advantage, it was simply the last instalment of a long-running debate in Britain about how to best regulate the grain trade. As Smith and later Malthus and Ricardo realized, the distributional effects of these policies were not always readily apparent. While the old system of corn bounties most obviously favoured the 'tenant' farmer, by ensuring a floor on the price of his grain, they might also benefit the landowner by encouraging his tenants to make capital improvements to the land they leased. Likewise the landowners themselves might be motivated to do so, or, as in the case of the Rochester Bridge Trust, might be impelled to experiment with different patterns of land use. The eighteenth-century British state was committed to monitoring both its inland grain markets and the market prices in its outports in order to reconcile competing demands and to ensure some measure of compliance with its regulations. Yet even after repeal of the Corn Laws, the state continued to collect the data and even greatly enlarged the number of markets under the requirement to report prices and quantities to the state. Eighteenth- and nineteenth-century statesmen knew that markets were social constructions that depended on community assent. When North American agriculture came on-stream in the 1850s and 1860s, a similar commitment to monitoring grain markets could be seen, though the function was largely performed by the exchanges themselves, at least until the 1920s when the Grain Futures Administration was established. These early, quasi-technocratic experiments have bequeathed future generations with remarkably robust data sets, which we have only begun to explore. To the extent that these markets were shaped by sectoral competition and multiple interdependencies, researchers should expect to find that they are internally structured. Characterizing those structures is the next challenge.

Given the size and internal coherence of the data set, there is also an unprecedented opportunity to test the suitability of certain advanced econometric techniques, used for modern financial assets, to historical commodities markets, thereby exploring their wider utility. Models developed by Hashem Pesaran (Holly, Pesaran and Yamagata, 2010) and Adrian Pagan (Dungey, Martin and Pagan, 2000) for housing markets and bond markets respectively can be used to investigate the temporal and spatial dispersion of price shocks emanating from London in a subset of the data (wheat prices and quantities for a sample of 12 of 150 market towns from 1836–42). In a different vein, a separate pilot study on volatility clustering on the 1836–42 data has already confirmed the well-known sensitivity of GARCH models to lower frequency (weekly) data (Coffman and Gao, 2012). It should be possible to refine the analysis to understand the asymmetric character of price shocks, thereby estimating the 'stickiness' of agricultural prices in this period (Lim and McNelis, 2008; Dungey *et al.*, 2008; Dungey *et al.*, 2010). This will, in turn, improve understanding of the economic incidence of the Corn Laws. Related studies of market integration, business cycles, and the changing relationships between substitute goods (wheat, rye and oats) over the century in question should reveal a great deal about the living standards of the urban labouring classes.

6. Conclusions

Sweeping verdicts about the political economy of grain markets in eighteenth- and nineteenth-century Britain and twentieth-century America have all too often been assumed rather than scrutinized thoroughly. The success of the Anti-Corn League in winning repeal of the Corn Laws has left many modern scholars with the view that there is nothing left to say. Worse still, influential writers such as Thomas Picketty and Arthur Goldhammer have mistakenly claimed that Malthus and Ricardo had 'virtually no genuine statistics at [their] disposal' (Picketty and Goldhammer, 2014, p. 5). Efforts by scholars such as Ha-Joon Chang (2007) to contest the received view have been at least as polemical and ideologically motivated, and have promoted the notion that economic rents earned by protective tariffs financed industrialization, even going as far as to afford that view the status of 'occult knowledge' Coffman and Ormrod, 2014). In the American case, Progressive-era rhetoric about the presumptively pernicious role of speculators has found new resonance during the financial crisis, which was preceded in part by a massive commodities bubble and renewed concerns about global food security.

The vapidness of these discussions have served to obscure the much more pressing need to understand the sectoral interdependencies between the primary and secondary sectors in both rapidly developing economies and advanced economies. Fortunately, the data sets afforded by the Corn Returns and by the activities of the North American grain exchanges make it possible to give such explorations a solid empirical base. Whatever populist caveats about Ricardian economics or the use of econometrics by mainstream economists, two of the greatest intellectual achievements of the economics discipline owe their genesis to the attempts by contemporaries – whether Smith, Malthus and Ricardo, or Holbrook Working and his colleagues at Stanford and the USDA – to understanding their worlds. We could do worse than follow in their footsteps.

REFERENCES

Adrian, L. (1977) 'The Nineteenth Century Gazette Corn Returns from East Anglian Markets', *Journal of Historical Geography*, 3.3, pp. 217–36.
(1978) 'The Nineteenth Century Gazette Corn Returns', *Journal of Historical Geography*, 4.3, p. 293.
Baker, D. A. (1970) 'The Marketing of Corn in the First Half of the 18th Century', *Agricultural History Review*, 18.2, pp. 97–115.
(1981) *Agricultural Prices, Production and Marketing, with Special Reference to the Hop Industry: North-East Kent, 1680–1760*, New York: Garland.
Barnes, D. G. (1930) *History of the English Corn Laws 1660–1840*, London: Routledge.
Bensel, R. F. (2000) *The Political Economy of American Industrialization, 1877–1900*, Cambridge: Cambridge University Press.
Beveridge, W. (ed.) (1939) *Prices and Wages in England from the Twelfth to the Nineteenth Century*, London: Longmans; New York: Green.
Brunt, L., and Cannon, E. S. (2013) 'The Truth, the Whole Truth, and Nothing But the Truth: The English Corn Returns as a Data Source in Economic History, 1770–1914', (April) NHH Dept. of Economics Discussion Paper No. 09/2013.
Cardinale, I., and Coffman, D. (2014) 'Economic Interdependencies and Political Conflict: Towards a Structural and Historical Approach to Taxation', *Economia Politica. Journal of Analytical and Institutional Economics*, 31.3 pp. 277–300.
Carter, C. A., and Giha, R. (2007) 'The Working Curve and Commodity Storage under Backwardation', *American Journal of Agricultural Economics*, 89.4, pp. 864–72.
Cecchetti, S. G. (1992) 'Prices During the Great Depression: Was the Deflation of 1930–1932 Really Unanticipated?', *The American Economic Review*, 82.1, pp. 141–56.
Chang, H.-J. (2007) *Bad Samaritans: The Myth of Free Trade and the Secret History of Capitalism*, New York: Bloomsbury Press.
Coffman, D. (2013) *Excise Taxation and the Origins of Public Debt*, London: Palgrave Macmillan.
Coffman, D., and Gao, Y. (2011) 'Capitalizing Costs: The Excise and Industrialization, a Case Study of the Brewing Industry', unpublished working paper.

(2012) 'Volatility Clustering in the English Corn Returns: A Pilot Study using GARCH models', unpublished working paper.

Coffman, D., and Ormrod, D. (2014) 'Corn Prices, Corn Models and Corn Rents: What Can We Learn from the English Corn Returns?', in M. Allen and D. Coffman (eds.) *Money, Prices, and Wages: Essays in Honour of Nicholas Mayhew*, Studies in the History of Finance, London: Palgrave Macmillan.

Deane, P. (1979) *The First Industrial Revolution*, Cambridge: Cambridge University Press.

Dungey, M., Fry, R., Gonzàles-Hermosillo, B., and Martin, V. L. (2007) 'Contagion in Global Equity Markets in 1998: The Effects of the Russian and LTCM crises', *The North American Journal of Economics and Finance*, 18.2, pp. 155–74.

Dungey, M., Martin, V. L., and Pagan, A. R. (2000) 'A Multivariate Latent Factor Decomposition of International Bond Yield Spreads', *Journal of Applied Econometrics*, 15.6, pp. 697–715.

Dungey, M., Milunovich, G., and Thorp, S. (2008) 'Unobservable Shocks as Carriers of Contagion: A Dynamic Analysis Using Identified Structural GARCH', NCER Working Paper Series 22, National Centre for Econometric Research, Brisbane.

(2010) 'Unobservable Shocks as Carriers of Contagion', *Journal of Banking & Finance*, 34.5, pp. 1008–21.

Fairlie, S. (1969) 'The Corn Laws and British Wheat Production 1829–76', *Economic History Review*, n.s. 22.1, pp. 88–116.

Fay, C. R. (1932) *The Corn Laws and Social England*, Cambridge: Cambridge University Press.

Federico, G. (2005) 'Not Guilty? Agriculture in the 1920s and the Great Depression', *Journal of Economic History*, 65.4, pp. 949–76.

Fleetwood, W. (1707) *Chronicon Preciosum: Or an Account of English Money, the Price of Corn, and Other Commodities for the Last 600 Years*, London: C. Harper.

Fox, K. A. (1986) 'Agricultural Economists as World leaders in Applied Econometrics, 1917–33', *American Journal of Agricultural Economics*, 68.2, pp. 381–6.

Glyn, A. (2006) 'The Corn Model, Gluts and Surplus Value', *Cambridge Journal of Economics*, 30.2, pp. 307–12.

Gerschenkron, A. (1962) *Economic Backwardness in Historical Perspective*, Cambridge, Mass.: Harvard University Press.

Hamilton, J. (1992) 'Was the Deflation During the Great Depression Anticipated? Evidence from the Commodity Futures Market', *The American Economic Review*, 82.1, pp. 157–78.

Holly, S., Pesaran, M. H., and Yamagata, T. (2010) 'A Spatio-Temporal Model of House Prices in the USA', *Journal of Econometrics*, 158.1, pp. 160–73.

Hoffman, G. W. (1937) 'Past and Present Theory Regarding Futures Trading', *Journal of Farm Economics*, 19.1, pp. 300–12.

(1941) 'Grain Prices and the Futures Market: A 15-year Survey, 1923–1938', Washington: *USDA Technical Bulletin* 747.

Houghton, J. (1969) *A Collection, For Improvement of Husbandry and Trade*, London, Nos. 1–582, 1692–1703 (Farnborough, reprint).

Lim, G. C., and McNelis, P. D. (2008) *Computational Macroeconomics for the Open Economy*, Cambridge, Mass.: MIT Press.

MacKenzie, D. A. (2006) *An Engine, Not a Camera: How Financial Models Shape Markets*, Cambridge, Mass.: MIT Press.

McNally, D. (1988) *Political Economy and the Rise of Capitalism: A Reinterpretation*, Berkeley: University of California Press.

Ormrod, D. (1985) *English Grain Exports and the Structure of Agrarian Capitalism 1700–1760*, Hull: Hull University Press.

Ormrod, D., Gibson, J. M., and Lyne, O. (2011) 'City and Countryside Revisited. Comparative Rent Movements in London and the South-East, 1580–1914', Studies in Economics 1117, Department of Economics, University of Kent.

Petty, W. (1662) *A Treatise of Taxes and Contributions*, London (written and published anonymously).

Picketty, T., and Goldhammer, A. (2014) *Capital in the Twenty-First Century*, New York: Belknap Press.

Quadrio Curzio, A. (1986) 'Technological Scarcity: An Essay on Production and Structural Change', in M. Baranzini and R. Scazzieri (eds.) *Foundations of Economics*, Oxford and New York: B. Blackwell, pp. 311–38.

(1990) 'Rent, Distribution and Economic Structure: A Collection of Essays', *Quaderni IDSE*, 1, Milan: ConsiglioNazionale delle Ricerche-CNR

(2011) 'Resources and Economic Dynamics, Technology and Rents', *Quaderni Cranec*, Milan: Vita e Pensiero.

Quadrio Curzio, A. and Pellizzari, F. (1999) *Rent, Resources, Technologies*, Berlin: Springer.

Quesnay, F. (1758) *Tableau Économique*, Versailles. (Also published as *Quesnay's Tableau Economique* [based on the 3rd French edn] edited with new material, translations and notes by M. Kuczynski and R. L. Meek, London: Macmillan; New York: A. M. Kelley, for the Royal Economic Society and the American Economic Association, 1972.)

Rostow, W. W. (1960) *The Stages of Economic Growth: A Non-Communist Manifesto*, Cambridge: Cambridge University Press.

(2014) 'Can Inflation Expectations be Measured Using Commodity Futures Prices?', *Cambridge Working Paper in Economic and Social History*, no. 20, August, http://www.econsoc.hist.cam.ac.uk/docs/CWPESH%20number%2020%August%202014.pdf.

Scott, J. (2003) 'Good Night Amsterdam', Sir George Downing and Anglo-Dutch Statebuilding' *English Historical Review*, 118(476), pp. 334–56.

Sewell, M. (2011) 'History of the Efficient Market Hypothesis', London: *UCL Research Note*, RN/11/04.

Shelton. R. (2008) 'Practical Economics in Eighteenth-Century England: Charles Smith on the *Grain Trade and the Corn Laws, 1756–1772*', *Historical Research*, 81 (214), pp. 636–62.

Smith, A. ([1776, 1778] 1976) *An Inquiry into the Nature and Causes of the Wealth of Nations*, General Editors R.H. Campbell and A.S. Skinner, Textual Editor W.B. Todd, vol. I, Oxford: Clarendon Press.

Thirsk, J. (ed.) (1985) *The Agrarian History of England and Wales, vol. V, 1640–1750, and vol. VI, 1750–1850* (ed. by G. E. Mingay, 1989), Cambridge: Cambridge University Press.

van Tielhof, M. (2002) *The 'Mother of All Trades': The Baltic Grain Trade in Amsterdam from the Late 16th to the Early 19th Century*, vol. 3, Leiden: Brill.

Vamplew, W. (1978) 'The Nineteenth Century Gazette Corn Returns: A Word of Warning', *Journal of Historical Geography*, vol. 4.3, pp. 291–3.

Wakita, S. (2001) 'Efficiency of the Dojima Rice Futures Market in Tokugawa-Period Japan', *Journal of Banking and Finance*, 25.3, pp. 535–54.

Williamson, J. (1990) 'The Impact of the Corn Laws Just Prior to Repeal', *Explorations in Economic History*, 27.2, pp. 123–56.

Working, H. (1934) 'Prices of Cash Wheat and Futures at Chicago since 1883', *Wheat Studies of the Stanford University Food Research Institute*, 11:3, pp. 75–124.

(1942) 'Quotations on Commodity Futures as Price Forecasts', *Econometrica*, 10.1, pp. 39–52.

(1958) 'A Theory of Anticipatory Prices', *The American Economic Review*, 48.2, pp. 188–99.

(1960) 'Note on the Correlation of First Differences of Averages in a Random Chain', *Econometrica*, 28.4, pp. 916–8.

4   The classical theory of rent

Heinz D. Kurz and Neri Salvadori

1.   Introduction

In this chapter the mathematical properties of a model in which only one commodity is produced will be studied. The commodity is assumed to be a pure consumption good. Hence, there is no produced means of production, or capital good, used in the production of the commodity.[1] In accordance with this setting of the problem we shall be concerned only with land and human labour as factors of production. Using the terminology of Eugen von Böhm-Bawerk ([1889] 1959) and Knut Wicksell ([1901] 1934) we may speak of 'non-capitalistic production'.[2] In what follows the single produced commodity will be called 'corn'.

Land is taken to be the only external force at the service of man. Land is a special natural resource. Economists generally distinguish between *renewable*

---

[1] Ever since the inception of systematic economic analysis economists have attempted to improve their understanding of certain phenomena by comparing two situations: one in which the problem under consideration is absent and one in which it is present. This method was used, for example, by Adam Smith in chapter VI of book I of *The Wealth of Nations*, in which he invoked the concept of an 'early and rude state of society which precedes both the accumulation of stock and the appropriation of land' (Smith, [1776] 1976, vol. I, p. 65). This device was meant to prepare the ground for a better understanding of the role of private property in modern, i.e. 'commercial', society. His main concern was with clarifying the role of capital ('stock') in the process of production, income distribution and economic growth. This method, whose characteristic feature is that it makes use of counterfactuals, is widely used in economics.

[2] Economic systems that produce without and with capital goods, and the transition from the former to the latter, are analysed by Johann Heinrich von Thünen in *Der isolirte Staat* (The Isolated State, 1826). Thünen's contribution had a considerable impact on major representatives of the 'Austrian' theory of capital and interest, in particular Eugen von Böhm-Bawerk and Knut Wicksell. In his *Positive Theorie des Kapitales* (Positive Theory of Capital) ([1889] 1959, book II) which formed the second part of his magnum opus *Kapital und Kapitalzins* (Capital and Interest), Böhm-Bawerk counterposed what he called the 'capitalist process of production', which utilizes and (re)produces means of production, and the 'non-capitalist' process, which does not. The latter transforms non-produced or 'original' factors of production, or rather factor services, directly into consumable output, while the former does so with the help of capital goods which are internal to the production process. The factor services contemplated are labour and land services. This distinction was adopted by Knut Wicksell both in his *Über Wert, Kapital und Rente* (Value, Capital and Rent, [1893] 1954) and in volume I of his *Föreläsningar i nationalekonomi* (Lectures on Political Economy, [1901] 1934).

and *exhaustible* natural resources. A resource is called renewable if constant periodic removals from or uses of it can be indefinitely prolonged. A renewable resource is called depletable (non-depletable) if the level of its exploitation or use affects (does not affect) the productivity or quality of the resource. Arable soil is a renewable resource that can be depleted and, as history shows, has often been depleted by use. However, in economics there is a long-standing tradition of treating land as a non-depletable resource. Thus, in his theory of rent David Ricardo refers to 'the original and indestructible powers of the soil' (Ricardo [1817] 1951, vol. I, p. 67). We shall, in what follows, adopt this view, keeping in mind that it implies a bold abstraction. That is, we shall assume that the cultivation of land does not alter the quality of the land. In addition, we shall assume that the land available is already in a cultivable state. Otherwise we would have to consider cultivable land as a produced means of production, which would introduce the problem of capital (which we want to circumnavigate in this chapter). We first distinguish between two simplified cases:

1. There are several different qualities of land available, but there is just one process of production for each quality of land.
2. There are several processes of production, but all available land is of uniform quality.

In both cases the amount(s) of land(s) are taken to be given (and finite). A subcase of (i) concerns plots of homogeneous land that, however, are located at a smaller or larger distance from the 'village' or 'town' where the corn is consumed. In this subcase differences in quality are exclusively due to differences in location relatively to the centre of consumption. Case (i) leads to the concept of *extensive diminishing returns* in corn production and to the related concept of *extensive rent* (a subcase of which is *rent due to location*); case (ii) leads to the concepts of *intensive diminishing returns* and *intensive rent*.[3] We shall then deal with the general case in which there are several qualities of land and several alternative processes to cultivate each quality of land. While land need not be of uniform quality, it will be assumed for simplicity that labour is. Perhaps this is expressed too strongly, since in order to be able to set aside the problem of the heterogeneity of labour we only have to assume that

---

[3] The principles of extensive and intensive rent can be traced back to the beginnings of classical political economy. The concept of rent due to advantageously situated land is spelled out as early as William Petty (1662). A clear notion of extensive rent was elaborated by James Anderson (1777a, 1777b), a contemporary of Adam Smith. The theory of rent was further developed by Thomas Robert Malthus (1815), Edward West (1815) and David Ricardo. Ricardo's exposition of extensive and intensive rent in his *Essay on Profits* (1815) and in his *On the Principles of Political Economy and Taxation* (1817) was more carefully set out and clearer than anyone else's. This is why the theory of rent is commonly associated with his name.

there is a uniform wage rate for all kinds of labour performed. In accordance with the homogeneity assumption all the labourers are regarded as possessing the same physical and mental strength and the same skills.[4] These skills have to be conceived as naturally given, otherwise the problem of capital would enter the system of production by the back door, so to speak, in the sense of human capital.

Both land and the power to perform labour are assumed to be *private property*. We are neither concerned with forms of social organization characterized by collective or common property of natural resources nor with forms characterized by slavery. Hence all agents could be described in terms of their property in their own capacity to work and their landed property. It is not assumed that landed property is equally distributed among the members of society. Since we concern ourselves only with questions of 'functional' rather than 'personal' income distribution, the attention will focus on what determines the wages of labour and the rent(s) of land.

Agents are assumed to act in a self-interested way, which means in the present context that they attempt to maximize their income in terms of corn. In addition, it will be assumed that there is *free competition*, characterized by the absence of substantial barriers to entry and exit with regard to the three types of market of the simple economy under consideration: the corn, the labour and the land (or real estate) market. Free competition and maximizing behaviour involves that producers will try to produce as cheaply as possible, i.e. they will try to minimize unit costs. We shall assume *cost-minimizing* behaviour on the part of producers. Despite the fact that agents are assumed to act in a self-interested way, we will dispense from behaviours of the agents tending to limit competition or to take advantage of special conditions in a strategic way. In particular we do not consider the case in which landowners collude in order to act as a single monopolist on their resource or that they merge for the same reason or take advantage of the distribution of plots in order to get more corn. The distribution of plots of land among landowners is not considered.[5]

Obviously, every owner of a factor of production faces the following alternative: to use the factor for productive purposes or not to use it that way. The second alternative presupposes that there exist alternative uses of the factor. For example, a landowner could retain a part of his land as a promenade or hunting ground. However, this would run counter to the assumption that there is only a single commodity produced in the economy. Hence it is implicitly assumed that there is no use of land other than employing it in corn production. As a further implication the *reservation price* of the use of

---

[4] It would be easy to take into account merely quantitative differences in physical strength by reckoning in terms of some 'efficiency' units of labour.

[5] The reader interested in the last of these problems may consult Salvadori (2004).

land is zero. The reservation price is that price for the use of land, or rent, at which the landowner is just indifferent to renting or not renting his land. It is a kind of minimum price, which in our case is zero.

While the assumption of a zero reservation price for the use of land is rather strong, it would be unreasonable to assume a zero reservation price for the use of a person's capacity to work. In order for the worker and his family to be able to survive, they have to consume, and if they do not own land and yield a rent they have to earn their living by selling their labour power. A worker cannot work, at least not for a long time, unless he is paid a wage that is high enough to allow him to reproduce his capacity to work and support his family. The latter condition has to be met in order to guarantee the continued existence of the workforce as a whole. In classical economics it was assumed that in the long run the reservation price of labour reflects a minimum subsistence level, which may be taken as given with regard to a particular society in a particular historical period. We shall follow this procedure and assume that the reservation price of labour in terms of corn is positive. We shall not attempt, however, to specify the subsistence level. We shall simply assume that all economic systems studied in this chapter satisfy the condition that the corresponding wage rates are larger than or at most equal to that level.

Production is taken to be a time-consuming process. The length of the production period is assumed to be uniform across all different qualities of land and all alternative methods of production available to cultivate them; we shall call that period of production a 'year'. Wages and rents will be paid to workers and landlords respectively at the end of the year. The assumption of *post factum* payment is necessary in order to avoid that wages or rents represent 'capital' advanced at the beginning of the production period and discounted forward at a given rate of profit (rate of interest). If corn was produced by labour, land *and* corn, and therefore there was no further commodity, nevertheless the rate of profit (rate of interest) would have to be introduced into the analysis. This is so since the payment of the input corn cannot be made *post factum* unless also the revenue from the sale of the produced corn is postponed by one period. In any case the payment for a commodity available at the *beginning* of the year cannot be done at the same time of the payment for *the same commodity* available at the end of the year.

Attention will focus on positions of the economy characterized by a uniform wage rate and a uniform rent rate for each particular quality of land. These positions, or *systems of production*, involve the conditions necessary for the maintenance of a self-reproducing state of the economy, i.e. the reproduction of the extant economic relations. The method of analysis is *long-period* rather than short-period. Making use of the method of *comparative statics*, we compare different systems of production with one another. We shall not, however, study the dynamics that lead from one system to the other. The chapter illustrates

Knut Wicksell's dictum that 'the problems of production and distribution cannot be separated, but are essentially one; production is not a technical problem only, but technical and economic at the same time' (Wicksell [1901] 1934, p. 106).

While the wage rate will always be positive, given the positivity of the reservation price of labour, the rent per acre of a given quality of land will be positive if and only if that quality of land is 'scarce'. It is indeed an analysis of the problem of the *scarcity* of natural resources such as land that is the main concern of this chapter. In order for a natural resource to be scarce from an economic point of view it is obviously not enough for that resource to be given in finite supply. What matters is that the resource must be in *short* supply. A resource that is not in short supply is just a free gift of nature. Whether a particular natural resource will be scarce depends of course on a variety of factors – in the case of our simple model: on the amount of corn to be produced, given the endowment of the economy with land(s) of given quality and quantity and the technological alternatives from which producers can choose. Apparently, the scarcity of a natural resource is not something that can be *assumed* at the outset: it rather ought to emerge as a result of the analysis, given the data of the problem under consideration. The assumption of a zero reservation price for the use of land in combination with that of free competition amongst landlords imply that no quality of land can yield its proprietor a positive rent unless that land is scarce.[6]

The only relative prices dealt with are the wage rate and the rents per acre, or rent rates, in terms of corn. Alternatively, we can consider the price of corn and the rent rates in terms of the wage per unit of labour. In the former case corn serves as the standard of value or *numéraire*, in the latter the wage. Taking corn as the numéraire involves setting the price of corn, p, equal to unity: $p = 1$. Similarly in the case in which all value magnitudes are expressed in 'wage units' (J. M. Keynes), here the wage rate, w, is set equal to unity: $w = 1$. The analysis will be carried out in terms of the following three premises. We take as given

1. the total amount of corn to be produced in the economy;
2. the quantity (quantities) of land of given quality (qualities) available in the economy that can at most be employed in the production of corn; and

---

[6] Hence, only rent due to scarcity will be dealt with, whereas no form of 'absolute rent' will be considered. In the *Principles* Ricardo develops his argument in terms of the assumption of 'free competition', i.e. he sets aside the problem of absolute rent or rent conceived, as it was by Adam Smith, as a monopoly price. This becomes clear in his discussion of the cause(s) of rent: 'If all land had the same properties, if it were unlimited in quantity, and uniform in quality, no charge would be made for its use, unless where it possessed peculiar advantages of situation. It is only, then, because land is not unlimited in quantity and uniform in quality, and because in the progress of population, land of an inferior quality, or less advantageously situated, is called into cultivation, that rent is ever paid for the use of it' ([1817] 1951, p. 70).

3. the alternative methods of production from which cost-minimizing producers can choose.

On the basis of these givens or 'data' or 'independent variables' the following
'unknowns' or 'dependent variables' will be determined:

(α) the methods (or processes) of production, and the levels of their operation,
by means of which the requested amount of corn will be produced in a
cost-minimizing way;
(β) the distribution of the product amongst workers and landowners, that is,
the wage rate and the rent(s) of land(s), both in terms of corn.

We carry out this exercise for different amounts of corn to be produced: this
allows us to identify the impact of changes in one of the independent variables,
that is, datum (a), on the dependent variables (α) and (β).

As the reader will have recognized, the intention of this chapter is to present
the main principles of the theory of rent in a simple framework. Why to do this
in a volume aiming at expounding and appraising the scientific programme of
Alberto Quadrio Curzio? First of all, Quadrio Curzio deserves the credit for
having further developed the theory of rent, especially extensive rent, starting
from Sraffa (1960). His book (Quadrio Curzio, 1967) was the main source
under consideration in the field and was read not only by Italian, but also
foreign scholars. Both of us benefitted a great deal from studying it. It was a
great service to the international community of scholars that the main results of
the book were then published in English (Quadrio Curzio, 1980). Another
reason that is close at hand is the following: As all his writings show, Quadrio
Curzio was always concerned with rendering the argument as clear as possible,
and if simplifications helped in the interest of conveying the main message
without thwarting its content, he used them. What matters is not only that
economists come up with new results, which he did in various areas of
research, but also that they put them forward in a way that can easily be
grasped by the audience, which he also did. We therefore feel entitled to follow
him in this second regard and present the theory of extensive and intensive rent
for beginners in economics.

The composition of this chapter is the following. In Sections 2 and 4 two
special models are investigated. Section 2 deals with the principle of extensive
rent, Section 4 with that of intensive rent. Section 3 investigates some properties of the extensive rent model. These properties are amongst the main results
that Alberto Quadrio Curzio elaborated in his contributions of 1967 and 1980.
Section 5 generalizes the models presented in the previous sections. Section 6
asks whether further generalizations are possible and emphasizes that no such
generalization is possible, if capital (produced means of production) is
involved. Section 7 concludes the discussion.

2.   Extensive diminishing returns (extensive rent)

Consider an economy that produces only corn. At the beginning of the production period labourers cultivate the land and at its end they harvest the crop. There is no commodity input in production. Corn is the only means of subsistence (food) to support the population. The production technology can be represented, in abstract terms, as a set of processes. Each process can be described as follows:

$$t^* \text{acres of land } i \oplus l^* \text{ hours of labour} \rightarrow b^* \text{ bushels of corn.}$$

The symbol '$\rightarrow$' stands for the 'black box' in which labourers working for l^* hours at a given intensity of work on t^* acres of land of quality i generate b^* bushels of corn during a yearly production cycle. The symbol '$\oplus$' indicates that both inputs, i.e. land of quality i and labour, are required to produce the given output of corn. The period of production separates the moment when labourers start to work from the moment when the harvesting is accomplished. We will assume that returns to scale with regard to each process are constant. With this assumption the production process can be represented as:

$$\frac{t^*}{b^*} \text{ acres of land } i \oplus \frac{l^*}{b^*} \text{hours of labour} \rightarrow 1 \text{ bushels of corn.}$$

or, for short,

$$t_i \oplus l_i \rightarrow 1.$$

In this section it will be assumed that there are n different qualities of land, named 1, 2, ..., n, and for each quality of land there is exactly one process producing corn. Table 4.1 provides the list of the existing processes. Obviously the existing qualities of land (and corresponding processes) can be numbered in such a way that $l_1 \leq l_2 \leq \ldots \leq l_n$. Let us first assume that $l_1 < l_2 < \ldots < l_n$. The case in which $l_i = l_{i+1}$, some i, will be considered later. Let G be the amount of corn produced and let T_i be the existing amount of land of quality i.

Table 4.1 *Technical features of production processes (extensive rent)*

	land inputs				labour		corn
processes	1	2	...	n	labour		corn
(1)	t_1	—	...	—	l_1	$\rightarrow$	1
(2)	—	t_2	...	—	l_2	$\rightarrow$	1
...	...	...	...	...	...	$\rightarrow$	...
(n)	—	—	...	t_n	l_n	$\rightarrow$	1

If land of quality i is cultivated, the following equation must be satisfied:

$$t_i q_i + w l_i = 1,$$

where q_i is the rent per acre (or rate of rent) of land of quality i and w is the wage rate. Moreover, it is assumed that no process can yield a surplus. Otherwise all farmer-capitalists would prefer to operate the surplus yielding process. Therefore it is assumed that

$$t_j q_j + w l_j \geq 1. \qquad (j = 1, 2, \ldots, n)$$

Obviously $w > 0$ and $q_j \geq 0$. If no quality of land is scarce, competition amongst landlords drives the rent for each quality of land down to zero. In such a situation with land of quality i being cultivated the wage rate w must satisfy the equation

$$w l_i = 1,$$

that is, the wage rate equals the inverse of the labour input coefficient associated with the process of production employed on land of quality i which, in turn, equals the *productivity of labour* on that kind of land.

If $i \neq 1$, then a surplus can be generated by operating process (1) since by assumption $l_1 < l_i$. Hence, if landlords get nothing from letting their land, then only land 1 can be cultivated since all farmers would want to employ land 1. Since in this circumstance land 1 is not scarce, G must be lower than T_1/t_1, which gives the maximum amount of corn producible on land of quality 1. As we have established, in this case all rent rates must equal zero and

$$w = w_1 := \frac{1}{1}.$$

Assume now that $T_1/t_1 < G < T_1/t_1 + T_2/t_2$. Corn cannot be produced by using land of the first quality alone, then, if effectual demand is to be met, a process $(j) \neq (1)$ must be operated. Let process $(j) \neq (1)$ be operated, then $w l_j \leq 1$ and therefore $w < w_1$. If, moreover, process (1) is not operated, $q_1 = 0$, and process (1) generates a surplus. This is a contradiction and, therefore, process (1) must be operated. If process (1) is operated, then it must hold that $t_1 q_1 + w l_1 = 1$. That is,

$$q_1 = \frac{1 - w l_1}{t_1}, \qquad (1)$$

where the wage rate $w < w_1$ is to be determined. If equality (1) is satisfied, then land 1 is certainly fully used. In fact, if land 1 was not fully used, then landlords would bid down q_1: a contradiction. If land 2 is used, only part of it is cultivated since $G < T_1/t_1 + T_2/t_2$. Therefore the rent rate of land

2, q_2, must equal zero because of the competition amongst landlords who own land 2. If $(j) \neq (2)$, then w is so low that process (2) generates a positive surplus: a contradiction. Hence, of necessity only lands of quality 1 and 2 are cultivated. In the present case land of quality 2 is what is conventionally called *marginal* land, which is the quality of land which is cultivated, but not fully used. (Conversely those qualities of land which are fully used are called *intra-marginal*.) As a consequence of the fact that land 2 is marginal

$$w = w_2 := \frac{1}{l_2}$$

$$q_1 = q_{12} := \frac{l_2 - l_1}{t_1 l_2}$$

$$q_k = 0, \qquad (k = 2, 3, \dots, n)$$

where q_{12} is the rent rate paid to the owners of land 1 on the assumption that land 2 is marginal.[7]

In general, if

$$G_{i-1} := \sum_{h=1}^{i-1} \frac{T_h}{t_h} < G < G_i := \sum_{h=1}^{i} \frac{T_h}{t_h},$$

the same argument shows that lands 1, 2, ..., $i - 1$ are fully used; land i is used, but only partially, and the wage rate and the rates of rent are determined as follows:

$$w = w_i := \frac{1}{l_i} \tag{2a}$$

$$q_h = q_{hi} := \frac{l_i - l_h}{t_h l_i}, \qquad (h = 1, 2, \dots, i) \tag{2b}$$

$$q_k = 0, \qquad (k = i, i+1, \dots, n) \tag{2c}$$

In fact, the requested amount of corn cannot be produced by using only the first $i - 1$ qualities of land. Hence, if that amount of corn is to be procured, a process (j), $j \geq i$, must be operated. Let process $(j) \neq (1)$, (2), ..., $(i - 1)$

---

[7] 'When in the progress of society, land of the second degree of fertility is taken into cultivation, rent immediately commences on that of the first quality, and the amount of that rent will depend on the difference in the quality of these two portions of land' (Ricardo [1817] 1951, p. 70). Since in Ricardo's view 'The value of corn is regulated by the quantity of labour bestowed on its production on that quality of land, or with that portion of capital, which pays no rent', the famous dictum follows: 'Corn is not high because a rent is paid, but a rent is paid because corn is high' (1951 p. 74). Hence, in the case of extensive diminishing returns rent is not a component part of the price of a commodity as Adam Smith had wrongly contended.

be operated, then $wl_j \leq 1$ and therefore $w < w_{i-1}$. If, moreover, process (h), $h = 1, 2, \ldots, i - 1$, is not operated, $q_h = 0$, and process (h) generates a surplus. This is a contradiction and, therefore, process (h) must be operated. If process (h) is operated, then it must hold that $t_h q_h + wl_h = 1$. That is,

$$q_h = \frac{1 - wl_h}{t_h}, \qquad (3)$$

where the wage rate $w < w_{i-1}$ is to be determined. If equality (3) is satisfied, then land h is certainly fully used. In fact, if land h was not fully used, then landlords would bid down q_h: a contradiction. If land i is used, only part of it is cultivated since $G < G_i$. Therefore the rent rate of land i, q_i, must equal zero because of the competition amongst landlords who own land i. If $j > i$, then w is so low that process (i) generates a positive surplus: a contradiction. Hence, by necessity only lands $1, 2, \ldots, i$ are cultivated. As a consequence equations (2) hold. Two special cases remain to be analysed.

1. The first case refers to a constellation where several processes employ the same amount of labour per unit of product, that is *the case in which two or more lands are marginal*. In order to simplify the exposition, let us assume that $l_1 < l_2 < \ldots < l_i = l_{i+1} < \ldots < l_n$. In this case, if $G_{i-1} < G < G_{i+1}$, then both lands i and $i + 1$ may be cultivated and therefore they are both marginal. The remainder of the analysis is unchanged. The fact that when one of the two is marginal also the other is does not mean that they have always the same rent unless $t_i = t_{i+1}$.

2. The other special case is the one in which $G = G_i$, that is, *the case in which the marginal land is fully utilized*. In this case competition amongst landlords who own the marginal land need not be enough to bid the respective rent rate down to zero. It is possible that the marginal land yields its proprietors a positive rent (though this is not necessarily the case). As a consequence the number of processes operated may *fall short* of the sum of the number of commodities produced (in our case: one) plus the number of the qualities of land paying a rent: thus prices, rents and wage rate cannot be fully determined and they may assume any level within a closed and bounded range:

$$w_{i-1} \leq w \leq w_i$$
$$q_{hi} \leq q_h \leq q_{h,i+1} \qquad (h = 1, 2, \ldots, i)$$
$$q_k = 0. \qquad (k = i + 1, \ldots, n)$$

Finally, we can assert that if the quantity of corn produced is not larger than G_n, then there is a positive wage rate and there are nonnegative rates of rent, such that the economy can produce that quantity of corn.

The results presented in this section can also be illustrated with the help of a *production function*. When we do so, we consider the amount of labour (instead of the gross product of corn) as the independent variable. In the present context this is possible since there is a monotonic relationship between these two magnitudes. Consider Figure 4.1 where along the horizontal axis we measure the amount of labour employed L and on the vertical axis the amount of corn produced G, where

$$L_i = \sum_{h=1}^{i} \frac{T_h l_h}{t_h}$$

The production function has the form of an increasing polygonal whose slope is not increasing. In order to see this, consider that if λ_i labourers operate process (i), then the quantity of corn produced with this process is $y = \lambda_i/l_i$ and the extension of cultivation on land i is $\tau_i = (t_i/l_i)\lambda_i$. Since $\tau_i \leq T_i$ by the assumption concerning the availability of land i, then $\lambda_i \leq (l_i/t_i)T_i$. The first segment of the polygonal refers to process (1), whose slope $(1/l_1)$ is the highest. It is the choice of the cost-minimizing farmers to operate only this process when total production is small. If $L = (l_1/t_1)T_1$, production can be increased only by operating another process on another quality of land. Once again the farmers choose to operate process (2), whose segment has a slope $(1/l_2)$, which is the highest apart from process (1). And so on.

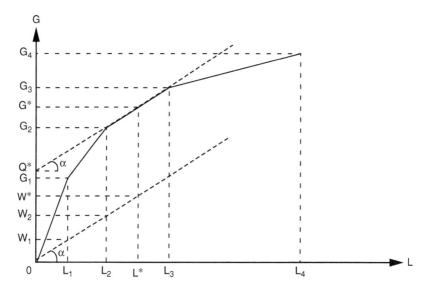

Figure 4.1 The production function for extensive rent

Thus, the slope of the production function along the i-th segment equals the *marginal product of labour*, i.e. the increment in total corn output associated with a small increment in total labour input, and coincides with the output-labour ratio on land i and with the wage rate that process (i) can pay if no rent on land i is paid. In a cusp of the polygonal the slope is not defined, but can vary in a range. As we have seen earlier, this is a consequence of the fact that the marginal land is fully cultivated. A straight line tangent to a point of the production function has a slope equal to the wage rate, whereas the vertical intercept of this straight line gives the sum total of rents paid on the different cultivated lands. The production function can be represented by

$$G = G(L).$$

The figure can also be used to illustrate the cost-minimizing solution of the problem under consideration. For example, with $G = G^*$, total employment will be equal to $L = L^*$ and lands of quality 1, 2 and 3 will be utilized: L_1 units of labour will be employed on land of quality 1 producing G_1 units of corn, $L_2 - L_1$ units of labour on land of quality 2 producing $G_2 - G_1$ units of corn, and $L^* - L_2$ units of labour on the marginal land, that is, land of quality 3, producing $G^* - G_2$ units of corn. The real wage rate will be given by $\tan \alpha$, that is, the labour productivity on marginal land ($1/l_3$). Total wages will be given by $W^* = G^* - Q^* = L^* \tan \alpha$, and total rents by $Q^* = G^* - W^* = G_2 - W_2$. Total rents on land of quality 1 and land of quality 2 will be given by $Q_1^* = G_1 - W_1$ and $Q_2^* = (G_2 - G_1) - (W_2 - W_1)$, respectively, and could be represented in the diagram inserting another straight line of slope α passing through the point (L_1, G_1); obviously, $Q^* = Q_1^* + Q_2^*$.

3.   Order of fertility and order according to rent per acre

In Section 2 an existence condition for an extensive rent model has been developed. It has also been shown that the different qualities of land can be ranked according to the order in which they are taken into cultivation. This order will be called the *order of fertility*. What matters with regard to this order are the cost-minimizing ways to produce ever larger amounts of corn: as the effectual demand for corn rises, more and more qualities of land have to be cultivated. The order of fertility reflects the sequence according to which the different qualities of land are taken into cultivation.

A related, but different, way of ranking the different qualities of land is their ranking according to the rent they yield per acre, i.e. the rate of rent; we may also talk of the *order of rentability*. In early contributions to rent theory it has commonly been assumed that the order of fertility and of rentability coincide. This is certainly true in some special cases, especially when all methods of production available to cultivate the different plots of land exhibit the same amount of land (acreage) needed per unit of output,[8] but not in general.

Obviously, all fully cultivated types of land yield a higher rent per acre than those types which are not fully used. Therefore the order of fertility has some influence on the order of rentability. However, even though land of quality i will be taken into cultivation prior to land of quality j, it is possible that the rent per acre accruing on land i is smaller than the rent per acre on land j when land of quality k, $k > j$, is marginal. In this section we will clarify this point by means of a graphical tool. The same tool will also be used in the following section. If land h is cultivated, then w and q_h need to satisfy the following equation:

$$t_h q_h + w l_h = 1. \tag{4}$$

Equation (4) represents a straight line in the (q_h, w) plane. This straight line will be called the q_h−w relationship. Similarly with regard to each $h = 1, 2, \ldots, n$. These q_h−w relationships ($i = 1, 2, \ldots, n$) may even be drawn in the same diagram, keeping of course in mind that q_h is the rent *per acre* of land of quality h. Hence the intersection of the q_h−w relationship and the q_h−w relationship ($h \neq k$) can sensibly be interpreted only in the following way: at the corresponding wage rate land of quality h and land of quality k yield the same rent *per acre*. This being said, the n straight lines (4) can be drawn as in Figure 4.2, where $n = 3$.

In Figure 4.2 the wage rate corresponding to a constellation in which land of quality h is marginal is given by the intersection of the q_h−w relationship with the horizontal axis. The rent rates on the intramarginal lands associated with such a constellation are then found on the q_k−w relationships ($k < h$). Thus, in the case in which none of the lands is scarce ($G < T_1/t_1$), i.e. land 1 is marginal, the wage rate would be equal to w_1 and no quality of land would yield its owner a positive rent. If $T_1/t_1 < G < T_1/t_1 + T_2/t_2$, then the rate of rent obtained by an owner of land of quality 1 equals $q' > 0$, whereas no other quality of land is able to yield a positive rent. But if $T_1/t_1 + T_2/t_2 < G < T_1/t_1 + T_2/t_2 + T_3/t_3$, then the rate of rent obtained on land of quality 1 is $q'' < q'''$, where q''' is the rate of rent obtained on land of quality 2. This is a consequence of the fact that in the example depicted the q_1−w relationship cuts the q_2−w relationship at a wage rate lower than w_3. It goes without saying that the

---

[8] A case of this type has been studied by Johann Heinrich von Thünen in *Der isolirte Staat* (1826): plots of homogeneous land on which corn is grown are located at different distances from the market place, i.e. the 'town', where the output of corn is consumed. Ricardo also expressed the view that the order of the different plots of land according to 'fertility' corresponds to the order according to the associated rents per acre, such that the 'most fertile' land always yields the highest rent per acre, the second-best land the second highest, and so on; see Ricardo ([1817] 1951, p. 70). This view was also shared by Marx ([1894] 1959, p. 665).

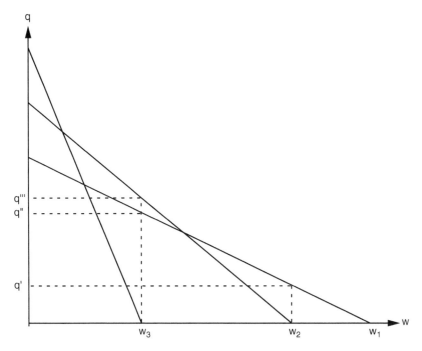

Figure 4.2 The relationships between rent rates and the wage rate

location of the q_h–w relationships reflects the magnitudes of the production coefficients with regard to labour and land.

4.   Intensive diminishing returns (intensive rent)

We now turn to the case in which land is assumed to be of uniform quality; the available amount totals T units (acres). There exist n processes to produce corn, which are given in Table 4.2. Obviously, the existing processes can be numbered in such a way that $l_1 \leq l_2 \leq \ldots \leq l_n$. With no loss of generality we can even assume that $l_1 < l_2 < \ldots < l_n$. In fact if $l_i = l_{i+1}$, some i, then either $t_i < t_{i+1}$ or $t_i > t_{i+1}$ (otherwise the two processes would be indistinct). In the former case process $(i + 1)$ would be dominated by process (i); the reverse would be true in the latter case. The dominated process could be dropped, since it would never be operated. We can also assume that $t_1 > t_2 > \ldots > t_n$. In fact if it were not so, then there would be a process producing the same amount of corn and utilizing both a larger amount of land and a larger amount of labour than another process. Clearly, the former process would be dominated by the latter. As a consequence, $T/t_1 < T/t_2 < \ldots < T/t_n$. That is,

Table 4.2 *Technical features of production processes (intensive rent)*

processes	land	labour		corn
(1)	t_1	l_1	$\rightarrow$	1
(2)	t_2	l_2	$\rightarrow$	1
...	...	...	$\rightarrow$	...
(n)	t_n	l_n	$\rightarrow$	1

the maximum amount of corn that can be produced with process (i) is smaller than the maximum amount of corn that can be produced with process $(i + 1)$.

If process (i) is operated, then the following equation must be satisfied:

$$t_i q + w l_i = 1,$$

where q is the (uniform) rent rate and w is the wage rate. It is assumed that no process can yield a surplus, otherwise all farmers would prefer to operate it. That is,

$$t_j q + w l_j \geq 1. \qquad (j = 1, 2, \ldots, n) \qquad (5)$$

Obviously, $w > 0$ and $q \geq 0$.

If $G < T/t_1$, then land is not scarce and competition amongst landlords rules out a positive rent. Of course, only process (1) will be operated. This part of the analysis is identical to the corresponding part of Section 2. But if $G > T/t_1$, land is in short supply. Let us first assume that $T/t_1 < G < T/t_2$. Apparently none of the other processes, i.e. processes 2, 3, ..., n, can be operated alone. In fact if they could, then land would not be scarce and the rent rate would be zero. As a consequence process (1) would yield a surplus if the wage rate would be determined by the operation of any of the other processes. If processes (h) and (k), $h < k$, are both operated, then

$$t_h q + w l_h = 1$$

$$t_k q + w l_k = 1.$$

Solving for w and q we get

$$w = \frac{t_h - t_k}{l_k t_h - l_h t_k} > 0, \qquad (6a)$$

$$q = \frac{l_k - l_h}{l_k t_h - l_h t_k} > 0. \qquad (6b)$$

Since $q > 0$, the available land must be fully cultivated. This can be the case only if processes (h) and (k) are operated in such a way that the amount of corn produced with process (h), $G_h \geq 0$, and the amount of corn produced with process (k), $G_k \geq 0$, are such that[9]

$$G_h + G_k = G,$$
$$t_h G_h + t_k G_k = T,$$

that is,

$$G_h = \frac{T - t_k G}{t_h - t_k}, \tag{7a}$$

$$G_k = \frac{t_h G - T}{t_h - t_k}, \tag{7b}$$

In order for a positive solution to obtain, $h = 1$ and $k > 1$. Moreover, process (k) has to be chosen in such a way that w and q as determined by equations (6), with $h = 1$, must satisfy also inequalities (5). We can continue the exposition by using Figures 4.3a and 4.3b, which give two possible examples of a set of 3 q-w relationships ($n = 3$). It deserves to be noted that in the case of intensive rent the qualification added in the previous section regarding the possibility of drawing the q-w relationships in the same diagram is not necessary, since now q is the rent rate relative to the *same* quality of land. Because of the chosen order of processes the q-w relationship which cuts the horizontal axis at the highest level of w corresponds to process (1); the q-w relationship which cuts the horizontal axis at the lowest level of w corresponds to process (3); the remaining q-w relationship corresponds to process (2).

In both Figures 4.3a and 4.3b, if $G < T/t_1$ and, as a consequence, land is not scarce, the wage rate is given by point A, in which the q-w relationship relative to process (1) cuts the horizontal axis. With $T/t_1 < G < T/t_2$ inequalities (5) are satisfied only on the upper envelope of the q-w relationships, whereas equations (6), with $h = 1$, are satisfied only in points in which the q-w relationship relative to process (1) cuts another q-w relationship. Obviously, both these properties hold in a unique point only (otherwise the q-w relationship relative to process (1) would cut more than one other q-w relationship *on the envelope*). This point is point B in Figure 4.3a and point D in Figure 4.3b.

---

[9] As Sraffa (1960: chapter XI) stresses, the scarcity of land is generally reflected in the co-existence of two or more processes producing the same commodity. In the pure case of *extensive* diminishing returns, in which there is only one process for the production of corn on each quality of land, different qualities of land will be used side by side in order to produce the amount of corn required. If there were no scarcity, cost-minimization would imply that only one quality of land (and only one method of production), i.e. the one that allows production of the commodity at lowest cost per unit, would be used, and there could be no rent. In the pure case of *intensive* diminishing returns, in which there is only one quality of land but a variety of methods of production to cultivate it, 'the only evidence of [the] scarcity [of land] to be found in the process of production is the duality of methods' (1960; p. 76).

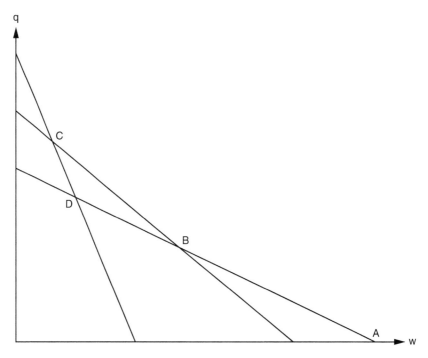

Figure 4.3a The q-w relationships (example 1)

Assume now that $T/t_2 < G < T/t_3$. If in the previous analysis $k > 2$, as in Figure 4.3b, then no change is required: the increased production of corn can be effected by operating processes (1) and (k) – and, indeed, with no other pair of processes. If, on the contrary, in the previous analysis $k = 2$, as in Figure 4.3a, then another pair of processes must be operated: even if the whole land was to be cultivated with process (2), the amount of corn G could not be produced. This new pair of processes will be indicated again with letters h and k ($h < k$). This pair must satisfy equations (6) and inequalities (5). Moreover, since $q > 0$ because of equations (6), also equations (7) must be satisfied. This implies that process h must be either process (1) or process (2). But process (1) has no other segment of its q-w relationship on the envelope; hence of necessity $h = 2$. As a consequence, we have to find on the envelope the unique point in which process (2) cuts a q-w relationship other than the one corresponding to process (1). In Figure 4.3a this is point C. In general, each cusp on the envelope of the q-w relationships determines levels of w and q compatible with the co-existence of two methods of production employed in the production of the given amount of corn, where $T/t_h < G < T/t_k$ and (h) and (k) are the processes whose q-w relationships determine the cusp on the envelope.

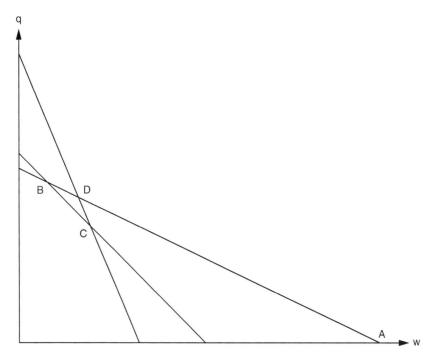

Figure 4.3b The q-w relationships (example 2)

It remains for us to investigate the case in which $G = T/t_k$, where (k) is one of the processes contributing to the envelope. In this case only one process will be operated on the entire land. As a consequence, w and q are not fully determined, but can vary in a range. The possible values of w and q are exactly those values of the q-w relationship relative to process (k) which are on the envelope. Hence the *outer envelope* of the q-w relationships is the *q-w relationship for the economy as a whole*. Finally, we can assert that if the quantity of corn in effectual demand is not larger than T/t_n, then there are levels of the wage rate and the rent rate such that the economy can produce this quantity of corn.

The model presented in this section can be interpreted as a formalization of the concept of intensive rent as it was used by Ricardo, among others. When $G < T/t_1$ the amount of corn produced can be increased through the gradual extension of process (1). As soon as the whole area is cultivated, the production of corn can be increased through the gradual extension of the second process contributing to the outer envelope of the q-w relationships (call it process (k_1)) at the expense of process (1) $(T/t_1 < G < T/t_{k_1})$: this requires that the rent rate rises to the point where processes (1) and (k_1) can both be operated. As soon as process (k_1) is used to cultivate the whole area the production of corn can be increased only if the rent rises to the point where process (k_1) and the third process on the envelope of the q-w relationships (call it process (k_2)) can both be operated. Then, once again the amount of corn produced can be increased through the gradual extension of process (k_2) at the expense of process (k_1) $(T/t_{k_1} < G < T/t_{k_2})$. And so on. Note that both process (n) and process (1) contribute to the envelope for sure.

Exactly as in Section 2, the results of this section can again be illustrated with the help of a *production function*. It is constructed in an analogous way and also has the same properties. A brief sketch must suffice. In order to simplify the exposition, assume that s processes $(2 \leq s \leq n)$ contribute to the envelope and $n - s$ do not. Drop the $n - s$ processes, which do not contribute to the envelope, and renumber the remaining processes from 1 to s. Then the G_i depicted in Figure 4.1 equals T/t_i $(i = 1, 2, \ldots, s)$; the L_i depicted in Figure 4.1 equals $(l_i/t_i)T$ $(i = 1, 2, \ldots, s)$. The slope of each segment of the production function does not give the output-labour ratio, but still gives the real wage rate.

5.   A generalization

In the previous sections we have studied two simple cases. A more general analysis includes in a single model at the same time several qualities of land and several processes for each quality of land. A formal presentation could be given with the help of linear programming, but we refrain from doing it here. A simple sketch of the argument must suffice.

If total production is small enough, only one method of production will be employed, that which maximizes output per worker. Total output can be increased by gradually extending the cost-minimizing method to the entire available amount of the quality of land (call it quality 1) utilized by this method. In Figure 4.4 the maximum output to be produced with this method is given by G_1; the corresponding employment of labour on land of quality 1 is L_1; tan α gives both the output-labour ratio and the wage rate. A further increase of output can take place either by taking into cultivation another quality of land (call it quality 2) or by gradually replacing the first method of production by another one which utilizes the same quality of land but produces more corn per acre by employing a larger quantity of labour per unit of output. Farmers will choose the cheapest method available, which is the one that allows the highest slope. If the cheapest method available happens to be that one utilizing land of quality 2, then in Figure 4.4 the maximum output to be produced with this method is given by $G_2 - G_1$; the corresponding employment on land of quality 2 is $L_2 - L_1$; tan γ gives both the output-labour ratio and the wage rate. On the contrary, if the cheapest method available is

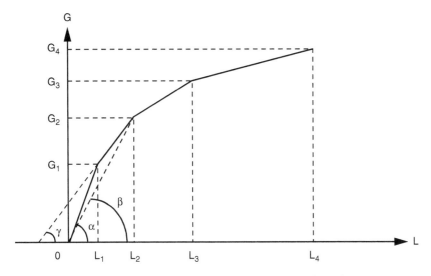

Figure 4.4 The production function for extensive and intensive rent

another method utilizing land of quality 1, then in Figure 4.4 the maximum output to be produced with this method is given by G_2; the corresponding employment is L_2; $\tan \beta$ gives the output-labour ratio and $\tan \gamma$ the wage rate when processes (1) and (2) are both operated.

Similarly, a further increase of output can take place either by taking into cultivation yet another quality of land or by gradually replacing (one of) the operated process(es) of production by another one which utilizes one of) the same quality (qualities) of land but produces more corn per acre at a still higher labour input per unit of output. Once again farmers will choose the cheapest method available.[10]

Even if returns to scale are assumed to be constant from a technological point of view, the scarcity of land is reflected in returns that are *decreasing*:

diminishing returns must of necessity occur because it will be the producer himself who, for his own benefit, will arrange the doses of the factors and the methods of use in a descending order, going from the most favourable ones to the most ineffective, and he will start production with the best combinations, resorting little by little, as these are exhausted, to the worst ones. (Sraffa, [1925, p. 288], 1998, p. 332).

---

[10] In an extreme case there is a continuum of processes and/or a continuum of different qualities of land such that both the production function and the supply function can be drawn as continuously differentiable functions. This would be the case if $G = G(L)$ is the production function, then $G'(L) > 0$ and $G''(L) < 0$. Similarly, if $p = p(G)$ is the supply function, then $p'(G) > 0$.

6.   Is a further generalization possible?

In the previous section we have shown how it is possible to describe the choice of technique as a function of the (net *and* gross) product of corn under the form of a production function. We want to stress, however, that this is not possible when capital is involved, even if capital has just the form of corn (as seed). In fact, if corn is produced by means of labour, land *and* corn, we have both to distinguish between net and gross product and to take into account a further variable, the rate of profit. The consequence is that the function that we can construct between labour employed and net product of corn does not need to be increasing and concave, and for the production of a given amount of net product more than one solution may exist for a given rate of profit.[11] Further, since costs of production now depend on the level of the rate of profit, so does the order of fertility: while it was naturally determined in the cases discussed in Sections 2 and 5, it now no longer is, but may change with a change in the level of the rate of profit, and this makes the difference.[12]

7.   Concluding remarks

This chapter has first and foremost a pedagogical aim: to present the principles of extensive and intensive diminishing returns, and thus extensive and intensive rent, in as simple terms as possible. These principles Alberto Quadrio Curzio dealt with in a number of contributions. Our construction is meant to complement his in the hope and expectation that it proves useful in teaching these important principles to beginners in economics. Although the chosen framework is very simple indeed – corn is produced by means of labour and land(s) only – some of the results might come as a surprise and were in fact not anticipated in the earlier literature and others are even disputed in the most recent literature. We show, in particular, that in the conditions given an aggregate production function for corn can be constructed both in the case of extensive and in the case of intensive diminishing returns and a fortiori also in the more general case that combines both kinds of returns. This latter result was disputed by Morishima (1989) in a criticism of Luigi Pasinetti's paper on Ricardo's theory of profits and differential rent (Pasinetti 1960). In addition we show that other than in extremely special cases there is no presumption that the

---

[11]   A numerical example was provided by Freni (1991). See also Kurz and Salvadori (1995, p. 313, exercise 7.7).

[12]   The locus classicus of the dependence of the order of fertility on the rate of profit as well as the fact that the order of fertility need not coincide with the order of rentability is Quadrio Curzio (1967, 1980). It is, however, interesting to note that Sraffa in his hitherto unpublished papers had anticipated these results.

order of fertility will coincide with the order of rentability, a view advocated by authors from David Ricardo and Johann Heinrich von Thünen to Karl Marx. Finally it is emphasized that no production function can generally be built up as soon as there are produced means of production, or capital goods, employed in the production of corn. Even the case in which there is only seed corn allowed for can be shown to typically create difficulties in the regard under consideration. Therefore the reader must not consider our argument as supportive of the use of aggregate production functions. It should rather be read against the background of Spinoza's *determinatio est negatio*.

REFERENCES

Anderson, J. (1777a) *Observations on the Means of Exciting a Spirit of National Industry*, London: Thomas Cadell; Edinburgh: Charles Elliot.
    (1777b) *An Inquiry into the Nature of the Corn Laws*, Edinburgh: Mundell.
Böhm-Bawerk, E. v. (1889) *Kapital und Kapitalzins. Zweite Abteilung: Positive Theorie des Kapitales*, Innsbruck: Wagner (4th edn 1921, Jena: Fischer).
    (1959) *Capital and Interest*, 2 vols. Translation of the 4th edn of Böhm-Bawerk (1889), South Holland, Ill.: Libertarian Press.
Freni, G. (1991) 'Capitale tecnico nei modelli dinamici ricardiani', *Studi Economici*, 44, pp. 141–59.
Kurz, H. D., and Salvadori, N. (1995) *Theory of Production: A Long-Period Analysis*, Cambridge: Cambridge University Press.
Malthus, T. R. (1815) *An Inquiry into the Nature and Progress of Rent*, London: John Murray.
Marx, K. (1959) *Capital*, vol. III, Moscow: Progress Publishers. English translation of Das Kapital, vol. III, ed. by F. Engels, Hamburg: Meissner, 1894.
Morishima, M. (1989). *Ricardo's Economics. A General Equilibrium Theory of Distribution and Growth*, Cambridge: Cambridge University Press.
Pasinetti, L. L. (1960) 'A Mathematical Formulation of the Ricardian System', *Review of Economic Studies*, 27.2, pp. 78–98. Reprinted in Pasinetti (1974).
    (1974) *Growth and Income Distribution. Essays in Economic Theory*, Cambridge: Cambridge University Press.
    (ed.) (1980) *Essays on the Theory of Joint Production*, London: Macmillan.
Petty, W. (1662) A Treatise of Taxes and Contributions. Reprinted in Petty (1986).
    (1986) *The Economic Writings of Sir William Petty*, ed. by C. H. Hull, 2 vols., Cambridge 1899: Cambridge University Press. Reprinted in one vol., New York: Kelley.
Quadrio Curzio, A. (1967) *Rendita e distribuzione in un modello economico plurisettoriale*, Milan: Giuffrè.
    (1980) 'Rent, Income Distribution, and Orders of Efficiency and Rentability', in Pasinetti (1980), pp. 218–40. Reprinted in Quadrio Curzio (1990), pp. 21–47.
    (1990) *Rent, Distribution and Economic Structure. A Collection of Essays*, Milan: IDSE.
Ricardo, D. (1815) 'An Essay on the Influence of a Low Price of Corn on the Profits of Stock', in D. Ricardo (1951–1973), vol. IV.

(1817) *On the Principles of Political Economy and Taxation*, in D. Ricardo (1951–1973), vol. I.

(1951–1973) *The Works and Correspondence of David Ricardo*, 11 vols., ed. by P. Sraffa with the collaboration of M. H. Dobb, Cambridge: Cambridge University Press.

Salvadori, N. (2004) 'Is Ricardian Extensive Rent a Nash Equilibrium?' in R. Arena and N. Salvadori (eds.) *Money, Credit and the Role of the State: Essays in Honour of Augusto Graziani*, Aldershot: Ashgate, pp. 347–58.

Smith, A. (1976) *An Inquiry into the Nature and Causes of the Wealth of Nations*, 1st edn 1776, vol. II of *The Glasgow Edition of the Works and Correspondence of Adam Smith*, ed. by R. H. Campbell, A. S. Skinner and W. B. Todd, Oxford: Oxford University Press.

Sraffa, P. (1925) 'Sulle relazioni fra costo e quantità prodotta', *Annali di Economia*, 2, pp. 277–328.

(1960) *Production of Commodities by Means of Commodities. Prelude to a Critique of Economic Theory*, Cambridge: Cambridge University Press.

(1998) 'On the Relations between Cost and Quantity Produced', in Pasinetti L. L. (ed.), *Italian Economic Papers*, Bologna: Il Mulino; Oxford: Oxford University Press, pp. 323–63; translation of Sraffa, P. (1925). Reprinted in H. D. Kurz and N. Salvadori (eds.) (2003) *The Legacy of Piero Sraffa*, Cheltenham: E. Elgar.

Thünen, J. H. v. (1826) *Der isolierte Staat in Beziehung auf Landwirtschaft und Nationalökonomie*, Stuttgart: Gustav Fischer (2nd edn 1842).

Wicksell, K. (1901) *Föreläsingar i Nationalekonomi*, vol. I, Lund: Berlingska Boktrycheriet.

(1934) *Lectures on Political Economy*, vol. I, London: George Routledge & Sons. Translation of Wicksell (1901) by E. Classen and edited, with an introduction, by Lionel Robbins.

(1954) *Value, Capital and Rent*. Translation of Wicksell (1901), London: George Allen & Unwin. Reprinted (1970), New York: Kelley.

West, E. (1815) *An Essay on the Application of Capital to Land*, London: John Hopkins Press.

5   Profit, productive rent and parasitic rent

Pier Carlo Nicola

1.   Introduction

The economic categories of wage, profit and rent have always been the bases on which to build the theory of the distribution of income over a given time period. The term 'rent' (in Ricardo's terminology) is the payment to the landlord for the use of land to produce commodities, while 'wage' is paid to workers for their productive services, and 'profit' is the reward for the use of means of production different from land and labour. But in all economies, past and present, whether capitalistic or centralized, there is also a second type of 'rent', which may be defined as 'unproductive' or 'parasitic', received by those individuals contributing nothing to the production of national income and which is spent by these recipients in order to buy a quota of the national income. In this chapter, land is grouped with all other production factors[1] and the corresponding payment is included in the category of profit, while the term 'rent' is understood in a totally unproductive meaning.

Profits and Ricardian rent have been thoroughly considered in the economic literature, and their mutual relationship investigated in particular by Alberto Quadrio Curzio (see especially his two theoretical monographs dated 1967 and 1975). The aim of this chapter is to present a formal model analysing, in a limited and unconventional context within the framework of economic growth models, what economic theory can offer on the issue of *unproductive rent*. Before entering the main theme of this chapter, it is useful to recall some excerpts by Quadrio Curzio on rent:

As it is well known, the so called residual theory of distribution is grounded on the notion of net profit (or surplus) and on the idea that its division among various categories of income (wages, profits, rents) occurs according to a given sequence ...' (Quadrio Curzio 1967, p. 9; author's translation)

---

[1] Very likely the distinction between land and other production factors different from labour is motivated by the fact that the total amount of original land is finite, while all other capital goods can be increased by production.

And:

It is our aim to insert a theory of rent into a modern taxonomy of the residual theory of distribution. (Quadrio Curzio 1967, p. 9; author's translation)

It seems useful to state that the present chapter may be placed inside the sphere of the marginal theory of income distribution; for the sake of simplicity the term 'rent' in the meaning of Quadrio Curzio is here assimilated to 'profit', by considering land on a par with every other material input. It is also useful to underline a distinction, important in our opinion, between the model here presented and the theory stemming from the fundamental contribution by Solow (1956) and independently by Swan (1956). It is the assumption that the saving propensity, s, is a constant. Because under standard assumptions in Solow's model all *per capita* variables converge to a stationary state, many economists studied how to make s endogenous, by choosing its value so that in a stationary state *per capita* consumption may be maximized. This particular state of the economic variables is called by Phelps (1961) a state of 'golden age'. The problem is: who chooses the unique value of s ? This agent must be a meta-operator from outside the economic system. In fact the model that we shall put forward here requires the participation of a meta-operator; his presence is thus to be considered not as an *ad hoc* addition, at least with reference to the existing macroeconomic literature.

After this Introduction, Section 2 points out what is meant by the terms 'profit' and 'rent'; Section 3 presents a model somewhat different from the models inspired by Solow's contribution previously quoted. In Section 4 an exemplification is put forward, while a dynamic version of the model is contained in Section 5. Finally, Section 6 concludes this short chapter.

2.   Profit and rent

From a social viewpoint, wages are the quota of national income on which everybody has nothing to question. Socially speaking, profits do not seem to be so well received, at least according to an ethical and/or social viewpoint. Profits are inescapable in every decentralized economy, because they are the main source for investment. Rents are very often regarded as negative, as they subtract a share of national product from profits, and worse still from wages, with the consequence of reducing the potential rate of investment and growth of the economy. The main purpose of this note is to verify, by means of a formal model, these principles, not always accepted from a theoretical point of view. Rent is here understood as the share of national product (the so called GDP) spent by their owners, whatever their legal rights, without any contribution by them to the production of commodities and services. There are at least two types of rent.[2] At one extreme we find the treasury bonds inherited by a consumer with no role whatsoever in economic activity, the interests of which are wholly consumed by him. At the other extreme we find pension payments, received by retired workers for their past contribution to the production process, a sort of delayed wage payment. The rent considered in this chapter is of the first type; hence it may be named unproductive or parasitic, and every person receiving such an income is rightly called *rentier*. It is also important to underline that the model presented here is applicable to a decentralized economy, where both profits and capital have a full right of existence. Of course, wages and labour are even more 'normal': these economic categories are unavoidable both in decentralized and in centralized economies.

3.   An elementary macroeconomic model

Let Y mean the value of total production (for instance measured on an annual basis) in a given economy, which is obtained by applying an aggregate production function, $F : \mathfrak{R}_+^2 \to \mathfrak{R}_+$ whose factors of production traditionally are the amount of labour applied, N, and the quantity of capital, K. Thus, the well-known relation

$$Y = F(N, K) \tag{1}$$

holds true. As usual, F is assumed to satisfy the following conditions: its first and second partial derivatives are continuous; additionally both the first partial derivatives are positive; and F satisfies the two equalities $F(0,K)=0$ for every K and $F(N, 0)=0$ for every N. Moreover, the second order partial derivatives of F are negative, or $F_{NN}(N, K) < 0$ and $F_{KK}(N, K) < 0$ for all values of N and K.

Production is distributed in three shares: wages, W, profits, P, and rents, R; thus the following relation holds true

$$Y = W + P + R. \tag{2}$$

From now on we start introducing some differences with respect to the traditional macroeconomic theory, and assume that all wages are devoted to the supply of labour[3] according to the formula[4]

---

[2] As already underlined in Section 1, the term 'rent' is here considered to be a residual category, namely everything which is not wage nor profit, and not in the Ricardian definition of 'that portion of the produce of the earth which is paid to the landlords for the use of the original and indestructible power of the soil' (Ricardo 1951, p. 67; 1st edn 1817).

[3] W being an unknown, the labour supply, N, becomes an endogenous variable, differently from what happens in many macroeconomic models where the labour supply is an exogenous variable.

[4] More generally, one could write $N = g(W)$, where g is a differentiable and strictly increasing function satisfying $g(0) = 0$.

$$N = aW \ (a > 0). \tag{3}$$

Namely: when wages increase, and hence also the material means on which individuals live increase, the quantity of labour increases. Correspondingly, profits generate new capital, according to the formula[5]

$$K = bP \ (b > 0). \tag{4}$$

Thus, we can write (1) as follows:

$$Y = F \ (aW, \ bP), \tag{5}$$

which shows that production is entirely obtained from wages and profits, while unproductive rent plays no role in the production process. But such a rent receives a *quota* in the distribution of the product. Thus, we can assume that c is a parameter, where $0 < c < 1$; therefore

$$R = cY. \tag{6}$$

It then follows that relation (2) becomes

$$F \ (aW, \ bP) = W + P + cF \ (aW, \ bP); \tag{7}$$

an equation in the only variables W and P, which can be written as:

$$F \ (aW, \ bP) = \frac{1}{1-c} (W+P). \tag{8}$$

From (8), it looks quite clearly that R may be thought of as a residual category of income; contributing to expenditure, according to relation (6), but having no impact on production, as it appears from (5). The problem to be considered here is the following one: how may we select wages and profits in order to maximize production?[6] Hence we are, with respect to the choice of the saving rate, in the same situation as Section 1 of this chapter. Moreover, we might recall that another variant of Solow's model inspired a number of scholars (for instance Koopmans, 1965) to extend the model so as to maximize *per capita* utility. This being the case, a meta-agent must be introduced, sometimes considered to be the Government, which in the present model introduces the following Lagrangian function:

$$L(W, \ P, \ \lambda) = F \ (aW, \ bP) + \lambda[W + P - (1-c)F \ (aW, \ bP)], \tag{9}$$

where λ is the Lagrange multiplier. Assuming F to be quasi-concave, a necessary and sufficient condition to obtain the constrained maximum of F is

---

[5] More generally, it is possible to set $K = h(P)$, where h is a differentiable and strictly increasing function, satisfying $h(0) = 0$.

[6] Of course, we are compelled to assume that there is a meta-agent, either the invisible hand or the market or the auctioneer, responsible for the maximizing process.

the vanishing of both the first order partial derivatives of L. By denoting these derivatives with F_N and F_P we have:

$$aF_N + \lambda - \lambda(1-c)aF_N = 0, \tag{10}$$

$$bF_P + \lambda - \lambda(1-c)bF_P = 0. \tag{11}$$

From this system we immediately obtain

$$aF_N(aW, bP) = bF_P(aW, bP), \tag{12}$$

which with equation (7) allows us to calculate the optimum values for W and P, and thus for $N=aW$ and $K=bP$. Relation (12) states the equality, under equilibrium conditions, between the marginal productivities of labour (i.e. the wage rate) and capital (i.e. the profit rate). This equilibrium condition is totally independent of the value taken by rent, R. But R, due to the distributive condition (2), plays a part in income distribution, and so it plays an important role in sustaining expenditure. Hence, it is also possible to state that this type of rent cannot be considered entirely parasitic: after all, buying jewellery contributes to the increase in national income.

Back to formula (12), one may note another important point in the model put forward, which is not to be found in traditional macroeconomic models without a maximization process. In fact relation (12) unequivocally states, without any doubt, that when the aim is the maximization of the gross domestic product, then the distribution of GDP between wages and profits must take a specific value. At least from an ideal point of view, the conflict of interest between the social classes of workers and capitalists is fully bypassed!

4.   An example

To fully understand the results of the previous model, let us assume that the production function is of the Cobb-Douglas type, namely $(W, P) \to F$ $(aW, bP) = (aW)^\alpha(bP)^\beta$ where α and β are positive parameters subject to $\alpha+\beta<1$.[7] By this choice, and after the needed manipulations, relation (12) becomes

$$\frac{W}{P} = \frac{\alpha}{\beta}. \tag{13}$$

By substituting $W = (\alpha/\beta)P$ into (2), after the necessary manipulations and writing $v=(1-c)a^\alpha b^\beta(\alpha/\beta)^\alpha > 0$, we obtain the following equilibrium values:

---

[7] This inequality guaranties that the solution of the previous constrained maximum problem effectively supplies the unique maximum.

$$\hat{P} = \left(v\frac{\beta}{\alpha+\beta}\right)^{\frac{1}{1-\alpha-\beta}} \tag{14}$$

and thus

$$\hat{W} = \frac{\alpha}{\beta}\left(v\frac{\beta}{\alpha+\beta}\right)^{\frac{1}{1-\alpha-\beta}}. \tag{15}$$

One may note that these formulae contain the term $1-c$, associated with the unproductive rent. Due to this condition, *ceteris paribus*, the values of W and P are smaller than in the case of $c=0$, i.e. when there is no unproductive rent. This fact confirms that the present form of rent is unproductive.

5.   Dynamic elements

In this section our aim is to present a dynamic version of the model; time, t, is expressed by the sequence of non-negative integers, $t=1, 2, 3, \ldots$, where $t = 0$ is considered to be the starting moment, while period t runs from $t - 1$ and t. To avoid formal complications, let us assume that capital has the form of circulating capital; as a consequence, in every period capital is proportional, according to the parameter b introduced in Section 3, to profits. The starting data are expressed by the positive quantity Y_0, namely by the production obtained in the time period preceding the first one, at the disposal of the economy to be distributed among individuals and for production purposes during period $t = 1$; moreover, given are also the values W_{-1} and P_{-1}. Thus, we have $Y_1 = F(aW_1, bP_1)$ and $W_1 + P_1 + R_1 = Y_0$. More generally, in every period t we have

$$Y_t = F(aW_t, bP_t), \tag{16}$$
$$W_t + P_t + R_t = Y_{t-1}. \tag{17}$$

Moreover:

$$R_t = cY_{t-1}. \tag{18}$$

From these three equations we obtain:

$$W_t + P_t = (1-c)F(aW_{t-1}, bP_{t-1}). \tag{19}$$

Given the values W_{t-1} and P_{t-1}, the value of W_t and P_t are obtained, as in Section 3, so to maximize production, Y_t. By writing the Lagrangian as in Section 3, the necessary manipulations yield the following result:

$$aF_N\ (aW_t, bP_t) = bF_P\ (aW_t,\ bP_t),\qquad(20)$$

which is to be associated with (19).[8] Recursively, from relations (19) and (20) we obtain the optimal sequences

$$\{W_t\}_{t=1}^{\infty},\ \{P_t\}_{t=1}^{\infty},\ \{R_t\}_{t=1}^{\infty}\qquad(21)$$

and moreover the sequence of GDP values, $\{Y_t\}_{t=1}^{\infty}$. The dynamic system has, of course, a stationary solution, expressed by the optimal values obtained in Section 3. In order to simplify the analysis we shall confine ourselves to the study the convergence to the stationary equilibrium of the values of the three sequences (21) for the example considered in Section 4. In this case it follows:
$F(aW, bP) = (aW)^{\alpha}(bP)^{\beta}$. Thus, (20) is $W_t/P_t = \alpha/\beta$, and equation (19) can be written as:

$$W_t + P_t = (1 - c)(aW_{t-1})^{\alpha}(bP_{t-1})^{\beta}$$

by substituting for W_t the value $(\alpha\ /\ \beta)\ P_t$, the next expression is obtained:

$$(1 + \alpha/\beta)P_t = (1 - c)(a\alpha/\beta P_{t-1})^{\alpha}(bP_{t-1})^{\beta}$$

that is

$$(1 + \alpha/\beta)P_t = (1 - c)(a\alpha/\beta)^{\alpha}b^{\beta}(P_{t-1})^{\alpha+\beta}$$

Therefore:

$$P_t = AP_{t-1}^{B}\qquad(22)$$

where we have set $A = \frac{\beta}{\alpha+\beta}(1 - c)(a\alpha/\beta)^{\alpha}b^{\beta} = \frac{\beta}{\alpha+\beta}v$, a positive parameter, and $B = \alpha + \beta$. Note that (22) is a finite difference equation of the first order, and non-linear because we have $B = \alpha + \beta < 1$. By recursion, from (22) we obtain $P_1 = AP_0^{B}, P_2 = AP_1^{B} = AA^{B}P_0^{2B}$, and in general

---

$$P_t = A^{1+B+B^2+\ldots+B^{t-1}} P_0^{Bt} \quad (\mathrm{t} = 1, 2, 3\ldots). \tag{23}$$

Recalling that $B < 1$ for $t \to \infty$ the exponent of A takes the value $1/(1 - B)$, while the exponent of P_0 goes to zero; thus, we obtain

$$P_\infty = A^{\frac{1}{1-\alpha-\beta}} \tag{24}$$

a value totally independent from the starting condition, P_0, but uniquely dependent from the parameters A e B. Being $W_t/P_t = \alpha/\beta$, from formulae (23) and (24) we have, respectively,

$$W_t = \frac{\alpha}{\beta} A^{1+B+B^2+\ldots+B^{t-1}} P_0^{Bt} \quad (\mathrm{t} = 1, 2, \ldots, t), \tag{25}$$

and

$$W_\infty = \frac{\alpha}{\beta} A^{\frac{1}{1-\alpha-\beta}}. \tag{26}$$

To conclude, from the values P_∞ and W_∞ we immediately obtain Y_∞, namely

$$Y_\infty = (aW_\infty)^\alpha (bP_\infty)^\beta = \left(\frac{\alpha}{\beta}\right)^\alpha a^\alpha b^\beta A^{\frac{\alpha+\beta}{1-\alpha-\beta}}. \tag{27}$$

It is important to note that the *one-period* equilibrium values, expressed by relations (14) and (15), are those, respectively, of the limit values given by relations (24), (26) and (27). We might stress, once again, in analogy with the one-period case that the values obtained are all dependent from the factor $1-c$, which increases when c decreases. So that when there is no unproductive rent $(c=0)$, wages, profits, and production take larger values, period after period and for $t=\infty$. Thus, capital accumulation is hampered by unproductive rent. While we have considered here only the formal issues of the problem, it is clear that, by means of statistical data, econometric estimates of time series are possible in order to provide values of the parameters of the model, in particular of c, thus measuring the incidence of parasitic rents on the economy. It is obvious that without a formal model applicable to specific data, every discussion on profits and on both types of rents remains a mere academic exercise.

6.   Conclusions

This chapter modifies somewhat the traditional framework of macroeconomic models, by introducing the category of those who receive unproductive rents (the so called *rentiers*), individuals who spend their incomes without taking part in the production of the goods defining the GDP. Of course, as we have pointed out at the beginning, in the real world there are also individuals receiving *Ricardian* rents, as landlords who own and provide an important factor of production, i.e. land. In the model here developed, they are considered on a *par* with capitalists, and their incomes are rightly included in the category of profit. Many of us think that socially speaking profits are not to be valued more than rents, be they productive or parasitic. The model put forward here goes against this viewpoint and shows how in every decentralized economy profits are important as wages are, differently from unproductive rents. Thus, the category of profit has an ethical value, more or less like wages,[9] while unproductive rents cannot deserve such a positive opinion. Once more, it seems useful to underline that, thanks to the constrained maximization of GDP, as considered in Section 3, the class contest between workers and capitalists may be resolved by means of the mathematical calculus, which objectively states the optimal distribution of production between wages and profits.

One of the purposes of the present chapter has been to clarify the distinction, frequently absent in writings of economics scholars, between profit and unproductive rent. It is, in my opinion, a distinction conceptually very important, which is useful for underlining that profit is important as an economic category. Its social adequacy ought to be promoted in all capitalistic economies.

I fully appreciate that we ought to include this analysis in the wider conceptual environment of the theory of economic development, while the model here proposed belongs to the narrower domain of economic growth theory. As a partial justification for this, I wish to remember the recent contribution by Velupillai (2010) on development economics, in opposition to growth economics. Given that development theory is much less formalized than growth theory, it seems to me that often development theory has produced more heat than light, Schumpeter allowing.

REFERENCES

Koopmans, T. C. (1965) 'On the Concept of Optimal Economic Growth', *Pontificiae Academiae Scientiarum Scripta Varia* (Study Week on the Econometric Approach to Development Planning), 28, Vatican City, pp. 225–87.

Malinvaud, E. (1965) 'Croissances optimales dans un modèle macro-économique', *Pontificiae Academiae Scientiarum Scripta Varia* (Study Week on the Econometric Approach to Development Planning), 28, Vatican City, pp. 309–78.

Phelps, E. S. (1961) 'The Golden Rule of Accumulation', *American Economic Review*, 51, pp. 638–2.

Quadrio Curzio, A. (1967) *Accumulazione del capitale e rendita*, Bologna: Il Mulino.

---

[9] If profits are zero there are no investments, and so there is no capital at the disposal of the economy; hence, production is zero. Indeed, in real economies there are no production processes activated only by means of labour.

(1975) *Rendita e distribuzione in un modello plurisettoriale*, Milan: Giuffré.

Ramsey, F. P. (1928) 'A Mathematical Theory of Saving', *Economic Journal*, 38, pp. 543–59.

Ricardo, D. (1951) *On the Principles of Political Economy and Taxation, vol. I of Works and Correspondence of David Ricardo*, ed. by P. Sraffa, Cambridge: Cambridge University Press (1st edn 1817; 2nd edn 1819; 3rd edn 1821).

Solow, R. M. (1956) 'A Contribution to the Theory of Economic Growth', *Quarterly Journal of Economics*, 70, pp. 65–94.

Swan, T. W. (1956) 'Economic Growth and Capital Accumulation', *Economic Record*, 32, pp. 334–61.

Velupillai, K. V. (2010) 'Development Economics without Growth Theory', *Economia Politica*, 27, pp. 9–52.

Part II

Structural dynamics: resources and multi-sectoral linkages

6   Limits, resources and distributional trade-offs: structural constraints and opportunities

Albert E. Steenge

1.   Introduction

Input–output (IO) analysis offers a detailed insight in economic structure in terms of production, consumption and value-added. Production takes place in sectors, ranging from agriculture to industry and services, producing a single, characterizing product. Consumption, as exercised by households, business and government investors or foreign countries, is determined by various external mechanisms. Value-added is described in terms of the inputs of so-called primary or non-produced input factors, such as various types of labour or capital. Prices are expressed in terms of the embodied amounts of those primary factors. Built-in is the property that the total value of exogenous final demand is equal to total value-added, which means that the primary factors can buy the national product.

Central in IO methodology is the focus on the so-called multiplier matrix, which gives the relation between (shifts in) final demand, total production, and total factor use. It enables policymakers to focus on employment programs, to calculate required imports, et cetera. A most important feature here is the role of the so-called fixed input coefficients assumption. Fixed coefficients mean that if final demand changes (and in the absence of technical change), there are no economies of scale if production is increasing, and neither are there increasing costs. A theoretical foundation – to a certain extent – for the fixed coefficients assumption is provided by the well-known Non-substitution Theorem. This theorem goes back to a number of contributions in Koopmans (1951). It says that if alternative technologies are available, changes in final demand will not induce changes in the existing set of technologies, provided a) there is only one primary factor, say homogeneous labour, and b) this factor is available in sufficient quantities to produce the desired final demand bundle.

The model effectively tells us that, given unlimited availability of labour, any final demand bundle can be produced. However, what will happen if that primary factor is available only in certain amounts? And what will happen if more than one primary or non-produced factor should be distinguished – each of which also is available only in limited amounts? We then definitely will run into a new kind of problem and into situations of scarcity-related problems of distribution and allocation.

In fact, little is known about what may happen if the (single) primary factor is in short supply. To contribute to the discussion of this type of problem, we shall in this chapter focus on a special type of scarcity phenomena in the open static Leontief model. This model provides the core structure of IO methodology, and will function, for us, as a platform to systematically discuss particular situations that may arise, and the various ways of facing them. We shall propose a decomposition that allows us to analyse the interdependencies between primary inputs, intermediate inputs and consumption patterns in a novel way. We shall proceed here by concentrating on 'real wage bundles'. Working with these bundles allows us to rewrite the open static Leontief model in terms of an alternative model where 'commodities are being produced by means of commodities', much in the Sraffian spirit (Sraffa, 1960). This transcription, as we shall show, allows us to derive exact analytical relations between the various interdependent sectors within an economy in times of changes in overall circumstances.

With the basic model to be introduced in the next section, we aim to put forward a number of points, i.e.:

1. To distinguish between what we shall call 'internal structure' and 'scale',
2. To show that scarcity issues can be discussed in terms of balances within this internal structure,
3. That policy issues can be structured in the form of 'trade-off curves' based on the open static Leontief model.

We shall start with a brief discussion of the standard model in Section 2. In Section 3 we shall introduce the notion of augmented input coefficients matrices and in Section 4 discuss trade-offs enforced by some of the big issues of today, such as emerging resource scarcity or various manifestations of climate change. In between, we shall give a number of numerical illustrations using the same numerical values throughout.[1]

2.   The standard model

2.1   The open model

We shall start with a short introduction to the open static Leontief model (OSLM for short). We have,

---

[1] Quadrio Curzio and Pellizzari (1999) follow a road quite different from ours in modelling resource scarcity, thereby focusing on aspects that we cannot discuss in the present contribution, such as the relation between final demand, rent and technology. For a discussion involving those aspects, we refer to that publication.

$$x = Ax + f \tag{1}$$

where $A = [a_{ij}]$ is the n x n matrix of input coefficients, a_{ij} standing for the input of commodity i per unit of output of commodity j. Matrix A is assumed to be nonnegative, with Perron-Frobenius or dominant eigenvalue $\lambda(A)$ smaller than 1. This eigenvalue can be interpreted as a measure of what can be called the productivity of the economy under study; later on we shall come back to this property. We shall distinguish only one primary or non-produced factor, to be identified as homogeneous labour. We have,

$$L = v'x \tag{2}$$

where $v' = [v_j]$ is the 1 x n vector of labour input coefficients. The standard approach proceeds by solving x from (1)

$$x = (I - A)^{-1}f \tag{3}$$

where I is the identity matrix and $(I - A)^{-1}$ the multiplier matrix. Subsequently, total employment is obtained from substitution in (2):

$$L = v'x = v'\,(I - A)^{-1}f \tag{4}$$

The corresponding price equation is

$$p' = p'A + wv', \tag{5}$$

p' standing for the 1 x n vector of equilibrium prices. The wage rate w can be expressed in any appropriate numeraire and can be set equal to unity. Built-in is now

$$p'f = wv'x = wL \tag{6}$$

That is, the value of the final demand bundle is equal to the wage sum. Prices p' are obtained from (5) as:

$$p' = wv'(I - A)^{-1} \tag{7}$$

We see that any shifts in the wage rate w are straightforwardly absorbed in the price system, there is no influence on relative prices, neither on the real sphere. We also see that each final demand bundle f can be produced, provided a sufficient amount of labour is available.[2]

So, the static model informs us that, given sufficient supply of labour (the non-produced factor), any final demand bundle f can be produced. Now, how

---

[2] Further discussion of the standard model can be found in major textbooks and monographs devoted to particular topics. See e.g. Miller and Blair (2009), Nakamura and Kondo (2009) or Duchin (2009).

could scarcity or specific 'supply limits' enter and be analysed? To structure the discussion we shall assume below that the economy is self-sufficient in the sense that it can reproduce itself without requiring any inputs from outside the economy, or without requiring the outside world for disposing of superfluous materials or substances.

Looking at what we said a bit earlier about $\lambda(A)$ (i.e. the dominant eigenvalue of matrix A), we might – as a first observation – expect the presence of an inverse relation between the size of $\lambda(A)$ and (some standardized form of) the size of net output. If so, a decreasing $\lambda(A)$ would imply a potential increase in net output possibilities, and *vice versa*. In the next sections we shall try to make this type of intuition more precise. As we shall see, the notion of equilibrium, in the (IO) sense of equality of the bundles of total outputs and total inputs, is central to our argument.

3.   Internal structure and scale

In this section we shall focus on what we shall identify as an economy's 'internal structure'. As a first step, however, we shall go to an IO model which has *no* surplus. The reason for doing so is that the logic of providing a central place to the equilibrium notion we referred to (i.e. equality of the bundles of total outputs and inputs) is more directly illustrated using another IO model, i.e. the *closed* static Leontief model (CSLM). The model is closed in the sense that final demand, i.e. labour's consumption bundle in the open static model, is not exogenously determined anymore, but has been reduced to just another production process, producing 'labour' or 'labour force'. Also here is a standard form, given by a deceptively simple-looking equation

$$x = Mx \qquad (8)$$

Matrix $M = [m_{ij}]$ is an n x n matrix of input coefficients of the same type as matrix A in the previous section. However, M has a special property, i.e. its Perron-Frobenius eigenvalue is equal to unity. This means that the economy needs all inputs to reproduce itself. In other words, there is no surplus that can be used for consumption or other purposes without endangering the capacity for reproduction.

We shall use the CSLM to introduce a distinction between what we shall call the economy's 'internal structure' and its 'scale of operation'. The internal structure is given by the sum of the matrix of intermediate input coefficients and a matrix that stands for imputed real wage coefficients.[3] The scale of

---

[3] Because there is no explicit reference to the real wage, in this section the internal structure is simply given by matrix M.

operation is given by vector x. This vector being an eigenvector of matrix M, the scale of operation can be varied without changing M. We see, e.g., that the internal structure stays unchanged for increasing (or decreasing) x. That is, x may increase to $(1 + \alpha)x$, where α can be positive or negative, thereby assuming that the term $(1 + \alpha)$ will remain positive. There are no economies of scale, as also is clear from the accompanying price equation,

$$p = pM \tag{9}$$

We observe that we can rewrite the equations (8) and (9) as

$$(I - M)x = 0 \tag{10}$$

and

$$p(I - M) = 0 \tag{11}$$

From (10) and (11) we have that the columns of matrix $(I - M)$ are interdependent. This implies

$$|I - M| = 0 \tag{12}$$

That is, the determinant of matrix $(I - M)$ is 0. For us, equation (12) is interesting in that it provides a simple and transparent way of analysing the internal structure of an economy. We can see this using a small 2 x 2 example. Let us write

$$M = \begin{bmatrix} m_{11} & m_{12} \\ m_{21} & m_{22} \end{bmatrix} \tag{13}$$

This gives

$$|I - M)| = 1 - m_{11} - m_{22} + m_{11}m_{22} - m_{12}m_{21} = 0 \tag{14}$$

That is, the interdependencies in the economy under consideration can be expressed in terms of relations between the sectoral input coefficients. A number of points should be noticed here. First, we see that there is no explicit distinction between intermediate and primary inputs. Therefore, we can speak of a situation where 'commodities are being produced by means of commodities'. In this sense, the model is identical to Sraffa's 'production for subsistence' model (Sraffa, 1960, ch. 1). Second, we immediately observe that if the number of sectors increases, the above expression will soon become extremely complex. Third, we also observe that the elements of matrix $(I - M)$ are interdependent in a particular way. That is, if one of the elements of M changes, one or more of the remaining ones must also change if the property of uninterrupted reproduction is to be preserved.

4.   Augmented input coefficients matrices

In this section we shall show that the OSLM can be discussed in terms of the concepts of the previous section, i.e. internal structure and scale of operation. However, before we are able to do so, we have to reformulate the model. Equations (8) and (9) described an economy in terms of one matrix (i.e. M or, equivalently, I – M) and one vector (i.e. x) which represented the scale of the system. If we look at the OSLM of Section 2, the situation is different, and we cannot immediately recognize a property such as the equality of the bundles of inputs and outputs – which we used to identify the scale of operation in the CSLM. However, there is a way to proceed. To this end, we shall borrow part of the structure of the CSLM by linking the consumption vector f to the row vector v' of direct labour input coefficients.

The argument involved is basically the same as in the CSLM. In the OSLM of Section 2, only one primary factor, labour, is distinguished, supplied by the household sector, which is the single category consuming the economy's net output bundle. In the absence of foreign trade, domestic saving and similar factors, this means that the consumption bundle per head, f/L, is equal to the real or 'physical' wage bundle, also per head.[4] Recalling that w in equation (5) stands for the wage received per head, and calibrating the value of w at 1, we obtain:

$$w = p'(f/L) = 1 \qquad (15)$$

(Thus, $wv'x = p'(f/L)v'x = [(p'f)/L]L = p'f$). This means that we may write the price equation as

$$\begin{aligned} p' &= p'A + p'(f/L)v' \\ &= p'(A + (f/L)v') \end{aligned} \qquad (16)$$

from which we observe that the elements of the standardized, final deliveries vector now appear as part of the economy's *cost* structure. Correspondingly, we have for the real output system

$$x = (A + (f/L)v')x \qquad (17)$$

So we have rewritten the model given by equations (1), (2) and (5) in terms of two equations where p' and x stand for, respectively, the left and right hand Perron-Frobenius eigenvectors of matrix

---

[4] Each element of the column vector f/L is obtained by dividing the corresponding element of f by L, a scalar. The term 'physical' wage is used here to stress that the wage is presented in terms of the commodity bundle that workers consume, paid for out of their money wage. We assume thereby that workers have homogeneous preferences and do not save.

$$C \equiv A + (f/L)v' \tag{18}$$

From equations (16) and (17) we have that the dominant eigenvalue of matrix C is equal to 1. It is useful to also have a compact notation for the wage part of matrix C. With

$$B \equiv (f/L)v' \tag{19}$$

we have

$$p' = p'(A + B)^5 \tag{20}$$

Correspondingly, we find:

$$x = (A + B)x \tag{21}$$

with $Bx = [(f/L)v']x = f$, using (2) and (19). We observe that, interpreted in this way, matrix C is comparable to matrix M in Section 3. Both are matrices of input coefficients, of an n-sector economy in equilibrium. C has two components, matrices A and B, one of which (i.e. matrix B) has shrunk to zero in M.

We should observe here that the transcription of the nominal wage (as in equation (15)) into real wage bundles per head opens up the possibility to formulate also this model in terms of 'commodities being produced by commodities'. The labour inputs are still present, evidently, but expressed in terms of the remuneration labour receives in exchange for its productive inputs.[6]

We can rewrite (21) as

$$[I - (A + B)]x = 0 \tag{22}$$

From (22) we have that, like the columns of matrix I – M, also the columns of matrix I – (A + B) are interdependent. This implies that its determinant must be equal to 0, i.e.:

$$|I - (A + B)| = 0 \tag{23}$$

So, we observe that any Leontief system satisfying the equations in Section 2 also satisfies equation (23), with $w = p'(f/L) = 1$.

At this point we should mention that adding 'intermediate' and labour costs is quite well-known in certain specializations. For example, Seton (1977, p. 17), in discussing Marxian production systems, points out that the sum A + B sometimes is referred to as the economy's 'augmented technology', representing the total cost of each output unit to the producer. Pasinetti (1977, appendix to ch. V) used a similar construct in discussing the structure of

---

[5] So matrix B is the outer product of the column vector f/L and the row vector v'.
[6] For a discussion of this line of argument in a Leontief-Sraffa income distribution context, see Steenge and Serrano (2012).

particular Marxian inspired models. However – as far as we know – such constructs have never been employed to study trade-offs of the type we shall be dealing with in the next section.

Now let us return to equation (23). As mentioned, it informs us about the precise functional relationship between the parameters representing the technology (i.e. the elements of matrix A and row vector v'), the households consumption preferences as given by the elements of the column vector f, and the required labour input L. If we treat these as *variables* the value of which is to be determined by as yet undefined mechanisms, equation (23), in its most general form, can be interpreted as an equation in $n^2 + 2n + 1$ variables.[7] Given the platform offered by equation (23), we now have a number of options. We can, as in the standard approach of Section 2, proceed by fixing the technology parameters and the final demand vector, and ask the usual questions regarding the relation between final demand f and total output x.

However, many other questions can be asked. In fact, equation (23) offers a novel way of analysing the interdependencies in a multi-sector economy. We have seen that the requirement of (simple) reproduction leads to a rule (expressed by equation (23)) which enables us to trace the consequences of a shift in any (input) coefficient for any subset of the model's other coefficients. The cause of such shifts can be found in a number of underlying processes. For example, as already indicated, if technology would improve, the real wage per head (i.e. the bundle f/L) can be raised. If the physical wage would decline, possibilities would arise for other policy options, etc. We shall further discuss these issues in the next section.

As we may see, equations (20) and (21) provide information on the cost structure (as represented by matrix C) *and* on the independently to be discussed scale of the system (as represented by the vectors p' and x). Thus, cost or input structure and scale of operation are separated in a way that the standard methodology, as represented by equations (1) – (5), cannot accomplish.

There is an additional point that requires attention here. We have worked with an *open* model to introduce factor scarcity, a typically 'exogenous' phenomenon. However, to analyse the options open to an economy confronted with scarcity, we have transcribed the model into a model closely related to Leontief's *closed* one, in fact, a variant where 'commodities are produced by commodities' (see Sraffa, 1960). The distinction between open and closed models has a long history in economic analysis (see e.g. Quadrio Curzio and Scazzieri, 1986). However, the economics of scarcity may mean a re-consideration of many themes and sub-themes; further work here definitely is required.

---

[7] We recall that matrix A has n^2 potentially different elements and matrix B $2n + 1$.

5.   The 'internal structure' matrix

So, the introduction of the 'augmented coefficients' matrices offers us the possibility to study the economic system in terms of a set of interdependencies *different* from those given by the standard static models. As we have signalled, these interdependencies allow us to study the consequences of a change in one or more technology parameters or consumption related coefficients for the entire system. By now, some illustrations of the proposed method are asked for.

Suppose we have a three-sector economy with the following technology:

$$A = \begin{bmatrix} 0.15 & 0.25 & 0.05 \\ 0.20 & 0.05 & 0.04 \\ 0.10 & 0.25 & 0.50 \end{bmatrix}$$

and

$$v' = \begin{bmatrix} 0.20 & 0.30 & 0.05 \end{bmatrix}$$

Final demand is given by

$$f = \begin{bmatrix} 150 \\ 100 \\ 250 \end{bmatrix}$$

Straightforward calculation using equation (3) gives

$$x = \begin{bmatrix} 270.373 \\ 189.503 \\ 648.826 \end{bmatrix}$$

and

$$L = v'x = 143.367$$

From its components (i.e. respectively the column and row vectors f and v', and the scalar L) we now can compose matrix B. We have

$$B = \begin{bmatrix} 0.209 & 0.314 & 0.052 \\ 0.140 & 0.230 & 0.035 \\ 0.349 & 0.523 & 0.087 \end{bmatrix}$$

So, finally, we obtain C = A + B as

$$C = \begin{bmatrix} 0.359 & 0.564 & 0.102 \\ 0.340 & 0.259 & 0.075 \\ 0.449 & 0.773 & 0.587 \end{bmatrix}$$

where we should note that $\lambda(C) = 1.000$ (as it should).

Now let us take a closer look at the structure of interdependencies within this economy. Suppose we are interested in the effect of a particular form of technological change on the consumption possibilities. If we model technological advance by a decrease of certain elements of A, we would expect certain elements of matrix B to increase because they stand for (standardized) final demand. The reason is simple: if total employed labour stays the same, this quantity of labour can produce – under the changed circumstances – increased final output f. As we shall see, our procedure will produce an exact result on this type of relation.[8]

We shall proceed by introducing a change in one set of coefficients and see which effects this has on a specified set of other coefficients. We shall start in a very general way by multiplying each element of A by the parameter α and each element of B by the parameter β. Opting for $\alpha < 1$ can in this context be interpreted as introducing a technological improvement that can be expected to result in increased consumption possibilities for an unchanged labour force. So we consider a new 'internal structure matrix' obtained by attributing weight coefficients α and β to the input coefficients matrices A and B, respectively. Let $C(\alpha,\beta)$ stand for this new matrix, with

$$C(\alpha, \beta) = \alpha A + \beta B \qquad (24)$$

Imposing equilibrium (i.e. $\lambda(C(\alpha,\beta)) = 1$), we immediately have $|(I - C(\alpha,\beta))| = 0$. Introducing $\alpha < 1$, we shall see that means $\beta > 1$, i.e. labour obtains a larger real wage. More complex trade-off mechanisms can straightforwardly be investigated based on the admittedly still rather simple scheme offered by equation (24). (Note that the corresponding output vector will change, in general.)

Now let us consider which trade-offs between (lowered) inputs and (increased) final consumption (per head) are possible in the economy under consideration. Calculation gives:

$$|I - C(\alpha, \beta)| = 1 - 0.700\alpha - 0.506\beta + 0.043\,\alpha^2 + 0.119\alpha\beta$$
$$+0.020\alpha^3 + 0.025\alpha^2\beta$$

Figure 6.1 gives the relation between α and β in the equilibrium situation.

However, only a small part of Figure 6.1 is economically relevant. Let us consider this part somewhat closer. Figure 6.2 gives the details. We have:

Point (1,1) gives the initial situation where $\alpha = \beta = 1$. So we see that an increase in β only is compatible with a decrease in α. We also see that in the relevant part, the (negative) relation is almost linear. The two figures thus

---

[8] Consider here equation (14): a change in any of the four coefficients of M will have specific effects on the size of a subset of the other coefficients if the system is to remain in equilibrium (i.e. a state of simple reproduction).

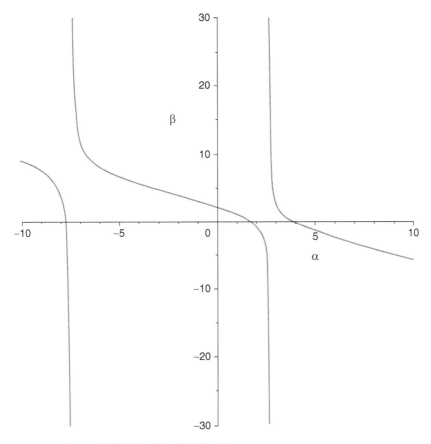

Figure 6.1 Graph of $|I - C(\alpha,\beta)| = 0$

contain a fundamental truth, i.e. that an improvement in living conditions (if we may translate an increase in final consumption in that way), without outside assistance, only can be realized if technology will be more efficient in terms of its input requirements. The formula we have derived then informs us about the precise shape of the relation between the core parameters.

We may 'zoom in' for additional detail. As a further exercise, let us take a look at the relation between an increase in final demand and a decrease in the required labour inputs for a specific sector. So let us consider the relation between growth in final demand, modelled as an increasing α in the consumption term αf and a β which stands for shifts in the direct labour input of the second sector (so v' becomes a function of β):

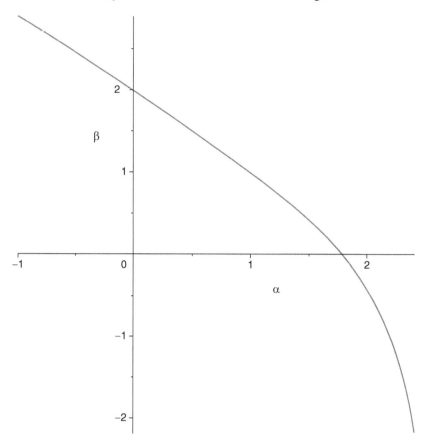

Figure 6.2 Graph of the economically relevant part of $|I - C(\alpha,\beta)| = 0$

$$v'(\beta) = [0.20 \quad 0.30\beta \quad 0.05]$$

A change in the labour input coefficients means that each element of matrix B will change. With B written in terms of its components, we then have

$$C(\alpha, \beta) = A + \alpha(f/L)v'(\beta) \qquad (25)$$

Figure 6.3 gives the relation between α and β, again in the equilibrium situation.

So, less labour inputs (introduced via a lower value of β) corresponds to a higher value for α. (Alternatively, the influence of higher intermediate inputs – such as in situations of depletion of natural stocks – can be compensated by lower labour costs per unit.) However, there are more options, clearly. So, finally, let us also consider the relation between a shift in all elements of either a row or a column of matrix A (possibly after an innovation that affects systematically all

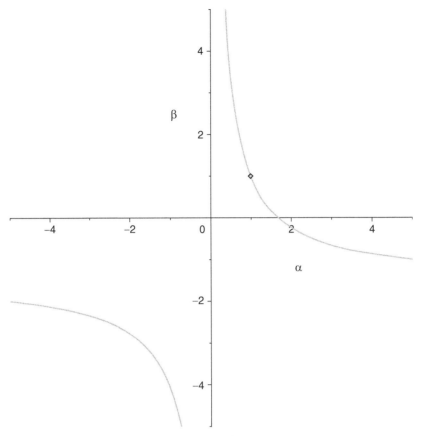

Figure 6.3 Graph of $|I - (A + \alpha(f/L)v'(\beta))| = 0$

elements in that row or column), and specific elements of the final demand vector. Let, successively,

$$D_1 = \mathrm{diag}(\alpha, 1, 1)$$

and

$$D_2 = \mathrm{diag}(1, 1, \beta)$$

and let our new internal structure matrix become

$$C(\alpha, \beta) = D_1 A + (1/L)D_2 f v' \qquad (26)$$

The resulting trade-off between α and β, again in equilibrium, is pictured in Figure 6.4.

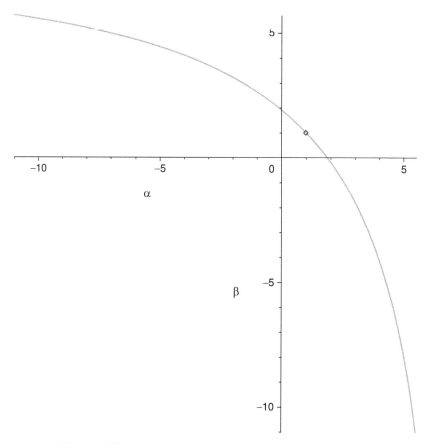

Figure 6.4 Graph of $|I - (D_1A + (1/L)D_2fv')| = 0$

Situations of resource scarcity can be modelled in several ways. One interesting way, clearly, is to consider the role of increasing technology-based costs. This can be done by considering the effect of increasing intermediate and/or labour inputs per unit and over time. Other exercises might focus on conditions to keep consumption levels within specific bounds against the background of deteriorating production circumstances.

6.   Crowding-out issues

Let us return now for a moment to equation (22). We have, up to now, discussed various systematic trade-offs between the two components of the system matrix $C = A + B$ and its variants. We have seen, e.g., that an increase in consumption per capita only can be realized if access is secured to new and more efficient technology.

We thus have seen that this model, though relatively simple, is able to provide insight in the fundamental trade-offs that are involved if some part of the coefficients-constellation is changed. Let us now for a moment consider a problem of a quite different scale. Many countries nowadays are confronted with big challenges, often of a nature or intensity that these countries have not met before. We may think here of the exhaustion of traditional energy sources, accelerated demographic change, or climate change in its various manifestations, all examples of new developments that introduce new and often unknown risks and, most likely, heavy price increases for many goods (see e.g. Okuyama, 2007).

Let us concentrate for a moment on energy sources such as oil or gas. One consequence of the first category of problems is that due to a mixture of geological, geographical or sociopolitical motives many areas that up to now were not heavily exploited now are, such as the polar areas, or the deep seas. This often goes hand in hand with increasing risks, which are not always properly recognized or dealt with (see, e.g., the backgrounds of the 2010 oil spill in the Gulf of Mexico).

For a country like the Netherlands climate change can be translated into rising sea level and accompanying challenges for the big-river systems. Safeguarding the country from flooding will mean that in the coming decades large investments in infrastructural change and protection will have to be made. The cost of these can be very substantial, on the order of magnitude of the national income.

Getting insight in the trade-offs that are involved will ask for a strategy that does justice to the particular case at hand. Below we shall propose a general way of looking at this relatively new class of problems, without venturing into the particularities of individual cases. Suppose that the arrival of the new class of problems means that new technologies must be developed, tried out and implemented. Suppose furthermore that it is possible to translate the costs of facing the new kinds of challenges into *additional* costs of producing the traditional commodities. That is, next to the two inputs categories we have distinguished up to now (as represented by the matrices A and B), we now have a new category that rather forms a challenge for the country as a whole, and not so much for the individual sectors and final demand and value-added categories.

In modelling terms this means that we should introduce an additional matrix, say T, next to the matrices A and B. So, we then obtain a new matrix C, which, just as before, must have dominant eigenvalue equal to 1 to guarantee that the economy can reproduce itself. This, however, means that if we keep the numerical values used earlier, the introduction of matrix T will cause a 'crowding-out' of the functions that matrices A and B stand for. We shall see what this means next.

So, let us say we have the following technology matrix, still to be 'calibrated',

$$T = \begin{bmatrix} 0.010 & 0.010 & 0.055 \\ 0.015 & 0.030 & 0.025 \\ 0.020 & 0.005 & 0.045 \end{bmatrix}$$

For matrix C, following the same procedure as before, we then have

$$C = \alpha A + YT + \beta B \tag{27}$$

where $\gamma > 0$ is an intensity parameter that indicates the level of intensity of the new program. The hybrid character of matrix T can be seen as follows. First, we can view matrix T as an extension of the 'old' input coefficients matrix A, writing

$$C = (\alpha A + YT) + \beta B \tag{28}$$

Or, secondly, we can view it as an extension of matrix B, by writing

$$C = \alpha A + (YT + \beta B) \tag{29}$$

From a computational point of view, both interpretations are equally acceptable. The 'crowding out' process means that we have to solve

$$|I - (\alpha A + \gamma T + \beta B)| = 0 \tag{30}$$

We recall that $\gamma = 0$ represents the original situation, before the introduction of the program; see Section 5 and Figures 6.1 and 6.2.

Below we have given γ the values 1, 3 and 5, respectively. Figure 6.5 gives the trade-offs between α and β that introduction of the program requires, where the numbers next to the curves in the economically relevant part of Figure 6.5 refer to the values of γ. We see that governing bodies in each case (i.e. for each value of γ) will have to find the right balance between α and β. Again we see that keeping up a particular standard of living (as defined earlier) will be difficult. In any case, one of the conditions will be technological innovation in the 'old' technologies to provide for sufficient room (by lowering α in equation (27)). We may think of several ways to visualize this, such as aid and assistance from third parties in obtaining and operating the new technology as represented by matrix T.

A final remark here should concern the pedigree of the method we have put forward in this contribution. An early example of the aforementioned approach can be found in Steenge (2004), in the context of a discussion of the costs of environmental policy employing Leontief's environmental model (Leontief, 1970). The model there is a standard IO model, extended with sub-matrices standing for the emission of pollutants and pollutant-specific abatement activities. The problem was to calculate the direct and indirect effects, in terms of outputs and prices, of environmental policy aiming at reducing emissions into

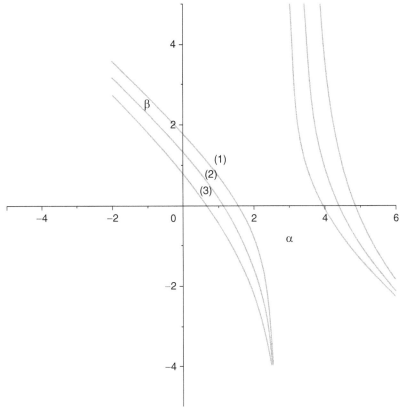

Figure 6.5 Graph of $\left| I - (\alpha A + \gamma T + \beta B) \right| = 0$

the environment. Matrix T there is basically the product of two matrices, A_{21} and A_{12}, standing for, respectively, the matrices of emission coefficients and input coefficients of the abatement industries, $A_{12}A_{21}$. The parameter α (see e.g. equation (8) in Steenge, 2004), is an intensity parameter similar to γ above. The general concept has been further explored in Steenge and Serrano (2012) in the context of a study of income distributions in Sraffa-based and Leontief-based input–output models. For further discussion on the origin of the approach, we refer to the same publication.

7.   Conclusion

In the previous sections we have discussed the structure of input–output models in terms of relations between the input coefficients and several types of other coefficients and parameters. We thereby have focused on a particular class of interconnections that exist in an economy that is able to reproduce itself, i.e. that produces just as much in terms of output as it needs in terms of inputs. We have introduced the notions of 'internal structure' and 'scale', represented by an augmented input coefficients matrix with dominant eigenvalue equal to 1 and the corresponding eigenvector, which has a double function, standing both for the vector of total outputs and the vector of total inputs.

In this contribution we have focused on an economy with a single primary factor, homogeneous labour, and have investigated situations where the supply of this primary factor is fixed. We showed that in this context it is possible to derive exact analytical relations between sets of selected inputs and outputs. That is, we were able – with a fixed amount of the scarce factor – to indicate precisely how large a reduction of inputs in particular processes should be to increase specific elements of the final consumption bundle.

The system we have proposed can be used to model the effects of many types of scarcities, particularly those involving resources being in short supply. Scarcities of the type we have considered lead to the necessity of trade-offs between commodity allocations: higher consumption demand will mean that fewer resources are available for industrial production activities. To obtain the actual trade-off curves, we considered a system determinant that is a function of all model coefficients *casu quo* parameters, and which must be 0 in equilibrium. By fixing certain parameters or coefficients, so-called trade-off functions between the remaining ones can be obtained. The graphs of a number of cases have been included (Figures 6.1 to 6.5).

We should point out that the methods we have proposed need further investigation. For example, we did not discuss prices and price implications of the various policy options modelled in terms of our structured matrices. However, there also are issues of a quite different nature. An important theme in multi-sectoral-based research concerns the distinction between closed and open systems. Probably most well-known is Leontief's open static model where exogenous mechanisms play a dominant role in explaining prices and outputs. Leontief's closed static model, on the other hand, only describes an economy capable of simple reproduction, without strong external impulses. In this chapter we have shown that there are interesting 'in-between' forms that allow novel insights into the interdependencies between processes of exchange, production and consumption. In fact, transcribing the open model into a model where 'commodities are produced by means of commodities' brings additional analytical tools to study situations of rapid shifts in national or global production systems. Future work can be expected to bring additional, exciting results.

REFERENCES

Duchin, F. (2009), Input-output Economics and Material flows, in S. Suh (ed.), *Handbook of Input-Output Economics in Industrial Ecology*, Dordrecht: Springer, pp. 23–41.

Koopmans, T. C. (ed.) (1951) *Activity Analysis of Production and Allocation*, Cowles Monograph 13, Wiley.

Leontief, W. W. (1970) 'Environmental Repercussions and the Economic Structure: An Input-Output Approach', *Review of Economics and Statistics*, vol. 52(3), pp. 262–71.

Miller, R. E., and Blair, P. D. (2009) *Input-Output Analysis: Foundations and Extensions*, 2nd edn, Cambridge: Cambridge University Press.

Nakamura, S., and Kondo, Y. (2009) *Waste Input-Output Analysis; Concepts and Application to Industrial Ecology*, Amsterdam: Springer.

Okuyama, Y. (2007) 'Economic Modeling for Disaster Impact Analysis: Past, Present, and Future', Introduction to Economic Modeling for Disaster Impact Analysis, special issue of *Economic Systems Research*, vol. 19(2): pp. 115–124.

Pasinetti, L. L. (1977) *Lectures on the Theory of Production*, New York: Columbia University Press.

Quadrio Curzio, A. and Pellizzari, F. (1999) *Rent, Resources, Technologies*, Berlin: Springer.

Quadrio Curzio, A. and Scazzieri, R. (1986) 'The Exchange-Production Duality and the Dynamics of Economic Knowledge', in M. Baranzini and R. Scazzieri (eds.) *Foundations of Economics, Structures of Inquiry and Economic Theory*, Oxford and New York: B. Blackwell.

Seton, F., (1977) 'The Question of Ideological Obstacles to Rational Price Setting in Communist Countries', Ch. 2 in Alan Abouchar (ed.) *The Socialist Price Mechanism*, Durham, NC: Duke University Press.

Sraffa, P. (1960) *Production of Commodities by Means of Commodities*, Cambridge: Cambridge University Press.

Steenge, A. E. (2004) 'Social Cost in the Leontief Environmental Model: Rules and Limits to Policy', in E. Dietzenbacher and M.L. Lahr (eds.) *Wassily Leontief and Input-Output Economics*, Cambridge: Cambridge University Press.

Steenge, A. E. and Serrano, M. (2012) 'Income Distributions in Input-Output Models', *Economic Systems Research*, vol. 24(4): pp. 391–412.

7 Producible resources and producibility prices in a dynamic Leontief-type model

Carlo D'Adda

1. Introduction

The idea that the production coefficient matrix (Leontief matrix) may be used to represent the relative size of the productive sectors of an economic system and at the same time to determine the prices of sectoral products always appeared to me prodigious and fascinating. In the economist's language it is common to say that the problem of price determination in the Leontief model is simply the 'dual' of the quantity determination problem. But when one proceeds from the elementary Leontief model to the dynamic one, the mentioned simple and elegant correspondence between direct and dual problem seems to vanish. The modelling of exchanges and sectoral interdependencies must address capital adjustment, namely plants, machinery, building constructions and inventories that become progressively needed to allow for the growth of production in the different sectors. One has consequently to do with a coefficient matrix that is more complex than the one of the static model where the problem of capital accumulation is ignored. At first sight it is not immediately clear how accumulation (that is generally financed by both retained earnings and stock issue) may have an influence over production prices. In reality the additions to sectoral capital stocks taken into account by the dynamic model ultimately represent costs that must be covered by market prices in order for growth to be sustainable[1].

2. Leontief models and capital accumulation requirements in an expanding economy

It is worth recalling shortly formulations of the static and of the dynamic Leontief model, both in quantities and in prices (the meaning of the symbols is given under the equations):

I wish to express my gratitude to Salvatore Baldone, who read a preliminary version of this writing and made precious suggestions. I am also obliged to Roberto Scazzieri, whose subsequent reading helped me to improve the clarity of several passages.
[1] Let me mention a paper of mine written many years ago: D'Adda (1966), specifically Section 4, p. 14.

$$q = A\,q + f = (I - A)^{-1}\,f \tag{1}$$

$$q = A\,q + K\,G\,q + c = (I - A - K\,G)^{-1}\,c \tag{2}$$

$$p = A'\,p + v = (I - A')^{-1}\,v \tag{3}$$

$$p_p = A'\,p_p + G\,K'\,p_p + w\,l = (I - A' - G\,K')^{-1}\,w\,l \tag{4}$$

Symbols:

A matrix of current inputs in sectoral production processes

a_{ij} generic element of A

A_j j-th column of A

c column vector of final consumptions of the sectoral products

c_j j-th component of vector c

f column vector of the final uses of the sectoral products

I diagonal matrix with elements equal to 1 on the principal diagonal

K matrix of capital stocks per unit of sectoral product

l column vector of the labour coefficients (for ex. labour hours) for sectoral product unit

p column vector of sectoral prices in the static model

p_p column vector of sectoral producibility prices in the dynamic model (cost of growth considered)

p_c column vector of sectoral capitalist prices in the dynamic model (interest on capital considered)

q column vector of sectoral products

g column vector of the sectoral products growth rates

G diagonal matrix of the sectoral products growth rates

r scalar representing the rate of interest

R diagonal matrix with elements equal to r on the principal diagonal

v column vector of sectoral added values (wages and other incomes per product unit)

w scalar representing the contractual wage per labour unit (assumed equal in all sectors)

$'$ transposition symbol

The reader must be warned that the present versions of the Leontief model involve simplifications as is usual in theoretical models. First of all the role of the State is not explicitly taken into account and taxes are disregarded. Therefore added value and prices are here intended as net of taxes. Population and labour force growth are implicitly assumed but are not explicitly in the models. Even if exogenous in the short run, population may be thought as endogenous in the long run. Note in addition that to be economically significant equations (1)–(3) and (2)–(4) must admit positive solutions for sectoral products and prices. Such a condition has obvious implications on the coefficients of **A** and **K** matrices, as well as on vector **g** of the sectoral growth rates.

As to consumptions, remark that in the dynamic model the components of vector **g** of the sectoral product growth rates are here intended as given numbers. For an elementary presentation of the model this is reasonable and permits to maintain light notation. Yet a more satisfactory formulation of the model should explain the dynamics of final consumptions and use equation (2) to determine sectoral products consistent with sectoral consumptions[2]. This means that in general the sectoral dynamics of the economy is not of the steady growth type.

With reference to the equations used to determine prices (equations 3 and 4) it is worth distinguishing clearly between static and dynamic models. In the first case the vector of prices is determined on the base of the added value coefficient vector and income distribution as such is disregarded. Sectoral prices are expression of the added value directly and indirectly contained in every unit of sectoral product (namely in inputs, inputs of inputs and so on). Of course if labour were to be the sole production factor, the overall labour cost would correspond to the total added value of the economy (national income), but in general other sectoral incomes join labour costs. Even so simply defined the notion of prices related to the static Leontief model is not trivial: it can be useful for practical purposes, for example to estimate the effects on sectoral prices of technical innovations or new collective agreements that change the added value per unit of sectoral product[3].

The dynamic model price equation raises an interesting question. Is it possible to give a meaning to matrix $(\mathbf{I} - \mathbf{A'} - \mathbf{G}\,\mathbf{K'})^{-1}$? The answer is *yes* if we recognize that in order for growth to be sustainable the cost of sectoral capital adjustments must be added to current production costs. Therefore we define *producibility prices* that include cost of current inputs, cost of the period sectoral capital additions[4] and cost of labour. More precisely in formulating

---

[2] I followed this way in D'Adda (1989). As suggested by Pasinetti (1965, 1977) in a context similar to the present one, an empirically robust theory allowing interpreting the long-run dynamics of sectoral final consumptions may be based on Engel's curves. More elaborate models could obviously be suggested for open economies.

[3] Little before the introduction of the value-added tax (VAT) in the EU, this notion of prices proved useful to estimate the consequences on current prices of that important fiscal innovation (Cavazzuti and D'Adda, 1972).

[4] In accounting practice depreciation of total capital stock, rather than capital stock additions, are imputed to production costs. But depreciation schemes represent ways of distributing the cost of capital stock additions over a number of years. And obviously in a given year several overlapping depreciation schemes are in function. Therefore what accounting practice imputes to production costs is a weighted average of current and past additions

equation (4) we assume that every sectoral price includes direct and indirect content of wages in direct and indirect inputs[5], yet the concept of *input* is generalized in view of a wider notion of *producibility*: production inputs are not only the ones represented by matrix $\mathbf{A}$ (*current* inputs), but also those corresponding to the product matrix $\mathbf{K}\,\mathbf{G}$ representing the additions to sectoral capital required for growth[6].

Note that in the dynamic model there is no more *one* final use vector that corresponds to *one* added value vector. Among the final uses it becomes necessary to distinguish between investments (endogenous) and consumptions (subject to evolution over time) and instead of an added value vector we find a labour cost vector. If we wish to reconstruct the whole added value vector we have to sum labour costs and sectoral investment costs: $\mathbf{w}\,\mathbf{l}\,+\,\mathbf{G}\,\mathbf{K'}\,\mathbf{p_p}$.

Finally, a remark on the short and long run. Intuitively we understand that individual firms, even if subject to long-run producibility conditions, may temporarily deviate from such conditions: to take advantage from favourable situations or to face unfavourable contingences (such as high or falling demand), to exploit temporary opportunities showing up on financial markets and the like. We are not interested in these circumstances that on the whole relate to the short run. Producibility is to conceive as a long-run condition that both the system and individual firms must observe in order to survive. The implication is that both fixed coefficients of technological matrices and also sectoral mark-ups should be taken as norms over a certain time horizon.

3.   Capitalist versus producibility prices

Note that no reference to interest[7] has been made so far: it may seem that we are thinking only of a situation that recalls planned and mixed economies. But if we want to focus on capitalist economies we have to take into account the fact that labour aided by capital (which is not a free good!) becomes more

---

to capital stocks. What we have done is treating capital additions as if they were current production inputs, disregarding depreciation of past investments: a simplification in view of the fact that in any case the whole cost of capital stock additions must ultimately be charged on production costs. Obviously the longer periods are, the smaller approximation is.

[5] If capital receives an interest, equation (4) must be changed. We come to this problem in the next section.

[6] The generic element of matrix $\mathbf{G}\,\mathbf{K'}$ is the product $k_{ij}\,g_j$ that indicates the capital requirement of product i needed to increase the production capacity of sector j according to the rate g_i.

[7] We don't distinguish between interest and profit by assuming, as often is done, that competition makes them coincide.

productive. This is why the availability of capital commands a price (rental)[8]. In this case our previous equation (4) must be changed by replacing the product matrix **G K'** with the product matrix **R K'** (**R** being a diagonal matrix with elements all equal to the rate of interest). In the following equation (4.1) we define a new vector $\mathbf{p_c}$ of sectoral *capitalist* prices that keep into account interest on fixed capital stocks[9] instead of capital additions for growth:

$$\mathbf{p_c} = \mathbf{A}^{'}\,\mathbf{p_c} + \mathbf{R}\,\mathbf{K}^{'}\,\mathbf{p_c} + w\,\mathbf{l} = (\mathbf{I} - \mathbf{A}^{'} - (\mathbf{R}\,\mathbf{K}^{'})^{-1}\,w\,\mathbf{l} \qquad (4.1)$$

In general, if we look at a modern capitalist economy, there is no reason to expect that producibility prices and capitalist prices at the sectoral level are the same (even though the order of magnitude of the rate of interest is comparable to the one of a sectoral growth rate). So in principle all the inequalities

$$p_{cj} > p_{pj}; \; p_{cj} = p_{pj}; \; p_{cj} < p_{pj}$$

are possible. Obviously in order for growth to take place in a capitalist economy if $p_{cj} \neq p_{pj}$ financial transfers from surplus sectors to deficit sectors must be envisaged.

It is time to raise the question of whether the concept of *producibility* prices is to be taken as purely theoretical, or purely restricted to the purpose of describing what used to happen in planned economies. The answer is *no*, because *planned economies* and *capitalist economies* are just expressions meant to indicate stylized theoretical situations. Reality often presents situations that are not so clear-cut. In the modern global world, big oligopolistic firms are probably the most relevant production structures. My impression is that our producibility prices strongly approach the prices decided by oligopolistic firms by means of mark-ups. These firms enjoy relevant market power, aim at growth more than at profits, are not particularly dependent on capital markets and can largely auto-finance their growth. From this point of view the dynamic Leontief-type model and producibility prices associated with it seem to offer interesting theoretical ground to justify diverse sectoral mark-ups on current production costs

---

[8] See Keynes (1936), Ch. 16, 'Sundry Observations on the Nature of Capital', II. Curiously, in my opinion, medieval canonists didn't perceive the similarity between interest on money capital (condemned) and rental on real capital (admitted): they both aid labour.

[9] An alternative formulation is possible, where interest is not charged only on fixed capital (as it is done here for simplicity), but also on circulating capital. In any case the presence of interest sets a more stringent constraint on the maximum sustainable sectoral growth rate of the system.

(i.e. current inputs plus direct labour costs). In our language the j-th sector mark-up may be defined as

$$m_j \equiv g_j \, \mathbf{p'_p} \, \mathbf{K_j})/(\mathbf{p'_p} \, \mathbf{A_j} + w \, l_j)$$

The fact that sectoral mark-ups differ is not surprising, since the growth rates of the sectoral products expressed by vector $\mathbf{g}$ are different by assumption and the sectoral capital stocks per product units differ for technological reasons.

4.   Who pays for growth?

In different institutional contexts the task of providing resources to allow for accumulation may be organized in different ways. It may be mainly realized by firm owners through retained earnings or by borrowing consumers' savings with financial intermediaries, as is usual in capitalist economies; it may be realized by the state as used to happen in centrally planned economies, or it may be managed by intermediate bodies between state and citizens as happened (and happens) in the so-called mixed economies. Different institutional decisions about the responsibility for accumulation imply correspondent decisions about income distribution mechanisms and incentives. What does not change is the fact that if society wants to grow, its productive sectors (and firms) must receive the resources needed to adjust the capital stocks. This implies that over time at the sectoral level the value of the provided financial resources must match the value of the required additions to the capital stocks.

Of course if society wants to promote efficiency a price for the use of capital (interest) must exist, even if in the real world, for different reasons, the rate of interest may not be as uniform as suggested by pure theory. Individual firms may get the mentioned resources by imposing a mark-up on current inputs, from government transfers, or a combination of these sources. If different financing patterns for growth continue to exist in a competitive environment they must ultimately imply similar costs, otherwise competition would make some of them disappear.

5.   Some classical problems involving the notion of direct and indirect labour inputs

Equations (3) and (4) of the previous section can easily be modified to revisit the classical problem of *labour value* in economic theory. To this purpose let us replace vector $\mathbf{v}$ of added value coefficients in equation (3) with vector $\mathbf{l}$ of direct labour coefficients and suppress the unit wage $\mathbf{w}$ in equation (4), then solve respectively for the vectors $\mathbf{p_L}$ e $\mathbf{p_{LL}}$ (labour value vectors in the static and dynamic model):

$$\mathbf{p_L} = \mathbf{A}' \, \mathbf{p_L} + \mathbf{1} = (\mathbf{I} - \mathbf{A}')^{-1} \mathbf{1} \qquad (5)$$

$$\mathbf{p_{LL}} = \mathbf{A}' \, \mathbf{p_{LL}} + \mathbf{G} \, \mathbf{K}' \, \mathbf{p_{LL}} + \mathbf{1} = (\mathbf{I} - \mathbf{A}' - \mathbf{G} \, \mathbf{K}')^{-1} \mathbf{1} \qquad (6)$$

The first equation of labour values fits closely the famous example in Adam Smith's *The Wealth of Nations* where exchanges of captured animals take place according to ratios that are proportional the total hunting time. If this barter economy is changed into a money economy in which current inputs are bought on the market with no growth and no markets for capital goods (hunters remaining the sole agents) everything is simple: labour values of the different sectoral products are adequately expressed by vector $\mathbf{p_L}$ (equation 5). The case of a growing economy with capital goods is slightly more complex: the components of vector $\mathbf{p_{LL}}$ (equation 6) express the total direct and indirect labour contained in current inputs, as well as the direct and indirect labour contained in the capital goods additions that have to adjust the sectoral production capacities. Obviously in both equations (5) and (6) the product of vector $\mathbf{1}$ of direct labour coefficients times the unit wage $\mathbf{w}$ permits to convert labour values into wage-prices (expression of total contained wages).[10] Such a conversion regards only the accounting units, leaving relative prices unchanged.

Let us remember that the notion of *labour value* was used by Marx to discuss his concept of worker's exploitation. Marx focused on the difference, in a capitalist economy, between *embodied* (directly and indirectly contained) labour and *commanded* (currently paid) labour, the difference between the two (embodied but not paid labour) being defined as *surplus labour* which was meant to represent a measure of exploitation.[11]

It may be interesting now to connect our notions of *capitalist* prices and *producibility* prices to the Marxian problem. Capitalist and producibility prices (equations 4 and 4.1) differ because of different cost inputations represented the product matrices $\mathbf{G} \, \mathbf{K}'$ and $\mathbf{R} \, \mathbf{K}'$. If $\mathbf{R} \geq \mathbf{G}$ capitalist prices are higher than producibility prices and the real wage is lower than it is in a purely producibility context. Note that in our *producibility* world speaking of *exploitation* is inappropriate because inputs intended for capital additions are determined by technological requirements, not by distributional choices. But if capitalist prices exceed producibility prices exploitation enters the stage. In this case the economy as a whole generates a share of interest income that exceeds the investment required to integrate the inherited sectoral capital stocks. Such an income excess may be subtracted from the purchasing power of wages by prices higher than those required by simple producibility. In this situation the

[10] With reference to equation (6) this takes us back to equation (4).   [11] Marx (1867), Ch. IX.

excess of interest income over investment for growth may be intended as a measure of the Marxian *exploitation*.

Finally let me remind that the notion of total (direct and indirect) labour contained in one unit of each sectoral product has been used by Pasinetti (1973) in his definition of production technology in terms of sole labour of a *vertically integrated sector* (i.e. integrated by 'fractions' of every other productive sector, so to be self-sufficient for the production of its own inputs, except labour).

6.   Concluding remarks on structural dynamics and economic policy

The term *structural dynamics* indicates generally the change over time of the technical coefficient matrices. Such dynamics is primarily due to scientific progress that leads to innovation in production techniques. A different and complementary approach to structural dynamics and technical change is due to A. Quadrio Curzio (see, in particular, Quadrio Curzio 1980, 1986), who examined the role of non-reproducible resources and rents on growth, prices, and income distribution. These instances of structural dynamics are of great interest, but lie outside the scope of the present contribution. Yet, when the technological matrices that we consider are of the 'augmented' type that we have taken into account, such for example the matrix $[\mathbf{A} + \mathbf{K}\,\mathbf{G}]$, a new kind of structural dynamics may be considered along with the technological dynamics strictly speaking. Attention must be focused on the sectoral growth rates of the $\mathbf{G}$ diagonal matrix. In a realistic context, as we have noted, the dynamics of sectoral growth and capital accumulation is ultimately led by the growth of sectoral consumptions. Therefore a distinct (dated) diagonal matrix $\mathbf{G_t}$ is likely to correspond to every dated consumption vector $\mathbf{c_t}$[12].

Finally, a look to economic policy: Is there any influence of economic policy on the time path of prices in the Leontief dynamic model? The area in which the otherwise spontaneous price dynamics is likely to be modified by policy is the one of fiscal policy. The state may choose the growth rate of public consumptions, corresponding to some of the consumption categories of the model; at the same time the government budget constraint implies some form of taxation of all other sectoral consumptions (because ultimately resources must be subtracted from private consumptions to permit public consumptions). As usual the taking of resources may be done on individual incomes (wages and interests on capital stocks) or on final distribution of consumption goods (as in the case of VAT). For the reasons explained earlier the 'natural' price dynamics is obviously affected.

---

[12] See Appendix.

Appendix

This appendix aims to clarify why, under realistic hypotheses, the growth rates of sectoral products that appear in the diagonal matrix $\mathbf{G}$ are likely to change over time. For this purpose let's assume that the vector of sectoral consumptions of period t is

$$\mathbf{c_t} = (\mathbf{I} + \mathbf{D})^t \, \mathbf{c_0} \qquad (A1)$$

where $\mathbf{D}$ represents a diagonal matrix having non zero elements d_i equal to the growth rates of sectoral *consumptions* (that we take as known) and $\mathbf{c_0}$ represents a vector of initial consumptions. The Leontief sectoral production vector at time t may therefore be expressed as a function of the vector of sectoral consumptions at time t:

$$\mathbf{q_t} = \mathbf{A}\,\mathbf{q_t} + \mathbf{K}\,(\mathbf{q_t} - \mathbf{q_{t-1}}) + (\mathbf{I} + \mathbf{D})^t \, \mathbf{c_0} \qquad (2.1)$$

Now express $\mathbf{D}$ as the sum of its diagonalized column vectors $\mathbf{D_j}$

$$\mathbf{D} \equiv \mathbf{D_1} + \mathbf{D_2} + \dots$$

Define in addition c_{j0} as the column vector having c_{j0} as j-th component and zero otherwise. So we can write:

$$\mathbf{q_t} = \mathbf{A}\,\mathbf{q_{1t}} + d_1\,\mathbf{K}\,\mathbf{q_{1t}} + (\mathbf{I} + \mathbf{D_1})^t\,\mathbf{c_{10}}$$
$$+\mathbf{A}\,\mathbf{q_{2t}} + d_2\,\mathbf{K}\,\mathbf{q_{2t}} + (\mathbf{I} + \mathbf{D_2})^t\,\mathbf{c_{20}} + \dots$$

where $\mathbf{q_{1t}}, \mathbf{q_{2t}}, \dots$ represent production vectors required to deliver $c_{1t}, c_{2t}, \dots$ as final sectoral consumptions. The total sectoral products vector may consequently be expressed as a sum of addends, each corresponding to a subsystem at its turn corresponding to one of the sectoral consumption growth rates[13]

$$\mathbf{q_t} = (\mathbf{I} - \mathbf{A} - d_1\,\mathbf{K})^{-1}\,(\mathbf{I} + \mathbf{D_1})^t\,\mathbf{c_{10}}$$
$$+(\mathbf{I} - \mathbf{A} - d_2\,\mathbf{K})^{-1}\,(\mathbf{I} + \mathbf{D_2})^t\,\mathbf{c_{20}}$$
$$+\dots \qquad (A2)$$

Note that at time t $\mathbf{q_t}$ is an endogenous vector and $\mathbf{q_{t-1}}$ is known; consequently also the growth rates of the sectoral products ($\mathbf{g}$ vector and $\mathbf{G}$ matrix) are endogenous variables, changing over time. We understand that in the very long run the sectoral structure of the whole system asymptotically approaches the one of the subsystem

---

[13] I have taken this decomposition from Mathur (1964).

corresponding to the dominant growth rate. Since the growth rates of sectoral products don't remain constant over the time sectoral prices change as well.[14]

REFERENCES

Cavazzuti, F., and D'Adda, C. (1972) 'Imposta sul valore aggiunto e prezzi: un'applicazione dello schema input-output', *Note economiche*, 5–6, pp. 176–87.

D'Adda, C. (1966) *La funzione del consumo nel modello di Leontief* (a report to the Italian National Research Council, Study Group on Distribution, Technical Progress and Economic Development), mimeo.

(1989) 'An Economy of Industries and Its Aggregate Representation', *BNL Quarterly Review*, 168, pp. 97–107.

Keynes, J. M. (1936) *The General Theory of Employment, Interest and Money*, London: Macmillan.

Leontief, W. W. (1941) *The Structure of American Economy 1919–1939*, New York: Oxford University Press.

(1966) 'Input-Output Analysis 1965' in W. W. Leontief *Input-Output Economics*, New York: Oxford University Press, pp. 134–55.

Marx, K. (1867) *Das Kapital, Kritik der politischen Ökonomie*, Hamburg: Verlag von Otto Meisner.

Mathur, P. N. (1964) 'Output and Investment for Exponential Growth in Consumption – An Alternative Formulation: and Derivation of Their Technological Upper Limits', *Review of Economic Studies*, 31.1, pp. 73–6.

Morishima, M. (1958) 'Prices, Interest and Profits in a Dynamic Leontief System', *Econometrica*, 26.3, pp. 358–80.

Pasinetti, L. L. (1965) 'A New Theoretical Approach to the Problems of Economic Growth', Vatican City: Pontificia Accademia Scientiarum Scripta Varia, 28, Part. II, pp. 1–126.

(1973) 'The Notion of Vertical Integration in Economic Analysis', *Metroeconomica*, 25, pp. 1–29. Reprinted in L. L. Pasinetti (ed.) (1980) *Essays on the Theory of Joint Production*, London: Macmillan; New York: Columbia University Press.

(1977) *Lectures on the Theory of Production*, London: Macmillan; New York: Columbia University Press.

Quadrio Curzio, A. (1980) 'Rent, Income Distribution and Orders of Efficiency and Rentability', in L. L. Pasinetti, (ed.), *Essays on the Theory of Joint Production*, London, Macmillan, pp. 219–40. Reprinted in H. D. Kurz and N. Salvadori (eds.), *The Legacy of Piero Sraffa*, Cheltenham, UK: E. Elgar, 2003, vol. II, pp. 311–41.

(1986) 'Technological Scarcity: An Essay on Production and Structural Change', in M. Baranzini and R. Scazzieri (eds.) *Foundations of Economics. Structures of Inquiry and Economic Theory*, Oxford and New York, Basil Blackwell, pp. 311–38.

---

[14] This result doesn't cope with the finding of prices independent of the scale of production and final output composition in a dynamic Leontief model (Morishima, 1958). The reason is that different notions of price are considered. Moreover a situation in which the **g** vector changes over time is a transitory one, in the wait (no matter how long) that asymptotic equilibrium is reached.

8   The transformative potential of input–output economics for addressing critical resource challenges of the twenty-first century

Faye Duchin

1.   Introduction

The size of the global economy – by any measures of population, resource extraction, production, consumption and pollution – has grown enormously, with the widely shared expectation that it will grow larger still, while the planet's geophysical resource base does not expand and its ability to absorb wastes is already being tested. Associated with this expansion of the world economy are dense and growing interconnections among geographic regions at different stages of economic development and material standards of living. These interconnections quickly link events taking place in one area to repercussions in others and, although they have spread prosperity, it remains highly uneven. We have seen how climate events and government policies that affect local agricultural production can have rapid impacts on global food prices. With the steep increase in quantity and variety of financial transactions, a financial crisis originating in a single country has spread widely and deeply throughout the global economy and affected it substantially. One can anticipate future shortages of resources, such as fresh water and platinum group metals, accompanied by sharp increases in their prices that bring windfall scarcity rents for the highest-quality endowments. Given the ongoing acquisitions of large tracts of land and long-term access to raw materials throughout the developing world, concerns abound about the future size, distribution and disposition of these rents. Scenario analysis can help analyse likely eventualities and the impacts of possible strategies to avoid disastrous outcomes.

Input–output economics is uniquely suited to analysing problems surrounding resource dependence, economic interdependence, and distribution of income and wealth, as well as strategies for addressing them. Economic analysis in these areas is today largely reliant on neoclassical economic theory as reflected in computable general equilibrium (CGE) models of the global

I am grateful for many conversations on related topics with Carlos Lopez-Morales and acknowledge support provided by the U.S. National Science Foundation's CNH grant #1115025, *Impacts of Global Change Scenarios on Ecosystem Services from the World's Rivers.*

economy. Input–output economics and models have the potential to transform economic analysis of resource challenges in three major ways. First, it is designed to analyse changes that involve substantial departures from current practices in response to novel situations, rather than only marginal adjustments to an external change to arrive at a new equilibrium. Second, it does not rely on standard behavioural assumptions that assume a narrow definition of rationality on the parts of decision makers. These notions about rational behaviour formally preclude critically important initiatives such as adopting technologies that may be costly in the short term, citizens' preferences for less pollution over more consumption, or government policies and international agreements that improve the allocation of resources. Third, it readily accommodates process-level information about technological alternatives and their reliance on resources, whether the latter are priced or not.

The remainder of this chapter is divided into five sections. Section 2 identifies distinctive features of input–output economics that characterize the basic input–output model and need to be maintained in all conceptual extensions. Reasons why further development of input–output theory has attracted less attention than data compilation and empirical analysis are discussed in Section 3. Section 4 expands the concept of factors of production from labour and capital to include any number of resources – just as it includes many sectors and products – as central to new theorizing. Section 5 describes the logic behind several existing model extensions. These include a model of the world economy based on the logic of comparative advantage, a systematic approach to waste management for recovery of secondary resources, and a multi-period dynamic framework to provide infrastructure and other forms of built capital and the funding for it. Section 6 concludes by identifying priority areas for further theoretical development.

2. Features of input–output economics

2.1 The basic input–output model and "Big A" matrices

The basic input–output model consists of two matrix equations, $(I - A) x = y$ and $(I - A') p = v$, where the columns of the matrix A quantify the technologies in terms of intermediate inputs, y and x are the vectors of final demand and output, and v and p are the vectors of value-added (factor costs) and prices of goods. Typically A, y and v are specified for a given scenario, and one solves for output (x) and prices (p). For alternative scenarios, one may assume changed values for technologies or final demand and obtain new values of x and p. These changed assumptions reflect choices attributable to the actors. However, no specific objectives are identified, and there are no constraints as to how much output can grow.

The final demand vector y describes the levels and composition of private consumption, government spending, investment, and imports and exports, while the vector v of value-added quantifies the payments by each sector to factors of production (per unit of output); these distinguish labour earnings, returns on built capital, and (in principle although unfortunately not in fact in most databases) resource rents. The properties of the A matrix, and in particular of the matrix $(I - A)^{-1}$, for relating x to y and p to v, have been amply described in other places. Also amply noted are several limitations of this model. First, all the components of y and v must be specified exogenously rather than being determined by the model. As a consequence, the framework cannot assure consistency between components of y and v, for example between household consumption outlays and worker earnings, or between exports and imports. Also, while the solution values for x and p are consistent with the technological assumptions, and therefore with each other in the sense that p'y = v'x, there is no reciprocal impact between changes in demand and in unit prices of products. It is well understood that extensions to the basic input–output framework are needed to achieve 'closure' in these and other variables in order to expand its explanatory scope. To achieve closures that are more than symbolic requires that they be based on theory relating the variables one to another. In later sections I will describe input–output models closed for international trade, waste management and investment. However, the most common closures still take the familiar form of a square matrix and its inverse. Rather than being based on theoretical considerations, this form of closure is selected for convenience of calculations.

Without exception, the first efforts at closure of the basic input–output model for any exogenous variable has involved expanding the original square A matrix by adding a column and a row to form a larger square matrix that I call a Big A matrix and denote A_B. The new column and row are assumed to bear the same relation to each other as in the case of any production sector in the economy; consequently, the Big A matrix is manipulated in the same equations as the simple A matrix by forming the inverse $(I - A_B)^{-1}$. Households, for example, can be represented like a production sector, with input coefficients for consumption in the column and labour coefficients in the row, on the assumption that when more or less labour is required, then consumption will accordingly rise or fall. This assumption is implicit in forming the inverse associated with a Social Accounting Matrix, where the institutions (such as households) are treated like production sectors. An early dynamic model was actually called the 'dynamic inverse' (Leontief 1970) with both intermediate and capital coefficients organized in a Big A matrix. In an important area of contemporary analysis, a Big A matrix incorporating substantial detail about bilateral trade flows is the basis for multiregional input–output (MRIO) data-bases. The resulting MRIO models are truly input–output models by all the criteria defined in this chapter and make it possible to examine a deeper structure behind the data at hand. However, they are typically not well suited for *ex ante* scenario analysis, as the standard manipulation of the additional rows and columns implies relationships that held in the base year but can not be expected to hold, in general, under other circumstances. The matrix A_B in the case of MRIO, for example, combines not only region-specific matrices of technologically determined requirements but also the shares of a region's imports supplied domestically and by each trade partner in the absence of an underlying theory of interregional trade.

2.2   Multidimensionality of goals, options, and outcomes

Economics is the field that evaluates a society's options for allocating scarce resources for consumption, production and exchange so as to achieve specific objectives. Contemporary practice of economics relies on models and methods to quantify the extent to which particular options contribute to realizing the goals. Like mainstream neoclassical economics, input–output economics takes a system-wide perspective in terms of measurable quantities and associated prices and is capable of producing numerical answers to various kinds of questions. However, input–output economics is sufficiently open-ended to allow for societies to have multiple objectives, to allow for objectives and preferences – and their relative importance – to change over time, and to accommodate alternative actions with multiple outcomes that need not be reduced to a money value or any other single measure, precluding a unique ordering of the outcomes by their desirability. Other schools of economic thought also take exception to oversimplified behavioural assumptions of mainstream theory (e.g. ecological economics, behavioural economics, evolutionary economics, institutional economics), but input–output economics is alone among them in offering an alternative framework for quantitative analysis, one that both is well established and provides a flexible base for further conceptual development.

2.3   Meso-level actors and actions

From the simplest to the most elaborated model formulation, input–output economics conceptualizes an economy in terms of *groupings* of its major actors, namely households including individuals who are both workers and consumers and sectors comprised of firms employing similar input structures to produce comparable outputs. Households classified within a particular socio-economic category generally have patterns of consumption and employment that are far closer to each other than to those of households in different socio-economic categories, and the comparable observation holds for firms in the same sector. This *mesoeconomic*, or medium-level, focus contrasts with the handful of aggregate variables that are the basic conceptual units of mainstream macroeconomics as well as with the individual consumers and individual firms of microeconomic theory. Theorizing that attempts to root macroeconomic reasoning in the decisions of the individual actors entirely bypasses the meso-level decision makers in households, industries and government agencies, all of which may produce and consume goods and own factors of production. The choice among technologies and the decision to invest reflect the circumstances affecting an entire sector of the economy and can be conceptualized at that level. Furthermore, the options available to a sector are also meso-level in that each decision involves a specific combination of factors of production and intermediate or consumer goods, not trade-offs between two individual inputs.

The structural building blocks of input–output economics are the technologies utilized in production. Technologies are described in terms of process-level inputs per unit of output, such as magnitudes of seed, chemicals and land required to produce a ton of wheat in a particular region and the change in yield when a given amount of water is applied by sprinkler irrigation. Columns of such coefficients are quantified for the past from business records (the source of official input–output tables), while for the future technical experts can provide projections for alternative technologies such as incorporation of drip irrigation, the use of cooling towers to reduce thermal pollution or entirely new technologies, for example, wind power for generating electric power. This approach to representing a sector's technology in terms of its inputs from other industries, and its outputs to them, accounts for the ability to track interdependencies among sectors. Statistical offices still produce input–output tables and coefficient matrices exclusively in money values, but it is easy to see that mixed units also satisfy the logic of the basic model and all its extensions and offer the substantial advantage of explicitly distinguishing changes in quantities from changes in unit prices. Mixed units also enable in-depth communication with engineer and natural scientist colleagues about changes in resource availability, processing and fabrication, which are their foci of concern.

The parameters that dominate mainstream models, by contrast, are elasticities that quantify the percentage change in one variable assumed to follow from a percentage change in another. A key example is the elasticity of substitution, which measures the ease of substituting capital and labour for each other in a production function, in which output is a function of only these two variables. When intermediate inputs (considered as a single input, when they are included at all) and natural resources (again, usually represented as a single variable when included) are added, a "nested" procedure is employed to determine substitutions. The number of inputs is always quite small, as the nested production functions approach quickly becomes unwieldy. Armington elasticities are used to govern the substitution between a domestically produced product and its imported counterpart, and then in nested fashion to determine the amounts imported from different trade partners. All elasticities must be inferred from (past) relationships among the changes in the variables in question, a pair of variables at a time, on the assumption that the substitutions are independent of each other, or separable. The use of elasticities as *ex ante* parameters require the assumption that, to the extent that the changes reflect other unspecified variables, their omission does not appreciably change the elasticity. The challenges in quantifying elasticities are well known: some believe that their measurement can be refined through better measurement techniques, but input–output models are based on the conviction that columns of technical coefficients are better choices than elasticities for parameterization.

A hallmark of input–output models is the fact that, not only the choice among alternative technologies, but *all options* available to the meso-level actors are represented at the same meso-level of detail, even when the scope for decisions extends well beyond that of the basic model. This means, for example, that a sector's investment demand is specified at the level of individual capital goods in a dynamic input–output model, not as an aggregate money amount; and the investment goods ordered by a sector at one point in time match those produced by other sectors, adding with a time lag to production capacity in the using sector. This commitment imposes a strong consistency requirement on extensions to the basic input–output model and in turn offers assurance of consistency among the quantities and prices of goods produced, traded and consumed.

2.4   Physical feasibility and price duality

The input–output representation of production technologies aims to achieve physical plausibility. Each technological alternative is compiled as an exogenous column of coefficients, whether it is the average technology used in that sector or one of several choices for endogenous determination of how much is produced by each option (in a choice-of-technology model). When the choice is endogenous, it is based on consideration of entire input structures: the obviously strong complementarity among most inputs makes this a more realistic choice than allowing substitution between two inputs, one pair at a time. Physical feasibility must also respect limits in factor endowments. Challenges surrounding the representation of resource stocks are discussed next.

2.5   Compatibility among model closures

The development of input–output economics proceeds by progressive 'closure' of the basic model, where each closure makes endogenous some category of final demand or some factor used in production by structuring additional relationships among variables. The logic governing these relationships may be made explicit by adding new equations, by adding new assumptions to scenarios, or using a mixture of both. Even after model extensions, however, input–output models make more substantial use of exogenous assumptions than do neoclassical equilibrium models; input–output models rely heavily on the narrative describing a scenario in cases where explanatory theory is deemed to be lacking. This is the reason, to take a simple example, that consumption demand is almost always exogenous and scenario-dependent in an *ex ante* input–output analysis: consumption preferences change for many reasons beyond changes in incomes and relative prices, such as changes in diets in rich countries away from animal products towards more plant-based ones because they are healthier and less resource-intensive. There is nothing to be gained from attempting to construct formal equations to predict such changes in behaviour: they are better viewed as alternative scenarios.

Input–output theorizing is the basis for a new model of international trade (world model), the choice among alternative technologies within a single region (choice-of-technology model), waste generation and waste management (waste input–output model), and investment in built capital (dynamic model). The world model is based on a generalized theory of comparative advantage; in addition to the familiar variables, it requires exogenous variables measuring factor endowments and endogenous variables quantifying scarcity rents. The choice-of-technology model is based on the same logic as the world model, optimization subject to factor constraints; its representation requires no variables or parameters besides those identified for the world model, and it is achieved for each individual region through the device of a rectangular in place of a square interindustry coefficient matrix. The logic behind the waste input–output model is that wastes generated in one sector in an economy can after processing be employed in the same or another sector, but the match must be made at the level of specific resources. An extensive supplementary database is needed to represent resource inputs, wastes generated, technologies for processing wastes and sectoral technologies with the potential to absorb recovered resources. A comparative static analysis can represent an economy at several points in time, with decision makers taking decisions at each time step that reflect scenario assumptions for that period. A dynamic model links these time steps by requiring investment to maintain the capacity of the capital stock in place in each sector and offering sector-level decision makers the possibility to expand its capacity. It requires an additional matrix of coefficients showing the sectoral composition of input requirements to expand each sector's capacity and an associated matrix of time lags for each such input, measuring how far in advance that component needs to be purchased. Each of these models, described in more detail in this chapter, requires establishing the logical relationships and defining any new variables and parameters before quantitative information can be compiled into databases.

To be compatible, theories must not contradict each other, but meeting this criterion is not sufficient to assure their integration in a single model. In fact, integrating the individual models just mentioned requires both further conceptual extensions and the compilation of new kinds of data. Consider the requirements for extending a one-region dynamic model to a dynamic model of the world economy, or alternatively of making a one-period model of the world economy dynamic. A dynamic model of one region will require (among other conditions) that sector-level retained earnings plus loans from financial intermediaries cover the costs of investments. Extension to the world economy requires additional logic, and additional data, to distribute one region's excess earnings among domestic and foreign investment prospects.

3. Development of input-output theory

Several characteristics of all input–output models were described in the last section: potential for multidimensionality of goals, options, and outcomes; meso-level of analysis; physical feasibility and price duality; and model closures supplemented by scenario narratives and scenario assumptions. Each extension beyond the basic input–output model represents a conceptual extension – a theory of trade in the case of a world model, the relations between the generation and effective recovery of wastes for a model with recycling, and a theory of investment for a dynamic model. If it has the characteristics identified, the result is an input–output model. These logical extensions are not unique: there is more than one way to realize any particular conceptual extension. Nonetheless these extensions comprise theories, and they should be called theories, to signal and emphasize the fact that input–output economics is more than a collection of data and an expanding toolkit, and to identify and prioritize the areas requiring new theory development to guide the formulation of model extensions.

3.1   Input–output economics and neoclassical economic theory

Over the course of the last century professional economists have perfected the integrated conceptual edifice of neoclassical economics to describe how an economy operates to achieve growth through exchanges among well-informed individuals in unobstructed markets. It is assumed that decision makers have stable, rational preferences among options; individual consumers maximize utility (consumption) while individual producers maximize profits; and market prices adjust to equilibrate demand and supply by allocating scarce factors most efficiently. Researchers working in different areas develop specialized theories relevant to their parts of the domain that may depart in particulars from a pure version of neoclassical theory, but they are at least tacitly supportive of the overall neoclassical program for a variety of reasons. However, while CGE models make use of input–output databases, they fully adhere to the basic neoclassical assumptions of complete information, competitive markets, and the standard motivations associated with rational behaviour of individual consumers and individual firms. Even within the input–output community, some researchers embrace CGE models as a way of embedding some of the attributes of input–output economics within an *ex ante* model of the global economy that is based on standard neoclassical theorizing. This is one approach to extending the scope of the basic input–output model.

Starting with Professor Leontief, however, many input–output economists find the ground rules of neoclassical theorizing unnecessarily restrictive in that many potentially desirable consumer and producer choices would have to be deemed 'irrational' by those criteria. When it comes to representing the choices among distinct technologies and the associated reliance on resources, the advantages of a mesoeconomic representation are clear – at least to many engineers and natural scientists. This fact can perhaps provide the incentive for also considering the advantages of less restrictive behavioural assumptions and a wider range of criteria for evaluating options.

Setting out the basic precepts of the program of input–output economics, and identifying the distinct component theories as input–output theories, has been slow to be realized for several reasons. Over many decades Wassily Leontief developed and used input–output models to evaluate ways of addressing what he saw as the critical problems of the twentieth century: reducing income gaps among countries, the reallocation of resources from military to civilian objectives, evaluating the adequacy of global endowments of resources, and examining prospects for employment and incomes of workers facing labour-saving technological changes. To support these investigations, he chose to encourage the compilation of data over theoretical development for two reasons. Since his approach to empirical analysis depends on the availability of a highly structured and detailed database, institutionalizing the collection of these data was indispensable for input–output economics to flourish. He focused on data also because of his conviction that theorizing must start from facts and proceed by direct interaction with empirical analysis, by contrast with more abstract, data-free theorizing that he associated with "pure theory" in the neoclassical program (Leontief, 1971).

Professor Leontief's second priority was to promote interdisciplinary collaboration that would afford input–output economists access to the specialized knowledge needed for the representation of technologies. He also advocated scenario formulation and interpretation that transcends mathematical formalisms or overly simplified assumptions analyzed with any model including the input–output model. He especially singled out engineers as collaborators, who would be necessary partners for a deeper understanding of the production processes actually utilized in different sectors and their technological alternatives (Leontief, 1953).

Today, less than two decades after Professor Leontief's death, his two main *desiderata* (focus on data and interdisciplinarity) have been achieved even more emphatically than he might have imagined. Input–output data for the global economy are now compiled on a regular basis by statistical agencies around the world and continue to be expanded in size and scope. More recent is the development of several ambitious databases of the world economy that include not only input–output data at unprecedented levels of regional and sectoral detail, but also a great deal of environmental data organized in classifications and units that facilitate their use in combination with the economic information (a recent special issues of *Economic Systems Research* is devoted to global multiregional input–output databases). Input–output economics has sought and achieved a greater degree of interdisciplinarity in representing technologies than other approaches to economics, benefitting from the substantial recent influx into our community of researchers in industrial ecology with expertise in process-level life-cycle assessment and material flow analysis. These researchers are attracted by the ability to absorb descriptions of specific resources, products, processes and technologies into a systemwide analytic framework. Their vital contributions continue to improve the quantity and quality of input–output data and expand the range of questions addressed in the input–output literature. The International Society for Industrial Ecology now has sessions at its conferences, and subject editors for its scholarly journal, expressly devoted to input–output analysis.

3.2 Why input-output theory development lags

The realization of Professor Leontief's priorities is a historically significant achievement, and productive work along these lines continues to expand. Unfortunately, however, the further development of input–output theory has not only failed to keep pace with this burst of activity, but what is more, its absence is barely noted because its importance tends to be overlooked. Potential theorists of input–output economics have in my opinion been inadequately engaged in providing the kinds of conceptualizations needed to address the great challenges of the twenty-first century in part because the authors of empirical studies have failed to articulate their needs. Industrial ecologists have championed the value of mixed units and hybrid analysis but still work exclusively with only the basic model, represented by a square Big A matrix, although possibly a very large one with many new types of components, that is inverted to yield multipliers that measure the amount of output required to satisfy a unit of final demand. While multipliers and the kinds of *ex post* decomposition analyses they make possible comprise a substantial portion of input–output analysis today, there is also a critical need to carry out *ex ante* scenario analysis. Sometimes the *ex post* models are utilized for *ex ante* analysis without sufficient attention to the inadequacy of their parameterization for this changed purpose. The CGE model is often presented as an input–output model closed for the behavioural motives of agents. But these are neoclassical closures: for those who consider turning to CGE models, it is vital to clarify both the differences and the existence of alternative input–output formulations beyond the basic model. This will entail also actively encouraging theory building as the work of researchers who also build models and interpret the empirical significance of their data and results.

4.   Resources as factors of production

Factors of production are inputs that are indispensable for production but are not themselves produced in factories and offices, at least not in a single production period. Factor inputs are either immobile or at least distinctly less mobile than the products in which they are embodied. Often economists distinguish only built capital and labour as factors of production, and the only trace of factor inputs in an input–output table is limited to the earnings of these two factors in the form of value-added contributed by labour and by capital. Distinguishing more factors will require corresponding detail on factor earnings, namely distinguishing rents on scarce resources. Input–output studies have demonstrated the value of analysing an economy in terms of dozens or hundreds, possibly even thousands, of economic sectors producing goods and services. It is time to represent resources and other factors of production also at a mesoeconomic level of detail. Challenges surround the definitions and quantification of stocks of primary resources and endowments of built capital and infrastructure, technologies in place for resource extraction, and factor prices – especially rents accruing to scarce factors. The resources include fresh water, arable land, petroleum and other fuels, rare earths, platinum group and other metals, and fertilizer materials such as phosphate rock.

The quality of a resource endowment depends on geological, technological and economic considerations. These include, for example, the grade (or concentration) and accessibility of a deposit, the extraction techniques available, and the distance from processing facilities. Current sources of mineral reserves estimate for a given country the geologic endowment that could be 'economically extracted or produced at the time of determination' (USGS, 2010). In the case of petroleum, it is widely recognized that distinct technologies are required to extract reserves in, say, Saudi Arabia or the Canadian tar sands, even though both are by definition economic deposits (since they are in fact being exploited). Reserves of natural gas (and some other crucial resources such as lithium) have increased substantially due to the development of hydraulic fracturation, which makes them economic in this sense. Starting with selected resources of strategic importance, it is imperative to characterize at least major deposits in more detail by specifying qualitative attributes and technological requirements as well as quantities. The effects of changes in demand, endowments, technological choices, prices and scarcity rents will be far different for regions with high-quality endowments than those with low-quality stocks.

The distribution of resource rents between the owner of a resource, say a national government, and firms in the domestic or foreign extraction sector exploiting it, can exhibit huge discrepancies depending on the resource and negotiating power (e.g. see (Zacharia, 2010) and (Reuters, 2010) for divergent arrangements for Israeli gas and Chilean copper). The systematic compilation of information about resource royalties and rents in actual situations would provide not only empirical information but also guidance for scenario development.

A combination of resource depletion, increased demand, more stringent environmental protection, and intentional restrictions on exports is generating competition among importers, more aggressive extraction technologies (such as deep mining of the seabed) and higher extraction costs. At the same time, the accumulation of goods and infrastructure that no longer have economic value are waste products that could provide a secondary source of resources while also relieving pressures on landfills. Both resources and material wastes exhibit highly uneven global distributions, reflecting geophysical realities in the first case and the history of industrialization and the accumulation of wealth and material infrastructure in the latter. The ability to substitute primary, nonrenewable resources by recovered ones, or by renewable resources, has implications for material impacts of extraction and processing as well as international transfers of wealth. Expanding the set of factors of production poses data challenges that depend on expertise about the physical properties of resources and technologies for extracting, processing, fabricating, recovering and re-using or reprocessing them.

5.   Extensions: model closures and data requirements

A dynamic input–output model of the global economy with an adequate conceptualization of resource endowments and resource rents and offering technological alternatives for production, including the choice between primary and secondary resource inputs, can improve understanding of the nature of the resource crises we may face and ways for avoiding them. Many of the modelling and data requirements exist and are described in this section. Five features that distinguish the input–output modelling framework are identified and are maintained through all the conceptual extensions.

5.1   Closure 1: comparative advantage

I start with an input–output model of the world economy that determines the international division of labour and world prices by direct comparisons of costs of production using different technologies in different regions. The world model in question is based on a theory of comparative advantage, generalized to the case of any number of trading partners, sectors and factors of production (Duchin 2005). The scenario specifies consumption demand, alternative production technologies and factor endowments. Resources have two-part prices: one part is exogenous, assuring that resources with endowments that are not fully utilized can have non-zero prices. The model minimizes global factor use, rather than maximizing notions of welfare and utility (or consumption) and profits. A sector's output may be constrained by any one (or more) of the various factor endowments. Thus it may be a mineral endowment that is scarce, the resource could be abundant but the mine operating at full capacity, or fresh water needed for mining operation in short supply. When an endowment constraint is binding in some region, meaning that it is fully utilized and therefore scarce, an endogenous scarcity rent is earned and added to the exogenous price. The amounts of rents earned in a region depend upon the size of the divergences between a region's costs of production and that of the highest-cost producer (that actually produces) in each sector. The comparative advantage framework provides direct logical links among global demand (which puts pressure on endowments), exhaustion of regional factor endowments (which requires moving on to higher-cost producers), world prices of goods and regional factor earnings.

One extension of this theoretical framework is the endogenous determination of bilateral trade flows by taking the differential costs of transport from exporting regions directly into account in the cost comparisons (Strømman and Duchin, 2006). The full family of World Trade Models (WTM) and databases has been applied in a number of empirical studies, most recently focusing on future challenges surrounding food and agriculture and their reliance on water withdrawals and agricultural land.

Another extension of the World Trade Model incorporates the Rectangular Choice of Technology (RCOT) model (Duchin and Levine, 2011, 2012). In the case of a single region, a sector chooses the lowest cost among two or more alternative technologies. However, if this technology runs into a factor constraint before satisfying all demand for its product, the sector will simultaneously employ another one of its options if possible. The model is called rectangular because the matrix of intermediate coefficients includes only one row for the product in question but several columns, one for each technological option. The underlying assumption is that the user is indifferent to how the product was produced. The realization that an input–output matrix of intermediate outputs need not be square and invertible helps encourage other departures from accustomed practices. The RCOT specification for a single region is easily and fully incorporated into the model of the world economy. My colleagues and I make use of it in all our empirical studies, in particular allowing for crops to be grown by some combination of irrigated and rainfed technologies depending upon water availability under different scenarios.

5.2   Waste management and secondary sources of resources

Secondary resources are one output of a waste-management system focused on recovering useful materials from by-products and production wastes, obsolete infrastructure, and end-of-life products. The ability of material-using sectors to make use of reprocessed materials depends on product requirements, properties of the secondary vs. primary materials, and their relative prices. A body of work called Waste Input-Output (WIO) analysis, developed by Nakamura and Kondo (2002, 2009) includes a detailed database of technical information about material use and wastes, models for analysing the database, and empirical studies. The WIO database distinguishes dozens of resource inputs and wastes generated in each sector of the Japanese economy. It is quantified using process-level data (LCA inventories) in physical units and aligned with the sectors of the Japanese input–output table. The database also identifies the major treatment options used for recovering materials for reuse, indicates the portions of each waste treated in different ways and indicates the wastes that can be handled using each treatment technology. An extension of the framework is an optimization model that establishes a criterion for an optimal waste management and recycling program (Kondo and Nakamura, 2005). The objective function used in this case study maximizes GDP per unit of direct material input, but other formulations can be used in future research. The model constraints include limits on landfill capacity.

The incorporation of waste generation, waste treatment, and material recovery and reuse into an input–output modelling framework provides closure of the one-region model for wastes. Doing so further strengthens the linkage between LCA and input–output economics by directly incorporating into the model the end-of-life stage of a product's life cycle. It associates a detailed array of resources with the products in which they are embodied, and links these products with associated wastes and their prospects for reuse. The feasibility of this WIO program is now demonstrated. A conceptualization and database that extends the framework for a global perspective on wastes and recycling remains to be developed.

5.3   Investment and economic dynamics

Investment in a great deal of infrastructure and built capital of all types will take place over the next few decades in developing countries. One priority area is electrification, including construction of dam projects to supply hydropower, irrigation water and household needs. A related area is infrastructure for water delivery and sewage treatment. An important project is development of renewable energy sources intended for desalination of sea water, in particular in parts of the Middle East that are well endowed with solar radiation but water-scarce (World Bank 2012). Realizing such development objectives is a resource-intensive undertaking that will require funding from domestic and foreign sources. In many of the rich countries, infrastructure renewal is a high priority that is also resource intensive. For a single economy, both physical requirements and availability of funding can be evaluated using a dynamic input–output model. Many of these projects, very large dams for example, will have impacts on the provision of ecosystem services that need to be evaluated for comparison with the intended benefits.

Duchin and Szyld (1985) developed a dynamic input–output model for a single region that introduces sector-level production capacity as a variable and tracks its rate of utilization. In this framework, a sector invests for expansion when unused capacity is inadequate to meet anticipated future needs. The model provides an equally good representation for an individual sector that is contracting as for one that is expanding. The intertemporal structure of the model assures consistency between investment goods ordered at one time, their production in other sectors at different times (reflecting an exogenous lag structure) and their addition to capacity at yet another time. The duality between the dynamic quantity and price models assures consistency between funds available and funds spent on capital investment. The model is more successful for empirical analysis than Professor Leontief's dynamic inverse or its predecessors, which were restricted to a balanced growth path where all sectors must expand (or see their built capital turn back into intermediate goods and the intermediate goods into resources!), and in addition do so at the same rate. This model has been used in empirical studies, but its wider use is limited by a number of deficiencies, including but not limited to the paucity of data on capacity by sector and capacity utilization rates that meet more than minimal conceptual requirements.

To incorporate dynamics into an input–output model of the world economy requires the explicit representation of retained earning and savings in
each economy and a conceptual logic for their allocation domestically or
abroad. The explicit representation of the extent and distribution of the
international transfers of wealth associated with resource scarcity and
resource rents in the World Trade Model is a necessary but not sufficient
step towards representing the transfers associated with direct domestic and
foreign investment.

The representation of waste generation and material recovery requires
a dynamic framework to associate the stock-flow relationships in the accumulation of built capital and the portion of it available for recovery of secondary
materials, on the one hand, and of the drawdown of resource endowments
due to cumulative extraction, on the other, while also explaining the dual
relationship between associated costs and prices. This integration has not yet
been undertaken.

6.   Conclusions

This chapter focuses on the emerging resource challenges of the twenty-first
century and the development of an input–output framework for analysing ways
of responding to them. I identify the features of input–output economics that
distinguish it from mainstream economics in ways that make it well suited to
taking on this challenge. I provide a sketch of what exists and what is needed
in terms of theory, models and data to analyse alternative scenarios about
future population, lifestyle preferences, technologies and constraints (both
of physical origin and based on legislation). The objective is to examine
prospects for primary resource use, shifts in the international division of
labour, and the transfer of income, wealth and property ownership that could
be anticipated.

I argue that the effort expended for theory formulation and scenario development in input–output economics has been inadequate. This is true both for
historical reasons and because of ambivalence within our community about
the relation of input–output economics to neoclassical economics, where the
fundamental building blocks for theory already exist and there is less need
to develop the new skill of developing detailed narratives for scenarios. The
central challenge addressed in this chapter is to stimulate new work on
expanding the theory of input–output economics that is directly related to
extending the scope of existing models and, in turn, assuring conceptual
definitions of variables that match theoretical requirements. I identify as
priorities the need to treat all potentially scarce resources as factors of production and to develop a framework for describing their endowments in a particular economy. Four active areas of input–output development in theory, data

compilation and empirical analysis are discussed: the choice among alternative technologies, a model of the world economy, a waste input–output framework and a dynamic model. A related need is for a representation of the financial sectors that reveals their special role in the allocation of savings. In fact, there is no shortage of theoretical challenges to be taken on by those who agree that we have only begun to exploit the full potential of input–output economics.

We have entered the era of Big Data for Big Models, developed within highly organized, cross-disciplinary research communities that are supported by national and inter-governmental science agencies. Perhaps the earth system modelling community, which aims to understand the interactions among biogeochemical system components as the basis for predicting future climatic conditions, best exemplifies this phenomenon. Emissions of greenhouse gases and changes in land use are drivers for climate change scenarios that engage thousands of researchers.

Emissions and land use reflect many levels of decisions that are and will continue to be taken by human populations, and those decisions are interconnected with other choices regarding lifestyle preferences involving diets and mobility, recovery of secondary materials, and investment priorities to name only a few. It seems timely and critical for a research community to emerge around data and models of the world economic system that attempts to bring closure for the many socio-economic and material challenges that confront us. In this chapter I have tried to make the case for the features of input–output economics that distinguish it from neoclassical economics in defining its role within that community and to stress the need for a focus on theory development that is consistent with input–output economics. I have illustrated the potential with several existing input–output models. These could be combined, starting with the input–output model of the world economy with interdependent quantity and price models and stocks and flows of a vastly expanded set of resources. The model offers choices among alternative technologies at process-level detail; these options could include technologies for recovering secondary materials from wastes as an alternative to their primary material counterparts. Decisions governing the disposition of domestic and foreign investment could determine the nature of infrastructure and other built capital that remain in place for decades and examine the consequences of alternative sources of funding them. These phenomena hardly exhaust the aspects of the global socio-economic system that will be important determinants of the quality of life of future generations and that no doubt will eventually also be included in comprehensive models of this system.

I end with a reminder that one characteristic feature of input–output models is the simplicity that lies behind their logical transparency: all of the input–output models discussed earlier can be written in a very small number of matrix equations. Alongside the efforts to build and sustain Big Data and Big Models, it is vital to keep a safe place for developing and refining theory describing the logic behind specific aspects of the complex reality. In the final analysis, it is the power of theory that makes it possible to achieve transparency and simplicity without oversimplification.

REFERENCES

Duchin, F. (2005) 'A World Trade Model Based on Comparative Advantage with m Regions, n Goods, and k Factors', *Economic Systems Research*, 17.2, pp. 141–62.

Duchin, F., and Levine, S. H. (2011) 'Sectors May Use Multiple Technologies Simultaneously: The Rectangular Choice-of-Technology Model with Binding Factor Constraints', *Economic Systems Research*, 23.3, pp. 281–302.

(2012) 'The Rectangular Sector-by-Technology Model: Not Every Economy Produces Every Product and Some Products May Rely on Several Technologies Simultaneously', *Journal of Economic Structures*, 1.3, pp. 1–11.

Duchin, F., and Szyld, D. (1985) 'A Dynamic Input-Output Model with Assured Positive Output', *Metroeconomica*, 37, pp. 269–82. Reprinted in H. Kurz, C. Lager and E. Dietzenbacher (eds.) Input-Output Analysis, Cheltenham: E. Elgar.

Kondo, Y., and Nakamura, S. (2005) 'Waste Input-Output Linear Programming Model with Its Application to Eco-Efficiency Analysis', *Economic Systems Research*, 17.4, pp. 393–408.

Leontief, W. (1953) *Studies in the Structure of the American Economy*, New York: Oxford University Press.

(1970) 'The Dynamic Inverse' in A. Carter and A. Brody (eds.) *Contributions to Input-Output Analysis: Proceedings of the Fourth International Conference on Input-Output Techniques*, Amsterdam: North Holland, pp. 17–46.

(1971) 'Theoretical Assumptions and Nonobserved Facts', *American Economic Review*, 61.1, pp. 1–7. (Presidential address delivered at the eighty-third meeting of *The American Economic Association*, Detroit, Michigan, December 1970.)

Leontief, W., Carter A., and Petri, P. (1977) *The Future of the World Economy*, New York: Oxford University Press.

Nakamura, S., and Kondo, Y. (2002) 'Input-Output Analysis of Waste Management', *Journal of Industrial Ecology*, 6.1, pp. 39–63.

(2009) *Waste Input-Output Analysis: Concepts and Application to Industrial Ecology*, Berlin: Springer Verlag.

Reuters (2010) 'Chile Bill Ups Mine Royalty from 2018', *Mining Weekly*, September 1, www.miningweekly.com/article/chile-bill-ups-mine-royalty-from-2018-2010-09-01, accessed 15 September 2010.

Strømman, A., and Duchin, F. (2006) 'A World Trade Model with Bilateral Trade Based on Comparative Advantage', *Economic Systems Research*, 18.3, pp. 281–97.

United States Geological Survey (USGS) (2010) *Mineral Commodity Summaries*. Washington, DC: US Geological Survey.

World Bank (2012) *Renewable Energy Desalination: An Emerging Solution to Close the Water Gap in the Middle East and North Africa*, Washington, DC.

Zacharia, J. (2010) 'Offshore Gas Discoveries in Israel Prompt Squabbling over Royalties', *The Washington Post*, 29 August, 3 pp., www.washingtonpost.com/wp-dyn/content/article/2010/08/28/AR2010082803523.html, accessed 15 September 2010.

9 Capital mobility and natural resources dynamics: a classical-Keynesian perspective

Heinrich Bortis

1. Problem and plan

The aim of this chapter is to sketch the relationship between financialization and capital mobility, and structural change and the management of non-produced natural resources. In this relationship the interrelated phenomena of income distribution and employment level play a crucial role. This problem involves considering the functioning of the entire socio-economic system. To come to grips with this very complex subject matter, strong and solid theory is required. Classical-Keynesian political economy, grounded on the classical labour value principle and the surplus principle of income distribution, and on the Keynesian principle of effective demand, seems most appropriate. However, financialization and capital mobility in relation to structural change and managing natural resources are seen in an entirely different way in neoclassical economics and in classical-Keynesian political economy.

The neoclassical vision is based on Say's Law, implying that saving is always invested. In this view, financialization reflects an abundance of saving and capital mobility implies that saving is globally invested in an efficient way. Higher growth in all countries and regions would result. Economic structures basically result from market processes; non-produced natural resources are managed through a framework of intertemporal markets. The quantity of money can, in principle, be controlled by the Central Bank through the monetary basis consisting of high-powered money (coins and banknotes) and the reserve ratio on bank loans, both of which govern the extent of deposit creation.

In the classical-Keynesian view the close link between saving and investment is cut, and the paradox of thrift implies that, in principle, higher saving/income ratios are associated to lower investment volumes; this is valid in the short *and* in the long run, as emerges from the supermultiplier (Bortis, 1997, pp. 142–204). Given this, it may be attempted to unveil the mechanisms through which financialization and capital mobility lead on to increasing inequalities in income distribution, higher levels of involuntary unemployment, undesirable structural

Without implicating him, I am greatly indebted to Sergio Rossi for his most useful comments.

changes and an inappropriate management of non-reproducible resources. The analytical basis of the classical-Keynesian system of political economy is set forth in Bortis (2003) and put into a wider context of the social and political sciences and of history in Bortis (1997, 2012, 2013).

Since the neoclassical position is reasonably well known, we start by exhibiting some salient features of classical-Keynesian political economy. Section 3 deals with the significance of the real and the financial sectors from a classical-Keynesian perspective and with the coming into being of financialization. The central Section 4 pictures the interaction between both sectors in the light of the domination of the financial sector over the real sector brought about by financialization. Section 5 deals with some effects of financialization and global capital mobility on the real economy, specifically structural change and the management of non-produced natural resources. The chapter ends with some policy conclusions.

2.   Salient features of classical-Keynesian political economy

Keynes's thoughts on the crisis and unemployment started to take shape in 1932 and materialized in a small article entitled *A Monetary Theory of Production* (Keynes, [1933] 1973). Here Keynes suggests to complement neoclassical *real exchange theory*, where only relative prices are determined, with a *monetary theory of production*, where absolute prices prevail, to come to grips with the crisis and massive unemployment as well as with business cycles in general. The basic scheme picturing a monetary production economy, where money and finance as well as the social process of production are crucially important, is set out in the second volume of Marx's *Kapital* (1973, p. 31; 1st edn 1885):

$$M-C\ldots P\ldots C'-M' \text{ [orig. : } G-W\ldots P\ldots W'-G'] \qquad (1)$$

(*M*) now stands for money and the financial sector from which entrepreneurs may get their own and outside financial means to buy means of production in the widest sense (*C*): factory buildings and machines, primary and intermediate products and, last but not least, the labour force. Within the social and circular process of production (*P*) these means of production are transformed into final products (*C'*) – the social product – which have to be sold for money, with (*M'*) representing effective demand. In the course of Shackle's *Years of High Theory 1926–1939[–1960]*, Maynard Keynes and Piero Sraffa produced a theoretical twin revolution, which filled the above scheme of relation (1) with theoretical content. In his 1960 *Production of Commodities by Means of Commodities*, Piero Sraffa showed how, in principle, the prices of production were determined within the social and circular process of production (*P*) and how distribution (the rate of profits) was governed through the surplus principle. Maynard Keynes showed in his 1936 *General Theory of Employment, Interest and Money* that in a monetary economy effective demand (M') determines output (C') and employment through the multiplier relation. A macroeconomic equilibrium below the full employment level turned out to be possible, implying the existence of system-caused involuntary unemployment.

Keynes's and Sraffa's ideas have been taken up and developed by the post-Keynesians and the neo-Ricardians. One of the main problems was to work out a long-period theory of output and employment. This requires replacing investment, the short-period autonomous variable, with government expenditures and exports, which represent long-period autonomous variables in so far as these are institutionally determined. Given this, the long-period investment *volume* becomes an *institutionally determined* derived variable; however, *uncertainty* remains attached to *individual* investment projects, the question being as to which investment projects will be successful and which firms will survive in the long run. Subsequently, Luigi Pasinetti has elaborated a conceptual framework, providing the long-period basis to bring together, on the level of principles, Sraffa's classical theory of value and distribution and Keynes's theory of employment, interest and money (Bortis, 2012). On this Pasinettian basis, a system of classical-Keynesian political economy can now be erected (Bortis, 1997 and 2003). In this theoretical framework the *long run* is to be found in the *present* and is given by Ricardo's constant or slowly evolving magnitudes, that is, technology and institutions, which form a system made up of a material basis and an institutional superstructure. Given this, the technological-institutional system governs prices and quantities in the long run, forming thus a system-equilibrium.

In a monetary production economy the social and circular process of production (P) represents the core of the material basis and, as such, moves to the centre of analyses. The essence of this process can be brought out best as a specific form of the Leontief scheme (see Bortis, 2003, pp. 433–6). In a Marxian vein production may be seen as an interaction between man (labour) and nature (land). This gives

rise to distinguishing *three* kinds of basic goods absolutely necessary for production: land basics, labour basics, and labour-land basics. *Land basics* are primary products taken from nature, for example iron ore or crude oil, which are made ready for productive use in the form of steel or petrol respectively. Subsequently, land basics or primary goods are used to produce intermediate products: wheat, flour, leather, bricks for instance. Primary products and intermediate products represent part of the means of production that are converted into final products … *Labour basics* are *final* products and correspond to the socially necessary consumption goods required to maintaining persons active in the [productive or profit] sector … Finally, *labour-land basics* are machine tools, that is, machines to make machines, representing past labour, and enable the labour force operating in the profit sector to enter into contact and to interact with nature through the social process of production'. (Bortis, 2003, p. 433).

As pointed out in Bortis (2003, pp. 433–6), the primary land basics move between industries in horizontal interindustry models to produce, in a first stage, primary goods entering the production of all goods, as is pictured by Sraffa's model in which inputs and outputs coincide. Since the output of land basics enters the production of all intermediate and final goods, necessary technical relations exist between land basics and the final output. The prices of nature basics are thus determining the prices of final products. The triangular structure of the Leontief matrix now emerges. Sraffa's land basics are located in the upper left corner, intermediate products in the centre and final products in the lower right corner (Bortis 2003, pp. 434–5).

This view of the social process of production puts to the fore the fundamental role of nature basics taken from non-produced resources. In fact, economists such as François Quesnay and Alberto Quadrio Curzio see nature and land as a kind of basis upon which economic activities – mainly production in general and the production of the social surplus – take place, which enables societies to build up a political, legal, social and cultural superstructure (Quesnay, [1758] 1972; Quadrio Curzio, 1967). The central importance of production in scheme (1) in this section implies that the fundamental prices are the prices of production, governed by the conditions of production and income distribution, represented by the money wage rate and the rate of profits. Labour values turn out to be the essence of the prices of production and of market prices; the Kalecki-Weintraub macroeconomic price equation precisely embodies the labour value principle (Bortis, 2003, pp. 436–45). Distribution is now no longer a market problem: in a positive vein distribution is regulated by social and political forces; normatively distribution becomes an immensely complex problem of distributive justice, which represents the heart of social ethics. Here, the central problem is to determine a socially appropriate profit rate and a fair structure of wages (Bortis, 1997, pp. 158 ff.).

The normal or long-period level of output and employment in a monetary production economy is governed by the supermultiplier relation, picturing how output and employment are determined *in principle* by the various demand variables and parameters on the right-hand side of this equation (Bortis, 1997, pp. 142–204). Economic activity is set into motion by autonomous expenditures, government expenditures and exports, to bring about a cumulative process of demand and production of consumption and investment goods, which is strengthened by a relatively equal distribution of incomes and is dampened by imports. The determination of the volumes of *normal output and employment is equivalent to fixing the output and employment trend*, which is governed by the socio-economic *system*, that is, by technology and institutions located in the material basis and in the sociopolitical-cum-cultural superstructure of a society; around the trend cyclical fluctuations associated to the *behaviour* of firms and households occur (Bortis, 1997, pp. 204–20).

Normal output and employment are negatively linked with the size of the property share in income and a low propensity to consume, resulting from an unequal income distribution. Hence in Keynesian and classical-Keynesian theory, the close positive connection between saving and investment, characteristic for neoclassical theory, is cut as emerges from the macroeconomic equilibrium condition ($S=I$):

$$I = S = s\,Q = s\,Y \tag{2}$$

Here an increase in the saving/income ratio (s) will, as a rule, *reduce* economic activity, that is, output (Q) and employment (N). This might lead on to a lower volume of investment (I), implying a reduced accumulation of capital. This is crucial to analyse the phenomenon of financialization in a classical-Keynesian framework to which we now turn.

3.   Financialization in a classical-Keynesian framework

In a monetary production economy (scheme 1) there is always an exchange of money (M) and commodities, that is, labour (force) and means of production (C) and final goods (C'). Labour and means of production are bought and, subsequently, pass through the social process of production (P). Hence *new* values (C' or Q) are created in the *real* sector of an economy, Keynes's *industrial circulation* (Keynes, [1930] 1971, I, pp. 217–30). In the processes of circulation taking place within the real sector, money *represents* values, since it has no *intrinsic* value. However, once money leaves the real sector for the financial sector – Keynes's *financial circulation* – there is no longer any real equivalent and this money does, consequently, not represent any real values (Keynes, [1930] 1971, I, pp. 217–30). Given this, money circulating in the financial sector always looks for acquiring already *existing goods*, some of which are reproducible (houses, industrial equipment, or firms, to give instances), others are not reproducible (for example, land, natural resources or old masters); money circulating in the financial sector may also look for *already existing* financial titles, for example, already existing state bonds and stock.

A remark on the nature of money is to be made here. In the form of finance, *money* is *endogenous* since it may easily adjust to whatever part of the *given* investment volume the banks are ready to finance. However, in the course of the *process of production*, where goods are produced and incomes are created, finance (credits) is transformed into *money proper* and becomes in a way *exogenous* and, as such, *given*. Granting a credit increases the assets and liabilities side of banks. Making full use of the credits obtained runs the liabilities side down to zero. If loans are repaid, a change in the composition of the asset side of a bank would occur: the item *credits* would be reduced and the entry *cash* would correspondingly increase. Hence bank loans, if used productively by enterprises, lead on to *permanent* money creation. This means that the quantity of money (M) is given and is *not reduced* when loans are repaid.

Let us now consider the relationship between the real and the financial sector of a monetary production economy at the level of principles. Within the global financial system – global because of the worldwide mobility of financial capital – there is the quantity of money (M), made up of cash deposits and saving and term deposits, with coins and banknotes playing an *auxiliary* role. The fraction r of M, made up of cash deposits, circulates in the real sector, involving wages and business accounts. Obviously, (rM) represents 'the amount of cash held to satisfy the transactions- and [the short-term] precautionary motives' (Keynes, [1936] 1973, p. 199). A complementary fraction of (M), $(f = 1-r)$ to wit, circulates in the financial sector to buy commodities and real and financial assets with the aim of selling these with a profit or of deriving an income. Keynes denoted this quantity of money (fM) 'the amount of money held to satisfy the speculation motive' (p. 199). However, speculation is only one aspect of the quantity of money (fM); in fact, (fM) also represents the monetary wealth resulting from past savings and permanent money creation through the banks.

The quantity of money (fM) remains in the financial sector when wealth holders diversify their monetary wealth through buying *already existing* commodities (real estate, land, precious metals and the like), and *already existing* financial assets (shares, bonds). Now, the clue to understanding the interaction between the real and the financial sector is to examine the macroeconomic significance of saving in a monetary theory of production. Here the distinction between saving and finance is crucial. Banks provide finance. This is the *monetary* financing of investment (I) through bank credits and acquiring *new* shares or bonds by the banks (B) and through financial means of the enterprises themselves, for example reinvested profits; part of current or past saving may also participate in the financing of current investment, if households subscribe *new* shares or bonds. Let us denote the fraction of *current or new* saving used by firms and households to finance *current or new* investment by (bS). Hence the equation for the *monetary* financing of investment is:

$$B + bS = I \qquad (3)$$

Obviously finance *precedes* investment.

The equation for the *real* financing of investment (relation (2)) states that saving makes available the resources (labour, capital equipment and land) required to produce investment goods. And, crucially, with the real financing of investment through saving, investment *precedes* saving, which, in turn, *adjusts* to investment (*I*) through changes in output (*Q*) and employment (*N*). Thus, the whole sequence of monetary and real financing of investment is given by

$$B + bS = I = S = s\,Q \tag{4}$$

This relation shows that in a monetary production economy *investment* stands at the centre of events. The left-hand side pictures how, in principle, the *monetary* financing of investment goes on, the right hand side how, in principle, the *real* financing occurs. Hence, in relation (4), saving (*S*) on the right-hand side of investment has not the same meaning as (*S*) on the left-hand side. Since we consider *principles* only, no time lags occur.

Given relation (4), the total quantity of money (*M*) and the quantities of money in the real and in the financial sector (*rM* and *fM*) will seemingly remain constant since saving (*S*) moves from the real to the financial sector and vice versa for the financial means required for the monetary financing of investment (*I*). However, on account of definition (5) below the quantities of money (*M*) and (*fM*) will continuously grow in spite of the equality between (*I*) and (*S*), because the banks create money through granting credits. In principle, there is no upper limit to the credit volume the banking system can provide. There are, however, two important barriers to extending the credit volume. First, the Basel agreements prescribe that own capital to be held as a percentage of assets. Second and more importantly, according to classical-Keynesian theory, *the investment volume is strictly limited in the long run through long-period effective demand* as emerges from the supermultiplier relation (Bortis, 1997, relation (5), p. 144). It is likely that, in order to maximize profits, banks will attempt to finance as much of the new investments as possible with credits (*B*) at the expense of directly reinvested savings. This type of bank behaviour will be reinforced in the absence of reserve requirements and higher own capital–assets ratios. In equation (4) above, a higher volume of (*B*) implies a reduction of the coefficient (*b*), the fraction of savings directly used to finance new investments by firms and households; endogenous money creation (*ΔM*) increases as is evident from definition (5), if account is taken of relation (4):

$$\Delta M = B = (1-b)\,S = (1-b)\,I \tag{5}$$

The newly created amount of money (*ΔM*) implies that only a fraction of saving is required to finance investment:

$$\Delta M + (S-\Delta M) = I \tag{6}$$

Given this, savings amounting to (*ΔM*) flows into the financial sector.

We may mention here that *permanent* endogenous money creation also takes place if banks acquire government bonds to partly finance government deficits. The interest on government bonds represents an important source of revenue and profits for the banks. Probably, very large parts of these revenues are flowing into the financial sector to be invested in already existing real and financial assets and are, consequently, not transferred to the real sector in the form of financial means to finance *new* investment goods which are financed by new bank credits. This mechanism may get dangerous if the indebtedness of specific states becomes so important that bankruptcy threatens. Obviously, if some state goes bankrupt the existence of specific banks, having bought large quantities of government bonds, now among their assets, may be threatened, too. Important repercussions on parts of the banking system may be the consequence.

Moreover, if the Central Bank buys *new* state bonds *exogenous* money creation takes place. The newly created amount of money will in the first stage flow into the real sector; new incomes will be created and additional saving comes into being, part of which will leave the real sector for the financial sector. However, if the Central Bank buys *existing* state bonds, for example, in the course of a *monetary easing operation* aimed at maintaining low interest rates on state bonds to keep the government debt service at a low level, the additional exogenously created money will directly flow into the financial sector. Given this, budget deficits are, as one would expect, at the origin of monetary expansion through the banking system comprising banks and Central Banks. All in all, and if the world level is considered, the capacity of banks and central banks to create money simply seems immense.

As a consequence, the ratio *(fM/rM = f/r)* continuously grows. The evolution of the quantities *(rM)* and *(fM)* is indeed significant. In 2005 it has been estimated that in the last thirty years, that is from 1975 onwards, the quantity of money in the real sector *(rM)* has been multiplied by *four*, and the quantity of money in the financial sector by *forty*! To be sure, the total quantity of money has grown, too, but the main reason for this development is the increase of the relation *(f/r)*. It is very likely that, in the meantime, *(M)* and *(f/r)* have increased still more, also because of the massive interventions of the Central Banks to save 'too-big-to-fail' banks. If such interventions are financed by the taxpayer, 'good' money, originating from the real sector, where it was a representative of value, has been turned into 'bad' money, representing no values at all. In other words, *this money has clearly been frittered away*. To prevent this, bankruptcy has simply to go on in an orderly way: The own capital and parts of the very large deposits must be considered lost; however, it is absolutely necessary to entirely or partly guarantee deposits up to a socially acceptable amount. This may involve a temporary nationalization of banks.

The fact that more and more money is shifted from the real sector to the financial sector leads on to a *financialization* of the economy, implying that the financial sector increasingly dominates the real sector. Given this, let us now have a closer look at some interactions between real and financial sector and its consequences in a classical-Keynesian perspective.

4. Financialization and capital mobility related to interactions between the real and the financial sector

In Keynes's view, there are two principal activities in the financial sector, first, speculation, and, subsequently, enterprise or investment. Both activities are based upon (*fM*). In the case of speculation, part of this quantity of money is used to buy already existing real and financial assets (shares, land and real estate, precious metals, raw materials and energy products) in view of selling these at a higher price. The prices and their evolution are governed by the relative strength of *bulls* and *bears*, those speculating *à la hausse* and those speculating *à la baisse*. Part of the buying operations may be financed by bank credits, implying a *temporary* creation of money. This money creation is passing because the *repayment of credit* is equivalent to a *destruction* of money. If, at the end of a speculative bubble or in the course of a cyclical downswing, share prices decline generally, many debtors may not be in a position to repay credits. If this happens at a large scale, a bank crisis may ensue, touching the financial sector only, and leaving the real sector *in principle* unaffected. It is quite evident that speculation, Keynes's *casino capitalism*, may completely detach current share values from their real values as is governed by the normal profitability of enterprises. This kind of capital-ism may have serious negative effects on the real economy if there is an interaction between speculation and new (real) investment; indeed, the volume of new investments may be reduced if speculation leads on to unjustified declines in share prices: to finance new investment projects will become more difficult and long-term expectations may be negatively affected. Or, asymmet-ric knowledge, in some cases accompanied by fraudulent practices, may lead on to huge concentrations of monetary wealth. As a consequence, take-overs may increase, as do profits, which are paper profits arising from a redistri-bution of monetary wealth in the financial sectors; no values have been created. Distribution gets more unequal and, in a classical-Keynesian spirit, involuntary unemployment will increase and thereby affect the real sector.

As to investment, two types may be distinguished, that is, investments in the *financial* sphere involving investments in already existing assets, and invest-ments in the *real* sector, resulting in the production of *new* capital goods. Investments in the financial sector are also of two kinds, that is, normal and aggressive financial investment. With normal financial investment, the finan-cial sector is subordinated and ancillary to the real sector; shareholders would accept the dividends proposed by the management and would not attempt to influence short- and long-term policies of enterprises if management pursues an ordinary and normal strategy aimed at securing competitiveness and improving the market position of firms. However, with aggressive financial investments the financial sector dominates the real sector; may even happen that enterprises are damaged or eventually destroyed. In fact, speculation may result in unjustified rises of share prices. Now, to render sufficiently profitable an eventual investment, unfriendly take-overs may result in restructurations of these enterprises to render them even more profitable. Costs have to be lowered and dismissals are inevitable. The destruction of enterprises through 'asset stripping' is also due to aggressive investment linked with speculation.

Aggressive investments result in a more unequal income distribution. With high share prices, speculation requires large profits to render investment profitable. These profits are *real* profits since they arise from the creation of values in the real sector; in fact, they are part of the surplus created in the social process of production (scheme (1) in this chapter). If the object of investment is an enterprise in the production or service sector, high profits imply a pressure on wages. Rising inequalities in income distribution reduce the purchasing power of the population, effective demand declines and ultimately leads on to system caused involuntary unemployment (Bortis, 1997, ch. 4).

However, part of the financial system stands in the direct service of the real sector; services provided to the real sector by the financial sector might comprise commercial banking and granting credits to small and medium-sized enterprises, or traditional wealth management in the service of individuals and institutions, non-profit organizations, for example; moreover, some hedging is also required due to the permanent presence of more or less uncertainty about the evolution of prices, including of course the prices of natural resources and exchange rates. All these services of the financial sector in favour of the real sector are indeed normal and socially necessary.

As a rule, the individuals and institutions active in the financial sector *in excess* of the normal and socially necessary activities participate more or less intensely in draining the real sector of surplus, mostly without being conscious of it. Among these actors banks obviously play a pivotal role, since all transactions are carried out by banks, either for their customers, including hedge funds, or for the banks themselves. Since the banks and some big customers command the whole of the liabilities of banks, the entire quantity of money (fM) circulating in the financial sphere of an economy may, in principle, be put to use for excessive surplus extraction. This means that, through some large banks and hedge funds, the entire financial system may participate in excessively shifting money from the real sector to the financial sector. In theory, the actors in the financial sector presumably simply think along dominating *neoclassical* mainstream lines, being convinced of permanently allocating resources in an efficient way. In practice, most small and medium actors simply follow the general trend set by the big players regarding the composition of their portfolio. However, the trendsetters, that is, some large actors on the financial markets presumably know fairly well what they are doing. These big actors possibly also knew that they were considered too big to fail, wrongly so as has been suggested earlier.

Why do these problems with the financial sector arise, given the fact that the activities of this are in itself good in the social ethical sense? It is, in fact, normal that there should be markets for financial assets (bonds and shares), raw materials and energy resources, for old masters, and so on; and wealth management is an important financial sector activity. But these markets should ultimately enhance the proper functioning of the real sector. For example, if a non-profit organization wants to finance some project it should be able to sell financial assets it possesses at a good price. This implies that there must be buyers of these assets wishing to invest profitably money not needed at the moment, that is, to hold wealth in terms of specific financial assets. This implies that the quantity of money in the financial sector, $(fM)^*$ say, should be large enough to satisfy the *long-period* precautionary motive of households, firms, non-profit institutions, and of the state, that is, to hold monetary wealth and to provide for reserves and incomes to ensure the proper functioning of these institutions.

Given this, the problem of the financial sector can now be assessed. In the *classical-Keynesian* perspective, the *financial sector becomes increasingly an extractor of social surplus* through *financialization* because it is *far too large* compared with the real sector. *Too much money* circulates in the financial sector $[fM >> (fM)^*]$, subduing thus increasingly the real sector. Given this, 'monetary *production* economies' (scheme (1) in this chapter) tend to become 'monetary *finance* economies': more money is to be made out of money ($M'>M$). Instead of factories, *banks and hedge funds* will tend to dominate an economy as is particularly visible in economically underdeveloped and transition economies. As a result, financial transactions more and more dominate the production of goods and the rendering of services. In fact, the production and service enterprises in the real sector, whether listed at the stock exchange or not, have to maximize their short-term profits in order to maximize shareholder's values. Otherwise takeover threatens. Given this, all firms have to reduce costs, wage costs most importantly, to realize high and rising profits. Distribution gets more unequal and internal demand stagnates or declines. Exports are the only way out. This, in turn, leads to *a world war between workers and employees* through a downward pressure on wages, worsening working conditions and delocalizations. These processes are enhanced through the fact that real sector enterprises have to reinvest large parts of their profits in the financial sector because reduced effective demand also reduces investment opportunities in the real sector. The final result is a continuous downward pressure on living standards worldwide, accompanied by growing poverty and misery and an increasing number of the working poor. This process of financialization occurs because, in some or all banks of an economy, *traditional commercial banking becomes secondary* and *investment and private banking, complemented by the activities of the hedge funds, move to the fore*. This process goes on deterministically, driven by a dramatic excess of money (fM) above the socially necessary quantity of money, $(fM)^*$, circulating in the financial sector.

Let us, next, have a look at investment in the *real* sector, which, by definition, is *new* investment, resulting in increasing or maintaining the real capital stock. Indeed, if money located in the financial sector, also potential money such as bank credits, is used in a spirit of *enterprise*, then it will find its way to the real sector, if, for example, *new* shares, representing financial means to produce *new* investment goods, are bought. Hence new investment strongly links the financial sector to the real sector through determinating the *volume* of long-period trend investment as is determined by long-period effective demand (see Bortis, 1997, relations (5a) and (5b), p. 156; and Bortis, 2003, relation (19.39), p. 464). Uncertainty and expectations are related to *individual* investment projects only: which enterprises remain in the production system, which ones are squeezed out? The dramatic increase of the quantity of money in the financial sector (fM) has contributed to a growing inequality of income distribution and in increasing involuntary unemployment. This exerts a downward pressure on the long-period output and employment trend and hence on the trend investment volume. Real wealth is thus destroyed.

Real wealth is also destroyed in the course of a downswing of the business cycle, when firms go bankrupt. This has repercussions in the financial sector: share prices fall or, in the case of bankruptcy, stock is even wiped out; together with the breakdown of real estate values, disastrous consequences will occur for households as well as investment and pension funds. The banking system has the capacity to expand very quickly the credit volume in the cyclical upswing, enhancing thus the interaction between profits and investment, which is basic to the income effect of investment; in the downswing banks tend to reduce credits, accelerating thus the downswing. Hence the financial sector renders cyclical movements, accompanied by temporary wealth creation and destruction, more pronounced. However, the additional quantity of money created in the cyclical upswing through increased bank credits cannot be destroyed. This increases the quantity of money in the financial sector (fM); consequently, speculative bubbles may become more frequent and pronounced.

Keynes confirms the considerations taken up in this section: 'Depressions arise, Keynes wrote in his *Treatise on Money* [1930], when money is shifted from the "industrial circulation" into the "financial circulation"' (Skidelsky, 1992, p. xxiv).

5.   The impact of financialization and capital mobility on evolving structures and the management of non-produced resources

In a classical-Keynesian perspective financialization enhanced by capital mobility leads on to various structural changes so profound that a new type of society tends to emerge (Dembinski, 2008). Here the financial sector increasingly dominates the real sector. Individualism and egoism move to the fore; social institutions and the state are weakened and social relations in part disintegrate. Broadly since the 1970s there has been a dramatic ascendancy of the free-market system, as a doctrine and as praxis. Deregulation and privatization have become more and more widespread. *Homo oeconomicus* has become *homo financiarius*. Efficiency is established as the basic axiom of action, the maximum rate of return on equity emerges as the fundamental aim to be reached by the means of complex mathematical models and the insurance of risk (Dembinski 2008). Banks and hedge funds start to dominate the factory. The real sector moves into the service of the financial sector.

However, financialization enhanced by capital mobility also brings about profound structural changes in various socio-economic and technical spheres as well as in the domain of natural resources. There is, first, a change in the composition of the social product. The share of luxuries in the social product increases at the expense of necessaries, even in times of deep crisis. This is due to the rising inequality in income distribution, largely due to financialization. Significantly, since the breakdown of socialism, the sale of very expensive watches has increased enormously, luxury car production is booming, and so is the construction of splendid yachts. Or, exclusive and very expensive holiday resorts flourish because very rich people, frequently originating from so-called transformation, emerging or even underdeveloped countries, spend their holidays there. In rural areas and in cities privileged by climate and situation, the price of very well-located land soars; very expensive villas and flats are built; land, house and flat prices rise dramatically; the poor segments of the population cannot afford the high rents and eventually have to leave the regions or the cities in question. In general, a higher share of incomes has to be paid for rents; the demand for goods other than housing declines on account of a more unequal income distribution. In this context the role of sovereign funds must be mentioned, too; for example, financially strong countries are buying land in poor regions to increase the supply of food in their countries.

Moreover, financialization and capital mobility may also have an effect on the nature of technical progress. Indeed financialization requires that firms have to aim for short-term profit maximization in order to render financial investments profitable. This may lead to a neglect of long-term strategic thinking. Specifically, research and development expenditures may be reduced. Research is eventually carried out to a larger extent at universities or specialized institutes, and firms will have to buy inventions that may eventually be transformed into innovations. It is an empirical question as to how financialization affects the nature and the pace of technical progress.

Financialization primarily involves maximizing profits in the short run. This precisely goes on in the case of non-produced natural resources. Oil and mining fields are frequently in possession of very rich individuals, national and international oligarchies, multinationals or large finance groups and extraction goes on at a rapid pace and at relatively low prices. Nevertheless, huge profits arise out of trade gains made by intermediaries and by a pressure on the costs of extraction, wages in the main. Hence the management of resources is *not* based on a long-term conception involving sustainable development, but really aims at short-term profit maximization; as a consequence, the natural environment is negatively affected. In these circumstances the distribution of revenues is bound to be very unequal. Most of the profits realized on the extraction of natural resources flow into the financial sector with the negative effects on real-sector employment.

Most important, however, are the changes in the property structure in the production and service sector brought about by financialization and capital mobility. The service sector has to be taken in a very wide sense, including, for example, buying football clubs. In any case, mergers and acquisitions lead on to an increasing concentration of real capital. A few individuals and huge financial groups own ever larger parts of real capital, real estate and land. This leads to increasing inequalities in income distribution; and, in a classical-Keynesian vein, involuntary unemployment is bound to increase, too. Inequalities are particularly pronounced in poor and emerging countries; investment opportunities in the real sector are limited by small effective demand; consequently, finance capital frequently moves from poor and emerging countries to rich countries, enhanced by an insecure investment climate in the former. These effects of financialization represent a new kind of feudalism. Large parts of the social surplus produced in the real sector are transferred to the financial sector. In a way, the real sector feeds the financial sector, enhancing thus the profitability of money circulating in this sector. The ultimate aim is no longer economic, that is, increase wealth in the form of goods and services, but financial, making more money out of money by means of extracting surplus from the real sector.

The growing indebtedness of financialized societies, yet another type of structural change, proceeds on the background of growing inequalities of income and wealth distribution. We start by some remarks on public debt. With government expenditures determined by some socioeconomic-cum-political mechanism, public debt increases in the long run for two basic reasons; first, not enough taxes are paid, implying that saving is high because of an unequal distribution, which, second, leads on to involuntary unemployment, which, in turn, reduces output and incomes, and, as a consequence, tax receipts. Government bonds have now to be issued to finance the deficit. Banks grant credits to buy part of these bonds; this leads on to money creation; individuals and investment and pension funds looking for investment opportunities for their monetary wealth also acquire state bonds. These amounts of money flow, in the first place, into the real sector, contributing thus to producing goods, rendering services and creating incomes. Subsequently, part of the saving out of these incomes is squeezed out of the real sector into the financial sector according to the mechanism outlined earlier. The interest on government bonds bought represents an important source of revenue and profits for the banks, investment and pension funds as well as (wealthy) individuals. Probably, very large parts of these revenues flow into the financial sector to be invested in already existing real and financial assets. This mechanism may get dangerous if the indebtedness of specific states becomes so important that the servicing of the debt cannot be guaranteed and bankruptcy threatens. Obviously, if some state goes bankrupt the existence of specific banks, having large quantities of government bonds among their assets, may be threatened, too. Important repercussions on parts of the banking system may be the consequence.

However, households and firms may get indebted, too, and the financing of the debt may go on by the same mechanism as has just been pictured for the state. The growing indebtedness of states, households and firms also represents an important type of structural change occurring with large-scale financialization and capital mobility. To reduce public debt, a sale of national wealth, in the form of public transport and communication services for example, goes on actually. Increasing privatization, too, is a kind of structural change going on with increasing financialization, accompanied by growing capital mobility; in fact, privatization provides additional investment opportunities for finance capital. Privatization implies a reduction of the non-profit and, above all, of the public sector. Autonomous expenditures are reduced, for example, if educational institutions are privatized, mainly universities and grammar schools, and even primary schools; the tax-income rate (t) diminishes and, ideally, the consumption-income ratio (c) ought to increase correspondingly to enable families to finance the education of their children. However, an unequal distribution of incomes implies that the increase in (c) is, as a rule, not sufficient to compensate for the reduction of (t). Hence on the social side, access to education will be restricted. This hampers the middle class and very severely hits the lower classes. Social and economic inequality is bound to increase, and social mobility, essential for the renewal of intellectual, economic and political elites, is restricted. On the economic side, the saving ratio (s) increases and so does monetary wealth and financialization. In the main, (permanent) long-period unemployment, private and public deficits and debts will all increase.

Hence financialization and capital mobility bring about a new society, implying momentous structural changes. Monetary production economies are gradually transformed in monetary finance economies; in the spirit of Dembinski (2008) the financial transaction starts to dominate production. Banks and hedge funds increase more rapidly than real sector enterprises in the spheres of production and services. Moreover, financialization and capital mobility result in increasing inequalities in income distribution accompanied by growing involuntary unemployment. This results in a struggle for survival between individuals and social, ethnic and religious groups, which may lead on to conflicts; the ensuing social disorder will require a law-and-order state. Perhaps the most important social result of financialization is the weakening of the middle classes, implying a growing polarization of society: due to the existence of permanent involuntary unemployment, middle-class people have to accept increasingly precarious and badly paid jobs. On the political level, the parties of the centre decline, whilst extremist left-wing and, above all, right-wing political formations grow in strength. All in all, the traditional political, socio-economic and cultural elite is pushed into the background by an oligarchy grounded on monopoly-finance capital. The whole system is maintained and kept under control by the application of two very simple but robust City Principles frequently mentioned by Nicholas Kaldor. Both are based on the fact that inflation is the mortal enemy of finance, that is, of all elements of monetary wealth (cash, saving and term deposits, bonds and, in part, stock, most importantly). Given this, the first City Principle states that unemployment must at least equal 5 per cent; this is to keep the workers in check, to prevent wages from rising too strongly, and hence to prevent a cost-inflation. The second City Principle requires a balanced budget at a low level of government expenditures and taxes. This is to prevent demand-inflation. Moreover, lower taxes mean higher savings and additional possibilities to accumulate monetary wealth. Implementing both principles simultaneously is obviously a very efficient device to maintain the dominance of finance. The whole scheme is like putting an airtight seal on a steamer while ever increasing the heat. Explosion seems inevitable, eventually resulting in heavily damaging or even in the breakdown of the institutional system, which may mean heavy social disorder or, in extreme cases, even anarchy.

6.   Policy conclusions

The problem of financialization *cannot* be tackled through the *regulation of behaviour; the system must be changed*. The regulation of behaviour may be necessary in some instances, for example requiring a certain ratio of own means to bank assets; indeed such a regulation of behaviour can reasonably be implemented. However, it seems very difficult if not impossible to implement a tax on financial transactions, the famous Tobin tax, on a world level, as would indeed be required. What is badly needed is a *new economic and financial world order* along Keynes's 1944 Bretton Woods proposals: each country would have its own currency; international real and financial transactions would be carried out by means of a supranational currency, Keynes's Bancor. This system would enable each country to establish a current account equilibrium in the long run; financialization would be drastically reduced, and international capital movements would go on in an orderly way (Keynes, 1980). This implies reducing the size of the financial sector through special taxes on wealth and by channelling part of the money circulating in this sector (*fM*) back into the real sector, for example to preserve the cultural heritage and to establish foundations for cultural and scientific purposes. Indeed, in a Keynesian vein, to make more money out of money is socio-economically useless, even damaging, also because huge monetary wealth provides the big players in the financial sector with excessive economic, social and political power. Moreover, the size of the financial sector may be reduced through replacing the capital cover system through the *pay-as-you-go (or contribution) system*, putting thus pension schemes on a much more secure basis. As to the real economy, long-period incomes and employment policies along Keynes/Beveridge lines should bring about a fair distribution of incomes and eliminate system-caused involuntary unemployment, the theoretical basis being Classical-Keynesian Political Economy, the economic theory of the social doctrine of *Social Liberalism* (Bortis, 1997, 2003, 2012, 2013).

In the social liberal sense governing basically consists in setting up, or favouring the coming into being, of appropriate institutions and permanently maintaining their proper functioning, such as to preserve full employment and a fair distribution of incomes and wealth; the ultimate aim would be to bring about, as far as is possible for fallible human beings, harmonious proportions between the various spheres of the economy, society and the state. Needless to say, that this is a most difficult long-term task, requiring a very solid system of political economy and a vision of how a political society should look like. In the social liberal vision the state should, ideally, be of small and medium size to be governable, a fact already perceived by Aristotle. Given this, large states (Brazil, China, India, Russia, the United States) would have to decentralize substantially on the basis of the Principle of Subsidiarity. Moreover, since there is no tendency towards full employment, large free-trade areas are not appropriate; in fact, economic instability is likely to increase with the size of the free-trade area, also on account of the free flow of financial capital which favours bubbles in the financial sector and reinforces business cycles. However, stability within each country would produce stability on the continental and global levels. Hence Europe, and, in fact, the world should become a family of nations, eventually to be structured by historical-geographical federations which would deal with common problems of nations having a common history or belong together geographically. If stable, near full employment conditions, could be created within the European states and, in fact, in the world at large, the unrestricted mobility of individuals between countries and the free flow of capital would be no problem. In general, the presently dominating *external (outward directed)* development mechanism associated to free trade ought to be replaced by the *internal (inward directed) development mechanism;* here development would be driven by internal forces, basically private and public consumption, with the current account being in equilibrium at any level of exports and imports and with the rich countries providing assistance for poor through realizing an export surplus (Bortis, 1997, pp. 190–8 and ch. 6, specifically pp. 326–43).

The global management of natural resources would require a World Resources Agency, acting in the interest of present and future generations as well as in view of preserving the natural environment (Bortis 1997, pp. 337–8). This Agency ought to be created within the framework of the United Nations. Its central task would be to organize the husbanding of non-renewable raw material and energy resources in the present but also in the interest of future generations. At present the natural resources are controlled by individual states, and sometimes even by powerful interest groups. The uncontrolled squandering of resources resulting from this might lead the world to the brink of environmental collapse. In a world of ferocious competition with conflicts between power blocks permanently existing, it will be impossible to stop this misusing of resources. The starting point for managing appropriately the world's natural resources could be the propositions made by Sheikh Yamani in the 1970s already: Oil prices, and the prices of non-renewable resources in general should be fixed at a high level and the quantities extracted should be kept at the lowest possible level. Given this, alternative energies would become profitable, the natural environment would be largely preserved and, very importantly, precious non-renewable resources would be preserved for future generations. In this context, paying countries, mainly poor countries, for leaving raw materials and energy resources in the ground, to preserve these for future generations, is certainly an excellent idea.

REFERENCES

Bortis, H. (1997) *Institutions, Behaviour and Economic Theory – A Contribution to Classical-Keynesian Political Economy,* Cambridge: Cambridge University Press (paperback edn 2006).
    (2003) 'Keynes and the Classics – Notes on the Monetary Theory of Production', in L.-P. Rochon and S. Rossi (eds.) *Modern Theories of Money,* Cheltenham, UK and Northampton, Mass.: E. Elgar, pp. 411–75.

(2012) 'Toward a Synthesis in Post-Keynesian Economics in Luigi Pasinetti's Contribution', in R. Arena and P. L. Porta (eds.) *Structural Dynamics and Economic Growth*, Cambridge: Cambridge University Press, pp. 145–80.

(2013) 'Post-Keynesian Principles and Economic Policies', in G. C. Harcourt and P. Kriesler (eds.) *Oxford Handbook of Post-Keynesian Economics*, vol. II, Oxford: Oxford University Press, pp. 326–65.

Dembinski, P. H. (2008) *Finance: Servant or Deceiver? Financialization at the Crossroads*, London: Palgrave-Macmillan; original: *Finance Servante ou Finance Trompeuse?* Paris: Desclée de Brouwer, Editions Paroles et Silence.

Keynes, J. M. ([1930] 1971) *A Treatise on Money*, 2 vols., London: Macmillan.

([1933] 1973) *A Monetary Theory of Production*, reprinted in *Collected Works*, vol. XIII, *The General Theory and After, Part I: Preparation*, London: Macmillan, pp. 408–11.

([1936] 1973) *The General Theory of Employment, Interest and Money*, London: Macmillan.

(1980) *Activities 1940–44–Shaping the Post-War World: The Clearing Union*, Collected Writings, vol. XXV, London: Macmillan.

Marx, K. ([1885] 1973) *Das Kapital*, vol. II, Berlin: Dietz Verlag.

Quadrio Curzio, A. (1967) *Rendita e distribuzione in un modello economico plurisettoriale*, Milan: Giuffrè.

Quesnay, F. (1972) *Quesnay's Tableau économique*, edited, with new material, translations and notes by M. Kuczynski and R. L. Meek, London: Macmillan; New York: A. M. Kelley for the *Royal Economic Society* and the *American Economic Association* (1st edn 1758).

Shackle, G. L. S. (1967) *The Years of High Theory: Invention and Tradition in Economic Thought 1926-1939*, Cambridge: Cambridge University Press.

Skidelsky, R. (1992) *John Maynard Keynes, vol. II, The Economist as Saviour 1920–1937*, London: Macmillan.

Sraffa, P. (1960) *Production of Commodities by Means of Commodities. Prelude to a Critique of Economic Theory*, Cambridge: Cambridge University Press.

10   The chimera of a complete analysis of economic dynamics

Kumaraswamy Vela Velupillai

"Who are they?
. . .
Below the bounds
of this estate, through rainbowed cold, the rockheaded and cored
of bone, *the chimera our madness does not cease to reinvent*
and which we dare not think alive, crawls in a thick ooze.
Is it not good? The man pauses,
looks around—the sea undulated, sharpening and smoothing
all the grooves that history has graven on the sand — . . ."

Carol Frost: Chimera* (emphasis added)

1.   The complete analysis of economic dynamics

The final aim of the theory of the motions of a dynamical system must be directed toward the qualitative determination of *all possible types of motions* and of the interrelation of these motions. (Birkhoff, 1927, p. 189; italics added)

The obsession with the desire for a *complete analysis of economic dynamics*, is analogous to the classic – but forlorn – search for a 'qualitative determination of *all possible types of motions*', or to considering all possible sets and ending up with the (in)famous Russell paradox of considering all possible sets and wondering what to do about that class that is made up of those sets that are not members of themselves.

It is possible, perhaps even desirable, to separate the notion of *complete analysis* of any problem – not only in economics – and the idea of a complete economic dynamics, independent (at least in the latter case) of the feasibility of

The subject matter of this chapter is squarely within the research program of the Algorithmic Social Sciences Research Unit (ASSRU), at the department of economics, University of Trento. I have benefitted greatly from discussions with my resident fellow ASSRU members, Professor Stefano Zambelli, Dr Selda Kao and Dr V. Ragupathy. Alas, none of them agree to bear responsibility for the remaining infelicities, which must, therefore, be borne entirely by me.

* 'A mere *wild fancy*; an unfounded conception' (the ordinary modern use, italics added); also attrib. 1587, according to *The Shorter Oxford English Dictionary: On Historical Principles* (the first of two volumes of which are only 1280 pages in length!).

its complete analysis. Then Quadrio Curzio's wise injunction comes into its own (see Birkhoff above and Quadrio Curzio and Pellizzari, 1999, p. 240, italics added): '*Theory always* takes a specific definition of [an] economic system and *chooses a select set of tools and methods for its analysis.*' That 'set of tools and methods for its analysis', chosen by a 'theory taking a specific definition of [an] economic system' is often thought of as having achieved completeness – of analysis, of formalization, etc. Thus in the admirable volume of essays in honour of Augusto Graziani (Arena and Salvadori, 2004)[1], Wynne Godley claims (ibid., p. 143) to have built a Complete Keynesian Model (albeit a simple one!). Even more remarkably, in the same volume, Jean Cartelier claims that (ibid., p. 221; italics added): 'A *complete* demonstration of the existence of a Keynesian equilibrium in an Arrow-Debreu framework exists.'[2] Obviously Professor Cartelier, like most of the profession, has forgotten – or, more likely, is ignorant of the fact – that Glustoff (like his fellow general equilibrium theorists) 'chose a select set of tool and methods' to provide a so-called *complete* demonstration of the existence of a Keynesian equilibrium in an Arrow-Debreu framework. From the perspective of a different kind of mathematics, say computable or constructive analysis, this demonstration by Glustoff would not be considered complete[3]. This is precisely the point made by Quadrio Curzio – leaving aside the other injunction of taking 'a specific definition of [an] economic system', often unadaptable to the tools and methods of analysis being used.

To the best of my knowledge, the earliest attempt to seek a formalization of a notion of *complete economic dynamics* was in a classic contribution by Kuznets at the dawn of the era, which sought to integrate equilibrium theory with dynamics (Kuznets, 1930). On the other hand, all attempts, in every kind of economic theory, at formulating 'General Theories' – be it the *General Theory of Employment, Interest and Money* or *General Equilibrium Theory* – are

---

[1] In which there is also a fine, concise, summary of Quadrio Curzio and Pellizzari (1999).

[2] He then goes on to refer to the 1968 work of Glustoff, adding: 'It seems that no Keynesian has ever been aware of it.'! I am not sure who he means by 'Keynesians', but it was fairly well known among the cognoscenti working on varieties of fix price equilibria from the early 1970s all the way till that whole approach died the natural death it deserved to die of, by the early 1980s.

[3] The obverse side of this absurd Cartelier coin is the claim by Kaldor (1954, p. 53; italics added):

> *[I]t is not possible}* to make the [Schumpeter] story as a whole into a 'model' (meaning by a model the sum total of assumptions which are just sufficient – no more no less – together to provide the necessary and sufficient conditions for the generation of a recurrent cycle with a clear periodicity) without incorporating into it elements which would suffice by themselves to explain the cycle – without recourse to Schumpeter's own stage army of initiators and imitators, or even the very concept of technical progress.

> How does Kaldor know that 'it is *not possible* to make the [Schumpeter] story as a whole into a model'? Is this an 'impossibility theorem', *within some mathematical formalism* of theories and models?

efforts, always falling foul of Quadrio Curzio's previously mentioned wise injunctions at building *complete* theories and choosing a select set of tools and methods for their analysis, from which special theories are derived.

Consider the following *general* form of a differential-difference equation of differential order n and difference order m (Bellman and Cooke, 1963, p. 43):

$$F[t, u(t), u(t - \omega_1) \ldots, u(t - \omega_m), u'(t), u'(t - \omega_1) \ldots,$$
$$U'(t - \omega_m), \ldots, u^{(n)}(t), u^{(n)}(t - \omega_1) \ldots, u^{(n)}(t - \omega_m)] = 0 \quad (1)$$

Where: F and u are real functions of real variables, t; ω_i: real numbers, $\forall i = 1 \ldots m$, and n, m: integers.

Then it is easy to show that the endogenous macrodynamic business cycle models of Kalecki (1935), Lundberg (1937), Kaldor (1940), Hicks (1950) and Goodwin (1951b) can be derived from the above general form of a differential-difference equation. Now two simple questions can be posed:

1. In what sense can (1) be considered a *complete* formulation of endogenous business cycle theories? In other words, do differential, difference and mixed differential-difference equations encapsulate, completely, *all dynamic phenomena in economics*?
2. Even if we grant the above, is there *one unique mode of analysis* of such a system for which *completeness* can formally be defined?

In answer, first, to the second part of the first question, it is easy to construct an example of an algorithmic dynamical system that has not been shown to be reducible to the dynamics of a differential, difference or mixed differential-difference system of any generality. I have in mind here the *Goodstein Process* (cf. Goodstein, 1944 and Paris and Tavakol, 1993). As for an answer to the first part, nothing in dynamical systems theory indicates that there is any hope of characterizing the complete (sic!) dynamics of (1), when hardly any breach has been made towards even solving the second part of *Hilbert's 16th Problem* regarding even planar dynamical systems (Hilbert, 1902).

As for the second question, first of all there are many modes of analysis to *prove* the existence of a closed path using the *Poincarè – Bendixson theorem*, as applied, for example, to Kaldor (1940), some of which invoke Hilbert's notion of 'consistency implies existence', which fall foul of Gödel's results on *incompleteness* (Shapiro, 1997, p. 134)[4]. Moreover, it is by now well known that many special cases of (1) are subject to *undecidable dynamics* (Stewart,

---

[4] *A fortiori*, all orthodox mathematical general equilibrium theories are subject to the (second) *incompleteness theorem of Gödel* (Velupillai, 2009). I am afraid this also applies to formal Neo Ricardian Models of growth and distribution – although it is **not** applicable to Sraffa's own framework of analysis in his *magnum opus* (Sraffa, 1960).

1991), which implies that *no* constructive, algorithmic *methods* can lead to any kind of complete analysis, except in the world of non-applicable (i.e. non-empirical) classical mathematics.

2. If economic dynamics is algorithmic dynamics, then complete dynamics is a chimera

> But all the clocks in the city
> Began to whirr and chime:
> *O let not Time deceive you,*
> *You cannot conquer Time.*
> . . ...
> *Time watches from the shadow*
> *And coughs when you would kiss.*
> 'In headaches and in worry
> Vaguely life leaks away,
> *And Time will have his fancy*
> *To-morrow or to-day.*
> W.H. Auden: *As I Walked Out One Evening* (emphasis added)[5]

Change, in economics and in all the sciences, is considered synonymous with dynamics, at least since Newton and always in mathematical formalisms that invoke one or another form of dynamical systems theory – most commonly, almost trivially, in terms of differential, difference or mixed differential-difference systems of equations. These phantoms lead to the false dichotomy, in economics, mimicking that which originated in Newtonian mechanics, between statics and dynamics; between equilibrium and disequilibrium; and between stability and instability. Rarely does one think – at least not in economics – of *algorithms* as dynamic objects, implemented in time, imperative in their logical form and intrinsically constructive, in the strict mathematical sense of this word, especially in its *Intuitionistic*, Brouwerian versions. As affirmed in what he called the *First Act of Intuitionism*, Brouwer stated, in his *Cambridge Lectures on Intuitionism* uncompromisingly:

---

[5] St. Augustine's famous reflections on TIME, in Bk. XI of his Confessions, is worth remembering as we, in economics, think we can master it by one or another kind of formalization:

> What, then, is time? If no one asks me, I know; if I wish to explain to him who asks, I do not know. Yet I say with confidence, that I know that if nothing passed away, there would be no past time; and if nothing were coming, there would be no future time; and if nothing were, there would be no present time. Those two times, past and future, how are they, when even the past not now, and the future is not yet? But should the present always be present, and should it not pass into time past, it could not truly be time, but eternity. If then, time present– if it be time–only comes into existence because it passes into time past, how do we say that even this is, whose cause of being is that it shall not be, namely, that we cannot say what time truly is, unless because it tends not to be.

Completely separating mathematics from mathematical language and hence from the phenomena of language described by theoretical logic, recognizing that intuitionistic mathematics is an essentially languageless activity of the mind having its origins in the perception of a move of time. This perception of a move of time may be described as the falling apart of a life moment into two distinct things, one of which gives way to the other, but is retained by memory. (Brouwer, 1981, p. 4; in italics in the original)

The fundamental dichotomies in algorithmic mathematics – whether it be in its computable or constructive versions – is that between the halting and non-halting behaviour of a machine implementing an algorithm, between decidable and undecidable problems that an algorithm aims to solve, against the backdrop of the further dichotomy between the solvability or the unsolvability, easily or with difficulty, of a decision problem[6]. Six decades ago, at the pre-dawn period of what eventually became the algorithmic avalanche and the dominance of the computational[7] approach to economics, in both theoretical and empirical modes, Richard Goodwin's acute prescience led him to observe that:

In the continuing effort to erect a useful dynamics [in economics], we need all possible helpful sources or hypotheses. One such is the traditional mathematical device of solving equations by trial and error and its vigorous modern step-child the automatic computing machine or zeroing servo. It always takes time to solve an equation by approximative methods, and if our methods for determining the successive approximations are made analogous to the structure of economic decisions, then we may regard the sequence of steps as entirely parallel to an actual process of economic dynamics in time. The convergence of the approximations to the correct answer is the same as the dynamical stability of the economy.

   . . .

Hence a solution corresponds to an equilibrium value. Similarly we may regard economic dynamics as such a series of iterated trial solutions . . .

[C]ontinuous [economic] processes (with differential equations) may . . . be regarded as trial and error *methods of solution* to static equations. The reason why it is not so easy to see is that no human being can make continuous trials infinite in number. This gap in our grasp of the problem has been closed by the perfection of electronic and electro-mechanical computers . . . Such a machine is an exact analogue of a continuous dynamic process[8]. Therefore it seems entirely permissible to *regard the motion of an economy as a process of computing the answers to the problems posed to it.* (Goodwin, 1951a, pp. 1–2; italics added)

---

[6] Again, interpreted in its strict metamathematical sense. It may be useful to point out that standard optimization problems, as in economics and operations research are trivial special cases of decision problems.

[7] Not necessarily to be equated with the notion of *computability* in its recursion theoretic senses.

[8] Goodwin is, here, referring to analogue computers. However, such computers do not have more power, in the sense of computing beyond the *Turing Limit*, by 'breaking' the strictures of the *Church-Turing Thesis*. Hence, I shall assume we are working with ideal digital computing machines – i.e. *Turing Machines*– in the discussions of this section. These results are discussed, described and explained in Velupillai (2011).

In this perceptive conjecture, Goodwin suggests an equivalence between *algorithmic dynamics* and *economic dynamics*, mediated by viewing 'the motion of an economy as a process of computing the answers to the problems posed to it'. The false dichotomies pointed out earlier are replaced by those that are intrinsic to algorithmic dynamics.

Computation, problem, solvability and *dynamics* are all defined algorithmically.

However, algorithmic dynamics is replete with undecidabilities and incompleteness, in the strict metamathematical senses; it is also richly endowed with uncomputabilities in recursion theoretic senses. Moreover, carrying the suggested equivalences a little further, it would be natural to ask what kind of *problems* can be posed to 'such a machine' (or the economic system) and ask whether we can classify the 'posable' problems as *easy* and *hard*, on a sliding scale, first separating the *decidable* problems from the *undecidable* ones. Such questions lead immediately to structuring the data, which is the bridge between theory and empirical implementation, in terms of sets of numbers that are recursive, recursively enumerable and recursively enumerable but not recursive. These, then, lead to notions of recursive separability and inseparability, from which *naturally* paradoxical undecidable and uncomputable dynamics emerge, encapsulable even in the formalism of dynamical systems theory (Smullyan, 1993; Pour-El and Richards, 1989).

The classification of the *decidable problems* – i.e. classification of recursive sets – into a sliding scale, ranging from easy to hard – the domain of *computational complexity theory*[9] – say from *polynomial time computability* at the 'easy' end, all the way to the NP-*Complete* problems at the difficult end.

On the other hand, classification of undecidable problems – i.e. classification of non-recursive sets (of numbers) – requires the formalism of *oracle* (or *relative*) computations, *reducibilities* and a rigorous notion of *complete* (Davis, Sigal and Weyuker, 1994; Salomaa, 1985).

The idea of classifying *undecidable problems* in terms of the difficulty of *solving them* may seem like a contradiction in terms. However, this apparent 'contradiction' is resolved by means of Oracle Turing Machines, or using relative computations (Rogers, 1967; Davis, 1958). Thus, an undecidable problem P* is classified as being *at least as difficult* as another problem, P, if an algorithm, to which an Oracle is adjoined, implemented on an Oracle Turing Machine, that can solve P* can also be utilized to solve P. If the reverse process is infeasible, i.e. if the undecidable problem P, solved with an Oracle Turing Machine, cannot be used to solve P*, then the latter is, intuitively, considered 'more undecidable', or more difficult, than the former.

---

[9] Perhaps the interested reader could be referred to my attempt at providing a pathway into computational complexity theory (Velupillai, 2008) for the economist.

Definition 1:

Given two sets of arbitrary – i.e. not necessarily recursively enumerable sets – nonnegative integers, S and S*, if any algorithm for solving whether an element is a member of S* implies the existence of an algorithm for solving the membership problem for S, then we denote this by:

$$S \leq S^*$$
$$\text{If } S \leq S^* \ \& \ S^* \leq S, \text{ then } S^* \equiv S$$

Definition 2: Complete

If S* is a recursively enumerable set, and $\forall S$, also recursively enumerable sets, $S \leq S^*$, then S* is said to be **COMPLETE**.

Definition 3: m-reducible

S is *m-reducible* to S* *iff* $\exists$ a recursive function g s.t., $\forall i, j \in g(i)$ in case $g \in S^*$

Remark 1:

Every recursively enumerable set is *m-reducible* to the *Halting set*.

Thus the *halting problem for Turing Machines* is an alternative mode of tackling undecidability in the context of recursively enumerable sets and their membership problem. If the economic system's dynamics is to be interpreted as the trajectory of the path taken by a computing machine solving problems posed to it, then the data sets – in this case, economic data in the form of numbers – must be considered to be appropriately recursive. *Ad hoc* habits of assuming data to be generated from exogenous probability distributions, or worse, will have to be given up. In this way theory and empirical analysis are tied together within a unified algorithmic framework.

This notion of *complete* has, of course, nothing whatsoever to do with the loose, almost flippant, use of the word *complete* by economists, claiming to model this or that completely, or analyse a given model completely; not even anything to do with the notion of completeness in classical real analysis (for example the 'completeness of a metric space'); above all, nothing at all to do with the deep notions of completeness and incompleteness in metamathematics, due to the pioneering contributions of Thoralf Skolem and Kurt Gödel in the first third of the twentieth century.

If Kaldor can imagine an *Economics without Equilibrium* (Kaldor, 1985), I see no reason why, with a vision from an algorithmic point of view, I should not – or cannot – imagine an economics without the dichotomies that originated in the natural sciences and replace them with those that are intrinsic to a mathematics that is naturally adapted to implementing empirically the theoretical structures of economics.

3.   Towards undecidable, incomplete and uncomputable dynamics

An algorithmic vision of economic dynamics – or any kind of dynamics – entails a challenge of a qualitatively different kind from those that have become almost 'standard' in an analytically trivial sense. I am referring here to all the hype about complex dynamics, emergence and the like. The algorithmic vision forces the serious scholar of change as dynamics to come to terms with *undecidable* dynamics, *incomplete* dynamics and *uncomputable* dynamics. In the world of algorithmic dynamics, richly endowed with undecidabilities, incompleteness and uncomputabilities, the notion of optimization is meaningless. Instead, the framework is that of decision problems in its metamathematical algorithmic senses.

Completeness, even in mathematics, has become a weasel word; disentangling its many splendoured variations, showing its chimerical usage by pseudo-mathematical economists, is itself a difficult task, like that faced by a mycologist trying to classify mushrooms, as Vladimir Arnold suggested:

When you are collecting mushrooms, you only see the mushroom itself. But if you are a mycologist, you know that the real mushroom is in the earth. ..... In mathematics, the upper part of the mushroom corresponds to theorems that you see. But you don't see the things which are below, namely *problems, conjectures, mistakes, ideas*, and so on.

You might have several apparently unrelated mushrooms and are unable to see what their connection is *unless you know what is behind. And that's what I am now trying to describe.* This is difficult, because to study the visible part of the mathematical mushroom you use the left half of the brain (which deals with logic), while for the other part the left brain has no role at all, because that part is extremely illogical. It is therefore difficult to communicate it to others. But here I shall try to do it. (Arnold, 2006, pp.19–20; italics original in first paragraph and added in second paragraph)

Taking a cue from what I like to think of as Alberto Quadrio Curzio's fundamental precept – to recognize, explicitly, that '*theory always* takes a specific definition of [an] economic system and *chooses a select set of tools and methods for its analysis*'– I have tried to discuss what may be implied by selecting a particular set of tools and methods for the analysis of economic theory. I have tried to couple this to a vision of an economic system devoid of false dichotomies, those that have shackled economic theory for over two centuries. The price of the vision I advocate is the introduction of new dichotomies, but those that I think are natural to economic analysis in its mathematical mode.

However, anything I can contribute, to pay *homage* to the *aristocratic scholar-gentleman who is Alberto Quadrio Curzio* must, surely, be woefully inadequate from every point of view. Yet, I consider myself privileged to have been invited to do so, and – however inadequate – it is written with conviction and humility, knowing that the unattainable is also the impossible, but yet, with Tennyson's *Ulysses* (italics added):

'Tis not too late to seek a newer world.
...

It may be that the gulfs will wash us down;
It may be we shall touch the Happy Isles,
And see the great Achilles, whom we knew.
Tho' much is taken, much abides; and tho'
We are not now that strength which in old days
Moved earth and heaven, that which we are, we are,–
One equal temper of heroic hearts,
Made weak by time and fate, but strong in will
To strive, to seek, to find, and not to yield.

4.   A personal acknowledgement

Non-produced means of production [(NPMP)] influence prices and distribution, the relations between these two entities and production, the *continuous*[10] but *non-regular growth and dynamics of economic systems* and international trade. This [conviction that reality lies between the pessimism of Ricardo and the optimism of an eminent father of contemporary dynamic analysis] tells us that [NPMPs], in their coexistence with produced and reproduced means of production, influence the distribution of income and have effects that range from *a non-regular dynamic of economic systems*, which *continue* to grow, to special international economic relations. By following this path of *constructive research* it will also be possible to utilize part of the theories of production of Leontief, with its *formidable empirical content*, and of von Neumann. (Quadrio Curzio, 1980, pp. 219, 239; italics added)

My first encounter with one of Quadrio Curzio's brilliant writings was one that was bristling with implicit dynamics, although clothed in the impeccable and illuminating formalism of capital theory – and that was over three decades ago (Quadrio Curzio, 1980). Over the next two decades – and more – Quadrio has worked out the 'formidable empirical content' of the clearly set out theoretical research program (Quadrio Curzio and Pellizzari, 1999, 1996), 'following [a] path of constructive research', implicit in that classic, itself a continuation of a deeply original line of research, powerfully inspired in an unparalleled way by Sraffa's classic (Sraffa, 1960), that had begun at least as early as 1967 (Quadrio Curzio, 1967, 1975).

In a precisely definable sense of the consummation of a research program, 'following a path of constructive research' and endowing it with some 'formidable empirical content', the more mature Quadrio Curzio concluded almost with some resignation: 'In conclusion ... we recall some studies of economic dynamics just to remind us [of] the vast range and complexity of this field, and the *absence* of a *complete analysis of economic dynamics*' (Quadrio Curzio and Pellizzari, 1999, p. 240; italics added). Perhaps one should read 'absence'

---

[10] The unwary reader may be tempted to interpret 'continuous' in its ordinary (real analytic) mathematical sense, but the later phrase 'continue to grow' should dispel such a person of any such illusion.

as '*impossibility*'! Such a reading would be entirely consistent with the view of Siro Lombardini, summarized, I think with warm approval by Quadrio Curzio and Pellizzari (1999, p. 242; italics added):

> Lombardini ... reminds us that 'the' model of economic growth *does not exist*. ... Lombardini also reminds us that the mathematical *complexity* of these models always risk to transform theory in a pure formal exercise ... In conclusion ... Lombardini asks if there exists 'the true' theory of growth. His answer is *negative. Theory always* takes a specific definition of [an] economic system and *chooses a select set of tools and methods for its analysis.* But all definitions are partial and each tool or method can clarify some specific aspects of an economic system, *leaving aside others.*

These wise caveats by Quadrio Curzio are those of a scholar with a mastery of the history of thought, a supreme economist who has grappled with the conundrums of grounding empirical content in solid economic theory, a concerned policy analyst who sees the need for understanding the evolution of institutions, and a passionate advocate of the need to foster innovation and, therefore, to grasp the role of entrepreneurship in advanced industrial economies (Quadrio Curzio and Fortis, 2005, 2008). In these attempts at forging an eclectic vision for an enlightened society, Quadrio Curzio invokes, as if they were intimate friends with whom he converses regularly, the classics and the pioneering Italian pre-Classics (for example, Cesare Beccaria and Ferdinando Galiani), our neoclassical masters, and those of the interregnum who aimed to consolidate the classical framework – John Stuart Mill and John E. Cairnes – and some who went beyond, Karl Marx, and the giants of the twentieth century, from Wicksell and Schumpeter, to Keynes and Sraffa. There were the Scottish and the French enlightenments – and also the partial Italian ones, those of an old nation yet to be forged into a new country. These partial Italian contributions, particularly the *Lombard enlightenment*, are reflected in Quadrio Curzio's passionate commitment to the unified ideals of European values, against a backdrop of European unity and unified policy for research and innovation within a framework of evolutionary institutions, fostering entrepreneurship (Quadrio Curzio and Fortis, 2005, 2008)[11]

---

[11] In my review of the book by Lombardini (1996), which is summarized as in this section by Quadrio Curzio, I wrote (Velupillai, 1997, pp. 1260–1):

> In sum, these chapters are an elegant, but rigorous, plea for an amalgam of the visions advocated by Schumpeter and Simon on the foundations built by our classical and neoclassical predecessors. It is not about micro and macro with the former providing the underpinning for the latter. It is, rather, about entrepreneurs and innovation, about evolution and institutions, about adapting and computing, about procedures and policies, and about applying Marshall's epitaph in endogenising these features on the structures that we have inherited from Smith and Ricardo, from Walras and Pareto.

> *I would feel entirely comfortable in* characterizing Quadro Curzio's visions in the above vein, *to which my only addition would be the name of Piero Sraffa.*

I have often found myself remembering, and reminding my own students, when we are prone to indulge in flights of theoretical fancy and atheoretical empirical fantasies, precepts elegantly and concisely formulated by Quadrio Curzio, but in the unlikely context of 'the Gold Problem' (Quadrio Curzio, 1982, p.1): 'History and fantasy, scientific analysis and platitudes, present-day dicta and the beliefs of centuries past overlap and mingle in such a way as to render quite complex both an objective analysis and a detached reading of contributions which seek to be objective.' Alberto Quadrio Curzio, an *aristocrat* of theory, with a mastery of history and tradition – as Carlo Cipolla was, in a not unrelated field – combined majestically, as I, with my stunted scholarship and blinkered visions have understood, the visions of a Schumpeter with the theoretical purity of a Sraffa, and took that synthesis to new heights of formidable empirical and institutional scholarship. Lesser mortals like me can only wonder at, with admiration, and seek to emulate, the ideals of scholarship, institution-building and fostering of the evolution of tradition that Alberto Quadrio Curzio has made into an art, whilst also personifying its encapsulation in one, whole personality.

REFERENCES

Arena, Richard, and Salvadori, Neri (eds.) *Money, Credit and the Role of the State: Essays in Honour of Augusto Graziani*, London: Ashgate Publishing.

Arnold, V. I. (2006) 'From Hilbert's Superposition Problem to Dynamical Systems', in A. A. Bolibruch, Yu. S. Osipov and Ya. G. Sinai (eds.) *Mathematical Events of the Twentieth Century*, Berlin: Springer-Verlag, Moscow: PHASIS, ch.2, pp. 19–45.

Bellman, R., and Cooke, K. L. (1963) *Differential-Difference Equations*, London: Academic Press.

Birkhoff, G. D. (1927) *Dynamical Systems*, Providence, RI: American Mathematical Society.

Brouwer, L. E. J. (1981) *Brouwer's Cambridge Lectures on Intuitionism*, ed. by Dirk van Dalen, Cambridge: Cambridge University Press.

Davis, M. D. (1958) *Computability and Unsolvability*, London: Constable and Company, Ltd.

Davis, M. D., Sigal, R., and Weyuker, E. J. (1994) *Computability, Complexity, and Languages: Fundamentals of Theoretical Computer Science*, New York: Academic Press.

Goodstein, R. L. (1944) 'On the Restricted Ordinal Theorem', *Journal of Symbolic Logic*, 9.2, pp. 33–41.

Goodwin, R. M. (1951a) 'Iteration, Automatic Computers and Economic Dynamics', *Metroeconomica*, 3.1, pp. 1–7.

(1951b) 'The Nonlinear Accelerator and the Persistence of Business Cycles', *Econometrica*, 19.1, pp. 1–17.

Hicks, J. R (1950) *A Contribution to the Theory of the Trade Cycle*, Oxford: Clarendon Press.

Hilbert, D. (1902) 'Mathematical Problems', *Bulletin of the American Mathematical Society*, 8 July, pp. 437–79.

Kaldor, N. (1940) 'A Model of the Trade Cycle', *The Economic Journal*, 50.2, pp. 78–92.
    (1954) 'The Relation of Economic Growth and Cyclical Fluctuations', *The Economic Journal*, 64.253, pp. 53–71.
    (1985) *Economics without Equilibrium*, New York: M.E. Sharpe.
Kalecki, M. (1935) 'A Macrodynamic Theory of Business Cycles', *Econometrica*, 3.3, pp. 327–44.
Kuznets, S. (1930), *Secular Movements in Production and Prices: Their Nature and Their Bearing upon Cyclical Fluctuations*, Boston, Mass. and New York: Houghton Mifflin.
Lundberg, E. (1937) *Studies in the Theory of Economic Expansion*, London: P. S. King & Son.
Paris, J., and Tavakol, R. (1993) 'Goodstein Algorithm as a Super-Transient Dynamical System', *Physics Letters A*, 180, pp. 83–6.
Pour-El, M. B and Richards, J. I. (1989) *Computability in Analysis and Physics*, Berlin: Springer-Verlag.
Rogers, H. Jr. (1967) *Theory of Recursive Functions and Effective Computability*, New York: McGraw-Hill Book Company.
Quadrio Curzio, A. (1967) *Rendita e distribuzione in un modello economico plurisettoriale*, Milan: Giuffré.
    (1975) *Accumulazione del capitale e rendita*, Bologna: Il Mulino.
    (1980) 'Rent, Income Distribution, and Orders of Efficiency and Rentability', in L. L. Pasinetti (ed.) *Essays on the Theory of Joint Production*, London and Basingstoke: Macmillan, pp. 218–40.
    (ed.) (1982) *The Gold Problem: Economic Perspectives*, Oxford and New York: Oxford University Press.
Quadrio Curzio, A. and Pellizzari, F. (1996) *Risorse, tecnologie, rendita*, Bologna: Il Mulino.
    (1999) *Rent, Resources, Technologies*, Berlin: Springer-Verlag.
Quadrio Curzio, A., and Fortis, M. (eds.) (2005) *Research and Technological Innovation: The Challenge for a New Europe*, Berlin: Physica-Verlag.
    (2008) *The EU and the Economies of the Eastern European Enlargement*, Berlin: Physica-Verlag.
Salomaa, A. (1985) *Computation and Automata*, Cambridge: Cambridge University Press.
Shapiro, S. (1997) *Philosophy of Mathematics: Structure and Ontology*, Oxford: Oxford University Press.
Smullyan, R. M. (1993) *Recursion Theory for Metamathematics*, Oxford: Oxford University Press.
Sraffa, P. (1960) *Production of Commodities by Means of Commodities: Prelude to a Critique of Economic Theory*, Cambridge: Cambridge University Press.
Stewart, I. (1991) 'Deciding the Undecidable', *Nature*, 352, August, pp. 664–5.
Velupillai, K. V. (1997) 'Review of "Growth and Economic Development" by Siro Lombardini', *Journal of Economic Dynamics and Control*, 21, pp. 1259–62.
    (2009) 'Uncomputability and Undecidability in Economic Theory', *Applied Mathematics and Computation*, 215.4, pp. 1404–16.
    (2011) 'The Phillips Machine and the Epistemology of Analogue Computation', *Economia Politica – Journal of Analytical and Institutional Economics*, 27, Special Issue on the Phillips Machine, pp. 39–62.

11   Ricardian and Schumpeterian rents: fundamental ingredients for structural economic dynamics

Michael A. Landesmann

1.   Introduction

Rents play an important role in Ricardian economics[1] and in Schumpeterian analysis (in the latter it refers to transitory profits but we shall nonetheless use the notion of Schumpeterian rents[2]).

The notion is relevant in both streams of analysis as it emphasizes the issue of differentiation amongst producers or production activities within the same industry. In Ricardo it is the impact of limited quantities of non-producible inputs (which are themselves differentiated in productivity) that generates this differentiation. In Schumpeter it refers to differentiation in terms of technology (product and process) employed by different producers that reflect differences in technological or innovation capabilities.

In this chapter we shall explore the link between rent theory and structural economic dynamics. The crucial element in this link is the impact of rents on investment dynamics and further on 'endogenous' productivity dynamics.

We shall also point to the crucial position of rent theory in analysing *growth retarding and growth enhancing features* of structural features of an economic system.

This is the structure of the chapter: in the next section we point to important differences in the link between rent analysis and price theory in Ricardo and in Schumpeter. We then consider the link between rent analysis and investment dynamics. The analysis is then extended to analyse the usefulness of rent

---

[1] Although I shall in the following refer to Ricardian rent theory, Ricardo ([1817] 1951) is not the only originator of the rent concept in classical political economy but shares this claim with Malthus, West and Torrens as fully discussed in Luigi Pasinetti's chapter in this volume.

[2] Although I shall in the following refer to Schumpeterian 'rents', Schumpeter speaks of 'profit' instead of 'rent' as his notion of profits is a 'disequilibrium' concept, i.e. characterizing the state of an industry when full-scale imitation (of best technologies and products) has not yet been achieved and hence differentiation across producers characterizes an industry (Schumpeter, [1912] 1961). Once full imitation has been achieved, differentiation disappears and a new 'equilibrium' will be reached where these types of 'profits' will have disappeared. Because of 'disequilibrium profits' reflecting differentiation across producers (and of technologies and products) I shall refer to Schumpeterian 'rents' instead of 'profits' in the following.

concepts in analysing cross-industry dynamics. We further analyse additional distributional issues and how these affect overall system dynamics. Other issues discussed include the impact of limited availability of non-producible inputs on structural dynamics including the issue of induced and directed technological change. Finally we discuss institutional and political economy considerations that affect rent structures and economic dynamics.

2.   Link to price theory

Ricardian rent theory emphasizes the determination of industry price by the least productive producer ('marginal land' in the case of 'extensive rent' and the reduced productivity to produce higher levels of output through more intensive cultivation of the same land). Schumpeter, on the other hand, emphasizes the determination of pricing in an industry through the relative market power that the most productive/most innovative producer has in an industry. This market power is constrained by the ease of transferability/imitation of new technologies/new product designs, etc.

Furthermore, in Ricardo the ranges of emerging rents are determined by overall level of output to be produced by an industry, which determines the spectrum of differentiated lands to be taken into cultivation (in the case of extensive rent) or the levels of intensive use of the same piece of land (in the case of intensive rent).

In Schumpeter, the case of process innovation in an industry (leaving the product the same) is easier to analyse, so we take this case first. In some sense the case of process innovation is analogous to the Ricardian case: producers are differentiated in the cost effectiveness of the technologies they employ (taking input prices as given). However, the cut-off point that determines the range of processes that stay in operation (and those that will no longer be employed) depends on the price-setting outcome in an industry that is characterized by producers with differentiated market power; the least efficient producer still has to cover its costs just as in the Ricardian case. The literature suggests a number of ways to approach such price setting (e.g. Cournot vs. Bertrand models of oligopolistic competition), and the location and shape of the demand curve matters. As is the case with Ricardo, it is the producer (in Ricardo, the landowner owning the most fertile land) operating with the most efficient (least cost) technology who receives the 'rent'. As a new production technology disseminates across producers, the market power of the more efficient producers declines, the demand curve becomes more price elastic and – without a further process innovation – the degree of heterogeneity across producers declines in the industry.

In the Schumpeterian case of product innovation, it is again the location and shape of the demand curve facing a particular producer (with its elasticity parameter) that determines the pricing policy of the innovator. The more of a gap there is between the innovator and the existing producers (in product 'quality' or in the characteristics space) and the more consumers appreciate the innovative content of a new product, the more the demand curve shifts upwards, the lower the price elasticity and hence the higher the willingness to pay, and the higher the Schumpeterian rent. In this context, the issue of product differentiation (while in the Ricardo context a homogeneous output is assumed) opens up complicated issues of different producers potentially catering to different 'quality segments' of demand with different purchasing power. This co-determines the spectrum of producers that cater towards particular market segments (see e.g. Gabszewicz and Thisse, 1979, 1980) and thus the extent of heterogeneity of producers in an industry.

3.   Link to investment dynamics

The link between the structure of rents and investment dynamics is crucial for establishing the importance of rent theory for structural economic dynamics.

Let us first recapitulate the link between investment dynamics and the rent issue in Ricardo: Ricardo (and the other classical authors) analyses the situation when a particular sector is subject to the impact of the limited availability of a necessary non-produced input. That input is available in different quality grades (lands of different fertility). What does it mean with respect to the investment dynamic?

In Ricardo's 'extensive rent' case the investment dynamic is strictly determined by the limitations of the availability of lands of different types and the level of output to be produced: hence an increase in the level of output requires the cultivation of less fertile pieces of land, and the shares of overall investment that goes to the sector increasingly shifts towards the lower productivity (farming) entities. The reason is that lower productivity levels mean higher levels of inputs per unit of output and hence a higher investment requirement per unit of output.

In Schumpeter the opposite investment dynamic takes place in relation to his 'rent' (i.e. transitory profit) concept. Here the production entities with the higher productivity growth levels attract – over time – an increasing share of investment. The innovating firm (introducing a better product or better techniques of production) will show higher profits (the Schumpeterian 'rent') and will thus attract more investment. Depending on the determination of the industry price (see earlier) there can – and will in due course – also be negative net investment (due to non-renewal of existing capacity and scrapping) in the least productive enterprises.

In the Schumpeterian case, this investment dynamic can give rise to cumulative processes of differentiation across producers in terms of innovation rates and thus can widen the range of differentiated products and processes in an industry. That range is in turn determined by the structure of demand for different quality producers and pricing power of the technology leaders.

4.   Extending the analysis to interindustry dynamics

Applying the Ricardian situation to analyse cross-industry investment dynamics let us take the simplest case in which we distinguish between a sector with diminishing returns and one with constant returns (e.g. agriculture and manufacturing in the classical Ricardian setting, see for instance Pasinetti, 1960). Ignoring initially interindustry linkages between the two sectors, the evolution of demand for the two sectors will depend on income and price elasticities with regard to products produced by the two sectors. As the sector with diminishing returns will have to have recourse to less efficient production techniques, the relative price of its product will rise and this factor will lead to demand turning away from it. However, if this sector produces an essential commodity (in Ricardo's case the essential wage good, i.e. food) there will be a unit income elasticity with regard to its output and a low price elasticity. In this case, output composition will have to remain roughly constant and with increasing output levels overall, the investment share of the diminishing returns sector will increase. This is the argument behind Ricardo's gloomy picture of a move towards a 'stationary state'.

A similar type of analysis has been put forward by Baumol (1967) when he discussed the increasing strain that the provision of (essential) services (such as health and education) might impose on fiscal budgets. He argued that income elasticities for these types of services are high, while relative productivity growth rates are low in these sectors. Hence investment shares of these (low productivity growth) sectors will grow over time. If private budgets are not willing to cover the increasing relative costs of these sectors, the political pressure will build up to finance these from the public purse, hence the impact on State finances.

If we want to consider also the case when the two sectors also produce and use intermediate inputs, the role of rigidities in input composition – or in the parlance of neoclassical production theory, the substitution elasticities with regard to the use of different inputs – will come into play. Low substitution elasticities (in the extreme case a linear production technology) would mean that in spite of the rising relative costs of the intermediate input produced by the diminishing returns industry it will keep its 'real' share in the input composition of the different industries. It thus depends on how 'essential' the output of the diminishing returns industry is as an input for itself and for other industries, i.e. how 'rigid' production technologies are in the economy. This is equivalent to the relative 'rigidity' of demand structures alluded to earlier (expressed by high or unit income elasticities of demand for the produce of the decreasing returns or low productivity growth sector as well as low price elasticities).

Let us now extend the Schumpeterian analysis to the interindustry situation. Schumpeter's theory – as did Ricardo's dynamic theory – emphasized the differentiation within an industry across different producers (producing different products or using different production technologies). The analysis may be extended to the situation across industries that also produce different products. While one could make a qualitative difference between the case of product differentiation within the industry (see e.g. the models of monopolistic competition such as the one proposed by Dixit and Stiglitz, 1977) and different industries producing distinctly different products, it is basically an issue of the values of substitution elasticities applied in the two cases (high in the case of product differentiation within an industry, lower in the case of products supplied by different industries). A further analytical difference exists between the within-industry and the across-industry cases: in the within-industry case, quality (i.e. vertical) differentiation and hence demand segmentation matters, while in the cross-industry case one can assume a homogeneous demand function for the consumers for each of the industries' products.

Let us discuss the investment dynamic in the interindustry case in more detail: from empirical evidence it is clear that different (average) profits are being reaped in different industries in the normal dynamic of a capitalist economy. Since the classics this 'stylized fact' has attracted the attention of analysts. How should this stylized fact be approached? As an 'equilibrium' or 'disequilibrium' feature of the dynamics of a capitalist economy? In other words, in a Schumpeterian or in a classical (also 'new growth' theory) perspective?

The classical perspective is that different per-unit profits (mark-up rates) are compatible with an equilibrium situation where these different per-unit profits simply reflect different 'composition of capital' (Marx) or different fixed to variable cost requirements (new growth theory[3]) of different industries.

A Schumpeterian perspective characterizes differentiation of profits across industries (above and below the classical and new growth theory 'equilibrium'

---

[3] New growth theory utilizes the 'free entry' assumption so as determine the 'equilibrium' profits in different industries at levels that exactly cover total (i.e. fixed plus variable) costs. The Schumpeterian scenario would not want to pin down profit differentiation in this manner as it would ignore the rather differentiated innovation capacity (*ex ante*) of different producers and in different industries. This gives rise to differentiated profits above and below 'equilibrium' profits as long as perfect technology transfer or full imitation is not assumed.

profits) as reflecting the dynamic phenomenon of different rates of innovation (in product and process technologies) across industries.

The dynamic of Schumpeterian 'profits' or 'rents' across industries is a complex process. There are many elements that play a role here: substitution and income elasticities for the goods produced by the different industries (income elasticities are particularly emphasized in Luigi Pasinetti's well-known works; see Pasinetti, 1981, 1993); the market structures within each industry (which determine the pricing powers within each industry), which in turn are determined by within-industry product and process differentiation as well as institutional features that determine entry-barriers.

We can make a number of empirically sensible assumptions regarding profit/rent dynamic across industries:

1. Industries with higher innovation rates are likely to show wider spreads of productivity levels across producers within an industry. The reason for this is that innovation activity is a 'differentiating device' in a Darwinian sense. On the other hand, high innovation potential in an industry will also attract a high number of potential innovators who are attracted by the potential for Schumpeterian rents. Following a successful innovation, also a large pool of imitators who want to benefit from the existence of 'transitory' Schumpeterian profits will be attracted to that industry. Hence an industry with high innovation rates will be characterized by a high (initial) range of differentiation followed also by a higher rate of imitation and diffusion.

2. High innovation is likely to occur in industries that in principle are characterized by high income elasticities for its output (this provides an incentive for innovation). On the other hand, one has to take account of the fact that income elasticities are also a function of product innovation (of the rates and levels of 'quality jumps' in the wording of Grossman-Helpman type growth models, see Grossman and Helpman, 1991). Hence there is some circularity or cumulativeness here.

3. The prospect of innovation in high-income elastic areas attracts more 'potential innovators' and this is one of the reasons why new growth theorists would assume a higher pressure from the mass of 'free entrants' and also a higher pressure from 'imitators' in such industries, which would lead to the equilibrating forces that characterize their models. While the prevalence of these forces could lead to (*ex ante*) equilibration of profit rates across the different industries (as the steady-state cases in endogenous growth models usually assume) it does not lead to the disappearance of differences of Schumpeterian 'transitory' rent structures (above or below equilibrium profits) across different industries.

4. Just as we emphasized differences in income elasticities earlier, there is also the issue of different cross-industry substitution elasticities when

innovation rates are high in particular industries and low in others. Thus one would expect lower price elasticities in industries in which product innovation proceeds at higher rates ('reward for radical innovations') – which allows the charging of higher mark-up on costs. Schumpeterian rents are in this case a reflection of (temporary) 'scarcity', i.e. a limited number of suppliers that are able to offer radically new products.

5.   When and how do rents get shifted across industries?

As an introduction to tackling the issue of rent shifting across productive sectors, let us first discuss the distribution of rents within industries across different 'classes' of society.

In the Ricardian case, rents are straightforwardly retained by the owners of the differentiated non-producible input, i.e. the landlords. In the Schumpeterian case there is a possibility to have different distributions of Schumpeterian profits across different groups: e.g. workers and capitalists. The reason for this is that Schumpeterian rents are transitory and are defined as being above 'normal profits' (i.e. above average profits made in an industry). Hence the option opens up to have different distributions of such rents, e.g. between capitalists and workers or between different groups of workers (e.g. those involved in innovation activities and those involved in production). Since Schumpeterian profits/rents emerge from transitory dynamics (i.e. from the temporary advantages that producers have in terms of the efficiency of their production technologies or the characteristics of the products they supply), there is bargaining space over how these rents get distributed between different social groups.

There are implications for such different distributions of 'rents' across social groups: e.g. higher wages paid out to workers by the more innovative firms (or by more innovative industries) attracts 'better' workers (or allows employers to select them from a wider pool of applicants). Or relatively higher wages to employees involved in innovation activities will encourage more workers to apply for these activities than for production activities; again this will be reflected in differences in 'quality' between innovation and production workers. Similarly, higher returns on capital invested in high innovation (high productivity) firms will attract more capital (although the *ex ante* risk might also be higher and hence it will attract more risk-friendly investors, i.e. venture capitalists). All these compositional effects can have implications for further 'endogenous' innovation and productivity dynamics across the different industries.

The distribution of 'rents' between social groups may generate a 'shifting of rents' across sectors. Take the case where the accrual of 'innovation rents' leads to high wage growth in a particular sector earning a high share of these rents. In this case the share going to Schumpeterian 'profits' would be quite low and the consequences depend on the pattern of expenditure out of profits and out of wages. If, as can be well assumed, profits accrued in one industry are more likely to be spent in that industry (investment financed through retained earnings) while wages would be spent across sectors depending on workers' expenditure patterns, then obviously different distributions of Schumpeterian rents between workers and entrepreneurs within an industry will have an impact on the investment dynamic across sectors[4]. Similarly, if parts of Schumpeterian rents get differently distributed, e.g. between higher- and low-skilled workers in an industry (reflecting their relative bargaining positions), this can have differential impacts upon other industries through a wage drift (i.e. driving up wage rates of these particular workers also in other industries), which in turn affects industries with different skilled/unskilled labour ratios differently. Further examples can easily be elaborated.

We shall come back to another form of 'rent shifting' across industries when institutional and political interferences affect entry conditions (e.g. through licencing, quotas) or the price-setting in other ways in different industries (could be through direct price controls or pricing rules, or affecting the market structure of an industry in other ways e.g. protection).

6.   Rents due to non-producible inputs and links to the direction of technological change

Alberto Quadrio Curzio, a lifelong student of rent theory and of structural economic dynamics, focuses in many of his writings[5] on a specific issue in the rent-dynamics story: the impact which non-producible input constraints (he uses the term 'non-produced means of production' (NPMP)) have on the adjustment of production structures and thus on economic dynamics.

The first case of adjustment of productive structures to the presence of limited availability of NPMP is the one considered by Ricardo: as the overall level of activity of an economy expands, the sectors that require the use of NPMP will have to have recourse to worse qualities of the NPMPs and the overall rate of economic growth of the economy will suffer. This can be neatly shown in models in which input–output interdependencies across sectors are considered and in which the overall growth potential can be calculated as the economy 'traverses' adjusting its production structures to the uses of inferior qualities of NPMP and the overall potential growth rate suffers. Quadrio Curzio

---

[4] These issues of the distribution of Schumpeterian rents have been explored in a variety of dynamic multi-sectoral modelling exercises and in the context of closed and open economies in Goodwin and Landesmann (1996) and Landesmann and Stehrer (2006, 2007).

[5] See e.g. Quadrio Curzio (1986, 1990).

shows neatly in mathematical terms how such traverses can be described through decompositions into subsystems that show the parallel use of different qualities of NPMP where each of these decomposed subsystems is characterized by a different 'net output' and maximum potential growth rate. The overall economic system is a linear combination of such subsystems and in the course of the traverse the weights of these subsystems change. It is a fundamental generalization of Ricardo's own analysis of the impact of NPMP on economic growth and – in the prices-distribution space – of his theory of 'rents'.

Quadrio Curzio points also to additional features of such 'traverses'. For example, any change in techniques of production (as the economy is forced to utilize inferior qualities of NPMP) also means a change in the composition of input requirements. At each juncture of such a traverse, and depending upon the degree of flexibility of output structures, the changing input requirements might not match exactly the composition of output. Hence 'residuals' (surplus output) would be available, which remain either unused or might give rise to the start of other activities that could make use of such surplus output. The other possibility is that such 'residuals' get simply reflected in portions of under-utilized capacities. Hence important changes in productive structures rarely pass without phenomena of 'wastes' or 'under-utilized resources'.

The final and important step of the analysis is the impact that limited availabilities of NPMP (or 'technological scarcities' as Quadrio Curzio calls them) have on the invention and introduction of new techniques of production, hence of technological change. One incentive for such inventions or introductions of new activities can simply be the emergence of 'wastes' or 'under-utilized resources'. Another is the more fundamental one, to free the economic system from the constraints of the limited availability of NPMP themselves. In some sense, one can think of the entire history of humankind's inventive effort to be directed at overcoming such constraints. One form of overcoming such constraints is to invent PMP (produced means of production) that can take over the function of the NPMP in the same production activities; another is to invent entirely new activities that can replace the older ones and that are not constrained in the same way. An interesting feature of Quadrio Curzio's framework is that the analytical capture of the impact of NPMP on potential growth rates – which in some sense is a generalized form of Ricardo's 'rent' theory – allows to analyse the systemic incentives of overcoming 'technological scarcity' and hence specifies the incentive for 'induced and directed technological change'.

7.   Rents and institutional/legal barriers

There is another tradition in 'rents' analysis which emphasizes the role of institutional and political structures for the emergence of rents, their distribution across different social groups and their uses. The famous historical example is the classic analysis by Ricardo and other classical authors of the impact of the Corn Laws: protectionist barriers against the import of corn (the principal wage good in an explosive period of population growth) led to the need to bring an increasing range of inferior lands into cultivation (to produce enough food). This in turn leads to an increasing share of national income going to landlords and since this social group is more inclined towards conspicuous consumption rather than using an economy's net produce (a surplus of produce beyond the need of simple reproduction) to build up additional capacities and towards technological advance.

This type of analysis has been further developed in differentiated forms when analysing the impact of regulations, attempts to restrict entry (through protection or various forms of licencing), political interventions into price-setting, etc. on market structures in different industries, hence on the degree of competition by sector. The resulting impact on price and cost structures in turn influences the income flows to different social groups, in parts by influencing their relative bargaining positions within sectors towards each other. This influence also extends further to their dealings with political authorities who decide on public procurement, set the conditions for such procurements, decide on the allocation of licences and entry permits, subsidies, tax reliefs, etc. All of this opens up a complicated analysis of how regulations, different legal structures and direct political interferences influence price structures and quantity decisions by different producers in an interdependent economy. This influences the distribution of the economy's 'net product' across social groups (including those operating in the state sector itself). We are dealing here with instances of 'incidence analysis' already tackled by the classics (such as François Quesnay or David Ricardo; see e.g. Eltis, 2000) in their analysis of the impact of different types of taxes.

Whether it is appropriate to use the term 'rents' in this context (as done e.g. in the famous paper by Anne Krueger, 1974, on 'rent seeking') is not easy to judge. The analysis is, of course, different from the specific 'rent' concepts designed by David Ricardo or Joseph Schumpeter. On the other hand, it shows the distributional implications of certain institutional and legal set-ups as well as of direct political interventions. The main mechanism underlying such distributional impacts is via the differentiating impact on different – actual or potential – producers (e.g. incumbents and potential entrants). The distributional implications in turn impact on the growth dynamics (and on structural features) of economies. Hence in this sense, it relates to the core element in any rent theory – i.e. differentiation across producers – and covers the wider concern of Ricardo and the classics as well as of Schumpeter who analysed the relationship between price structures, their distributional implications, and further their impact on structural features and the dynamics of economic systems.

8.   Conclusions

We have tried to show that 'rents' are a crucial concept in the analysis of 'structural dynamics' of an economic system. This link has already been powerfully pointed out by Ricardo and Schumpeter. This chapter has attempted to show the differences between these two authors' approaches to rents and their impact on the dynamics of economic systems.

There is a very interesting twist in the comparison between Ricardo's and Schumpeter's theory of 'rents/profits'. One of the main differences between the two lies in the link between rents and investment dynamics. In the Ricardian case, the highest rents are received by the landlords owning the most fertile pieces of land. However, Ricardo does not assume that this would lead to a higher investment dynamic by these landlords but would simply be used for conspicuous consumption.[6] In fact since land of the highest fertility cannot be extended, there cannot physically be more investment in such types of land (or if it were to take place, it would incur diminishing returns as it would move towards the case of 'intensive rent'). For Schumpeter, in contrast, higher rents/ profits are obtained by the most innovative firms and higher rates of investment by these are not constrained by any physical limitations (as would be the case if they were dependent upon limited availability of non-producible inputs). Hence the rates of investment can be higher for those firms that brought the most innovative products to the market and/or use the most productive techniques of production. The uneven investment dynamics across the firm population[7] is the main mechanism of new products and superior techniques of production gaining higher shares of the market and being used more widely, i.e. being 'diffused'. This in turn drives, in Schumpeter, the mechanism of economic growth that proceeds (following the dynamics of 'transitory rents') in a fluctuating manner.

Rent analysis – although conceived in quite a different manner – thus occupies a central place in both Ricardian as well as Schumpeterian approaches to economic dynamics. The common element is the attention given by both authors and following contributions to the issue of 'differentiation' whether this is the result of constraints imposed by nature or of the ingenuity of man.

---

[6] In Quesnay's analysis, the importance of longer land tenure leases by farmers was brought into the picture, which would allow the tenant farmers to reap a higher share from the gains of productivity on land. This would provide an incentive to introduce better techniques of production. Quesnay thus provides a bridge to a Schumpeterian approach to rents or linking the issue of rents on land to potential technological change (see also Eltis, 2000).

[7] The overall investment dynamic is not only determined by the firms that bring new products to the market and introduce better techniques of production but also by the negative investment rates of the other firms – the least productive ones and the ones with the least desired older products – which are affected by the induced price dynamic and incur devaluation processes of their capital stock. The analysis can be extended, as discussed in an earlier section of this chapter to the interindustry case.

REFERENCES

Baumol, W. J. (1967) 'Macroeconomics of Unbalanced Growth: An Anatomy of Urban Crisis', *The American Economic Review*, 57.3, pp. 415–26.

Dixit, A. K., and Stiglitz, J. E. (1977) 'Monopolistic Competition and Optimum Product Diversity', *The American Economic Review*, 67.3, pp. 297–308.

Eltis, W. A. (2000) *The Classical Theory of Economic Growth*, 2nd edn, London and New York: Palgrave.

Gabszewicz, J. J., and Thisse, J. F. (1979) 'Price Competition, Quality and Income Disparities', *Journal of Economic Theory*, 20.3, pp. 340–59.

 (1980) 'Entry (and Exit) in a Differentiated Industry', *Journal of Economic Theory*, 22.2, pp. 327–38.

Goodwin, R. M., and Landesmann, M. A. (1996) 'Disaggregated Models of the Business Cycle', in M. Landesmann and R. Scazzieri (eds.) *Production and Economic Dynamics*, Cambridge: Cambridge University Press, pp. 304–43.

Grossman, G. M., and Helpman, E. (1991) *Innovation and Growth in the Global Economy*, Cambridge, Mass.: MIT Press.

Krueger, A. O. (1974) 'The Political Economy of the Rent Seeking Society', *The American Economic Review*, 64.3, pp. 291–303.

Landesmann, M. A., and Stehrer, R. (2006) 'Goodwin's Structural Economic Dynamics: Modelling Schumpeterian and Keynesian Insights', *Structural Change and Economic Dynamics*, 17.4, pp. 501–24.

 (2007) 'Income Distribution, Technical Change and the Dynamics of International Economic Integration', *Metroeconomica*, 58.1, pp. 45–73.

Pasinetti, L. L. (1960) 'A Mathematical Formulation of the Ricardian System', *The Review of Economic Studies*, 27.2, pp. 270–82.

 (1981) *Structural Change and Economic Growth: A Theoretical Essay on the Dynamics of the Wealth of Nations*, Cambridge: Cambridge University Press.

 (1993) *Structural Economic Dynamics: A Theory of the Economic Consequences of Human Learning*, Cambridge: Cambridge University Press.

Quadrio Curzio, A. (1986) 'Technological Scarcity: An Essay on Production and Structural Change', in M. Baranzini and R. Scazzieri (eds.) *Foundations of Economics. Structures of Inquiry and Economic Theory*, Oxford and New York: B. Blackwell, pp. 311–38.

 (1990) 'Rent, Distribution and Economic Structure: A Collection of Essays', *Quaderni IDSE*, 1, Milan, CNR.

Ricardo, D. ([1817] 1951) *On the Principles of Political Economy and Taxation*, Cambridge: Cambridge University Press, for the *Royal Economic Society*.

Schumpeter, J. A. ([1912] 1961) *The Theory of Economic Development: an Inquiry into Profits, Capital, Credit, Interest, and the Business Cycle*, translated from the German by R. Opie (1961) New York: Oxford University Press.

12   Towards a structural political economy of resources

Ivano Cardinale

1.   Introduction

Non-produced resources play a fundamental role in shaping economic dynamics and distribution. The dynamics of technical and material relationships are embedded in economic and political relationships, which suggests the existence of a 'complex web of interests of the different social categories during the process of accumulation' (Quadrio Curzio and Pellizzari, 1999, p. 236).

This chapter outlines a framework to explore the role of economic and political relationships in the interplay of resources and economic dynamics. The heuristic strategy of the chapter is inspired by François Quesnay's ([1759] 1972) *Tableau Économique*, in particular for what concerns its coupling of economic and political analysis, rooted in the overlaps between sectors and social classes. However, this chapter departs from Quesnay's approach in two important ways. First, it makes use of modern tools and results that have been developed since Quesnay's work, such as the distinction between horizontal interdependencies and vertical integration (Pasinetti, 1973), the tools of traverse analysis (Hicks, 1973; Lowe, 1976; Scazzieri, 2009) and the models of multi-sectoral dynamics in the presence of non-produced resources (Quadrio Curzio, 1996). Moreover, as will be shown throughout the chapter, the relevant political-economic aggregations and cleavages of interests are not assumed at the outset, but are seen as a result of the process that the analysis uncovers.

This chapter is part of an ongoing research programme of 'structural political economy' (Cardinale 2012, 2015; Cardinale and Coffman 2014; Cardinale and Landesmann, 2015; Cardinale and Scazzieri, 2014), which deploys categories and tools of structural economic analysis as heuristics for uncovering the deep structure of economic interests in societies, and the relative positions of political

The framework of this chapter was initially formulated in the invited comment to the lecture of Balzan Prize winner Michael Grätzel at the second edition of Interlab, which took place at the University of Lugano, Switzerland, in October 2013. I would like to thank the International Balzan Foundation, the National Lincei Academy, and the Swiss Academies for inviting me, and the Interlab participants for their comments. I am grateful to Roberto Scazzieri for his insightful comments on several drafts of this chapter. The usual disclaimer applies.

groups that represent those interests. In the spirit of structural economic analysis, this chapter assigns central importance to the configuration of political interests that corresponds to the economic interests of industrial sectors. The aim is to investigate how the 'invisible but nevertheless very real ties' between industrial sectors within the 'general interdependence' of the economy (Leontief, 1941, p. 3) may provide the ground for sectors' construction of their own interests, thus shaping their interaction within the political arena. Industrial sectors clearly have economic interests, for instance in obtaining economic policies that favour them, and there is the possibility that they will seek some form of political influence to protect those interests. Industrial sectors can be either potential or manifest groups in Truman's (1962) sense. Truman distinguishes between potential interest groups, which are latent and could organize themselves under certain conditions, for instance if threatened, and manifest interest groups, which are already organized and exert active pressure on decision making. What matters for our purposes is the *possibility* that sectors seek some form of political influence. In fact, the purpose of this analysis is to explore the possibilities for conflict and cooperation between sectors that a given economic structure makes possible, independently of realized outcomes.

More specifically, the chapter aims to explore how the interplay of resources and dynamics influences the configuration of interests in a given society, by shaping the system of technical and material relationships in which political and economic relationships are grounded. Political and economic relationships in turn provide *conditions for possibility*, by defining the set of politically feasible choices among those that are made possible by technical relationships. Within that set, the specific constructions of groups' interests that emerge in a given society, which are influenced but not determined by material relationships, activate paths of structural dynamics that may differ across societies.

It is particularly important to investigate these issues in the context of the transition between resource bases, because of its profound effects on technical change and scarcities (Wrigley, 1962, 2010; Quadrio Curzio, 1975, 1986) and its implication for the dynamics of rents (Quadrio Curzio, 1967, 1980, 1987). In this chapter I outline two orders of conditions that allow the transition between resource bases. I first identify 'economic conditions', i.e. conditions concerning technical and material relationships that make the transition feasible. I then specify political-economic conditions, which concern the social and political relations, and which may or may not allow the economic conditions to be met. The fact that each set of economic conditions is associated to a set of political-economic conditions is the direct result of the coupling of economic and political analysis. I illustrate this framework with reference to a pressing problem that modern societies face – the dual objective of increasing energy supply while reducing carbon emissions to a level compatible with widely shared environmental objectives.

2.   Transition between resource bases: an interpretive framework

The first building block of the interpretive framework for the transition between resource bases can be taken to be a definition of the initial and final states, which can be usefully represented through input–output tables corresponding to the beginning and the end of the transition.[1] Input–output analysis originates in François Quesnay's ([1759] 1972) *Tableau Économique*, which described 'the circulation of money and commodities in relation to both the expenditure of revenue and the technical and social relationships between the two main sectors of the economy' (Vaggi, 2008; see also Phillips, 1955; Hishiyama, 1960; Candela, 1975; Vaggi, 1987; Pasinetti, 2002). Quesnay's insight was more recently built upon by von Neumann (1945), Sraffa (1960) and Leontief (1941), who saw his *Structure of the American Economy* as an attempt to construct a modern *Tableau* (see also Leontief, 1991; Samuelson, 1991).

An input–output table of the Quesnay-Leontief type breaks down aggregate output into the output of n industrial sectors (x_1 to x_n). Each line shows the output of a sector (e.g. 1) as an input into the other sectors (the input of good 1 into process 1, process 2, process 3, process n) and a final demand of good 1 (d_1). This representation allows visualizing the industrial sectors of the economy as well as the interdependencies among those sectors.

Let us illustrate the initial and final states with reference to the energy resource base. Synthesizing a wide consensus in the scientific community, Grätzel (2013) argues that societies face the dual objective of containing emissions while producing a sufficient quantity of energy, and proposes a 'stabilization triangle' as an analytical tool for combining energy-saving measures and increasing reliance on renewable energy sources. We can observe that implementation of a stabilization triangle potentially results in changes in many coefficients across the input–output table, both in the energy sector and in other sectors. More specifically, changes in the energy sector take place because starting new production processes related to renewable energy results in changes in the coefficients of inputs from other sectors. For example, as a growing proportion of energy is produced from windmills, the input of crude oil declines while the inputs necessary for the construction of windmills rise.

Changes in non-energy sectors take place because a reduced coefficient of energy input, resulting from energy-saving measures, is likely to require reorganization in production processes, hence also different coefficients of other inputs (Georgescu-Roegen, 1969; Scazzieri, 1993; Cardinale and

---

[1] Of course, the transition often implies that new production processes emerge. In order to preserve the heuristic value of comparing input–output tables, in this chapter I will assume that industrial sectors are defined in a way such that processes before and after the transition are aggregated within industrial sectors as initially defined.

Scazzieri, 2013). In fact, changes in the structure of production tasks may affect not only the input of energy, but potentially other inputs too (Scazzieri, 1993). Moreover, new tasks may make evident new functions, i.e. new possibilities for the transformation of matter (Cardinale and Scazzieri, 2013; Cardinale and Runde, 2014).

This suggests that implementation of a stabilization triangle is likely to cause widespread changes in technological relationships among sectors across the economy. On both historical and theoretical grounds, we can expect that this process drives structural change and economic dynamics (Jevons, 1865; Quadrio Curzio, 1986; Quadrio Curzio and Pellizzari, 1999; Wrigley, 1962, 2010). We can distinguish different mechanisms in this process. A 'direct' mechanism is the development of new production processes in the energy sector. An 'indirect' but no less important mechanism is that the resulting scientific and technological progress can find application in other parts of the production system, improving existing processes or creating new ones both within and outside the energy sector (Dosi and Nelson, 2010).

The framework outlined in this chapter proposes two sets of conditions under which the final state described can be reached. The first includes conditions that concern the feasibility of the final state, that is, the state of scientific and technological knowledge and organization of production processes that allows large-scale deployment of energy produced from renewable sources. The second set includes conditions concerning the *process* through which the final state can be reached – what is usually called the *traverse*. Each set of conditions can be further divided into economic conditions, which pertain to material and technical relationships, and political-economic conditions, which pertain to the social and political configurations that make it possible to meet economic conditions.

3.   The final state

Because the technology that characterizes the material relationships of the final state is often unknown at the initial state, an important class of economic conditions is related to technological exploration. For example, in the case of energy, Grätzel (2013) shows that current technology would not allow meeting energy needs from renewable sources alone.[2] Doing so would require wide-scale exploration of new technologies and their application within production processes. This would be an instance of exploration at the frontier

---

[2] This situation, in which a particular input (energy) is scarce because of the state of technology, is akin to what Quadrio Curzio (1986) defines 'technological scarcity', although the type of scarcity described in this case is not specifically due to limited availability of resources or impossibility to utilize residuals from other processes.

of technology, which is characterized by fundamental uncertainty regarding the outcomes of different trajectories of technological exploration (Dosi, 1982; Pich, Loch, and de Meyer, 2002; Dosi and Nelson, 2010; Janeway, 2012). In other words, it cannot be known in advance which technologies will prove economically viable. As a result, technological exploration needs to be based on trial and error, which is a wasteful process and has unpredictable results, because it requires developing technologies in parallel, many of which will not prove to be viable (Pich *et al.*, 2002). Crucially, the process takes place outside the logic of efficient allocation of resources, because of the impossibility to obtain reliable estimates of profitability (Janeway, 2012). Therefore, the financing of technological exploration often needs to be enabled by previous public spending that allows scientific and technological research decoupled from concerns about economic return. Investment in infrastructure and fundamental research are two cases in point.

The need to tolerate the allocative inefficiency inherent in technological exploration points to the necessity of a type of accountability of public spending that allows sacrificing allocative efficiency in view of the systemic benefits of structural change. This leads to considering the political-economic conditions that make it possible to finance technological exploration, and which may or may not be met in different contexts.

4.   Political-economic conditions concerning the final state

The category of 'systemic interest' (Cardinale, 2012, 2013) may be a useful analytical tool for investigating the conditions under which a given political-economic system is able to tolerate spending under fundamental technological uncertainty, and hence outside allocative efficiency. As a general principle, under conditions expressed by the determinant of the matrix of technical coefficients (the Hawkins-Simon conditions), the ability of the system to reproduce itself and produce a surplus – that is, its ability to grow – is compatible with different sectoral proportions (see Schwartz, 1961; Pasinetti, 1977). Therefore, the system could be preserved and grow with different relative weights of sectors. From the political-economic point of view, this means that there is potential for conflict between sectors: a sector might 'want' to grow relative to others, and, within limits, this would not compromise the viability of the system. For instance, let us consider a potential conflict of interest between two sub-sectors within the energy sector, producing energy from hydrocarbons and from renewable sources respectively. Policies aimed at decreasing the production of energy from hydrocarbons would favour the sub-sector that produces energy from renewable sources, by making the latter's output more attractive than before the policy was implemented. However, if the reduction is too wide, too abrupt, or more generally not implemented in a way compatible with conditions concerning the traverse, the fall in energy output could jeopardize the viability of the whole economic system, which could damage the renewable energy sector because of its interdependencies with other sectors. More generally, policies that favour certain sectors at the expense of others benefit the former only so long as the system remains within sectoral proportions that are compatible with its capacity to reproduce itself. Beyond those limits, the crisis of some sectors can also affect and damage other sectors through interdependencies.

The representation of the economy based on sectoral interdependencies thus highlights the possibility of conflict as well as the necessity to keep conflict within a systemically sustainable level – one that guarantees that the system as a whole is not jeopardized.[3] Therefore, each sector has a particular interest in its own survival and expansion, as well as a 'systemic' interest in the preservation of the system to which it belongs, which is itself necessary for its survival. Systemic interest derives from interdependencies and is a generalization of the traditional category of national interest (List, 1885; Morgenthau, 1954; Finnemore, 1996). In particular, systemic interest is a property of any system, be it regional, national or supranational, in which interdependencies are such that each interest group has to consider the preservation of the system in order to effectively pursue its own interest. It is worth reiterating that sectors may well constitute potential rather than manifest interest groups: whilst interests are grounded in the structure of the economic system, not every sector may be aware of them and act accordingly at the political level. As a consequence, it is possible that a system of interdependencies affords a systemic interest but the groups involved do not consider it as such in the construction of their own interest (Cardinale, 2012; Cardinale and Coffman, 2014).

This analysis suggests that the political feasibility of technological exploration outside allocative efficiency depends on the existence of a systemic interest in the public investment that is necessary for technological exploration, and which would in turn allow the system to embark on a trajectory of structural change in general, and a transition between resource bases in particular. This point can be illustrated by comparing the political sustainability of taxation in eighteenth-century Britain and France and the paths of economic development to which it can be connected. In Britain the extremely high levels of taxation were politically sustainable because they were perceived as serving the systemic interest of financing the fiscal-military state, whereas in France they were

---

[3] The political representation of economic interests, and the political conflict to which it gives rise, is a classic theme in political science (e.g. Truman, 1962; Buchanan and Tullock, 1962; Olson, 1965; Rogowski, 1987; Svallfors, 2007). By grounding groups' interests in the system of productive interdependencies, the approach pursued here makes it possible to explain not only political conflict, but also the limits on conflict imposed by the need to keep the system viable (Cardinale, 2015).

not, despite material conditions that might have been even more favourable than in Britain (Cardinale and Coffman, 2014). This also has implications for the kind of political accountability that prevails in different societies. Accountability that is inspired by allocative efficiency alone may hinder the political feasibility of a type of public spending that, whilst not being efficient from the allocative point of view, may still be necessary for structural change and thus potentially efficient in a dynamic sense.

5.   The traverse

In order for the final state outlined in this chapter to be reached, a further set of conditions needs to be analysed – those about the traverse, i.e. the transition between two different states. Economic conditions about the traverse derive from rigidities in the transition between production states. These can be of two types (Scazzieri, 2009). Rigidities of a vertical type are highlighted by studies of production as a sequence of stages of transformation (Smith, [1776] 1976; Lowe, 1976; Hicks, 1973). Such rigidities impose constraints on the time profile of production, and in particular require the 'availability of a sufficient amount of work-in-process materials at the different stages of the same vertically integrated process' (Scazzieri, 2009, p. 115). For example, producing a sufficient amount of energy from wind requires that, at any given period, a certain number of windmills be operational. Hence, energy cannot be produced in sufficient amounts until the mills are produced, which requires the parts to be produced, etc.

Rigidities of a horizontal type are made evident by studies of production as based on interdependencies between sectors (Ricardo, [1817] 1951; Leontief, 1941; Quadrio Curzio, 1996). Such rigidities impose constraints on the proportion between sectors, and more specifically, on 'the size of the capital fund reproduced in each accounting period' (Scazzieri, 2009, p. 115). For example, in order to produce a certain number of windmills, it is required that a certain capacity for the production of windmills be installed.

The case in which non-produced resources are used as inputs introduces the possibility of further rigidities, one of which is the combination of vertical and horizontal rigidities. In fact, residuals in one process can sometimes be used as inputs in other processes, so that vertically integrated subsystems are introduced within horizontal schemes of interdependencies (Quadrio Curzio, 1986). This implies that both vertical rigidities (relative to the availability of work-in-process materials of the 'right' kind at the appropriate stage of production) and horizontal rigidities (relative to the availability of a sufficient capital fund) are present in the transition between resource bases. Another element of potential rigidity in the traverse is suggested by Quadrio Curzio's (1990) distinction between technical and technological progress. The former refers to 'changes that bring about an increase in the physical efficiency of a single technique', whereas the latter indicates 'changes that bring about an increase in the physical efficiency of a compound technology' (Quadrio Curzio and Pellizzari, 1999, p. 208). The distinction suggests that increments in the efficiency of a set of interdependent techniques (a technology) require *structural compatibility* between techniques. Structural compatibility may be seen as imposing the requirement that increases in efficiency of different techniques be compatible with existing or emergent complementarities between techniques. However, it also suggests that technological progress can take place by improving compatibility, independently of efficiency improvements in techniques taken in isolation, for instance through the emergence of new techniques or through variation in proportions between techniques (see also Scazzieri, 2014).

6.   Political-economic conditions concerning the traverse

The political-economic conditions concerning the traverse derive from the interplay of technology, scarcities and rents. In fact, as technologies change, so do scarcities and rents associated with them (Quadrio Curzio, 1986; Quadrio Curzio and Pellizzari, 1999). Given the radical uncertainty concerning the direction of technical progress, uncertainty also surrounds the dynamics of scarcities and rents. This has important implications for how the interests of groups are determined. We can distinguish between 'static' and 'dynamic' implications. The latter derive from fundamental uncertainty concerning the trajectory of the traverse. The difficulty in envisioning the complex paths of scarcities that can emerge from uncertainty surrounding the directions of technological progress makes it problematic for economic groups to ascertain *ex ante* whether a certain policy is in their interest.

The 'static' implications are those that hold even in the absence of fundamental uncertainty. In particular, a given structure of economic interdependencies can give rise to different but equivalent representations of that structure, which highlight different interests (Cardinale, 2012). For example, Pasinetti (1973) shows that a given economy can be represented equivalently as a set of interdependencies between industrial sectors that exchange intermediate goods (a 'horizontal' representation) or as a set of final goods, each of which is produced through a series of interactions between several sectors (a 'vertical' representation). If a given group adopts a horizontal representation of the system to which it belongs, the 'particular' interest becomes salient, because a horizontal representation highlights the different sectors and the possibility of shifting value added from one to another. On the other hand, a vertical representation highlights systemic interest, as it suggests that every final good is produced by the system as a whole, through stages of fabrication that involve several industries. As analytically equivalent representations of the same objective configuration suggest different interests, a given system of interdependencies can give rise to alternative constructions of interests that are different but equally grounded (Cardinale, 2012).

As a result, a given system of technical and material relationships makes possible a set of dynamic paths, and creates the possibility for a set of possible configurations of interests, which are compatible with, but not determined by, technical and material relationships. This suggests the existence of a set of material possibilities, a subset of which is politically feasible *in principle*. In order to understand which dynamic path a given system *actually* embarks on, we need to consider the specific constructions of interests that emerge in a given historical context. Such constructions of interests, and the political decisions to which they give rise, can be seen as 'closing the system', thereby initiating a specific path of structural change among the many that are made possible by technical and material relationships. It is important to emphasize that the activation of a specific path is neither structurally determined, nor voluntaristic. It is not determined because of the multiplicity of constructions that are compatible with a given system of interdependencies. It is not voluntaristic because the interest of a group is developed within a given technical and material configuration, which *orients* the construction of interests along directions that are compatible with it (Cardinale, 2014). This suggests that a promising route for investigating the ways in which 'the system is closed' in particular historical contexts may be the co-determination of material relationships and the construction of groups' interests (Cardinale, 2013; see Bourdieu, 2000). An historical case study that could provide valuable insights in this direction is the comparison between eighteenth-century Britain and France. In fact, in Britain the construction of groups' interests took into account the systemic interest of financing the fiscal-military state, whereas in France it did not, despite material conditions that were arguably more favourable than in Britain (Coffman, 2013; Cardinale and Coffman, 2014).

The interplay of static and dynamic elements adds a new dimension to the discussion of systemic interest. In fact, not only is perception of systemic interest necessary for the final state to be desirable to sufficiently influential coalitions of groups – it is also necessary for each group to tolerate the uncertainty about who will be favoured along the traverse. In other words, perception of the systemic desirability – or inevitability – of the shift to a different resource base needs to overcome the uncertainty that concerns the outcome of the traverse for specific groups.

7.   Concluding remarks

This chapter has outlined a framework for analysing the transition from a resource base to another, distinguishing between economic and political-economic

Table 12.1 *Conditions for the transition between resource bases*

Conditions	Economic	Political-economic
Concerning the final state	Technological exploration requires tolerance of allocative inefficiency	Systemic interest in the creation of conditions for structural change
Concerning the traverse	Requirements about the time profile of production, the proportions between sectors, and the structural compatibility of techniques	Systemic interest that allows tolerance of uncertainty concerning which groups will benefit from the dynamics of rents

conditions, and in turn between conditions concerning the final state and the traverse. The framework has been illustrated with respect to the transition to large-scale deployment of renewable energy, although it can be applied to other transitions between resource bases. Four orders of conditions have been found, which are summarized in Table 12.1.

The framework suggests that, at any given moment, political-economic relationships are grounded in, but not determined by, technical and material relationships. The construction of groups' interests generates an interplay of conflict and cooperation, which in turn leads to political decisions that modify technical and material relationships in a way that may or may not be conducive to structural change and economic dynamics.

This chapter thus suggests that a fundamental element explaining the differences in structural dynamics across countries may lie in the configuration of political-economic systems, which may or may not afford the systemic interest that allows the public investment underlying technological exploration and embarking the traverse.

In conclusion, the framework outlined in this chapter points to the groundedness of the construction of groups' interests in the very system of interdependencies that those groups' choices aim at modifying. It thus opens up to the study of the interaction between structures and decisions in the transition between resource bases, as well as in processes of structural change more generally.

REFERENCES

Bourdieu, P. (2000) *Pascalian Meditations*, Cambridge: Polity Press.
Buchanan, J. M., and Tullock, G. (1962) *The Calculus of Consent, Logical Foundations of Constitutional Democracy*, Ann Arbor: University of Michigan Press.
Candela, G. (1975) 'Il modello economico di François Quesnay', *Giornale degli Economisti ed Annali di Economia*, 34 N. S., pp. 69–94.

Cardinale, I. (2012) *The Political Economy of Circular Interdependencies and Vertical Integration. Opening the Black Box of 'National Interest'*, Rochester, NY: Social Science Research Network.

(2013) *Structural Political Economy and the Economics of Institutions*, Rochester, NY: Social Science Research Network.

(2014) 'Beyond Constraining and Enabling: On How Social Structure Orients Action in Organisations,' unpublished PhD thesis, University of Cambridge.

(2015) 'Towards a Structural Political Economy of the Eurozone', in I. Cardinale, D. Coffman and R. Scazzieri (eds.) *The Political Economy of the Eurozone*, Cambridge, Cambridge University Press, forthcoming.

Cardinale, I., and Scazzieri, R. (2013) *Technology and Production: The Economic Analysis of Tasks, Functions, and Material Structures*, Working Paper, University of Cambridge.

Cardinale, I., and Coffman, D. (2014) 'Economic Interdependencies and Political Conflict: Towards a Structural and Historical Approach to Taxation', *Economia Politica. Journal of Analytical and Institutional Economics*, 31:3 pp. 277–300.

Cardinale, I., and Landesmann, M. A. (2015) 'Tradables, Non-Tradables and the Political Economy of the Eurozone', in I. Cardinale, D. Coffman and R. Scazzieri (eds.) *The Political Economy of the Eurozone*, Cambridge, Cambridge University Press, forthcoming.

Cardinale, I., and Runde, J. (2014) *Technology and Human Practices: Beyond Enabling and Constraining*, Working Paper, University of Cambridge.

Cardinale, I., and Scazzieri, R. (2014) 'The Political Economy of the Eurozone: Crisis and Prospects', *Rendiconti dell'Accademia delle Scienze dell'Istituto di Bologna, Classe di Scienze Morali*, pp. 207–16.

Coffman, D. (2013) *Excise Taxation and the Origins of Public Debt*, Basingstoke: Palgrave Macmillan.

Dosi, G. (1982) 'Technological Paradigms and Technological Trajectories. A Suggested Interpretation of the Determinants and Directions of Technical Change', *Research Policy*, 11, pp. 147–62.

Dosi, G., and Nelson, R. R. (2010) 'Technical Change and Industrial Dynamics as Evolutionary Processes', in B. H. Halland and N. Rosenberg (eds.) *Handbook of the Economics of Innovation*, vol. I, Burlington, Mass.: Academic Press, pp. 51–128.

Finnemore, M. (1996) *National Interests in International Society*, Ithaca, NY: Cornell University Press.

Georgescu-Roegen, N. (1969) 'Process in Farming versus Process in Manufacturing: A Problem of Balanced Development', in G. U. Papi and C. Nunn (eds.) *Economic Problems of Agriculture in Industrial Societies*, New York: St Martin's Press, pp. 497–528.

Grätzel, M. (2013) 'Energy Beyond Oil', Paper Presented at the Second Edition of Interlab, University of Lugano, Switzerland, 18 October 2013.

Hicks, J. (1973) *Capital and Time: A Neo-Austrian Theory*, Oxford: Clarendon Press.

Hishiyama, I. (1960) 'The Tableau Economique of Quesnay', *Kyoto University Economic Review*, 30.1, pp. 1–46.

Janeway, W. H. (2012) *Doing Capitalism in the Innovation Economy: Markets, Speculation and the State*, Cambridge: Cambridge University Press.

Jevons, W. S. (1865) *The Coal Question: An Inquiry Concerning the Progress of the Nation, and the Probable Exhaustion of Our Coal-Mines*, London: Macmillan.

Leontief, W. W. (1941) *The Structure of American Economy, 1919–1929; an Empirical Application of Equilibrium Analysis*, Cambridge, Mass.: Harvard University Press.

(1991) 'The Economy as a Circular Flow', *Structural Change and Economic Dynamics*, 2.1, pp. 181–212.

List, F. (1885) *The National System of Political Economy*. London: Longmans, Green.

Lowe, A. (1976) *The Path of Economic Growth*. Cambridge; New York: Cambridge University Press.

Morgenthau, H. J. (1954) *Politics among Nations: The Struggle for Power and Peace*. New York: Knopf.

von Neumann, J. (1945) 'A Model of General Economic Equilibrium', *The Review of Economic Studies*, 13.1, pp. 1–9.

Olson, M. (1965) *The Logic of Collective Action*. Cambridge, Mass.: Harvard University Press.

Pasinetti, L. L. (1973) 'The Notion of Vertical Integration in Economic Analysis', *Metroeconomica*, 25.1, pp. 1–29.

(1977) *Lectures on the Theory of Production*. New York: Columbia University Press.

(2002) 'Il Tableau Économique e le economie moderne', Paper Presented at Fondazione Mattioli, Milan, 9 October 2002.

Phillips, A. (1955) 'The Tableau Économique as a Simple Leontief Model', *The Quarterly Journal of Economics*, 69.1, pp. 137–44.

Pich, M. T., Loch, C. H., and de Meyer, A. (2002) 'On Uncertainty, Ambiguity, and Complexity in Project Management', *Management Science*, 48.8, pp. 1008–23.

Quadrio Curzio, A. (1967) *Rendita e distribuzione in un modello economico plurisettoriale*. Milan: Giuffrè.

(1975) *Accumulazione del capitale e rendita*. Bologna: Il Mulino.

(1980) 'Rent, Income Distribution and Orders of Efficiency and Rentability', in L. L. Pasinetti (ed.), *Essays on the Theory of Joint Production*, London: Macmillan, pp. 219–40.

(1986) 'Technological Scarcity: An Essay on Production and Structural Change', in M. Baranzini and R. Scazzieri (eds.) *Foundations of Economics: Structures of Inquiry and Economic Theory*, Oxford and New York: B. Blackwell, pp. 311–38.

(1987) 'Land Rent', in J. Eatwell, M. Milgate and P. Newman (eds.) *The New Palgrave. A Dictionary of Economics*, London: Macmillan, pp. 118–21.

(1990) 'Rent, Distribution and Economic Structure: A Collection of Essays', *Quaderni IDSE*, 1, Milan: CNR.

(1996) 'Production and Efficiency with Global Technologies', in M. A. Landesmann and R. Scazzieri (eds.) *Production and Economic Dynamics*, Cambridge: Cambridge University Press, pp. 105–39.

Quadrio Curzio, A. and Pellizzari, F. (1999) *Rent, Resources, Technologies*. Berlin and New York: Springer.

Quesnay, F. ([1759] 1972) *Quesnay's Tableau Économique*, Marguerite Kuczynski and Ronald L Meek (eds.), London: Macmillian; New York: A.M. Kelley, for the Royal Economic Society and the American Economic Association.

Ricardo, D. ([1817] 1951) *On the Principles of Political Economy and Taxation, vol. I of The Works and Correspondence of David Ricardo*, P. Sraffa ed. with the collaboration of M. H. Dobb, Cambridge: Cambridge University Press.

Rogowski, R. (1987) 'Political Cleavages and Changing Exposure to Trade', *The American Political Science Review*, 81.4, pp. 1121–37.

Samuelson, P. (1991) 'Leontief's "The Economy as a Circular Flow": An Introduction', *Structural Change and Economic Dynamics*, 2.1, pp. 177–9.

Scazzieri, R. (1993) *A Theory of Production: Tasks, Processes, and Technical Practices*, Oxford: Clarendon Press.

(2009) 'Traverse Analysis and Methods of Economic Dynamics', in H. Hagemann and R. Scazzieri (eds.) *Capital, Time and Transitional Dynamics*, London and New York: Routledge, pp. 96–132.

(2014) 'A Structural Theory of Increasing Returns', *Structural Change and Economic Dynamics*: 29.2, pp. 75–88.

Schwartz, J. T. (1961) *Lectures on the Mathematical Method in Analytical Economics*, New York: Gordon and Breach.

Smith, A. ([1776] 1976) *An Inquiry into the Nature and Causes of the Wealth of Nations*, Oxford: Clarendon Press; New York: Oxford University Press.

Sraffa, P. (1960) *Production of Commodities by Means of Commodities; Prelude to a Critique of Economic Theory*, Cambridge: Cambridge University Press.

Svallfors, S. (2007) *The Political Sociology of the Welfare State: Institutions, Social Cleavages, and Orientations*, Stanford: Stanford University Press.

Truman, D. B. (1962) *The Governmental Process: Political Interests and Public Opinion*, New York: Knopf.

Vaggi, G. (1987) *The Economics of François Quesnay*, London: Macmillan.

(2008) 'Quesnay, François (1694–1774)', in S. N. Durlauf and L. E. Blume (eds.) *The New Palgrave Dictionary of Economics*, Basingstoke: Nature Publishing Group, pp. 816–26.

Wrigley, E. (1962) 'The Supply of Raw Materials in the Industrial Revolution', *Economic History Review*, 15.1, pp. 1–16.

(2010) *Energy and the English Industrial Revolution*, Cambridge: Cambridge University Press.

Part III

Resources, institutions and social structures

13 Monetary analysis, financial innovation and institutions before the Industrial Revolution: a paradigm case

Lilia Costabile

We hope nevertheless that everyone will learn for the future the lesson that the financial economy and the real economy should never be split to a degree that the former could be perceived by the public as merely a «paper economy» or worse as a «waste paper economy». . . . These effects call for the role of Institutions which must never be neglected, in order to have well-functioning markets.

(Quadrio Curzio, 2008, p. 370)

1. Introduction

The assumption that there is a necessary connection between the real and the monetary/financial sides of the economy is a central theme of this volume. These two sides cannot be divorced, because their coordination and harmonization is a necessary condition for a well-functioning economic system. A 'paper economy', and the monetary/financial institutions that support it, can facilitate economic transactions because liquidity is a necessary ingredient of economic activity in a monetary economy. Nevertheless, when the virtuous circle between the monetary/financial institutions and the real economy is disrupted, the stage is set for economic disorder, with consequences that may go beyond the strictly economic realm and impact on the political and social spheres of human activity. The risks of such disruptions are so great that appropriate institutions should be devised in order to prevent their occurrence, thereby promoting well-functioning markets and healthy economic relations.

The integration of the monetary sector into the analytical framework of structural analysis has a double rationale. Firstly, structural analysis includes, and indeed requires, an understanding of how different sectors interact in shaping the evolution of the whole economy. Now, the financial/monetary sector has been an integral, important part of the economy since the Middle Ages. Consequently, this analytical framework would be incomplete without the analysis of the interactions between the real and the monetary/financial sectors of economic systems. In particular, one aspect of structural economic dynamics concerns technical progress. Financial innovation is the form that

213

technical progress takes in the monetary/financial sector of the economy. One of the earliest, most striking examples of financial innovation was the passage from a purely metallic money to fiduciary money at the initiative of appropriate institutions, and is the subject matter of the present chapter.

Secondly, one of the founding principles of structural analysis is the 'principle of antagonism-coexistence and synergy between scarcity and reproducibility' (Quadrio Curzio, 1986, p. 313). Antagonism can be turned into synergy by appropriate institutional development. A paradigmatic example of this principle is the antagonism-coexistence between the scarcity of the precious metals and the reproducibility of paper money. This chapter illustrates the aforementioned principle through the analysis of how the 'scarcity of (metallic) money' plagued economic systems in the early stages of modern economic growth, and how institutional development in this field provided a solution via the invention of paper money, which is easily reproducible.

The first aim of this chapter is to clarify what the coordination and harmonization between the real and the monetary/financial sides of the economy means, by elucidating the physiological role of liquidity in the economic mechanism, and the causes and consequences of a 'scarcity of money', or, in modern parlance, of liquidity constraints. The problem is illustrated by means of the historical example of the Kingdom of Naples between the second half of the sixteenth century and the first decades of the seventeenth century. At that time, there was intense debate among Neapolitan economists concerning the causes of severe money shortage in the Kingdom, and the devices that could be implemented in order to remedy it. This example helps clarify how economies struggled with liquidity constraints at a time when metallic money was the dominant medium of exchange.

The second, related, aim of this chapter is to inquire into the ingenious remedies devised by economic agents in order to transform money scarcity into 'abundance'. The solution, in the historical example discussed here, was to invent an institution in charge of the creation of liquidity: the 'public banks of Naples', which, among the first in the Western world (De Rosa, 1955, 1958, 1987, 2002a, b), initiated the circulation of fiduciary money in the form of paper notes. These notes were nothing but the banks' 'promises' to honour their debts by paying the precious metals on demand. They were one of the greatest examples of financial innovation in economic history.

However, financial innovation is always a mixed blessing. The solution found in Naples was an effective remedy for the liquidity constraints then biting on the national economy and restraining economic transactions. Nevertheless, it opened the way to a system of interactions between the real and the financial sides of the economy more complex and, in some way, more dangerous than had existed before. The circulation of paper money was based on 'public faith', and one of the issues in this new, complex interaction was the 'convertibility' of paper money into the metallic money to which debtors' 'promises to pay' referred. A betrayal of public faith thus became possible, via 'inconvertibility'. While in the historical conditions of the time disciplining factors restrained debtors' ability to renege on their own debts, the seeds had been sown for more serious convertibility problems in the future. This is illustrative of the principle that in the dynamics of economic systems the interactions between the real and the monetary/financial side of the economy never reach a standstill. Financial innovations may provide helpful solutions for the growth of the economy, but they often do so by imposing new instability costs, which then require new solutions, in an endless chain.

The chapter is structured as follows. Sections 2, 3 and 4 are devoted to three protagonists of the debate on the money shortage in the Neapolitan Kingdom in the first decades of the seventeenth century: Antonio Serra, Marc'Antonio De Santis and Giovan Donato Turbolo. In order to shed further light on the historical context, Section 5 adds another cause of the money shortage to those analysed by these three economists. Section 6 explains how the 'invention' of paper money as a substitute for metallic money in domestic circulation solved the problem. The process started when the 'public banks of Naples', owned by well-respected charities based in the Kingdom's capital, started to produce bank money; and, as we will see, it was reinforced when the government effectively transformed this private paper money into fiat money. Section 7 concludes by suggesting that the issue of convertibility raised by the invention of paper money was to become a more serious problem in the twentieth century, when the fiduciary circulation was extended to the world economy, and a paper currency became the international means of payments.

2.   Antonio Serra

At the beginning of the seventeenth century, Neapolitan economists were investigating the causes of the money shortage in the Kingdom and were warning the authorities against its consequences. In particular, a lively debate flared up among three of them: Antonio Serra, Marc'Antonio De Santis and Giovan Donato Turbolo.

It would be a mistake to interpret these debates as merely reflecting their protagonists' 'bullionist' fancies. Their preoccupation with the scarcity of money did not reflect a confusion between money and wealth, nor did it imply their unduly concentration on the 'sphere of exchange' rather than production. The rationale for their concern is now well-established in the literature: in a monetary economy the smooth operation of production activities requires that liquidity constraints do not bite. The underlying reason is that no commodity other than those performing the role of money is accepted in this economy as means of payments. Whilst in barter economies, 'any commodity can be offered directly in exchange for any other commodity', in monetary economies 'transactions necessarily involve intermediate monetary transactions' (Clower, 1967, pp. 4–5), which means that would-be buyers need to offer money – not goods, services or assets – for the goods, labour services, capital goods and assets that they wish to purchase.

It is for this reason that the relationships between money and the 'real economy' need to be investigated. And it is not by chance that Keynes – whose theoretical work may be interpreted as a far-reaching attempt to differentiate monetary economies from barter economies – proposed a rehabilitation of mercantilist economic writers. Put briefly, he did not accept the idea 'that the mercantilist argument is based, from start to finish, on an intellectual confusion', and he was convinced that there was an 'element of scientific truth in mercantilist doctrine' (Keynes, [1936] 1973a, ch. 23, pp. 334–5). In similar vein, in what follows I investigate the element of scientific truth in, and also the historical truth underlying, the arguments put forward by the Neapolitan economists at the beginning of the seventeenth century in order to explain the scarcity of money and their denouncement of it, their diagnoses, and their policy recommendations.

Let us start with Antonio Serra from Cosenza. This mysterious writer, while imprisoned in the Vicaria jail of Naples,[1] produced his book *A short treatise on the causes that can make kingdoms abound in gold and silver even in the absence of mines (Breve trattato delle cause che possono far abbondare li regni d'oro e d'argento dove non sono miniere)* (Serra, [1613] 1973).[2] His entire book was an answer to the question of how to explain, and remedy, the scarcity of money that plagued the Kingdom, which was then part of the Spanish Empire's system of Viceroyalties.[3]

Serra's main point was that the problems of the Kingdom of Naples were rooted in the sectorial composition of its production structure, or, as we would say today, in its product-mix. In other words, what was to blame was the Kingdom's unfavourable economic specialization, which determined an efflux of the precious metals towards its commercial partners.

With regard to the production of tangible goods, Serra thought that the main cause of the Kingdom's disadvantage in international trade was its

---

[1] Did he take part in Tommaso Campanella's conspiracy to establish a republic in Calabria, then part of the Spanish-dominated Kingdom of Naples? Or was he, less heroically, merely guilty of counterfeiting? The doubt has not been resolved, and probably never will be: many regard his involvement in the revolt led by Campanella as a myth, while it is not known whether or not the Antonio Serra jailed on indictment for counterfeiting was 'our' writer.

[2] Rosselli (1995, 2000) and Zagari (1995) are interesting presentations of the debate between Serra and De Santis. An English translation of Serra's work has now been published with the title *A Short Treatise on the Wealth and Poverty of Nations* (Serra, 2011). The book is edited by Sophus Reinert, who has written a long and well-documented introduction.

[3] The Spanish domination of Southern Italy lasted for two centuries, from 1502 to 1707.

underdeveloped manufacturing sector, a problem made more serious by the scant entrepreneurship of its inhabitants (Serra, [1613] 1973, pp. 172–3). By way of comparison, he referred to the abundance of manufacturing activities as the main advantage of cities like Venice. In order to investigate this problem, Serra produced one of the earliest examples of structural analysis, centred on the structural characteristics of manufactures as opposed to agricultural production. First of all, the manufacturing industry was able to multiply its products 'with proportionally less expense' (Serra, [1613] 1973, p. 172), a point that many commentators (e.g. Schumpeter, 1954, p. 258; Reinert, editing Serra, 2011; Thirlwall, 2011, pp. 6–7) have interpreted as an early formulation of the law of increasing returns to scale, as opposed to decreasing returns in agriculture. Secondly, industry yielded more reliable profits than agriculture, because of both its independence from the weather and the less perishable nature of its products. This analysis of the characteristics of manufactures as opposed to agriculture, as well as to mining, sets Serra apart from contemporary writers as a theorist of structural analysis, because he introduced the principle of antagonism/coexistence between reproducibility (of manufactured goods) and the scarcity of natural resources as the main factor in the process of economic dynamics.

The Kingdom's unfavourable product specialization was the main reason for its disadvantage in international trade. Serra noticed that the Kingdom was also at a disadvantage in the service sector because, owing to its 'very bad' peripheral geographic position (as the hand of the Italian peninsula's 'arm' projecting into the Mediterranean sea), it could not become a site of *trafico grande* (great trade), i.e. develop as a hub of international trade as Venice had done, nor could it give rise to a transport industry (Serra, [1613] 1973), pp.174–5). In addition, Serra also acknowledged the role of the Kingdom's external debt, which explained both the (high) interests paid on the public debt instruments held by foreigners and the repatriation of profits on foreign investment.

As a consequence of the cumulative operation of these disadvantages, he argued, the monetary flows out of the kingdom exceeded monetary inflows. This explained the drain on the country's stock of metallic money.

A very interesting aspect of Serra's approach was the importance that it gave to institutions, to the point that they played a more important function in the efficient functioning of the economic system than the other 'accidents', such as the abundance of manufactures, 'great trade', and the quality of people. Good government was 'the most powerful of all in making the kingdom abound in gold and silver, for it may be described as the efficient cause and superior agent of all the other accidents' (ibid., p.176). He praised republican governments because of the institutional continuity that they provided. Kings lasted for fifty years at most, and the kingdom's policies and strategic objectives would then change with the advent of the new monarch. In republics, by contrast, the coexistence of old and new generations in the governing institutions, such as the Senate, ensured strategic continuity and – simultaneously – the constant rejuvenation of the governing body. Venice was again the example to admire, and possibly to imitate (ibid., pp. 176–7).

We may sum up Serra's position by saying that good institutional design is the main foundation of a healthy economic system: good government would create the conditions and provide the incentives for developing a modern manufacturing sector and, through this channel, generate a positive external account, which in its turn would make the kingdom rich in silver and gold 'even in the absence of mines'.

3.   Marc'Antonio De Santis

Serra presented his book as a confutation of the arguments put forth by Marc'Antonio De Santis's two *Discourses*, published in 1605. He thought it still useful to comment upon, and strongly criticize, those arguments although eight years had already passed since their publication, and in spite of the failure of De Santis's proposed law, or *Prammatica*, which had been enacted but then soon repealed.

Serra's polemical attitude, coupled with the unconditional support given to him by Ferdinando Galiani against De Santis more than 150 years later in his rather sweeping comments on the controversy between the two men (Galiani, 1780, p. 340),[4] determined the unfortunate undervaluation of De Santis's contribution to economic analysis. A more dispassionate analysis shows that, notwithstanding the failure of his policy recommendations, there was a grain of truth in his analysis as well.

De Santis had proposed completely different views than Serra's on the origins of the outflow of the precious metals from the Kingdom. He did not consider the roots of the problem as originating in the sectorial composition of production on the real side of the economy, which he regarded as quite competitive in the international context. The agricultural specialization, he argued, only meant that foreigners could not do without imports from the Kingdom, which were, so to speak, 'necessary goods', while, on the contrary, the domestic citizens could do without at least some of the imported goods. This advantage was so strong, he maintained, that the country could have easily confronted an appreciation of its currency and still keep its privileged position in international trade. De Santis, like Serra and Turbolo (see next section), was aware of the repatriation of rents and profits earned by foreigners

---

[4] Galiani admitted that he had relied upon Serra's renderings of De Santis's *Discourses*, the original of which he had been unable to find.

on their investments in the Kingdom, which weakened the latter's position. Nevertheless, all things considered, his basic argument was that, even so, there was no outflow of metallic money to be expected from these items in the Kingdom's international transactions.

The culprit, he argued, was the structure of the financial market, which favoured the continuing export of the precious metals. In this context, differently from Serra, he interpreted the liquidity constraint impairing the productive capacity of the Kingdom as a consequence of the malfunctioning of the monetary/financial markets, rather than as a consequence of its 'product mix'.

Let us consider De Santis's analysis of financial markets in detail. He explained the money outflow as a consequence of the co-existence of two distinct means of international payments, namely silver coins and 'letters of exchange'. The latter introduced a larger wedge between the equilibrium and the market exchange rates than would be the case in their absence. An incentive was thus created to send silver coins out of the country, both to finance commercial transactions and to speculate on that wedge.

His starting point was the definition of the equilibrium level of the exchange rate as that level at which the flow of precious metals into and out of the country would come to a full stop (De Santis, 1605a [1973], p. 132). According to De Santis, to establish this equilibrium exchange rate was a very important practical objective, because at this level there would be no drain on the country's stock of silver coins, and the liquidity constraint impairing the Kingdom's production activities would be relaxed.

How, then, would this equilibrium level of the exchange rate be determined? De Santis referred to the metallic content of currencies as the basis for its determination (ibid., pp. 138–9). In other words, the equilibrium level of the bilateral exchange rate was determined by the mint par between any two national currencies. The legal par corresponded to the mint par under some reasonable simplifying assumptions.[5] Thus, at the theoretical level, the equilibrium exchange rate was determined by the demand for and supply of metallic money, which would bring it into equality with the underlying mint parity[6].

De Santis was well aware of the institutional settings under which financial markets operated at this time. He explained that the actual process whereby exchange rates were set took place in the 'Piacenza fair'. Here a restricted number of well-respected merchants fixed the exchange rates, having taken

---

[5] Firstly, an adjustment should be made for differences in the metal content of the different coins, as determined by seignorage (Rosselli, 1995; 2000). Secondly, transport costs of the precious metals should be added to the metal par.

[6] As we know from later theoretical developments, the equilibrating system would work though 'arbitrage'. This would remedy any discrepancy between the exchange rate and the mint par between any two currencies.

into account the conditions of demand of, and supply for, all the currencies in the system. These exchange rates then served as the basis for individual bargaining in local markets.

De Santis described the fixing process in Piacenza as 'fair', because the merchants in charge usually 'took the rule' from the markets, by which he meant that they respected the actual conditions of demand and supply (ibid., p. 123). Thus, he thought the Piacenza fair was the place were the *equilibrium* exchange rates between national currencies were established, as if the wise merchants supervising the fixing process were acting like a sort of Walrasian auctioneer. The problems of the Neapolitan economy, then, did not originate in the Piacenza fair, but in the decentralized markets for 'letters of exchange', where the market exchange rates were determined on the basis of local bargaining.

Letters of exchange were the means of payments that local merchants could use to settle their international accounts as an alternative to cash payments. By buying a letter of exchange in Naples in exchange for the local currency (the silver carlino, or its multiple, the ducat), a Neapolitan merchant would be entitled to a given amount of the foreign currency in the foreign country (e.g. florins in Florence) where he had to make international payments.

In Naples the sellers of letters of exchange, whom De Santis called '*negotianti*', were very few. Consequently, as it happens in oligopolistic markets, they were able to manipulate the price of these letters through collusive practices. And it was obviously in their collective interest to set the price of these letters (the 'price of the exchange') as high as possible; or, to put it the other way around, it was in their interest to quote the local currency at the lowest possible level. Thus, the market power of these *negotianti* determined a systematically high price of the exchange and, accordingly, a systematically depreciated carlino.

This systematic depreciation, De Santis thought, was the cause of the continuous outflow of silver coins plaguing the Kingdom of Naples. This happened because the 'price signals', as we would call them today, worked in an unfavourable direction: firstly, for Neapolitan importers of foreign goods, sending cash abroad was more convenient than buying letters of exchange at an overpriced exchange rate. Secondly, it was convenient for foreigners to make their payments into the Kingdom by means of cheap letters of exchange, rather than more expensive carlinos. Consequently, they sent pieces of paper, rather than silver coins. Finally, speculators, expecting a further depreciation of the carlino, sent cash out of the Kingdom in order to repatriate it later at a profit.

As a consequence of his diagnosis, De Santis refused to think of the exchange rate as a price set by the forces of demand and supply in a competitive market. Because the market for letters of exchange was vitiated by an oligopolistic element on its supply side, he proposed that the exchange rate be administered via legislation, rather than left prey to manipulation by the rapacious *negotianti*. This was his proposed remedy for stopping the silver efflux and solving the 'scarcity of money' problem in the nation.

A few remarks may be useful to understand De Santis's point in comparison to Serra's position. Serra, as we have seen, considered structural analysis as limited to the real side of the economy, and therefore concentrated on the sectorial imbalances between manufacturing production and agriculture. In this field, he reached very high theoretical standards, unequalled at his time. But De Santis, too, was making a very interesting point: even an otherwise healthy economic system (as he, for right or wrong, regarded the Kingdom's economy to be on its real side) can be disrupted by a faulty financial structure. Because of lack of competition in the financial sector, the price to be paid by local traders for the services of financial intermediation was higher than their cost. Consequently, the *negotianti* earned rents, resulting in an exchange rate different from its equilibrium level. These rents weighted heavily on the national economy, paradoxically turning its competitive advantage in production into a continuing drain on its monetary base.

Thus, De Santis's contribution was to show that the structure of financial markets interacts with the real side of the economy in determining the overall economic performance of countries. Although De Santis's analysis was inspired more by his practical preoccupations as a merchant than by purely theoretical motivations, his investigation of the role of financial markets as an integral part of the economic process marks an important step forward in economic analysis.

4.   Giovan Donato Turbolo

Yet another interpretation was proposed in a series of *Discourses* written between 1616 and 1629 by Giovan Donato Turbolo, head officer (*gran maestro*) of the Royal Mint in Naples. Firstly, Turbolo was well aware of the role of money as a means of payments, and the consequent need for a monetary circulation adequate to the needs of domestic trade: 'very important for the public and for contracts in the Kingdom is the quantity of coins, which facilitates trade and the collection of revenues by both the King and private individuals' (Turbolo, 1629, p. 320: this sentence is part of a speech originally given in 1619).[7]

---

[7] '... importa molto al pubblico e alla contrattazione del regno la quantità di monete, la quale facilita li negozj e l'esazione dell'entrate sì regie come de' particulari'. In 1629 Turbolo published in book form a collection of speeches given on various occasions between 1619 and 1629.

Secondly, like Serra, he was convinced that the drain on the country's silver stock was determined by both the high volume of imports and the huge amount of interests and rents to be paid abroad (Turbolo, 1616, p. 290): in 1619, he estimated the Kingdom's annual deficit at two million ducats (Turbolo, 1629, p. 354). Given this large external deficit, it was no wonder that the national currency was depreciating; and because there was no reason to expect a reversal in the current situation, it could not but undergo further depreciation in the future. This depreciation was 'unavoidable'. However, contrary to De Santis, Turbolo thought that a depreciated currency was favourable to the balance of payments, for two reasons.

First, a weak currency stimulated exports, as the example of the merchant Stefano Saluzzo from Genoa had clearly shown: at an exchange rate set at 170, he had exported from the Kingdom clothes and merchandises for more than 200,000 ducats in that year 1619, with great advantage for the State, thanks to the duties paid at customs. And Saluzzo certainly would not have been able to do that at an exchange rate of 160 (Turbolo, 1629, p. 313).

Second, because rents and interests were now paid out in a devalued currency, the real value of the service of the country's external debt was reduced. And if foreign debtors objected to this, they should be reminded that they had better 'maintain their debtors', as the Kingdom was declining and in need of help (Turbolo, 1629, pp. 304–5).

Turbolo's analysis, although not developed in details, is perhaps the clearest of the three reviewed thus far: if you cannot avoid the deficit, then let your currency depreciate, thus bringing some relief via both increased exports and the reduced burden of the external debt. After all, this recipe is still followed today by important nations, such as the United States, a country indebted in its own currency. However, in a system of international payments based upon metallic money, the situation was more complicated than in today's 'paper' system, because a persistent deficit would produce a continuous drain on the country's silver stock. And this was in fact the problem with the Kingdom's money stock.

Turbolo had a diagnosis for the drain and a remedy for it. The problem, he argued, derived from the high silver content of the national currency, which had not been adjusted to the rise in the market exchange rate.[8] Because silver for the coinage was imported, the price paid by Neapolitans to buy silver abroad had been rising with the market exchange rate. However, the silver content of the Neapolitan coins had remained unchanged. Thus, when the Neapolitan mint bought a given weight of silver abroad at a market rate of, say, 170 *carlini*, and then melted it into coins, that weight of silver

---

[8] Turbolo also informs us that the basis for conversion of silver coins into gold scutes was 1 ounce (22 carats) of gold = 1 *libbra* of silver for *carlini*.

was worth only 130 Neapolitan *carlini*. 'Thus I have seen silver bought and coined at a lower price than it had cost ... and because of this abuse more than 400,000 ducats have been lost' (Turbolo, 1629, p.31). That is where the outflow of silver from the country originated. The nation had been willing to suffer the loss by keeping its money 'good' – that is, better than the currencies of the foreign countries – because it would have been dishonourable to devalue its silver coin. But reducing the silver content of the national currency was the only remedy by which the silver outflow could be curbed. Thus, Turbolo's was an early argument for debasement or 'raising the coin' (*alzamento*), as it came to be called in the literature.

The difference between Turbolo's position and those of his fellow economists, Serra and De Santis, can now be clearly seen. For Serra, there was still hope of turning the current account deficit into a surplus by adopting measures acting on the real side of the economy (education, industrial investments, good government, etc.). But, differently from Turbolo, he did not contemplate the positive effects of a currency depreciation on exports. De Santis, by contrast, proposed legislative intervention on the financial side of the economy, via realignment of the market exchange rate with the underlying mint par, in order to cut financial rents and curb speculation, which he considered the main causes of the drain on silver reserves. Turbolo's recipe was also monetary in nature. But his remedy reflected his more pessimistic diagnosis: currency depreciation was so deeply rooted in the weaknesses of the national economy, and in the burdens imposed upon it by foreign economic domination, that the only remedy was to accept that depreciation and bring the mint parity into line with the market parity, which was the reverse of what De Santis had proposed.

5.   Spanish fiscalism

Our three authors (perhaps for reasons of prudence) did not comment on a fourth cause of the continuous silver outflow. To a large extent, the scarcity of money was due to Spanish fiscal policy, which in its turn was necessitated by the financial needs of the empire, particularly to finance the wars in which Spain was involved: against the French, against Algeria and Tunisia, against pirates, etc. In order to meet these needs, Spain imposed harsh taxes on the Kingdom. Between ordinary and extraordinary taxes, millions of ducats left the country between 1520 and 1647 (De Rosa, 1987, chs. 1 and 2).

Moreover, in order to raise the money to be sent to Spain as taxes and 'donations', the Neapolitan government was forced to sell the sources of public income (*entrate*)[9] to foreigners (Venetians, Florentines, Genoese, and

---

[9] By selling these sources, the government earned the present value of the expected tax revenues, discounted at the current interest rate (De Rosa, 1987, pp. 14–5).

the Roman Church, which also extracted ecclesiastical rents from the Kingdom), thus generating a further drain on domestic money in the form of interest and rent payments abroad, as denounced by our three writers. These historical circumstances explain why, in the words of a modern writer, the crisis in the Kingdom 'was complex and difficult, and certainly not endogenous' (De Rosa, 1987, p. 102).

Thus we have four alternative accounts of the scarcity of money in the Neapolitan Kingdom: Serra's 'real' interpretation was in opposition to the one put forward by De Santis, which blamed financial rents and speculation. Turbolo combined real and financial analysis in his diagnosis, and proposed a remedy consisting in a change in the legal parity. Moreover, the 'fiscal' interpretation has been borne out by the historical facts. My aim here is not to ascertain whether one explanation is better than the others; nor the extent to which they may be regarded as complementary rather than alternative (the fiscal interpretation, in any case, is certainly not in contrast with any of the others). Rather, my point is that the intense debate just described reflects a money shortage that was a historical fact, rather than the phantom produced by the fevered imaginations of 'Bullionist' writers identifying money with wealth.

Official documents in 1581, 1587, 1590, 1592, 1594, and many years afterwards, complained of a 'great scarcity of cash' (*gran penuria di denari contanti*), and they also recorded that the silver coins exiting the country were melted at the mints of foreign cities, such as Ancona, and transformed into foreign coins (De Rosa, 1987, pp. 95–8). To remedy this constant drain, silver had to be imported from Spain and paid for either in cash or by the sale of future government revenues, only to be transformed by the mint into coins that would soon again leave the Kingdom. Yet, as we know, if money is the means of payment, money is needed to finance every economic transaction.

Thus, given the serious shortage of money afflicting the Kingdom for so many years, the internal circulation might be seriously impaired, and economic activity might consequently come to a complete halt. This, however, did not happen. Deflation, on the other hand, was not recorded until many years later, and it was a cure worse than the disease. How, then, were Neapolitans able to circumvent the problem?

6.   The invention of fiduciary money

The Neapolitan solution is a remarkable example of financial innovation, one of the most momentous in monetary/financial history: the invention of a substitute for metallic money, of which such a 'great scarcity' was felt. Starting in the second half of the sixteenth century, both in the capital and in the Kingdom at large, silver coins were substituted by paper money, the ingenious invention of the Neapolitan *banchi pubblici*. From 1570, when the Monte di

Pietà (founded in 1539) started to function as a bank, to 1600, six public banks were established in Naples. The *banchi pubblici* were not state-owned: they were private banks, and we will presently see who their owners were. They were 'public' only in the sense that their operations were guaranteed by the state and were subject to some degree of public regulation.

The public banks introduced paper money in the form of deposit certificates called *fedi di credito*, which is an interesting term, given that *fede* means both 'statement' and 'trust' or 'faith'. Thus, the deposit certificate stated both that the owner had deposited such and such amount of money at the bank, and that he was trustworthy because he was in credit with the bank for that amount. Indeed, the public banks worked as great builders of trust in economic transactions, and more generally in the societal network, because they themselves were trustworthy. One may read this, for instance, in the high praise given to 'our banks' in Galiani's *Della Moneta* ([1780] 1963, pp. 278–80), which extolled the credit enjoyed by 'our banks', the great honesty of their administrators, their 'religious' scrupulosity in saving the coins deposited in their vaults, their ability to 'multiply money', and, last but not least, their readiness to give back cash on demand[10].

It was because of trust that the *fedi di credito* become generally accepted as means of payments, and circulated, from hand to hand, in endless payment rounds. This was a great relief: the larger the trust in paper money and, consequently, the greater the amount of deposit certificates circulating in the system, the less was the amount of metallic money needed for circulation. This happened because the demand for cash was reduced: people brought the deposit certificates received in exchange for their goods back to the banks, in order to register their transactions on the banks' books, but they did not ask to convert these certificates into silver coins. Thus, whilst in theory the *fedi di credito* were convertible on demand, in fact they functioned as such good substitutes for silver money that 'everything is paid for at the Bank with a sign, without cash', as an anonymous Genoese writer remarked in 1605 in his critique of De Santis, who conscientiously reported all the arguments made by his critic (De Santis, 1605b, p. 147).

The public banks of Naples were able to create liquidity because they were trustworthy debtors: their deposit certificates were in fact nothing but statements notifying the amounts of hard cash that the public banks owed their creditors, namely the depositors, and pledging that they would pay cash for

---

[10] Another author interested in the banking system was the Neapolitan economist Carlo Antonio Broggia, who in his books commented on their operations. He was also invited to write down his suggestions for the institution in Mannheim of a bank guaranteed by the prince, based upon the model of the public banks of Naples (see Broggia, 2004, particularly pp. 1–41; also Broggia, 1743, pp. 389–420). On Broggia's monetary thought see also the introduction by Graziani (2004).

that debt on demand. Technically, they functioned as a fractional reserves system, creating liquidity as a multiple of the silver reserves that they held in their coffers, according to the rules of a modern multiplier. At times, the public banks were even recorded as having issued *fedi di credito* without any previous deposits of cash (De Rosa, 1987, p.62), thus anticipating the overdraft system which was to become common only centuries later.

One of the reasons why the public banks were so successful in gaining the trust of the population, and in redistributing this asset (as in fact it was) among their clients, was the support that they received from the state. This support culminated in 1584 when the state, by ordering that all payments to itself must be made with bank deposit certificates, *de facto* transformed this fiduciary money into legal tender. The course of paper money from private money to legal tender was thus completed in two decades.

Another reason for the banks' success was the nature of their owners, which were charities: two pawnbrokers (*Monte di Pietà* and *Monte dei Poveri*); four hospitals (Incurabili, S.Eligio, S. Giacomo e Vittoria, SS Annunziata), and one charity offering shelter to young women in need (*Casa Santa dello Spirito Santo*). They were highly regarded because of their support of the poor and needy, and also because in some instances they promoted scientific research in the health sector (Valerio, 2010). Trust in these charities was so deep that their pledge concerning the full metal backing of paper money was taken at face value, even if the coverage was at best partial, as we saw earlier. Antonio De Santis's words testify to the great respect enjoyed by these charitable institutions in their banking activities. Most importantly, they testify to his full acknowledgement of their role in relaxing the monetary constraint on economic activity. In response to the anonymous Genoese writer previously mentioned, who had suggested that 'payments by writing' may have aggravated the problem of money scarcity by concealing it, De Santis wrote:

Paying in cash what everybody owes to each other is impossible, given that the Kingdom abounds with business transactions; because what is paid into the Banks and withdrawn from them in one day could not be paid in one month in the form of cash; and, since all Banks today belong to charitable institutions, which permit nobody to spend more than the amount for which they are creditors at the Bank, it does not follow what he says that all the payments are made at the stroke of a pen.[11] (De Santis, 1605b, p. 153)

---

[11] 'Il pagar tutti quel che l'un deve a l'altro in danari contanti, essendo il regno copioso di negotij, è pur impossibile; perché quel che si paga, e si riscote in un dì per Banchi, non si faria in un mese di denari contanti; et essendo hoggidì tutti li Banchi di lochi pij, li quali a nissun fan spendere più di quel che son creditori in essi, non segue quel che dice, che tutti li pagamenti si fanno con una scritta' (De Santis, 1605b, p. 153).

7.   Conclusions: back to the future

Neapolitan citizens under the Spanish domination had to make do with a scarce and dwindling stock of metallic money. Like a leaking bucket, the Kingdom had to pay foreigners whatever amount of silver it coined, whether in payments for imports, rents, taxes or as 'donations' to finance the Spanish wars. They solved the problem with paper money, which became accepted by virtue of both the reputation of its issuers, the public banks of Naples, and the state's authority. By means of this device, they made that scarce stock of silver adequate to the needs of the domestic circulation: an ingenious solution which enabled them to conduct the Kingdom's 'abundant' business transactions even in the presence of a severe money shortage.

There is no question that the Neapolitan invention of paper money, an outstanding example of financial innovation, was a major achievement in history. Its main benefit, in Naples as elsewhere, was a closer integration between the monetary and the real sides of the economy, which set economic activity free from the constraints imposed by the precious metals. But its benefits should be weighed against its costs in terms of both instability and the economic power conferred upon the producers of paper money. One example is their power to renege on their own debts, by suspending convertibility.

Since that period, banks have always oscillated between trust building and trust betrayal: on the one hand, they have built trust by producing generally accepted means of payments which relax the liquidity constraints biting on economic transactions; on the other, they have betrayed the public trust when they have refused to honour their promises to pay by declaring banknotes irredeemable.

At the time in history that we have been dealing with in the present chapter, discipline was imposed on debtors by the national boundaries within which the circulation of paper money was restricted, because the liquidation of *international* payments still required metallic money. Consequently, the power to declare one's own debt inconvertible did not extend beyond the national borders.

Hence, whilst the Neapolitan banks could sometimes renege on their own domestic debt by refusing to convert paper into the precious metals, currency inconvertibility in international transactions was not an option for the Kingdom, a peripheral state in the international economic and political order of the time. The discipline of the external constraint was not relaxed by the ingenious invention of paper money.

The circulation of paper money still had a long way to go in the following centuries, gradually extending its benefits and costs beyond national borders to the international economy. Eventually, inconvertibility became an option for the central power in the economic and political landscape of the twentieth century. When, starting in July 1961, US liabilities to foreigners surpassed their gold reserves (Meltzer, 2009, p. 394), the remedies originally devised included the proposal to 'internationalise the provision of world currency and to eliminate the special role of the dollar' as suggested by Tobin. Others proposed a devaluation of the dollar in terms of gold (just as Turbolo had proposed for the Neapolitan carlino in terms of silver), while still others suggested a revaluation of the partner countries' currencies.

The solution that eventually prevailed – inconvertibility followed by a pure dollar standard – meant the transformation of the international currency into pure 'fiat' money, or, as others have put it, the establishment of a pure debt-credit relationship among countries (Quadrio Curzio, 1982, p. 12; and also 1981). This was a new sort of financial innovation by which the liquidity constraint on the international economy ceased to bite, and in the issuing country discipline in international economic transactions became just a memory of the past.

The passage to full inconvertibility in the international monetary system set the scene for the new forms of interactions between the real and the financial side of the world economy that we have witnessed in recent years (Quadrio Curzio, 2008; Quadrio Curzio and Miceli, 2010; Costabile, 2007, 2009, 2010, 2011). As we have observed before, structural analysis of evolving economic systems would be incomplete without a full understanding of the significance of these new, complex interactions.

REFERENCES

Broggia, C. A. (1743) *Trattato de' tributi, delle monete, e del governo politico della sanità. Opera di stato, e di commercio, di polizia e di finanza: molto, alla felicità de' popoli, alla robustezza degli stati, ed alla gloria e possanza maggiore de' principi, conferente e necessaria*, Naples: Pietro Palombo.

(2004) *Il Banco ed il Monte de' Pegni. Del Lusso*, Introductions by L. De Rosa and A. Graziani, transcription and critical edn by R. Patalano, Naples: Edizioni la Città del Sole per l'Istituto Italiano per gli Studi filosofici.

Clower, R. (1967) 'A Reconsideration of the Microfoundations of Monetary Theory', *Western Economic Journal*, 6.1, pp. 1–8.

Colapietra, R. (1973) *Problemi monetari negli scrittori napoletani del Seicento*, Rome: Accademia Nazionale dei Lincei.

Costabile, L. (2007) 'Current Global Imbalances and the Keynes Plan', *Working Papers*, wp156, University of Massachusetts at Amherst: Political Economy Research Institute.

(2009) 'Current Global Imbalances and the Keynes Plan: A Keynesian Approach for Reforming the International Monetary System', *Structural Change and Economic Dynamics*, 20.2, pp. 79–89.

(2010) 'The International Circuit of Key Currencies and the Global Crisis:
Is there Scope for Reform?', *Working Papers*, wp220, University of
Massachusetts at Amherst: Political Economy Research Institute.

(2011) 'Review of Quadrio Curzio and Miceli's (2010) *Sovereign Wealth Funds.
A Complete Guide to State-Owned Investment Funds*', *op. cit.*, *Journal of
Economics*, 104.1, pp. 91–4.

De Rosa, L. (1955) *I cambi esteri del Regno di Napoli dal 1591 al 1707*, Naples:
Banco di Napoli, Biblioteca del 'Bollettino' dell'Archivio Storico.

(1958) *Gli antichi banchi napoletani e l'odierno Banco di Napoli*, Naples:
Banco di Napoli.

(1987) *Il Mezzogiorno spagnolo tra crescita e decadenza*, Milan: Il Saggiatore.

(ed.) (2002a) *Gli inizi della circolazione della cartamoneta e i banchi pubblici
napoletani*, Naples: Istituto Banco di Napoli-Fondazione.

(2002b) 'Gli inzi della circolazione della cartamoneta e i banchi pubblici napoletani',
in A. De Rosa (ed.) *Gli inizi della circolazione della cartamoneta e i banchi
pubblici napoletani, op. cit.*, pp. 437–59.

De Santis, M. A. (1605a) *Discorso di Marc'Antonio De Santis intorno alli effetti che fa
il cambio in Regno*, Naples: Appresso Costantino Vitale, in Colapietra (1973),
pp. 111–41.

(1605b) *Secondo Discorso di Marcantonio Santis intorno alli effetti che fa il
cambio in Regno. Sopra una risposta, che è stata fatta avverso al primo*,
Naples: nella stamperia di Felice Stigliola, a Porta Reale, in Colapietra, pp.143–62.

Eichengreen, B. (1995) *Golden Fetters: The Gold Standard and the Great Depression,
1919–1939*, New York: Oxford University Press.

Galiani, F. ([1780] 1963) *Della moneta e scritti inediti*, with introduction by
A. Caracciolo and ed. by A. Merola, Milan: Feltrinelli.

([1780] 1977) *On Money: A Translation of Della Moneta by Ferdinando Galiani*,
trans. P. R. Toscano, University of Chicago: Published for Dept. of Economics
by University Microfilms International.

Graziani, A. (2004) 'Introduction' to C. A. Broggia, *Il Banco ed il Monte de' Pegni.
Del Lusso, op. cit.*, pp. XV–XXIX.

Heckscher, E. F. (1935) *Mercantilism*, London: George Allen and Unwin, 2 vols.

Keynes, J. M. ([1936] 1973a) *The General Theory of Employment, Interest and Money*,
London: Macmillan. Reprinted in D. Moggridge (ed.) The Collected Writings of
J.M. Keynes, vol. VII, London: Macmillan.

(1973b) *The Collected Writings of J.M. Keynes: Preparation, Vol XIII, The General
Theory and After*, ed. by D. Moggridge, London: Macmillan.

McKinnon, R. I. (1993) 'The Rules of the Game: International Money in Historical
Perspective', *Journal of Economic Literature*, 31.1, pp. 1–44.

Meltzer, A. H. (2009) *A History of the Federal Reserve*, vol. 2, book 1, 1951–1969,
Chicago and London: The University of Chicago Press.

Musi, A. (1991) *Mezzogiorno spagnolo: la via napoletana allo Stato moderno*,
Naples: Guida.

Quadrio Curzio, A. (1967) *Rendita e distribuzione in un modello economico
plurisettoriale*, Milan: Giuffré.

(1981) 'Un diagramma dell'oro tra demonetizzazione e rimonetizzazione', *Rivista
Internazionale di Scienze Economiche e Commerciali*, 28.10–1, pp. 915–40.

(ed.) (1982) *The Gold Problem: Economic Perspectives*, Oxford: Oxford University Press.

(1983) 'Alternative Explanations', in J. A. Kregel (ed.) *Distribution, Effective Demand and International Economic Relations, Proceedings of a Conference held by the Centro di Studi Economici Avanzati, Trieste, at Villa Manin Passariano, Udine*, London and Basingstoke: Macmillan, pp. 142–52.

(1986) 'Technological Scarcity: An Essay on Production and Structural Change', in M. Baranzini and R. Scazzieri (eds.) *Foundations of Economics. Structures of Inquiry and Economic Theory*, Oxford: B. Blackwell, pp. 311–38.

(2004) 'Introduction', in A. Quadrio Curzio (ed.) *La globalizzazione e i rapporti Nord-Est-Sud*, Bologna: Il Mulino, pp. 7–17.

(2008) 'Foreword' to Reflections on the Crisis 2007–2008, *Economia Politica. Journal of Analytical and Institutional Economics*, 25.3, pp. 369–70.

Quadrio Curzio, A., and Miceli, V. (2010) *Sovereign Wealth Funds: A Complete Guide to State-Owned Investment Funds*, Petersfield, Hampshire: Harriman House.

Rosselli, A. (1995) 'Antonio Serra e la teoria dei cambi', in A. Roncaglia (ed.) *Alle origini del pensiero economico in italia. Moneta e sviluppo negli economisti napoletani dei secoli XVII-XVIII*, Bologna: Il Mulino, pp. 37–58.

(2000) 'Early Views on Monetary Policy: The Neapolitan Debate on the Theory of Exchange', *History of Political Economy*, 32.1, pp. 61–82.

Schumpeter, J. A. (1954) *History of Economic Analysis*, London: George Allen & Unwin.

Serra, A. ([1613] 1973) *'Breve trattato delle cause che possono far abbondare li regni d'oro e d'argento, dove non sono miniere con applicazione al regno di Napoli'*, Naples: Lazzaro Scoriggio, reprinted in R. Colapietra (1973), pp.161–228. Another edition is in P. Custodi (ed.) *Scrittori Classici Italiani di Economia Politica*, Parte antica, Tomo I, Milano: Destefanis, pp. 1–179.

([1613] 2011) *A Short Treatise of the Wealth and Poverty of Nations*, ed. by S. A. Reinert, London and New York: Anthem Press.

Thirlwall, A. P. (2011) 'Balance of Payments Constrained Growth Models: History and Overview', University of Kent School of Economics Discussion Papers, May, KDPE 1111.

Triffin, R. (1985) 'The Myth and Realities of the So-called Gold Standard' in B. Eichengreen (ed.) *The Gold Standard in Theory and History*, New York and London: Methuen, pp. 121–40.

Turbolo, G. D. (1616) *Discorso della differenza et inegualità delle monete del Regno di napoli, con l'altre monete di potentati convicini, e della causa della penuria di esse. Con l'espediente per lo aggiustamento, et abundanza sì delle monete di Regno, come di forastiere. Per beneficio publico*, Naples: nella stamperia di tarquinio Longo, 1616, as reprinted in R. Colapietra (1973) *Problemi monetari negli scrittori napoletani del Seicento, op. cit.*, pp. 289–97.

(1629) *Discorso sopra le monete del Regno di Napoli. Per la renouatione di esse monete, ordinata & eseguita nell'anno 1622. E degli effetti da quella proceduti. E se il cambio alto sia d'utile o danno a' Regnicoli. Diuerse relationi, e copie d'altri discorsi, dati fuora nell'anni 1618, 619 & 620 pertinenti alla medesima materia*, s.l., reprinted in R. Colapietra (1973), *Problemi monetari negli scrittori napoletani del Seicento, op. cit.*, pp. 299–376.

Valerio, A. (ed.) (2010) *L'ospedale del Reame. Gli Incurabili a Napoli. Storia e arte*, Naples: Il Torchio della Regina Editore.

Zagari, E. (1995) 'Moneta e sviluppo nel "Breve Trattato" di Antonio Serra', in Roncaglia (ed.) *Alle origini del pensiero economico in italia. Moneta e sviluppo negli economisti napoletani dei secoli XVII-XVIII*, Bologna: Il Mulino, pp. 15–36.

14 Institutions, resources and economic growth in transition processes: the case of Russia

Constanze Dobler and Harald Hagemann

1. Introduction

The analysis of the interplay between material and technological linkages is central to the analysis of resource-constrained economies undergoing structural economic dynamics (see e.g. Quadrio-Curzio, 1986, and Quadrio-Curzio and Pellizzari, 1999). In particular, the relationship between material and techno-logical linkages highlights the classical theme of the analysis of structural change, i.e. the relationship between changes in the economic structure and the adjustment of an existing institutional set-up compatible with such changes. Historical processes of structural change illuminate the importance of the rela-tionship between the structural composition of the economy, the distribution of agents among different institutional clusters and the overall growth performance of the economy. Institutions are the 'Carriers of History' (David, 1994), i.e. institutions are a decisive constraint upon growth and structural change. This has been an important insight in development economics where economists such as Albert Hirschman have identified the connection between political and economic progress and emphasized that certain institutional changes are clearly favourable to a process of sustained economic growth. The work of North (1990, 2005) and others has shown the importance of institutions and institutional changes for economic performance. This also holds in particular for post-socialist transition economies, where a radical shock therapy neglecting the existing institutions – and the importance of the search and evolution of the right institutions for the completely different reality of everyday life – has proven a failure (Rodrik, 2000). Initially, authors such as Przeworski and Limongi (1993) have pointed out that there is no simple answer to the question whether democracy fosters or hinders economic growth and that a credible commitment to economic growth may be difficult to achieve under autocratic rule, in which there is a high probability that the society will be plundered, as well as with democratic insti-tutions in which too much weight may be given to a more egalitarian distribution of income and wealth with possibly detrimental effects on growth.

From an institutional economist's point of view the countries of the former Soviet Union depict one lucky accident that allows special research possibilities.

The often discussed matter of institutional transformation with all its perils can be observed by means of Russia and its cohorts. There, we have a dramatic systemic change from one of the dominating sociopolitical directions of the twentieth century – Communism – to the other – Capitalism. Hence what is often discussed in theory did actually happen on the ground of the former Soviet Union: the shift of a complete system, that is, the transition from a centrally planned to a market economy. This systemic change is interesting for institutional economics in several ways. Institutions as the rules of the game are thought to influence a country's economic development path (Acemoglu, Johnson and Robinson, 2005). Now, countries differ regarding their level of economic development and regarding their institutional environments. Hence, the crucial question is whether certain institutions are generally more growth-supportive than others and thus yield higher growth rates and higher development levels in the long run. The crux is that a country's institutional environment depicts a complex entity with myriads of institutions and other factors influencing each other. Hence, the political and economic institutions of an economically successful country might not cause the same results if applied in another country. Institutions depend on history, culture, religion, geography, and reverse causalities. During the time of Soviet transition, mainstream economic opinion was that institutional transformation is possible. Hence, free-enterprise institutions could be implemented in every country and would then lead to economic growth and development. The necessary modifications were summarized in the 'Washington Consensus'. The complex dependencies that exist between institutions and other exogenous and endogenous factors were ignored.

Empirical evidence, however, proved that things were not so easy. It looks as if many institutions cannot just be transplanted into certain societies, although they might support efficient outcomes in other economies. Whether the transformation of institutions is possible or not seems to depend on a country's history and culture, that is, on its roots and established morals, worldview and traditions (Boettke *et al.*, 2008; Landes, 1998). Hence, the rule of law cannot be easily installed in a country that has no tradition of law and property. Rule of law, property rights, division of power and other institutions, which have evolved in the Western countries, may not be simply transplanted to other historical, cultural and institutional environments (Hedlund, 2005; Huff, 2003; Jacob, 1997; Lipsey *et al.*, 2005). Therefore, the former Soviet Union depicts a kind of natural experiment where institutional economists can observe what happens if systems change and transition is conducted rapidly or gradually.

The current chapter emphasizes the transition in Russia and the role institutions played before and during the process. It broadly describes the developments of the last two decades. In Russia, first a Big Bang approach was applied. Transition was conducted all of a sudden, omitting important underlying reforms. This practice should function as a shock therapy. After the institutional vacuum would be established, new growth-promoting free-market rules would come into play and foster development. However, since Russian GDP per capita and thereby living standards deteriorated dramatically in the years after the collapse of the Soviet Union in December 1991, the plan did not work. At any rate, since then Russian economic indicators recovered and partly achieved their pre-1991 levels at the end of the last decade. Therefore, we have to examine whether Russia at least made its way to a path of sustained growth (Lipsey *et al.*, 2005). One characteristic of recent Russian economic history is that – in remarkable contrast to the economic growth process in China – Russia in the 1990s went back to a 'pre-manufactory' stage of economic growth based on primary resource exports.

2.   Signs of structural change

Economic transition describes the process of change from a centrally planned to a free-market economy. Centrally planned or socialist economies are characterized by heavy industry, state-owned enterprises, physical management systems, and underdeveloped service and finance sectors (Ickes and Ofer, 2005). Hence, privatization and structural change are central elements of economic transition. Therefore, the current chapter first demonstrates some core indicators of the Russian economy and then explores whether structural change is observable since 1991.

According to the World Bank classification, the Russian Federation belongs to the group of high-income economies.[1] Development of GDP per capita can be observed in Figure 14.1. In 1990, Russian GDP per capita amounted for US$5,685. After the breakdown of the Soviet Union in 1991, per capita income continually decreased, reaching its lowest point in 1998 with US$3,300. After 1998 a recovery began. The 1990-level, however, was not reached until 2006 – that is fifteen years after the end of the Soviet Union. This, however, was not the original intention of economic transition. Living standards and therefore GDP per capita were thought to increase right from the start of the reforms.[2]

Figure 14.2 depicts GDP per capita growth rates. Between 1990 and 1998, GDP per capita on average fell by-6.10 per cent per year. The average yearly growth rate of the period between 1999 and 2008 amounted to 7.29 per cent. After the financial crisis of 2008, however, the growth rate in 2009 accounted for -7.79

---

[1] World Bank classification: Country and Lending Groups; [online] available at: http://data.world-bank.org/about/country-classifications/country-and-lending-groups [accessed 2 April 2014].
[2] GDP per capita is measured in constant 2005 US$; World Development Indicators, The World Bank.

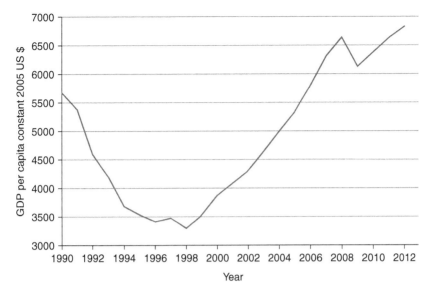

Figure 14.1 Russian GDP per capita in constant 2005 US dollars
Data Source: World Development Indicators.

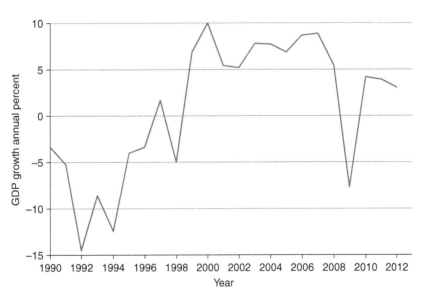

Figure 14.2 Russian GDP per capita growth annual per cent
Data Source: World Development Indicators.

per cent and 4.15 per cent in 2010. The average GDP per capita growth rate between 1990 and 2012, however, is merely 0.914 per cent. Hence, on average, almost no growth in GDP per capita can be observed within a time span of twenty years. Russian growth until 2006/07 can be described as mere recovery.

Another critical point regarding living standards in Russia in the phase after the breakdown of the Soviet Union is the development of the GINI-index, which increased from 0.289 in 1992 to 0.418 in 2013, indicating a growing gap in income distribution.[3] Income disparities may form social and political tension, especially in the Russian regions (Hagemann and Kufenko, 2013).

Since economic transition describes the change from a centrally planned to a free-market economy, several modifications of the structure of the economy should be observable during and after the phase of transition. Employment shares, for example, are a sign for structural change. In 1992, according to Goskomstat, 14 per cent of total employment was registered in agriculture. The value decreased to 9.5 per cent in 2013. In industry, employment dropped from 29.6 per cent in 1992 to 15.1 per cent in 2012, and in services employment increased from 31.5 per cent in 1992 to 54 per cent in 2012. According to World Bank data, unemployment in the Russian Federation rose from 5.3 per cent in 1992 to 13.0 per cent in 1999. In the 2000s, the unemployment rate was decreasing up to 5.5 per cent in 2012.[4] Value-added as percentage of GDP in agriculture decreased from 17 per cent in 1990 to 3.9 per cent in 2012. In industry, value-added decreased from 48 per cent in 1990 to 36 per cent in 2012, and in services an increase from 35 per cent in 1990 to 60.1 per cent in 2012 is observable.[5]

Net inflows of foreign direct investment (FDI) increased from 0.25 per cent of GDP in 1992 to 4.5 per cent in 2008. FDI then, however, dropped to 2.5 per cent in 2012. These indicators indeed refer to structural change, which usually comes along with decreasing employment and value-added rates in agriculture and industry and increasing shares in services.

Transition had an effect on enterprises, as can be seen in Figures 14.3–14.6. Accordingly, the market capitalization of listed companies as percentage of GDP rose from 0.05 per cent in 1991 to 115.64 per cent in 2007. Afterwards it crashed to 23.91 per cent in 2008 due to the financial crisis, but recovered to 43.41 per cent in 2012. The total value of stocks traded as percentage of GDP also increased from 0.07 per cent in 1994 to 58.05 per cent in 2007, 33.85 per cent in 2008, and 36.34 per cent in 2012. The turnover ratio of stocks traded increased from 11.14 per cent in 1996 with

---

[3] Relevant data taken from Goskomstat. The measure for GINI-coefficient for 1992 was taken from Litvinov (1999).
[4] Data taken from Goskomstat.
[5] Value added as percentage of GDP, World Development Indicators, The World Bank.

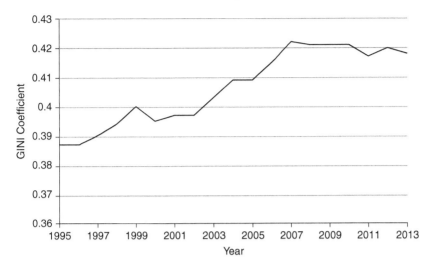

Figure 14.3 Increasing income inequality in Russia
Data Source: Goskomstat.

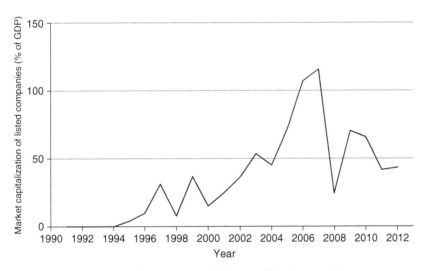

Figure 14.4 Russian market capitalization of listed companies, per cent
of GDP
Data Source: World Development Indicators.

several ups and downs to 87.64 per cent in 2012. The number of total
businesses registered increased from 1,609,423 in 2000 (first year for
which data are available) to 3,267,325 in 2007.[6]

---

[6] All data are taken from the World Development Indicators, The World Bank.

3.   The early years

These indicators, however, indicate signs of structural change. According to Ickes and Ofer (2006), structural change proceeded too slow and still lacks behind the respective expectations. Hence, '[Russian] enterprises continue to produce the wrong products, with too many workers and in the wrong place' (Ickes and Ofer, 2006, p. 1). This statement hints at the low productivity of the Russian economy, which is a legacy of its Soviet past. Soviet economic performance has almost never been as successful as predicted. At least under Reform Communism (1953–1991) official Soviet as well as Western data were overestimated. On the contrary, Angus Maddison's data of GDP and GDP per capita (Maddison 2001, 2003) demonstrate an almost continuous decrease compared to the US level (see also Rosefielde, 2007, pp. 145–60; Rosefielde and Hedlund, 2009, pp. 78–91). Hence, the Soviet Union never caught up to the United States but was falling behind in GDP per capita, at least during the Cold War. This is not surprising since centrally planned economies and the Soviet strategy of physical systems management lacked sufficient attention for the demand side. Therefore, demand and supply were not equilibrated, and prices and wages were fixed by the respective bureaucratic bodies. Emphasis was on heavy industry and within that, on arms production. Therefore, although it can hardly be proven with statistical facts, since the respective data are not available, probably a negative factor productivity growth was haunting Russia for decades. However, after the collapse of the Soviet Union, Russia

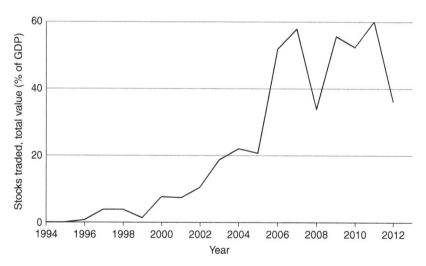

Figure 14.5 Russian stocks traded; total value of GDP, per cent of GDP
Data Source: World Development Indicators.

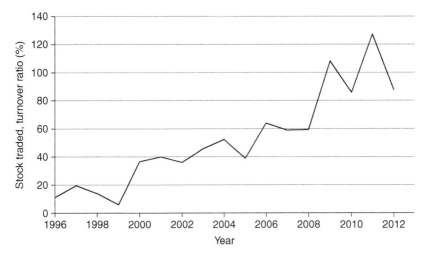

Figure 14.6 Russian stocks traded turnover ratio, per cent
Data Source: World Development Indicators.

was not able to bury its past. This is not surprising from an institutional point of view. Institutions, understood as informal mental models and belief systems and, more practically, as formal rules like the political or legal system of a state or certain laws, cannot be easily changed, added or omitted. Transition in Russia meant more than merely adapting some economic rules. The political, legal, economic, and at best the societal system had to be modified heavily. This is a difficult task, the more so since transition should be conducted 'overnight'.

Emphasis of the so-called shock therapy was on macroeconomic stabilization, price liberalization and finally privatization. Their implementation neglected two important aspects. First, the inherited institutional structure was not sufficiently adapted. Hence, the reforms were realized without implementing the rule of law and therewith an independent judiciary, democracy, and certain civil rights such as freedom of the press. Secondly, in reality the reforms conducted differed considerably from what was officially decided and written down.

Liberalization inter alia meant that prices, which were fixed by the governmental bureaucracy until then, were liberalized on 2 January 1992. It was hoped that this step would fill the retail traders' shops and would enable the population to buy the necessary goods. Furthermore, price liberalization would force productivity since the consumers would determine which goods to produce. First individual one-man firms were allowed in May 1987 and private cooperative enterprises were introduced as a form of organization in May 1988; however, during liberalization establishment of private trade, private enterprise and manufacture was enforced with legislative basis on a larger

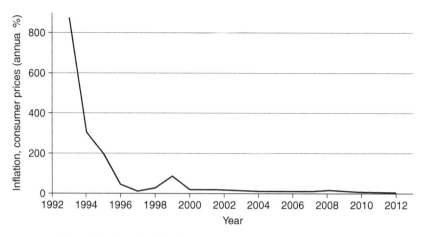

Figure 14.7 Russian inflation, consumer prices, annual per cent
Data Source: World Development Indicators.

scale. Subsidies to state enterprises and farms were cut. Barriers to foreign
trade were decreased to allow foreign imports with which the indigenous
producers had to compete.

It was overlooked that firm managers who were educated in fulfilling state
directives did not have a clue about efficiency, productivity and profit maximization. Firms suddenly had to deal with the fact that the state reduced
subsidies and did not fulfil its role as reliable purchaser anymore. Price
liberalization led to a much higher inflation than expected. Fixed incomes
and pensions of workers, pensioners, widows, etc. lost value and therefore,
living standards decreased drastically.

The central bank's expansive monetary policy, which was introduced to
finance the state's debts, mainly inherited from its Soviet past, exacerbated
inflation. The expansive supply of money and credit in 1992 and 1993 let the
rouble devaluate. The situation ended in the well-known hyperinflation that hit
Russia in the 1990s. The development of the inflation rate is depicted in
Figure 14.7. Enterprises lost their production plans and additionally the state
as reliable purchaser. For decades the firms' existence had been based on
physical systems management. They got their production plans from the
appropriate authority that told them what, how, and which quantity to produce.
Wages were fixed by the state; hence, enterprises never had to calculate on
labour and other input costs. After a time of interfirm credit lending supported
by the central bank in 1991 and 1992, which further boosted inflation, the
government restricted credit expansion to state-owned firms (Robinson, 1999).
Since the firms, instead of decreasing production, were producing inventory

stocks, the credit crunch resulted in monetary shortages. Many firms had to be shut down. This had far-reaching consequences. Often, a certain firm was the only employer in the region, like in cases of the so-called mono-cities ('*mono-goroda*'). Therefore, a region's whole working-age population got unemployed at once. The Soviet enterprises were not only mere employers, they also covered many social services. Industrial firms dealt with their employees' housing, health service, education and other social functions. Furthermore, the state was heavily in debt and not able to pay wages or pensions and had to cut the few services that existed. Altogether, the 1990s were characterized by a severe decrease in living standards and social indicators. A more thoughtful plan for transition that incorporated these issues could have resulted in a better outcome. In reality, Russia's economic transition ended in circa 3.4 million premature deaths between 1990 and 1998 and in impoverishment of large parts of its population (Rosefielde, 2001).

Macroeconomic instability in the first half of the 1990s was due to a sudden price and exchange rate liberalization, high and growing government debt, excessive money expansion, the resulting devaluation of the exchange rate and hyperinflation. Since 1993, however, macroeconomic stability became a main target. A restrictive monetary and fiscal policy was implemented, interest rates were increased, credits restricted, and subsidies reduced.

Polterovich (1995, p. 277) argues that the negative results of the shock therapy, which were unforeseen by proponents and opponents alike, are not only due to monopolies and incompetence to perform in a market economy but that, above all, 'it was the particular "cooperative" structure of relationships and interests that had been established during the process of the evolution of the Soviet enterprise that was a root cause of the economic crisis'. He calculates that labour collectives in industry, construction, trade, and consumer services, gave work to more than 50 per cent of the employed population in 1992. 'The economic "battle" that took place in that year consisted of the struggle between the liberally oriented government and the labour collectives (including their managers), the latter of which regarded the government's reform program as an encroachment upon their wages; their jobs; and their rights to use, manage, and own principal funds' (Polterovich, 1995, pp. 266–7). The resistance of labour collective enterprises to the austere credit and monetary policies of the government and their continued practice of reliance on governmental help contributed to economic inefficiency and social injustice. Workers were suffering most in all those sectors that could not develop markets for their final products – such as health, culture, education, the arts and sciences – and therefore could not follow the double-strategy of raising output prices and delaying payments to suppliers in the interenterprise debt crises which developed.

These economic and political struggles and conflicts that would come to exist had not been considered before by the Russian and foreign inventors of the 'shock therapy'. However, looking back at the Soviet history, this is something that could have been expected. At any rate, it was not, and political fights endured after the coup that ended Gorbatchev's reign and brought Boris Yeltsin into the leading state position. The replacement of Yegor Gaidar as Prime Minister by Viktor Chernomyrdin complicated things for the economic reformers since economic and political pragmatism entered the stage (Robinson, 1999). The never-abolished Russian properties of networks, relationships, authoritarianism and rent-granting defined daily business. Yeltsin's plan for re-election necessitated this strategy. However, it was not incorporated in mainstream economic modelling of transition. Political struggles continued to influence economic development in several ways. Policy, economy, and business got mixed up by the implementation of the respective personnel, especially from the banking sector, in political positions. Lobbyism affected every sphere of governmental decisions, such as subsidies granted to certain sectors, possibilities of tax evasion, or unfairly gained profits from privatization. In this way, lobbyism and rent-granting had an influence on the budget deficit, since they inhibited policies of debt reduction and a restructuring of the state budget. Especially the intertwining of banks and politics caused problems. The hyperinflation caused a demonetization of the economy that left the commercial banks as the only liquid actors. Therefore, the state relied heavily on the banks to finance the budget deficit. To reduce the budget deficit, the lax taxation system had to be reformed and tax evasion reduced. However, strict taxation would hit the banks and the industrial firms (which were partly owned by banks) particularly hard. Therefore, the government was filled by internal power struggles while the President had his re-election in mind. The banks' linkages with the government can be demonstrated with the appointment of Vladimir Potanin and Boris Berezovsky in 1996. Again in 1997, Anatoli Chubais and Boris Nemtsov became part of the government while Vladimir Potanin had to leave. Boris Berezovsky and Vladimir Potanin became two of the Yeltsin-era Russian oligarchs. Their places in government simplified enforcing their interests. The entanglements between banks and government had far-reaching consequences regarding the second wave of privatization and the 1998 currency crisis.

4.   Privatization

Privatization was conducted in two steps. The first privatization program, the 'voucher' privatization, started in 1992. Beforehand, retail shops and other small enterprises were just transferred to the employee(s). Then, it was decided which of the large enterprises, with thousands or tens of thousands of employees, should be privatized. Here the struggle started. The firms to be sold within the voucher program were the more or less worthless, inefficient enterprises whose production until then was planned via physical systems management. On a free market, those enterprises were valueless. The remaining high-value enterprises, often those exploiting natural resources, stayed in the hands of the state for the present. The firms taking part were transformed into stock companies. The stock was managed by property funds until the auctions were put into practice. However, the insider dominance that characterized the privatization process already started before the first firm was privatized with specifying the rules for the distribution of shares. It was decided that 51 per cent of the enterprise shares should be sold to worker collectives at favourable prices. Hence, a majority of the shares went directly to insiders – that is, worker collectives and former managers (Hedlund, 2001). The remaining shares were to be open for purchase by the Russian citizens. Therefore, every Russian was provided with a voucher worth 10.000 roubles in nominal value, so every Russian individual should have been able to purchase an enterprise-share using her or his voucher at the upcoming auctions. In reality, however, due to hyperinflation vouchers lost almost all their value. Additionally, since people did not trust the program and thought it would not take place anyway, vouchers were traded at street kiosks for the price of a bottle of vodka or were sold cheaply to speculators. When the auctions at last took place in 1993/1994, the outcome was quite dubious. Some auctions were announced only shortly before they started, they were conducted at places far apart and access could be restricted via arrangements with the police or the security services. Hedlund (2001), referring to Lieberman *et al.* (1995), states that '80% of the capital [of the enterprises that participated in the voucher privatization], had either remained in the hands of the state or gone straight to enterprise management and the worker collectives' (pp. 230–1). Hence, already the voucher privatization ended in ownership dominated by insiders and therefore by the former managers.

The second step of privatization took place in 1995–97 and should have privatized the high-value oil, natural resource, and telecommunication companies. This part of the privatization, however, was influenced by the political struggle penetrating the government. The commercial banks played an important role since they were the last liquid actors that could help the government shoulder its high debt burden. The privatization deal known as 'loans for shares' was as follows: the shares of the enterprises were given to the banks as collateral. In return, the state got credit from the banks to finance the budget. In case the credit was not repaid by August 1996 the banks were allowed to hold auctions and sell the enterprise shares. The credit was never repaid and the banks sold the firms under value to insiders, often themselves. Treisman (2010, p. 1) provides examples of various tricks (see case of the oil company Surgutneftegaz) used by the red directors to eliminate the competition during the auctions.

The political context becomes clear when we look at the relevant dates – the loans were made before the 1996 election, but the auctions took place

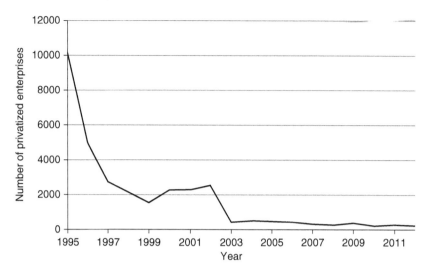

Figure 14.8 Privatization waves of the state-owned enterprises
Data Source: Goskomstat.

afterwards. That way the potential buyers and the bankers had a reason to support Yeltsin's re-election campaign and to inhibit a return of the Communists. The buyers, however, were probably selected long before the auctions occurred and often the lenders more or less sold the shares to themselves at low prices (Hedlund, 2008; Treisman, 2010). It is often argued, and in some cases it is in fact true, that the loans-for-shares auctions led to the emergence of the Russian oligarchs, who thus were able to buy lucrative enterprises at low prices. The economic outcome of these developments is discussed controversially. Patronage, manipulation and insider trading led to a form of privatization that differed from what was intended by Russian and Western reformers. However, Woodruff (2004, p. 92) points out that some of the distortions incorporated in the privatization programs were wanted by the Russian reformers and their Western advisors. They must have been aware that the Soviet managers would try to strip assets and to self-enrich themselves. Therefore, they wanted to give the managers an advantage in acquiring shares and in controlling enterprises to force them to join the new competitive environment and to produce according to efficiency criteria. However, if this were true, it seems to have been a naïve plan, ignoring the Soviet managers' past and environment they had to deal with up to then.

At any rate, the Russian privatization program is often described as a betrayal of the Russian population, as plundering and theft (Hedlund, 2001, 2008; Rosefielde, 2007). It has been argued that the oligarchs owe their wealth to the loans-for-shares auctions and these oligarchs inhibit the development of free-enterprise institutions such as secure property rights, contract law and independent judiciary. Guriev and Rachinsky (2005), however, find that only a few oligarchs owe their wealth to the auctions, including, for example, Roman Abramovich, Mikhail Khodorkovsky, Vladimir Potanin, Vagit Alekperov and Vladimir Bogdanov. The rest of the 627 owners considered in the study got rich in different ways. Most of them, however, already belonged to the old Soviet *nomenklatura* (red directors), or they were able to take an advantage of the power struggles and reform efforts of the 1980s and 1990s. The authors further figure out that the oligarchs' enterprises are more productive than other Russian firms. Yet, oligarchs do not support free-enterprise institutions. Treisman (2010) also demonstrates that oligarchism as it appeared in Russia is not a unique phenomenon in emerging markets and can take on even greater dimensions as is the case, for example, in Mexico. Obviously, the winners in the loans-for-shares privatization were the red directors, who took advantage of their positions to accumulate more wealth.

5.   On the way to the 1998 crisis

In 1996–1997, however, the Russian economy was characterized by strong connections between the government and the banking sector. The government was unable to collect taxes and hence, to pay its bills. Therefore, the strange relationship with the banking sector was a necessity. Wages were not paid, living standards decreased and industries were provided with non-monetary subsidies in the form of fuel. This contributed to the demonetization of the economy and the emergence of a barter system, and it further decreased the government's ability to raise taxes (Robinson, 1999, p. 550).

The lack of deeper institutional reforms, coupled with events in Asia, contributed to the Russian currency crisis of 1998. The Asian crisis might have hit Russia anyway; however, the prevalent structures were responsible for its severity. Political struggles, lax tax collection, hyperinflation, demonetization of the economy and a high fiscal deficit had a share in Russia's extreme downturn in 1998/1999.

Reformists politically lost ground in 1994, when Yegor Gaidar and Boris Fedorov resigned from government after the Duma elections. The growing influence of lobbyists had affected state finances, tax collection and subsidies. Since many of the bankers that gained influence owned stakes in the privatized enterprises, they were busy inhibiting a more severe tax system. Lax tax collection, on the other hand, led to a further decrease in state revenues and to an increase of the budget deficit. Non-monetary subsidies, primarily fuel, worsened the situation and further contributed to the demonetization of the economy. In October 1994 the rouble collapsed, inflation further shot up and in 1995 a fixed exchange rate corridor was implemented.

Since many members of the Soviet *nomenklatura* were part of the new banking sector and had close ties to the government, both sides were already mingled. The state needed the banks to finance its deficit. The banks, on the other hand, used their influence to gain an advantage in the upcoming loans-for-shares auctions. Hence, the state further lost its ability to collect taxes, paid non-monetary subsidies to the industry and continued to run into debt. Commercial banks invested in treasury bills and hence helped the government to finance its deficit. On the other hand, they influenced the loans-for-shares auctions and inhibited the formation of market prices for the firms to be sold. Then, they prevented the government from tax collection and therewith exacerbated the state's financial situation. The banks supported Boris Yeltsin during his re-election campaign and in 1996, after the election, two from their ranks, Vladimir Potanin and Boris Berezovsky, became members of the government. It was discovered that the only way to cover the state's debt was through international finance. However, to attract international investors, the state needed regular revenues to create confidence. Besides opening the bonds market to foreigners, a stronger tax collection was enacted. This led to a conflict between the state and the banks. Vladimir Potanin was released from government, whereas Anatoli Chubais and Boris Nemtsov were brought in. These policy changes as well as anti-inflationary actions led to an international upgrading of Russia's solvency. Exports of natural resources, especially fuel, resulted in a balanced foreign trade. Oil was sold at a high price on the world markets. The World Bank and the IMF promised further assistance. Inflation decreased from 131 per cent (1995) to 11 per cent (1997) (Chiodo and Owyang, 2002). Limitations for foreign investors on the bond markets were removed. In 1997 the market for short-term government bills almost exploded. Within one year foreigners tripled their holdings of government bonds and foreign cash financed 56 per cent of the government's deficit (Robinson, 1999, p. 552). However, although from an outsider's point of view the situation seemed to improve, no real changes were made to the economy apart from bond markets. Tax receipts improved compared to the previous year, but the general trend did not change, and tax evasion and indebtedness even increased. Real wages were significantly lower than in 1991, and large parts of the workforce still suffered from wage arrears. The linkages between bankers and government were ravaged by conflicts since more severe tax laws affected the banks' interests. A scandal concerning the loans-for-shares auctions caused the degradation of Anatoli Chubais and ended in the dissolution of the government in March 1998. Prime Minister Victor Chernomyrdin was fired and replaced by Sergei Kiriyenko.

In 1997, prices for fuels and other natural resources began to fall on the world markets. The drop in prices resulted in a deterioration of the trade balance. The government crisis and the Asian crisis led to a decline in investors' confidence. In November 1997 the Russian central bank had to defend the rouble with almost US$6 billion. The short-term government bonds expired within a year and hence, investors started to withdraw their money. In August 1998, Russia announced a debt default, floated and therewith devalued the rouble, and suspended payments by banks to foreign lenders (Chiodo and Owyang, 2002; Kharas, Pinto and Ulatov, 2001; Robinson, 1999).

The crisis of 1998 can be attributed to the prevalence of weak economic fundamentals. Public debt problems, large parts of it inherited from the Soviet past, could not be solved with the political and economic structures at hand. After the break-up of the Soviet Union, the country was thrown in at the deep end without the necessary reforms of the economic, political and legal fundamentals. The omitted reforms, for example the introduction of secure property rights via an independent judiciary and the rule of law, made a solution to the debt problem and everything it incorporated – expansive monetary policy, hyperinflation, demonetization, real appreciation of the rouble, economic recession, and strongly decreasing living standards – impossible.

6.   A new decade – time for reform?

In the aftermath of the 1998 crisis, however, Russia exhibited a surprisingly fast recovery with an average growth rate of 6.7 per cent per year between 1999 and 2007 (Hanson, 2007, p. 869). Such a positive economic development after a severe crisis came unexpected. It is often argued that Russia's impressive growth performance in the 2000s is due to developments in the world markets for natural resources. Accordingly, the increasing oil price in particular enhanced Russia's economic growth, especially between 2000 and 2004. The economic downturn of the 1990s is described as 'transition recession' ('valley of tears'), which was overcome with the end of the crisis in 1998; thereafter Russia had performed relatively well compared to other transition countries until the 2008/9 crisis. However, according to Vinhas de Souza (2009), 70 per cent of Russia's economic growth since 1999 cannot be directly attributed to natural resources. A boom in services and construction contributed to the improved growth performance (Hanson, 2007). Although oil, gas and other natural resources might have had a limited direct effect on the growth rate, their indirect contribution is enormous. The revenues created in the natural resource sector went largely into the state budget and contributed to a fast decrease in external and internal government debt, which was less than 5 per cent of GDP in 2007. Furthermore, the natural resource revenues increased personal gains and enterprises' profits, driving domestic demand for consumption and investment. Therefore, Russia's government budget, its trade balance, and GDP in general depend on natural resource extraction and especially on oil production and exports. The fast economic upturn after the

1998 crisis can be contributed to increasing oil prices as well as to the fivefold devaluation of the Russian currency (Hanson, 2007, p. 870).[7] Still the early 2000s were characterized by an enormous increase in exports, especially oil. Ahrend (2006, p. 5) estimates that, between 2001 and 2004, 70 (45) per cent of the growth in industrial production can be attributed to the natural resource (oil) sector. The oil sector's direct contribution to GDP growth in 2000–03 was 24.8 per cent and its export share accounted for more than 50 per cent. Hence, at least until 2004 the oil sector strongly influenced GDP development.

The Russian government, however, dealt wisely with the growth benefits – mainly the oil windfalls – after the 1998 crisis. A Stabilization Fund was created that collected parts of the natural resource windfalls, which were then used to pay off state debt. Oil exports and rising oil prices resulted in an inflow of foreign currency, which the central bank used to build up the third-largest foreign-exchange reserves worldwide (Hanson, 2009, p. 25). Inflation was successfully brought down into the single-digit range in 2006 and the tax system was reformed (Hanson, 2007, p. 871).

Now there is concern that Russia might suffer from the 'Dutch Disease' phenomenon without a 'Polder model' yet in sight. Until 2008 natural resource exports drove up the rouble exchange rate while other sectors of the economy were losing competitiveness on world markets. These sectors are not able to catch up because the exchange rate pushes up the prices for Russian products.

The problem of Russia's oil and gas industry is its low technology level. Natural resource exports are not much processed and research-based high-technology production is also missing in other sectors. This, however, could also be a sign of the 'Dutch disease' (Hanson, 2007, p. 875). Investment shares are generally low and productivity gains can be traced back to the formerly under-utilized capital stock. After the 1998 crisis, many of the production facilities lay idle, so that production and productivity could be increased by using the idle capital stock. Therefore, even the oil sector might face future problems since necessary investments to keep up its production capacity are missing. 'Easy oil', that is oil extracted from fields with under-utilized capacity, has been running out for years, which might have contributed to the slowdown in oil production in 2004. The private oil firms did not make substantial long-term investment to adjust their production facilities to new technology levels. Investment was only conducted to absorb short-term gains. The reason for this behaviour may be due to the insecure situation regarding

---

[7] Zhuravskaya (2007) also emphasizes that the high commodity prices and the devaluation of the rouble 'provided Russia with extremely fortunate terms of trade'. Furthermore she states that 'Yeltsin's radical reforms of 1991–96 and, in particular, completion of privatization created necessary preconditions for the subsequent growth and, second, the effects of favorable external conditions were strongly supported by continuation of liberal reforms and responsible macro-economic policy during Putin's first term in power in 2000–2004' (p. 135, n. 10).

property rights. Since 2003 the government distinctly increased its influence in the oil sector by state-acquisition of oil firms. Examples are Yukos, which was overtaken by the state-controlled oil firm Rosneft, and Sibneft, which was bought up by Gazprom, a state-owned gas monopolist. State intervention was also observable in other sectors, for example electricity, arms production, automobile production, shipbuilding and nuclear industry (Ahrend, 2006, p. 7; Hanson, 2007, p. 877).

A result of the state intervention was a slowdown in the oil sector. Insecure property rights and under-utilized capacity inhibited long-term investments in the exploitation of new oil fields in the early 2000s. The Yukos affair caused an even more severe crisis regarding secure ownership rights and let the business climate deteriorate. Therefore, growth in oil exports have decreased since 2004. However, Russian exports are still governed by natural resources. According to Hanson (2009, p. 21), oil and gas were still responsible for 65.9 per cent of merchandise exports in 2008, while metals and coal added another 15 per cent.

At any rate, despite the slowdown in oil exports since 2004, the Russian economy in general has become more productive between 1998 and 2008. This is due to productivity increases of the labour force and the use of under-utilized capacities (Hanson, 2009, p. 12). The economic boost in 1999–2000 can be traced back to the severe rouble devaluation and increasing oil prices. The upturn between 1998 and 2008 must be attributed to additional factors. Resources were reallocated from heavy industry to the service sector and into new industries such as telecommunication (especially mobile phones) and software development. Employment shifts were observable from agriculture and manufacturing into construction, services, finances and trade. FDI provided more productive management skills, new technologies, machinery and equipment. Estimates exist that certify Russia a TFP growth of 3.3 to 4.7 per cent per year (Hanson, 2009, p. 13). However, Russia started from a low level. Hence, despite productivity increases its labour productivity is still only between one-fifth and one-third of the US level (Hanson, 2009, p. 19). The same is true regarding its production facilities and machinery. Russia is still unable to compete with low-wage manufactures from Asian countries.

Indicators positively highlight Russia's macroeconomic stability, its educational level and its market size (Hanson, 2009, p. 16). On the other hand, indicators measuring the *institutional quality* rate the country worse. In the World Bank's Doing Business 2014 report Russia achieves only the 92nd place out of 189 countries. The report measures business regulations and the security of property rights and hence, the quality of regulations influencing business activity. The World Economic Forum's Global Competitiveness Report 2013–14 (Schwab, 2013) paints a slightly different picture. In 2013–14 Russia is ranked 64th out of 148 countries, between Hungary and Sri Lanka. However, the index incorporates areas where Russia shows a better performance. This is the case regarding infrastructure (45), higher education and training (47), and market size (7). Russia exhibits a bad valuation regarding its institutions (121), especially property rights (133), judicial independence (119), burden of government regulation (120), reliability of police services (122) and protection of minority shareholders' interests (132). Still inflation depicts a major problem for the country's competitiveness (91), as well as its inefficient goods markets (126), and its underdeveloped financial markets (121). Russia's technology level is also badly rated (Schwab, 2013, p. 327). Hence, it can be stated that Russia's institutional development, as measured by the here-mentioned indicators, is economically inefficient and inhibits a better economic performance.

The 2008/9 crisis, however, hit Russia particularly – much harder than the other BRIC economies China, India and Brazil – due to Russia's relatively high integration into world markets and its export dependence. As helpful as these characteristics are in normal times, they make a country vulnerable to external crises. Furthermore, Russia experienced a capital flight after investors' confidence declined. Foreign creditors reclaimed their money, investors withdrew and Russian businessmen switched their assets from roubles into other currencies, mainly dollars and euros (Hanson, 2009, p. 27). All emerging economies were affected by capital withdrawals and investors staying away; Russia, however, was hit particularly hard. This can be traced back to the fact that both Russians and foreigners involved were conscious about the institutional environment. The financial sector is still underdeveloped. Most banks are controlled by the state; the stock market consists mainly of natural-resource based and state-controlled companies, and the turnover ratio is still relatively low. Even private Russian companies send their profits out of the state to offshore holding firms situated in other countries (Hanson, 2009). Hence, Russia's corrupt regime, its missing property rights, its absent rule of law, its interventionist government, and the knowledge that the state is the patrimony – enforcing its interests when necessary against all resistance – have made foreign and Russian investors and businessmen cautious.

Our investigation of the problems facing the Russian oil sector has pointed out the lack of investment into modern technology and the ensuing backwardness of extraction facilities. Here we can state an interesting parallel with a situation analysed by classical political economists in which rents generated by resource bottlenecks are not ploughed back in the production process in order to secure the capital facilities needed for intensive utilization of a 'mine', in Ricardo's terminology, or of an oil or gas field in the case of Russia. Strengthening innovative investment activities and an associated increase in the demand for higher skills, thereby not only stimulating incentives to acquire skills but also reducing Russia's extremely high number of expatriates with high skills, are an essential condition for future growth.

7.   Historical institutional reasons

Regarding the role of institutions in Russia's economic history of the last twenty-two years, almost everything that happened can be referred to the country's 'rules of the game'. Its ambitious transformation into a free-enterprise economy with the shock therapy at the beginning of the 1990s was permeated by the omission of institutional influences. The idea of fast liberalization and privatization without previous adjustment of the formal and informal rules might work theoretically. In reality, however, people's minds are inert and cannot suddenly adjust to efficiency criteria. The slow-moving informal and proto-institutions are persistent and subject to strong path dependence. Therefore, the transplantation of new formal institutions may be seriously distorted by the already well-established and path-dependent informal ones. For example, property rights were never sufficiently enforced in Russia. On the contrary, although Russian citizens were the owners of their assets, they were aware of the fact that the patriarch, whether the Grand Prince, the Tsar or the President, could always access their property. According to Pipes (1974), the Russian head of state had the same function as the patriarch of a family, with the family members being the Russian population: his wife and his children had rights to which everybody respected, but the patriarch could override them whenever he wanted to. The characteristics of Russian history, politics, and society were, and still are, that sovereignty has always been equated with ownership. Sovereignty and property were an entity and the sovereign owned everything within the realm. These patterns of a patrimonial state are still observable today due to an exercise of a centralized and virtually absolute power. This behaviour appeared in the 2000s, when the Russian state intervened repeatedly in private enterprise ownership and got hold of majority shares, no matter how. However, it was already observable earlier during the processes of privatization. The procedures were influenced by interest groups and the government, grabbing the most valuable entities themselves.

Other properties permeating Russian history, politics and society since early times are networks of patronage and nepotism. Nepotism could be partly explained by the absence of formal reputation mechanisms. Nevertheless, loyalty, informal connections and patronage relations, were historically much more important than efficiency and new investment opportunities (Buss, 2003, p. 36). Today, the strength of patronage networks depicts some of Russia's largest problems regarding its business environment. A good example is the hiring and firing of government members in the 1990s and 2000s, depending on which interest group was most influential and which policy was followed.

Regarding its formal institutional framework Russia never had a tradition of property rights and the rule of law. Secure property rights and the rule of law necessitate a third-party enforcement mechanism able to implement the rights against private persons or the state. Hence, the state has to subordinate itself to a constitution and to an independent judiciary. According to Hedlund (2001) the Russian state had never established law as an instrument to secure individual property and the individual *per se*. On the contrary, law was used as an instrument when favourable for the state. Hence, Russians always had to trust in personal relationships and social networks, but not in the state. Personal connections and patronage could help to achieve a certain goal, rather than law enforcement by an independent judiciary. Accordingly, Russia is characterized by 'the path dependent absence in Russian tradition of a state that is ready, willing and able to shoulder a role as legitimate guarantor of the rules of the game, and in the equally path dependent evolution of organizational responses and mental models that help economic actors in exploiting the opportunities for gain that are offered by such a weak state' (Hedlund, 2001, p. 227).

It can be stated that institutions as the rules that regulate social interaction, whether habits and conventions or formal laws and directives, influenced Russia's development since 1991 despite reform efforts appealing to rational behaviour and efficiency criteria. Nowadays the economic decline of the 1990s is called a 'transition recession' and describes the logical economic development after reform efforts transforming a planned economy into a market economy (Vinhas de Souza, 2009). Hence, the reforms caused a downturn and economic development took a u-shape. However, such a process was not intended by the Russian and Western architects of the 'shock therapy'. The term 'transition recession' emerged afterwards, when the empirical evidence required it. It would have been irresponsible anyway, to promote transition, being aware of the fact that it would cause an economic recession leading to the loss of millions of lives and impoverishing millions of people (Rosefielde, 2001). The original intention was that growth would take-off immediately after the implementation of the reforms.

The rule of law, protection of property, contracts, civil liberties, and state's separation of powers may not be realizable in every society, at least not overnight. The lack of certain proto-institutions and patrimonial traditions limit and distort institutional transplantation from the West to Russia. Therefore, even after the transition process, the path dependence will still prevail, making the country diverge from the original blueprints of the reformers of the 1990s. Hence, certain habits and patterns, regarding, for example, the role of the state, might never completely change. Still, development and growth are possible, as Russia demonstrated in the 2000s and might demonstrate in the near future. Despite the fear that the country could suffer from the 'Dutch Disease' – it certainly does – it might find a way to keep up its economic performance. Because of its export dependence, Russia will stay vulnerable to global crises. This necessitates a government that knows how to handle crises and how to stabilize the economy. At any rate, ups and downs cannot be prevented when a country is as dependent on natural resource exports as Russia is.

With only five years since the 2008/9 crisis, it is difficult to make assumptions about the economic future of Russia. It appears as if, again, Russia survived the crisis better than expected. Although the country was hit hard, effects on unemployment, for example, were less severe than expected. Real GDP growth in 2008 amounted to 5.2 per cent, followed by-7.8 per cent in 2009, 4.5 per cent in 2010, 4.3 per cent in 2011, 3.4 per cent in 2012 and 1.5 per cent in 2013 (OECD 2014). Hence, the recession following the crisis merely lasted for a year. Unemployment fell from 8.2 per cent in 2009 to 5.5 per cent in 2013. Most sectors experienced negative growth rates in 2009, but again positive growth since 2010. Similar to the 1998 crisis, oil prices and exports were responsible for at least some growth after the 2008/9 global economic crisis.

With a trend growth estimated of ca. 3 per cent in the next years the Russian economy is neither fully exploiting the potential offered by its wealth of natural resources nor by the high skill level of its population. Due to technological backwardness the energy-intensiveness of GDP remains one of the highest in the world. Although progress has been made in the gradual decline in the inflation rate since the late 1990s, with an estimated inflation rate of 6.6 per cent in 2013 Russia remains a relatively high-inflation economy.

8.   Conclusion

In their survey of the first decade of economic performance of post-socialist transition economies Campos and Coricelli (2002, p. 817) have provided us with 'the magnificent seven' stylized facts: (1) a major fall in GDP; (2) a massive reduction in the technologically outdated capital stock; (3) a massive reallocation of labour; (4) a collapse of CMEA trade and an almost complete structural reorientation of trade towards the leading international economies; (5) high costs due to a rise in unemployment and income inequality; (6) an institutional vacuum being created due to the collapse of the old communist regime; and (7) a rapid decline of industry and consequential major structural changes in the composition of output and employment.

In general this also holds for the Russian economy, with some modifications. Thus the rise of mortality rates of Russian men has been quite severe, whereas the institutional vacuum has been less pronounced in countries such as Poland, Hungary or the Czech Republic, which have a better basis for a historical and cultural path dependency towards a blueprint version of democratic Western institutions.[8]

---

[8] For a distinction of the two types of transition in Central and Eastern Europe see Zweynert and Goldschmidt (2006).

The output fall in the countries of the former Soviet Union was notably higher than in other post-socialist transition economies, not least because of institutional reasons. However, the shock therapy of the fundamentalist 'big-bang' approach, which relied on the imposition of an idealized version of Anglo-American institutions and neglected the existing institutions and a historical and cultural path dependency, has proven a failure and made things worse. Serious economists such as Kenneth Arrow (2000) have early on favoured a mixed strategy where a rapid entry of private-ownership activities into commerce and light industry and a massive start up of private services is combined with a more gradual transition process in the management of a declining sector of heavy industry by the government, which is also responsible for the provision of infrastructure in traffic and communication to private industry, and in particular for the restructuring and developing of the legal and financial institutions required for a modern viable economy. Institutional changes are path dependent and should try to avoid *institutional traps* (Polterovich, 2008), which are supported by cultural inertia and serious obstacles to economic reforms and to a better growth performance in transitional economies.

Although prospects might not look that bright regarding systemic reforms, especially concerning property rights, the rule of law, the business environment and the end of state interventionism, it is conceivable that Russia will go its own way – as it did before. Hence, it will not develop into a perfect free-enterprise economy and therefore, it will not satisfy efficiency criteria of economic theory. Russia will face some severe issues in the upcoming years. Its population, and thereby its labour force, is in decline. Its technology level is low and its research and development sector is not comparable with world standards. In general, Russia's economy, apart from the natural resource sector, is not competitive on world markets. Technologically, its natural resource sector is also uncompetitive, but still it produces urgently needed oil, gas and metals. Therefore it will keep on driving growth. The Russian government might implement some reforms, however, its general pattern will not change. Basic institutions cannot be easily modified, particularly not when they are rooted in certain convictions and habits that persisted for decades or centuries and peremeated the whole society. The level of Russia's growth rate will continue to depend on natural resource exports and it will be vulnerable to external economic crises. Living standards will probably stay behind those of highly developed industrial nations. Hence, Russia will not belong to the richest countries soon, but it will also not fail completely. In this sense, Russia might be described as a 'normal' middle-income country, whatever that means (Shleifer and Treisman, 2005). The term 'normal' requires that there is one true, normal standard development path, probably defined by a theoretical model. It suggests that the high-technology and high-income countries followed this path once they got there. Each country deviating from this standard path is 'abnormal'. According to Rosefielde (2005) this is the case for Russia, since it will not democratize and become a free-enterprise economy, soon. However, the classification into 'normal' and 'abnormal' countries seems rather odd. Any country follows its logical, normal development path. This path leads some of them to democracy, the rule of law, individualism and eventually to high technology levels and living standards. Other paths lead to autocracy, oppression, low growth and therewith low living standards[9]. Anyway, every path depicts a logical consequence of accidents that cannot necessarily be consciously influenced. Still it can be tried to improve a country's development pattern and hence, to improve its growth performance. But it cannot be transformed into a perfect copy of another country or into a model. Hence, Russia departs from certain models and other countries since its prerequisites and its institutional environment differs. Some factors influencing its economic performance may be improved; others are more difficult to change, as, for example, Russia's incomplete protection of formal property rights, the 'vertical' character of the Russian political system, and the resulting necessity of patronage relationships. These are difficulties that may inhibit the realization of its full growth potential.

REFERENCES

Acemoglu, D., Johnson, S., and Robinson, J. A. (2005) 'Institutions as the Fundamental Cause of Long-Run Growth', in P. Aghion and S. N. Durlauf (eds.) *Handbook of Economic Growth*, vol. 1B, Amsterdam: North Holland, pp. 1500–39.

Acemoglu, D., and Robinson, J. A. (2012) *Why Nations Fail: The Origins of Power, Prosperity and Poverty*, New York: Crown Business.

Ahrend, R. (2006) 'Russia's Post-crisis Growth: Its Sources and Prospects for Continuation', *Europe-Asia Studies*, 58.1, pp. 1–24.

Arrow, K. J. (2000) 'Economic Transition: Speed and Scope', *Journal of Institutional and Theoretical Economics*, 156.1, pp. 9–18.

Boettke, P. J., Coyne, C. J., and Leeson, P. T. (2008) 'Institutional Stickiness and the New Development Economics', *American Journal of Economics and Sociology*, 67.2, pp. 331–58.

Braguinsky, S. (2009) 'Postcommunist Oligarchs in Russia: Quantitative Analysis', *Journal of Law and Economics*, 52.2, pp. 307–49.

Buss, A. E. (2003) *The Russian-Orthodox Tradition and Modernity*, Leiden, Boston: Brill.

Campos, N. F., and Coricelli, F. (2002) 'Growth in Transition: What We Know, What We Don't, and What We Should', *Journal of Economic Literature*, 60.2, pp. 793–836.

---

[9] See Acemoglu and Robinson (2012).

Chiodo, A. J., and Owyang, M. T. (2002) 'A Case Study of a Currency Crisis: The Russian Default of 1998', *Review of the Federal Reserve Bank of St. Louis*, 84.6, pp. 7–18.

David, P. (1994) 'Why are Institutions the "Carriers of History"? Path Dependence and the Evolution of Conventions', Organizations and Institutions, *Structural Change and Economic Dynamics*, 5.2, pp. 205–20.

Goskomstat, data [online] available at: www.gks.ru and www.gks.ru/bgd/regl/b13_12/Main.htm [accessed 4 April 2014].

Guriev, S., and Rachinsky, A. (2005) 'The Role of Oligarchs in Russian Capitalism', *Journal of Economic Perspectives*, 19.1, pp. 131–50.

Hagemann, H., and Kufenko, V. (2013) 'The Political Kuznets Curve for Russia: Income Inequality, Rent Seeking Regional Elites and Empirical Determinants of Protests during 2011/2012', Discussion Paper Series *Globalizaztion and Employment*, 39, Stuttgart-Hohenheim.

Hanson, P. (2007) 'The Russian Economic Puzzle: Going Forwards, Backwards or Sideways?' *International Affairs*, 83.5, pp. 869–89.

(2009) 'Russia to 2020', Occasional Paper, *Finmeccanica Research Department*, Rome: Finmeccanica.

Hedlund, S. (2001) 'Property without Rights: Dimensions of Russian Privatization', *Europe-Asia Studies*, 53.2, pp. 213–37.

(2005) *Russian Path Dependence*, Abingdon, Oxon: Routledge.

(2008) 'Such a Beautiful Dream: How Russia Did Not Become a Market Economy', *The Russian Review*, 67.2, pp. 187–208.

Huff, T. E. (2003) *The Rise of Early Modern Science: Islam, China, and the West*, 2nd edition, Cambridge and New York: Cambridge University Press.

Ickes, B. W., and Ofer, G. (2006) 'The Political Economy of Structural Change in Russia', *European Journal of Political Economy*, 22.2, pp. 409–34.

Jacob, M. C. (1997) *Scientific Culture and the Making of the Industrial West*, New York and Oxford: Oxford University Press.

Kharas, H., Pinto, B., and Ulatov, S. (2001) 'An Analysis of Russia's 1998 Meltdown: Fundamentals and Market Signals', *Brookings Papers on Economic Activity*, 1, pp. 1–50.

Landes, D. (1998) *The Wealth and Poverty of Nations*, New York: W. W. Norton.

Lieberman, I. W., Ewing, A., Mejstrik, M., Mukherjee, J., and Fidler, P. (eds.) (1995) *Mass Privatization in Central and Eastern Europe and the Former Soviet Union. A Comparative Analysis*, Washington, DC: The World Bank.

Lipsey, R. G., Carlaw, K. I., and Bekar, C. T. (2005) *Economic Transformations: General Purpose Technologies and Long Term Economic Growth*, Oxford and New York: Oxford University Press.

Litvinov, V. A. (1999) Konzentrazia i differenziazia denezhnuh dohodov po gruppam naselenia [Concentration and differentiation of income according to population groups]. *Economic Journal of the Higher School of Economics*, Moscow, 2, pp. 226–37.

Maddison, A. (2001) *The World Economy: A Millennial Perspective*, Paris: OECD.

(2003) *The World Economy: Historical Statistics*, Paris: OECD.

North, D. C. (1990) *Institutions, Institutional Change and Economic Performance*, Cambridge: Cambridge University Press.

(2005) *Understanding the Process of Economic Change*, Princeton: Princeton University Press.

OECD (2014) *OECD Economic Surveys: Russian Federation 2013*, Paris: OECD.

Pipes, R. (1974) *Russia under the Old Regime*, London and New York: Penguin Books.

Polterovich, V. M. (1995) 'Economic Reforms in Russia in 1992: The Government Battles. Labor Collectives', *Journal of International and Comparative Economics*, 4, pp. 265–87.

(2008) 'Institutional Trap' in S. N. Durlauf and L. E. Blume (eds.) *The New Palgrave Dictionary of Economics. Second Edition*, New York and London: Palgrave Macmillan, pp. 369–74.

Przeworski, A., and Limongi, F. (1993) 'Political Regimes and Economic Growth', *Journal of Economic Perspectives*, 7.3, pp. 51–69.

Quadrio Curzio, A. (1986) 'Technological Scarcity: An Essay on Production and Structural Change', in M. Baranzini and R. Scazzieri (eds.) *Foundations of Economics. Structures of Inquiry and Economic Theory*, Oxford and New York: B. Blackwell, pp. 311–38.

Quadrio-Curzio, A., and Pellizzari, F. (1999) *Rent, Resources, Technologies*, Berlin, Heidelberg and New York: Springer.

Robinson, N. (1999) 'The Global Economy, Reform and Crisis in Russia', *Review of International Political Economy*, 6.4, pp. 531–64.

Rodrik, D. (2000) 'Institutions for High-quality Growth: What They are and How to Acquire Them', Cambridge, Mass.: NBER Working Paper 7540.

Roland, G. (2004) 'Understanding Institutional Change: Fast-Moving and Slow-Moving Institutions', paper presented at the Conference of Endogenous Institutional Change, Stanford University: Social Science History Institute; also published in *Studies in Comparative International Development* (2004) 38.4, pp. 109–31.

Rosefielde, S. (2001) Premature Deaths: Russia's Radical Economic Transition in Soviet Perspective, *Europe-Asia Studies*, 53.8, pp. 1159–76.

(2005) 'Russia: An Abnormal Country', *European Journal of Comparative Economics*, 2.1, pp. 3–16.

(2007) *The Russian Economy: From Lenin to Putin*, Oxford: B. Blackwell.

Rosefielde, S., and Hedlund, S. (2009) *Russia since 1980*, Cambridge and New York: Cambridge University Press.

Schwab, K. (ed.) (2013) *The Global Competitiveness Report 2013–2014*, Geneva: The World Economic Forum.

Shleifer, A., and Treisman, D. (2005) 'A Normal Country: Russia After Communism', *Journal of Economic Perspectives*, 19.1, pp. 151–74.

Treisman, D. (2010) '"Loans for Shares" Revisited', Cambridge, Mass.: NBER Working Paper 15819.

Vinhas de Souza, L. (2009) 'Russia's Recent Economic and Reform Performance and Remaining Reform Challenges', *Journal of the New Economic Association*, 1–2, pp. 207–22.

Woodruff, D. M. (2004) 'Property Rights in Context: Privatization's Legacy for Corporate Legality in Poland and Russia', *Studies in Comparative International Development*, 38.4, pp. 82–108.

World Bank (2013) 'Doing Business 2014: Understanding Regulations for Small and Medium-Size Enterprises', Washington, DC: The World Bank.

(2014) 'World Development Indicators (WDI) Online database', [online] available at: http://data.worldbank.org [accessed 31 March 2014].

(2014) Country and Lending Groups, [online] available at: http://data.worldbank.org/about/country-classifications/country-and-lending-groups [accessed 31 March 2014].

(2014) Russian Economic Report, 31, Washington, DC: The World Bank.

Zhuravskaya, E. (2007) 'Whither Russia?' A Review of Andrei Shleifer's *A Normal Country*, *Journal of Economic Literature*, 45.1, pp. 127–46.

Zweynert, J., and Goldschmidt, N. (2006) 'The Two Transitions in Central and Eastern Europe as Processes of Institutional Transplantation', *Journal of Economic Issues*, 40.4, pp. 895–918.

15 Institutions, resources and the common weal

Alessandro Roncaglia

1. Introduction

It is quite difficult to point to a specific time as marking the birth of political economy as a social science. There are good reasons to invoke the name of William Petty (1623–87) in this respect, and his political arithmetic; however, some important notions were already present in previous writings. Often, such notions first appeared with a somewhat vague meaning, and were increasingly closely specified at a later stage, especially when embodied in formal models of the economy. Scientific progress in economic analysis is connected to increasing precision in the definition of the concepts utilized in the analysis.[1] Quite often, though, what is left out in pursuing clear-cut definition is not irrelevant for a fuller grasp of the societies in which we live. In other words, we should keep in the back of our minds the multifacetedness of the original notions, although they are too vague for 'scientific' analysis, for they can provide useful reminders of the various different aspects involved in our general object of study; moreover, even if such aspects are better analysed separately, their interconnections may be very important.

There is thus, so to say, an 'internal' evolution in the connotation of the concepts utilized in economic analysis, connected to the pursuit of scientific progress in our analysis. Obviously, there is also an 'external' evolution, connected to historical events affecting human societies, which modify their inner structure in such a way as to require changes in the way we view and represent the economy and society.

One of the aspects that often come to light when considering the evolution of a concept is the relationship between the positive and normative side of our analytical efforts, between the 'objective' description of the state of affairs and

Thanks, with no further implications, are due to Carlo D'Ippoliti for his critical remarks on a first draft of this chapter.

[1] There are countless examples of this fact. For instance, the Ricardian problem of the invariant measure of value could only be solved (by Sraffa, 1960) by distinguishing, and keeping separate, invariance to changes in technology and invariance to changes in income distribution. Cf. Roncaglia (2009, pp. 78–94).

our desire to find out what we should do to improve the situation. Since we are not interested in a one-to-one mapping of reality, 'objective' description implies simplification, hence choices – quite often difficult ones – concerning what to take into account and what to leave out of our analysis. It is first of all through the definition of the concepts utilized in our analysis that such choices take shape, and it is through such choices that our interests, and hence our ethical position, come into play.

A basic concept in economic analysis, whose (very complex) evolution provides a test ground for the methodological issues previously mentioned, is the notion of the common weal. Considered a central issue for analysis of human societies in the sixteenth century, it is now more or less forgotten, possibly because of the difficulty of arriving at a clear-cut definition of the term, but its original content reappears, and has forever been reappearing in the history of economic thought, within other concepts and within different contexts.

Though certainly in a not univocal way, such a concept lies behind analysis of any specific issue, together with some elements of institutional background. Specifically, the common weal notion (as we shall see, quite a complex notion) involves aspect that is behind the very setting of the analysis: the relationship between theoretical analysis, with its unavoidable simplifying assumptions, and the ethical element that is the (often unrecognized) prime mover for the economists who try to understand the world in order to change it, whatever is the theoretical topic they deal with: natural resources and technical choice, value and distribution, or monetary and financial institutions.

Basic choices concerning the use of natural resources (specifically, land: either for cattle-raising or for crop-growing) constitutes, as we shall see in the next section, the testing ground for the early development of the notion of the common weal. Issues concerning institutions, technical choice and income distribution all come into play in the subsequent developments of the notion. The opposition between a 'subjective' and an 'objective' approach – with their well-known different ways of treating natural resources, scarcity and production[2] – reappear, also recently, in the opposition between the so-called economics of happiness and the common weal notion as illustrated later.

In the following pages we consider some aspects involved in the evolution of the concept of common weal, with no attempt at completeness – neither from the point of view of the history of economic thought, nor with regard to the many aspects included in the substantive content of the notion.

In Section 2 we recall an early instance of the use of this notion, the *Discourse on the Common Weal of This Realm of England* ([1581] 1893).

---

[2] Cf. Roncaglia (2001) on the differences between the classical (objective) and the marginalist (subjective) approach; and Quadrio Curzio (1967, 1975), Quadrio Curzio and Pellizzari (1996) for a theoretical 'objective' treatment of natural resources, technology and rent.

Subsequent sections are devoted to considering the different aspects of its substantive content, from the material idea of the common weal identified with the wealth of nations to the contemporary notion of happiness as the true aim of human behaviour. Thus Section 3 considers Smith's notion of the wealth of nations, focused on the material aspect of production, and his notion of self-interest, where the pursuit of material welfare is balanced with the ethical element of care for others. In Section 4 we discuss Bentham's reduction of the common weal to a monodimensional magnitude with his utilitarianism, and John Stuart Mill's criticisms, which in a sense bring us back to Smith's views. In Section 5, then, we consider marginalist-neoclassical individualism, with cursory consideration of Pareto's notion of optimality; commenting on its limits, we point out the absence from the marginalist approach of an equivalent to the notion of common weal, accounted for by its methodological individualism. Finally, Section 6 is devoted to discussion of some contemporary theories concerning aspects of the notion of common weal, such as the growing recourse to the notion of happiness and the notions of social capital or civil economy, and Amartya K. Sen's notion of development of capabilities.

2.   The original notion of common weal

Written in 1549 but first published only in 1581, the *Discourse of the Common Weal of This Realm of England* is a dialogue between a doctor, a knight, a merchant, an artisan (a capper) and a husbandman – representing the different classes of society and their different interests and points of view – dealing with the economic and social situation of England at the time. Long attributed to John Hales, it has also been ascribed to Thomas Smith or to William Stafford.[3]

The very title of the *Discourse* points to the common weal as the object of the analysis. No definition of it is given. Among cultured people, the implicit reference was possibly to the notion of *bonum commune*, present in the debate of the Late Middle Ages and early Renaissance on political institutions though extraneous to the corpus of Roman law.[4] In the *Discourse*, the notion of common weal acquires more precise connotations from the very content of the text itself.

---

[3] Cf. Lamond (1893) for the attribution to John Hales and Dewar (1969) for the attribution to Thomas Smith.

[4] A Florentine monk, the Dominican Remigio dei Girolami (d. 1319), who was lector of theology at Santa Maria Novella and may have been Dante's teacher, left among his many writings a manuscript treatise entitled *De bono comuni*, recently published under the telling title 'Dal bene comune al bene del comune' ('From the common weal [good] to the municipality weal [good]', Panella, 1985). Half a century earlier, Thomas Aquinas (c. 1225–74) discussed the *bonum commune* in connection with the natural law doctrine, in such a way as to reconcile social stratification with the equality of Christians before God (cf. Viano, 2010). For other references, cf. Maifreda (2012, pp. 160–2).

At the time of the *Dialogue*, English society was experiencing massive upheaval due to the enclosure revolution. The feudal regime of property meant political, juridical and economic domination by the landlord over the peasant-serfs in the context of a socio-economic set-up that guaranteed the serfs a life of mere subsistence through cultivation of plots of land (servile lands), the product of which went to meet their own subsistence needs, side by side with cultivation of the landlord's lands (*terrae dominicae*), and through the right, for instance, to gather – in the woods where the landlord asserted his exclusive right to hunt – wood to build their huts and heat them. The landlords, however, had discovered that cattle-raising was more profitable than crop-growing, in that it produced a greater surplus for themselves, largely thanks to the fact that it required fewer hands. (In modern terms, gross production fell but the difference between gross production and costs of production increased.) Thus gradually, but ever more relentlessly between the end of the fifteenth and beginning of the sixteenth century, the landlords proceeded to 'enclose' lands that had hitherto provided the traditional basis for subsistence for the serfs and their families, simply driving out those who were not needed to mind the cattle. So it was that multitudes lost their traditional means of subsistence. As a contemporary writer, Thomas More (1516, pp. 65–7), observed, sheep 'which are usually so tame and so cheaply fed, begin now … to be so greedy and wild that they devour human beings themselves and devastate and depopulate fields, houses, and towns'.

Enclosures were a social tragedy, but they also marked a step in the direction of modern property relations, conducive to higher productivity, accumulation and economic growth. Feudal relations gave way to private property, and a radical restructuring of agriculture – by far the most important sector of the economy at the time – was enacted. The way the change took place saw landlords ruthlessly utilizing their political strength to change the rules of the game to their own advantage, appropriating as their own private property what had originally been common lands over which they had political dominion but, in accordance with consuetudinary practice, together with responsibility for survival of the dominated classes.

The *Discourse* discusses this situation in precise terms. The situation is seen to be one of transition, and the simultaneous presence of positive and negative features in the process of transition is recognized, as well as a role of monetary disorders (the debasing of coins) in the accelerating pace of enclosures. The 'common weal' is precisely the standpoint from which the observer judges the positive or negative features of the transition; namely, in some vague sense, it points to what is good for the community as a whole: 'eche man, added to another, maketh up the whole bodie of the common weale' (Anonymous, [1581] 1893, p. 51).

There are two aspects to be stressed here. First, the point of view adopted in the *Dialogue* is that of the community as a whole rather than that of the sovereign. The latter was indeed the typical point of view for many – indeed, most – writings of the time and for a couple of centuries subsequently (the so-called mercantilist literature, a catch-all label for the political and economic writings of the long period of naissance of the nation-state). Indeed, as we shall see, Smith's notion of 'the wealth of nations', which can be considered as a radical departure from the previous dominant consensus viewpoint, has significant similarities with the point of view adopted in the *Discourse*. Second – and here is an important element distinguishing this from Smith's later notion – here the notion of the common weal embodies a strong ethical component, present in the culture of the time as the religious tenet that we are all sons (and daughters) of God so that we must care for each other.

The author of the *Discourse* to a certain extent accepts that the enclosures embody an element of progress, but is also well aware that they constitute a social tragedy. His point is that enclosures cannot be stopped by the law,[5] but the transition process should follow a path such as not to imply the ruin of the poor people ('an vndoinge of the poore commons', Anonymous, [1581] 1893, p. 53).[6] The common weal appears here to be a multidimensional notion, taking into account both the increase of net production and the social malaise it involved, the latter stemming from a very unequal distribution of the gains and losses among the different classes of society.

The problem which the *Discourse* tackles is how to pursue the common weal, interpreted in such a multidimensional way, while taking into account the conflicting interests of the different social classes. Obviously, this depends on the way the process of transition takes place, and this in turn depends on the choices of those who govern the process, both the sovereign and the landlords (represented by the Knight in the *Discourse*). It is up to them to follow such a path as to keep to a minimum the negative consequences of the enclosures. The author of the *Discourse* does not argue that such a course is in their own interest (as one might try to maintain invoking fear of a revolution), but refers instead to an ethical precept. In pursuing their interests, the *Discourse* says, the sovereign and landlords should also keep account of the common weal, namely the weal of the whole community: 'they may not purchase them seules profit by that that may be hurtfull to others. But how to bringe them that [they]

---

[5] 'Euerie man will seke wheare most advantage is, and they see theire is most advantage in grasinge and breedinge than in husbandrie and tillage, by a great deale. And so longe [as] it is so, the pasture shall [evere] encroche vpon the tillage, for all the laws that euer can be made to the contrarie.' (Anonymous, [1581] 1893, p. 53).

[6] The Doctor in the *Discourse* states that he does not oppose all enclosures, 'but only of such Inclosures as turneth commonly arable feildes into pastures; and violent Inclosures, without Recompence that haue right to comen therein' (Anonymous, [1581] 1893, p. 49).

would not doe so, is all the matter' (Anonymous, [1581] 1893, p. 50). And again, in a passage which foreshadows the notion of Pareto optimality, answering the Knight's argument that whatever is profitable to somebody is profitable to the common weal ('Euerie man is a member of the common weale, and that that is proffitable to one maie be proffitable to another, yf he would exercise the same feat'), the Doctor states:

that thinge which is proffitable to eche man by him seule, (so it be not preiudiciall to anie other,) is proffitable to the whole common weale, and not other wise; or els robbinge and stelinge, which percase is proffitable to some men, weare profitable to the whole common weale, which no man will admitt. But this feate of Inclosing is so that, wheare it is proffitable to one man, it is preiudiciall to manie'. (Anonymous, [1581] 1893, pp. 50–1)

What the doctor appears to suggest is that in a good society, where the common weal is pursued, the behaviour of the main agents must conform to a complex rule: pursuit of self-interest, but constrained by social responsibility. Implicit here, albeit in rudimentary form, is the complex notion of self-interest which, as we shall see, is developed two centuries later in the writings of Adam Smith, when we consider the *The Theory of Moral Sentiments* (1759) and the *The Wealth of Nations* (1776) as proposing a unified worldview.

3.   Smith's notions of wealth of nations and self-interest

Smith's notion of the wealth of nations is clearly set out in the very first lines of his *magnum opus*:

The annual labour of every nation is the fund which originally supplies it with all the necessaries and conveniences of life which it annually consumes, and which consist always, either in the immediate produce of that labour, or in what is purchased with the produce from other nations.

According therefore, as this produce, or what is purchased with it, bears a greater or smaller proportion to the number of those who are to consume it, the nation will be better or worse supplied with all the necessaries and conveniences for which it has occasion. (Smith, 1776, p. 10)

Thus Smith's notion of the wealth of nations more or less corresponds to what today we call per capita income, or in other terms to the standard of living of the citizens of the country under consideration. It is therefore a more restricted notion than the *Discourse*'s common weal, leaving aside the dimension of greater or lesser social inequality. At the same time, thanks to its clear-cut specification Smith is able to analyse it and show that it depends on two elements, productivity (product per worker) and the share of productive workers over population, and subsequently to analyse the factors that affect productivity – mainly the division of labour – and the share of the active population – mainly accumulation. Furthermore, Smith's notion has in common with the *Discourse*'s common weal notion reference to the point of view of the individual members of society, as opposed to the point of view of the sovereign, for whom the wealth of the nation corresponds to total and not to per capita product, as the ground for the military/political strength of the nation as well as the sumptuousness of the sovereign's court.[7]

Obviously, the fact that Smith's notion of the wealth of nations does not embody the ethical element implicit in the earlier notion of the common weal does not mean that Smith himself is uninterested in income distribution or social inequality. Far from it: Smith is clearly aware of the distributive conflict (in relation to which he stresses, for instance, the unbalance in bargaining power between the masters and the workers), as indeed he is of the negative social effects of the division of labour (an aspect for which he can be considered a precursor of the Marxian notion of alienation, and on account of which he proposes recourse to generalized free public education).[8] Quite simply, different issues need be considered separately in the analysis of society.

It is undeniable that Smith attributed great importance to the element of material welfare. Progress in the wealth of nations, in the specific sense of increase in per capita product, is considered by Smith as related to progress in civilization and in general well-being. Thus, for instance, Smith recalls that the habit of putting to death malformed children was widespread in primitive societies due to a level of productivity too low for workers to be able to produce enough for the subsistence of the unable, and points out that economic development is a prerequisite for the development of the arts.[9]

The idea of a civilizing role played by growing economic interchange – the idea of the *doux commerce* – was widely supported in the eighteenth century: Montesquieu, Hume, Condorcet and Paine all express ideas similar to Smith's. The opposite idea, namely that the market economy corrodes its own moral and cultural foundations (what Hirschman, 1982, p. 1466, calls

---

[7] As a matter of fact, the military/political strength of the nation is (also) somehow connected to per capita income, mainly – but not only – because of its connection with technology, especially military technology.

[8] Cf. Smith (1776, pp. 83–4 and pp. 781–2). On these issues cf. Roncaglia (2001 pp. 130, 149–54) and Roncaglia (2005).

[9] Cf. Smith (1759, pp. 209–11) and Smith (1983, pp. 136–7). Let us quote a few lines: 1. 'In general, the style of manners which takes place in any nation, may commonly upon the whole be said to be that which is most suitable to its situation. Hardiness is the character most suitable to the circumstances of a savage; sensibility to those of one who lives in a very civilized society.' (Smith, 1759, p. 209) 2. 'Opulence and Commerce commonly precede the improvement of arts, and refinement of every Sort. I do not mean that the improvement of arts and refinement of manners are the necessary consequence of commerce ... but only that it is a necessary requisite.' (Smith, 1983, p. 137)

'the self-destruction thesis'), found support at the time on the conservative side, reacting to Walpole and the Whig government who were favourable to progress for the market society, by revolutionaries such as Marx and Engels in the following century,[10] and by economists taking different standpoints such as Schumpeter and Hirsh in the twentieth century.[11]

Today we might prefer to stress other – more 'objective' – elements, such as the correlation, both over time and across countries, of per capita income with various dimensions of human development such as life expectancy, child mortality and literacy.[12] These other elements are also positively related to public expenditure on education, medical assistance, retirement provisions and support for the poor: in other words, the pillars of the welfare state.[13] While the welfare state is clearly beyond Smith's cultural horizon, there is nothing in his theoretical construction directly opposed to it; in fact, the idea that support for the poorer strata of society is not only morally good but also favourable to sound economic development can be found in Smith as well as Turgot, Condorcet and many other writers of the Enlightenment period.[14]

Thus, we can understand and sympathize with Smith's overall positive attitude to the wealth of nations in its material characterization, notwithstanding the recognized presence of negative implications. However, there are also good reasons for the opposite attitude, the idea of material growth as a positive aim for society being subjected to widespread criticism. A very important element, which did not loom large in Smith's times, is the environmental issue (which did, however, receive attention from John Stuart Mill a century after Smith).[15] This issue becomes increasingly important with growth in gross production and consumption, while at the same time, with famine and the worst aspects of poverty perceived as problems having more to do with income distribution than the level of per capita product,[16] economic growth appears less important for the issues that were central to Adam Smith.[17]

Another, more subterraneous element underlies negative attitudes towards assigning pride of place to the target of economic growth, namely the

---

[10] Marx and the Marxist tradition also reject the idea of a 'common weal' for a capitalist society (indeed, for all pre-socialist societies) where social classes basically differ in their interests. As we saw earlier, conflicts of interest are not denied by the *Discourse* or by Adam Smith: conflicts, even harsh ones, coexist with a basic 'consent' (as Hume, 1748, called it) considered as a necessary requisite for the development of a civilized society.

[11] Cf. Roncaglia (2001, pp. 85–7).

[12] Admittedly the correlation is far from perfect; analysing the outliers may prove very useful in showing the relevance of such factors as political democracy, absence of gender discrimination, public expenditure on education and the welfare state.

[13] Welfare expenditure is obviously positively related to, but by no means univocally determined by, per capita GNP.

[14] Cf. Roncaglia (2001, pp. 155–8).   [15] Cf. Mill ([1848] 1871, book IV ch. 6).

[16] On this cf. Drèze and Sen (1989).

[17] Cf. Fuà (1993) for a balanced critical presentation of the 'growthmania'.

corruption in customs and ethics engendered by unilateral focus on the pursuit of material wealth.[18] A persistent aspect in economic debate at all times, it is also implicit in the work of Adam Smith himself (in a passage in the *The Theory of Moral Sentiments*, which should be borne in mind when discussing the notion of happiness, in that once again it stresses its multidimensional character):

What can be added to the happiness of the man who is in health, who is out of debt, and has a clear conscience? To one in this situation, all accessions of fortune may properly be said to be superfluous; and if he is much elevated upon account of them, it must be the effect of the most frivolous levity. (Smith, 1759, p. 45)

Thus, two centuries after the *Discourse*, in Adam Smith the notion of the common weal gives way to the more specific notion of wealth of nations, focused on material production; however, the other elements intrinsic to the common weal do not disappear but, on the contrary, take on a clearer physiognomy and find an appropriate place in Smith's complex and balanced discourse on human societies.

Another nexus between the economic and ethical sides of the notion of the common weal is the relationship between selfishness and care for others in the motivation of each person's choices. As we saw, this aspect is already present in the *Discourse*, as a problem the solution to which is crucial for the pursuit of the common weal. Smith, as we shall briefly recall, provides a solution to this problem with a well-guarded notion of self-interest, not to be confused with mere selfishness. In order to understand this point, we must consider the two books published by Smith in his lifetime, the *The Theory of Moral Sentiments* (1759) and the *The Wealth of Nations* (1776), as complementary rather than opposite, focusing one on the ethical issue, the other on the material issue in the behaviour of human agents and the evolution of human societies.

The thesis of a contradiction between the two works prevailed for a certain time, constituting what was labelled *das Adam Smith Problem*.[19] According to this view, at first, in *The Theory of Moral Sentiments* Smith developed an ethical theory based on 'the moral principle of sympathy', more or less meaning (in the etymological sense of the word) the ability to share the feelings of others, while subsequently, in *The Wealth of Nations*, he relied on the basic assumption that individuals pursue their own personal interest. However, the idea of a contradiction between the contents of the two books is clearly absurd: Smith reprinted his first book after publishing the second one, introducing changes that, however, did not concern the basic idea of sympathy, thus showing that he himself saw no contradiction between it and his notion of

[18] References to the supporters of this thesis can be found in Hirschman (1982).
[19] Cf. Roncaglia (2001, pp. 121–6).

self-interest. Let us see how the apparent contradiction can be transformed into complementariness between the two notions.

In *The Theory of Moral Sentiments* Smith considers sufficiently widespread adoption of the ethic of sympathy (reinforced by the law and the police, since men are basically good but not perfect)[20] as a prerequisite for the very survival of human societies: 'Society ... cannot subsist among those who are at all times ready to hurt and injure one another' (Smith, 1759, p. 86).[21] Now, it is clear that such a prerequisite – namely the assumption that the market economy subsists in the context of a civilized society – also underlies the analysis of *The Wealth of Nations*. There (Smith, 1776, pp. 26–7) we find Smith's celebrated remark that 'It is not from the benevolence of the butcher, the brewer, or the baker, that we expect our dinner, but from their regard to their own interest' (with an implicit critique of his teacher Hutcheson's theory of benevolence). Quite simply, self-interest is not to be interpreted as perfect selfishness, but as constrained by adhesion to the ethic of sympathy, once again supported by the law and the police (as is stressed in the *The Wealth of Nations* as well, where Smith sees the administration of justice as a basic task of the State).[22]

Indeed, Smith's reliance on self-interest stems from his confidence in the self-governing capacity of individuals: 'Every man is, no doubt, by nature, first and principally recommended to his own care; and as he is fitter to take care of himself than of any other person, it is fit and right that it should be so' (Smith, 1759, p. 82). In other words, the free pursuit of personal interest is constrained, and addressed to society's common weal, both by an element external to the individual (the administration of justice) and an element internal to him ('sympathy' for his fellow human beings). Let us recall in passing that, from the context of Smith's discourse, it is clear that enforcement of the law is seen as a prerequisite for a civilized society and not – or at least not necessarily and not primarily – as an instrument of domination of the higher classes over the lower classes. The latter point of view found a place in the anarchist and Marxian traditions, while Smith (1776), with his characteristic concern for the multifaceted nature of humans and human societies, is also able to observe that

---

[20] 'The coarse clay of which the bulk of mankind are formed, cannot be wrought up to such perfection' (Smith, 1759, pp. 162–3). Twenty-five years later, this passage was echoed by Kant (1784, p. 130): 'From a twisted wood, such as that of which man is made, nothing entirely straight can come out. Only the approximation to this idea is imposed on us by nature'.

[21] Let us also recall the internal constraint – conscience – or, in Adam Smith's words, the 'impartial spectator', who is endowed with the same knowledge of the situation as the agent, and judges his or her actions from the point of view of the average citizen.

[22] Somewhat different from Smith's is the solution to the issue proposed a few years earlier by Muratori (1749), who distinguishes between the 'desire ... of our particular happiness' from 'another desire, namely that of the good of society ... namely public happiness'. (Muratori, 1749, p. 7) Cfr. Ricuperati (2010).

'Civil government, so far as it is instituted for the security of property, is in reality instituted for the defence of the rich against the poor, or of those who have some property against those who have none at all' (p.715). Obviously, there is a 'violence from below', which is dreadfully feared by the dominant classes; when we speak of a 'police state' we mean a state with laws forbidding any manifestation of dissent and the police enforcing compliance to these laws. But history also offers examples of 'violence from above', when the dominant classes utilize violence, even against existing laws, to subjugate the lower classes: the Fascist regime is an obvious instance.[23] Besides, common (non-political) violence is in general more damaging for the lower classes than for the rich, who have the means to defend themselves directly.[24]

4.   Bentham's greatest happiness principle

We should recall that when identifying the Smithian notion of the wealth of nations with per capita income we refer to a modern notion, which did not exist in Smith's times. We have to wait a couple of centuries more for the naissance and development of national accounting and for a precisely defined notion of national income as a monodimensional magnitude. Thus, the notion of the wealth of nations simply implied reference to material well-being in a rather general way.

A monodimensional translation of the wealth of nations in subjective terms was accomplished, in the same years that saw publications of Smith's *magnum opus*, by Jeremy Bentham with his 'greatest happiness principle'. According to Bentham (1776, p. 393), 'it is the greatest happiness of the greatest number that is the measure of right or wrong'. Literally taken, this implies two elements to be simultaneously maximized: 'greatest happiness' for the individual and 'greatest number' of happy individuals. However, Bentham assumes as a principle that all individuals are equal (as he is entitled to, since his aim is the construction of a normative theory, not a descriptive one), so that individual pleasures and pains can be algebraically added up in what Bentham calls 'felicific calculus',

---

[23] A lively picture of Fascist violence is provided for instance by Matteotti, in his writings and speeches in the two years preceding his assassination (Matteotti, 2009, 2011), or by Lussu (1945).

[24] The importance for the lower classes of the rule of the law, and the very connection between liberty and order, is stressed, for instance, in a letter by Sraffa to Gramsci: "The most pressing issue, taking precedence over any other, is one of 'freedom' and 'order': the others will come later, but for the time being they can be of no interest to workers". The letter was published anonymously in *L'Ordine Nuovo*, in April 1924 (Sraffa, 1924; my translation), and Gramsci drew the attention of his comrades to it. The story is told in Roncaglia, 2009, pp. 6–9. Matteotti explicitly and Sraffa implicitly suggest a sort of political exchange between democratic freedoms (implying the rule of the law) and renouncing to 'violence from below' in political and social conflicts.

implying maximization of a single magnitude, total social happiness. Bentham's great contribution was, of course, his consequentialist ethics, as opposed to the deontological ethics that in various forms had been the principle hitherto commonly adopted. With a good deal of simplification, we may state this opposition in the following terms. The deontological approach maintains that human actions are intrinsically 'good' or 'bad'; the terms for judgement of the intrinsic characteristics of each action must somehow or other be established, since peaceful coexistence within a community requires a common ethical ground. Apart from some fairly obvious instances (e.g. killing a person is bad, at least in peacetime), this is commonly obtained by recourse to some authority, be it religious commandments or the strength of traditions sanctioned by political authorities. Bentham's consequentialist approach, instead, maintains that any action can, with recourse to the felicific calculus, be judged on the basis of its consequences and their impact on the general happiness.[25]

In principle, the felicific calculus may be utilized to evaluate the impact on the general happiness of both individual actions and public policy choices. Bentham focuses on the latter, with a variety of proposals for 'rational' institutional set-ups. His main aim is the enactment of a legal code such as to achieve the supremacy of reason within human societies, the felicific calculus being the legislator's main tool. In Bentham's opinion, enlightened reason should drive all citizens to support the same institutions, and specifically those rationally designed by him; in practice, realization of the "rational" legal code is entrusted to the enlightened prince. This may even imply an authoritarian turn, which is common in Enlightenment culture among those favouring the ésprit de systeme; within the Enlightenment, this tendency was opposed by advocates of the critical rather than constructive role of reason, the ésprit de finesse; Voltaire, for instance, is a well-known advocate of this position, but Adam Smith is also to be recalled in this context.[26]

---

[25] Needless to say, such a clear-cut dichotomy between the two approaches is simplistic and hides many a problem. As pointed out by Sen (1991), on the one hand deontological theories are often open to recognition, at least indirectly, of the importance of the consequences of actions, while on the other hand consequentialist theories commonly retain some elements of a priori judgment.

[26] Clear expression of this latter position, in opposition to the Physiocrats, seen as 'men of the system', was supplied by Galiani (1770, p. 55): 'Nobody ever makes a mistake without a reason. Thus everybody wants to follow reason and experience, but if you follow an idea reasonable in itself and rely on an experience or a true and demonstrated fact, but which does not fit in – is not applicable to the case at hand – you think you are doing well, and you are wrong'. Or again: 'Nothing in politics can be pursued to the extreme. There is a point, a limit up to which good is greater than evil; if you pass beyond it, evil prevails over good. [This point . . .] only the sage knows how to find. People feel it by instinct. The man in power needs time to find it. The modern economist does not even suspect it' (Galiani, 1770, p. 233; perhaps we should add that by 'modern economists' Galiani refers to the Physiocrats, then known as les économistes).

The idea that we can rely on the felicific calculus to solve our ethical problems and any problem of choice, be it individual or concerning policy issues, has a basic prerequisite: a full knowledge of the pleasures and pains consequent upon any action must be possible, and all sorts of pleasures and pains must be comparable on the same quantitative scale. This is, in fact, Bentham's basic tenet, and it is on this tenet that John Stuart Mill exercises his critical powers.

Mill does not reject consequentialist ethics. Quite the contrary: he supports it as superior to deontological ethics, because of the latter's authoritarian, traditionalist nature. However, he also stresses that the felicific calculus cannot be applied in many important instances, since pleasures and pains of different sorts are not comparable. Specifically, there are different levels of pleasure – elevated and commonplace pleasures, for instance, such as the pleasure derived from reading poetry and enjoyment of a card game.[27] And there are the 'tragic' issues (those that constitute the basic structure of Greek tragedies) where choosing is so painful as to be practically impossible – love for one's country versus love for one's family, obeying a religious duty versus survival of a son, and so on. In essence, what Mill stresses is that the practical application of consequentialist ethics is no easy task, and certainly not one that involves univocal answers.

This is most important on two accounts. First, the idea of the perfect rational scheme (and the associated idea that such a perfect scheme can be entrusted to an enlightened prince, with all its authoritarian implications) falls away. Second, this implies a basic critique of attempts to import into the realm of economics the principles of felicific calculus, which are discussed in the next section.

5. Resources, common weal and methodological individualism: the case of marginalist economics

Bentham, and the supporters of a consequentialist ethics, did not offer a theoretical treatment of the relationship between utility and value. When considering the issue, they limited themselves to the vague observations, common since classical antiquity, to the effect that scarcity and utility determine exchange value. In fact, theoretical treatment of the issue requires substantive changes in the Benthamite notion of the felicific calculus.

First of all, there is a change in perspective, from the pursuit of the common weal (the 'greatest happiness' principle) to analysis of individual behaviour.

---

[27] 'It is better to be a human being dissatisfied than a pig satisfied; better to be Socrates dissatisfied than a fool satisfied. And if the fool, or the pig, are of a different opinion, it is because they only know their own side of the question' (Mill, 1861, p. 281).

The individualistic turn was so strong that the Smithian notion of self-interest discussed earlier came to be identified with the mono-dimensional notion of selfishness. Simultaneously, the subjectivist turn was so strong that the leading exponents of the new economics denied the interpersonal comparability of pleasures and pains.[28]

Second, Mill's criticism regarding the existence of different kinds of pleasure and pain was circumvented either by assuming – as Jevons did –[29] that economics only refers to the lowest kinds of human activity, those having to do with the satisfaction of mere material needs, or more often by simply ignoring it. In fact, since the satisfaction of both 'higher level' and 'lower level' desires implies buying goods and services, Jevons's suggested solution cannot be accepted.

Third, the notion of the common weal remains, but constrained into the straightjacket of Pareto optimality: namely, a situation such that no individual can improve his or her position without a worsening for somebody else.[30] The so-called fundamental theorems of welfare economics link the optimal position of the economy to perfect competition, specifying that i) each competitive equilibrium is Pareto-optimal and ii) each Pareto optimum corresponds to a competitive equilibrium.

This would have allowed for identification of the common weal with the institution of perfectly competitive markets for all goods and services: the Gospel of the invisible hand of the market (a thesis erroneously attributed to Adam Smith).[31] However, if we consider the precise nature of these fundamental theorems, we can reach a different conclusion. They only point to a 'local' optimality: general equilibrium theory shows that it is impossible to demonstrate the uniqueness of competitive equilibrium, so that any specific solution, interpreted as the optimal point to which a competitive market leads, can be far inferior to other optimal points, and even to non-optimal points in the vicinity of other equilibriums. Moreover, the theorems hold only under very specific assumptions (such as convexity of individuals' preference sets and of production sets, so that increasing returns to scale, so common in reality, are ruled out). Stability too – namely a tendency to an optimal equilibrium from any nearby point – cannot be held as a general property even in perfectly competitive markets.

---

[28] In the Introduction to *The Theory of Political Economy*, Jevons (1871, p. 85) clearly states that in it 'There is never, in any single instance, an attempt made to compare the amount of feeling in one mind with that in another. I see no means by which such comparison can be accomplished.'

[29] 'It is the lowest rank of feelings that we here treat. The calculus of utility aim to supplying the ordinary wants of man at the least cost of labour' (Jevons, 1871, p. 93).

[30] As we saw earlier, the Doctor of the *Discourse* utilizes a similar notion only as a critical tool, in order to criticize the Knight who had left out the distributive effects of the enclosures.

[31] Cf. Roncaglia (2005).

As a general principle, methodological individualism cannot lead to any useful proposition endowed with general validity applying to the economy as a whole.[32] This means that even specified in the very restrictive sense of the 'maximum utility principle' the common weal turns out to be a notion on which marginalist/neoclassical economics has nothing to say. Since the invisible hand of the market proves to be nothing but a myth, identification of the common weal with a perfectly competitive market economy is a mere rhetorical tool for ideological propaganda.

## 6.	A few notes on the current debates: common weal, non-producible resources, happiness and civil society

If we renounce to the 'maximum utility principle', we are driven back to the old idea of the common weal as a multidimensional notion. In this direction, we can here briefly consider some apparently similar but basically different notions present in contemporary debate: the notions of happiness and the civil economy, human development, social capital and civic development. The notion of 'happiness' has been developed within the conceptual framework of the traditional marginalist/neoclassical approach, although presented as critical towards mainstream economics.[33] The element of critique lies in rejection of a restricted 'economicist' view, based on the individual (selfish) pursuit of material well-being. Thus, happiness is pursued through various drivers, such as the family, work, liberty, health, friends, personal values and riches, within a lifestyle more open to a community dimension. The persistent element is the subjective/individualist viewpoint, and hence a hedonist interpretation of individual behaviour.

This latter element must be kept in mind: happiness economics implies some economics, namely some theorizing. The case is different if we refer to happiness in a general way, as the aim of human behaviour. For instance, a declaration on the inalienable right of the citizens to the pursuit of happiness is famously embedded in the American Declaration of Independence. There, it corresponds to a declaration on the individuals' right to pursue their own chosen life objectives; it is implied neither that happiness can be measured nor that maximum happiness can be operationally defined.

More recently, dissatisfaction with the materialist measure provided by per capita GNP has driven researchers in the new 'happiness' field to endeavour in attempts to construct indexes of happiness and/or to analyse its determinants. Such measures differ from the 'human development index', which we shall briefly consider later, in that they stress the

---

[32] For a discussion of the limits of mainstream economics, cf. Roncaglia (2011).
[33] Cf. for instance Layard (2005).

subjective viewpoint of individuals, as expressed in opinion surveys. Some national statistical institutions have been happy to embrace the new happiness notion, since the statistical exercise to measure it opens new and interesting research areas. However, it is quite clear that happiness is a composite notion, like the common weal, and that it is best illustrated by looking at its constituent elements, while the construction of aggregate indexes is more of an exercise in communication than an addition to our knowledge of the situation.[34]

The notion of human development, sufficiently well established by now, is in certain respects different from the notion of happiness discussed earlier. Both are, of course, multidimensional notions; moreover, their dimensions are partly the same (material well-being remains a component of both; health and a low crime rate also enter both notions). However, 'human development' is directly opposed to 'happiness' in that the former notion points to an objective viewpoint rather than a subjective one. Its foundation is provided by Amartya Sen's notion of 'capabilities',[35] which expand on the notion of per capita GDP by taking into account elements (correlated with GDP, but not perfectly) empowering humans to pursue their own ends. As developed in a series of studies and embodied in the human development index, the notion of capabilities includes an income aspect (per capita income and its more or less unequal distribution), health (life expectancy at birth, infant mortality and so on) and education.[36]

The notion of 'social capital' (more or less meaning civic traditions, sociability) and the associated notion of 'civic development' have also taken on an important role in the contemporary debate.[37] However, they should be distinguished from the notion of the 'civil economy' as suggested in a series of writings by Zamagni and others (and hinted at in Pope Benedict XVI's recent

---

[34] Cf. the *Report by the Commission on the measurement of economic performance and social progress* (Stiglitz, Sen and Fitoussi, 2010). While the *Report* is commonly cited in connection with the measurement of happiness, it refers in fact to 'well-being'.

[35] Cf. for instance Sen (1985), Nussbaum and Sen (1993).

[36] Cf. the yearly *Human Development Reports* of the United Nations Development Programme (UNDP) prompted by Mahbub ul Haq. The convention adopted in the construction of the human development index (simple arithmetical mean of its main components) has been criticized by Casadio Tarabusi and Palazzi (2004).

[37] Cf. Putnam (1993, 2000); Sylos Labini (1989, 2000). Putnam's treatment of sociability implies an element of ethical judgement (with the distinction between 'bridging' and 'bonding' social capital), which is also important in Sylos Labini's notion of civic development. In fact, typical Italian traditions, such as the so-called amoral familism (illegally favouring relatives) or the mafia or political clienteles, point to the need to discriminate among types of sociability, according as to whether they are conducive to or damaging for civic development. Among the forerunners of the notion of civic development we may recall Cesare Beccaria, Pietro Verri and Carlo Cattaneo (cf. Quadrio Curzio, 2007, pp. 43–56 and 101–14). On the role of subsidiarity for civic development, cf. Quadrio Curzio (2002).

epistle).[38] The first notion concerns the presence of non-egoistic motivations for human action and points to the simultaneous presence of a complex set of motivations, namely in the direction of the Smithian notion of self-interest discussed earlier. The 'civil economy' notion, on the other hand, points to the existence of a third sector – represented mainly by the voluntary work associations – characterized by altruistic behaviour, side by side with the public (state) and the private sector of the economy, the latter characterized by selfish behaviour. The third sector – the civil economy – is considered essential to the good functioning of the economy and society. However, the distinction between the civil economy and the market (private) economy implies a great – indeed, an excessive – simplification of the motivations for human action, which are never fully selfish nor fully altruistic, and avoids the crucial issue of striking the right balance between the different motivations. Of course such a balance can be different as occurring between different individuals, partly at least depending on the kind of activity involved; in any case, as Smith shows, it is also required for self-interested agents, or in other words for the private sector of the economy without which a market economy cannot subsist. Thus, the mere existence of a third sector, useful as it may be, cannot in itself constitute the solution to keep society on the right track of civilized life.

7.   Summing up

To sum up, the sixteenth-century notion of common weal, primitive and vague as it was, embodies an essential element, namely its multidimensional nature, which has been re-evaluated in present-day debates. In essence, the common weal notion appears as a criterion for evaluation: the common weal is pursued, or obtained, whenever we pursue, or obtain, a 'good' situation for society as a whole. Thus economic well-being (per capita income) matters, but also its sufficiently egalitarian distribution, as well as other elements such as – in casual order – peace, personal security, a healthy natural environment, political freedoms, culture, solidarity and so on. In a global context, we might add, pursuit of the common weal implies – possibly, first and foremost – consideration of the underdevelopment issue.

The monodimensional specifications that the notion of common weal received, such as the Smithian notion of the wealth of nations, are useful – even very useful – if we recognize their limits and utilize them – as Smith

---

[38] Cf. for instance Zamagni (1998), Bruni and Zamagni (2004); for a critique, cf. Roncaglia (1998). In Pope Benedict XVI's Encyclical letter *Caritas in veritate*, cf. § 39. The Encyclical letter, however, also encompasses other lines of reasoning; a more extended treatment of such themes – such as subsidiarity and development, democracy and social justice, social capital and human development – can be found in Quadrio Curzio and Marseguerra (2007, 2008, 2009).

did – in a context open to taking other relevant elements into account. However, we must retain a distinction between subjective and objective notions: the former (from the maximum utility principle to the notion of happiness) are connected to marginalist/neoclassical economics, while the latter are derived from the objective Smithian notion of the wealth of nations. Failure to perceive this distinction is a drawback in the debate: when dealing with a multidimensional notion, interpreting its dimensions entails clear specification of the underlying vision of the economy and the society.

Taking into account the multidimensional nature of the common weal notion, then, implies – as we saw earlier, in the case of the *Discourse* – recognizing the social implications of fundamental choices such as those concerning the use of the basic natural resource, land. The issue here is not the scarcity of the natural resource, as in mainstream economics, but the institutional and social context in which its use is decided. The relationship between technical choice, economic progress and income distribution should then be considered not in search for an univocal solution to the unavoidable conflicts of interest (even less for denying their existence), but in search for a 'common understanding' around possible ways of composition of these conflicts.

REFERENCES

(Page references in the text refer to the last of the editions quoted below.)

Anonymous ([1581] 1893) *A Discourse of the Common Weal of This Realm of England*, new edn. by E. Lamond, Cambridge: Cambridge University Press (written 1549).

Benedict XVI (2009) *Caritas in veritate*, Encyclical letter, www.vatican.va/ holy_father/benedict_xvi/encyclicals/documents/hf_ben-xvi_enc_20090629_caritas-in-veritate_en.html.

Bentham, J. ([1776]) 'Fragment on Government', in *The Works of Jeremy Bentham*, 9 vols., ed. by J. Bowring, Edinburgh and London: William Tait-Simpkin and Marshall & Co., 1843–59, vol. 1, pp. 221–95. Reprinted in *'A Comment on the Commentaries' and 'A Fragment on Government'*, ed. by J. H. Burns and H. L. A. Hart, London: Athlone Press, 1977.

Bruni, L., and Zamagni, S. (2004) *Economia civile*, Bologna: Il Mulino.

Casadio Tarabusi, E., and Palazzi, P. (2004) 'Un indice per lo sviluppo sostenibile', *Moneta e Credito*, 57, pp. 123–49.

Dewar, M. (1969) 'The Authorship of the "Discourse of the Commonweal"', *Economic History Review*, 19.2, pp. 388-400.

Drèze, J., and Sen, A. K. (1989) *Hunger and Public Action*, Oxford: Clarendon Press.

Galiani, F. (1770) *Dialogues sur le commerce des blés*, Londres: no publisher. Reprint ed. by F. Nicolini, Milan-Naples: Ricciardi, 1959; Italian transl., *Dialoghi sul commercio dei grani*, Rome: Editori Riuniti, 1978.

Hirschman, A. (1982) 'Rival Interpretations of Market Society: Civilizing, Destructive or Feeble?', *Journal of Economic Literature*, 20.4, pp. 1463–84.

Hume, D. (1748) 'Of the Original Contract', in *Three Essays: Moral and Political*, Edinburgh: Kinkaid and London: Millar. Reprinted in E.C. Miller (ed.) (1985) *Essays, Moral, Political, and Literary*, Indianapolis: Liberty Classics, pp. 465–87.

Jevons, W. S. (1871) *The Theory of Political Economy*, London: Macmillan (2nd edn. 1879; reprint Harmondsworth: Penguin Books, 1970).

Kant, I. (1784) 'Idee zu einer allgemeinen Geschichte in Weltbürgerlicher Absicht', *Berlinische Monatsschrift*, 4, pp. 385–411. Italian transl.: *Idea di una storia universale dal punto di vista cosmopolitico*, in I. Kant, *Scritti politici*, Torino: Utet, 1956, 3rd edn 1995, pp. 123–39. (English transl., *Perpetual Peace*, ed. by M. Campbell Smith, New York: Garland, 1972.)

Lamond, E. (1893) 'Introduction' to Anonymous 1581 (*A Discourse of the Common Weal of This Realm of England*, new edn by E. Lamond, *op. cit.*), pp. ix–lxxii.

Layard, R. (2005) *Happiness*, Harmondsworth: Penguin.

Lussu, E. (1945) *Marcia su Roma e dintorni*, Torino: Einaudi.

Maifreda, G. (2012) *From Oikonomia to Political Economy*, Farnham: Ashgate.

Matteotti, G. (2009) *Scritti economici e finanziari*, 2 vols, S. Caretti (ed.), Pisa: Pisa University Press.

(2011) *L'avvento del fascismo*, S. Caretti (ed.), Pisa: Pisa University Press.

Mill, J. S. ([1848] 1871) *Principles of Political Economy*, 7th edn, London: John W. Parker.

(1861) 'Utilitarianism', *Fraser's Magazine*, 64, pp. 383–4. Reprinted in J. S. Mill and J. Bentham (1987) *Utilitarianism and Other Essays*, ed. by A. Ryan, Harmondsworth: Penguin Books, pp. 272–338.

More, T. (1516) *Utopia*. Louvain: T. Martens. English transl., *Utopia*, in E. Surtz and J. H. Hexter (eds.) The Complete Works of St. Thomas More, vol. 4, New Haven: Yale University Press, 1965; reprint 1979.

Muratori, L. A. (1749) *Della pubblica felicità oggetto de' buoni principi*, Lucca. Reprinted in C. Mozzarelli (ed.) (1996) *Della pubblica felicità, oggetto de' buoni prìncipi*, Rome: Donzelli.

Nussbaum, M., and Sen, A. K. (eds.) (1993) *The Quality of Life*, Oxford: Oxford University Press.

Panella, E. (1985) 'Dal bene comune al bene del comune: i trattati politici di Remigio dei Girolami nella Firenze dei Bianchi-Neri', *Memorie domenicane*, 16, pp. 1–198.

Putnam, R. D. (1993) *Making Democracy Work*, Princeton: Princeton University Press.

(2000) *Bowling Alone. The Collapse and Revival of American Community*, New York: Simon & Schuster.

Quadrio Curzio, A. (1967) *Rendita e distribuzione in un modello economico plurisettoriale*, Milan: Giuffrè.

(1975) *Accumulazione del capitale e rendita*, Bologna: Il Mulino.

(2002) *Sussidiarietà e sviluppo*, Bologna: Il Mulino.

(2007) *Economisti ed economia*, Bologna: Il Mulino.

Quadrio Curzio, A., and Marseguerra, G. (eds.) (2007) *Intrapresa, sussidiarietà, sviluppo*, Milan: Scheiwiller.

(2008) *Democracy, Institutions and Social Justice*, Milan: Scheiwiller.

(2009) *Social Capital and Human Development*, Milan: Scheiwiller.

Quadrio Curzio, A., and Pellizzari, F. (1996) *Risorse, tecnologia, rendita*, Bologna: Il Mulino.

Remigio dei Girolami [A. D. 1300] *De bono comuni*. Ed. in E. Panella (1985), *op.cit.*, pp. 123–68.

Ricuperati, G. (2010) 'Pubblica felicità, uguaglianza nella legge, costituzionalismo, diritti dell'uomo. Innovazioni settecentesche ed eredità dell'Illuminismo', in *Bene comune e interesse pubblico, Quaderni laici*, 2, pp. 29–52.

Roncaglia, A. (1998) 'Comment', in Gandolfo, G. and Marzano, F. (eds.) *Economic Theory and Social Justice*, London: Macmillan, pp. 242–6.

(2001) *La ricchezza delle idee*, Roma-Bari: Laterza; English edn: *The Wealth of Ideas*, Cambridge: Cambridge University Press, 2005.

(2005) *Il mito della mano invisibile*, Roma-Bari: Laterza.

(2009) *Piero Sraffa*, Houndmills: Palgrave Macmillan.

(2011) 'Macroeconomie in crisi e macroeconomie in ripresa', *Moneta e Credito*, 64 (254), pp. 115–33.

Sen, A. K. (1985) *Commodities and Capabilities*. Oxford: Oxford University Press.

(1991) *Money and Value: On the Ethics and Economics of Finance*, Rome: Edizioni dell'Elefante.

Smith, A. (1759) *The Theory of Moral Sentiments*, London: A. Millar; critical edn by D. D. Raphael and A. L. Macfie, Oxford: Oxford University Press, 1976.

(1776) *An Inquiry into the Nature and Causes of the Wealth of Nations*. London: W. Strahan and T. Cadell; critical edn by R. H. Campbell and A. S. Skinner, Oxford: Oxford University Press, 1976.

([1761] 1983) *Lectures on Rhetoric and belles lettres*, ed. by J. C. Bryce, Oxford: Oxford University Press.

Sraffa, P. (1924) 'Problemi di oggi e di domani', letter to A. Gramsci, *L'ordine nuovo*, 1.3–4, p. 4.

(1960) *Production of Commodities by Means of Commodities*, Cambridge: Cambridge University Press.

Stiglitz, J. E., Sen, A. K., and Fitoussi, J. P. (2010) *Report to the Commission on the Measurement of Economic Performance and Social Progress*, www.stiglitz-sen-fitoussi.fr.

Sylos Labini, P. (1989) 'Sviluppo economico e sviluppo civile', *Moneta e Credito*, 42 (167), pp. 291–304.

(2000) *Underdevelopment. A Strategy for Reform*, Cambridge: Cambridge University Press.

Viano, C. A. (2010) 'I filosofi e il bene introvabile', *Bene comune e interesse pubblico. Quaderni laici*, 2, pp. 5–27.

Zamagni, S. (1998) 'Social Paradoxes of Growth and Civil Economy', in G. Gandolfo and F. Marzano (eds.) *Economic Theory and Social Justice*, London: Macmillan, pp. 212–36.

16   Development, capabilities and institutions

Stefano Zamagni

> The furrow will be straight [and the crop abundant] if the two horses dragging
> the plough proceed at the same speed.
>
> (Plato, *Phaedrus*)

1.   Introduction

Both economists and social scientists tend to share an awareness of the need, indeed the urgent need, to establish indices of the well-being of a nation or a community that go beyond the traditional measure of gross domestic product (GDP), without excluding the latter nevertheless. This awareness was a familiar one to classical economists, from A. Smith to J. S. Mill. The Marginalist Revolution, in the second half of nineteenth century, side-lined the well-being dimension, substituting it with the notion of (cardinal or ordinal) utility. To the neoclassical paradigm, economics should limit itself to optimal individual choice and efficient resource allocations. All the rest, in particular personal well-being and its components (values, culture, beliefs, social norms) should be treated as exogenous primitives. One major consequence of such a methodological stance is that the huge neoclassical literature dealing with economic growth is almost obsessed by the role that the misallocation of resources has in explaining the path of structural dynamics of a country. It is certainly true that the way in which the stock of physical capital, labour and human capital are allocated across firms, industries and within firms determines the economy's overall level of production and ultimately of welfare. However, what this literature tends to underrate is the importance of explaining why people living in society should seek to achieve the optimal resources allocation. If people do not perceive that such a goal will improve their well-being – which is not the same thing as welfare – the optimal allocation of resources will never be achieved.

I am grateful to Mauro Baranzini and Roberto Scazzieri for helpful comments and their valuable encouragement. The usual disclaimer applies.

279

In the last decade or so, a growing number of studies incorporate endogenous cultural change and the notion of well-being into economic models. This comes after a belated recognition that the notion of integral human development includes three fundamental dimensions: the material, the social-relational and the spiritual. While GDP tends to measure the first of these three aspects of well-being, it is plainly incapable of accounting for the other two. And since the three dimensions are related among them in a multiplicative, rather than an additive, manner, one cannot assume that an increase in material well-being may in some way 'compensate' for a reduction in relational and/or spiritual wellbeing. As Plato's famous metaphor, cited at the beginning of this chapter, clearly points out, integral human development requires that the aforesaid three dimensions proceed at the same pace.

As an example to clarify the point, consider the case of economic irrelevance. People are deemed to be economically irrelevant if their actions do not contribute, in any way, towards the production of wealth. Irrelevance is clearly perceptible today in the new face of an emerging social degradation, a phenomenon evident above all in the workplace. The removal of millions of people from productive activity is not just evidence of an inefficient allocation of resources, and hence of a loss of aggregate output (i.e. of GDP), but introduces into our advanced societies a real rationing of freedom, as von Hayek himself recognized in his *The Constitution of Liberty* (1960). Indeed, it is by now clear that people who remain unemployed for long periods of time suffer psychologically, a suffering that has nothing to do with their reduced income, but with their capacity to act and to learn. In terms of Sen's capabilities approach, this means that long-term unemployed people's ability to function is modified, in the sense that their actual ability to carry out previously set tasks is reduced drastically – a circumstance that no official statistic about GDP will ever be able to reveal. This implies that placing at the same level the availability of an income from work and that same income from a transfer (such as unemployment pay, minimum guaranteed income, etc.) signifies a negation of human identity. When values such as self-esteem or personal autonomy are at stake it is not a matter of indifference to know the sources of one's income. As Margalit (2000) acutely observed, it is not enough to struggle to create a just society. A more important goal is a 'decent society', that is, a society that does not humiliate its members by distributing benefits and advantages, but at the same time denying them their identity. When this happens, as history teaches us, the weakening of social norms of behaviour and the spread of cynical practices become inevitable phenomena. In situations of this kind, the GDP of a country may indeed rise, and with it material well-being, but certainly not the degree of integral human well-being.

Today, it is recognized that modern economic development did not derive principally from the adoption of more effective incentives or from the availability of new resources, but rather from the creation of a new culture. The idea that incentives or efficient allocations will generate positive economic results regardless of the prevailing culture is simply baseless, since what makes the difference is not the incentives *per se* but the way agents perceive and respond to them. And reactions depend precisely on the specificity of the cultural matrix conceived as a set of organized beliefs. (See McCleary and Barro, 2006; Guiso, Sapienza, Zingales, 2006; Jones, 2013)

A recent contribution attempting to overcome the strictures of the still prevailing mode of analysing the relationship between production and structural dynamics is the *Report by the Commission on the Measurement of Economic Performance and Social Progress*, edited by J. E. Stiglitz, A. K. Sen, and J. P. Fitoussi (2010) and submitted on 14 September 2009 to the French President Sarkozy. The main thesis of the Report is that GDP has serious limits as an indicator not only of social progress but also of economic performance. This is due to the fact that it is based solely on the economy's product, forgetting the other two dimensions of society's well-being. It follows that it is not enough trying to perfectionate the GDP indicator on technical grounds. What is needed is a change of the current way to represent the economic process: a change centred on the notion of sustainable well-being. In turn, this implies a redefinition of 'production boundaries' to include those non-market processes enhancing the quality of life. (Think of defensive consumption, domestic care, leisure, families' self-consumption, etc.) An important and, to a certain degree, decisive contribution in this direction has been made by the theoretical and empirical studies in the area of economics of happiness, dating back to the pioneering work in 1974 of Richard Easterlin, the discoverer of the well-known 'happiness paradox'.

In this chapter, I shall question the still prevailing approach to happiness studies based on a subjective notion of happiness and consisting in the identification and measurement of the major determinants of happiness (i.e. income, unemployment, inflation, personality traits, socio-demographic and political and institutional factors). A considerable number of researchers are by now wary of using subjective evaluations of well-being (SWB) as the basis for national and cross-national comparisons of well-being. They are unsure that a given question can mean the same thing in different languages. They also worry that the answers are likely to fluctuate with whim, mood and personality. Such critical remarks are certainly relevant, but to me they are not of decisive importance. A more fundamental critique is the one that focuses on the nature of the subjective metrics for assessing human well-being. I will speak in favour of eudaemonic analyses of happiness based on a version of the capabilities approach (CA) in the sense of A. Sen and M. Nussbaum (Alkire, 2002). The eudaemonic approach heavily relies upon the Aristotelian concept of the good life and appeals to the common shared intuition that there is more to life than a mere balance of pleasure and pain, along Benthaminian lines. Authenticity, self-actualization, participation and purpose in life are elements of the lay concept of well-being.

I believe that the happiness research program will increase its grasp on reality and as a consequence will contribute to solving not few of the serious problems of present times, if it manages to mingle with the categories of the CA. The core of the CA is its focus on what people are effectively capable of doing and being. The basic idea advanced by this approach is that people should have more freedom to live the kind of life they have reason to value. It follows that the CA is not insensitive at all to mental states such as desire–fulfilment or happiness. Rather, what the CA claims is that people's capabilities to function come 'before', in a logical sense, considerations of the type 'how subjectively happy you feel' or 'how happy you are these days'. This is tantamount to say that capabilities, ontologically speaking, 'precede' subjective declarations of well-being. In this specific sense one can talk of complementarity between the two approaches, a statement that finds some support in the most recent work by Kahneman and Riis (2005). Recognizing that both the subjective conception of well-being and the eudaemonic one are both valuable and insightful, Kahneman indicates that the important issue in happiness research is to move from the exclusive concern with the 'remembering self' (the self that keeps score and maintains records) to the 'experiencing self' (the self that draws happiness on immediate introspection). Kahneman's proposal to start exploring the well-being of the experiencing self applies both to the SWB and eudaemonic approaches.

My argument rests on four grounds. The first one is concerned with the distinction between happiness and utility. The conflation of the two notions has given rise to endless misunderstandings and unproductive disputes among scholars. Secondly, Section 3 clarifies that freedom of choice does not imply freedom of being able to choose for the fundamental reason that choosing does not necessarily imply consenting. My third ground addresses the question whereby a fruitful approach to happiness should include a genuine understanding of the notion of relationality. Indeed, persons cannot be happy in solitude – whereas one can be a utility maximizer even in complete isolation. Finally, starting from the concept of inexpressive laws, I suggest why it is necessary to consider the role played by institutions, both political and economic, in the pursuit of public happiness.

This chapter was written in honour of Alberto Quadrio Curzio, whose scientific work constitutes an important benchmark for all those who refuse to accept the idea that economics is merely a question of calculation. The 'paradigm of the three Ss' (in Italian: *Sussidiarietà, Solidarietà e Sviluppo* – Subsidiarity, Solidarity and Development), which he formulated and effectively applied in various different contexts – including, noticeably, the process of European unification – is the clearest example of his peculiar approach to economic theorizing (see Quadrio Curzio, 2002; 2007).

2.   Happiness versus utility

My first ground has to do with a semantic problem. The term 'utility' has become so ambiguous as to cause great confusion in happiness research. 'I take the terms happiness, utility, well-being ... to be interchangeable' (Easterlin, 2004, p.1176). 'If utility is whatever represents an individual's preferences, the question arises: is the one that an individual prefers always the one that is better for him? In other words, is it necessarily good for a person to have what he prefers'? (Broome, 1991, p. 4). The answer provided by Benthamian economic theory is that a person always prefers what is better for him or her. To recall, to Bentham utility refers to the hedonic dimension of experience: each moment is characterized by the quality and intensity of pleasure or pain. Yet, contemporary axiomatic utility theory, following Robbins's lead, makes no assumption that people are self-interested. All it assumes is preference consistency. 'So far as we are concerned' – wrote Robbins in his famous *Essay* (1935, p. 34) – 'our economic subjects can be pure egoists, pure altruists, pure ascetics, pure sensualists or – what is much more likely – bundles of all these impulses'. So, how can the same word 'utility' possibly stand for an individual's preferences and at the same time for the individual's good? Which meaning should one choose? If one proposes the first meaning – utility as preference – one cannot use happiness and utility as interchangeable terms. On the other hand, if one proposes the second meaning, one needs to specify what constitutes a person's good and in this case the reference to his or her capabilities becomes unavoidable. (See more on this in Zamagni, 2005.)

Following Broome (1991), I propose to use the term 'utility' to represent an individual's preferences and to reserve the term 'happiness' to denote the good of a person. In this sense happiness is a component of well-being. Macpherson (1973) was among the first to anchor well-being to the existence of a plurality of essentially human capabilities, such as our ability to acquire knowledge, to think and act rationally, to make moral judgements, and to develop our own capabilities, i.e. to flourish in the Aristotelian sense. Macpherson takes the existence of such capabilities as a 'value postulate, in the sense that rights and obligations can be derived from it without any additional value premise' (Macpherson, 1973, p. 53). He argues that this is so because 'the very structure of our thought and language puts an evaluative content into our descriptive statements about humanity' (p. 54). It is certainly possible to evaluate capabilities differently and to proceed to revising their ordering as time goes by. Yet, because they are about common aspects of our humanity, there is something quite *objective* about the notion of well-being that cuts across other differences that may exist between individuals. Macpherson opposes curtailed, narrow conceptions of what it is to be human, and of what the constituents of well-being are. His view is that humanity's essence is 'not as a consumer of utilities, but as a doer, a creator, an enjoyer of broad human attributes' (p. 4). Macpherson's ideas foreshadow the CA developed later by A. K. Sen and M. C. Nussbaum.

The meaning of integral human development must focus on the well-being of individuals and must be seen in terms of both its subjective and objective components. According to the former one, 'well-being encompasses three different aspects: cognitive evaluations of one's life, positive emotions ... and negative ones' (*Report*, p. 216). On the other hand, the objective perspective identifies the 'objective conditions and opportunities available to the population' that determine the 'capabilities of people, i.e. the extent of their opportunity set and of their freedom to choose among this set the life they value' (ibid., p. 15). Both approaches provide relevant information about people's quality of life: that is why they should be kept united. The ultimate focus of economic development has of course always been human development, but too often this has become obscured by too narrow concentration on expanding the supply of commodities. Capabilities and commodities are certainly linked ones to the others, for example through the distribution of income, which affects the degree to which the basic needs of the population are satisfied, and through the system of entitlements that determine to what extent specific needs in society are met. But commodities and capabilities are distinct categories and should be kept differentiated if one wants to enhance and expand the well-being production boundaries.

A revealing example of how self-reported happiness, i.e. the subjective component of well-being, may conflict with the objective one can be found in a work by Sen (2002) comparing the lives of people in Bihar, Kerala and the United States. Bihar is the poorest state in India, while Kerala is the Indian state that has invested more than others in the field of education. Predictably enough, life expectancy is lowest in Bihar and highest in the United States, with Kerala falling somewhere in between. However, the rates of self-reported illness are paradoxical, as they are low in Bihar and very high in the United States. Kerala combines the greatest longevity and the highest rate of self-reported illness of all the Indian States. It seems that the more people are exposed to health care, the sicker they feel. What, then, is the relationship between perceived and observed health? It seems that the achievement of longer and, by all objective measures, healthier lives, may result in those lives being increasingly dominated by feelings of illness (more on this question can be found in Nussbaum, 2011).

I would like to conclude this section by pointing out that reducing happiness to utility, as is done in standard economic theory, would lead to a paradoxical outcome: the negation, in actual fact, of the individual. In fact, the word 'individual' has a meaning in a social context that emphasizes individual differences, and differences can emerge only within a social context of interpersonal interaction. Put in another way, individualism, understood as self-differentiation from others, has a meaning only when there are others around us with whom comparison is possible. After all, communitarianism, as a specific and particular form of collectivism, differs from individualism only in one thing: the 'self' is a collective self ('my group'; 'my nation'; 'both'). However, in neither case can we escape the same conclusion. What changes is that the subject analysed is in the one case the single individual, and in the other case the group or society as a whole. It follows that the rational choice model, a true pillar of mainstream economics, is in reality an atomistic model, rather than an individualistic one as it is commonly believed. Indeed, it is a model that has taken over the perspective of Leibniz's *Monadology*, according to which human beings are seen not as interacting individuals, but as self-sufficient monads who do not need to relate to others. Frank Knight's well-known assumption of independence – an assumption that is still central to economic theory – succinctly expresses this position: 'It is assumed that every member of society acts only as an individual, [actually, as a monad] in total independence of all other agents' (Knight, 1933, p. 17). This position has been reiterated more recently by Robert Lucas: 'I prefer to use the term "theory" in a very narrow sense, to refer to an explicit dynamic system, something that can be put on a computer and run. This is what I mean by the "mechanics" of economic development – the construction of a mechanical, artificial world, populated by the interacting robots that economics typically studies'! (Lucas, quoted in Frydman and Goldberg, 2011).

3.   Freedom of choice does not necessarily imply consent

I now move to the second ground on which my argument lies. The subjective approach to well-being would pose no serious problem if we could take it for granted that in our market economies the mere act of choosing would *always* imply the agent's consent. If such an assumption were warranted, it would be possible to conclude that to choose is to consent to the consequences of the choices made. If so, that agent would be happy, *coeteris paribus*, since he or she obtains what he or she wants.

Unfortunately, the assumption in question is a very weak one, since there are many cases of significantly constrained volition in economic life that give one reason to believe that the constraints on an agent's choices may matter in the analysis of individual happiness. The point is that the notion of freedom of choice does not include the range of constraints the agent is faced with. Only if the agent could also choose (or contribute towards choosing) this set of constraints, would it then be true that 'to choose is to consent to'. Scitovsky points to the difference between being free to choose among alternatives in a *given* set, and being free also to choose the set of alternatives itself. 'People exercise freedom of choice whenever they use money to pay for goods and services and are free to decide what to pay and in what quantities. That freedom must not be confused with consumer sovereignty. The consumer is sovereign insofar as his choices influence the nature and quantity of the goods and services produced' (Scitovsky, 1976, p. 7).

It follows – as Peter (2004) argues – that I may certainly choose freely without, however, consenting to the consequences of my choice. 'The fact that people choose to sell their organs does not imply that they have consented to the institutional arrangements that confront them with such alternatives. Or that a woman who gets married may not have consented to the gender relations on which the institution of marriage is based' (p. 4). In situations of this type, an expansion of freedom of choice does not guarantee an increase in the happiness index; indeed, it may even reduce it. (By the way, this is a further mode to explain the 'happiness paradox'.) The tendency in economic theory to focus on people's choices, whilst neglecting to analyse constraints, elevates the freedom to choose between given alternatives to freedom *tout court*.

Yet, as Sen (1997) has, among others, repeatedly noted, the opportunity set an individual is presented with is as important to evaluating his or her freedom as is his or her decision-making autonomy. Indeed, it is not true that the preferences economic agents seek to maximize on the market have as their exclusive objects the goods that enter their choice sets. The way in which those objects are chosen is also relevant, since people attribute value to the possibility itself of acting (hence of choosing) on the basis, e.g., of their moral or social convictions. It is perfectly coherent for me to say that option x is superior, according to my preference ordering, to option y – perhaps because x contains a greater quantity of all goods than y – but if buying x contradicted my personal moral code, I could decide to buy y. Taking into account these types of consideration implies rejecting the tenet according to which 'goods are goods' and so that 'more is always better than less'. This is never the case when object of preference is also the *act* of choice and not simply what is chosen. It is not irrelevant for the consumer to know or not to know where the goods he or she is consuming came from or how they have been produced.

In arguing that freedom consists in the ability to achieve self-determined ends, Sen incorporates a substantive claim into his analysis of freedom: an agent's freedom is directly linked to what opportunities he has to realize his ends. As one can see, such a position differs considerably from the one taken by Posner (1981) when he writes: 'It is my contention that a person who buys a lottery ticket and then loses the lottery has consented to the loss so long as there is no question of fraud or duress' (p. 94). Posner thus assumes that the choice situation fully describes all the features of a proposal that may need justification through consent. The notion that choice expresses consent is symptomatic, however, of any theory that confines all evaluation to a single value function, as is the case with rational choice theory. Since utility depends on the alternatives that can be obtained, the evaluative exercise is exhausted by the choice from a given set of alternatives. In other words, since there is no basis for any other form of evaluation, a choice that does not involve duress or fraud is thus perceived as an act of consent (Peter, 2004).

Furthermore, even granting that to choose means to consent, the absence of coercion is neither a necessary, nor a sufficient, condition for happiness. Indeed, there are many examples of systems where consent (i.e. lack of coercion) does not lead to happiness. Most of these examples concern externalities; many others concern the phenomenon of endogenous changes in preferences. Let us consider the latter case. In such situations, actions taken to increase an individual's capabilities can be justified even on strictly libertarian grounds. Assume that the agent is in possession of complete information: he or she knows how his or her preferences will change in the future. Can it be that the agent is nevertheless at a disadvantage? Yes! The disadvantage of having endogenous changes in tastes lies in the fact that even with perfect information and perfect foresight, the agent may be forced by rationality to follow a course of action which, by the agent's own standards, is inefficient. As Yaari (1977) has shown, if in an exchange process, an agent although endowed with perfect information is in a position where behaving inefficiently is the only rational thing to do, then this exchange process is ethically flawed. Thus intervention by society to correct or mitigate this flaw is fully warranted from the perspective of the individual's well-being.

It may be of interest to note that the SWB approach to happiness poses no conceptual problem in so far as preferences are taken to be exogenous and stationary. The very distinction introduced by Kahneman between 'experienced well-being' and 'remembered well-being' is meaningful if, and only if, preferences remain constant over time. Whenever the 'moment preferences' undergo a process of endogenous change, the notion itself of moment utility, which is the basic element of 'experienced well-being', loses most of its explicative power. In particular, it makes no sense trying to derive total utility from the integration of momentary utilities. Yet it is a well-known fact that preferences do indeed change endogenously. The CA tells us why this happens in reality. Considering people's capability to operate 'in a normal way' in society as a goal introduces a strongly relational element to the concept of well-being. Aristotle's account of the human good was explicitly linked to the necessity to 'first ascertain the function of man' – explains Sen – 'and then to explore life in the sense of activity as the basic building block of normative analysis' (Sen, 1999, p.73).

This consideration turns on the increasing dissatisfaction with the way in which the principle of liberty is commonly interpreted. There are three constituent dimensions to freedom: autonomy, immunity and opportunity. Autonomy means freedom of choice. One is not free if one is not in a position to choose. Immunity means lack of coercion by outside agents. This is the negative freedom in the sense of yes, it is 'I' (according to Sir Isaiah Berlin). Opportunity, i.e. capability, means the capacity to choose, to actually attain the objectives that individuals set themselves. One is not positively free if he or she is never able to realize, at least partly, his or her life plan. A famous maxim by W. Goethe is of particular importance here: 'Treat a human being for what he is and he will remain what he is. Treat a human being for what he can and must be and he will become what he can and must be'. Goethe's maxim introduces the dimension of *possibility* – hence of capabilities – that is, of what persons can be. Responding to people as they can be implies taking account of their capability to flourish and to develop as individuals. However, the maxim also contains the concept of necessity. What a person has to be refers to the project of the person that each one of us tends to be, a project where each one aims at recognizing him/herself and at being recognized by others (within the context of labour relations, for example, the maxim implies that people are to be treated in such a way that their identity as moral agents is acknowledged and respected).

4.   Relationality and happiness

In a rightly famous essay, Romano Guardini writes: 'The human person cannot understand himself as if closed within himself, because he exists in the form of a relation. Although the person is not born from an encounter, it is certain that he becomes real only in the encounter' (Guardini, 1964, p. 90). If human beings discover themselves in interpersonal relationships, and fulfil themselves in their relations with others, it follows that their fundamental need is one of relationality. If we think about it, the demand for a better quality of life goes well beyond the simple demand for goods 'made well'. Rather, it is a demand for care, for participation – in other words, for relationality. The quality we increasingly hear about today does not just involve consumer products, but also (and perhaps above all) human relations. If it is true, as I believe it is, that the quality of life is measured along the axis of freedom, perceived as the possibility of self-realization, whereas increases in per-capita income only point to individuals' greater spending power, then it is equally true that interpersonal relationships are real goods, and as such cannot be excluded from economic discourse.

What is characteristic of the human person is relationality, the fact that the other becomes a *you*. If my being in relation to another can only be justified in terms of opportunity – the opportunity to obtain consensus or to resolve conflicts, as the neo-contractualist school of thought would have it – I shall never be able to escape from the 'unsociable sociability' Kant spoke of. In this case, I shall of course be free in the sense of self-determination, but certainly not in the much weightier sense of self-realization, since freedom as self-realization requires relating to others as a value in itself. If it is true that today no one is any longer prepared to dissolve his or her 'I' into any kind of 'we', it is equally true that the alternative cannot be the social atom, so dear to individualist thinking, but an 'I-person' who does not accept dissolving into any kind of mechanism, even if it is an efficient one like the market.

It follows that the full realization of personal identity cannot be limited to mere respect for the freedom of others, as liberal–individualistic philosophy, for which living together is an option, would have it. We know, in fact, that for each of us this is just not the case. The choice is never between living in solitude or living in society, but between living in a society according to one set of rules or another. The radical perception of freedom claims that it is simply not enough to think of individuality by leaving out relationships with others. If it is true that personal identity derives from our relationships with others, then reducing happiness to utility would prevent us from gaining a proper understanding of a fundamental element of personal well-being.

That interpersonal relations make a significant positive contribution to happiness is now a widely accepted, well-known fact. Yet, interpersonal relations are not analysed in economic theory. They are simply taken for granted, as if they were a particular kind of preference, specifically, the preference for interpersonal relations. It follows that interpersonal relations are treated as if they were one of the market fundamentals, along with technology and natural resources.

Today it is a well-documented fact that several transactions in our societies are based on the principle of reciprocity (Bruni and Zamagni, 2007). It is widely acknowledged that reciprocity entails deep relational aspects that cannot be adequately accounted for by strict instrumentality. Consider a situation in which I decide to reciprocate another person's action. From an individualistic perspective, I may have both instrumental reasons and 'communicative' reasons to do so. In a rational choice set-up, the only way to account for those reasons is to use them as an argument of my objective function. However, an interpersonal relation is characterized both by the linked persons and by the nature of their link. It is common practice in economics to represent the utility function of an individual who has relations with others in the form: $U_i = f(Y_i, R_i)$, where R_i denotes the i's preference to maintain relations with others. However, this is a very simplistic way of representing interpersonal relations, since it forgets the fact that a relationship always affects (either positively or negatively) the well-being of both parties.

To clarify this point, consider the two different kinds of relations: the 'I-it' and the 'I-You' relations. The former is the everyday relation of a human being with the things surrounding that person. Here, the self confronts an external object world and proceeds to give this world shape and meaning. The I-it relation is one of detachment and mastery, and is regulated by purely technical interest in manipulation and control. In the I-You relation, on the contrary, 'I' appears as a person and becomes conscious of him/herself as subjectivity. Therefore, the relationship with the 'You' is immediate. The 'I-You' relation established a new type of entity, a 'We'. The point is well expressed by Nagel (1970) in his famous essay on the possibility of (true) altruism, when he writes: 'Altruism depends on a recognition of the reality of other persons, and the equivalent capacity to regard oneself as one individual among many ... Altruism is not a feeling' (Nagel, 1970, p. 3). A few pages later he adds: 'The general thesis to be defended concerning altruism is that one has a direct reason to promote interests of others, a reason which does not depend on immediate factors such as one's own interests or one's antecedent sentiments of sympathy and benevolence' (Nagel, 1970, p. 16).

What is the ultimate foundation of interpersonal relationships? The principle of self-preservation. My fundamental aim that I be preserved in time cannot be achieved if I isolate myself from others. I need other human beings to judge whether I am worth preserving. Do they have grounds for doing so? They certainly do, since they themselves need to be recognized by me as worth preserving. In needing the same form of recognition, I act as a mirror. Preservation of the self is the outcome of this interaction. The original resource a human being can offer to another is the capacity to recognize the worth of the other to exist, a resource that can only be produced if it is shared. In this way, recognizing other human beings as ends in themselves, and recognizing the same human beings as means to the end of preserving oneself, are united. The good of self-preservation is achieved. The fact that recognizing others brings about the reciprocal recognition that oneself needs, does not make this attitude merely instrumental. Oneself is constituted by the recognition thereof by the other. A person's capacity to calculate the means needed to achieve a given end depends on the achievement of reciprocal recognition. This is why one can say that mutual recognition is basically antecedent to self-interest. Before becoming a possible means for individual ends, the interaction with others appears as an end in itself. Individual ends themselves emerge because such interaction is possible. Recognition of the other person's reality and the possibility of putting yourself in his or her place is of essential importance. Another person's interests are someone else's interests as much as yours are.

One simple way of summarizing this argument is to say that while one cannot be happy in isolation, a lonely person can be a perfect utility maximizer. Yet the fact is that the SWB approach, by conflating happiness and utility, is unable to see that happiness has fundamentally to do with relationality. This is the price one has to pay for accepting utilitarianism as one's own theoretical horizon. Consider the following passage from J. Bentham's *opus magnum*: 'The community is a fictitious body, composed of the individual persons who are considered as constituting as it were its members. The interest of the community is, what? – the sum of the interests of the several members who compose it' (Bentham, 1789; I, IV).

The economic importance of relationality is clearly understood by Akerlof (1997), who recognizes that 'social decisions' affect, and are affected by, one's social network, and are induced, and in turn determine, one's social distance from other individuals and groups, and thus shape an individual's social identity. Bourdieu (1979) in the field of sociology, together with Akerlof and Kranton (2000) in the economics sphere, extensively document the fact that by shaping an individual's social identity, social decisions are a major determinant of his or her future preferences and choices. This means that if we reduce reciprocity to the maximization of *given* preferences, we certainly miss its real significance. The concept of 'socially provided goods' (cfr. Sacco, Vanin and Zamagni, 2006) is of some relevance in this regard. The peculiar feature of socially provided goods is that they are not provided by either the market or the state, but rather by social interaction. Examples of socially provided goods include friendship, social approval, social identification, mates and social status. Evidently, such goods differ from standard commodities, since they directly shape human relationships. One consequence of the fact that they are provided through social interaction, is that an individual's decision to purchase is not sufficient to obtain such goods, since their enjoyment does not depend solely on individual choices, but also on a whole series of characteristics of social interaction, such as other people's behaviour, identity and motivation, and the rules, relational networks and opportunities to be found in the social environment.

We can distinguish between two basic motivational orientations vis-à-vis other people: the 'positional' and the 'relational'. A relational orientation corresponds to the desire to get closer to someone else, whereas a positional orientation corresponds to the desire to gain a better position than others on a given scale. While an interaction based on 'relationality' generates 'relational goods', an interaction based on 'positionality', with its prevalence of competitive behaviour, generates 'positional goods'. Contrary to what one might expect, these two orientations are not opposed to one another in any trivial way. For example, the desire to share one's life with a given partner may generate the need to win the social competition to get that partner, and a relational orientation towards the members of the upper class may just be the flip side of a general positional orientation. In other words, both positional competition and relational attitudes may be either pursued *per se* or instrumentally: a good position may serve to gain desired relations, and certain relations may serve to gain a higher social position. Needless to say, all this has a lot to do with the issue of well-being:

the relational orientation entails, apart from very specific contexts, a greater potential for well-being than the positional one.

Notwithstanding the fact that the majority of works on the economics of human relations are very recent, the discussion of positional and relational orientations, and of their connections with public happiness, goes back a long way to the early debates among the founding fathers of political economics and of moral and political philosophy. Two key figures in such debates were Hobbes (1651) and Rousseau (1762). For the former, in the 'state of nature' human relations are characterized by violence, and the need for self-preservation from the *bellum omnium contra omnes* leads to a social contract and to the attribution of power to a superior 'artificial person', the State. Therefore, Hobbes might be seen as the modern father of a 'positional' view on human beings. The following passage is self-explanatory: 'By art is created that great Leviathan called a commonwealth or State (in Latin, *Civitas*) which is but an artificial man' (Hobbes, 1651, Introduction). In contrast, Rousseau develops a radical criticism of competitive passions and desire for distinction, based on the fact that they produce a division between being and appearing. His solution lies in the refusal of competition in favour of the re-discovery of the authenticity of the self. Moreover, he thinks that the origins of competitive passions and false identity lie in social relations, rather than in 'pre-historical' human nature. Hence, the internal transformation of the individual is the prelude to the transition from a society based on competition, to a community based on solidarity and *philia*. We could see Rousseau as a modern interpreter of a 'relational' conception of human beings.

Although somewhat stimulating, simplistic interpretations of this kind tend to be misleading, because they may give the idea that relational orientations are intrinsically always 'good', while positional ones are intrinsically always 'bad'. That the matter is more complicated than this has been clear since the times of Mandeville (1714) and Tocqueville (1835), at least (for a thorough and illuminating discussion of this point, see McCloskey, 2008). We need to uncover factors that determine whether, and under what conditions, positional orientation undermines relational orientation in our contemporary societies. In pursuing this aim, we need to adopt a rather broader account of human motivation than is normally found in the advocates of the SWB approach. It is not possible to analyse whether particular institutional arrangements inhibit or encourage the production of happiness, unless the latter is recognized as an important, independent category, that is, unless we move away from the narrow confines of *homo oeconomicus*.

Placing sustainable well-being at the centre of the reproduction process of society constitutes a major step towards a conceptualization of the functioning of the economy and of its structural dynamics where market production is seen to be part of a broader concept of production that also includes non-market goods such as relational goods (Gnesutta, 2013).

5.   Inexpressive laws and public happiness

Finally, I come to the fourth reason why the happiness approach should go hand in hand with the CA. It is widely accepted that there are three types of rules required by any society, regardless of time or place, in order to maintain social order. They are: legal norms, which are an expression of the coercive power of the State, the enforceability of which is dependent upon penalties and sanctions; social norms, which are the result of conventions and traditions, the enforceability of which depends on shame that always accompanies the stigmatization of deviant forms of behaviour (loss of social status and social reputation); and moral norms, which are associated with the prevalence of clearly defined cultural matrices (religious and non-religious), breach of which triggers a feeling of guilt in the individuals concerned. It was the American anthropologist Ruth Benedict (1946) who first distinguished the civilization of shame from the civilization of guilt, and in doing so affirmed the belief that the transition from the first to the second type of civilization represented genuine moral progress. Such a view is supported by the American philosopher Bernard Williams, who wrote that while '[t]he most primitive experiences of shame are connected with sight and being seen', guilt 'is rooted in hearing, the sound in oneself of the voice of judgement' (Williams, 1993, p. 89).

The fact is that the culture of modernity has eroded the relational foundations of values, which have ended up acquiring an increasingly private standing. By subjectivizing values through their reduction to the level of mere individual preference, this culture has undermined the social weight that such values have always possessed. The idea of freedom as the freedom of the isolated individual has deprived the sense of guilt of its proper function, and has led to the prevalence of the sense of shame. As Lal (1999) clearly points out, there are basically two types of non-legal norms governing self-interested forms of human behaviour: those based on the feeling of shame, which are in turn based on external social sanctions; and those based on the feeling of guilt, which depend on the conscience of the individual. Lal shows that in those societies where the culture of shame prevails, the social order tends to be established from above, with managerial-type measures based on principles of public rigour; in those societies founded upon the feeling of guilt, on the other hand, the institutional arrangement is founded on citizens' interiorized moral norms.

The question is: what kind of relationship is there between these three types of norms? If the norms that are promulgated 'run counter' to social norms and/ or to the moral norms prevailing within that society, then not only will the former fail to produce the desired results, but what is worse, they will undermine the credibility and/or the acceptability of the other two categories of norms, thus threatening the stability of the social order itself. This is the case whenever society is facing 'inexpressive laws', that is, laws that fail to express the prevailing social and moral norms. Unfortunately, current economic theory continues to remain silent on the question of the relationship between the three types of norms. With few rare exceptions, the subdivision of intellectual labour is such that jurists deal exclusively with laws, sociologists solely with social rules, and ethicists with moral rules. Thus it is not difficult to understand why a great deal of legal norms are of the 'inexpressive' variety (Carbonara *et al.*, 2010). It is easy to imagine the perverse effects due to inexpressive laws. An illuminating example can be found in the paper by Guiso *et al.* (2006). With specific reference to the European Union crisis, the authors show that if voters of different countries are called to interact to solve a problem of common interest, the political elites may find it impossible to agree on efficient policies since they are bound by a 'conformity constraint' that requires them to advance policies that do not go against those norms, even though in so doing the well-being of the citizens is not enhanced at all.

The question arises spontaneously: what is it that determines the degree of law inexpressivity in a given society at a given time in history? The answer is not to be found in the methods of legislating, i.e. in the technicalities of law making, nor in the lack of resources. Rather, it rests on the prevailing political-institutional set-up. It is widely acknowledged that the differences in the economic and social performance of diverse countries depends largely on the differing quality of the institutional capital within those countries, even when they possess similar levels of physical and human capital. In fact, despite the lasting importance of geographical-natural factors, and of human capital, the institutional arrangements of a country are, today, the one factor that more than any other accounts for the quality and intensity of the process of human development. Political institutions, i.e. the rules of the political game according to the famous definition by Douglas North, determine the distribution of political power in society. In turn, political institutions give birth to the economic institutional set-up. Following the distinction introduced by Acemoglu and Robinson (2012), institutions can be either inclusive – those fostering human progress and economic activity – or extractive – those designed to extract income and wealth from a large portion of society to benefit a small elite. The prevalence in a given community of extractive institutions is the major factor determining the production of inexpensive laws. Once created, these laws tend to persist generating vicious circles reinforcing each other over time, unless a radical change brought about by reactive social forces modifies the incumbent social equilibrium. (Think for a typical, although not unique, case to the Glorious Revolution (1688) in England, showing that vicious circles, although resilient, are not unbreakable.)

In view of the above, it comes to no surprise that the well-being of people, in both of its components – subjective and objective – heavily depend on the type of laws that are being enacted within society. As Bar-Gill and Fershtman (2004, p. 349) have pointed out: 'Legal rules do more than provide incentives; they change people'. A vast survey conducted recently by the World Bank in thirty-seven countries (see: www.govindicators.org) supplies an important empirical confirmation of the link between the degree of law expressivity and an index of public well-being. Over 100 years ago, Lawrence Lowell, the President of Harvard University, argued that: 'Institutions are rarely murdered; that meet their end by suicide ... They die because they have outlived their usefulness or fail to do the work that the world wants done' (*Inaugural Address*, 10 October 1909). Perhaps, quite a number of political and economic institutions today need to be put on suicide watch.

6.   *In lieu* of a conclusion

The main message I want to convey is the following. It is by now a well-acknowledged fact that market economies are in keeping with many cultures, conceived as traceable patterns of behaviour or, more generally, as organized systems of values. In turn, the type and degree of congruence of market systems with cultures tends to affect not only the overall performance of the systems themselves but also the quality of life of people. Thus one would expect that a culture of extreme individualism will produce different results from a culture where individuals, although also motivated by self-interest, give importance to the principle of reciprocity. In the same way, a culture of cooperative competition will certainly produce different results from a culture of confrontational, i.e. positional competition, in terms of the value production process. It is time to start building bridges between the set-up of an economic system and its institutional framework. As suggested by Scazzieri (1997, p. 2): 'Current research in structural economic dynamics has introduced a distinction between the "natural" and the "institutional" features of a dynamic path, thus calling attention upon the critical linkages between structural change and its institutional (or "moral") prerequisites'.

However, cultures are not to be taken for granted. Cultures respond to the investment of resources in cultural patterns, and in many circumstances it may be socially beneficial to engage in cultural engineering. Indeed, the quality of performance of an economic system also depends on whether certain conceptions and ways of life have achieved dominance, albeit a precarious one. Contrary to what many economists continue to believe, economic phenomena possess a fundamental interpersonal dimension. Individual behaviour is embedded in a pre-existing network of social relations that cannot be thought of as a mere constraint; rather, they are one of the driving factors that prompt individual goals and motivation. People's aspirations are deeply conditioned by the conventional wisdom about what makes life worth living.

One of the fundamental questions that surfaces in dealing with this type of problems is the following: should not efficiency be the criterion by which to gauge the institutional set-up of society? If so, would it not be true to say that the existing rules of the game and current consumer models have proven to be more effective than others? The question is a complex one, and it cannot be addressed fully here. For our present purposes, suffice it to say that the answers to the foregoing questions are both negative for two key reasons. Firstly, the concept of efficiency – as used in economics – is not a primitive notion, since it derives from Bentham's utilitarian principle, which is neither an economic principle nor the only possible criterion by which to assess efficiency. Therefore, efficiency is not a neutral evaluation criterion, and it is certainly not an undisputable principle by which to measure market efficiency. In fact, market economies existed well before utilitarian philosophy made inroads into economic discourse. The second reason is that efficiency does not take account of the social externalities of economic activity, whether positive or negative. Consider a scenario in which the goal of efficiency is achieved in opposition to that of liberty. If positive liberty is sacrificed in the name of efficiency, what will guarantee the sustainability of the market order over the course of time? The market cannot last long without liberty, as John Hicks (1969) always insisted in highlighting.

I would like to conclude by recalling the fact that the early history of economics was characterized by the centrality of the happiness category. Political economy was essentially seen as the 'science of public happiness'. It was only with the acritical acceptance of utilitarianism within economic discourse during the latter half of the nineteenth century that the category of utility completely superseded that of happiness. And since then economics managed to be referred to as the 'dismal science' (Zamagni, 2014). A passage from the letter Vilfredo Pareto wrote to his colleague and friend Maffeo Pantaleoni on 30 July 1896 is revealing in this regard: 'I am more and more convinced that no study is more useless than that of Political Economy. Tell me, had this science never been studied, would we be in a worse state than the present? All our Political Economy is a vaniloquium'. I honestly believe that economists should not accept that economic discourse be reduced to a vaniloquium. All in all, this is the clear admonition stemming from the precious teaching and scholarship of Alberto Quadrio Curzio.

REFERENCES

Acemoglu, D., Robinson, J. (2012) *Why Nations Fail: The Origin of Power, Prosperity and Poverty*, New York: Crown Business.

Akerlof, G. (1997) 'Social Distance and Social Decision', *Econometrica*, 65.5, pp. 1005–28.

Akerlof, G., and Kranton, R. (2000) 'Economics and Identity', *Quarterly Journal of Economics*, 115.3, pp. 715–53.

Alkire, S. (2002) *Valuing Freedoms: Sen's Capability Approach and Poverty Reduction*, Oxford: Oxford University Press.

Bar-Gill, O., and Fershtman, C. (2004) 'Law and Preferences', *Journal of Law, Economics and Organization*, 20.2, pp. 331–52.

Benedict, R. (1946) *Il crisantemo e la spada*, Turin: UTET.

Benson, B. (1985) *Il cammino della felicità*, Turin: Einaudi.

Bentham, J. (1789) *An Introduction to the Principles of Morals and Legislation*, London: T. Payne.

Bourdieu, P. (1979) *La distinction. Critique sociale du jugement*, Paris: Editions de Minuit.

Broome, J. (1991) 'Utility', *Economics and Philosophy*, 7.1, pp. 1–12.

Bruni, L., and Zamagni, S. (2007) *Civil Economy*, Oxford: Peter Lang.

Carbonara, E., Parisi, F., and van Wangenheim, D. (2010) 'Inexpressive Laws', *Minnesota Legal Studies Research Paper*, 8.03.

Easterlin, R. (2004) 'Explaining Happiness', *Proceedings of the National Academy of Sciences*, 100, pp 1176–83.

Frydman, R., and Goldberg, M. (2011) *Beyond Mechanical Markets, Beyond Mechanical Markets*, Princeton: Princeton University Press.

Gnesutta, C. (2013) 'Sustainable Well-being as an Economic Indicator: A Challenge for Economic Analysis', *Rivista Italiana degli Economisti*, 18.2, pp. 253–89.

Guardini, R. (1964) *Scritti Filosofici*, Milan: Vita e Pensiero, vol. II.

Guiso, L., Sapienza, P., and Zingales, L. (2006) 'Does Culture Affect Economic Outcomes?', *Journal of Economic Perspectives*, 20.2, pp. 23–48.

Hayek, F. A., von (1960) *The Constitution of Liberty*, Chicago: Chicago University Press.

Hicks, J. (1969) *A Theory of Economic History*, Oxford: Clarendon Press.

Hobbes, T. ([1651] 1954) *Leviathan*, London: Dent & Son; London: Andrew Crooke.

Jones, C. (2013) 'Misallocation, Economic Growth and Input-Output Economics', in D. Acemoglu, M. Arellano and E. Dekel (eds.) *Advances in Economics and Econometrics*, Cambridge: Cambridge University Press, pp.419–56.

Kahneman, D. and Riis, J. (2005) 'Living and Thinking About it: Two Perspectives on Life', in F. A. Huppert, N. Baylis and B. Keverne (eds.) *The Science of Well-Being*, Oxford: Oxford University Press, pp. 285–304.

Knight, F. H. (1933) *The Economic Organization*, Chicago: The University of Chicago. Reprinted (1951) New York: A. M. Kelley.

Lal, D. (1999) *Unintended Consequences. The Impact of Factor Endowments, Culture and Politics on Long-Run Economic Performance*, Cambridge, Mass.: MIT Press.

Macpherson, C. B. (1973) *Democratic Theory*, Oxford: Oxford University Press.

Margalit, A. (2000) *The Decent Society*, London: Macmillan.

McCleary, R. M., and Barro, R. J. (2006) 'Religion and Economy', *Journal of Economic Perspectives*, 20.2, pp. 49–72.

McCloskey, D. (2008) 'Adam Smith; the Last of the Former Virtue Ethicists', *History of Political Economy*, 40.1, pp. 43–71.

Nagel, T. (1970) *The Possibility of Altruism*, Princeton: Princeton University Press.

Nussbaum, M. C. (2011) *Creating Capabilities: the Human Development Approach*, University of Chicago, mimeo.

Peter, F. (2004) 'Choice, Consent and the Legitimacy of Market Transactions', *Economics and Philosophy*, 20.1, pp. 64–89.

Posner, R. (1981) *The Economics of Justice*, Cambridge: Harvard University Press.

Quadrio Curzio, A. (2002) *Sussidiarietà e Sviluppo. Paradigmi per l'Europa e per l'Italia*, Milan: Vita e Pensiero.

(2007) 'Riflessioni sul liberalismo comunitario per lo sviluppo italiano', in A. Quadrio Curzio and M. Fortis (eds.) *Valorizzare un'economia forte*, Bologna: Il Mulino, pp. 361–87.

Robbins, L. (1935) *An Essay on the Nature and Significance of Economic Science*, 2nd edn, London: Macmillan.

Robeyns, I. (2005) 'The Capability Approach: A Theoretical Survey', *Journal of Human Development*, 6.1, pp. 93–114.

Sacco, P., Vanin, P., and Zamagni, S. (2006) 'The Economics of Human Relationships', in S. C. Kolm and J. M. Ythier (eds.) *Handbook of the Economics of Giving, Altruism and Reciprocity*, Amsterdam: North Holland, pp. 695–730.

Scazzieri, R. (1997) 'Civil Society and Structural Change', paper presented at the Conference *India: Nationalism, Democracy, Development, Multiculturalism*, University of Bologna, 28.11.1997.

Scitovsky, T. (1976) *The Joyless Economy*, Oxford: Oxford University Press.

Sen, A. K. (1997) 'Maximization and the Act of Choice', *Econometrica*, 65.4, pp. 745–79.

(1999) *Development as Freedom*, New York: Random House.

(2002) 'Health: Perception Versus Observation', *British Medical Journal*, 324 (7342), pp. 860–1.

(2009) *The Idea of Justice*, London: Allen Lane.

Stiglitz, J. E., Sen, A. K., and Fitoussi, J. P. (2010) *Mismeasuring Our Lives*, New York: The New Press.

Williams, B. (1993) *Shame and Necessity*, Berkeley, Los Angeles, Oxford: University of California Press.

Yaari, M. E. (1977) 'Endogenous Changes in Tastes: A Philosophical Discussion', *Erkenntnis*, 11, pp. 157–96.

Zamagni, S. (2000) 'Economic Reductionism as a Hindrance to the Analysis of Structural Change', *Structural Change and Economic Dynamics*, 11.1–2, pp. 197–208.

(2005) 'Happiness and Individualism: A Very Difficult Union', in L. Bruni and P. L. Porta (eds.) *Happiness and Economics*, Oxford: Oxford University Press, pp. 303–35.

(2014) 'Public Happiness in Today's Economics', *International Review of Economics*, 61.2, pp. 191–6.

17   Conquering scarcity: institutions, learning and creativity in the history of economic ideas

Pier Luigi Porta

1.   Introduction: resource scarcity and institutional dynamics

The relationship between scarcity of resources and the institutional set up of any given economic system is a complex one. For it could be argued that, in certain cases, scarcity itself is relative not only to the structure of human needs but also to the way in which institutional relationships determine the quantity and utilization patterns of the resources available at any given time and across time. The purpose of this chapter is to highlight the relationship between scarcity and creativity in the history of economic thought, and to explore the manifold routes that have been proposed in order to 'conquer scarcity' through institutional change. The chapter starts by setting the ground of the analysis by examining the intellectual setting of the Enlightenment and its manifold approach to the relationship between scarcity and institutional change. Against this background, the chapter examines the Italian 'civil economy' tradition by emphasizing its contribution to the foregrounding of institutional dynamics as a major trigger of human creativity, and therefore as a major condition favouring the overcoming of resource scarcity in human societies. The implications of this case study in the history of economic thought are further explored by investigating the influence of the 'civil economy' tradition upon the recent reappraisal of classical political economy and by calling attention to the distinction between its Smithian and Ricardian strands. A section of concluding remarks brings the chapter to a close.

2.   Sketching the European context

A necessary preliminary to the analysis of the relationship between creativity and scarcity in economic thinking is an overall image of the *European context* concerning the economic studies through the modern age. In a bird's eye view we shall try to outline a few specific characteristics that appear to be of special

A preliminary draft of this chapter was discussed at the XIV Annual Conference of ESHET, Amsterdam, 25–28 March 2010. I am grateful to the participants for a number of valuable insights and interesting comments, which have contributed to improvement of my work. No one else but the author shares responsibility for remaining errors or shortcomings.

significance in highlighting the rise and the influence of the Italian school. Through the modern age the main issue across the board of the economic discipline and of economic analysis (in Schumpeter's sense of the word) is the focus on *wealth*. Parallel with the study of wealth and wealth attainment, there is a whole set of inquiries into the *motivation to human action*, which gradually come to an intersection with the search on wealth.

If we take, as a random example, the *Handbook of Economic Growth*, even such editors as do not care much for the history of analysis venture to note that 'interest in economic growth has been an integral part of economics since its inception as a scholarly discipline'.[1] Indeed it is perhaps among the few undisputed facts of the history of the discipline that what distinguishes the economic discipline through the modern times is its focus on the question of aggregate *wealth*. Defining the *nature* of wealth, in the first place, and suggesting ways to *improve* and increase wealth overall turn into some of the few essential problems of the modern discipline that gradually came to be universally called 'political economy'. Wealth will certainly remain, along with distribution, one of the principal problems of the whole of the so-called classical political economy. That, of course, also explains why Adam Smith wrote an inquiry into the *nature* and *causes* of the *wealth* of nations, rather than simply a treatise of *principles* of political economy. Political economy can be described as a long series of endeavours to solve what is sometimes mentioned as the 'mystery' of economic growth.[2]

In ancient times, wealth had been originally conceived to be *instrumental* to happiness: through the modern age, instead, wealth turns into an end in itself or, rather, *the* end of *economic policy*; and it is economic policy, in modern times, that provides the main source of inspiration in the construction of the discipline of *political economy*.

The transformation takes place particularly during the sixteenth and seventeenth centuries and extends well into the eighteenth century. It entails a transition from an idea of possessive *acquisitiveness*, based on commerce in a zero-sum game (Mercantilism), to one of *productivity*, based on primary production and on circulation (Physiocracy), to approach, as a further step, a line of thinking based on *creativity*, founded on learning and on human and social capital (classical approach). It is here, at this third *classical* stage, that the study of wealth and the study of motivations come together. It is not only a matter of a study of *material* wealth, but it is a matter of judging satisfaction. One of the novelties of the classical approach is the unusually large space given to the analysis of the *motives to action* and to the *analysis of institutions*. This last strand of thinking finds its typical personification in Adam Smith, as the unwitting 'founder' of the 'Classical School' in economics, even if it can

---

[1] See *Handbook* etc. (Aghion and Durlauf, 2005, pp. xi and following).   [2] Helpman (2004).

be shown that Smith's contribution could hardly be understood independently of other strands of the Enlightenment movement.[3] It is in that context that an analysis of such issues as *trust, relationality versus sociality* and *institutions* acquires vital significance.

3.   A first case study: economic analysis in the Italian Enlightenment

The notion of *civil economy* surfaces in the Neapolitan School as an offspring both of the intellectual contributions of the previous generation of Neapolitan thinkers – especially Giambattista Vico, Paolo Mattia Doria and Pietro Giannone – and of a new political situation created by the accession to the throne of Charles of Bourbon who would be king for over twenty years towards the middle of the century. The Neapolitan school is entirely dominated by notions of sociality and social relations as the foundation of a social order. This as an issue is full of philosophical and even theological implications. For instance, Vico's *Scienza nova* may be seen as a preparation of the ground for the ensuing generation of civil economists by making the point that the development of a notion of sociality inspired by a hedonic canon does not by itself clash with the recognition of a role for divine providence.[4]

On the practical side of policy the role of Bartolomeo Intieri and his ideals and plans of reform are important; their direct influence on Genovesi, who came to be part of the circle around Intieri, is well-known. Genovesi develops a research program focused on theology and society, which includes a positive stand on free trade and a positive appreciation of luxury. His view of the social order is already much more sophisticated compared with the Mercantilist view.

It is, however, when we extend the analysis to the Milanese group, under the leadership of Pietro Verri, that we can fully appreciate the importance of civil economy as a canon of the economic discipline in its influence, especially on the Scottish Enlightenment and on the subsequent developments of the Italian tradition of Political Economy down to the present day.

The Milanese experience derives its origin from a compelling *practical* need for understanding the facts and the phenomena affecting the economy and for producing a design of interventions, which would become the frame of the famous reforms in eighteenth-century Italy. It goes back to the experience of a

---

[3] While it used to be common in the past to associate Smith's analysis with the Smith-Ricardo-Marx line of descent (emphasizing distribution) or with the Smith-Marshall or even the Smith-Walras-Pareto strand (emphasizing allocation and equilibrium), it is nowadays far more common to see Smith as the child of the Enlightenment movement, and in particular of the cross fertilization of the Italian and Scottish Enlightenment. The latter course of thinking does place a special emphasis on economic growth, knowledge and learning on one side, and on institutions on the other side.

[4] See in particular Robertson (2005).

generation before Verri, a generation that includes (among others) Pompeo Neri (1706–76), the Florentine civil servant who had served in Milan especially during the 1750s. Besides the practical aims of the reformers, Milan hosts an important intellectual movement. Much of that is about the notion of 'public happiness', as it is testified by Verri's lifelong work linking together happiness, pain and pleasure and political economy. This is particularly evident from Verri's *Discorsi* of 1781, a work which makes perfectly clear the parallel between the administrative work and the philosophical reflection.[5] To Pietro Verri in particular *political economy* is the true new science of politics and of civil society.

Pietro Verri, as a thinker and a political economist, is first and foremost an eminent representative of eighteenth-century eudemonistic philosophy. At the same time any view on him as a political economist would not be complete if we excluded his practical inclination as an applied economist and a reformer, bearing the mark of exquisitely Lombard traits, within the Austrian Empire after Aix-la-Chapelle under the reign of Maria Theresa and, later, of her children Joseph and Leopold. The intellectual inspiration of the Milanese thinkers and their ideal masters were in Paris, London, in the American Provinces and more generally in all places where political experience or ideological critique more clearly pointed towards a new social order, an order (it is important to notice) no longer founded on princely despotism.

If we consider Pietro Verri in that light, then his whole approach and his political economy show a very substantial coherence with his constitutionalism. Verri's continuing conscious efforts are entirely in the constitutional sense. In Pietro Verri's conception the role of competition and of the market are linked up as the bases of his overall view of the *civitas* or civil society. Verri's political economy, in other words, amounts to a 'science of the legislator', which owes a great deal to Montesquieu in France and to Locke and Hume in Britain. The *legislator* – as distinguished from the politician – is the public figure who establishes the constitutive links of civil society.[6] In Montesquieu the safeguard against despotism depends on the potential for developing a government as a *limited* power under the supreme authority of the law. However, the supreme authority of the law cannot be established in the absence of independent institutions – the *pouvoirs intermédiaires* – to which the law itself attributes identity and powers. A widespread canon in political philosophy suggests a parallel between one of the most celebrated chapters of the *Esprit des Lois* – the sixth of the eleventh book, namely 'De la constitution

---

[5] Now vol. III (2004) of the *Opere di Pietro Verri*, Edizione Nazionale, general editor C. Capra, 2003–2010 onwards.

[6] See Porta and Scazzieri (2002). On the distinction of the legislator and the politician, see Winch (1996, pp. 33–123).

d'Angleterre' – and another text on the division of powers, which had been produced half a century earlier and which is also well-known – the twelfth chapter of the second treatise on government by John Locke, 'Of the Legislative, Executive, and Federative Power of the Commonwealth'. Both of these texts deal with the English constitution. It is significant that Locke and Montesquieu are, in general, among the most important sources for Pietro Verri. Concerning his constitutional view of the polity, this, as an intellectual connection, qualifies Verri's conception in a fundamental way.

The intellectual experience of Verri shows that the anti-absolutist doctrine – in which the power of the government or of the sovereign is limited by the law, and society subsists on the basis of a relationship of trust[7] – has definite connections with the rise of political economy as an intellectual development. Political liberty is defined by Verri in terms of civil liberty. By the name of *political liberty*, he states meaningfully, we should mean the opinion that each citizen has about self-possession and the possession of whatever is his own and the freedom to make use of such assets at his own pleasure insofar as he does not trespass the laws made by the legitimate authority. Law's empire is defined by him to be *il più dolce, il più benefico impero*, the sweetest and most beneficial empire.[8]

Liberty – much as in Montesquieu (xi, iv) – is defined by Verri as subjection to the laws (to which also the sovereign is subjected). The great art of the legislator – in Verri's premise – is to know how to *ben dirigere la cupidigia degli uomini*, or channel the cupidity of men to the proper direction. Thereby the citizens' *utile industria*, useful industry, is revived: for example, by emulation and habit useful citizens themselves are multiplied. They compete and strive to get rich by supplying the country with better goods at a lower price. Verri goes on to maintain that liberty and competition – made possible by good laws – are *l'anima del commercio*, or the secret life of commerce. Liberty *nasce dalle leggi, non dalla licenza*: liberty comes from the laws, not from license. It follows therefrom that the inner life of commerce lies in the security of property founded on clear, not arbitrary, laws and that monopolies, or exclusive privileges, are the outright opposite of a spirit of commerce.[9]

---

[7] That is Locke's conception of limited government. 'Men' – Locke writes – 'give up all their Natural Power to the Society which they enter into, and the Community put the Legislative Power into such hands as they think fit, with this trust, that they shall be goven'd by *declared Laws*' (*Second Treatise of Government*, § 136, 137).

[8] See the essay 'Sulla interpretazione delle leggi', published in *Il Caffè* (1993 edn, pp. 700, 703). In celebrating the sovereignty of the law, he writes: '[Le leggi] non conoscono parzialità, non hanno affetti; sode, immutabili, ordinano lo stesso ad ognuno' (laws have no bias nor partiality; hard, immutable, they order the same to everyone). This is Verri's idea of the guarantee against unjust privileges and the *ognuno* here should be taken to include the sovereign.

[9] See Verri's 'Elementi del commercio', now in *Edizione Nazionale*, vol II.1, 2006. The original manuscript, which dates back to 1760, was later (1764) published with few alterations in *Il Caffè*

We find here the building blocks of the paradigm of the *economia civile*. It may be useful to recall here what Schumpeter argues about the fundamental sources of economic thinking such as they can be detected by analysing the historical experience of the development of economic ideas. Three points are relevant in Schumpeter's treatment:

1. The significance and the historical primacy of the Natural law philosophy as a source of economic analysis.
2. The influence of Political Arithmetic or the empirical-inductive notion of episteme.
3. The fundamental role of Economic policy in inspiring and shaping economic analysis.

In the Italian *modern* tradition the first point acquires great importance, largely – but not exclusively – through a sophisticated utilitarian framework. However it is important to realize that in the Italian tradition the moral content of economic analysis does not simply boil down to some form of utilitarian calculation, but it involves some kind of *qualitative judgement* of the hedonic experience. The 'tension', as it were, between happiness and liberty is thereby resolved precisely through the canon of *economia civile*.

4.   A second case study: the Anglo-Italian School vis-à-vis the Italian tradition of *economia civile*

An overview of the formation of the Italian tradition requires us to go back to the eighteenth century. An analysis of its development during the nineteenth and twentieth centuries would involve the treatment of the following authors and schools, only cursorily mentioned at this stage.

1. Romagnosi and Cattaneo (nineteenth century): in particular Cattaneo's conception of the 'morality of industry', implying an essential role for economic dynamics and for creativity, is a significant pillar of the whole idea of the *economia civile*.
2. The economists of the *Risorgimento* (Manzoni, Rosmini, Mazzini, P. Rossi, Ferrara, Cavour, Minghetti, Cernuschi, etc.).
3. The Historical School and the *Methodenstreit* in Italy (nineteenth to twentieth centuries).
4. The Italian School of Public Economics or *Scienza delle finanze*. Pareto.
5. The interwar period and the influence of Luigi Einaudi: the survival of the Italian liberal tradition in Economics.

(see the 1993 edn, pp. 35–6) and reprinted in the celebrated *Custodi Collection* early in the nineteenth century (vol. xvii, pp. 323–35).

6. Political economy in Italy in the latter half of the twentieth century.
7. The leading themes of the *civil economy*: ethics, society and institutions; economic dynamics; and the History of economics as part of Economics itself.

A sketch of the main schools of the post-war period would include at least Giacomo Becattini, Alberto Bertolino, Giovanni Demaria, Giorgio Fuà, Siro Lombardini, Luigi Pasinetti, Alberto Quadrio Curzio, Michele Salvati, Sergio Steve and Paolo Sylos Labini. Italy is the case of a country where the interest that economists have shown for the history of the discipline has been stronger than perhaps in any other country; this is a tendency that continues today. Riccardo Faucci, in his book on Italian economic thought (Faucci, 2000) explicitly brings out some of the general lines of his own reconstruction. Two characteristics of the Italian background stand out in Faucci's opinion:

1. A strong connection between *thought and action*, economics and policy, and positive and normative seems to be typical of the Italian tradition.
2. Further, another characteristic of the tradition is the link between *political economy and ethics*. It is interesting to see the large extent to which these two 'styles of thought', as Faucci writes, are pervasive through the narrative. The characteristics brought out by Faucci's book mean that in the Italian tradition there are strong forces leading to *contextualize*, i.e. putting the analysis in its proper empirical and historical context, on one side; additionally there is the widespread need to *go beyond* pure economic analysis in order to understand the real motivations of economic action. Under both respects economic analysis appears to intersect historical interests, whether of factual or intellectual history.[10]
3. The two characteristics above are conducive to what another author (Bellanca, 2000) has represented as the hallmark of the Italian tradition, namely to be focused on 'economic dynamics and institutions'.

Introducing the reader to the Italian tradition generally, Faucci then lists three economists – Ferdinando Galiani, Vilfredo Pareto and Piero Sraffa – among the greatest. These are names, in a sense, *beyond good and evil*; names *from the Italian tradition* that also belong to political economy *as such*. Still, even for a full understanding of them, it is important to put them also in their proper context and analyse their background. It would be interesting to discuss the extent to which those names embody and give actual expression to the characteristics just mentioned as typical of the Italian tradition. In the present context we single out the case of Sraffa.

---

[10] See Bertolino (1979); Becattini (2002). It could be documented, for example, that such and similar characteristics of the Italian tradition emerge also from the numerous studies of the Florence group through the studies of Alberto Bertolino to the developments by Giacomo Becattini and Piero Barucci and their associates.

The influence of Piero Sraffa (1898–1983) was of course pervasive for many years in contemporary economic thought, particularly so in the Italian context especially during the 1960s until the early 1980s. Piero Sraffa had become the central figure of the so-called Anglo-Italian school. There is today a widely felt need for retrospective appreciation of the significance of the contribution of the Cambridge school of political economy, particularly in its Anglo-Italian developments. Moreover it is a special feature of the Cambridge tradition that it has itself developed relevant justifications of its own for historical-analytical research. It is commonly accepted that the Cambridge school took off with Marshall, later to become centred on Keynes and later still, under Keynes's pupils, it continued to exert a significant influence, both in theoretical and applied economics, through much of the post-war period.[11] It is particularly through the latter stage that the *Anglo-Italian* component of the Cambridge school became prominent and developed – especially under the spread and influence of Piero Sraffa's contributions – a characteristic bent for the history of economic thought. This is a moot question that has some general bearing on the place of the history of economic thought in its relationship with economic research and teaching and possibly also on the future of the history of economic thought (HET) as a discipline, as some have recently argued (as we shall see presently). Thus this seems a subject where the Italian tradition can be analysed in its relation with the development of a successful strand of economic analysis. The question is interesting also because the Anglo-Italian line of thought, superficially considered, would rather appear as a decided break with the Italian tradition. It is now high time to reconsider the issue.

5.   A digression into the Cambridge intellectual tradition of economics

An appreciation of the case of Piero Sraffa and the Anglo-Italian branch of the Cambridge school in the Italian post-war context would imply reference to a fairly large literature. Fortunately enough E. Roy Weintraub recently edited a book on the problematic *future* of the History of Economics as a discipline, in which also the Italian case is discussed. It so happens that the authors of the article on the Italian case have chosen to single out and focus almost exclusively on a specific line of economic thinking within the Anglo-Italian school. This treatment of the Italian case is perfectly suited to our purposes in the

---

[11] Becattini (1990) gives a full idea of the various strands of the Cambridge school. In Bruni and Zamagni's view (2004, see later) the Cambridge tradition spans the space from Malthus to J.M. Keynes. See also Roncaglia (2006).

present chapter; its singularity is appropriate in order to critically discuss the view of the Anglo-Italian school.[12]

The Italian paper in Weintraub's book starts from a description of the state and retrospect view of what the history of economic thought in Italy has been through the post-war years. More particularly the declared purpose is to 'look at the peculiar Italian way of doing HET, which germinated in the late 1960s, blossomed in the mid-1970s, and withered away in the early 1980s, involving people who considered themselves and were generally perceived as economists rather than historians of economic thought' (Marcuzzo and Rosselli, 2002, p.98). In the authors' opinion what was peculiar of the Italian case 'was a way of doing the history of economics *as if* doing economics' with an approach 'characterized by two essential features: (1) the primary role assigned to textual exegesis; and (2) the almost exclusive attention given to great economists (who did not, however, reach ten in number)' (Marcuzzo and Rosselli, 2002, p. 99). Of the style in question the paper proceeds to provide three examples: Marco Lippi's 1979 book on Marx (*Value and Naturalism in Marx*), which first appeared in Italian in 1976; Pierangelo Garegnani's 1978 'Notes on Consumption, Investment, and Effective Demand' (first presented in Italian at a much earlier date); and finally Luigi Pasinetti classic 1960 'Mathematical Formulation of the Ricardian System' and 1977 *Lectures on the Theory of Production* – the latter first produced in Italian at an earlier date. In the background there is the Cambridge School: in Italy 'Marx and Sraffa were highly influential from the late 1960s to the early 1980s' (Marcuzzo and Rosselli, 2002, p. 102) owing to, *first*, the prestige of Piero Sraffa in attracting Italians to Cambridge and, *second*, the brain drain from almost any discipline towards economics, a massive drift taking place in the wake of the 1968 disturbances. Through these channels – it is argued – the HET developed as a discipline 'as part of a program to build an alternative economic theory ... and became synonymous with doing non-mainstream economics'(Marcuzzo and Rosselli, 2002, p. 104).

However, the story continued, interlacing Cambridge with Marx, Sraffa and Italy, and suddenly came to an end in the subsequent years, as soon as 'a number of people distanced themselves from previously held views'. Recantation became fashionable and quite often recantation sounded as betrayal and opportunism: people sometimes changed their heroes (typically, 'for instance, Hayek rather than Keynes'). The result of such and similar moves was to make the HET the culprit. The HET came to be 'seen as "antique collecting", possibly a subject for social conversation but hardly a professional field in an economics department. ... In conclusion, in Italy, too, doing HET is now

---

[12] Marcuzzo and Rosselli (2002). Weintraub's book is the 2002 companion volume to *History of Political Economy*.

seen simply as *not* doing economics, or better, doing second-rate economics' (Marcuzzo and Rosselli, 2002, p. 106).

Should this narrative be taken literally, one would have to conclude that the case of Sraffa and the Anglo-Italian school both embody and lead to a very different view of the basic characteristics of the Italian tradition, compared to the picture outlined in the opening sections of the present chapter. However, this chapter proceeds to show that the story has a different reading, which leads to highlighting the basic characteristics of the Italian tradition and, more generally the fact that the Italian tradition has a very strong and recognizable continuity in the research line of *economia civile*.

This narrative, in fact, closely reflects the *particular experience* of the so-called school or group of Modena, active approximately from 1968 to the early 1980s. What we argue here is that a concentration of attention upon the *Modena school* does not make full justice to the history of economics in Italy along the Cambridge tradition. The leading characteristics of the *Modena school* are in fact a reflection of the need and the purpose to revive a neo-Marxian tradition: it is precisely as a result of *that* purpose that the characteristics of the Modena school come to coincide with the two features of being based on textual exegesis and on a limited number of great masters.[13]

With Marco Lippi, the *first example* given in this chapter, we are confronted with a scholar turning to Economics from his initial choice of Mathematics. The important thing in the present context is Lippi's strict adherence to the two aforementioned criteria of attributing the highest importance to textual exegesis and to a restricted number of major historical figures. Lippi's work was highly regarded in many quarters and Lippi himself was then among the young scholars who aimed at qualifying themselves as historians of economic thought in addition to being economists. However, he later reverted to his original interest in quantitative techniques and became a distinguished econometrician.

6.   Sraffa's theory of production

The *second example* concerns the scholarly contribution by Pierangelo Garegnani. His scientific work was absorbed by the effort of continuing the work of the Cambridge School especially through the interpretation of Sraffa's contribution. What distinguishes Garegnani among other scholars working along the same broad intellectual tradition is his ambitious construction of

---

[13] On the experience of the Modena school, see the largely autobiographical discussion by Fernando Vianello, one of its leading figures, in Vianello (2004). It is perhaps to be emphasized that the discussion on the *Modena school* in the present chapter is *not* meant to involve the *whole* group of economists who have been teaching and doing research at the Faculty of Economics in Modena through the years following its foundation in 1968. This chapter is only meant to provide a critical evaluation of a peculiar approach to the history of economic thought within the Anglo-Italian line.

the new and definitive Sraffian paradigm. It is not the place here to revisit Piero Sraffa's scientific biography. While a complete knowledge of his literary remains is still lacking, a debate has set in through recent years especially on the formative stages and the construction of Sraffa's scientific contribution. A useful collection of papers on the subject is offered by the September 2005 issue of the *European Journal for the History of Economic Thought*, from which we now take a few examples in order to illustrate the point.

Pierangelo Garegnani (2005, p.453) maintains that a '*turning point*' (emphasis added) occurs at an early stage (soon after the mid-1920s) in Piero Sraffa's thought: from a critical appraisal (in content and tendency turning on the negative) of the neoclassical conception of the system in its Marshallian version, Piero Sraffa goes on to a more constructive approach and starts his own attempts at building up a new theoretical construction on the foundation of 'physical real costs', while psychological costs (in the Marshallian sense) are criticized. Luigi Pasinetti's (2001) essay contains a discussion on Piero Sraffa's literary remains at the Wren Library in Cambridge. He argues that the extant documents suggest a reconstruction of *continuity* in a constant attempt by Sraffa to develop a unique research program. Sraffa proceeds by gradually concentrating on a retreat to the essential preconditions for a critical appraisal of mainstream economics, or (as he wrote) on a '*prelude*' (emphasis added) to a critique of economic theory.

The interpretation of Sraffa's research programme proposed by Luigi Pasinetti provides our third example. In this connection, one should first emphasize that Pasinetti's aim is primarily not to propose an interpretation of the central contributions of classical political economy, but to draw freely from the classical tradition in order to develop a new dynamic theory.[14]

Pasinetti himself has repeatedly stressed the point; for example the preface to Pasinetti (1981) describes very effectively the intellectual climate of the Cambridge school during the post-war years and makes an explicit acknowledgement to that school as the source of his theory. Nevertheless, it remains perfectly clear that his theory remains *his own*, and cannot in any sense be reduced to a *purely* interpretative exercise. Thus, though it is perfectly understandable that in a discussion of the Cambridge tradition Pasinetti should be included among its most distinguished representatives, at the same time it must be emphasized that Pasinetti's analysis is not primarily an exegetical exercise.

The above is particularly relevant when the history of economic thought is at stake. Classical economic analysis, of course, provides the foundation of Luigi Pasinetti's theoretical framework. The opening pages of Pasinetti (1993), for example, convey an idea of what *classical* analysis is meant to represent.

---

[14] This kind *difference* in Pasinetti's contribution is perceptively brought out by Luigi Spaventa (see Spaventa, 2004, p. 576).

The main authors referred to – Smith, Malthus, Ricardo, Marx and others – are clear landmarks of the line of economic thinking pursued in the book. However, and more important, in Pasinetti's view the study of the classics is primarily to stimulate constructive theoretical work. The main point is that, far from seeing the function of the history of thought in a purely retrospective sense, a notion of what the frontier of current analysis actually *is*, in Pasinetti's conception, can only be acquired through the awareness and fully fledged openness to the historical-analytical background. At the present time, when analysis and history increasingly appear to drift apart, Pasinetti goes the other way round and shows directly, through the development of *his own* theoretical contribution, that the Schumpeterian paradigm of the history of economic analysis is well alive and how fruitful it can be made to be. In this sense Pasinetti's scheme lives on the *integration of analysis and history*; it thus also comes to represent, normatively, a model in method of what analysis should be. It would prove *impossible* to understand Pasinetti's scheme abstracting from the *historical* component of it. If we wish to establish a paradigm of Cambridge style history of economics, Pasinetti's theory – with particular reference to his schemes of structural dynamics – shows the open and innovative side of that tradition precisely in the use he makes of the historical-analytical material. Pasinetti's works show that he is developing a classical perspective on technical progress and on the consequences of human learning, a perspective where 'economic dynamics and institutions' play a fundamental role.[15]

At the same time, we should stress in the present context that Pasinetti's dynamic theory, together with its historical-analytical components, seems entirely consistent with some basic continuities of the Italian economic tradition, where the emphasis on 'thought for action', as it were, had very frequently implied a direct and deep interest in economic dynamics.[16] The argument here should take into account also Pasinetti's emphasis on the *institutional* side of his theory, which is also an aspect in line with the practical and applied character of the Italian tradition, as emphasized by Faucci and Bellanca (see earlier).

This same argument applies even when such a sensitive issue as the theory of *value* is at stake. As it is well-known Pasinetti discusses at length the significance of a 'pure labour model'. As he argues, the 'logical process of generalization' should proceed further in this field and 'this can be done precisely through a very logical and indeed complete generalization of the pure labour theory of value'.[17] In this way the theory of value is put at the centre of the stage; but it is a theory of value that must be judged from its fruits and it is *not* an end in itself:

---

[15] For a fuller treatment see Porta (1998), which provides a first attempt at a reconstruction of Pasinetti's economic thought in a history of analysis perspective. See also Porta and Scazzieri (2008).

[16] See Bellanca (2000).   [17] Pasinetti (1986, p. 426).

If this theoretical construction stands the consequences are far-reaching in economic theory. For, it would imply a revolutionary change even in economic methodology, in terms of a separation of those economic relations that are to be investigated at a *normative* level (giving a complete content to the classical notions of natural features of an economic system) from those relations that are to be investigated at a *behavioural* level, on rules and criteria that are no longer constrained by the limitations of the individualistic and competitive scheme of traditional economic theory, though being capable of absorbing it. (Pasinetti, 1986, p. 426)[18]

This as a perspective is firmly rooted in the history of economics as well as in *history* itself. 'The relevance of history to economics' – Baranzini and Scazzieri wrote (1986, p. 50) – 'is strengthened by the role of learning processes in human activity'; this emerges strongly from Pasinetti's theory in which 'human beings are able to learn from past experience and to communicate among themselves the results of their learning activity'.[19]

In his contribution to a volume on the economics of happiness Luigi Pasinetti (Pasinetti, 2005a) discusses the issue of happiness in the classical economists and their acknowledged shift from happiness to wealth. This contribution illustrates very clearly Pasinetti's idea of a classical approach to political economy. Pasinetti acknowledges that, with their focus on wealth, the classical economists did narrow the scope of their analysis; at the same time the economists of the classical school were able to sharpen their tools and offer more coherent inquiries, while at the same time keeping their horizon wide open to a whole range of factors in their explanation of the working of the economy. Pasinetti adds that 'a Classically-inspired framework is favourable to the adoption of theories which are conceived from the outset in a dynamic setting. These kinds of theories would consider novelty, creativity, and human learning not as a perturbation of a (statically conceived) equilibrium, but as the essence itself of the basic movements of modern economies for which human beings must face the task of continuous adaptation' (Pasinetti, 2005a, p.341). This line of analysis makes the emergence of appropriate notions of 'common good' and of 'public happiness' possible in a natural way within the classical context of analysis.

What is argued here is that Pasinetti's method of analysis and dynamic theory do provide an example of the *Cambridge style* of doing the history of economic thought conceived as the work of an *economist*, which is in fact the Schumpeterian sense of the history of economic analysis. It is possible to add here that this kind of 'Schumpeterian' use of the history of economics was indeed

---

[18] We do not enter here into a discussion of the meaning of the *natural features* of an economic system. It should only be recalled here that the point is fully treated in Pasinetti (1981, 1993). See also Porta (1998) and Porta and Scazzieri (2008).

[19] Pasinetti (1981, p. 22).

entirely shared by Sraffa himself.[20] Particularly in introducing his 1928 lectures on the theory of value,[21] Piero Sraffa emphasizes that, in order to understand the (then) current theory of value, it is necessary to have some knowledge of its history. To Sraffa history is not only necessary for a proper understanding of the origin of the theory, as it is obvious, more than that the historical-analytical perspective is necessary to appreciate the significance of the theory and above all to see exactly the scope and purpose of the theory and the nature of the problems it is designed to solve. These words express very clearly the main justification for the study of the history of the discipline by the practitioners themselves in the case of Economics: and the main reason, in fact, is that we cannot indeed identify the present-day frontier of the discipline without some considerable degree of historical analysis.[22] In Sraffa's time there were those – much as nowadays – who thought that the history of economic doctrines should only be a history of 'true' doctrines. Piero Sraffa criticizes that view very neatly, by observing that such a conception of the discipline implies absolute certainty of what are the 'true' doctrines; it further implies a belief in the final character of present-day theory. This is probably the most relevant point: the latter-day frontier of the discipline is not an absolute to be explained in purely logical terms, but it requires to be understood in context. Sraffa's own achievements as an economist provide of course a signal instance of a fruitful way of combining historical-analytical research with advanced theory.

On the other hand, whenever the analysis reduces to textual exegesis and concentrates on a restricted number of authors, this is a sign that historical-analytical research is not open-ended, but it increasingly risks turning into a sterile business of justifying a pre-conceived theoretical *status quo*. This is in line with the diagnosis of the crisis of HET in the Italian context, such as it is given in the paper on Italy in Weintraub's book, and it is a curious nemesis indeed that a risk of that kind should have affected precisely some of the most brilliant minds in non-mainstream economics in Italy. To that extent, indeed, the history of economic thought in Italy has turned into a comparatively unattractive discipline. Fortunately, however, as we have seen, the discipline has also taken other and different routes and has shown its merits in the Italian context, both in general terms and within the Anglo-Italian tradition itself. In other words, we might conclude that the Cambridge legacy is much closer to the Italian style than the Modena school.

---

[20] Though Sraffa is singled out by Faucci (as we have seen) in his 'Trinity' of the outstanding authors of the Italian tradition, his credentials for belonging to that tradition have been so far insufficiently treated in the relevant works, Faucci included. The present chapter is a very preliminary attempt to indicate how the gap might come to be filled. On the issue, see Sylos Labini (2004, especially ch. 2).

[21] The Lectures were first delivered in 1928 and are to appear (shortly, it is said) in the first volume of Sraffa's works to be published by Cambridge University Press.

[22] See Porta (1992).

7.   **Learning, creativity and institutions: conquering scarcity through a structural dynamics point of view**

At various points in this chapter I have considered the development of a tradition of economic tradition rooted in creativity and learning rather than in the overwhelming influence of scarcity constraints. As we have seen, there are reasons to believe that one important element of this intellectual tradition is attention to the structural analysis of economic systems, and in particular to the structural dynamics of economic systems. Piero Sraffa's intellectual development can be understood (although the point has not been developed in the present chapter) as a result of a typical Italian way of studying Marx's economics, which through the years produces the basis for theoretical developments along new directions, unforeseen to Sraffa himself, but for which he was conscious to have provided the prelude.[23] Another important strand of that tradition is the critical attitude to the self-interest theory of economic behaviour, which was expressed already at the times of classical economics by scholars such as Gian Domenico Romagnosi (Romagnosi, 1827), and was recently taken up by economists calling attention to the pre-classical lineage of 'civil economy' (Bruni and Zamagni, 2004).

A recent reappraisal and reformulation of some fundamental themes of the civil economy tradition may also be found in the contributions of the Florence economics school, and particularly in the works of Alberto Bertolino, Giacomo Becattini and Piero Barucci.[24] We trust that the references, given in the course of this chapter, may be sufficient to present the reader with an idea of the impressive scientific work that is being done in many quarters. What is more significant in the present context is not only that a number of strands in those developments are indeed the offspring of a new reading of the history of economic thought and particularly of the Italian tradition, but also that a new reading of the history of economic thought is the real source of many such developments, even when they are the result of the work of scholars relatively unaware of those historical roots. The fact remains, at any rate, that this is a field where – much as in the case of the

---

[23] I have developed this point in a communication to a meeting on Italy and *the Cambridge School of Economics* at the *Accademia Nazionale dei Lincei* in Rome, March 2009. There are other examples that follow the same pattern. In particular Alesina and Tabellini's *political economics* arises from a radicalization of Buchanan's theory of public choice, itself largely inspired by the Italian tradition. When converted into an endogenous theory of institutions, as it happens with its transformation into political economics, the theory changes entirely its characteristics. The case of *political economics* is discussed in a paper in preparation.

[24] For a recent effective contribution on the idea of an Italian tradition, see Becattini (2002, pp. 3–70). Latter-day illustration of the meaning and contents of the Italian tradition abound. A non-exhaustive list should include, besides Giacomo Becattini, Paolo Sylos Labini, Siro Lombardini, Claudio Napoleoni, Federico Caffè and others.

Cambridge tradition, as we have seen – historical awareness is likely to play an invariably significant and often decisive role.

Let us finally consider the relationship between the contribution of Luigi Pasinetti and the intellectual tradition discussed in this chapter. In this connection, we may note that Pasinetti's approach complements the tradition of institutional economics emphasizing creativity and learning over scarcity constraints. This is partly due to the fact that the latter tradition focuses upon 'thought for action', which has so frequently implied, both in a distant and in a more recent past, a direct and deep interest in economic dynamics.[25] The argument here should take into account also Pasinetti's emphasis on the institutional side of his theory, which is an additional aspect of his model of the economy, and which happens to be in line with the practical and applied character of the Italian tradition. Paolo Sylos Labini, in one of his late contributions, singles out Pasinetti's analysis on vertical integration and technical progress as one of the main routes for a 'return to the Classics'.[26] In his recent book Pasinetti maintains that the foundations of his analysis lies in the *separation theorem*, and states that: 'we must make it possible to disengage those investigations that concern the foundational bases of economic relations – to be detected at a strictly essential level of basic economic analysis – from those investigations that must be carried out at the level of the actual economic institutions' (Pasinetti, 2007, p. 275). Investigations of the former type consider fundamental economic relationships detected independently of specific behavioural patterns and institutional set-ups. This level of investigation, which Pasinetti calls 'natural', allows for the determination of economic magnitudes 'at a level which is so fundamental as to allow us to investigate them independently of the rules of individual and social behaviour to be chosen in order to achieve them' (Pasinetti, 2007, p. 275).

What I wish to contend here is that this approach, adopted by Pasinetti, embodies the essence of what has been called 'civil economy' (*economia civile*) in the Italian tradition. This is a tradition that is widely revisited today through a number of contributions by economists and historians of ideas. I should recall here that Genovesi's works do indeed give rise to a line and a style of economic thought in Italy that exhibits continuity from the eighteenth century down to the present day. Among the recent studies on *civil economy* I should single out a contribution by Alberto Quadrio Curzio in a recent book

---

[25] The special characteristics of the Italian tradition have been made the object of recent renewed interest and close investigation. See Bellanca (2000); also Faucci (2000); Ciocca and Bocciarelli (1994).

[26] Paolo Sylos Labini (2004).

of his, which is especially useful in highlighting the *continuity*, through Italian economic thought and analysis, of the 'civil economy' perspective.[27] So, it is hardly surprising that Alberto Quadrio Curzio himself, in treatment of the formative experience of Italian economists in the post-war years, finds important elements of the Italian tradition precisely in Pasinetti's analysis.[28] In particular, as a significant element of what 'civil economy' means, let us recall that Pasinetti's natural economic system is definitely *not* aimed at endogenizing the institutions, even if it 'has the power to give indications for institutional blueprints. It has the power to clarify the aims pursued by the institutions and in so doing to set the priorities in institutions building' (Pasinetti, 2007, p. 325).

Mauro Baranzini and Geoffrey Colin Harcourt, in introducing the Pasinetti *Festschrift* published in 1993,[29] have rightly called Luigi Pasinetti the 'senior heir of the Cambridge Post-Keynesian School'. In the book *Structural Dynamics and Economic Growth*, edited by Richard Arena and myself (Arena and Porta, 2012), William Baumol recalls the initial drift of Luigi Pasinetti, together with Spaventa, on structural dynamics. 'It is indeed a very fruitful development' – Baumol argues – 'one that has usefully been taken in Keynesian directions, but whose spirit can also take us far along other significant avenues'.[30]

Indeed this probably captures best the spirit of Pasinetti's intellectual legacy: for his analysis is much wider in scope than is commonly allowed. It opens up new vistas rooted both in the Cambridge and in the Italian tradition alike,[31] and at the same time goes well beyond the horizon of both. More particularly it opens the way to an understanding of the new views on social justice and on the welfare state, which are objects of current political discussion in many countries today.

REFERENCES

Aghion, P. and Durlauf, S. N. (2005) (eds.), *Handbook of Economic Growth*, vols. 1 and 2, Amsterdam: Elsevier.
Agnati, A., Montesano, A., and Porta, P. L. (eds.) (1994) *Momento analitico e momento civile nell'esperienza dell'economista. Saggi di economia di Tullio Bagiotti*, Padua: Cedam.

---

[27] See in particular Quadrio Curzio (2007) and Quadrio Curzio, Rotondi and Talamona (2007). The whole book by Quadrio Curzio can be read as an illustration of the Italian tradition in the perspective outlined here.
[28] See Quadrio Curzio and Rotondi (2004, esp. pp. 406–7).
[29] Baranzini and Harcourt (1993).   [30] Baumol (2012).
[31] Syrquin (2012), for example, aptly calls attention to the relative merits of Kuznets' approach compared to Pasinetti.

Albertone, M. (ed.) (2009) *Governare il mondo. L'economia come linguaggio della politica nell'Europa del Settecento*, Annali della Fondazione Feltrinelli, 43, Milan: Feltrinelli.

Arena, R. and Porta, P. L. (2012) (eds.), *Structural Dynamics and Economic Growth*, Cambridge: Cambridge University Press.

Bagiotti, T. (1974) 'Economia ed economisti in Italia', in A. Agnati. A. Montesano, and P. L. Porta (eds.) *Momento analitico e momento civile nell'esperienza dell'economista, op. cit.*, pp. 319–36.

Baranzini, M., and Harcourt, G. C. (1993) 'Introduction' in M. Baranzini and G.C. Harcourt (eds.) *The Dynamics of the Wealth of Nations. Growth, Distribution and Structural Change. Essays in Honour of Luigi Pasinetti*, London: Macmillan, pp. 1–42.

Baranzini, M., and Scazzieri, R. (eds.) (1986) *Foundations of Economics. Structures of Inquiry and Economic Theory*, Oxford and New York: B. Blackwell.

Barucci, P. (2009) *Sul pensiero economico italiano (1750–1900)*, ed. by R. Patalano, Naples: Istituto Italiano per gli Studi Filosofici.

Baumol, W. J. (2001) 'Priceless Value (Or Almost So). Misunderstood Concerns of Marx and Ricardo", in E. L. Forget and S. Peart (eds.) *Reflections on the Classical Canon in Economics. Essays in Honor of Samuel Hollander, op. cit.*, pp. 224–40, (2012) 'Growth: Toward a Structural Endogenous Macromodel', in R. Arena and P. L. Porta (eds.) *Structural Dynamics and Economic Growth, op. cit.*, pp. 125–34.

Becattini, G. (ed.) (1990) *Il pensiero economico: temi, problemi e scuole*, Torino: Utet. (ed.) (2002) *I nipoti di Cattaneo: colloqui e schermaglie tra economisti italiani*, Rome: Donzelli.

Bellanca, N. (1997) *Economia politica e marxismo in Italia. Aspetti della economia politica italiana tra Otto e Novecento*, Milan: Unicopli. (2000), *Dinamica economica e istituzioni. Aspetti dell'economia politica italiana tra Ottocento e Novecento*, Milan: Angeli.

Bertolino, A. (1979) *Scritti e lezioni di storia del pensiero economico*, ed. by P. Barucci, Milan: Giuffrè.

Bianchini, L. (1845) *Della scienza del ben vivere sociale e della economia degli stati*, Palermo: Stamperia di Francesco Lao.

Bruni, L., and Porta, P. L. (eds.) (2005), *Economics and Happiness. Framing the Analysis*, Oxford: Oxford University Press.

Bruni, L., and Sugden, R. (2000) 'Moral Canals: Trust and Social Capital in the Work of Hume, Smith and Genovesi', *Economics and Philosophy*, 16.1, *pp.* 21–45.

Bruni, L., and Zamagni, S. (2004) Economia civile. Efficienza, equità, felicità pubblica, Bologna: Il Mulino. (2007) *Civil Economy. Efficiency, Equity, Public Happiness*, Bern: Peter Lang.

Caffè, il (1993; 1st edn 1764–66), G. Francioni and S. Romagnoli (eds.), Torino: Bollati Boringhieri.

Capra, C. (ed.) (1999), *Pietro Verri e il suo tempo*, 2 vol., Milan: Cisalpino. (2003–2010) *Opere di Pietro Verri, Edizione Nazionale*, Rome: Edizioni di Storia e Letteratura.

Ciocca, P. L., and Bocciarelli, R. (eds.) (1994) *Scrittori italiani di economia*, Roma-Bari: Laterza.

Faucci, R. (2000) *L'economia politica in Italia. Dal Cinquecento ai nostri giorni*, Torino: UTET Libreria.

(2014) *A History of Italian Economic Thought*, London and New York: Routledge.

Forget, E. L., and Peart, S. (eds.) (2001) *Reflections on the Classical Canon in Economics. Essays in Honor of Samuel Hollander*, London and New York: Routledge.

Garegnani, P. (2005) 'On a Turning Point in Sraffa's Theoretical and Interpretative Position in the late 1920s', *The European Journal of the History of Economic Thought*, 12.3, pp. 453–92.

Garofalo, G., and Graziani, A. (eds.) (2004) *La formazione degli economisti in Italia 1950–75*, Bologna: Il Mulino.

Genovesi, A. (2005) *Delle lezioni di commercio o sia di economia civile con Elementi del commercio*, M. L. Perna (ed.) Naples: Istituto italiano per gli Studi Filosofici (1st edn 1765–67).

Gui, B., and Sugden, R. (eds.) (2005) *Economics and Social Interactions. Accounting for Interpersonal Relations*, Cambridge: Cambridge University Press.

Helpman, E. (2004) *The Mystery of Economic Growth*, Cambridge, Mass.: Harvard University Press.

Kolm, S. (1994) 'The Theory of Reciprocity and the Choice of Economic Systems', *Investigaciones economicas*, 18, pp. 67–95.

Loasby, B. (2002) 'Review of Porta and Scazzieri', *The European Journal of the History of Economic Thought*, 9.3, pp. 489–92.

Marcuzzo, M. C., and Rosselli, A. (2002) 'Economics as History of Economics: the Italian Case in Retrospect', in E. R. Weintraub (ed.) *The Future of the History of Economics, op. cit.* pp. 98–109.

Nussbaum, M. (1986) *The Fragility of Goodness*, Cambridge: Cambridge University Press.

Pasinetti, L. L. (1974) *Growth and Income Distribution. Essays in Economic Theory*, Cambridge: Cambridge University Press.

(1981) *Structural Change and Economic Growth. A Theoretical Essay on the Dynamics of the Wealth of Nations*, Cambridge: Cambridge University Press.

(1984) *Dinamica strutturale e sviluppo economico. Un'indagine teorica sui mutamenti nella ricchezza delle nazioni*, Torino: Utet.

(1986) 'Theory of Value – A Source of Alternative Paradigms in Economic Analysis', in M. Baranzini and R. Scazzieri (eds.) *Foundations of Economics. Structures of Enquiry and Economic Theory, op. cit.*, pp. 409–31.

(1993) *Structural Economic Dynamics. A Theory of the Economic Consequences of Human Learning*, Cambridge: Cambridge University Press.

(2001) 'Continuity and Change in Sraffa's Thought: An Archival Excursus', in T. Cozzi and R. Marchionatti (eds.) *Piero Sraffa's Political Economy. A Centenary Estimate*, London: Routledge, pp. 139–56.

(2005a) 'Paradoxes of Happiness in Economics', in L. Bruni and P. L. Porta (eds.) *Economics and Happiness. Framing the Analysis, op. cit.*, pp. 336–44.

(2005b) 'The Sraffa-Enigma. An Introduction', *European Journal of the History of Economic Thought*, 12.3, pp. 373–8.

(2007) *Keynes and the Cambridge Keynesians. A Revolution to be Accomplished*, Cambridge: Cambridge University Press.

Porta, P. L. (1992) 'The Present as History in Economic Analysis', in A. Salanti (ed.) *History of Economic Thought: How and Why*, Bergamo: University of Bergamo, pp. 31–4.

(1998) 'Structural Analysis in Retrospect. A Note on Luigi Pasinetti's Structural Economic Dynamics', *Storia del pensiero economico*, 35, pp. 43–60.

(2009) 'What Kahneman Could Have Learnt from Pietro Verri', in R. Arena, S. Dow and M. Klaes (eds.) *Open Economics. Economics in Relation to Other Disciplines*, London: Routledge, pp. 48–70.

Porta, P. L., and Scazzieri, R. (1997) 'Towards an Economic Theory of International Civil Society: Trust, Trade and Open Government', *Structural Change and Economic Dynamics*, 8.1, pp. 5–28.

(2002) 'Pietro Verri's Political Economy: Commercial Society, Civil Society, and the Science of the Legislator', *History of Political Economy*, 34.1, pp. 83–110.

(2008) 'A Revolution To Be Accomplished. Keynes and the Cambridge Keynesians', in *Economia politica. Journal of Analytical and Institutional Economics*, 3, pp. 455–80.

Porta, P.L., R. Scazzieri, and A.S. Skinner (eds.) (2001) *Knowledge, Social Institutions and the Division of Labour*, Cheltenham and Northampton: E. Elgar.

Quadrio Curzio, A. (ed.) (1996) *Alle origini del pensiero economico in Italia. Economia e istituzioni: il paradigma lombardo tra i secoli XVIII e XIX*, Bologna: Il Mulino.

(2007) 'Cesare Beccaria e Pietro Verri: l'economia civile per il governo della "cosa pubblica"', in A. Quadrio Curzio (ed.) *Economisti ed economia. Per un'Italia europea: paradigmi tra il XVIII e il XX secolo*, Bologna: Il Mulino, pp. 43–56.

Quadrio Curzio, A., and Rotondi, C. (2004) 'Sulle ricerche di economia politica in Cattolica' in G. Garofalo and A. Graziani (eds.) *La formazione degli economisti in Italia, op. cit.* pp. 361–422.

Quadrio Curzio, A., Rotondi, C., and Talamona, M. (2007) 'L'identità e l'eredità economico-civile di una Accademia plurisecolare', in A. Quadrio Curzio (ed.) *Economisti ed economia. Per un'Italia europea: paradigmi tra il XVIII e il XX secolo*, Bologna: Il Mulino, pp. 117–52.

Quadrio Curzio, A., and Scazzieri, R. (eds.) (1977–1982) *Protagonisti del pensiero economico*, 4 vols., Bologna: Il Mulino.

Robertson, J. (2005) The Case for the Enlightenment. *Scotland and Naples 1680–1760*, Cambridge: Cambridge University Press.

Romagnosi, G. (1827) 'Quesito. Il modo usato da alcuni scrittori di oggidì nel trattare le Dottrine economiche è forse plausibile', *Annali Universali di Statistica*, 13, pp. 23–30.

Roncaglia, A. (2006) *The Wealth of Ideas*, Cambridge: Cambridge University Press.

Sacco, P. L., and Zamagni, S. (1996) 'An evolutionary dynamic approach to altruism', in F. Farina, F. Hahn and S. Vannucci (eds.) *Ethics, Rationality and Economic Behaviour*, Oxford: Oxford University Press, pp. 265–300.

Spaventa, L. (2004) 'Il gruppo CNR per lo studio dei problemi economici delle distribuzione, dello sviluppo e del progresso tecnico', in G. Garofalo and A. Graziani (eds.) *La formazione degli economisti in Italia 1950–75, op. cit.*, pp. 555–78.

Sraffa, P. (1928) *16 Lectures in Michaelmas term 1928–29 'Advanced Theory of Value'*, Ms, Cambridge: Trinity College.

Sylos Labini, P. (2004), *Torniamo ai classici: produttività del lavoro, progresso tecnico e sviluppo economico*, Roma-Bari: Laterza.

Syrquin, M. (2012) 'Kuznets and Pasinetti on the Study of Structural Transformation: Never the Twain Shall Meet', in R. Arena and P. L. Porta (eds.) *Structural Dynamics and Economic Growth, op. cit.*, pp. 69–87.

Vianello, F. (2004) 'La Facoltà di Economia e Commercio di Modena', in G. Garofalo and A. Graziani (eds.) *La formazione degli economisti in Italia 1950–75, op. cit.*, pp. 481–534.

Weintraub, E. R. (ed.) (2002) *The Future of the History of Economics*, Durham and London: Duke University Press.

Winch, D. (1978) *Adam Smith's Politics. An Essay in Historiographic Revision*, Cambridge: Cambridge University Press.

(1996) *Riches and Poverty: an Intellectual History of Political Economy in Britain, 1750–1834*, Cambridge: Cambridge University Press.

Zamagni, S. (ed.) (1995) *The Economics of Altruism*, Aldershot: E. Elgar.

Part IV

Resources, industrial change and the structure of the world economy

18 Resources, industrial transformation and the structure of the world economy

Moshe Syrquin

1. Introduction

In the neglected Haynes Lectures of 1964 (published as *Postwar Economic Growth: Four Lectures*), Simon Kuznets summarized some of the emerging results of his monumental work on Modern Economic Growth (MEG) and used them to speculate on diversity, interdependence, war, conflict and cooperation among nations. It was an unusual Kuznets study – speculative rather than precise and quantitative. The tone and the approach clearly reflect the horrors of World War II and the palpable threats of oppression and aggression of communist totalitarianism.

Modern Economic Growth, the epoch characterized by a widespread application of science-based technology to production dating back to the late eighteenth century, resulted in a sustained increase in income, population and productivity and in widespread structural changes. However, it was also the case that most of mankind had not yet tapped the potential of economic growth provided by modern technology – even though the per capita product of most was probably higher already than it had been in the nineteenth and early twentieth centuries. No one was more appreciative than Kuznets of the benefits brought about by MEG but he was also keenly aware of its potential for conflict and destruction. In these essays he appears cautiously pessimistic reflecting on the threat of communism to world peace and stability and on the limited spread of the process of Modern Economic Growth with the resulting increased divide among rich and poor nations.

In this chapter I summarize some of Kuznets' arguments in his 1964 lectures and then update the analysis, taking into account the changes in the geopolitical environment over the past fifty years, primarily the end of the Cold War, the spread of globalization, and the rise of China and other Asian economies. In a final section I review various projections of expected changes in the global economy to 2050 and the main challenges such changes pose for conflict and cooperation.

2.   Highlights from Kuznets' 1964 study

Excluding the very small countries (Andorra, Monaco, etc.) there were more than 100 nation-states in the early 1960s. Kuznets began by pointing out the wide diversity among these countries with respect to size, natural endowments, performance (income per capita or labour productivity), economic structure, political organization and other aspects of their historical heritage (e.g. social institutions, conceptions of their role in the world, notions about relations of man to man and man to nature). Such diversity underlies the potential for conflict, a potential still painfully vivid in the experiences of only a few years earlier.

Looking back at the tumultuous previous half century Kuznets observed that diversity had widened while ties of interdependence strengthened, hence intensifying the potential for strain. The intensification of interdependence could be seen in an increase in accessibility (fall in transport costs), an increase in the dependence of underdeveloped on the developed countries, and in the intense hostility of communism that increased the (negative) interdependence between the United States and the USSR.

3.   Changes since Kuznets wrote

Much has changed since Kuznets wrote his 1964 study. The main source of diversity and conflict disappeared or was drastically reduced with the end of the Cold War, even if the 'end-of-history' moment was to be a brief one.

3.1   Politics and economics

The three decades after 1960 were dominated by intense block rivalry. The cataclysmic fall of Soviet Communism in 1989 upended the patterns of cooperation and rivalry and gave rise to short-lived utopian mirages of 'end-of-history' and peace dividends. A spillover came in the form of German reunification and a more unified (for a while) European Union with twenty-seven members up from the six original founders in 1958. East–West block rivalry was much diminished (again, for a while) but was soon replaced by a new clash of civilizations, and the spread of terrorism and weapons of mass destruction (WMDs).

The golden age of growth in Europe came to a halt with the first OPEC oil shock in 1973, an event which reestablished the command over natural resources as a crucial geopolitical factor. The subsequent great inflation with high unemployment (stagflation) led to the Volcker–Reagan–Thatcher disinflation that sent interest rates skyrocketing and helped trigger the Latin America debt crisis of the 1980s – a prelude of things to come in increasingly integrated global financial markets.

Industrialization and rapid growth spread now to new countries that began to be known by a variety of continuously changing terms and acronyms[1] (NICs, SICs, emerging, and BRICs among others). Among the giant economies in Asia, Japan as 'Number 1' became an almost obsessive preoccupation in the United States just as Japan was entering a long protracted period of stagnation. China and India enacted wide economic reforms and growth took off, impressively in China and more modestly and with some delay in India.

By 1960 most developing countries had adopted some variant of the Import Substitution Industrialization strategy behind high walls of protection and extensive planning. Yet, the continuing reduction in transaction cost led to increased interdependence soon to become ubiquitously referred to as globalization. Transport and communication costs declined but increasingly so did tariffs and various non-tariff barriers (NTBs). Developing countries shifted from import substitution to export promotion, liberalization and privatization – a set of policies that became known as the Washington Consensus. However, protectionist sentiments have not vanished, especially where income distribution has widened and where the increased competition from low-wage countries is strong.

3.2   Diversity and interdependence

Up to 1989 the proliferation of new countries continued but there were also important secessionist attempts: the break-up of Pakistan leading to the creation of Bangladesh and the unsuccessful revolt in Biafra. After 1989 former communist countries broke up, peacefully in Czechoslovakia but not so in Yugoslavia. The nation-state is increasingly contested with a larger role now for IGOs, NGOs, IFIs, MNCs, etc. They threaten sovereignty but with only limited effective success even if outwardly it does not appear so. The world has become more interdependent. This has manifested itself in two main aspects, both reflecting the rise of Asia:

1. The shift of the centre of gravity of economic activity from West (Europe) to East (China and other Asian countries), and a political shift from the Atlantic to the Pacific. The shifts reflect the vigor of Asia and the decline in Europe with the United States mostly maintaining its weight or even increasing it as the superpower that straddles both oceans.
2. A more connected world with increased participation from a growing number of members. That is, globalization advances not just at the intensive margin where existing links are strengthened but also at the extensive margin whereby new participants are added as well as new areas become open to trade by the advance of technology

---

[1] Amusingly reported by Alan Beattie in the *Financial Times* (2011).

Table 18.1 *Share of global production by major regions, 1820–2006*

Share of global production *(Percentages)*	1820	1913	1950	1973	2006
Western Europe	23.0	33.0	26.2	25.6	17.7
Australia, Canada, United States and New Zealand	1.9	21.3	30.7	25.3	22.7
Japan	3.0	2.6	3.0	7.8	6.2
Asia (except Japan)	56.4	22.3	15.5	16.4	36.4
Latin America	2.2	4.4	7.8	8.7	7.7
Eastern Europe and the former Soviet Union	9.0	13.4	13.0	12.9	6.0
Africa	4.5	2.9	3.8	3.4	3.3
World	100.0	100.0	100.0	100.0	100.0

Source: Inter-American Development Bank (IADB) (2009), table 1.1

Table 18.2 *Product per capita 1820–2006 by major regions*

Product per capita, region *(In USD according to 1990 PPP)*	1820	1870	1913	1950	1973	2006
Western Europe	1,204	1,960	3,457	4,578	11,417	21,098
Australia, Canada, United States and New Zealand	1,202	2,419	5,233	9,268	16,179	30,143
Japan	669	737	1,387	1,921	11,434	22,853
Asia (except Japan)	577	548	658	635	1,225	4,606
Latin America	692	676	1,494	2,503	4,513	6,495
Eastern Europe and the former Soviet Union	686	941	1,558	2,602	5,731	7,000
Africa	420	500	637	890	1,410	1,697
World	667	873	1,526	2,111	4,091	7,282

Source: Inter-American Development Bank (IADB) (2009), table 1.1

(e.g. pollution rights, radio spectrum) or by shifts in societal norms (e.g. pollution rights today, possibly human organs in the future).

4.   The rise of Asia

Table 18.1 illustrates the shift in the centre of gravity of the global economy towards the East[2]. The table also shows the earlier retreat of Asia in the nineteenth century and its rise over the past thirty years.

Western Europe and its offshoots were by 1820 already significantly wealthier (as measured by product per capita) than Asia (see Table 18.2).

---

[2] References to East and West are as seen from Europe of course. Even these terms of relative location may be affected by the shift of the economic centre of gravity.

The income gap between regions was relatively low and increased by a large amount during the next 180 years. The United States and other European offshoots were richer but given their relatively small population their combined share in global production was less than 2% in 1820. Western Europe's share was a much higher at 23% but the undisputed giant was Asia, its share of global output exceeding 56%. This pattern changes drastically over the nineteenth century – Asia's share plummets while both Europe and the United States advance steadily.

By the end of World War II the United States emerged as the largest industrial power. In the following fifty years the dominant trend was the rise of Asia, first with Japan's fast rise to the point of having been seen as a realistic challenger to the American primacy, and later with the emergence of the first and second tier East Asian 'tigers' (South Korea, Taiwan, Hong Kong, Singapore, Malaysia, Thailand and Indonesia). Over the last twenty-five years, China and India have moved to centre stage, with the rise of the former eclipsing everything that came before.

4.1 China/India as 1750 leaders: the big divergence

It is difficult to appreciate the extent to which the rise of China has been unprecedented. There are no cases of countries growing at or above 10 per cent per year consistently for over two decades and certainly no case of a very large country being able to do so. The commodity lottery may enable a small country to rapidly grow for a number of years, but no one could have predicted this happening in a vast region with a population of over 1 billion people. And yet, the rise of China has often been interpreted as simply a normal (and therefore expected?) return to the pattern of the late eighteenth century making up for lost ground during the long hiatus. China and India were the largest economies in the seventeenth to eighteenth centuries. But that was in pre-MEG times. Their economic structure was mostly rural and agricultural with low productivity. There was little urbanization and industry, and certainly almost no manufactured exports. Trade was very low and internal markets not much integrated, and there was certainly no extensive science-based application of technology to production – the hallmark of Modern Economic Growth.

4.2 Measurement issues: purchasing power parities or exchange rates?

The economic distance between, say, China and the United States appears much smaller when measuring their outputs at PPPs (Purchasing Power Parities) than at ERs (exchange rates). At PPPs, and with the current growth rates, China will catch up with the United States at a much earlier date than at ERs. PPP converted outputs are the figures used in most of the international comparisons, yet not everyone agrees that *for this type of comparisons* the PPP figures are the most relevant. Richard Cooper has been arguing for some time that for trade figures ERs are more relevant[3]. PPPs are much influenced by services and Baumol's disease. World trade and international accounts are conducted in ERs not in PPPs. PPP differs from ER primarily because of the price of nontradables. For tradables ER may be a better guide; industrial production and weapons (two key inputs into measuring power) are tradables. The qualitative differences in nontradables (including manpower, military or civilian) may be much greater precisely because there is no market test and competition. Cooper has been recently joined by Stanley Fischer who argues that 'PPP numbers ... are seriously misleading ... It is the dollar values that represent the current weight of countries in the international economy' (Fischer, 2006, p. 180).

5.   Interconnectedness

Over the last fifty years the world has become significantly more interconnected.

As a share of global output, trade is now at almost three times the level in the early 1950s, in large part driven by the integration of rapidly growing emerging market economies. The expansion in trade is mostly accounted for by growth in noncommodity exports ... [and it] is also characterized by growing regional concentration. (IMF, 2011, p. 4).

Recent studies of the network of world trade have documented the significant increase in trade links and the changes in the structure of the network itself. (See for example IMF, 2011, and De Benedictis and Tajoli, 2011). Some of the salient results from these studies are: The World Trade Network has indeed changed in the past decades; in particular, the trading system has become more intensely interconnected. From 1960 to 2000 the increase in trade linkages has been fairly widespread, reducing the role of hubs in the network (De Benedictis and Tajoli, 2011). Table 18.3 shows the substantial increase in trade flows over the period.

A noteworthy development is the increase in South-South trade illustrated in Table 18.4.

Most of the South-South trade increase is due to the growing importance of Asian trade. First, the share of Asia in world merchandise exports went up from 15% in 1973 to 29% in 2009 (WTO, 2010, p. 11), and second, more than half of these higher exports are intra-Asia trade. No other region comes close to Asia in its weight in total trade and less so in its contribution to South-South trade (WTO, 2010, table I.4).

---

[3] See, for example, Cooper (2005).

Table 18.3 *Trade flows' intensities*

	1950	1980	2000
Countries reporting trade flows	60	143	157
Total number of flows	1,649	8180	11,938
Value of total imports	1,585	19,529	34,100
(million US$ at constant prices)			
No of flows making up 90% of trade	340	894	855
No. of export markets: median	24	52	67
No. of import markets: median	27	64	71.5

Source: Abstracted from table 1 in De Benedictis and Tajoli (2011), p. 142.

Table 18.4 *South–south trade in world trade, 1955–2009*

Year	Total ($ billions)	Share in World Trade	Share in Developing Country Trade	Developing Country Share in World Trade
1955	5.8	7.1	25.3	28.0
1985	126.1	7.8	30.2	25.8
1990	208.5	7.4	35.5	20.7
2009	2,020.9	17.3	45.9	37.8

Source: Athukorala, P. (2011) *South-South Trade: An Asian Perspective*, ADB Economics Working Paper Series No. 265, July.
1955–1985: Only transactions between industrial and developing countries are included; based on UNCTAD database,1990–2009: Compiled from UN Comtrade database.

A further sign of the increase in interconnectedness and in the complexity of the globalization process are the longer global supply chains. The increase in the vertical specialization in production stretching across several countries was spurred by lower trade barriers, and by the declines in transportation and communication costs.

The recent expansion of global and regional trade has also been driven income convergence (see the next section). Contrary to the earlier pessimism of prominent British economists such as Robertson and Keynes (see Syrquin, 2005a for references), much of the expansion in world trade took the form of intraindustry trade among countries with an increasingly similar composition of their factor endowments. The expansion of intraindustry trade between 1985 and 2009 was particularly noted in countries integrated in a supply chain, such as China, Thailand and Mexico[4].

---

[4] IMF (2011), p. 9. Intraindustry trade was originally a puzzle for the simple Heckscher-Ohlin approach but not so for the relatively neglected approach of Linder (1961) that stressed the importance of *similarity* of incomes and consumption patterns.

Table 18.5 *Annual growth rates of GDP and of per capita GDP at constant PPPs*

	GDP – PPP		GDP per capita – PPP	
	1990–2000	2000–2010	1990–2000	2000–2010
Advanced economies	**0.049**	**0.038**	**0.040**	**0.032**
Emerging and developing economies	**0.060**	**0.081**	**0.041**	**0.067**
Developing Asia	0.090	0.102	0.075	0.090
Latin America and the Caribbean	0.052	0.054	0.036	0.040
Middle East and North Africa	0.055	0.071	0.034	0.042
Sub-Saharan Africa	0.042	0.076	0.014	0.049

Source: International Monetary Fund (2011) *World Economic Outlook Database*, April.

6.   Implications of the reallocation

The large changes in the global economy among regions and countries since Kuznets wrote and especially in the last two to three decades have some immediate implications and some more remote and speculative ones for the prospects for conflict and cooperation that were the guiding point for the Kuznets lectures of 1964.

6.1   Convergence

Over the last two decades the developing countries have been growing faster than industrial countries. It seems that the much lamented limited spread of MEG has, finally, began to reverse leading to a noticeable convergence in incomes, especially among countries that have integrated themselves into the global economy (see Table 18.5).

Timothy Taylor (2011) refers to the Great Factor Price Equalization in the wake of the fall of Communism, the rise of the internet and sporadic progress in institutional development in the emerging-market countries. In the last two decades or so the global labour force has virtually doubled in size, a change that augurs well for the newly globalizing countries even while leading to rising tension in the richer countries where growth is lower or has slowed down or even stagnated. It will put to the test the profession of solidarity among peoples especially in the more communitarian and cosmopolitan Europe.[5]

---

[5] The current climate in the Euro-crisis area and beyond does not augur well for global solidarity.

Table 18.6 *Contributions to global GDP growth, 1970–2015 (per cent)*

	US	Other advanced countries	China	Rest of the World
1970–1985	18	36	4	42
1985–2000	24	38	15	23
2000–2010	15	21	24	40
2005–2015	10	14	33	43

PPP Basis (per cent, three-year moving averages)
Source: World Bank (2010) *World Economic Outlook*, April 2010. www.imf.org/external/pubs/ft/weo/2010/01/#ch1fig

6.2   Structural changes

The central fact for the structure of the global economy has been the reallocation of the centre of economic activity from Europe and the Atlantic towards Asia and the Pacific.

Sectoral composition of output and trade: Beginning in the late 1960s deindustrialization (in relative terms) has taken place in all advanced countries while in Asia and other emerging countries a rapid rise of industry was observed, in part related to the disaggregation of the chain of production and the increase in the intraregional network of trade.

The faster growth rate in emerging countries coupled with the intensification in the industrialization process there has resulted in a substantial reallocation of manufacturing output towards the group of emerging countries. This trend already observed and analysed by Chenery in 1977 was turned into one of many UN 'Targets' – The Lima target – under which developing countries were to account for approximately a quarter of world industrial production by the end of the century[6]. Ironically, this became one of the precious few targets actually achieved but only after the prescribed UN engineering approach was abandoned.

Engines of growth: The 'South' is no longer a passive participant in global growth. In the last decade China accounts for a larger share of global growth than either the United States or other advanced countries as a group (see Table 18.6). This does not only reflect the recent financial crisis but it is the continuation of a decades-long process. China can no longer take the world economy as a given within which it can choose its best strategy but it has rather become an important player determining the shape of the world economy. This creates incentives for China to contribute to the stability and smooth expansion of the system.

---

[6] According to the 'Lima Declaration and Plan of Action on Industrial Development and Co-Operation' adopted in 1975 by the Second General Conference of the UN Industrial Development Organization in Lima, Peru.

Table 18.7 *World carbon dioxide emissions by region (million metric tons carbon dioxide)*

		Projections	% of World total	
Region/Country	2005	2035	2005	2035
United States	5,974	6,320	21	15
OECD Europe	4,398	4,107	16	10
China	5,558	13,326	20	31
Total World	**28,306**	**42,392**	**100**	**100**

*Middle East, Africa, and Central and South America
Source: U.S. Energy Information Administration (2010) *International Energy Outlook 2010*, p. 154, www.eia.gov/oiaf/aeo.

Structure of global trade: The rapidly industrializing developing countries, especially China and other Asian countries, 'demand proportionately more industrial raw materials, energy and food products, as opposed to manufactured consumer goods and non-tradable services. Hence with the growing importance of developing countries as an engine of growth, this is likely to sustain the high increases in commodity prices that occurred in 2010 over the forecast horizon' (World Bank, 2011, p. 55). These changes affect in different ways different regions and countries. As a simple and rough approximation producers of commodities in high demand by China (and other Asian countries) have benefitted while those mostly in competition with the Chinese manufactured exports have suffered. The apparently superior performance of Brazil over Mexico over the past one to two decades can largely be explained applying this simple taxonomy.[7]

Emissions: The differential growth and reallocation of production towards countries where industry is in the process of expanding has also implications for global CO_2 emissions. Even if all the developed countries including the United States were to adhere to the Kyoto parameters, the amount of emissions would inexorably continue to grow for the foreseeable future. The U.S. Energy Information Administration (2010) forecasts that shortly after 2020 China will account for a larger share of global CO_2 emissions than the United States and the OECD (Europe) *combined*. The amount of emissions forecasted for China in 2035 are three times the OECD's level in 2005 and account for over 30 per cent of the forecasted world total (Table 18.7).

Liberal democracy: The expected significant decline in the weight of the EU15 countries in global GDP does not augur well for the future of liberal democracy around the world. Who might take up the slack as representatives

---

[7] A recent IADB (2011) report entitled 'One Region, Two Speeds?' shows two distinct clusters of experiences labeled the 'Brazilian cluster' and the 'Mexican cluster'.

of liberal democracy? For Fogel (2007) the answer is mostly Asia, especially India and the SE6 where democracy prevails (Taiwan, Korea, Indonesia and Singapore and, to a lesser extent so far, in Thailand and Malaysia). His optimism seems a bit premature. According to the Economist Intelligence Unit (EIU, 2010, p.2) in 2010 the majority of countries and most of the world's population lived under regimes that were not fully democratic.

More than 35 per cent of the world's population still lives under authoritarian rule (with China accounting for a large share of them). The wave of democratization that began in the mid-1970s and intensified after 1989 seems to have come to a halt or even gone into a retreat. Even in Europe the financial crisis has had a negative impact on democracy. Beyond Europe, there has been backsliding on previous progress in Russia and its neighbors, in Sub-Saharan Africa, in Turkey, and in the new populist regimes in Latin America. In the most authoritarian region in the world, the Middle East and North Africa, the high hopes for the 'Arab Spring' proved woefully premature.

Regarding the prospects for mid-century we note that among the ten countries expected to grow the fastest between 2009 and 2050 (PwC, 2011) we find several populous authoritarian regimes (Vietnam, Nigeria, China, and Saudi Arabia).

7.   Shifts in the relative positions of nations

The rise of Asia, the end of the Cold War, and America's entanglement in wars in Asia has prodded a renewed thinking on overstretching and the decline of empires and on economic primacy. Two contradictory approaches interpret these events thus: The first one stresses the inevitability of the decline in the United States and predicts dire consequences for the world system unless the decline is graciously accepted, giving ample room to the emergent new *number one* whose identity has variously changed over the past three decades. A second approach sees also a potential for great distress in the global system unless the United States is willing to assert its still considerable economic and military preeminence.

The recent rise of China and other Asian countries suggests to many the imminent displacement of the United States as the leading, or sole, superpower. This echoes similar predictions in the not too distant past about the rise of Japan, of fortress Europe, etc. They proved to be more a wish to ascertain the decline of the United States than a realistic assessment.

During the Cold War it was the common view that the USSR was going to surpass the United States. The question was only *when*[8]. In the late twentieth

---

[8] In Samuelson's influential textbook over a period of three decades one finds a graphical prediction of the year at which the USSR would overtake the United States. The date was about twenty-five years into the future and it kept shifting forward in successive editions without any posterior adjustment to the strong prior (illustrated in Syrquin, 2005b).

century it was Japan's turn to be number one. When it stalled and the United States took off in the 1990s the search was on. Then it was ascertained that the twentieth century had been the US century and the twenty-first was going to be Europe's century[9]. It is now China's turn.

More important than who is number one might be the ability to cope with decline (Kindleberger, 1996). Differential economic growth implies that economic shares in world totals change, resulting at times in changes in economic leadership. Scholars of international affairs, ever since the classical statement of Jacob Viner in his 'Power versus Plenty' (1948), have argued against drawing too sharp a distinction between international economic and security affairs.

7.1   League mentality and measurement of performance

Before the twentieth century changes in economic primacy would only become clear long after the fact as the meager and partial statistics accumulated, or through some decisive event such as a military victory. The development of national income accounts, and their institutionalization as measures of performance officially sanctioned by the UN and its agencies, increasingly led to a narrow focus on GDP (total and per capita) and its rate of growth as measures of economic power to the almost exclusion of any other measures with the exception of military data. The availability of (more or less – probably less) comparable figures on GDP across countries, widely diffused, have created a league mentality where the position of a country in the pecking order becomes a national objective and an element of national pride.[10]

7.2   Measurement of relative power

The almost obsessive tracking of the relative rise of China and other Asian countries equates economic size with political and economic power. This core concept in international politics is largely absent from the economic literature (except for market power usually within a country or Marxian studies).

In realist approaches in international relations the main elements of state power considered are the sizes of the population, the territory, the economic (GDP) and military strength. A group of analysts at RAND (Tellis, 2000)

---

[9] Two examples: *The 20th Century Was American, But This One Will Be Europe's* [Mary Dejevsky in the *Independent* / UK, 9 January 2001] and *Why Europe Will Run the 21st Century* [Mark Leonard, Fourth Estate, 21 Feb 2005].

[10] And since the position of a country relative to various official thresholds can determine, for example, access to concessional aid, this creates an incentive to gaming the system. Similar comments apply, *mutatis mutandis*, to incentives for creative accounting to become eligible for, say, the Euro club.

argues that the postindustrial world requires new ways to assess national power and calls for the inclusion of additional measures to reflect soft power, ideational resources, etc. This post-modernist hollowing of the analysis inevitably concludes with the demotion of the United States.

7.3   On most items the dominance of the United States is paramount

GDP: even when measured in PPP (less relevant for relative weight in the global economy) China is still years away from catching up with the United States in terms of total GDP and many decades away in terms of per capita GDP. China is and will remain a very poor country for quite some time. Figure 18.1 and Table 18.8 show comparative data on military expenditures and demography relevant for the assessment of relative power.

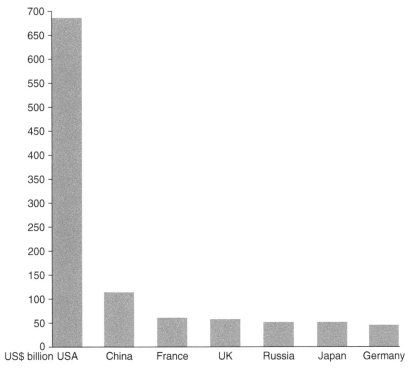

Figure 18.1 The world's top 7 largest military budgets in 2010
Data Source: Wikipedia, 'List of countries by military expenditures'
http://en.wikipedia.org/wiki/List_of_countries_by_military_expenditures,
(accessed 27 November 2011).

Table 18.8 *Population in 2010 and UN projections to 2050*

Country	2010	2050	2050/2010	2010	2050
World	**6896**	**9306**	**1.35**	**100.0**	**100.0**
China	1341	1296	0.97	19.5	13.9
India	1225	1692	1.38	17.8	18.2
United States	310	403	1.30	4.5	4.3
4 EU countries[a]	*268*	*279*	*1.04*	*3.9*	*3.0*
Russian Federation	143	126	0.88	2.1	1.4
Japan	127	109	0.86	1.8	1.2
Latin America	590	751	1.27	8.6	8.1
Sub-Saharan Africa	856	1960	2.29	12.4	21.1
Western Asia	232	395	1.70	3.4	4.2

[a]Germany, France, United Kingdom, and Italy
Source: Population Division of the Department of Economic and Social Affairs of the United
Nations Secretariat (2011) *World Population Prospects: The 2010 Revision*, 29 November, http://
esa.un.org/unpd/wpp/index.htm.

Military: China is huge and the regime is still capable of commanding and deploying waves of soldiers, as they did in Korea in the early 1950s. But the superiority of the United States in military expenditures and the quality differential is still overwhelming. The EU countries are a shadow of their former self; even if the five largest EU countries were to pull and coordinate their military resources their combined spending would add up to less than 14 per cent of the world total.

Demography: The UN projections of population in Table 18.8 show that in 2050 India, China, the United States, Nigeria, Indonesia and Pakistan are each expected to be as large as the four largest EU countries combined. In Russia, Japan, Germany, Italy *and* China the population in 2050 is expected to be lower than today. The one-child policy succeeded in making China an outlier among less developed countries. India will become the most populous country in the world and the United States will evidence only a moderate decline in its share of the world's total. Large increases in population are expected in Africa and the Middle East – one the poorest region and the other a region sustained by oil wealth.

The US demographic composition between working-age people versus dependents is relatively favourable when compared to most developed economies and China (see Syrquin, 2012).

Technology: A recent report on R&D and other technology indicators from the National Science Board (*Science and Engineering Indicators 2010*) documents a pattern of continued US leadership in technology, especially on patents, R&D expenditures and high-tech production. But there is also evidence of strong catching up on the part of China; its share of global high-tech goods exports more than tripled between 1995 and 2008 making China the single largest exporter of such products. It is still the case, however, that the United States remains the number one destination of foreign students worldwide (OECD, 2011).

Resources: Energy resources were for long the weak point in the US position since the 1970s. This, however, has been changing rapidly thanks to the exploitation of underground shale formations[11]. Between 2006 and 2010 US shale gas production nearly quintupled, accounting for almost a quarter of US natural gas production. The reserves of the US Northeast's Marcellus Shale formation is likely the world's largest unconventional natural gas reserve. The prospects for the United States seem to be radically changing from large importer of natural gas from unsavory sources to a once improbable future as an energy exporter.

To sum up, the overall picture is far more complex than the simple one portrayed by declinists.[12]

8.   The structure of the world economy: perspectives and prospects

The rise of China has come to dominate the discourse about the global economic and political systems. A key question then becomes whether the extraordinary fast growth of China is sustainable. After two decades of intense attention to the growth and transformation of the Chinese economy it is not easy anymore to appreciate the extent to which they were unprecedented and unexpected, putting into question many long-held beliefs. There is no precedent of *sustained very fast growth* for decades in a *very large country*.[13] Large countries have low trade shares especially if they are not oil exporters. The share of exports in GDP in 2012 was 14% in the United States, 15% in Japan and 27% in China (World Development Indicators, table 4.8, http://wdi.worldbank.org/table/4.8). No totalitarian country has been able to sustain fast growth for decades without major turmoil or worse.

8.1   Can fast growth persist?

Once again we find two camps with very different outlooks. The first one focuses on the spread of rent seeking behaviour and corruption, and the resulting

---

[11] This section is based on 'The FP Top 100 Global Thinkers', in the December 2011 issue of *Foreign Policy*, entry on Terry Engelder, Gary Lash and George P. Mitchell selected for 'upending the geopolitics of energy'.

[12] Samuel Huntington (1988) first used the term in his critique of Paul Kennedy's overstretching thesis in *The Rise and Fall of the Great Powers*.

[13] Japan's experience between 1950 and 1975 comes closest but it started from a much higher income in 1950.

political instability to predict that these developments will inevitably limit or halt China's growth. Other scenarios that may result in a slowdown[14] include over investment and the possibility of a downturn with higher unemployment, the inefficiencies of the SOEs (state owned enterprises), a collapse of the banking system, inflation, lack of democracy and inequality. Then there is also the observation that individual country growth is mean-reverting.

But there are others, Robert Fogel for example, who question this and, so far, seem to be right. Fogel (2007) is confident that: 'in 2040, the Chinese economy will reach $123 trillion, or nearly three times the output of the entire globe in the year 2000'. Fogel expects that by 2040 China will become superrich with a per capita income twice that of the EU15. This is almost beyond comprehension; it cannot just be more of the same but will involve huge reallocations and new products.[15] But how is this phenomenal transformation supposed to come about? For Fogel the main factors would be a continuation of the very high gains from inter-sectoral shifts, which account for fully one-third of the fast growth so far, the enhancement of the quality of labour through education, and a limit of control by central government based on the accepted policy called 'market preserving federalism', which promotes competition among local governments, constrains rent seeking and provides incentives to innovation.

Fogel is not alone in his bullish forecast: Boltho (2004) and Martin Wolf (2008) for example, stress that GDP per head in China is only a tenth of US levels at PPP giving it still plenty of room for catch up. Then there is also the widespread belief in China that living conditions have improved, contributing to political stability. In the experience of fast growers in the past there have been many false overtakes or aborted take-offs. Willem Buiter (now Citigroup Chief Economist) and Rahbari argue that:

'This time it's different': many EMs have either opened up already or are expected to do so, and have reached a threshold level of institutional quality and political stability. For poor countries with large young populations, growing fast should be easy: open up, create some form of market economy, invest in human and physical capital, don't be unlucky and don't blow it. Catch-up and convergence should do the rest. (Buiter and Rahbari, 2011, p. 1)

8.2   Challenges

Kuznets saw in the growing interdependence among progressively more diverse countries a source for potential benefits but also for tension and

---

[14] Fogel (2007) and Rogoff (2008).

[15] Over 70% of the goods in a contemporary consumption basket are in categories that have seen major changes (but are still recognizable – e.g. watches) or radical changes (e.g. appliances, medical care, transportation) since the beginning of the nineteenth century (Nordhaus, 1998).

conflict. In this section I discuss three main areas with significant potential gains from cooperation but also large potential for conflict: the realignment of the balance among nations, the increased scarcity in resources and food, and the issue of global governance.

8.2.1   Realignment of the balance among nations   Looking beyond the current financial crisis we can expect a continuation of the recent differential growth performance: high growth in Asia spreading (maybe) to other areas, and low growth in most advanced countries. These trends will pose two major challenges: accommodating the rise of very large and still very poor economies and, within countries, adjusting to the structural changes implied in the high and low growth patterns in an increasingly interconnected world economy.

In the 1964 lectures Kuznets pointed to the limited spread of MEG as a source of conflict. Now the source of conflict has become the long awaited spread of MEG to parts of Asia and Latin America. The adjustment to the newcomers would be easier if rich countries were to grow at their post-war historical rates. As discussed later this seems unlikely for the near future. Other challenges posed by the rise of China and other Asian countries were already mentioned earlier.

The second challenge – adjusting to the structural changes implied in the high and low growth patterns – brings us to the question: is growth the normal? For China the question is about the realization of a potential (which is not automatic). Catch up is a potential source of growth for follower countries but its realization is a different story, a point often emphasized by Kuznets. But for countries closer to the technological frontier – the United States, much of Western Europe, and Japan – the question is mostly an unexamined one. Peter Bauer stressed that 'Poverty has no causes. Wealth has causes' as in the title of Adam Smith's opus: *An Inquiry into the Nature and Causes of the Wealth of Nations*, but his remains a minority view since the rise of Development Economics as a field. The anomaly to be explained is the increased prosperity of the last 250 years, not the lack of growth that was the fate of humanity for millennia. Modern Economic Growth is a very recent phenomenon.

Fifty plus years of fast growth, on the heels of the sustained if slower growth from the mid eighteenth century on, have led us to accept growth as the normal state of affairs. Fifty years of growth theory has hammered in the concept of steady state balanced growth even if totally ahistorical and close to a contradiction. Steady (more or less) growth has by now been internalized into our discourse and worse into our expectations and institutions. Without it pension plans become insolvent, deficits explode, debt ratios grow unbounded and we find ourselves in the midst of a crisis worsened by those expectations.

In spite of the textbook presentation that regards growth as the normal, and with it the enormous progress achieved over the past two centuries, expectations of stagnation and of *Limits to Growth* abound; at times they become salient and are articulated by leading economists. I mentioned earlier the pessimistic forecasts for the American economy at the end of World War II that were based on the 'secular stagnation' thesis that saw stagnation as the result of an expected fall in aggregate demand after demobilization, the closing of the frontier and the exhaustion of investment opportunities. Rapid population growth in LDCs and OPEC's sharp increase in oil prices around 1970 generated a burst of apocalyptic predictions: mass starvation in Asia, exhaustion of oil and other natural resources, and massive species extinction. Fertility declines and the green revolution were not foreseen then and neither was the extraordinary economic growth of China and other Asian countries (Fogel, 2005).

Writing about today's global imbalances Martin Wolf (2010) borrows a page from the past when he writes: 'the notion of a savings glut is not right. It might be better thought of as an *investment dearth*. This is true of the high income countries in particular' (p. 65, italics added).

For long-term growth the crucial factor is, to quote Kuznets, the 'increasing stock of technological knowledge' (1964, p. 79). In the 1964 lectures he writes that it is impossible to quantify the stock of technological knowledge or to trace the consequences of its accumulation especially as they are spread out extensively over time and lead to unknown and unforeseeable paths. 'there is no tested theory that traces the path from basic science to the emergence of technological innovations, to their gradual spread through the production system' (1964, p. 81). Thus, successful performance in one decade may be a reflection of previous technological innovations making their mark with a lag due to slow spread in adoption and implementation or to a previously unsuitable institutional environment.

We lack a solid theory of the determinants of TFP so we proceed with partial theories. Over the last three decades the income of the median American household has not kept up with the expectations based on previous performance. Tyler Cowen (2011) labeled this experience 'The Great Stagnation' and attributed it to the slowdown in the rate of technological change combined with the exhaustion of the 'low hanging fruit' from previous innovations. Not only has long-term productivity growth declined but many of the recent innovations are more geared to private goods that benefit few, unlike earlier public goods with much-diffused impacts. Compare the employment generated by car production versus that of *Google* or *Facebook*.

Granted that technological breakthroughs are not foreseeable, the prospects are not bright. In a summary of his report for the Council on Foreign Relations, Spence (2011) shows that of the roughly 27 million jobs created in the American economy between 1990 and 2008, close to 98 per cent were created in the nontradable sectors, led by government and health care (with retail, construction, and hotel and restaurant industries also contributing significantly to job growth). Meanwhile employment barely grew in manufacturing, engineering, and consulting services.

Then there are those that go the other route and forecast accelerating growth. In its extreme version – the singularity approach – it predicts exponential growth for an indefinite future enabled by machine intelligence on a human level (Hanson, 2008). Still extreme but closer to the mainstream, Brian Arthur (2011) argues that digitization is creating a second economy that will lead to the biggest change since the Industrial Revolution. One final example, firmly within the mainstream, is the study by Brynjolfsson and McAfee (2011) where, contra Tyler Cowen, they argue that productivity growth is accelerating and that we are entering a third industrial revolution fuelled by computers and networks. The possibilities envisaged are vast but their realization is not automatic. Brynjolfsson and McAfee are not optimistic about the employment prospects unless institutions catch up with the speed of technological change. 'The root of our problems is not that we are in a Great Recession, or a Great Stagnation, but rather that we are in the early throes of a Great Restructuring' (2011, Kindle Locations, 170–1). 'As technology accelerates … so will the economic mismatches undermining our social contract' (2011, Kindle Locations, 452–4). Which takes us back to a crucial Kuznets theme: structural change is conflictual, and barring the proper institutions (such as a state as an agent for conflict resolution) engenders opposition that can hamper or stop growth.

8.2.2   Resources/food   Access to food, to energy sources and to other raw materials has always been an important strategic element in the global economy. The nineteenth century search for secure sources was a key factor in the quest for empires. Malthusian fears of population growth outstripping the production of food spurred the relentless search for secure sources of supply. Neo-Malthusian predictions of imminent exhaustion of oil and other natural resources have reversed the target from secure supply to limiting consumption, with little to show so far for the vociferous advocacy.

While Malthusian fears still seem unwarranted it is nevertheless the case that the sudden acceleration of growth in very populous countries is causing demand to outstrip supply of many commodities, leading to an increase in prices (beneficial to Brazil and Argentina, less so to Mexico and much of the developing world). A growing consensus, that goes beyond the 'chicken little' [*the sky is falling*] club, is emerging that for many prices of commodities we can expect an upward trend for some time to come. Rogoff (2005) argues that these trends will have:

huge implications for the global balance of power. Indeed, perhaps no other aspect of economic globalization will pose greater challenges to world leaders over the coming decades ... Will the rebalancing of global economic power that results from this destabilize world politics? World War I, of course, was partly set off by Germany's concern that the other colonial powers had locked up too large a share of world oil and commodity supplies. Similarly, in World War II, Japan feared for the stability of its foreign supplies of oil and other natural resources. Will similar tensions arise between resource-challenged China (where even water scarcity is a problem) and the West?

Similarly the US National Intelligence Council in *GLOBAL TRENDS 2025* argues that 'unprecedented economic growth, coupled with 1.5 billion more people, will put pressure on resources—particularly energy, food, and water— raising the specter of scarcities emerging as demand outstrips supply.' A recent study in *Nature* is optimistic about the prospects of food production but adds that 'we face one of the greatest challenges of the twenty-first century: meeting society's growing food needs while simultaneously reducing agriculture's environmental harm'(Foley and *al.*, 2011, p. 337). Trade-offs may yet come to be recognized.

8.2.3   Global governance   The challenges of accommodating rising new powers in an environment of slow growth and of resource scarcity, as well as the many other areas where the interaction among countries may be fraught with conflict, have all elicited calls for improved global governance.

The lowering of global barriers has resulted in many more friction points; it has become increasingly difficult to remain an isolated island. The emergence of many new countries and actors and the wider dissemination of information create a greater potential for perceived exclusion in global decision making; exclusion related to changes in the global distribution of power and wealth. The call for governance often amounts simply to demands for better function- ing, more transparency, and wider representativeness of existing practices and institutions such as the World Trade Organization and the Security Council of the United Nations. At other times it goes further, calling for a world government.

With the thickening agenda and increased congestion at the table, coordin- ation has never been more important. But the belief that there are world solutions to be achieved by global governance or, by default, by international law is a chimera. The growing literature on the supply of global public goods – a key component of global governance – mostly ignores that there are funda- mental differences in preferences among countries (and regions, and individ- uals) and a wide potential for conflict. It is not just differences in marginal evaluations and willingness to share the burden of an activity desired by all, formidable obstacles in themselves, but in the more fundamental question of conflicting evaluations as to whether the provision of a particular public good is desirable or not. Security, freedom and culture come to mind. In a world of increased differentiation it ignores subsidiarity and local knowledge.

The importance of national self-interest and the consequent primacy of great powers were forcefully argued in International Studies more than three decades ago by Krasner (1976) who regrets in his essay the excessive attention paid to transnational forces at the expense of the still-dominant role of the great powers. The global community as represented by the ubiquitous Global Civic Society (e.g. NGOs, epistemic communities, policy networks and transnational social movements) is leading to a 'world civic politics' where nation-states are contested and nonstate actors (IGOs, NGOs, IFIs, MNCs, etc.) become more prominent. They threaten sovereignty but with only limited effective success; their high level of engagement and of public activity demonstrate existence but it should not be taken as a measure of impact. Smaller states and nonstate actors often affect the process but not necessarily the outcome (Drezner, 2007). The utopian outlook that envisages a harmonious style of global governance is an extrapolation from the experience of the European Union to the world. The emergence of a postmodern system of security in Europe is seen as the desirable and likely future for the world.[16]

Given 'the configuration of state interests, the distribution of state power, the logic of collective action, and asymmetric information ... some global problems may simply be unsolvable' (Goldsmith and Posner, 2005, p. 225).

REFERENCES

Arthur, W. B (2011) 'The Second Economy', *McKinsey Quarterly*, October, www.mckinseyquarterly.com/The_second_economy_2853.

Athulorala, P. (2011) *South-South Trade: An Asian Perspective*, ADB Economics Working Paper Series, 265, July.

Beattie, A. (2011) 'When is a Bric not a Bric? When it's a Victim', *Financial Times*, 22 January.

Boltho, A. (2004) 'China; Can Rapid Economic Growth Continue?', *Singapore Economic Review*, 49, pp. 255–72.

Brynjolfsson, E., and McAfee, A. (2011) *Race Against the Machine: How the Digital Revolution is Accelerating Innovation, Driving Productivity, and Irreversibly Transforming Employment and the Economy*, Digital Frontier Press, Kindle edn.

Buiter, W., and Rahbari, E. (2011) 'Global Growth Generators: Moving beyond Emerging Markets and BRIC, *Global Economics View*, 21 Feb. 2011', Citi Investment Research & Analysis, www.econ.uzh.ch/faculty/groupzilibotti/Conferences/2011Nov21Demo/E_Rahbari.pdf.

Chenery, H. B. (1977) 'Transitional Growth and World Industrialization', in B. Ohlin, P. Hesselborn and P. Wijkman (eds.) *The International Allocation of Economic Activity*: Proceedings of a Nobel Symposium, pp. 457–90.

---

[16] Robert Cooper, in *The Breaking of Nations* (2003), extols the European system but he also recognizes the encroachment of chaos on the civilized world – from around it and within it. See also Syrquin (2010).

Cooper, R. N. (2003) 'The Breaking of Nations: Order and Chaos in the Twenty-First Century', *Atlantic Monthly.*
    (2005) 'Whither China?' *Japan Center for Economic Research Bulletin*, September, pp.1–11.
Cowen, T. (2011) *The Great Stagnation: How America Ate All The Low-Hanging Fruit of Modern History, Got Sick, and Will (Eventually) Feel Better*, eBook.
De Benedictis, L., and Tajoli L. (2011) 'The World Trade Network', *The World Economy*, 34, pp.1417–54.
Drezner, D. W. (2007) *All Politics Is Global: Explaining International Regulatory Regimes*, Princeton: Princeton University Press.
Economist Intelligence Unit (EIU) (2010) *Democracy Index 2010: Democracy in Retreat*, http://graphics.eiu.com/PDF/Democracy_Index_2010_web.pdf.
Fischer, S. (2006) 'The New Global Economic Geography', in *The New Economic Geography: Effects and Policy Implications*, Kansas City: Federal Reserve Bank of Kansas City, pp. 177–94.
Fogel, R. W. (2005) 'Reconsidering Expectations of Economic Growth After World War II from the Perspective of 2004', *IMF Staff Papers*, 52, pp. 6–14.
    (2007) 'Capitalism & Democracy in 2040', *Daedalus*, Summer, 136, pp. 87–95.
Foley, J. A., and al. (2011) 'Solutions for a Cultivated Planet', *Nature*, 478, 20 October, pp. 337–42.
Goldsmith, J. L., and Posner, E. A. (2005) *The Limits of International Law*, Oxford: Oxford University Press.
Hanson, R. (2008) 'Economics of the Singularity', *IEEE Spectrum*, June, pp. 37–42.
Huntington, S. P. (1988) 'The U.S.: Decline or Renewal?', *Foreign Affairs*, 6.2, pp, 76–96.
Internation Monetary Fund (IMF) (2011) 'Changing Patterns of Global Trade', *Strategy, Policy, and Review Department*, 15 June.
Inter-American Development Bank (IADB) (2009) *Honoring the Past, Building the Future: Fifty Years of Development in Latin America and the Caribbean*, Washington, DC.
    (2011) *One Region, Two Speeds?: Challenges of the New Global Economic Order for Latin America and the Caribbean*, A. Izquierdo and E. Talvi Coordinators, Washington, DC.
Kindleberger, C. P. (1996) *World Economic Primacy: 1500–1990*, Oxford: Oxford University Press.
Krasner, S. D. (1976) 'State Power and the Structure of International Trade World Politics', *World Politics*, 28, pp. 317–47.
Kuznets, S. (1964) *Postwar Economic Growth*, Cambridge, Mass.: Harvard University Press.
Linder, S. (1961) *An Essay on Trade and Transformation*, New York: Wiley.
National Intelligence Council (NIC) (2008) *Global Trends 2025: A Transformed World*, Washington DC, www.dni.gov/nic/NIC_2025_project.html.
National Science Board (2010) *Science and Engineering Indicators 2010*, Arlington, Virg.: National Science Foundation (NSB 10–01).
Nordhaus, W. D. (1998) 'Quality Change in Price Indexes', *Journal of Economic Perspectives*, 12.1, pp. 59–68.
OECD (2011) *Education at a Glance 2011: OECD Indicators*, OECD Publishing. http://dx.doi.org/10.1787/eag-2011-en.

Population Division of the Department of Economic and Social Affairs of the United
    Nations Secretariat (2011) World Population Prospects: The 2010 Revision, 29
    November, http://esa.un.org/unpd/wpp/index.htm.
PwC (2011) *The World in 2050: The Accelerating Shift of Global Economic Power:
    Challenges and Opportunities*, PwC economics, www.pwc.co.uk/economics.
Quadrio Curzio, A., and Fortis, M. (1996) 'Growth and Productive Structure.
    A Medium-Term Perspective', in B. Colombo, P. Demeny and M. F. Perutz (eds.)
    *Resources and Population. Natural, Institutional, and Demographic Dimensions
    of Development*, Study Week on Resources and Population, 17–22 November
    1991, Oxford: Clarendon Press-Pontificia Academia Scientiarum, pp. 137–56.
Quadrio Curzio, A. (2008) 'The EU 27 Integration and the Economic Relationship with
    the East. An introductory analysis', in A. Quadrio Curzio e M. Fortis (eds.), *The
    EU and the Economies of the Eastern European Enlargement*, Heidelberg:
    Physica-Verlag, pp. 1–25.
Rogoff, K. (2005) 'Who's Dependent Now?', *Project Syndicate*, www.project-
    syndicate.org/commentary/rogoff10/English.
    (2008) 'China May Yet be the Economy to Lose Sleep Over', *Financial Times*, 5
    February, p. 9.
Spence, M. (2011) 'Globalization and Unemployment: The Downside of Integrating
    Markets', *Foreign Affairs*, 90.4, pp. 28–41.
Syrquin, M. (2005a) 'Globalization: too Much or is it too Little?', *Economia Politica*,
    22.1, pp. 25–42.
    (2005b) 'Too Much Globalization or Is It Rather too Little?', in A. Cassetta (ed.)
    Increasing Complexity in International Relations: Economy, Politics and Values,
    The Leading Scholars' Program 2004, ASEI, Milan: Catholic University.
    (2010) '27 Countries in Search of a Project: A Skeptical View from Outside Europe',
    Economia Politica, 27.3, pp. 389–93.
    (2012) 'Changes in the Economic Structure of the World Economy', Working Paper
    No. 3/2012, Turin: ICER, www.icer.it/docs/wp2012/ICERwp03–12.pdf.
Taylor, T. (2011) 'Longer Global Supply Chains', Blog post *The Conversable
    Economist*, 19 August, http://conversableeconomist.blogspot.com/2011/08/
    longer-global-supply-chains.html.
Tellis, A. J., Bially J. L., Layne, C., McPherson, M., and Sollinger J. M. (2000)
    Measuring National Power in the Postindustrial Age, RAND Corporation, www.
    rand.org/pubs/monograph_reports/MR1110.html#toc.
U.S. Energy Information Administration (2010) *International Energy Outlook 2010*,
    www.eia.gov/oiaf/aeo.
Viner, J. (1948) 'Power Versus Plenty as Objectives of Foreign Policy in the
    Seventeenth and *Eighteenth Centuries*', *World Politics*, 1, *pp.* 1–29.
Wolf, M. (2008) 'Response to Kenneth Rogoff's "China may yet be the economy to
    lose sleep over"', *Financial Times*, 5 February, p. 9.
    (2010) *Fixing Global Finance*, Baltimore: Johns Hopkins University Press.
World Bank (2010) World Economic Outlook, April, Washington, DC, www.imf.org/
    external/pubs/ft/weo/2010/01/#ch1fig.
    (2011) *Global Economic Prospects: Navigating strong Currents*, January,
    Washington, DC.
World Trade Organization (WTO) (2010) *International Trade Statistics 2010*, Geneva.

19 Transformation and resources in the 'new' geo-economy

Marco Fortis

1. Introduction

Structural change in the dynamics of the World Economy can be analysed from many points of view. In this chapter we will combine two schemes of comparison across different areas and countries: that among GDPs, manufacturing outputs and products in international trade (Section 2); and that among industrial raw materials consumption (Section 3).

The core of this analysis is the second scheme, this being a field investigated at length by the present writer in the 1980s and 1990s. In fact previous works of mine have analysed the long-term trend of natural resources in global models (Fortis, 1981) and studied the raw materials consumption with reference to three broad situations: economic cycles (Fortis, 1988, 1990), different economic development stages (Fortis, 1993a, 1993b, 1993c) and single-commodity country (Fortis, 2006).

This is an applied research line strictly connected with the theoretical analysis of Alberto Quadrio Curzio[1], who worked for a long time on natural resources and raw materials (Quadrio Curzio 1967, 1975, 1980, 1986, 1990, 1996; Quadrio Curzio and Pellizzari, 1996, 1999). Quadrio Curzio did research on structural theory, changes in technologies, technical progress, and what he called technological scarcities, composite technologies (Quadrio Curzio, 1986, 1990) and global technologies (Quadrio Curzio, 1996), assigning a fundamental role to natural resources and raw materials both in comparative static (or better uniperiodal) and in dynamic schemes. He also made a remarkable contribution on the price-distribution relationship, with a central

---

[1] The author of this chapter was a pupil of Alberto Quadrio Curzio's, who supervised his dissertation in 1980. Since then he has been involved in manifold collaborative projects with him, both as coordinator of Nomisma's *Materie prime*, a journal directed by A. Quadrio Curzio, and as a colleague in research and teaching at the Economic Analysis Research Center (*Cranec*, set up by Quadrio Curzio) of the Catholic University, where the Political Science Faculty was presided over by Quadrio Curzio for twenty-one years. Since 1999 I have also been the coordinator of Fondazione Edison, whose scientific committee is chaired by Quadrio Curzio and where the analysis of production and technology is the core research field. See www.fondazioneedison.it.

role of rent systems connected with the previous dynamics of productions and technologies (see previous quotations and Quadrio Curzio, 1998). On the whole his contribution has been pioneering because it was initially conceived when most theories of growth and distribution disregarded such aspects (for a sum up see Quadrio Curzio, 2011).

Building on this theory much of my research has dealt with raw materials and commodities (see the works aforementioned) within a stylized scheme that is much closer to that of the 'old political economy' than to that of the 'new rigorous' one (which is often incapable of explaining the long-term dynamics of economies). On these issues I have also collaborated with Quadrio Curzio, starting with the Journal *Materie prime* founded in 1980 (Prodi, Quadrio Curzio, Fortis, 1980),which was titled *Innovazione e Materie prime* from 1990 up to 1993 when the publication ceased (for this joint research program see Quadrio Curzio, 1993). Among the collaborative works with Quadrio Curzio in these fields we mention the researches on industrial raw materials and the ones on innovation and resources (Quadrio Curzio and Fortis, 1986, 1996; Quadrio Curzio, Fortis and Zoboli, 1993).

This explains the common interests and complementarity in the analysis of raw materials and of their utilization in industry between this research programme and the one initiated and developed by A. Quadrio Curzio over many years.

2.   Traditional economic indicators of world development

This section is on the more traditional dynamics of GDPs, of manufacturing outputs and of international trade. This approach tells us that over the past few decades the world has been changing rapidly, with the fast growth of the Asian economies and especially of China. Up to twenty-five years ago most statistics provided details mainly on the economy of the 'Western world', which was a geo-politic, rather than a geographic concept. At that time the 'Western world' included West Europe, North and South America, as well as Australia and Japan. The statistics did sometimes go as far as to survey the economic situation of the former USSR and of its satellite countries (areas relatively closed to trade with the 'Western world'), while the rest of the world was considered almost exclusively as a 'residual area', a scarcely significant and marginal reality of our planet.

Everything changed over quite a short time and that residual area is becoming overwhelming in the economic figures when compared with the 'old advanced world', even if Russia and the Central and Eastern European countries are added to the 'Western' countries. Asia, the new big emerging world area, has a larger population and records bigger consumptions of food and many industrial raw materials than the 'old advanced world'. In two or three decades it is destined to overcome it also in global income and energy consumption.

2.1   World GDP: the 'overtaking' by China and India

The best known forecasts of the last few years on the long-term development of the world GDP and of the GDPs of the major countries are those made by Goldman Sachs (Wilson and Purushothaman, 2003) and those of the economist and historian Angus Maddison, published by the OECD (Maddison, 2007). The former are projections in US dollars at the 2003 exchange rates; the latter, instead, are in 1990 US dollars and compare the GDP size of the various countries assuming purchasing power parity. According to these latter estimates, the GDPs of the big emerging countries such as China and India are considerably larger than they appear from the figures compared in accordance with the usual exchange rates.

Goldman Sachs' projections became famous because they were centred on a more or less imminent 'overtaking' of the G-6 countries (United States, Japan, Germany, UK, France and Italy) by the GDPs of the so-called BRICs (Brazil, Russia, India and China). According to Goldman Sachs:

- China's GDP will surpass Japan's as early as in 2016;
- By 2023 China's GDP will surpass the aggregate GDP of the four major European countries,
- By 2039 India's GDP will surpass the aggregate GDP of the four major European countries; by the same year the aggregate GDP of the four BRICs will surpass the G-6 GDP;
- By 2041 China will be the largest world economic power because its GDP at current prices will surpass that of the United States.

The dates of the new Asian powers 'overtaking' the United States and Europe in Maddison's projections are much closer than Goldman Sachs's forecasts because the GDP values of the countries involved are expressed in US dollars at purchasing power parity. This way allowance is made for the different domestic price levels in the emerging countries vis-à-vis the major advanced countries. The emerging countries' GDPs, expressed as 'volumes' through purchasing power parity, appear bigger than they would be if they were simply converted into the respective national currencies at current exchange rates in US dollars, the usual international comparison currency. In 2003, for example, according to Maddison, China's GDP at current exchange rates would have been only 15 per cent of that of the United States, while at purchasing power parity it was already as big as about three-fourths of the American one (Maddison and Wu, 2007).

We have analysed Maddison's projections and compared, for the sake of convenience, two broad blocks of countries:

- the 'old advanced world' after the fall of the Berlin Wall, consisting of the United States, West Europe, Japan, the other 'ancient' capitalist economies such as Canada and Oceania, plus the USSR and the former Soviet countries, and East Europe;
- Asia, excluding Japan.

A comparison between 1952, 1990 and the 2030 projections shows that:

- in 1952 the 'old advanced world' accounted for little less than 73% of the world GDP. West Europe held 26% and the United States about 27.5% of the world total;
- in 1990 the 'old advanced world' share of the world GDP decreased, though not dramatically, to about 65%, against Asia's growth, above all in the 'other Asian countries', which include the more dynamic economies of South Korea, Singapore, Taiwan and the Middle East;
- as a result of the growth of the new Asian giants, between 1990 and 2030 the 'old advanced world' will suffer a real collapse with its world GDP share dropping by more than 24 percentage points from 65% to 41%. As a matter of fact Asia's growth will be huge, fuelled especially by China and India. Note that, according to Maddison's projections, China's GDP will be surpassing that of the United States as early as in 2015;
- Asia's total share (excluding Japan) of the world GDP will be rising from 23% in 1990 to 50% by 2030; China's share, in particular, will be rising from 7.8% to 23.8%. India's share of the world GDP will increase considerably, too, from 4% to more than 10%;
- the share of the rest of the world (Latin America and Africa), in contrast, will record a slight decrease to less than 10%.

2.2   The evolution of world manufacturing output and product trade

According to the *Centro Studi Confindustria* (CSC), the economic research centre of the Confederation of Italian Industry, deep changes took place in the geo-economy of the world manufacturing output in the decade from 2000 to 2010. In the year 2000 (Table 19.1) the United States still held 24.8% of the world manufacturing output expressed in current US dollars, followed by Japan with 15.8%. China ranked third, with a share in manufacturing output of 8.3%, followed by Germany (6.6%), Italy (4.1%) and France (4%).

By 2007, after only seven years, the power relationship had been overthrown. The United States still ranked first, but its share in the world manufacturing output was down to 18.2%, while China, jumping to 14.1%,

Table 19.1 *Manufacturing production in the most important G-20 countries (% share of the world manufacturing production in current U.S. dollars)*

Rank		2000	Rank		2007	Rank		2010
1	United States	24.8	1	United States	18.2	1	China	21.7
2	Japan	15.8	2	China	14.1	2	United States	15.6
3	China	8.3	3	Japan	9.0	3	Japan	9.1
4	Germany	6.6	4	Germany	7.5	4	Germany	6.0
5	Italy	4.1	5	Italy	4.5	5	India	3.7
6	France	4.0	6	France	3.9	6	Republic of Korea	3.5
7	United Kingdom	3.5	7	Republic of Korea	3.9	7	Italy	3.4
8	Republic of Korea	3.1	8	United Kingdom	3.0	8	Brazil	3.2
9	Canada	2.3	9	India	2.9	9	France	3.0
10	Mexico	2.3	10	Brazil	2.6	10	Russian Federation	2.0
11	Brazil	2.0	11	Canada	2.2	11	United Kingdom	2.0
12	India	1.8	12	Russian Federation	2.1	12	Canada	1.7
13	Turkey	0.9	13	Mexico	1.9	13	Indonesia	1.6
14	Australia	0.8	14	Turkey	1.1	14	Mexico	1.6
15	Indonesia	0.8	15	Indonesia	1.1	15	Australia	1.0
16	Russian Federation	0.7	16	Australia	0.9	16	Turkey	1.0

n.a. = not available
Source: Centro Studi Confindustria (2011)

surpassed Japan. Germany, Italy and France maintained their fourth, fifth and sixth places, respectively, as manufacturing producers, while South Korea rose quickly and surpassed Great Britain, which was seventh after France. By 2010 the situation had radically changed again. China reached the top position with a share in world manufacturing output of 21.7%, surpassing the United States. After Japan and Germany, which held the third and fourth positions as manufacturers, India and South Korea rose rapidly to the fifth and sixth positions, respectively. Both surpassed Italy and France. Italy ranked seventh while France was surpassed also by Brazil and went down to the ninth place. Great Britain lost three positions and ranked eleventh, preceded also by Russia.

Parallel to these developments of the world manufacturing output were those of world trade in manufactured products[2]. In 1980 the ranking of the

---

[2] According to the ITS (WTO International Trade Statistics) definition, 'manufactures' refer to iron and steel, chemicals, other semi-manufactures, machinery and transport equipment, textiles, clothing and others consumer goods (excluding foods). See: World Trade Organization (2011, pp. 188–9).

world export of manufactured products (Table 19.2) saw Germany at the top, followed by the United States; Japan was third, France fourth, Great Britain fifth and Italy sixth. China was only seventh. In 2009, after only thirty-nine years, China had become the 'world factory' and was ranked first as world exporter of manufactured products. All the other advanced countries lost one position, with the exception of Great Britain, which lost three and was surpassed also by South Korea, while Italy held its sixth place.

The changes in the ranking of foreign trade surpluses from manufacturing were even more shocking (Table 19.3). Among the G-20 countries, in 1980 Japan recorded the largest foreign trade surplus in manufactured products, followed by Germany, Italy and the United States. In 2009 the top position was held by China, followed by Germany. Japan lost two positions and ranked third. South Korea, which was only seventh in 1980, attained the fourth position in 2009, surpassing Italy, now fifth.

In the meantime, in 2009 the United States, Great Britain and France recorded deficits in manufacturing product trade, i.e. their imports were much bigger than their exports. This is because these countries either lost many of their manufacturing specializations or relocated them massively to other countries, mainly to China. It is worth stressing that in 2009 only five G-20 economies had a foreign trade surplus in manufactured products: China, Germany, Japan, South Korea and Italy.

3.   The dynamics of industrial materials consumption: 1980–2010

This section deals with the consumption figures of the main industrial raw materials, which are used as indicators to measure the structural dynamic change. In particular, we will be analysing the consumption of eleven main industrial materials (six non-ferrous metals, steel, wood-based panels, rubber, packaging paper and paperboard as well as plastic materials) and will be comparing the figures with those covering the evolution of the world manufacturing output with a view to measuring the shifting of its centre of gravity from North America and Europe towards Asia. The period under examination spans from 1980 to 2010 and focuses especially on raw materials consumptions in the G-20 countries.

The world manufacturing output data at current prices probably underestimate the goods volumes really produced in many emerging countries. In order to better understand the extent of the change that occurred in world manufacturing output it is useful to analyse the consumption of eleven major industrial materials in the G-20 countries over the last few decades. The consumption figures were reconstructed with reference to four years: 1980, 1990, 2000 and 2010.

Table 19.2 *Exports of manufactured goods of the G-20 countries: 1980–2009 (billions of current US dollars)*

1980		1990	
Germany	162	Germany	376
United States	142	United States	290
Japan	123	Japan	275
France	81	France	161
United Kingdom	79	Italy	148
Italy	65	United Kingdom	147
Canada	30	Canada	73
Korea, Rep.	16	Korea, Rep.	61
China	9	China	44
Brazil	7	Mexico	25
India	5	Brazil	16
South Africa	5	India	13
Mexico	4	Indonesia	9
Australia	4	Turkey	9
Argentina	2	South Africa	8
Turkey	1	Australia	7
Saudi Arabia	1	Saudi Arabia	4
Indonesia	0	Argentina	4
Russian Federation	-	Russian Federation	-

2000		2009	
United States	649	China	1.125
Germany	483	Germany	970
Japan	450	United States	800
France	273	Japan	508
United Kingdom	233	France	383
China	220	Italy	339
Italy	212	Korea, Rep.	323
Canada	176	United Kingdom	257
Korea, Rep.	155	Mexico	172
Mexico	139	Canada	157
Indonesia	37	India	107
India	33	Turkey	78
Brazil	32	Russian Federation	64
Russian Federation	25	Brazil	58
Turkey	22	Indonesia	47
South Africa	20	South Africa	32
Australia	15	Saudi Arabia	23
Argentina	9	Australia	23
Saudi Arabia	6	Argentina	18

Source: compiled by the author on data from WTO, *Statistics Database*, http://stat.wto.org.

Table 19.3 *Manufactured goods trade balance of the G-20 countries: 1980–2009 (billions of current US dollars)*

1980		1990	
Japan	98	Japan	175
Germany	65	Germany	123
Italy	21	Italy	35
United States	18	Korea, Rep.	16
United Kingdom	9	Brazil	4
France	9	China	2
Korea, Rep.	6	Argentina	0
India	0	India	0
Turkey	−2	Turkey	−5
Brazil	−3	South Africa	−5
China	−3	Mexico	−7
Argentina	−6	Indonesia	−8
Indonesia	−7	France	−11
South Africa	−7	Saudi Arabia	−15
Australia	−11	Canada	−20
Canada	−11	United Kingdom	−23
Mexico	−12	Australia	−25
Saudi Arabia	−24	United States	−85
Russian Federation	–	Russian Federation	–

2000		2009	
Japan	237	China	450
Germany	120	Germany	288
Korea, Rep.	57	Japan	222
Italy	50	Korea, Rep.	137
China	50	Italy	70
India	10	India	−9
Indonesia	6	South Africa	−11
France	5	Turkey	−11
South Africa	1	Indonesia	−11
Russian Federation	−6	Argentina	−16
Brazil	−9	Mexico	−16
Mexico	−11	France	−31
Argentina	−13	Brazil	−39
Turkey	−16	Saudi Arabia	−53
Saudi Arabia	−16	United Kingdom	−79
Canada	−25	Canada	−85
United Kingdom	−42	Russian Federation	−89
Australia	−44	Australia	−92
United States	−319	United States	−321

Source: compiled by the author on data from WTO, *Statistics Database*, http://stat.wto.org.

The utilization of the consumption data of raw materials and industrial materials as statistical indicators in the study of growth problems and economic cycles has a long tradition in economic analysis. Spiethoff, too, used the 'iron consumption parameter' as an analytical instrument (Spiethoff, 1925). Tugan Baranovsky did the same in his *Les crises industrielles en Angleterre* (Tugan Baranovsky, 1913).

The basic industrial products selected for this analysis are the most representative in a number of manufacturing productions. Some of their consumption takes place in the construction industry (steel consumption, for example), not in the manufacturing industry. Therefore, when observing the basic product consumptions in the emerging countries, the actual manufacturing activity may be overestimated due to the effect of the building industry on the demand of materials. However, the wide range of materials considered allows this aspect to be toned down, thus avoiding excessive overestimates of the shares of the various countries in the world manufacturing output.

To start with, we consider the six main non-ferrous metals: copper, aluminium, lead, zinc, tin and nickel. The strategic role of these materials in the development processes is not less important than that of steel and was thoroughly analysed both with reference to the dynamics of economic cycles (Fortis 1988) and to the 'stage of growth' theories (Fortis 1993a, 1993b[3], 1993c). Non-ferrous metals are suitable for a variety of uses in the various manufacturing industry sectors, in addition to the building industry. Some of them, like aluminium, are also tied to the household consumption cycles because of their utilization in packaging. For all these reasons the consumptions of non-ferrous metals are also extremely significant 'real' indicators of the trend in the most advanced economic systems. In addition, they make it possible to highlight particular manufacturing specializations in different countries or at particular historical stages of their development, while in some of our studies (e.g. Fortis, 1988) we also underlined the relationship between copper consumption, GDP and industrial output in a number of countries and in Italy.

The role of non-ferrous metals in the centuries-old process of economic development has been of major importance. It is almost impossible to imagine electrification and telephone communications between the end of the 1800s and the beginning of the 1900s without thinking of the essential role of copper as a conductor. Likewise we cannot imagine the development of 'mass

---

[3] Giorgio Fuà's great interest in raw materials consumption as indicators of structural changes in economy and in the economic development stages of nations spurred him in 1993 to ask the author of this chapter to conduct the study *Stadi della crescita e consumi di materiali industriali: l'esperienza dell'Italia e dei maggiori Paesi avanzati* published in the *Studi sullo sviluppo* series of the Economics Department of the University of Ancona.

consumption' in the United States in the 1920s and elsewhere in the following decades of the last century without thinking again of copper, with its increasing and widespread applications in the building industry, in the transportation industry and in consumer goods; or of lead and its usage in car batteries and as antiknock in gasoline; or of tin, as essential in welding as nickel is in the production of industrial steels and superalloys; or of zinc and its applications in the steel industry and in the production of brass (a copper-zinc alloy), the latter being another crucial material for its applications in mechanics and constructions (taps and valves). As regards aluminium, it is the non-ferrous metal with the largest consumption quantities at present, as it has become progressively fundamental in many sectors, from the building industry to packaging, from means of transportation to mechanics.

Another material considered in our analysis is crude steel. The same comments apply here as made in connection with non-ferrous metals. It is a material of major importance because of its use both in the manufacturing industry (automotive, machinery and mechanical products) and in the construction industry. Equally important in manufacturing processes are rubber (natural and synthetic), used in tyres and miscellaneous products, including piping, gaskets, shoe soles etc., as well as wood-based panels, available in a wide range of types with broadly diversified features and applications, used in the building and furniture industry and plastic materials.

In our analysis we consider the overall consumption of seven plastic materials: Low-Density Polyethylene (LDPE), Linear Low-Density Polyethylene (LLDPE), High Density Polyethylene (HDPE), Polypropylene (PP), Polyvinyl Chloride (PVC), Polystyrene (PS) and Polyethylene Terephthalate (PET).[4] Finally, we consider the consumption of wooden panels, very important in a number of industries, as well that of packaging paper and cardboard, another significant indicator of the manufacturing activity levels in a country.

The analysis is focused on the major trends and on the structural changes that occurred in the G-20 countries in the last thirty years, with the rising importance of the emerging countries as basic product consumers in the industrial manufacturing processes.

The main results are set forth hereunder.

---

[4] The utilization range of these seven plastic materials is very wide and they often compete with one another, especially in packaging. LDPE and LLDPE are used mainly in packaging, but also for cable sheathing and flexible hoses. PP is used in packaging (bottles, trays, plastic film) but also in the auto industry (bumpers, interior components) and in the manufacture of piping, chairs, apparel, carpeting and sanitary products such as diapers. PS is used in the manufacture of rigid consumer goods (CD cases, cutlery, dishes, tableware, cups, etc.) and in packaging. PVC is used in piping for buildings (roof gutters and drinking water piping), in window sections, roller shutters, and vinyl flooring as well as for packaging and stationery as rigid or plasticized film. PET is used in the manufacture of bottles and food packaging trays.

First of all it is observed that the United States, in 1980 the first world consumer of nine basic products out of eleven, preceded by the former USSR only in steel and zinc, lost the top place as user of industrial materials in 2010 and was replaced by China. The final overtaking by China took place between 2000 and 2010, but as early as in the year 2000 the Asian giant had surpassed the United States in the consumption of three materials (zinc, tin and steel) and held second place in the world consumption of as many as seven other basic products. By 2010 the overtaking had occurred in all the eleven materials examined. It should be emphasized that in the consumption of the seven single main plastic materials considered, in 2010 China recorded higher figures than the United States in six of them. Only in PET consumption was the top position still held by the United States, though by a small margin.

The structural change appears to be epoch-making also if the quantities used by China are examined. In 2000 China still used 64% copper, 75% rubber, 62% plastic materials and 55% packaging paper and paperboard compared with the United States. By 2010 China was already using four times as much copper as the United States, three times as much rubber, almost twice as much plastic materials and one-a-half times as much packaging paper and paperboard. All that took only ten years and gives a precise idea of the dramatic changes in world manufacturing output. China's overtaking of the United States in manufacturing production is probably one of the major economic changes in the entire economic history of humankind and among the fastest ever occurring.

It is worth stressing Russia's loss of importance, from the 1990s onwards, i.e. after the break-up of the USSR, in world consumption of raw materials, while Japan kept the second place in world consumption of industrial materials after the United States for a long time before the amazing rise of China as a new manufacturing power.

Japan's overtaking by China in industrial materials consumption, instead, took place between 1990 and 2010. In addition, South Korea came considerably closer to Japan in the basic industrial products consumption list between 2000 and 2010. A remarkable performance was recorded also by Germany, which in 2010 preceded Japan in the consumption of copper, lead and wood-based panels. As regards the main plastic materials, it should be underlined that in 2010 Germany, though preceded by Japan in total plastics consumption, ranked higher than Japan in LDPE, HDPE and PVC.

It is interesting to notice that, in Europe, Italy is preceded only by Germany in the use of industrial materials, a place continually maintained from 1980 to 2010. Despite the rise of the emerging countries, Italy also kept over time a good position in basic product consumptions among the G-20 countries, while France declined remarkably. The distance between Germany and Italy did not grow much, while the gap between Germany and France grew visibly between 2000 and 2010.

Two large emerging countries recorded a growing importance in world consumption of basic products in the period under consideration: India and Brazil. While in 1980 and 1990 Brazil preceded India as a raw material consumer, the latter country made a big jump in the world ranking of industrial material consumption between 2000 and 2010, surpassing even Brazil. Also South Korea, thanks to a strong acceleration in the last two decades, has surpassed Brazil in industrial material consumption. So now India and South Korea come immediately after China, the United States, Japan and Germany in the world list of basic products consumers.

In 2010 South Korea jumped right after Germany in material consumption, and by 2010 was already using more nickel, zinc, lead and steel than Germany.

As regards Italy, South Korea overtook this country in industrial materials consumption between 2000 and 2010. In 2010 South Korea used more primary aluminium, copper, zinc, lead, nickel, tin, steel, paper and paperboard as well as rubber than Italy, while Italy preceded South Korea only in the consumption of wood-based panels and plastic materials.

Again in 2010 also Brazil surpassed Italy in basic product consumption. Brazil's lead over France is even sharper, while it is worth remarking that Turkey is now more important even than Great Britain in industrial material consumptions.

In order to sum up the results of our analysis we built a rough consumption index for the eleven materials under examination. The index results from the average of the positions held by each economy in the consumption list of each basic product, always using the nineteen countries of G-20 as reference. The index is rather simple: if a country is the first consumer among G-20 for all eleven basic products, like China in 2010, its index is 1, i.e. equal to $(1 \times 11)/11$. The index ranges between a maximum value of 1 (if a country is the most important consumer of all the eleven raw materials) and a minimum value of 19 (if a country is the least important consumer of all the eleven raw materials). The twentieth G-20 member, the European Union, is not included.

Table 19.4 shows the rankings of the major raw material consumer countries in 1980, 1990, 2000 and 2010 according to our indicator. The following comments can be made.

From 1980 to 2000 the United States was always the top world consumer of raw materials. By 2010 China jumped to the top position, with higher consumptions than the United States in all the materials considered. In 1980 the USSR ranked second after the United States and in 1990 was third after the United States and Japan. After the collapse of the Soviet Union, Russia did not hold any leading position in the list of world consumption of basic products any more, and ranked between the eleventh and the ninth positions. Japan, with the temporary exception of 1990, was always third in raw material utilization, Germany was fourth. In 2010 the United States was still more

Table 19.4 *Index of consumption of 11 industrial materials: average of the places held by each G-20 country in the 11 raw materials rankings, 1980–2010*

Rank	1980	Index	Rank	1990	Index
1	United States	1.2	1	United States	1.2
2	Former USSR	2.5	2	Japan	2.2
3	Japan	2.6	3	Former USSR	3.6
4	Germany	3.9	4	Germany	4.1
5	France	5.6	5	China	4.9
6	Italy	6.3	6	France	6.8
7	United Kingdom	6.8	7	Italy	6.8
8	China	7.9	8	United Kingdom	7.5
9	Canada	9.1	9	Republic of Korea	8.6
10	Brazil	9.2	10	Canada	10.4
11	Australia	11.9	11	Brazil	10.9
12	Mexico	12.2	12	India	11.3
13	India	13.2	13	Mexico	12.7
14	Republic of Korea	13.6	14	Australia	14.3
15	South Africa	13.9	15	South Africa	15.2
Rank	**2000**	**Index**	**Rank**	**2010**	**Index**
1	United States	1.4	1	China	1.0
2	China	2.0	2	United States	2.2
3	Japan	3.0	3	Japan	3.5
4	Germany	3.7	4	Germany	4.5
5	Republic of Korea	5.6	5	Republic of Korea	5.6
6	Italy	6.9	6	India	6.5
7	France	7.3	7	Brazil	7.6
8	United Kingdom	9.0	8	Italy	7.8
9	Brazil	10.1	9	Russian Federation	10.6
10	Canada	10.6	10	Turkey	10.8
11	Russian Federation	10.9	11	France	11.5
12	India	11.0	12	Mexico	12.2
13	Mexico	12.1	13	Canada	12.6
14	Australia	14.5	14	United Kingdom	13.1
15	Turkey	14.5	15	Indonesia	13.6

Source: compiled by the author on data from World Bureau of Metal Statistics' Bulletins and Yearbooks (various years), World Steel Association's Yearbooks (various years), FAOSTAT database, International Rubber Study Group's Statistical Bulletin (various years), ICIS Consulting 2012.

important than Japan in the consumption of nine basic products out of eleven, while Japan ranked before Germany in eight raw materials. After these countries, South Korea climbed from the fourteenth position in raw material consumption held in 1980 to the fifth place in 2010. In 2010 Germany still preceded South Korea in the consumption of seven raw materials, while South Korea preceded Italy in nine materials.

Over the three decades from 1980 to 2010 Italy, France and Great Britain lost some places, Italy, however, fewer than the other two countries. In 2010 India and Brazil preceded Italy, which went down to the eighth position as raw material consumer. In the same year India preceded Brazil in the consumption of eight basic products vs. three where Brazil was more important. In turn, Brazil has a slight lead over Italy as user of basic products: six raw materials vs. five.

A sharper drop appears in raw materials consumption by France, down to the eleventh place in 2010, and by Great Britain, down to the fourteenth position. In 2010 Italy preceded France in nine materials out of eleven. In 2010 France was surpassed also by Russia and Turkey: both countries precede France in seven materials out of eleven. Russia, however, is more important than Turkey, preceding it in seven materials out of eleven. Finally, in 2010 Great Britain was preceded also by Mexico and Canada.

4.   Conclusions: raw material consumption as a fundamental indicator of dynamic structural change in the world economy

Raw material consumption shows clearly that the distribution of world manufacturing output has radically changed over the past ten to fifteen years, with the growth (beside the traditional developed countries) of new leaders such as China, South Korea, India and Brazil and with new outsiders such as Mexico and Turkey quickly moving up. Some substantial structural changes clearly appear both from the figures on manufacturing output value and from the consumption data of the main basic products used in the production processes. Both types of statistics show that the major world manufacturing producers in 2010 were, in decreasing order: China, United States, Japan, Germany and South Korea.

The figures analysed in this chapter undoubtedly prove China's absolute record, South Korea's rising role and the powerful growth of some emerging economies, such as India and Brazil, in world manufacturing output and primary commodity consumption. Over less than ten years the United States lost its manufacturing leadership, which was taken over by China. Japan maintains its prominent position in Asia, while Germany and Italy remain the two most important European manufacturing producers.

REFERENCES

Assomet (various years) *I metalli non ferrosi in Italia. Statistiche*, Milan: Assomet.
    (1996) *I metalli non ferrosi. 50 anni di storia italiana*, Bergamo: Edimet.

Centro Studi Confindustria (CSC) (2011) 'Effetti della crisi, materie prime e rilancio manifatturiero. Le strategie di sviluppo delle imprese italiane', *Scenari industriali*, 2, June.

Faostat, *Faostat Database*. http://faostat3.fao.org/home/E.

Fortis, M. (1981) 'Modelli globali e scenari di sviluppo mondiale', *Energia*, 2.2, pp. 32–57.

(1988) *Prodotti di base e cicli economici*, Bologna: Il Mulino.

(1990) *Dinamiche settoriali e indicatori di sviluppo. L'economia italiana dal 1950 al 1990*, Bologna: Il Mulino.

(1993a) *Competizione tecnologica e sviluppo industriale. Fasi dell'economia mondiale dal 1850 al 1990*, Bologna: Il Mulino.

(1993b) 'Stadi della crescita e consumi di materiali industriali. L'esperienza dell'Italia e quella dei maggiori Paesi avanzati', *Studi sullo sviluppo-Quaderni*, 4, Ancona: Università di Ancona.

(1993c) 'Economic Growth and the Intensity of Use of Industrial Materials', in A. Quadrio Curzio, M. Fortis and R. Zoboli (eds.) *Innovation, Resources and Economic Growth*, Berlin and Heidelberg: Springer-Verlag, pp. 83–99.

(2006) 'Il ruolo strategico dei metalli non ferrosi nel sistema produttivo italiano: produzioni, attività di trasformazione, filiere', in *Materie prime rinnovabili e risorse per il nostro futuro*, Milan: Assomet, pp. 6–29.

ICIS Consulting (2012), *Statistics Database*.

International Rubber Study Group (various years), *Rubber Statistical Bulletin*, London: IRSG.

Maddison, A. (2001) *The World Economy: A Millenial Perspective*, Paris: OECD.

(2007) *Chinese Economic Performance in the Long-Run*, 2nd edn, Paris: OECD.

Maddison A., and Wu, H. X. (2007) *China's Economic Performance: How Fast Has GDP Grown; How Big Is It Compared with the USA?*, www.ggdc.net/Maddison/articles/China_Maddison_Wu_22_Feb_07.pdf.

O'Neill, J. (2011) *The Growth Map. Economic Opportunity in the BRICs and Beyond*, New York: Penguin Books.

(1980) *Presentazione di un Rapporto trimestrale sulle materie prime*, Bologna: Nomisma.

Quadrio Curzio, A. (1967) *Rendita e distribuzione in un modello economico plurisettoriale*, Milan: Giuffrè.

(1975) *Accumulazione del capitale e rendita*, Bologna: Il Mulino.

(1980) 'Rent, Income Distribution and Orders of Efficiency and Rentability', in L. L. Pasinetti (ed.) *Essays on the Theory of Joint Production*, London: Macmillan, pp. 219–40. Reprinted in H. D. Kurz and N. Salvadori (eds.) (2003) *The Legacy of Piero Sraffa*, Cheltenham (Mass): E. Elgar, vol. II, pp. 311–41.

(1986) 'Technological Scarcity: An Essay on Production and Structural Change', in M. Baranzini and R. Scazzieri (eds.) *Foundations of Economics*, Oxford and New York: B. Blackwell, pp. 311–38. Reprinted in H. Hagemann, M. A. Landesmann and R. Scazzieri (eds.) (2003) *The Economics of Structural Change*, Cheltenham: E. Elgar, vol. II, pp.138–65.

(1990) 'Rent, Distribution and Economic Structure. A Collection of Essays', *Dynamics-Quaderni IDSE*, no. 1, Milan: CNR.

(1993) 'Innovation, Resources and the World Economy. A Survey on Twelve Years of Contributions through Two Journals', in *Innovazione e Materie Prime*, II, no. 2–3, pp. 5–20.

(1996) 'Production and Efficiency with Global Technologies' (with Appendices by C. F. Manara and M. Faliva), in M. A. Landesmann and R. Scazzieri (eds.) *Production and Economics Dynamics*, Cambridge: Cambridge University Press, pp. 105–39.

(1998) 'Rent', in H. D. Kurz e N. Salvadori (eds.) *Elgar Companion to Classical Economics (ECCE)*, Cheltenham: E. Elgar, pp. 289–93.

(2011) 'Resources and Economic Dynamics, Technology and Rents', Quaderno CRANEC – *Centro di Ricerche in Analisi Economica e Sviluppo Economico Internazionale*, Vita e Pensiero, Milan, November 2011. English edition of 'Risorse e dinamica economica, tecnologia e rendite', in *Gli economisti postkeynesiani di Cambridge e l'Italia*, Atti dei Convegni Lincei, n. 261, Rome: Accademia Nazionale dei Lincei, Scienze e Lettere Editore Commerciale, pp. 409–32.

Quadrio Curzio, A., and Fortis, M. (1986) 'Industrial Raw Materials: A Multi-Country Multi-Commodity Analysis, 1971–1983', in P. Ferri and G. Ragazzi (eds.) Adjusting to Shocks. A North-South Perspective, Studies in Banking and Finance, *Supplement to the* Journal of Banking & Finance, 4, pp. 99–107.

(1996) 'Growth and Productive Structure. A Medium-Term Perspective', in B. Colombo, P. Demeny and M. F. Perutz (eds.) *Resources and Population. Natural, Institutional, and Demographic Dimensions of Development*, Study Week on Resources and Population, 17–22 November 1991, Oxford: Clarendon Press – Pontificia Academia Scientiarum, 1996, pp. 137–56.

(2005) *Research and Technological Innovation*, Heidelberg: Physica Verlag.

Quadrio Curzio, A., Fortis, M., and Zoboli, R. (1993) *Innovation, Resources and Economic Growth*, Berlin: Springer.

Quadrio Curzio, A., and Pellizzari, F. (1996) *Risorse, tecnologie, rendita*, Bologna: Il Mulino. English edn (1999) *Rent, Resources, Technologies*, Berlin: Springer-Verlag.

Rostow, W. W. (1960) *The Stages of Economic Growth*, Cambridge: Cambridge University Press.

(1978) *The World Economy. History and Prospect*, London and Basingstoke: Macmillan.

Schumpeter, J. A. (1977) *Il processo capitalistico. Cicli economici*, Torino: Boringhieri.

Spiethoff, A. (1925) 'Krisen' in L. Elster, A. Weber and F. Wieser (eds.) *Handwörterbuch der Staatswissenschaften*, Jena: Verlag von Gustav Fischer, vol. VI., pp. 8–91.

Tugan Baranovsky, M. I. (1913) *Les crises industrielles en Angleterre*, Paris: Giard et Brière.

Wilson, D., and Purushothaman, R. (2003) *Dreaming with BRICs: The Path to 2050*, Global Economics, 99, October, Goldman Sachs.

World Bureau of Metal Statistics (various years) *World Metal Statistics Bulletin*, Ware, Hertfordshire: WBMS.

World Metal Statistics Yearbook, Ware, Hertfordshire: WBMS.

World Steel Association (various years) *Steel Statistical Yearbook*, Bruxelles: World Steel Association.

World Trade Organization, *Statistics Database*, http://stat.wto.org.

(2011) *International Trade Statistics 2011. Composition, Definitions and Methodology*, pp. 188–9.

20   Developmental state and structural economic dynamics: necessity of industrial structure

Sunanda Sen

1.   Introduction

This chapter seeks to situate the experiences of developing countries in the context of the structural relations as prevail within and across those nations, especially, in the age of globalization. Analysis of the changing structure in these economies relates to the interaction between the state, the shifting class alliances within and across nations, and the changing face as well as command of capital therein. The present chapter draws attention to the horizontal integration of agents as above in the context of developing economies, following studies of structural dynamics[1]. It helps to unfold the circular flow as well as the mutually dependent relations between social groups that remain responsible for the pattern of accumulation as well as the related class alignments in these countries over time.

2.   On regime changes in developing countries

Documenting the changes in the economic and the societal patterns of nations that gained political independence at end of World War II, one comes across some major structural breaks, especially as have taken place since the last decade of the previous century. These changes have unplugged the earlier pattern of governance in these nation states, which in effect has substituted the state directives accommodating the socially oriented developmental goals by a set of policies that facilitate the working of markets. These structural breaks incorporated a set of parallel changes in institutions, often with compliance of the state apparatus, thus smoothening the process of regime changes. The pattern, in our judgment, unfolds a story as to how the goal of development in these countries has been pushed to the backstage in the process.

Analyzing the similar changes in the advanced economies, it is possible to relate the systemic capitalist crisis, including the recent one, to the structural changes and the evolving institutional patterns under capitalism. The

---

[1] Baranzini and Scazzieri (1990, pp. 227–333).

repercussions in the developing region connect, once again, to the changing economic and social parameters therein, with processes similarly led by finance and technological changes.

Discontinuities in the pattern of governance in the developing economies goes back to the ending of colonial subjugation and the formal surveillance and domination by the ruling imperial nations in the middle of the last century. The changes as followed comprised of some initial efforts in these newly independent states to pursue the multiple aspirations of their own people. This agenda included some degree of national control over their basic economic activities, in a bid to achieve economic sovereignty along with economic and social advances for domestic citizens in general. Within the newly independent countries, there also evolved an implicit social contract, which embodied the economic aspirations as well as the social norms and traditions of their own citizens. By and large these at least provided a platform for further action in the same direction.

As for India and similar other countries that had parliamentary democracy, a formal commitment as aforementioned soon became politically important to the ruling state. However, the modest growth and limited industrialization as was achieved turned out as inadequate in terms of delivering a pace of development that reached the majority. In absence of adequate purchasing power and jobs for the population at large, the scale economies that could be backed by an expanding home market failed to come into being. In the long-run these countries missed the opportunities to transform into a developmental state proper that would take care of distribution along with growth.

Despite the limited success in achieving their developmental goals, countries as aforementioned were able to achieve a certain degree of self-reliance in terms of the range of products manufactured within the country. With the public sector taking the initiative, as in India, to set up basic industries such as steel, cement and even pharmaceuticals, the country was enabled to initiate what came to be described as a 'mixed economy'; one which also had, with limited state planning, the potential for shaping up as a developmental state that catered to all. In India the early attempts to attain the nationalist goal of industrialization were embedded in the *Nehruvian* vision to achieve self-reliance along with a socialistic pattern of society. This was reflected in a narrow but expanding role of the public sector in providing or subsidizing some basic facilities to people at large, a process which, however, got disrupted later, especially with the launching of major economic reforms in the country by the beginning of the 1990s.

The spate of economic nationalism with an urge for industrialization continued in India during the 1970s with policies initiating state-led regulations. Those included nationalization of banks and the insurance sector, state trading, controls over monopolistic practices, abolition of the managing agency system and privy purses in princely states, introduction of public distribution in food grains and limited measures of land redistribution in specific states, the last two in a bid to address the rising poverty as well as armed uprising among the masses in the countryside. In coming years exchange control in the external sector was consolidated with the Foreign Exchange Regulation Act (FERA), which was enforced to prevent leakages of foreign exchange and money laundering. A brief spell of the above regime, which can be labelled as a 'regulationist' one, continued with a populist pro-poor agenda and some degree of industrialization during the next few years.

The regulationist regime, in terms of a socialist or at best a developmental frame, of these countries came to an end by the mid-1980s. Interestingly, the shift coincided with the re-inventing, in advanced economies, of conservative neoliberal doctrines and its application, especially with the application of Monetarism to tackle the spiralling inflation that had emerged. The neoliberal doctrines also advocated an end to controls while championing the cause of free markets on grounds of economic rationality as well as efficiency. The end-results of these moves was the dismantling of the welfare state in the West and its replacement by a minimalist and conservative state.

There soon emerged a consensus on policies to be recommended to the developing nations which was in accordance with the leading multinational trading and financial institutions. These included the 'Washington Consensus', resonating in turn the paradigm shift as had already taken place in institutions and state policies of the advanced countries. Loans offered by these multilateral institutions such as the IMF or World Bank were inevitably beset with hard conditionality that compelled the developing countries to follow a contractionary monetary and fiscal policy and to open up and deregulate their respective economies, by scrapping controls in different markets. The changes signalled an incarnation, in the developing countries, of a new policy regime that by and large was consistent with the neoliberal macro-framework propounded by the advanced economies and the international financial institutions.

An explicit agenda with a neoliberal shift in economic policies was observable in India as the country accepted the conditional loan package from the IMF in 1981. Strict limits were imposed on fiscal deficits as a proportion of the GDP and several deregulatory measures followed in a few years, relating to trade, technology and finance. Policies facilitating liberalization continued during the successive years and were acceptable to different ruling parties that came to power, each bent in pushing further a market-oriented neoliberal policy.

Economic reform in 1991 became the main agenda of the ruling Congress Party in India that regained control of the central government during that year. Depleted official reserves, large deficits in balance of payments, and sharp declines in GDP growth all demanded urgent attention. Economic reforms were considered as the panacea and a cure-all to combat the economic crisis that had engulfed the country. Changes in economic policies scrapped the prevailing institutions relating to controls and regulations, on trade, technology, finance and even labour. By mid-1990s there was almost an implicit consensus or unanimity among the majority of political parties in India represented in the Parliament regarding the need to continue with the reforms process. As we pointed out earlier, these policies were backed by the neoliberal doctrines of growth via efficient market that were an accepted mainstream position.

The new strategy of opening up also changed the class alliances within the developing countries. Thus the national bourgeoisie that earlier was for industrialization in protected home markets was now more for alliances with foreign capital in activities dealing with finance and technology, often with a marked degree of dependence on imported inputs including technology. In general the local bourgeoisie was by this time in favour of a conciliatory move towards foreign capital.

One witnesses today, for India and other developing countries, a marked influence of the global financial and trading institutions in the making of national policies. The guiding principles as are followed by these institutions all originate from the neoliberal doctrines, as described earlier. Pressure also has mounted up from the powerful interest groups of external capital and technology to adopt policies that suit their interests. The measures include, among other things, cuts in fiscal spending (often at cost of social expenditure), privatization of the public sector enterprises even with profitability, deregulation of the domestic capital market, scrapping of industrial regulations, removal of trade barriers across countries, removal of labour market rigidities by reforms that push labour market flexibility, inflation targeting by means of monetary squeeze and fiscal cuts and also the lifting of controls on external payments and receipts. In general these measures are geared to strengthening the forces of the market while reducing the state machinery to a minimalist one.

The changing norms and policies in the developing countries went hand-in-hand with noticeable reorientations of their institutions. As it could be expected, privatization and a minimalist state were considered the prime harbingers of an efficient allocation and utilization of resources in these economies, which can also bring in the maximum possible growth. Based on the philosophical foundations of methodological individualism, the *Benthamite* logic of free markets provides the basis for the much-celebrated optimality principle formulated by Vilfredo Pareto back in the 1920s.

3.   Dominant finance in overpowering markets

Contemporary capitalism in the advanced and the less developed regions today is identified with the opening up of markets, an institution that has overpowered the state or other public organizations in the majority of those countries. The new mantra of the market has pushed the state to the backstage, thus limiting state spending in the social sector, which includes aid to schools, hospitals, and subsidies on housing, fuel, transport, electricity and the like that remain important for the poorer sections of society. With markets pitching the prices as well as transforming the quality of goods and services, even when supplied by state enterprises, the developmental or social content of growth has been eroding very fast. Thus the ability of markets to instil the positive effects of globalization, as claimed in theories that relate to an efficient growth process, has failed to be fulfilled, especially in terms of the experiences of the majority of developing nations. The current crisis in advanced countries in terms of financial upheavals, real stagnation and unemployment narrates a parallel story, of market-led destitution for a sizeable population. A neoliberalist appeal to free markets, when it concerns finance, is laden with the class interest of those whose assets primarily consist of financial claims in the market. Sections of people as aforementioned are often described as *rentiers* who subsist on income from financial assets rather than on income generated by current productive activities.[2] Owners of these assets usually have a stake in the stock markets where shares are traded and also in the credit and foreign exchange markets. The standard manuals of trading tell us that stock traders can profit (or even make losses) only in uncertain markets with price volatility. Thus for markets that are stationary or even stable, chances for traders to win (or even lose) are at their minimum, leaving them no possibilities to fetch profits/losses as a consequence of stock-price movements. It thus works to the advantage of finance, and in particular for the *rentiers* (who live on income from financial assets), when controls are removed in the financial sector and markets are volatile with fluctuations in prices and volume traded. With the lifting of controls on capital flows, the *rentiers* of today include the foreign institutional investors (FII in short) as well, having a stake in the movements of stock markets in the emerging markets that are now an integral part of global finance.

Opportunities of fetching handsome returns in capital markets around the world lent an elevated status to finance capital in terms of an authority in the global economy. Thus started the push for deregulated finance with pro-finance economic policies, in a manner which often was passive and even detrimental to the interest of industry. The changed set up of global capital had its influence on economic policies in developing countries as well, especially with their close links to global capital flows. We have outlined later in this chapter how global dominance of finance has made it mandatory for the

---

[2] Epstein and Power (2003).

developing countries to chart out a path of finance-led regime, which has often been opposed to growth in the real economy and fair distribution.

Viewed from a classical Marxian perspective, the market as an institution can be seen as an instrument to promote the expansion of capitalist production processes. Thus capitalism is made possible as the free market enables production to be based on wage labour, commodity production, exchange and capital accumulation[3]. From this angle advances of the market are treated as a necessary pre-requisite to a capitalist expansionary process. Markets provide a run up to transformations to competitive capitalism by compulsions, on the part of capital to improve productivity and in the process to extract surplus (labour) value by employing labour who works at low wages (equivalent to necessary labour) for survival.

Differences, however, exist within the Marxist circle on the historic and institutional specificities of capitalism (as a form of production, exchange and distribution) and the role of markets as an adjunct to capitalism. For the school led by Immanuel Wallerstein and Gunder Frank, markets remain central in bringing about a world system of trade and exchange, as happened since a period as early as the sixteenth century. The process, according to them, also heralded the advent of capitalism.[4] For other Marxist scholars such as Maurice Dobb, trade, exchange and markets, while necessary, are not sufficient to warrant a path of capitalist expansion via accumulation. Thus trade can be there even with serfdom or its variations that limit the accumulation and expansionary effects of the market. As pointed out, in absence of wage labour, commodity production for exchange and the ability of capitalists to accumulate by using surpluses from wage labour, it is not possible to have an expanded reproduction that makes for capitalism.[5]

However, these positions, while relevant in the context of the accumulation process under advanced capitalism, cannot be applied to the developing or the least developed countries where production and exchange are subject to several non-market relations. Interestingly the mainstream theorists often hold such aspects as responsible for the backwardness of these countries. The call for liberalization and opening of markets thus follows as a logical cure-all for low growth and underdevelopment.[6]

It may be relevant here to point out that to understand the dynamics of capitalist accumulation in market economies, which today include the developing countries, one has to rely beyond the standard tools of economics. As can be found in the classic work of Karl Polanyi[7], there exist, in all societies, a set of protective as well as countervailing forces that regenerate and sustain the 'mutually supportive relations' within it. As capitalist expansion enlarges the

---

[3] Dobb (1946).   [4] Sweezy (1950) and Wallerstein (1974).   [5] Ibid. See also Khan (2005).
[6] See for a short review Sen (2007).   [7] Polanyi (1944).

sphere of the market, it tends to subordinate the society and destroy the social fabric with standardized 'capitalist values, body and soul' as embedded in the culture of the global market. This violates both the basic human nature as well as such requirements of indigenous people as are fundamental and intertwined with family, community and social relations. In terms of this position, unlimited expansions of the capitalist system and the market, while capable of generating growth and accumulation, also cause 'dispossession, displacement and human degradation'.[8] Markets (with their adjunct, which is capitalism) in this alternate view are sustainable only when 're-embedded' in society with attempts on part of institutions including the state to act in a manner that conforms to the preferences of the society. It is usually done by regulating and stabilizing the market economy to achieve some degree of political legitimization. For Polanyi the 'commodified' land and labour goes against nature and generates 'fictitious' commodities that eventually bring a 'countermovement' to re-embed the market to the society.

Markets, as described earlier, have come up in a large number of countries today, often carrying the label of 'emerging economies'. For the majority of these countries, and in particular, for the developing countries, the expanding market has often remained 'dis-embedded' from society. Often the process generates reactions (countermovements) from what is described as civil society (which may include political parties as well as non-governmental organizations outside the seat of power). These can take the form of social and political protest movements and even political struggles/resistances. Reactions as these, while impairing the pace of market orientation of the society, can also help the market itself by bringing up to the surface what all are acceptable to the society at large. Described by Polanyi as a 'double movement',[9] the process is one that is but expected in a functioning democracy. The above, especially in its sequential arguments relating to 'countermovements' has been subject to questionings from different quarters.[10] However, one cannot undermine the role of 'civil societies' as institutions in these economies, which has been assuming a major role in contesting the limitations of a market-led economy. Their role, as we mention later in this chapter, is no less in advanced countries.

There remain, however, considerable discrepancies between what all are sought after in terms of the social and political movements within a country and the realm of what are actually achieved. The mediating role provided by the state here assumes a great degree of significance in these liberal market economies, with the state subject to an 'existentialist contradiction', between unfettered competition and expansion of capitalism on the one hand and the political necessity of sustaining a minimalist façade of a mutually supportive

---

[8] Levitt (2005).   [9] Polanyi (1944). See also Levitt (2005).   [10] Munck (2014).

and self-reinforcing society on the other. Rejecting this position, neoliberal mainstream policies continue to treat the market as the sole arbiter, using the narrow economics of supply and demand. Here it ignores the role of social institutions that shape up the civil society. Continuing with the impact of the market-led growth process in advanced, and especially in the developing countries, one can mention the changing composition of output, use of technology and the distributional pattern of output in these economies. The range of commodities offered by the market in this deregulated phase of capitalism have introduced, in developing countries, a variety of sophisticated goods that in terms of quality are comparable to those available in global markets. While these changes in the production pattern fulfil the much awaited and sought after changes in the consumption basket of the elite, these remain as unaffordable luxuries for the poor and those who are not so rich. These are the sections of population in these countries who are forced to opt out from these up-markets, not as voluntarily options but due to a lack of their purchasing power. Such actions cannot be classified as acts of 'voluntary exchange' and rational choice, as professed in the theory of the so-called free markets! Moreover these new products often need an upgrading of technology, which is usually labour displacing. Finally, a large and rising share is enjoyed as *rentier* income by those who hold stocks of equities, real estates and even commodities as sources of unearned income. Arguments as these put to serious doubts the claim, in mainstream theory and policy, that technology is a free public good that needs to be developed under patent protection.

4.   The meltdown in global markets: the great recession of 2008

There erupted, by the third quarter of 2008, a serious upheaval in the global financial markets, leading to a crisis which, once again, brings to a disbelief the mythical content of precepts offered in mainstream economic doctrines. The dramatic turn of events was, however, preceded by rapid fluctuations and rising turnovers in financial markets, much of which can be related to the steady pace of deregulation in those markets.

Financial market opening had a big push in the advanced economies in 1999 when the prevailing segregation between the banking and security markets under the Glass-Steagall Act of Roosevelt administration (1933) was repealed in the United States. This was achieved with the passing of the Financial Services Modernisation (Gramm-Leach-Billy) Act, which abolished the earlier compartmentalization of the financial markets for securities for other banking activities. In UK a similar change, described as 'big bang', in the financial market removed in 1986 the prevailing barriers across the credit and security market.

Deregulation of the financial market suited the interest of agents in these markets who were already engaged in the all-encroaching global security market, accommodating the free flow of finance across countries. As it may be guessed, security transactions were closely linked to the operations of the Trans-national Corporations (TNCs), both originating from the same set of advanced countries. With the security market gaining prominence, banks by this time were in no position to continue with credit flows as major channels of business, especially after the near collapse of the financial market at end of the debt-crisis, affecting countries in South America during the early 1980s.

The financial market went through a transformation, especially in developing countries, which by now were faced with limited options to obtain flows of official aid. It may be mentioned here that till the 1970s the latter had served as the main conduit of external finance to these areas. Global finance in the direction of developing countries was, by now, mostly from private sources, financing long-term bonds, direct foreign investments and short-term portfolio capital. Flows as such were ready to come to these outlying territories as long as private investors considered these countries to have 'financial viability', anchored on a steady pace of deregulation of the financial sector to cover domestic banks, security markets, overseas finance and the exchange rate of domestic currency.

With uninterrupted transactions in the deregulated global financial markets, which generated considerable uncertainty, instruments were devised to ward off risks by providing hedges against the latter. New instruments, known as derivatives, were innovated in the financial markets, often with direct connivance from the authorities in power. In this both the market as well as the so-called regulators seem to have been continuing with a shared faith on what they considered as 'modern financial theory', which was grounded on the belief that 'all available information is incorporated into market price, and that there exists complete arbitrage between the different financial instruments'.[11] As pointed out, this confidence in market finance 'was converted into practices, routines and computer programs of portfolio management ... using sophisticated statistical methods that are beyond the grasp of laymen'.[12] Thus, in the so-called modern financial theory, the source of profit was considered to lie in the skilful management of a set of assets and liabilities.[13] In this one could witness what has been described as an unprecedented degree of 'financial division of labour', which accompanied the emergence of new institutions. Those included 'the rise to power of credit rating agencies, pension funds and money managers, the creation of ever more complex financial instruments

---

[11] Boyer (2008).   [12] Ibid.   [13] Ibid.

defining as many specializations of financial agents ... and risk is spread to those who have the will and wherewithal to assume it'.[14]

Looking back at the evolving pattern of the crisis in the financial sector of the global economy and its growing intensity by end of the last decade, one can identify an underlying passive acceptance or at best, some inaction on part of the regulatory authorities on related matters. Examples include the role of the Comptroller of Currency in the United States in creating the notion of Too Big to Fail (TBTF) banks, making it nearly manadatory for the Federal Reserve to shoulder its responsibilities vis-à-vis the large banks as 'a lender of last resort'.[15] The move for creating the priviledged TBTF category of banks, initiated some thirty years back, was supported by the Federal Deposit Insurance Corporation of the country. One can also mention the Savings and Loan crisis and the protection offered to the relatively bigger units by monetary authorities. Responses as these clearly facilitated the pace for concentration as well as reckless investments, by large banks and other financial institutions that were favoured. Those institutions were increasingly involved in the markets for derivatives, entering into contracts such as forwards, futures, options and the like. Use of these hedging instruments worked to minimize risks as long as the market was stable and there was trust or confidence in these transactions. However, often the greed of making more money led agents to speculate in future markets of stocks, currencies or even commodities. And investments in the financial sector continued to be profitable as long as there was trust in the financial market, on operations that included *Asset-backed Securities* (ABS) and the *Credit Default Swaps* (CDS).

As for the CDS, those transactions were initiated in a limited scale by the Morgan Trust in 1997. The device soon assumed much bigger proportions in the derivative market over the next few years, especially with its attractive options in transferring (insuring) default risks. Those transactions entailed the sale of an ABS in the form of a CDS to a counterparty that insured the possible loss in asset value in the market on payment of regular insurance fees from the seller.[16] The counterparty insurer (buyer of CDS), however, could be in trouble when a large number of those turned red, a situation that involves proportionate payment obligations.[17] In fact the collapse of Lehman Brothers in September 2008 indicated such a situation, which in turn was followed by a massive bailout by the Fed of AIG, which was nearly insolvent with its large holdings of insured assets that carried little worth in the market. The large-scale bailing out of financial institutions as above indicates the weight of TBTF in the US financial market. It may be pointed out here that none of these ABSs including

---

[14] Ibid.   [15] Shull (2012).
[16] www.investopedia.com/terms/c/creditdefaultswap.asp#axzz1ujOF9QdQ.
[17] Nersiyan and Wray (2008).

the swap deals under the CDSs were subject to any regulation by the monetary authorities. Sometimes deals were enforced indirectly, as for example, with US Secretary of the Treasury Paulson pushing Fannie May and Fredie Mac, two major financial firms, into holding toxic assets in the collapsing mortgage market of 2008.[18] One may observe that the authorities in such cases were ready to put up with a consensual approach while shouldering the expenses (of course at cost to taxpayers) as were needed for emergency bailouts.

A scenario as above, with a passive acceptance of the ruling state authority of the on going financial engineering in search of higher short-term returns, has been identified in the literature as situations of a 'predatory state'. This implies that the state uses 'the existing institutions as devices for political patronage ... [and is] aligned with financial de-regulation'.[19] As is well-known, finance by the time of the sub-prime crisis was already dominated by aggressive practitioners in the financial markets who were familiar with the art of 'originating and distributing mortgages that were plainly fraudulent'. By then the state had already sent clear signals to the financial sector that the deregulatory wave is going to continue. In such predatory states there was also an implicit alliance between the public and the private sector, with the state relinquishing its role in crucial sectors of the economy, including health and education. Arrangements such as these also provided added space for marketization of public goods.

The lull in the US property market and the related crash in financial markets in 2008 led to a contagion that spread to other parts of the advanced economies as well as to the developing region. The spate of uncertainty that was rising in deregulated markets also resulted in a massive increase in the use of derivatives, which made investments in the real sector unattractive in terms of relative profitability.

As for official policies, especially in the United States, which aimed to mitigate the impact of the crisis, one notices an underlying pattern that confirms the predator character of the state. One can here mention the quick responses by US President George Bush to the subprime crisis and the successive bankruptcies of major financial institutions in the country. The measures included the Troubled Assets Recovery Program (TARP) of October 2008, which offered purchases of tarnished assets from financial institutions. Later the monetary authorities tried to bail out several US financial institutions, especially after a failure to act led to the bankruptcy of Lehman Brothers, a major investment bank. The cumulative sum deployed to rescue the ailing financial system since the onset of the crisis has been around $11 trillion as committed funds by 2011, of which the rescue package to AIG alone amounted to $182 billion. Other categories of rescue packages included

---

[18] Galbraith (2010).   [19] Ibid.

programs designed to revive the housing market and to prevent foreclosures by earmarking large sums of funds.[20] Responses to mitigate the financial crisis also included a series of regulatory proposals in the United States to address, among others, consumer protection, executive pay, financial cushions or capital requirements for banks. In January 2010, US President Obama proposed additional regulations that were to limit the ability of banks to engage in making speculative investments that fail to benefit the bank customers.[21] The major legislation initiated by the Obama administration included the Dodd-Frank Wall Street Reform and Consumer Protection Act of 2010, which aimed at the elimination of the TBTF problems. In effect it also targeted an end to bailouts causing losses to taxpayers. The pattern of implementation, however, has evoked criticisms as to whether the Act will also eliminate the growth of large banking companies and thus the need for further bailouts in future.[22]

While in the United States the bailout and related measures to protect the financial sector somehow worked in achieving temporarily what these measures sought to do, the real sector continued to be in disarray. After some early signs of recovery in the fall of 2009 and spring of 2010, economic growth in the United States started slowing down again. With jobs generated by the private sector negligible, US unemployment was at 5.9% in October 2014 as compared to 7.3% in October 2013 according to the US Bureau of Labor Statistics. Counting the number of unemployed who are outside the organized sector, the picture is even worse. The crisis spread to Europe with a similar impact on the real sector in terms of output growth and employment.

During the initial years after the onset of crisis, a package of spending along with tax cuts was introduced in the United States in early February 2009. Known as the American Recovery and Reinvestment Act (ARRA), it was expected to create or save approximately 3.5 million jobs by the end of 2010. The expenditure and tax cuts included in the legislation were expected to provide relief to low-income and vulnerable households, while at the same time supporting aggregate demand. It has been pointed out that the stimulus required per new job created was much higher than final outlay by those who got jobs. This was because consumption spending was already constrained by the large outstanding household debt and, also, a part of additional consumption could be absorbed by cheaper imports from abroad. The recent plans to directly inject liquidity in the credit market as a measure of Quantitative Easing also may be subject to the same limitations, *viz.*, of potential leakages via imports and the deflationary impact of outstanding debt.

---

[20] CNN Money.com's bailout tracker at www.CNN.com.   [21] Ibid.   [22] Shull (2012).

In a number of countries in Southern Europe and in Ireland the crisis in the financial and the real economy took a serious turn by 2010 with credit rating agencies downgrading a number of countries below investment grade. To avoid bankruptcy those countries accepted loans with hard conditionality from public sources such as IMF and the European Union. The mandatory fiscal discipline and the related austerity have been reducing further the output and employment growth rates in those indebted countries, as happened with the Latin American debtors in the early 1980s. The impact on developing countries this time was naturally even more deleterious with the squeezed export earnings and related consequences.

5.   Analysing the sequences in the crisis

Analyzing the functioning of the financial sector in recent years, which include the changing institutions in advanced as well as in the developing economies, the pattern can be explained by relying on economist Hyman Minsky's characterization of deregulated financial markets and its built-in tendencies towards an 'unstable economy'. The outcome has evolved around these sources of new-fangled credit, especially, with involvement of banks in the security market under universal banking, and the rise of what has been described as 'shadow banking'. Minsky drew attention to the fact that in the new institutional setting, banks and non-bank financial entities can follow an 'originate and distribute' model, which involves a re-packaging of assets and their sales. In this the shifting of risks to counterparties generates more profits than is possible from the simple 'commitment models' that rely on the rate spread at the loan officer's desk.[23] These practices, according to Minsky, make for higher profitability in market-based funding, as compared to bank-based leveraging of projects. In the changing scene banks got increasingly involved in the security markets. Thus there prevails, as pointed out, a 'symbiotic relation' between the universalized financial structures (which contrasts the earlier pattern of segregated banking) and the related securitization of financial instruments.[24]

Elaborating further, the easy access to credit, which made the recent financial boom, was needed to cover leverages for hedging as long as the expected income on assets was adequate to cover (hedge) the mandated interest and repayment liabilities. However, hedging often gave way to speculation when the realized income from the assets fell short of the payment liabilities. Attempts were then made to 'roll-over' past debt and continue speculating. Finally a state arose, as in the recent crisis, when payment liabilities could only be met by additional borrowing, a typical case of 'Ponzi finance' as described

---

[23] See Wray and Tymoigne (2008).   [24] See Minsky (2008).

by Minsky.[25] With a declining state of confidence in the market on value of assets held by lenders, dealings in the financial markets came to a grinding halt, leading to big holes in the balance sheets of the concerned counterparties and heralding the onset of a typical *ponzi* situation. It may be relevant at this point to highlight the point that *ponzi* finance is another name for fraudulent behaviour on part of financial agents, as can be seen in the various scams and related acts in recent times.[26] The alternative position offered here in line with *Minskian* analysis is to look at the uncertainty-ridden trail of financial markets, the route of which often deviates from the predictions of the private 'market makers'. Such a state clearly plagued financial markets in the United States in the fall of 2008. By this time the real economy in most advanced economies, including the United States, were already going through a phase of low growth and unemployment. A crash in the financial sector gave an added jolt to the stagnating economy, which plunged into a deeper recession as a consequence.

Looking at the transformed pattern of institutions in the context of securitization, one needs to draw attention to the changing character of money and credit as has taken place in the meantime, especially with credit flows from banks and non-bank financial intermediaries no longer constrained by the value of reserves and capital held under a fractional reserve system. The changes considerably lowered the weight of central banks in the credit market to protect credit, as was evident in the recent financial crisis with credit flows under 'shadow banking' no longer under the surveillance of the monetary authorities. This is because such credit flows by and large drive the leveraging of the ABSs, which in turn is made possible by the expanding derivative markets. In such situations the traditional devices used by the monetary authorities, which include a raise in interest rates to control inflation, might even lead to a collapse of stock prices and hence to a financial crisis rather than to a state of financial stability.

We may add here that with innovations in the financial markets providing lucrative returns on short-term financial transactions, equities bought and sold in the primary market as Initial Primary Offers (IPOs) fetch much lower rates. These assets, sold earlier as IPOs, are usually transacted later in the secondary market where these are no longer backed by physical assets.[27] Looking back at the boom-bust cycles, finance in its upswing, while creating myriads of financial claims and liabilities, thus becomes increasingly distant from the real

---

[25] Ibid.   [26] Sen (2009). See also Black (2005).

[27] We need to mention here that the multiplicity of financial assets as rely on derivatives, while originating from the *same* base in terms of specific real activities (or 'underlying'), do not expand the base itself. Instead, it amounts to a piling up of claims that are linked to the same set of real assets. As it has been pointed out, 'From a Wall Street point of view capital assets are valuable not because they are productive in a physical sense but because they yield profits' (Minsky, 1986, p. 204).

economy. An expansionary financial market thus does not necessarily generate corresponding expansions in real terms, while the growing disparity between the two may finally disrupt the financial boom itself, as happened of late in the world economy.[28] The financial boom never imparted proportionate growth in the remaining part of these economies, as was evident in the low average growth rates of GDP in the OECD nations all through those years when the financial sector was performing at its peak.

Efforts on part of monetary authorities to rejuvenate their respective ailing economies have generated rather limited results in advanced countries. Beyond helping to temporarily arrest further downslides in the financial sector in terms of bankruptcies and closures of financial institutions, the measures have not remedied the structural weaknesses of the system as are related to tendencies that relate to short-termism and speculation. Rather it has become clear that no amount of financial bailouts and monetary injections can bring back the system to a stable and sustainable order unless the caveats within the system are addressed squarely. Even policy measures like the American Recovery andand Reinvestment Act (ARRA) to create employment in the United States failed to address the cutbacks in levels of consumption of households as a result of their state of indebtedness in the financial markets. The large injection of credit via recent *Quantitative Easings* (QEs) in the United States may also not be effective if those lead to capital outflows in response to the higher interest rates overseas, and more so, with domestic rates in the United States falling as a consequence of the credit injection.

Developing countries, experiencing similar contractions in home demand as a result of the squeeze in wage share (of GDP) under labour flexibility, have often relied on export-oriented policies, which in turn did demand further disciplining of labour in a bid to save on labour costs. However, the shortfall in domestic demand could hardly be compensated by rising values of exports to the crisis-stricken advanced countries, which, as pointed out earlier, were experiencing low growth rates even before the onset of the recent crisis. Not much space was thus left for expansions in the real sphere of the developing countries by relying on the domestic or the export market, with the latter already subject to contractions as a result of the crisis. As for the financial sector, financial reforms and liberalization, which preceded the crisis in advanced countries, also hit hard the developing countries. The impact included the abrupt changes in the flow of capital, and especially those with short-term duration. Major changes that resulted included the additional responsibility of the monetary authorities in the management of their exchange rates in the floating rate regime. In addition their stock markets were subject to

---

[28] Palley (2010).

added degrees of volatility, largely with the uncontrolled flows of short-term capital. Problems such as these were linked to the liberalization of the capital account, a measure that continues to be questioned from different circles.

With the opening of their capital markets the developing countries attracted large flows of short-term capital, which entered these markets under high profit expectations. Much of these flows were deployed in the secondary markets of equities and also in the property as well as commodity future markets. Uncertainty and rising prices in real estate as well as in the commodity market attracted investments by fund managers in search of high profits. As a consequence there have been sharp increases in prices, both in property markets as well as in commodities, especially in fuel and food, in recent times.

State policies in the developing countries often actively encouraged these transactions, by providing tax reliefs, say on capital gains and on dividends, as in India. The high returns on those transactions generally were a drag on incentives to lock in funds as long-term investments in the slow-growing real sector. Incentives to invest in the secondary markets, however, were strong with fluctuations in stock prices and their returns, which was common in markets with capital account opening. As we have mentioned earlier, speculation by nature is rife in markets only when it is fluid.

In India, which is one of the foremost emerging markets after China, frequent upheavals were witnessed in the secondary markets for stocks, especially since the country opened its capital market to Foreign Institutional Investors (FIIs) in 1993. The turnover in the main stock markets located in Mumbai is today quite large as compared to what it used to be earlier. With uncertainty much higher than before in financial markets, trading as well as returns in the derivative market have naturally gone up. Even transactions in the secondary spot market are today at least ten times the volume transacted as Initial Public Offerings (IPOs) or private placements in the primary market for capital, a picture that tells us a story of slow-growth rates in the real sector.

For India and for a few other emerging economies, inflows of short-term capital from FII sources along with other sources of capital including FDIs have contributed to steady increases in the country's official exchange reserves. The stock, at around $300 billion at present, covers more than six months of average monthly imports of the country. With both non-factor income (mainly due to software exports) and remittances from abroad (mostly from workers in the Middle East) adequate to cover the payments due for interest and royalties etc. on foreign assets in India since some time, there has not been a major drag on exchange reserves in the recent past to meet the current deficits on trade. However, the reserves have been occasionally utilized to support the rupee rate from time to time, due to sudden outflows of short-term capital. On the whole India's central bank has so far been able to steer clear of a currency crisis by managing the real exchange rate of the rupee (for trade competitiveness) and a stable nominal value (for stability of financial assets in Indian currency held by foreigners). This, along with the rising level of exchange reserves, has lent credence to the image of India as a fast growing 'emerging economy'. A picture as above, however, excludes the very recent turn in India's balance of payments, with widening current account deficits, which are due to the continuing global slump and with the sudden outflows of FII held capital in the country, much of which is due to instability of global finance.

Accumulation of large official reserves in the high-growth economies of China and India have caused some spill-over effects which tend to constrain the management of their monetary policies. This happens when excess capital account inflows, as remain after financing the respective current account deficits, contribute to the rising reserves that provide sources of expansions in M2. To counter the inflationary effects, the monetary authorities often initiate inflation targeting by using monetary-fiscal measures, which may conflict with goals set for domestic growth and distribution, especially while curbing credit for investment and consumption in the domestic economy.[29] Monetary stabilization also puts pressure on governments to finance fiscal deficits through marketized borrowing, which in turn expands the internally held debt obligations with a rise in interest earnings by those who lend against the government bonds. The distributional implications of above include higher earnings of rentiers' capital on the one hand and an imbalance in the budgetary provisions on the other, with expenditure on interest liabilities taking over other items such as social sector spending.

Financial opening in developing countries has thus led to a restructuring of financial flows both within and across national territories. Transactions in the external sector have been dominated by spurts in private capital inflows with a considerable volume of short-term investments in the secondary stock market. Developments as above are beset with possibilities of sudden withdrawals of those funds and also with the frequent fluctuations in stock prices and volume traded, both of which have become endemic to the system. A run in the stock market, leading to a fast depletion of official reserves and a concurrent depreciation of the local currency, are some of the likely hazards. While the deregulated financial market makes it easy and lucrative to buy financial assets in the up-market of hot money in the stock market (or real estates and commodities market) the process, as we point out, does not generate real assets in the first round. Incentives to make quick money by toeing the line of the Keynesian 'animal spirit' may thus dampen the prospects of productive investments in the economy as may generate growth.

---

[29] See Sen (2014).

One more aspect of freeing the financial market by developing countries relates to the distribution of credit within their respective economies. As we mentioned earlier, opening up of the financial market along with a compliance to the norms set by the international financial institutions such as the Bank for International Settlements (BIS) has made it customary for banks in India to advance credit to profitable channels of investments. Often this is due to the exclusion of large sections of borrowers who do not qualify in terms of the BIS risk-adjusted credit ratings followed by banks.[30] This has continued to widen the economic disparities in countries such as Brazil and India while at the same time retarding the prospects of higher growth in sectors that are no less relevant.

It will be useful at this point of our analysis to distinguish the short-term factors that explain the flare-up of the recent financial crisis (with its spill over to the real sector) from the long-term structural changes that relate to policies, institutions, and the composition of output as well as the pattern of distribution in these economies. In our judgment those long-term changes can also be held partially responsible for the financial boom followed by the recent mayhem in the financial markets.

A major source of the long-term structural changes as have taken place since the 1970s relates to a rising gap between labour productivity and real wages in most countries. Use of labour-displacing technology as well as labour-market flexibility in these countries since the mid-1980s explain a large part of the gap. Competitive pressures consequent on globalization of commodity and financial flows led to further compressions of labour costs, which could be easily accommodated within the norms of the flexible labour-market policy. Similar pressures also led to an upgrading of technology with rising capital-labour ratios, which considerably reduced the wage share in aggregate output. It thus remained a vicious circle with cuts in wage bill and the related shortfalls in aggregate demand preventing expansions in output and employment, which further squeezed such demand.

6.   Conclusions

Looking back, one notices a systematic transformation in the power structure currently prevailing in the world economy with 'new capital' aligned to finance in its various forms. Such a change has replaced the authority of the state and the related regulations by liberalized markets in different spheres of these economies. This change has gone in with a meteoric rise in the weight of finance, both as an activity and as a commanding power over the economy,

---

[30] Sen and Gottschalk (2010).

which includes the state apparatus. Market-led economies, in advanced as well as in developing regions, have in the process generated the new genre, 'new capital' that deviates sharply from the earlier patterns of Fordist capital accumulation in advanced nations or even from the state-led developmental perspective of the post-colonial nations in the periphery.

These changes have gone in with marked transformations in institutions that promote this new avatar of finance-led capitalism in different parts of the world, which include the developing countries. In advanced countries the state has, in a relinquishing mood vis-à-vis markets, demonstrated a benign oversight of the negatives inflicted by big corporations on the wider public. Such as this has been the case in what has been described earlier as 'predator states',[31] in terms of the collusive arrangements of the state with corporate regimes controlled by 'new capital'. Changes in institutions relating to the financial sector has initiated, in addition to the steady dismantling of regulations, innovation of new products in the financial industry by agents operating in the sphere of 'high finance'. A parallel process has progressed in developing countries with dominance of finance and the growing authority of the market. As for monetary authorities in the new regime, the primary goal in policies has hovered around inflation targeting, which often demands sales of 'marketized' government securities. Between gains via stock markets in equities and commodity futures, and the rising interest income for those holding government bonds, there has been a rise in the share of what is described as 'unearned' or 'rentier' income in these economies. The rising share for the new class of non-wage earners has been matched by the squeeze in wage shares of GDP that followed wide-ranging deregulation in labour markets. It led to the dissolution of institutions such as labour laws and trade unions, which previously protected some of the labour rights including wages. While distribution of income has been predominantly in favour of those in command of financial and real assets deployed in brisk trading, stagnation in employment and wages have reflected the dismal state of people beyond the charm circle.

The long-term stagnation in living standards and employment of people was subject to further shocks as the world economy, including the developing area, was hit by crises of serious magnitude by 2007–08. Waves of protests, organized by the civil society against big capital and international financial and trading institutions, confirm a Polanyi-type 'double-movement' process. These are echoed in the demonstrations against WTO policies of free trade in Seattle (1999) and the 'Occupy Wall Street' movements in crisis-torn economies of the United States and Europe as well as the rise of new parties like the Aam Admi Party (AAP) in India, which seeks to fight corruption. These reflect the

---

[31] Galbraith (2008).

transformations in the structure of the economy and society, mirroring the aspirations from people who never shared the gains of high finance during its good times and who bear the increasing misery and destitution as a result of the crisis emanating from dominant finance.

These transformations have touched the social and economic fabric of developing countries. Rise of finance as the relatively dominant form of activity in terms of profitability has reduced the weight of the real sectors including agriculture and industry, both of which still provide the main source of jobs and income. Speculation on financial assets has even spread to the realm of commodities and property markets, offering quick returns to those who are active in handling such activities including future trade in commodity markets. Sharp increases in prices of food in particular have hit hard the poor who include masses of unemployed and semi-employed in the vast unorganized economy of the rural and urban areas. Monetary policy, geared to 'inflation targeting', has sometimes resulted in credit squeeze with high interest rates, which has proved unaffordable in terms of industrial expansion.

As it has been the case with the advanced economies, state directives in the developing countries have been guided by almost a blind faith on the efficacy of neoliberal policies. Sometimes the moves have been influenced by pressures from outside, as for example, with the conditional loan packages of the IMF or even in its absence (as in India) by unofficial dictates from credit-rating institutions (e.g. S&P or Moody's) or the Bank for International Settlement, trying to ensure what is reckoned as 'financial stability'. In effect such stability caters to the balance sheet of private financial institutions and corporates, many of which are staked by capital from global markets. While markets in these developing economies are usually shared between local and global capital, it is usual for the national bourgeoisie as well as the ruling state to share the enthusiasm for the 'order' approved by global capital and by the multinational trading as well as by the financial institutions.

On the whole, the dynamics of the structural transformations have rendered development as well as welfare of people less of a priority relative to other goals that have been prioritized in the prevailing regimes led by 'new capital' all over the world economy.

REFERENCES

Baranzini, M., and Scazzieri, R. (eds.) (1990) *The Economic Theory of Structure and Change*, Cambridge: Cambridge University Press.

Black, W. (2005) *The Best Way to Rob a Bank Is to Own One: How Corporate Executives and Politicians Looted the S&L Industry*, Austin, Tex.: University of Texas Press.

Boyer, R. (2008) 'History Repeating for Economists: An Anticipated Financial Crisis', Prisme 13, November, Paris: Cournot Centre for Economic Studies.

Dobb, M. (1946) *Studies in Development of Capitalism*, London: Routledge.

Epstein, G., and Power, D. (2003) 'Rentier Incomes and Financial Crises: An Empirical Analysis of Trends and Cycles in Some OECD Countries', University of Amherst: PERI (mimeo).

Galbraith, J. K. (2008) *The Predator State*, New York: The Free Press.

    (2010) 'The Great Crisis and the American Response', *Policy Brief* 112, Annandale-on-Hudson, NY: Levy Economics Institute of Bard College.

Khan, M. H. (2005) 'The Capitalist Transformation', in K. S. Jomo and E. S. Reinhart (eds.) *The Origins of Development Economics: How Schools of Economic Thought Have Addressed Development*, New York: Zed Books, pp. 69–80.

Levitt, K. (2005) 'Karl Polanyi as a Development Economist', in K. S. Jomo (ed.) *Pioneers of Development Economics. Great Economists on Development*, London and New York: Zed Books, pp. 165–80.

Minsky, H. (1986) *Stabilizing an Unstable Economy*, New Haven: Yale University Press.

    (2008) 'Securitization' with preface and afterword by R. Wray, in *Securitization, Policy Brief*, Policy Note 2, Annandale-on-Hudson, NY: Levy Economics Institute of Bard College.

Munck, R. (2014) 'Globalisation, Labour and the Polanyi Problem: Or the issue of Counter-hegemony', in S. Sen and A. Chakrabarty (eds.) *Development on Trial: The Shrinking Space for the Periphery*, Hyderabad: Orient BlackSwan, pp. 259–83.

Nersiyan, Y., and Wray, R. (2008) 'The Global Financial Crisis and the Shift to Shadow Banking', Working Paper 587, Annandale-on-Hudson, NY: Levy Economics Institute of Bard College.

Palley, T. (2010) 'The Limits of Minsky's Financial Instability Hypothesis as an Explanation of the Crisis', *The Monthly Review*, 61.11, pp. 28–43.

Polanyi, K. (1944) *The Great Transformation*, Boston: Beacon Press.

Sen, S. (2007) *Globalisation and Development*, New Delhi: National Book Trust of India.

    (2009) 'Speculation, Scams and Frauds: Theory and Facts', *Economic and Political Weekly*, 44.12, pp. 21–7.

    (2014) 'Global Financial Flows and National Autonomy: China and India', in S. Sen, *Dominant Finance and Stagnant Economies*, New Delhi: Oxford University Press, pp. 263–300.

Sen, S., and Gottschalk, R. (2010) 'Prudential Norms for the Financial Sector: Is Development a Missing Dimension? The Cases of Brazil and India', in R. Gottschalk (ed.) *The Basel Capital Accords in Developing Countries: Challenges for Development Finance*, London: Palgrave Macmillan, pp. 16–33.

Shull, B. (2012) 'Too Big to Fail: Motives, Countermeasures, and the Dodd-Frank Response', Working Paper 709, Annandale-on-Hudson, NY: Levy Economics Institute of Bard College.

Sweezy, P. (1950) 'The Transition from Feudalism to Capitalism', *Science and Society*, 14.2, pp. 134–57.

Wallerstein, I. (1974) *The Modern World System*, New York and London: Academic Press.

Wray, R., and Tymoigne, E. (2008) 'Macro-economics Meets Hyman Minski: The Financial Theory of Investment', Working Paper 543, Annandale-on-Hudson, NY: Levy Economics Institute of Bard College.

21 Resources, institutional forms and structural transformation in the BRICKs: the 'hybrid model of late capitalism'

Andrea Goldstein and Keun Lee

1. Introduction

The interplay between technical progress, investment in human and physical capital and institutions generates structural transformations along time and geographical lines (Quadrio Curzio *et al.* 1994).[1] In this chapter we examine a crucial policy issue associated with the governance of long-term structural change. At the centre of the on going recomposition of the global economy stands the changing ecology of large global companies (Goldstein, 2013). Data presented in this chapter show that 'the periphery' accounts for a rising share of the world's largest companies, in fact its weight in this universe is even larger than for global GDP or trade. An interesting feature of big business in the periphery – and more specifically in the BRICK economies of Brazil, Russia, India, China and Korea that are the focus of our chapter – is that there has been amazingly little convergence towards the Western model. The public company with dispersed ownership, separation of ownership and control, and contestable control that dominates in the United States and most of Europe is largely absent in the BRICKs. The 109 companies that constitute the pinnacle of BRICK corporate power in 2012, and henceforth a potent symbol of their economic and political success, are owned either by

For providing inputs to earlier versions of this chapter, the authors thank the anonymous referees. The views expressed in this article are those of the authors and do not necessarily represent the views of, and should not be attributed to, any of the institutions to which they are affiliated.

[1] More generally we may say that in half a century of thinking and writing on the global economy, Alberto Quadrio Curzio has shown constant interest in the evolution of economic diversity and interdependence and the resulting patterns of global cooperation, competition and conflict (e.g. Quadrio Curzio, 1983). Over this period globalization has emerged as a forceful force driving the destiny of national economies, with some of them proving better than others at seizing the opportunities offered by falling barriers, accelerating trade in goods and services and raising factor mobility. From this standpoint, 'shifting wealth' (OECD, 2010) – i.e. the dramatic rise of post-WTO China and other emerging economies – is arguably the most momentous change in the first decade of the twenty-first century. A very positive development indeed, especially when seen against the clash of civilizations – an extreme version of the conflicts that have worried Quadrio Curzio in his social and scholarly engagement (Quadrio Curzio and Marseguerra, 2010) – that many influential analysts were predicting after 9/11.

governments or families. Furthermore, the overwhelming majority of them are organized as diversified groups, with a core business and a myriad of more or less connected secondary activities. And this is also true for Korea, which we consider to be the catch-up country *par excellence*, in fact the only emerging economy to 'graduate' to high-income OECD status.[2]

The article examines this transformation in contrast to two extreme literature strands: dependency theory that expected local private entrepreneurship and state-owned enterprises (SOEs) to play an ancillary role to multinationals and neoliberal thinking that expected globalization to result in an absolute convergence of business models towards the Anglo-American paradigm of the focused company with widespread ownership and little, if any, state involvement. We argue for the relevance of a 'capability-based view' in explaining the BRICKs' catching-up development process, going beyond the sometime-sterile controversy on the respective role of governments and markets in economic development and focusing instead on the mechanisms that allowed countries to strengthen the capability of (large) firms, induce (differently sustained) growth and promote development. The analysis of this 'hybrid model of late capitalism' pays attention to the relationship between institutions, society and the economy, i.e. the dimensions of structural tranformation that we have discussed many times with Alberto Quadrio Curzio.

We proceed as follows. In Section 2, we first sketch the arguments that made dependency theorists pessimistic about the prospects of autonomous development in the periphery and neoliberals adamant that the forces of globalization would eliminate distinctive national models of capitalism. We then present a glimpse of an alternative view. Section 3 presents basic data on big business in the BRICKs to show its ring share in the global economy, as well as its main ownership, organizational and strategy traits. This allows us to highlight that there is much greater continuity than could be expected in view of the major changes that have interested the BRICKs in the 1990s–2010s period – from privatization and trade and financial liberalization, to the emergence of new industries and customers. That BRICK capitalism nowadays takes a variety of forms shows an institutional and organizational adaptability that contrasts with most expectations. In Section 4, we propose an explanation for these developments that links ownership and organizational strategy of big business, on the one hand, with the needs of fast upgrading and catch-up that are central in the current phase of BRICK development. We conclude with some policy observations, focusing on the need to rapidly adapt the hitherto successful model of

---

[2] Mexico joined the OECD before, but is not a high-income country. Similarly, Turkey was a founding member, but is not a high-income country. In fact, since the OECD started a round of enlargement in 1994, Korea is the only new member to join the Development Assistance Committee of aid donors.

big business, state- and family-led industrialization with the emerging reality of globalization, start-up entrepreneurship and open innovation.

2.   What place for large companies in economic development? Left, right and centre

Firms as such have never enjoyed pride of place in traditional accounts of economic development. Most scholars have shown greater interest in macro-economic 'framework conditions', including high-end institutions, than in the nuts and bolts of turning scarce resources into goods and services that can serve local and foreign customers. As a result, most models treat firms as largely identical in terms of size, ownership and control, with the important caveat that over time private came to be preferred to state.

However, there also exists a tradition of scholarship, especially Schumpeterian economics, that emphasizes firm heterogeneity as one of the essential features of capitalism (Nelson, 1991, 2009). One aspect of heterogeneity is size differences, and this chapter focuses on big businesses, following Schumpeters' earlier insight on their importance. From the literature, we can list several reasons for the new importance of big businesses, at least for middle- and high-income countries.

First, economic history has provided evidence that when economies take off, the number of big businesses also increases to exploit economies of scale and scope (Chandler, 1959, 1977, 1990). Second, big business contributes to and accelerates innovation in several ways. Large companies can incur high fixed costs for R&D, which may result in innovations and productivity growth (Pagano and Schivardi, 2003). For emerging economies, most technological change is closely related to the rise of big businesses, as shown by Pack and Westphal (1986) for Korea and Lee et al. (2011) for China. Jung and Lee (2010) also found that Korean firms have caught up with Japanese ones (in terms of total factor productivity) more quickly in sectors that are dominated by large firms and are more exposed to world market competition. This size–innovation link is consistent with the early insight of Schumpeter (1934, 1942), who stated that big businesses tend to put more resources towards generating innovation, consequently spurring national economic growth.

Third, globalization has reinforced the importance of big businesses. With very few exceptions, the world's largest companies have become multinational or transnational firms and now play a central role in global value chains (Gereffi et al., 2005). Notably, global value chains governed by large firms have improved inventory management and made production processes more efficient (Iacoviello et al., 2011). This improvement, in turn, has reduced GDP volatility and resulted in greater macroeconomic stability. Such theoretical expectations are confirmed by econometric testing – big businesses have a significant and positive effect on both economic growth and stability in economic growth (Lee *et al.*, 2013).

The next step in our argument is that ownership of large enterprises counts (Amsden, 2009). We don't live in a world of perfectly competitive markets, where access to inputs, technology and marketing channels is the same for all firms. The real world is made of oligopolistic markets in which firms compete on the basis of hard-to-acquire proprietary assets and competencies. In this regard, the success of entrepreneurial and dynamic domestically owned enterprises in the periphery challenges the pessimism with which local business was still seen two or three decades ago.

Let us first start with introducing two different views on the big businesses in the periphery.

On the 'left' side, imperialism theories, originating in the works of Lenin and Hilferding, saw 'comprador capitalists' in Third World countries as corporate lackeys serving the interests of an international capitalist class and henceforth considered very unlikely the emergence of genuine, independent entrepreneurs committed to national transformation. In the words of dos Santos (1970) 'industrial development is strongly conditioned by the technological monopoly exercised by imperialist centers' (p. 233) and 'the industrial and technological structure responds more closely to the interests of the multi-national corporations than to internal developmental needs (conceived of not only in terms of the overall interests of the population, but also from the point of view of the interests of a national capitalist development)' (p. 234).

Other dependency scholars took a less dim view in general, but yet their 'recognition of the strengths of local capital ... does not revive the national bourgeoisie as the hero of industrialization' (Evans, 1979, p. 281). In the periphery[3], nations remain in a stage of dependent development because 'they are recipient rather than source countries of foreign investment [and] are on the receiving rather than the originating end of product innovation and new production techniques' (Gereffi and Evans, 1981, p. 31).

On the 'right' side, another strand of the literature characterized indigenous capitalism in the periphery, state- or family-owned, as rent-seeking, but was open to the possibility that they could develop, if only they converged to a Western ideal–type of the firm and the business system. Two decades ago, the victorious end of the Cold War seemed to some to herald the emergence of a pleasant global economy, in which heterogeneity and differences were on the way out, homogeneity and convergence towards the Washington Consensus and *laissez faire* capitalism on the way in. Yoshihiro Francis Fukuyama wrote that 'the century ... seems at its close to be returning full

---

[3] Or the semiperiphery, but for the sake of simplicity (and also in line with Amsden's use of the term 'the rest' to designate countries outside the Triad) we use periphery.

circle to where it started ... an unabashed victory of economic and political liberalism'.[4] Privatization and the demise of the entrepreneurial state figured highly in John Williamson's Washington Consensus catalogue, in particular insofar as promoting state enterprises to countenance the lack of a strong indigenous private sector 'is again a nationalistic motivation and hence commands little respect in Washington'.

The view that there is only one way to organize economic activity extended in fact also to private business. It was Paul Krugman, of all people, who reminisced: 'I am (just) old enough to remember the conglomerate-building era of the 1960s, an era that ended so badly that many thought the word 'synergy' would be permanently banned from the business lexicon' (Krugman, 2000). In sum, the destiny of the world of global business seemed to belong to public companies combining limited liability, professional management, and 'corporate personhood'.[5] Intriguingly, proponents of the global system theory, such as Leslie Skair who accepted that the national bourgeoisie in the countries of the Third World was growing fast, still expected 'national, regional and First World–Third World differences between transnational corporations [to] diminish over time' (Sklair and Robbins, 2002, p. 97).

As will be shown in the next section, two forms of corporate organization have been successful, and thus dominated business systems in the periphery: family conglomerates and state-owned enterprises. This fact is a strong challenge against both the rightist convergence view and leftist dependency view. First, regarding the convergence view, an important countervailing evidence is the survival of conglomerates or business groups in emerging economies despite globalization and market reforms. Thus, the 'rightists' fail to acknowledge that firms are and continue to be heterogeneous in their structure, strategy and ownership (Nelson, 1991, 2009), and what matters most is not necessarily the development of market institutions but the co-evoluton of market institutions and firms.

Second, regarding the dependency view, an important countervailing evidence is the success of several periphery countries, such as Korea as well as China, India and Brazil, in nurturing globally successful companies despite increasing integration with the world economy. The dependency view downplayed the ability of governments in association with SOEs in implementing activist policies that use and manage rents in a productive way and prevent them from leaking out of national boundaries. Markets are never perfect and thus allow activist governments and their agents room for maneuvering.

---

[4] As we were writing this chapter, Fukuyama encouraged 'contemporary conservatives [to] get over their ideological aversion to the state'!

[5] 'The bid engine that couldn't', *The Economist*, 19 May 2012.

In what follows, we first turn to the situation of big business in the BRICKs (Section 3), before we attempt a fuller theoretical interpretation of their main characteristics in Section 4.

3. Big business in the BRICKs

3.1 The combined share

From only 23 in 1994 and 38 in 2005, the number of BRICK entries in *Fortune Global 500* has skyrocketed to 109 in 2012. This increase is much more spectacular for China, which had 73 companies in 2011, compared to only 3 in 1994. At this stage, China has more entries than any other country except the United States, as it surpassed Japan in 2011. Russia, India and Brazil had only zero, 1 and 2 companies respectively in 1994. These days each of them has more or less than 10, similar to Italy or Canada although still lower than the number for the three largest European countries (Germany, France and the UK), which have 30 to 40 entries each. In addition, the largest firm in each BRICK – always the same and invariably an oil company – has constantly climbed the global rankings. As far as headquarters are concerned, only Tokyo and Paris host more Global 500 companies than Beijing. (See Table 21.1.)

The combined share of BRICK countries in *Fortune Global 500* has increased from a mere 3% of all entries in 1994 to 23% in 2013 (Figure 21.1). The slope of the graph shows that the trend is accelerating; the increase was more pronounced in the 2000s than in the 1990s.

3.2 Ownership: the importance of the state

Regarding the ownership of big business in the BRICKs, Table 21.2 shows that the universe of the 100 largest companies remains absolutely dominated by domestic firms, including in Brazil, which is the least 'national' of the BRICKs.[6, 7] The share of foreign firms are negligible, except in Brazil where it

---

[6] Analyzing responses of large business to global change therefore amounts to an ambitious programme of research at any latitude, in the face of uneven access to data and information. When it comes to the analysis of large emerging economies, and the BRICKs in particular, limitations are even greater. To the extent that this chapter is based on four different rankings of large companies and that there is great variance in data coverage, the findings are indicative only. Nonetheless, the general contours are clear.

[7] Obviously this finding must be interpreted with a lot of caution, in view of the exclusion of foreign companies from the Chinese ranking, but it also reflects the fact that most inward FDI over the past fifteen years or so has been export-directed. With a lower degree of precision, in all likelihood no foreign firm other than the car makers (which are joint ventures and for which such data are not available) generates sufficient China sales to qualify for the top 100 listing. Sales of five of the world's largest companies with large operations in China range from US$7.5 billion

Table 21.1 *BRICK companies in Fortune Global 500 (number of companies and global ranking of the largest company)*

	Brazil		Russia		India		China		Korea	
	Number of entries	Global ranking of largest	Number of entries	Global ranking of largest	Number of entries	Global ranking of largest	Number of entries	Global ranking of largest	Number of entries	Global ranking of largest
1994	2		0		1		3		8	
2005	3	125	3	139	5	170	16	31	11	39
2006	4	86	5	102	6	153	20	23	12	46
2007	5	65	4	52	6	135	24	17	14	46
2008	5	63	5	47	7	116	29	16	15	38
2009	6	34	8	22	7	105	37	9	14	40
2010	7	54	6	50	8	125	46	7	10	32
2011	7	34	7	35	8	98	61	7	14	22
2012	8	23	7	15	8	83	73	5	13	20
2013	8	25	7	21	8	88	89	4	2	14

Source: *Fortune* (various years)

Table 21.2 *Top 100 companies' sales in the BRICKs, by ownership*

	Brazil	Russia	India	China	Korea
Domestic	57.32	91.53	96.83	100.00	87.89
Government	*28.02*	*51.74*	*47.96*	*95.25*	*11.23*
Private groups	*29.30*	*39.79*	*41.02*	*4.75*	*76.12*
Independent			*7.85*		*0.54*
Foreign	38.83	3.67	3.17	..	6.70
Joint Ventures	3.85	4.81	..	..	5.41
Total	100	100	100	100	100

Source: Goldstein (2013)

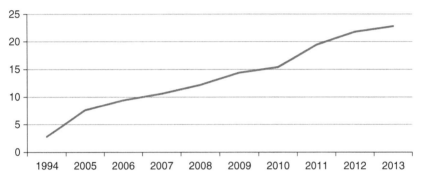

Figure 21.1 Combined share of BRICK entries in *Fortune Global 500*, 1994–2010.
Source: *Fortune* (various years).

is 38%. On the other hand, SOEs have very substantial shares in all BRICK countries (China 95%, Russia 52%, India 48%, and Brazil 28%), although it is much smaller in Korea (11%). Korea has a business scene dominated by a few large domestically owned enterprises, which are largely independent from multinational corporations in terms of financing, production and marketing (brand) (Lee *et al.* 2010). However, many of these private firms, including SK Telecom, POSCO (Pohang Steel), Korean Air, and Woori Bank, were state-owned before they were privatized in the mid-1980s.

Further stories from each country follow.

First, in India, among the top eleven in 2010, there were seven state-controlled enterprises (four in petroleum, one each in banking, mining and power), and the energy and petrochemical private group ranked 2nd in

for Wal-Mart to US$3.1 billion for Nestlé, with Siemens, General Electric and Procter & Gamble falling in between; 100th–ranked Beijing Railway had sales of US$8.3 billion.

Reliance Industries. The two largest manufacturing companies among the top eleven are Tata Motors (5th) and Tata Steel. Maruti Suzuki was the largest foreign-owned company and ranked 19th only. Among the world's largest multinationals, only in the case of Unilever has India always been a very important location (Jones, 2005, pp. 169–74).

Second, in Russia there are six oil companies (including state-owned Gazprom, Rosneft and Surgutneftegaz) among the top nineteen companies by turnover. The Kremlin has turned scattered companies into national champions. Rosneft took over most of Yukos from Mikhail Khodorkovsky, once Russia's richest man, and Gazprom bought Sibneft from Roman Abramovich. There is an equivalent number of mining and minerals conglomerates (controlled by oligarchs such as Mikhaïl Prokhorov, Alexeï Mordachov and Roman Abramovich) born from the ashes of Soviet *kombinaty*, together with seven services companies. It is only in the 20th position that one could find a manufacturing firm, TAIF, and in 32nd a foreign-owned entity, Ford.

Third, Brazil is yet another reality, more heterogeneous. In 2010 the two largest firms were in the petroleum industry, Petrobras (upstream) and BR Distribuidora (downstream), both controlled by the state albeit listed on the stock exchange and with sizeable stakes in the hands of private investors. Volkswagen in the 5th place was the largest multinational and four more, all European (Fiat, Ambev, Shell, and Vivo), were in the top ten, together with three private, Brazilian firms, including Vale in 3rd place. These seven multinationals, plus the four next largest (General Motors, Walmart, Arcelor Mittal and Ford), make more than 9% of their global sales in Brazil. There are four other local corporations ranked between 11th and 20th. While business groups exist, they are far less important and widespread than in India.

Table 21.3 *Varieties of state capitalism in China*

Typology	Characteristics	Examples
Large SOEs	Operate in capital-intensive sectors, as monopolies or oligopolies; minority stakes sold in IPOs on foreign exchanges.	ICBC, China Construction Bank, China Mobile, Unicom, CNPC
Joint ventures	Foreign MNEs given market access in exchange for technology	Shanghai Volkswagen, DHL Sinotrans
Private companies with some state influence	Often in new markets with no SOEs	Huawei, BYD, Geely, Chery
Companies backed by publicly-owned investment funds	Investors include foreign private equity and venture capital funds, as well as city and province governments	Shanghai Environment, Nanhai Development, Digital China

Source: 'Capitalism Confined', *The Economist*, 3 September 2011.

Fourth, in China, all entries bar five (Huawei, Ping An Insurance, Haier, Suning Appliance and Gome) correspond to state-owned enterprises. Petrochina and China Mobile alone recorded aggregate 2009 profits that were higher than for the 500 largest private companies in China! In fact not a surprising result when considering that China Mobile and two other state-owned companies, China Unicom and China Telecom, carve out the huge and very lucrative telecom market (in India, which is comparable in size, there are more than a dozen national operators), or that the price that Petrochina pays for land is well below the market value. Control by the government is never far away. This model provides the government with continuing control of enterprises critical to the functioning of the economy. In particular, it facilitates the execution of big capital projects such as high-speed railways, steel plants, telecommunications networks and ports.

In China state influence takes a variety of forms (Table 21.3). The Chinese Communist party maintains a lot of power even in those national champions such as Haier or Lenovo, that are usually put forward as examples of private entrepreneurship (McGregor, 2010). In addition, the People's Liberation Army has historically been involved in several business ventures, many of which are organized as business groups.

In China, under the impulse of SASAC (State-owned Assets Supervision and Administration Commission), property right management of Chinese SOEs changed significantly in recent years. More than 1,000 large SOEs, controlling high-quality assets, have listed either locally or internationally. SASAC typically owns 100% of the shares in the holding company. The holding company in turn owns a smaller proportion of shares in the listed subsidiary. For instance Petro-China, with a listing on the New York Stock Exchange, is the international division of China National Petroleum Corporation. In the overwhelming majority of cases, the public sector has remained the largest shareholder: among the 100 largest listed companies, when the state is the largest shareholder its stake is on average almost 50% (Bianco, 2010). In fact, out of 1,453 A-share companies listed on the Chinese stock market in 2007, as few as six were widely held, with contestable control (Amit *et al.*, 2010).

3.3 *Organization: the importance of conglomerates and business groups*

Another important feature of big business in the periphery is the strong presence of conglomerates or business groups, controlled either by families or states. While business groups are heterogeneous compared with the Anglo-Saxon style of specialized firms, we also see heterogeneity within business groups across the BRICKs.

Big businesses from China are mostly state-owned business groups, as analysed in Seo *et al.* (2010). This study shows that business groups account for more than half of firms listed on stock markets and show similar behaviour as other typical business groups. At the same time China's business groups have their own unique characteristics that reflect the socio-economic context of post-reform China. They have emerged not only as a response to market failures but also as an initiative of the government (Lee and Jin, 2009). As a result, they are state-owned and managed by hired managers (who respond to the state and the Party).

In India, among the top 100, the majority belongs to diversified family-controlled business groups which operate according to a different logic than traditional Western companies, with less emphasis on short-term financial returns. Such business affiliates account for more than 70% of corporate sector assets. Religion and ethnicity played an important role: as late as in 1997, fifteen of the twenty largest industrial houses were of *vaishya* or *bania* trading caste, and eight were Marwari.

Notable examples of conglomerates, or business houses, are Tata and Reliance. The Tata group has dozens of firms in almost every sector, each of them applying a series of group-wide principles established in more than a century of existence (Goldstein, 2008). Managers often rotate across different firms and other functions are performed centrally. The combined revenues of the six Tata firms (6th-ranked Tata Motors, 8th Tata Steel, 20th TCS in ICT, 40th Tata Power, 68th Tata Comm and 71st Tata Chemicals) equal 10% of the top 100 sales.

Korea is an extreme example as all big businesses are business groups, all of them controlled by families except POSCO (the world's third-largest steel maker), which is a state-owned business groups with tens of affiliates in several business areas. In Russia, industry-led financial-industrial groups (FIGs) emerged early in the privatization process. Bank-led FIGs emerged later, in relation to auctions initiated by President Yeltsin favoring (some) buyers.

The prevalence of business group structure implies that the degree of separation between ownership and control in the BRICKs remains much lower than in most OECD countries, although it has somewhat increased. In Brazil, the largest shareholder had a 50.3% stake in 2004, marginally declining to 49.2% in 2008 (Aguilera *et al.*, 2012); for Russia, the largest direct shareholder owns 46.2% and the percentage of voting shares tied up in blocks over 5% is, on average, 70.7% (Chernykh, 2008); in India, ownership is concentrated with Indian promoters, who together with persons acting in concert held on average around 34% of total outstanding shares from 2001 to 2006 (Kaur and Gill, 2009). In Korea, the degree of separation in typical family-controlled business groups is high as in general the family controls operating subsidiaries through cascading pyramids and circular arrangements.

3.4   A summary

In theory, the landscape of big business in the BRICKs at the end of the 2010s should bear little resemblance to the 1990s. Globalization, structural reform (especially privatization), reregulation, continuing government promotion and 'financiarization' have all shaped decisively the emerging corporate giants. In practice, however, path dependence and deliberate policy action have combined to maintain most of the ownership and structure (and at least some of the strategy and governance) that prevailed in the previous period.

To summmarize, big business in the BRICKs equals domestic capital (foreign-owned enterprises are important but not dominant in Brazil, marginal in Korea, India and Russia, and absent in China), with a towering presence of state ownership and business groups. In terms of ownership and control, the government continues to exercise wide-ranging control (or influence in Korea) over the industrial sector through a mix of legislation and ownership (including of banks and financial institutions that invest in commercial organizations).

Insofar as economies of scale and scope dominate other consideration, in a country where oil and gas account for 20% of GDP and 60% of exports, 'Russian capitalism would have been concentrated even if the Kremlin had not been so ruthless'.[8] The reach of the state has further expanded since 2008: VTB Bank, for instance, acquired 50% plus one share of the DON-Stroy Group in 2009. Russian Technologies rolled up hundreds of state companies, many of which had little to do with technology, into a vast conglomerate. As a result the Russian state once again controls the commanding heights of the economy – only this time through share ownership and cajoling, rather than directly.

Similarly, the Brazilian state has also kept control over Petrobras even after floatation. In other cases it has replaced direct with indirect government ownership through the Brazilian National Development Bank (BNDES) and its investment subsidiary (BNDESPar), and swapped majority for minority ownership by acquiring shares in a broad spectrum of different companies – the model of 'Leviathan as a minority shareholder' (Lazzarini and Musacchio 2012).

In fact, this is not different from the situation in the early 1990s, when state ownership (although in most cases they were legally ministerial departments) was the only form of production in China and Russia, and accounted for 44% of the total turnover of the largest firms in Brazil (Siffert and Souza e Silva, 1999). With the exception of Brazil – where there were 27 foreign firms among the top 100 – subsidiaries of foreign multinationals played almost no role in the heights of corporate power. In the universe of big business, private companies, listed or unlisted, were in practice a residual category. The main shareholders in both Brazil and India were families, representing 27% of the 100 largest companies in Brazil.

---

[8] 'State Capitalism is Not All the Same', *The Economist*, 21 January 2012.

4.   Explaining big business in the BRICKs: co-evolution of firms and the environment

As documented in the previous section, big business in the BRICKs have grown dramatically over the past three decades, but not necessarily in the way that scholars and pundits expected. Companies have responded vigourously to the challenges and opportunities of globalization – as the dependency theory did not anticipate. But they have done so in their own terms, maintaining tight control and ownership arrangements, persisting with diversification and developing new forms of interaction with governments. While the traditional view focuses on market institutions acting as a force for selection and thus homogenization, reality shows that SOEs and business groups continued to thrive as they adapted to the changing business environment (Choo *et al.* 2009). Even when SOEs and conglomerates list on the stockmarket, they do little to constrain the power of controlling shareholders (the state or the family). The current shape and state of big businesses in the BRICKs can be used to re-assess the two prevailing views from the left and the right and to suggest alternative interpretations.

First, the survival, when not further growth, of conglomerates or business groups in emerging economies despite globalization and market reform challenges the convergence view. Business groups (some of which can be state-owned) are defined as collections of firms bound together in some formal and/ or informal way and by an intermediate level of binding; that is, they are neither bound merely by short-term strategic alliances nor legally consolidated into a single entity (Granovetter, 1995). They are considered to be responses to market failures in emerging economies: business groups internalize market functions to overcome imperfections in capital, labour, raw materials, components, and technology markets (Goto, 1982). This view predicts that, once market institutions mature, business groups eventually disappear. Consequently, a world of more homogenous firms is conceived. This view was very powerful during the Asian financial crisis as it was able to explain the collapse of many family-owned conglomerates in a region that was seen as a hub of crony capitalism.

However, this theory is insufficient to explain the evolution since the early 2000s and the continuing prosperity of business groups across emerging Asia. For example, Korean business groups, or Chaebols, showed serious problems in the 1990s, with declining and worsening performance due to excessive investment. During the crisis-and-restructuring period they improved financial management, diverted money from cash cows to new industries that might take a long time to produce results, and thus were born again in the 2000s as successful global players. Choo *et al.* (2009) and Lee *et al.* (2010) argue that enhanced technological capabilities and the correction of previous mistakes, such as over-investment, allowed the turn-around in the post-crisis period.

The improving performance of Korean business groups is also a puzzle to the agency cost view from the finance literature, because of the variance of their behaviour despite all sharing the same ownership and governance structure. Their cases show that the change in the surrounding market mechanism alone cannot explain fully the destiny of the firms, as these keep evolving and responding to changes in the environment. A study of state-owned business groups in China (Seo *et al.* 2010) also finds firm-level factors to have a stronger explanatory power than market-level ones in explaining the dynamic shift of relative performance of business groups in China.

Second, the emergence of companies from the periphery capable of joining the ranks of global big business counters the scepticism of the dependency theory regarding the role of the state. As highlighted in the previous section, state ownership remains an important feature of large corporations in the periphery. When the private sector was probably too weak to compete against foreign MNCs, governments implemented activist policies and supported SOEs through rents (over natural resources but also over promising markets). While in general such rents are regarded as bad or inefficient for economic growth, in most emerging economies governments have preferred to distribute them to domestic firms, rather than allowing MNCs to acquire them and leak them out of national borders. In a productive setting with some discipline device in force, rents could play the role of effective incentives and source for investment funds.

In this sense, we argue that an evolutionary, new Schumpeterian approach that emphasizes capability formation and co-evolution of firms and market is more relevant to the study of big business than either the convergence thesis predicted by the market-primacy view or the dependency view. What the business systems in emerging economies have in common is that they have proven efficient from a 'capability-based view' of national catch-up development (Lee, 2012). The idea of development of firm capability over time should be quite relevant in understanding the growth of firms in emerging economies.[9] Kock and Guillen (2001) consider the diversification of business groups from developing economies as a way of using their own unique capability or resources, which Amsden and Hikino (1994) defined as 'project

---

[9] A related but distinct body of literature, referred to as the 'dynamic capabilities perspective', is concerned with the mechanisms by which firms accumulate and dissipate new skills and capabilities (Teece *et al.*, 1997). This perspective builds on the same principles of resource heterogeneity, but is more focused on the dynamics of capability development than on stocks of capabilities at any given point in time. According to Teece *et al.* (1997), dynamic capabilities are firms' ability to integrate, build and reconfigure internal and external competences to address rapidly changing environments.

execution capability'. This capability refers to the skills required to establish or expand operating and other corporate facilities, which can later lead to the eventual accumulation of sector-specific know-how, especially when the projects tend to fall more within the same areas.

Lee and He (2009, pp. 280–1) describe a dynamic path of capability development by business groups in such terms:

In the early stage, business groups are less capable, and pursue rent-seeking behaviour, and any market winning capabilities should be more about how to build, maintain and utilize their connections and network with the government, which is in charge of key resource allocation. During the second stage, these business groups diversify into whatever related or unrelated sectors they think promising or profitable owing to market demand or government industrial policy, thereby accumulating project execution capability which is not very sector-specific. In the third stage, with diverse sectors, they can expect some integration benefits associated with horizontal integration among less related sectors or vertical integration, which is more sector-specific. Such integration would be a significant advantage in the environment with input market deficiencies, and also helps companies maintain better quality, efficient coordination and punctuality than the level possible through outsourcing. Finally, they could develop technological innovation capability, which is very specific to certain technological areas or knowledge and which can be represented by patents or totally new products. The vertical integration stage preceding the innovation stage makes sense because increased interaction between buyers and sellers can enhance technology development.

Building firm-level capability has been the crucial factor in the economy-wide technological catch-up in the dynamic emerging economies over the past two decades (and possibly for a longer period in the case of Korea, which has combined continuous upgrading within the same industries and successive entries into new promising industries). The strategies for learning and developing a knowledge base (i.e. technology and brands) have been numerous, ranging from reverse and forward engineering (e.g. through university spin-off firms) and learning from foreign direct investment, to the promotiong of in-house Research and Development (R&D), public and private R&D consortium, and international mergers and acquisitions (M&A) (Goldstein, 2007; Lee and Mathews, 2012). Firm growth in peripheries has depended on the ability to acquire such diverse resources – basic ones such as financial, physical and human capital and higher-level resources such as managerial skills and R&D – and SOEs and business groups have been particularly successful in this. Samsung Electronics and the Samsung group more broadly is a good example of the four-stage evolution (Lee and He, 2009).

It is the very rise of the BRICKs that can be explained by the strong growth and presence of big businesses (Lee et al., 2013). Other middle-income emerging economies may be registering slower growth performance because they do not have a sufficient number of *Fortune 500* companies, and in fact have fewer of them than the size of their economy would predict.

5. Policy implications

The BRICK economies have recorded impressive growth rates over the past decade and the role of big business has been crucial in this regard. The process of economic development, however, is inherently dynamic and unstable and new challenges continuously emerge. In this section we consider whether the BRICK model, and in particular its reliance on state activism (arguably much greater in the BRICs than in Korea), is acceptable, or at least compatible, in today's global environment. With no pretence of being exhaustive, nor of ranking such challenges in importance, some of them are discussed in the following paragraphs.

First, the quantitative and qualitative role of the state in the economy remains a source of contention. This is especially true in the case of China, where many reformers have asserted that 'the state [sector] is advancing and the private retreating'. Weakening the grip of SOEs is needed in order to prevent the country from eventually falling into a 'middle-income trap' of much slower growth. Control over SOEs should be taken over by new independent bodies that would hand over dividends to the state budget and gradually reduce the level of state ownership. Of course tackling economic reforms would affect powerful vested interests, such as SASAC.[10] But it is made all the more necessary by the expansion by China's SOEs into international markets and higher-profit areas, where they benefit from privileged conditions, jeopardize the principle of 'competitive neutrality' and generate recurring friction.

More broadly, in systems where lines between Party, state and business are blurred, a second and related challenge has to do with opacity in private-public interactions, bad corporate governance and lack of competition. In China and Russia there have been numerous episodes where prominent business people have accused political leaders of trampling on the law and property and human rights, attacking their competitors and taking whatever they want in order to enhance their power.[11] A few recent Brazilian cases are also illustrative. In 2009 president Lula accused the management of Vale of laying off workers

---

[10] 'According to a Chinese newspaper, *21st Century Business Herald*, SASAC wrote to the finance ministry arguing that the proposal to scale back state ownership was unconstitutional' ('The Bees Get Busy', *The Economist*, 3 March 2012).

[11] Recent examples include the Khodorkovsky-Yukos saga and the death of Sergei Magnitsky, the lawyer working for Hermitage Capital, in Russia; the incarceration of Huang Guangyu, founder and former CEO of retail appliance and electronics dealer Gome Electronics, and the Bo Xilai scandal in China.

during the global crisis and purchasing large vessels to ship iron ore to Asia, instead of investing in integrated steel mills in Brazil. The government eventually removed Roger Agnelli from his post as CEO of Vale despite his outstanding record and is trying to force Petrobras to use expensive local equipment suppliers despite doubts about their competence.

Third, the strategy of making huge strategic investments, even to the point of losing money for the sake of creating national champions and entire new industries, may be necessary to solve a market failure and substitute for financial intermediaries that are not doing their job properly, but it puts private companies at a severe disadvantage. The big question is whether this structure is less useful, and even counterproductive, when the country becomes more integrated into the world economy. If all countries were to implement state capitalism to accumulate a foreign currency surplus, this would result in a 'fallacy of composition'; another danger is that the big groups will rig the market in their favour and inhibit the emergence of specialized players.[12] To prevent such an outcome, a financial system that gives start-ups easy access to capital is essential, as well as a vigorous competition policy. In fact it is not sufficient to uphold competition, it is necessary to understand the implications of business groups, cross-shareholdings and interlocked directors in this regard (Kogut, 2012).

In this context, making the case that big business is essential for economic growth should not mean ignoring the role of small and medium enterprises (SMEs). National competitiveness critically hinges on the successful functional and territorial integration between SMEs and large enterprises (Fortis and Quadrio Curzio, 2006). Too much dependence on (few) very large firms may be counterproductive for economic growth. If these big firms come to monopolize the markets in which they operate, their managers might not feel sufficient pressure to innovate contrary to Schumpeter's expectations. Large powerful companies can also lead to the adoption of policies that hinder growth (Grossman and Helpman, 1994). In addition, market dominance by big businesses and their absorption of excessive resources might become a barrier against entry by new SMEs.

Fourth, even with substantial concentrated (State or family) ownership, corporate governance has been improving (especially in terms of disclosure and investor protection) in each BRICK. Reforms were initially mostly a formal-legalistic process, which with time have become more substantial as institutions (Stock Exchanges and government regulators) showed stronger commitment. Allocation of control, however, remains less dynamic than in more advanced market economies and the enforcement of rights is not always sufficient to protect minory shareholders and indeed other stakeholders.

---

[12] We owe this point to Jorge Arbache.

Diversification may also be motivated by expropriation – in Indian groups affiliates are found to engage in activities away from their core business to serve as destination points for funds tunneled from a group's core activity. This should be a cause of concern insofar as dispersed shareholder firms are typically better managed (Bloom *et al.*, 2011).

A note of cautious realism is needed here. There is a great deal of path dependence of corporate structure – the one that an economy has at any point in time depends in part on those that it had at earlier times (Bebchuk and Roe, 1999). In the case of China and Russia, their corporate ownership structures after fifty (pre-WTO era) and seventy-five years of socialism gave some stakeholders both the incentives and the power to impede changes, i.e. *de facto* privatization. In Brazil and India, corporate rules that favoured the formation of business groups also reinforced the latter's power to resist pressures to converge.

Fifth, the rapid globalization of BRICK firms through take-overs may well have thrilled cheerleaders and corporate patriots, but the rate of success has not been equally spectacular. *The Economist* has examined the four largest Indian deals for which enough information is available.[13] Gross operating profits (EBITDA) have risen in one case only, while in the others earnings have failed to generate an adequate return on capital. Most Indian dominant shareholders dislike issuing equity and firms have fiddly holding chains, thus raising the risk of being too convoluted and puny to handle large foreign deals. The problems of Chinese overseas investment have been documented in many studies. Even Samsung, which came almost from nowhere to become the world's largest electronics company, has had a poor track record in M&As.[14]

The learning curve in overcoming the liability of foreignness has always been very steep and the growing importance of M&A as entry mode adds post-merger integrations issues to the equation. Psychic distance between Russia, India and China, on one hand, and OECD economies, on the other, is rather high and generates reciprocal bafflement at practices such as taking long holidays or making 'facilitation' payments. In fact the greater success of Brazilian and Korean MNEs is explained by the greater role of foreign MNEs in the domestic economies and managers' greater experience with cross-cultural deals.

6.   Conclusions

The findings of this chapter, combined with the recent literature on business groups and state capitalism, suggest that diverse factors are involved in determining the ecology of large firms and the performance of diverse forms

---

[13] 'Running with the bulls', 3 March 2012.
[14] More details in 'To Keep Tech up, Samsung Acquires', *Joongang Daily*, 23 July 2012.

of firms in different countries. Moreover, these diverse forces that keep firms heterogeneous are as strong as the forces promoting homogeneity. By doing this they also challenge the rigid determinism that would always confine corporations in the periphery to occupy a secondary position, while in reality it is their success, very often made possible by pro-active state policies, that have changed the geography of the world economy.

We argue that it is time to upgrade or restate the market imperfection thesis in predicting the performance of business groups and SOEs over a longer period. Without sustained and policy-induced capability-building, standard liberalization measures (capital and trade liberalization, privatization etc.) alone cannot bring sustained catch-up as these often result in short-run, but ultimately temporary, export booms. While the maturing of market institutions must have affected the performance of business groups, some business groups have built up new capabilities to adapt to the new environment and have become freed from the 'law' of long-term decline. In a sense, these results can be considered consistent with the thesis of market failure as it shows that difference factors (e.g., technological capability) have been important in different institutional settings.

A business system dominated by SOEs and business groups can play a crucial role in generating the world-class big businesses that are fundamental in the catching-up stages, but their role should change and in fact decrease as economies move closer to the frontier. The best BRICK example is clearly Korea, which used to have a large number of SOEs until the mid-1980s, at which point the private sector had grown enough to take over the commanding heights of the economy and SOEs could be privatized. Against this background and in view of the practical difficulty of generating world-class big business in the periphery, we can suggest that establishing SOEs can be an effective strategy at the early stage of development, while at later stages privatization is a more effective strategy. China seems to provide a good case for this observation.

Of course, once business groups become so powerful new policy challenges emerge. It is important to avoid abuses of marker power, without constraining the actions of big businesses so much as to weaken their ability to generate innovation in the oligopolistic sectors that dominate the global economy. This will undoubtedly be one of the crucial dilemmas to keep policymakers in China and other large emerging economies awake in coming years.

REFERENCES

Aguilera, R., Kabbach de Castro, L. R., Lee, J. H., and You, J. (2012) 'Corporate Governance in Emerging Markets', in G. Morgan and R. Whitley (eds.), *Capitalisms and Capitalism in the Twenty-First Century*, Oxford: Oxford University Press, pp. 319–44.

Amsden, A. H. (2009) 'Firm Ownership, FOEs, and POEs', *WIDER Research Paper*, No. 2009/46.

Amsden, A. H., and Hikino, T. (1994) 'Project Execution Capability, Organizational Know-how and Conglomerate Corporate Growth in Late Industrialization', *Industrial and Corporate Change*, 3.1, pp. 111–47.

Amit, R., Ding, Y., Villalonga, B., and Zhang, H. (2010) 'The Role of Institutional Development in the Prevalence and Value of Family Firms', Harvard Business School, *Working Papers*, No. 10–103.

Bebchuk, L. A. and Roe, M. J. (1999) 'A Theory of Path Dependence in Corporate Ownership and Governance', *Stanford Law Review*, 52.1, pp. 127–70.

Bianco, M. (2010) 'Corporate Governance in China: A Changing Model?', presented at the Banca d'Italia Workshop 'The Chinese Economy', Venice, 25–7 November.

Bloom, N., Genakos, C., Sadun, R., and Van Reenen, J. (2011) 'Management Practices Across Firms and Countries', *HBS Working Papers*, No. 12–052.

Chandler, A. D. Jr. (1959) 'The Beginning of Big Business in American Industry', in R. S. Tedlow and R. R. John, Jr. (eds.) *Managing Big Business*, Boston, Mass.: Harvard Business School Press.

   (1977) *The Visible Hand: the Managerial Revolution in American Business*, Cambridge, Mass.: Belknap Press of Harvard University Press.

   (1990) *Scale and Scope: the Dynamics of Industrial Capitalism*, Cambridge, Mass.: Harvard University Press.

Chandler, A. D. Jr, Amatori, F. and Hikino, T. (eds.) (1997) *Big Business and the Wealth of Nations*, Cambridge: Cambridge University Press.

Chang, H.-J., Lee, K., and Lin, J. Y. (2005) 'Late Marketisation versus Late Industrialisation in East Asia', *Asia-Pacific Economic Literature*, 19.1, pp. 42–59.

Chang, S.-J., and Choi U. (1988) 'Structure and Performance of Korean Business Groups: A Transactions Cost Approach', *Journal of Industrial Economics*, 37.2, pp. 141–58.

Chernykh, L. (2008) 'Ultimate Ownership and Control in Russia', *Journal of Financial Economics*, 88.1, pp. 169–92.

Choo, K., Lee, K., Ryu K., and Yoon, J. (2009) 'Performance Change of the Business Groups in Korea over Two decades: Investment Inefficiency and Technological Capabilities', *Economic Development and Cultural Change*, 57.2, pp. 359–86.

dos Santos, T. (1970) 'The Structure of Dependence', *American Economic Review*, 60.2, pp. 231–6.

Evans, P. (1979) *Dependent Development. The Alliance of Multinational, State, and Local Capitalism in Brazil*, Princeton, NJ: Princeton University Press.

Fortis, M., and Quadrio Curzio, A. (eds.) (2006) *Industria e distretti. Un paradigma di perdurante competitività italiana*, Bologna: Il Mulino.

Fukuyama, F. (1989) 'The End of History?', *The National Interest*, Summer, pp. 3–18.

   (2012) 'Conservatives Must Fall Back in Love with the State', *Financial Times*, 14 July.

   (1981) 'Transnational Corporations, Dependent Development, and State Policy in the Semiperiphery: A Comparison of Brazil and Mexico', *Latin American Research Review*, 16.3, pp. 31–64.

Gereffi, G., Humphrey, J., and Sturgeon, T. (2005) 'The Governance of Global Value Chains', *Review of International Political Economy*, 12.1, pp. 78–104.

Goldstein, A. (1999) 'Brazilian Privatization in International Perspective: The Rocky Path from State Capitalism to Regulatory Capitalism', *Industrial and Corporate Change*, 8.4, pp. 673–711.

——— (2006) 'State-owned Enterprises, Privatization and Industrial Policy', in P. Bianchi and S. Labory (eds.) *International Handbook on Industrial Policy*, Cheltenham: E. Elgar.

——— (2007) *Multinational Companies from Emerging Economies: Composition, Conceptualization and Direction in the Global Economy*, Basingstoke: Palgrave.

——— (2008) '"Emerging Economies" transnational corporations: the case of Tata', *Transnational Corporations*, 17.3, pp. 85–108.

——— (2013) 'Big Business in the BRICs', in J. Mikler (ed.) *Handbooks of Global Policy: Global Companies*, Oxford and New York: Wiley Blackwell, pp. 53–74.

Goto, A. (1982) 'Business Groups in Market Economy', *European Economic Review*, 19, pp. 53–70.

Granovetter, M. (1995) 'Coase Revisited: Business Groups in the Modern Economy', *Industrial and Corporate Change*, 4.1, pp. 93–130.

Grossman, G. M., and Helpman, E. (1994) 'Protection for Sale', *The American Economic Review*, 84.4, pp. 833–50.

Guillen, M. F. (2000) 'Business Groups in Emerging Economies: A Resource-Based View', *Academy of Management Journal*, 43.3, pp. 362–80.

Iacoviello, M., Schiantarelli, F., and Schuh, S. (2011) 'Input and Output Inventories in General Equilibrium', *International Economic Review*, 52.4, pp. 1179–213.

Jones, G. (2005) *Reinventing Unilever*, Oxford: Oxford University Press.

Jung, M., and Lee, K. (2010) 'Sectoral Systems of Innovation and Productivity Catch-up of Korean Firms with the Japanese Firms', *Industrial and Corporate Change*, 19.4, pp. 1037–69.

Kaur, P., and Gill, S. (2009) 'The Effects of Ownership Structure on Corporate Governance and Performance: An Empirical Assessment in India', Panjab University Business School.

Kock, C. and Guillen, M. (2001) 'Strategy and Structure in Developing Countries: Business Groups as an Evolutionary Response to Opportunities for Unrelated Diversification', *Industrial and Corporate Change*, 10.1, pp. 77–113.

Kogut, B. (ed.) (2012) *The Small Worlds of Corporate Governance*, Boston, Mass.: The MIT Press.

Krugman, P. (2000) 'Media Mania', *The New York Times*, 12 January.

Lazzarini, S., and Musacchio, A. (2010) 'Leviathan as a Minority Shareholder: A Study of Equity Purchases by the Brazilian National Development Bank (BNDES), 1995–2003', HBS Working Paper, No. 12–101.

Lee, K. (2012) 'How Can Korea be a Role Model for Catch-up Development? A "Capability-based View"', in A. K. Fosu (ed.), *Achieving Development Success: Strategies and Lessons from the Developing World*, Oxford: Oxford University Press, pp. 25–49.

Lee, K., and He, X. (2009) 'Project Execution and Vertical Integration Capability of Business Groups: Samsung Created in Korea, Replicated in China', *Asian Business and Management*, 8.3, pp. 277–99.

Lee, K., Jeeb, M., and Eun, J.-H. (2011) 'Assessing China's Economic Catch-up at the Firm-Level and Beyond: Washington Consensus, East Asian Consensus and the Beijing Model', *Industry and Innovation*, 18.5, pp. 487–507.

Lee, K., and Jin, X. (2009) 'The Origins of the Business Groups in China: An Empirical Testing of the Three Paths and the Three Theories', *Business History*, 51.1, pp. 77–99.

Lee, K., Kim, B.-Y., Park, Y.-Y., and Sanidas, E. (2013) 'Big Business and Economic Growth: Finding a Binding Constraint for Growth by a Country Panel Analysis,' *Journal of Comparative Economics*, 41.1, pp. 561–82.

Lee, K., Kim, J.-Y., and Lee, O. (2010) 'Long-term Evolution of the Firm Value and Behavior of Business Groups: Korean Chaebols between Weak Premium, Strong Discount, and Strong Premium,' *Journal of Japanese and International Economies*, 24.3, pp. 412–40.

Lee, K., and Mathews, J. (2012) 'Firms in Korea and Taiwan: Upgrading in the Same Industry and Entries into New industries for Sustained Catch-up,' in J. Cantwell and E. Amann (eds.), *The Innovative Firms in the Emerging Market Economies*, Oxford: Oxford University Press, pp. 223–48.

Lee, K., and Temesgen, T. (2009) 'What Makes Firm Grow in Developing Countries: An Extension of the Resource-Based View', *Journal of Technological Learning, Innovation and Development*, 1.3, pp. 139–72.

Lin, J. (2012) *New Structural Economics: A Framework for Rethinking Development and Policy*, Washington, DC: The World Bank.

McGregor, R. (2010) *The Party: the Secret World of China's Communist Rulers*, London: Penguin.

Musacchio, A., Lazzarini, S., and Bruschi, C. (2012) 'Do CEOs of State-Owned Enterprises Matter? Evidence from Brazil, 1973–1993', mimeo.

Nelson, R. (1991) 'Why Do Firms Differ and How Does it Matter', *Strategic Management Journal*, 12.S2, pp. 61–74.

(2009) 'Why Do Firms Differ and How Does it Matter? A Revisitation', *Seoul Journal of Economics*, 21.4, pp. 607–19.

OECD (2010) *Shifting Wealth*, Paris: OECD.

Pack, H., and Westphal, L. (1986) 'Industrial Strategy and Technological Change: Theory versus Reality', *Journal of Development Economics*, 22.1, pp. 87–128.

Pagano, P., and Schivardi, F. (2003) 'Firm Size Distribution and Growth', *Scandinavian Journal of Economics*, 105.2, pp. 255–74.

Penrose, E. T. (1959) *The Theory of the Growth of the Firm*, New York: John Wiley.

Quadrio Curzio, A. (1983) 'Primary Commodity Prices, Exhaustible Resources and International Monetary Relations: Alternative Explanations', in J. A. Kregel (ed.) *Distribution, Effective Demand and International Economic Relations*, London: Macmillan, pp. 142–52.

Quadrio Curzio, A., Fortis, M., and Zoboli, R. (1994) *Innovation, Resources and Economic Growth*, Berlin-Heidelberg: Springer.

Quadrio Curzio, A., and Marseguerra, G. (eds.) (2010) *Values and Rules for a New Model of Development*, Milan: Fondazione Centesimus Annus – Pro Pontifice, Libri Scheiwiller.

Schumpeter, J. A. (1934) *Theory of Economic Development: An Inquiry into Profits, Capital, Credit, Interest, and the Business Cycle*, Cambridge, Mass.: Harvard University Press.

(1942) *Capitalism, Socialism and Democracy*, New York: George Allen & Unwin.

Seo, B.-K., Lee, K., and Wang, X. (2010) 'Causes for the Performance Change of Business Groups: Market-level vs. Firm-level Factors in China,' *Industrial and Corporate Change*, 19.6, pp. 2041–72.

Siffert, N. F., and Souza e Silva, C. (1999) *Large Companies in the 1990s: Strategic Responses to a Scenario of Change*, Rio de Janeiro: BNDES.

Sklair, L., and Robbins, P. T. (2002) 'Global Capitalism and Major Corporations from the Third World', *Third World Quarterly*, 23.1, pp. 81–100.

Teece, D. J., Pisano, G., and Shuen, A. (1997) 'Dynamic Capabilities and Strategic Management' *Strategic Management Journal,* 18.7, pp. 509–33.

Teece, D. J., and Winter, S. G. (1984) 'The Limits of Neoclassical Theory in Management Education' *American Economic Review*, 74.2, pp. 116–21.

Williamson, J. (1990) 'What Washington Means by Policy Reform', ch. 2 in *Latin American Adjustment: How Much Has Happened?*, Washington: Institute for International Economics.

Yudanov, A. (1997) 'Large Enterprises in the USSR – the functional disorder', in A. D. Jr. Chandler *et al.* (eds.) *Big Business and the Wealth of Nations, op. cit.*, pp. 397–432.

22   On manufacturing development under resources constraints

Antonio Andreoni

1.   Introduction

Manufacturing development and resources constraints are linked by a complex array of structural relationships which have been unfolding in a variety of ways in different countries since the Industrial Revolution. Resource constraints are *sector specific* and affect production tasks within each sector in more or less deep ways according to the production units involved and relative levels of aggregation at which economic systems are operating. This implies that, at each stage of structural change and according to the countries' different patterns of specialization, resources constraints (or abundance) will affect economic systems differently. Ultimately problems of resource scarcity tend also to acquire an international character and, as such, become a geopolitical and multi-polar issue, to the extent countries become integral parts of the increasingly modularized global manufacturing system.

Within this complex and inherently dynamic architecture, interdependencies across sectoral value chains are the main channels through which resource constraints affect countries' manufacturing development trajectories. The aim of this chapter is to show firstly how multi-sectoral models of production in which resource constraints are structurally integrated offer critical analytical tools to unpack such complexity. In disentangling the relationships between manufacturing development and resource constraints, the chapter then focuses on the way in which the 'manufacturing apparatus' transforms the nature of scarcity by making it a 'relative' phenomenon functionally linked to incremental as well as disruptive technological changes. Building on an analytical-historical reconstruction of countries' structural learning trajectories, the

The author is grateful to Hassan Akram, Ha-Joon Chang, Eoin O'Sullivan, Roberto Scazzieri and Bill Wicksteed for comments and discussions. This chapter was presented at the Global Young Academy Annual Conference 'Natural Resources in a Finite World', Santiago de Chile, 21–24 May 2014. The author gratefully acknowledges the support of the President's Council of the *Accademia Nazionale dei Lincei*, Rome, and in particular of the President of the Class of Moral Sciences Alberto Quadrio Curzio. The Centre for Science, Technology and Innovation Policy acknowledges the support of the Gatsby Charitable Foundation.

chapter points out the inter-sectoral nature of 'technological scarcity' but also how scarcity induced technological innovations may trigger cumulative technological transformations across sectors.

An understanding of these resource-led structural dynamics provides fresh lenses to investigate the political economy of resource constraints at the national and international level. Going beyond the dominant 'resource curse' debate, the chapter concludes by sketching a number of specific policy implications. In particular, the lack of alignment of manufacturing, technology and resource policies (and, thus, the missed opportunity of creating and capturing value through resource-triggered complementarities over time) is identified as the main constraining factor for countries at both initial and more advanced stages of manufacturing development.

2.   Unfolding interdependencies in manufacturing development: opening the black box of resource constraints

Manufacturing development is the most dramatic and pervasive structural transformation that countries experience along their economic growth path. It consists of the creation and sustained expansion of production activities across different industrial subsectors, from resource based manufacturing activities towards increasingly technologically complex ones. Not only does manufacturing development trigger a process of industrial structural change, it also induces an increasing interconnectedness of the manufacturing base with the economic activities in other sectors such as agriculture, mining, construction and services (Ames and Rosenberg, 1965; Baranzini and Scazzieri, 1990; Andreoni, 2013).

Throughout this manufacturing development process, production interdependencies take different forms. They involve input–output multi-sectoral relationships, but also a variety of linkages among the technologies adopted in different sectors and manufacturing subsectors. In their unfolding, these interdependencies and linkages are shaped by a number of *structural tensions* such as rigidities, bottlenecks and indivisibilities in production structures (Kalecki, 1976; Kaldor 1985; Landesmann and Scazzieri, 1996; Andreoni, 2014); complementarities, horizontal and vertical externalities (Scitovsky, 1954; Hirschman, 1981; Dahmen, 1988); and disproportional variations in technological coefficients and natural resource constraints (Quadrio Curzio, 1967; Pasinetti 1981). As a result of these structural tensions, manufacturing development is intrinsically characterized by disproportional dynamics and various forms of dualism, that is, dynamic processes of cumulative differentiation within and across countries (Spaventa, 1959).

The way in which natural resource scarcities constrain national manufacturing development was at the core of the classical economic debate. The dialectic between 'almost unlimited producibility' à la Smith and 'scarcity' à la Malthus and Ricardo (in its absolute and relative forms respectively) defined the two main axes along which economists have disentangled the structural dynamics of manufacturing development.

Building on the Smithian idea of 'absolute dynamic producibility', a number of structural economists developed multi-sectoral models in which the constraining role played by natural resources on increasing production scale remain mostly unexplored (Leontief, 1953; Pasinetti, 1981). Even in those cases in which natural resources were factored in (Leontief *et al.*, 1977; Kuznets 1965), there was a tendency to stress the idea that technologies are able to neutralize scarcity problems by shifting them to an 'indefinite' long term. In other words, these contributions underestimated the fact that resource constraints unfold *throughout* the manufacturing development process. Thus, the fact that technological change will neutralize resource constraints in the future does not guarantee that it will be able to do it over time along specific manufacturing development trajectories.

This overall attitude towards the problem of resource scarcity can be also found in classical development economists (e.g. Singer, 1950; Prebish, 1950; Hirschman, 1981). Although the manufacturing development process was at the core of their investigation, the relationship with the commodity sector was mainly explored in terms of whether resources were beneficial (or detrimental) to the process of industrial structural change. The commodity sector (especially hard commodities) was perceived as an enclave activity, that is, a sector relatively detached from the rest of the economic system and characterized by low technological development and relatively few linkages and spillovers. This is why, in contrast to classical economists, the early development economists formulated the hypothesis according to which the commodities-manufacturing terms of trade would have moved in favour of manufacturing (Harvey *et al.*, 2010).

The idea of 'relative scarcity' originally conceptualized in Ricardo opened a different line of investigation of manufacturing development under resources constraints. In particular the work started by Alberto Quadrio Curzio (1967 and 1986) was developed in a number of different ways (Quadrio Curzio and Pellizzari, 1999). These developments offered an open-structural framework to disentangle the way in which natural resources direct and shape different manufacturing development trajectories. With respect to the specific relationship linking multi-sectoral structural change dynamics, technologies and natural resources constraints, this framework introduced a critical distinction between *techniques* and *technologies*.

Within a multi-sectoral model, each technique relies on a certain natural resource and produces one raw material adopted in the production of all other commodities, both directly and indirectly. Technologies are the n techniques that have been activated, at whatever production scale is feasible given the constraints imposed by natural resource scarcity. Each technology is thus linked to the others through scarce natural resources at each point in time. More importantly, each technique is 'connected dynamically in the process of accumulation to other techniques. The dynamic process, therefore, occurs at variable rates over time and is uneven across commodities. This raises complex problems of structural compatibility between techniques and it generates some residuals, that is, net products that cannot be utilized in the process of accumulation' (Quadrio Curzio and Pellizzari, 1999, p.33).

From a manufacturing development perspective, this *compound technologies scheme* opens the black box of resource scarcity by pointing out the possibility that different compositions of techniques are bounded in scale and structure by resource constraints. In other words resource constraints become an integral part of the *manufacturing apparatus*, that is, the set of manufacturing production processes that rely on natural resources as factor inputs. Not only does resource scarcity become a structural problem, its dynamic character is also revealed. Resources are constraining forces involving all sectors at the same time and over time in both direct and indirect forms. This is why the activation of different orders of techniques along different countries' structural trajectories is no longer a simple matter of production and technological capabilities transformations.

3.   The resources-manufacturing matrix: compound production units, resources sector-specificity and shifting constraints

The adoption of a compound technologies scheme as the critical analytical core of a multi-sectoral model of manufacturing development is a powerful focusing device with respect to a specific set of complex dynamics.

The first of these is related to the relationship between production units, resources constraints and the time required for their renewability. Production processes take place within production units that may be identified at different levels of aggregation, such as the productive establishment, the constellation of establishments, the sub-sector, the sector and, finally, the production system as a whole (Andreoni and Scazzieri, 2013). Depending on the active production units and relative levels of aggregation at which the economic system is operating, a given natural resource may or may not be a constraint. For example, a certain endowment of natural resources may not constitute a constraint for a given sector while it can become a binding constraint as soon as more than one sector relies, both directly and indirectly, on the same type of natural resources. In fact, given a number of active production units operating at a certain level of aggregation, a relative scarcity problem may become absolute scarcity. Thus, resource bottlenecks may unfold at a certain point in time and along a certain country structural trajectory. Even when these natural resources are renewable, the time required for restoring them – i.e. *time renewability* – might be too long to satisfy the pressure that fast manufacturing subsectors may impose on a certain natural resource. This means that given fixed time renewability, production units may be affected by resource availability misalignments over time.

These resource-triggered structural tensions may hinder the pattern of structural change an economy is undergoing and, ultimately, it might force a shift towards a different structural trajectory. The new structural trajectory will be characterized by different 'compound technologies', that is, a different set of active techniques. Moreover as these new techniques will reshape the relationship between manufacturing production and scarcity, a new 'compound production units scheme' will also have to emerge. What we call here a *compound production units scheme* identifies the n active production units and relative levels of aggregation characterizing a multi-sectoral model of manufacturing development under resource constraints.

The complexity introduced by the consideration of different production units can be also extended to an open economy system. In this specific case it was observed how '[w]hat appears a relative scarcity for a single economic system could become historically an absolute scarcity for the planet as whole' (Quadrio-Curzio and Pellizzari, 1999, p. 6). In fact, even those countries that have been lagging behind in terms of their manufacturing development might indirectly face resource constraints in their early stages of industrialization. To the extent developing countries provide industrial value chains and networks at the regional and global levels with intermediate resource inputs, the relevant level of aggregation at which scarcity problems unfold in these countries becomes difficult to identify and delineate geographically. This implies that the political economy of resource constraints involves the domestic structural change and relative institutional-power dynamics as well as linkages among countries along different manufacturing development trajectories.

The second issue that emerges from opening the black box of resource scarcity is that there are different types of natural resources and that the relationships they have with each sector is not a linear one. In fact, it implies a complex set of direct and indirect relationships. Table 22.1 addresses this challenge by proposing a simple *resources-manufacturing matrix* whose architecture is defined by a taxonomy of natural resources (related to certain commodity sectors) and by a standard list of manufacturing subsectors.

Natural resources have been clustered here in three main groups, namely: *soft commodities* (mainly related to different agriculture products and industrial crops), *hard commodities* (including a number of materials coming from mining and quarrying) and, finally, *energy commodities* (both traditional sources such as coal, gas and crude oil, but also nuclear and renewables). Of

Table 22.1: *The resources-manufacturing matrix*

MANUFACTURING APPARATUS, NATURAL RESOURCES		Final consumption inputs	17RB Textiles	23LT Coke, ref. petroleum products & nuclear fuel	15RB Food & beverages	26LT Non-metallic mineral products	24MHT Chemicals & chemical prod (pharmaceutical included)	16RB Tobacco products	27LT Basic metals	20RB Wood products (furniture excluded)
SOFT COMMODITIES A: Agriculture, hunting & forestry B: Fishing	Industrial crops	▓	▓		▓		▓		▓	▓
	Wood	▓					▓			▓
	Cereals	▓			▓					
	Livestock	▓	▓		▓					
	Beverages & other fluids	▓			▓					
	Fisheries	▓			▓					
HARD COMMODITIES C: Mining & quarrying	Stone					▓				
	Sand					▓	▓			
	Precious metals								▓	
	Ferrous metals			▓			▓		▓	
	Non-ferrous metals			▓			▓		▓	
	Rare earths & metals			▓			▓		▓	
ENERGY COMMODITIES C: Mining & quarrying E: Electricity, gas & water supply	Coal			▓						
	Natural gas									
	Crude oil		▓	▓			▓			
	Nuclear	▓		▓						
	Renewables	▓								
Natural structural change pattern peaks (Real GDP per capita, 2005 US$)		**5,000**			**7,000**				**9,000**	

Source: Author

Inputs to industry												
D: Manufacturing												
18& 19RB	21– 22RB	21RB	28LT	36RB	31& 32MHT	25LT	34& 35MHT	29& 30MHT	33MHT	E: Electricity, gas & water supply industries	F: Construction industry
Wearing apparel, fur, leather & footwear	Printing & publishing	Paper & paper products	Fabricated metal products	Furniture; manufacturing n.e.c.	Electrical machinery & apparatus / Radio, TV & communication equipment	Rubber and plastic products	Motor vehicles, trailers & semi-trailers / other transport equipment	Machinery & equipment n.e.c. / Office, accounting & computing machines	Medical, precision & optical instruments		
	11,000	13,000					15,000	27,000			

course, some soft commodities such as palm oil may be used as energy sources and vice versa an energy-related resource such as crude oil is also used as a raw material (substituting industrial crops or livestock) in the wearing apparel and footwear subsector. Thus, there is a certain degree of substitutability among different types of resources.

Manufacturing subsectors have been grouped according to standard industrial codes (ISIC rev. 3) and by adopting a standard technological classification distinguishing Resource Based (RB), Low Tech (LT) and Medium-High Tech (MHT) manufacturing industries. Industries have been then listed along the horizontal axis following a specific sequence, that is, the one that is possible to obtain by tracking the 'normal structural change pattern' experienced by countries in their manufacturing development process. The GDP per capita levels at which the share of the individual manufacturing subsectors peaks in terms of share of total GDP was extracted from a number of empirical studies (Chenery and Syrquin, 1975; Alcorta, Haraguchi and Rezonja, 2013; UNIDO, 2013). The construction and electricity, gas and water supplies industries have been added as part of the secondary sector.

At each intersection of the matrix, a relationship between certain specific natural resources and certain industry subsectors is identified and highlighted in grey in Table 22.1 The manufacturing apparatus is constituted of two kinds of manufacturing subsectors. There are *transformative industries* that process, combine and modify the properties (and, thus, functions) of different kinds of natural resource commodities to obtain a number of raw industrial materials. These materials are then used by *manufacturing industries* to produce an array of intermediate and final products of different kinds (e.g. more or less resource dense). Finally there are a number of natural resources that are consumed with very little (almost no) processing or beneficiation.

This matrix does not pretend to show a full set of input–output flows. Instead it is aimed at considering the different unfolding interdependencies between manufacturing subsectors development and different types of resource constraints. Firstly, resource constraints are sector specific. Moreover, each resource may constraint sectors in more or less direct or indirect ways. For example, materials such as sand are used for producing semiconductors in a certain transformative industry (*direct resource constraint*); semiconductors are then used in the electronics sector to produce basic components such as transistors, cells and integrated circuits (*indirect resource constraint*). Of course, all sectors tend to be more or less directly dependent on energy commodities, although the type of energy source they rely upon may be different according to the technology adopted in the subsectors as well as the stage of economic development of the overall economic system.

The fact that certain sectors that are relatively more important at certain stages of economic development are also relatively more dependent (either directly or indirectly) on specific subsets of natural resources introduces three orders of complexity.

First of all, countries at different stages of structural change will be constrained by different combinations of direct and indirect resource constraints. The resource-manufacturing matrix shows how, at advanced stages of development, countries tend to become directly dependent on a number of natural resources such as rare earths and metals that are critical for the production of subsystems' components or technologies underpinning complex system products. The second problem is that these resources represent a binding constraint since an increasing number of countries enter certain subsectors and increase the production volume of certain complex system products to capture greater manufacturing value and increase their manufacturing resilience. With the exception of two subsectors (Food and Beverages, and Chemicals – including Pharmaceutical) the only manufacturing industries that maintain a contribution to GDP above 1 per cent (from their peak point until highest stages of economic development) are those with the highest scope for technological innovation. Finally, to the extent sectors become vertically disintegrated and modularized production tasks are undertaken by specialized production units in different regions and nations, resource constraints tend to affect countries in more direct or indirect ways according to their specialization patterns. In sum, countries are affected by *shifting resource constraints* along their manufacturing development and specialization patterns.

The last order of complexity is represented by the fact that resources constraints will be shifting also as a result of technical change. In fact, throughout its development, the manufacturing apparatus becomes increasingly able to develop techniques and activate technologies that do not simply shift resource constraints away but also reshape the frontier of production possibilities determined by them. In other words, the manufacturing apparatus changes the nature of resources constraints.

4.   The manufacturing apparatus: turning resources constraints into technological opportunities

The compound technologies scheme on which the previous section's analysis is grounded stresses the need for a truly structural understanding of the relationship linking 'resource scarcity' and 'technological scarcity' within a multi-sectoral production framework. This relationship is described as follows:

technical change (a phenomenon which includes both technical progress and the choice of techniques and technologies) due to choice of techniques is dependent not only on the degree of internal efficiency of each of the single techniques available, but also on the compatibility of the structures of the various techniques, which will be put successively into operation on account of the constraints imposed by the non-produced means of production (Quadrio Curzio, 1986, p. 336).

Given that the definition of techniques incorporates 'scarce natural resources' (this is what is meant by 'non-produced means of production'), resources constraints are structurally embedded in the multi-sectoral technical change dynamics described by this model. This means that technical change is triggered by material structural components of production. These are the constraining natural resources used as factor inputs in the manufacturing apparatus. In this sense, this approach is distinctively 'more structural' with respect to technical change than those multi-sectoral models in which technical change is triggered simply by exogenous production or consumer learning dynamics (e.g. Pasinetti, 1993).

Building on the original idea of 'induced invention' (Hicks, 1932) this model incorporates an idea of 'innovation scarcity', namely the possibility that innovations may be triggered by the scarcity of natural resources (Quadrio Curzio and Pellizzari, 1999). Models of induced innovation like the ones adopted to explain agricultural change (Ruttan and Binswanger, 1978; Quadrio Curzio and Antonelli, 1998; Andreoni, 2011) focus on the changes in relative prices of factors inputs. These alter the signals that the market sends to producers regarding their choice of techniques. Similarly, within a multi-sectoral model of production under resources constraints, the focus is on market prices and rents as specific signals of relative scarcity.

The learning dynamics that have historically led to scarcity-induced technological innovations, as well as broader disruptive technological changes, have been only partially analysed within this framework. Specifically, three main *stylized mechanisms* have been identified. Firstly, the extension of the boundaries of the locations where the natural resources are exploited often requires the development of new technologies (e.g. deep water oil drilling). Secondly, technological change allows the substitution of scarce resources with relatively more abundant natural resources. Finally, the reduction in the use of natural resources and primary commodities per unit of production is the result of the introduction of more efficient techniques that increase resource productivity.

However, in order to go beyond these stylized technical change mechanisms, the concept of *structural learning* appears useful as it allows us to understand in which specific ways, and along which learning trajectories, the manufacturing apparatus is able to turn resources constraints into technological opportunities. The concept of structural learning has been introduced to characterize the continuous process of structural adjustment triggered and orientated by existing productive structures at each point in time (Andreoni, 2014). In particular, the transformation of structural constraints such as resource bottlenecks and technical imbalances into technological opportunities is made possible by the existence of complementarities, similarities and indivisibilities acting as focusing devices within and across sectors.

The process of structural learning in any given sector may in fact develop an inter-sectoral character. In other words, complementarities (as well as innovations that can be applied to similar tasks performed in other productive activities) may spread from one sector or subsector to others, triggering a specific form of structural learning called *inter-sectoral learning*. The latter expression identifies a dynamic process of interlocking and mutual reinforcing technological developments that link the innovative patterns of two or more sectors in a relationship of complementarity and/or similarity. Given that many resources are intermediate inputs in many different manufacturing industries, scarcity-induced technological innovations may transform production activities across sectors. This also implies that one scarcity-induced technological innovation in one sector may be responsible of compulsive sequences of technological transformations across sectors. For example, during the last decade, a number of technical developments in multistage hydraulic fracturing and extended-reach horizontal drilling in a number of manufacturing industries have made the production of shale gas viable and revolutionized the energy sector in the United States. These complex technological systems were only partially triggered by market prices signalling the need to identify new energy commodities.

Economic historians have documented a number of cases of such structural learning dynamics, especially of the inter-sectoral type (Innis, 1957; Rosenberg, 1976, 1982, 1994, 1996; Wright, 1990; David and Wright, 1997). The analytical discussion of these cases is beyond the scope of this short chapter. However, a number of analytical points can be highlighted to show the complexities underpinning scarcity-induced structural learning trajectories and, thus, the relationship between resource scarcity and technological scarcity.

Let's take the structural learning trajectory of the United States as an example (Barnett and Morse, 1963; for more country examples see Wright and Czelusta, 2004; Best, 2001; Bianchi, 2013). In that case the development of the manufacturing apparatus did not merely allow for scarce resource substitutability. In fact, what is even more crucial is the fact that the *range of substitutability among materials* kept expanding over time (Rosenberg, 1976, p. 240). This phenomenon is responsible for an expansion of the range of compound technologies that the economic system can activate. The range of possibilities also tends to expand because manufacturing industries are not bound to specific resources *as such*, but rather to their specific properties and functions. If materials available in greater abundance can substitute the functions performed by other scarce resources, manufacturing industries will substitute them (Scott, 1962).

However, substitution processes require increasing rounds of fixed capital investments and equipment replacement. Without them the manufacturing apparatus is not able to use certain new materials or resources as inputs. Also, since '[t]oday's factor substitution possibilities are made possible by *yesterday's* technological innovations' (Rosenberg, 1976, p. 253), the substitution process made feasible by certain technical advancements might not be viable in historical time or might require a prolonged adjustment period. The possibility that certain feasible techniques are not activated as they do not satisfy conditions of contextual viability is strictly related to the distinction between techniques and technologies (see earlier). Structurally feasible trajectories (development patterns made possible by technological changes or because of resource scarcity) may never unfold in reality if they do not find a viable historical and institutional context (Andreoni and Scazzieri, 2013).

Manufacturing development is a process transforming the structural-technological production system as well as the set of social technologies – i.e. institutions – in which it is embedded. That institutions might be the ultimate constraint in manufacturing development was a point stressed by Simon Kuznets (1965, p. 208) when he said, 'It is the social and political obstacles that are likely to be more serious than our technological capacity', and then restated by Wassily Leontief *et al.* (1977, p. 6): 'The principal limits to sustained growth and accelerated development are political, social and institutional in character rather than physical'. The last concluding section of this chapter addresses the political economy of resources constraints and, thus, deals with the possibility to develop policies beyond resource, technological and institutional scarcity.

5.   Beyond resource, technological and institutional scarcity: the political economy of resources constraints

Today's political economy debate around natural resources constraints is built on a quite simplistic, linear and static understanding of the relationship between resource, technology and institutions. For example, in the context of developing countries, the 'resource curse' thesis has pointed out how natural resource abundance has adverse consequences for economic growth. Alongside various explanations (e.g. Dutch Disease), this thesis builds on the idea that natural resources (especially minerals) tend to be concentrated in 'point resources'. As a result, it is relatively easy to loot them (high risk of 'lootability' and rent capture).

This influential thesis has been recently challenged (Lederman and Maloney, 2007; Morris *et al.*, 2012). The reason why resource-abundant developing countries do not exhibit strong and sustained economic growth has to be found in their condition of 'technological and institutional scarcity', more than in their inescapable resource curse (Chang 2007, 2011). The structural trajectories followed by today's industrialized countries provide very clear historical evidence in support of this argument. In many country cases (e.g. the United States between 1870 and 1910) natural resource abundance was a 'socially constructed' condition (achieved through purposefully designed institutions and policies) more than a geologically preordained one (David and Wright, 1997, p. 203). In the opposite scenario, as stressed by Simon Kuznets (1953, p. 230), 'the have-not societies are poor because they have not succeeded in overcoming scarcity of natural resources by appropriate changes in technology, not because the scarcity of resources is an inexorable factor for which there is no remedy ... this is a matter of social organisation and not of bountifulness or niggardliness of nature'. Despite their different trajectories, these countries stylizations raise the same three fundamental challenges underlying the political economy of resource constraints and developmental policies (Chang et al., 2013; O'Sullivan et al., 2013). Let us look at them through the analytical lenses developed earlier in this chapter.

Countries who successfully developed their manufacturing apparatus (under resources constraints) adopted integrated policy packages combining manufacturing, technology (including institutional) and resource policies. Given the sector specificity of resources and the existence of technological interdependencies across sectors, policy packages have to match and, at the same time, transform the country's specific structural sets of compound technologies, institutions and natural resource constraints. Within a multi-sectoral system, this *transformative matching* can operate in different ways. By targeting different levels of aggregation of production activities, policies can change the compound production units scheme and, thus, the relative conditions of resource scarcity. The intensity as well as selectivity of these policies may vary substantially and can operate both *along* and *across* sectoral value chains. While some of the policies may simply introduce scarcity signals to induce market-driven technological innovation, others may change the rents appropriation mechanism and channel resources towards targeted sectors and technologies (both related and unrelated). The redistribution of resource rents across sectors changes power relationships across (but also within) the same interest groups (Khan and Jomo, 2001). At the same time, it may offer different economic actors a focal point of coordination that sets the conditions for a certain manufacturing development trajectory.

If the integration of manufacturing, technology and resource policies (given certain resources constraints) allows the full exploitation of complementarities among interdependent economic activities *in time*, the possibility of shifting natural resource constraints will depend upon the coordination of complementary activities *over time*. This is why the *synchronization* of resource, manufacturing and technological policies is even more critical than their integration at each point in time. *Policy synchronization* is not trivial as policymakers have to consider a plurality of policy targets and relative trade-offs among them over time. The composition of these trade-offs also generates structural tensions in the form of conflicts among and within interest groups. Moreover, with the expansion of the manufacturing apparatus and the unfolding of new interdependencies, policy synchronization becomes extremely complex as policies can affect both different resources types and manufacturing sub-sectors (Table 22.1). At the same time, a number of new value creation and value capture opportunities associated with shifting resource constraints may emerge. For example, a new technology today may allow the substitution of a certain scarce material in a product system (and complementary products or activities) tomorrow.

With the increasing interconnectedness of different countries' manufacturing apparatuses, specific sectoral trajectories of one country are increasingly intertwined with other countries' same (or different) sectoral trajectory. The same manufacturing sectors in different countries may be more or less directly competing for the same set of scarce resources and being affected by the same set of resource-related risks (Farooki and Kaplinsky, 2011). Because of the increasing dependence of many product systems on scarce resource-based platform technologies, even apparently unrelated sectors in different countries may be constrained more or less directly by the same natural resources. Recent technical studies identify a number of resource-related global risks, such as the increasing scarcity of minerals and metals and the consequent supply instability in specific sectoral value chains; the emergence of a number of disruption processes; the concentration of critical resources in a limited number of countries; finally, the fact that energy critical elements (ECEs) such as Tellurium, Germanium, Platinum and Lithium are now part of a myriad of high tech and environmental equipment, from smart phones, to solar panels to jet engine parts, wind turbines and hybrid cars (DOE, 2010; APS, 2011; EU 2011; Heck and Rogers, 2014).

Within this new complex and multi-polar resource scenario, the possibility of designing and implementing effective developmental policies increasingly depends on the availability of appropriate structural heuristics (Andreoni and Scazzieri, 2013). Among them, the multi-sectoral models of manufacturing development under resources constraints discussed in this chapter have pointed out the analytical and policy challenges posed by various forms of scarcity and the critical importance of embedding resources within structural dynamics frameworks. Not only do multi-sectoral production models allow unpacking structural dynamics of realized manufacturing development trajectories, they also point to the existence of alternative 'still-to-come' patterns. Without such form of structurally grounded virtuality, developmental ways of managing scarcity would remain unexplored.

REFERENCES

Alcorta, L., Haraguchi, N., and Rezonja, G. (2013) 'Industrial Structural Change, Growth Patterns, and Industrial Policy', in J. E. Stiglitz, J. Y. Lin and E. Patel (eds.) *The Industrial Policy Revolution II*, Basingstoke: Palgrave Macmillan, pp. 457–92.

Ames, E., and Rosenberg, N. (1965) 'The Progressive Division and Specialisation of Industries', *Journal of Development Studies*, 1.4, pp. 363–83.

Andreoni, A. (2011) 'Manufacturing Agrarian Change: Agricultural Production, Intersectoral Learning and Technological Capabilities', *DRUID Working Paper Series*, 11.13, pp. 1–36.

  (2013) *Manufacturing Development: Structural Change and Production Capabilities Dynamics*, PhD dissertation, University of Cambridge.

  (2014) 'Structural Learning: Embedding Discoveries and the Dynamics of Production', *Structural Change and Economic Dynamics*, 29.2, June, pp. 58–74.

Andreoni, A., and Scazzieri, R. (2013) 'Triggers of Change: Structural Trajectories and Production Dynamics', *Cambridge Journal of Economics*, 37, doi: 10.1093/cje/bet034. First published online 19 July 2013.

American Physical Society (APS) (2011) *Energy Critical Elements: Securing Materials for Emerging Technologies*, American Physical Society Report, Washington, D. C.: APS Press.

Baranzini, M., and Scazzieri, R. (eds.) (1990) *The Economic Theory of Structure and Change*, Cambridge, Cambridge University Press (pb edn 2012).

Barnett, H., and Morse, C. (1963) *Scarcity and Growth: The Economics of Natural Resource Availability*, Baltimore: Johns Hopkins University Press.

Best, M. (2001) *The New Competitive Advantage. The Renewal of American Industry*, Oxford: Oxford University Press.

Bianchi, P. (2013) *La Rincorsa Frenata. L'Industria italiana dall'Unità alla crisi globale*, Bologna: Il Mulino.

Chang, H.-J. (2007) 'State-Owned Enterprise Reform', UN DESA Policy Notes, New York: United Nations.

  (2011) 'Institutions and Economic Development: Theory, Policy and History', *Journal of Institutional Economics*, 7.4, pp. 473–98.

Chang, H.-J., Andreoni, A., and Kuan, M. L. (2013) 'International Industrial Policy Experiences and the Lessons for the UK', in A. Hughes (ed.) *The Future of UK Manufacturing: Scenario Analysis, Financial Markets and Industrial Policy*, London: UK-IRC.

Chenery, H. B., and Syrquin, M. (1975) *Patterns of Development 1950–1970*, Oxford: Oxford University Press.

Dahmen, E. (1988) 'Development Blocks in Industrial Economics', *Scandinavian Economic History Review*, 36.1, pp. 3–14.

David, P., and Wright, G. (1997) 'Increasing Returns and the Genesis of American Resource Abundance', *Industrial and Corporate Change*, 6.2, pp. 203–45.

DOE (2010) *Critical Materials Strategy*, Washington, DC: US Department of Energy.

EU (2011) 'On the Implementation of the Raw Materials Initiative', European Commission Report, COM (2013) 442.

Farooki, M., and Kaplinsky, R. (2011) *The Impact of China on Global Commodity Prices*, London: Routledge.

Harvey, D., Kellard, M. N., Madsen, J. B., and Wohar, M. E. (2010) 'The Prebisch-Singer Hypothesis: Four Centuries of Evidence', *The Review of Economics and Statistics*, 92.2, pp. 367–77.

Heck, S., and Rogers, M. (2014) *Resource Revolution*, New York: New Harvest.

Hicks, J. (1932) *The Theory of Wages*, London: Macmillan.

Hirschman, A. (1981) *Essays in Trespassing: Economics to Policy and Beyond*, New York: Cambridge University Press.

Innis, H. (1957) *Essays in Canadian Economic History*, Toronto: Ryerson Press.

Kaldor, N. (1985) *Economics without Equilibrium*, New York: ME Sharpe Inc.

Kalecki, M. (1976) *Essays on Developing Economies*, Atlantic Highlands, NJ: Humanities Press.

Khan, M., and Jomo, K. S. (eds.) (2001) Rents, Rent-seeking and Economic Development, Cambridge: Cambridge University Press.

Kuznets, S. (1953) *Economic Change*, London: W.W. Norton.

(1965) *Modern Economic Growth: Rate, Structure and Spread*, New Haven: Yale University Press.

Landesmann, M., and Scazzieri, R. (eds.) (1996) *Production and Economic Dynamics*, Cambridge: Cambridge University Press (2nd edn 2009).

Lederman, D., and Maloney, W. F. (2007) *Natural Resources: Neither Curse nor Destiny*, Washington DC: Stanford University Press.

Leontief, W. (1953) *Studies in the Structure of the American Economy*, New York: Oxford University Press.

Leontief, W., Carter, A.P., and Petri, P. (1977) *The Future of the World Economy*, Oxford: Oxford University Press.

Morris, M., Kaplinsky, R., and Kaplan, D. (2012) 'One Thing Leads to Another – Commodities, Linkages and Industrial Development', *Resources Policy*, 37, pp. 408–16.

O'Sullivan, E., Andreoni, A., Lopez-Gomez, G., and Gregory, M. (2013) 'What is New in the New Industrial Policy? A Manufacturing System Perspective', *Oxford Review of Economic Policy*, 29.2, pp. 432–62.

Pasinetti, L. L. (1981) *Structural Change and Economic Growth*, Cambridge: Cambridge University Press.

(1993) *Structural Economic Dynamics*, Cambridge: Cambridge University Press.

Prebisch, R. (1950) 'The Economic Development of Latin America and its Principal Problems', *Economic Bulletin for Latin America*, 7, New York: United Nations, pp. 1–59.

Quadrio Curzio, A. (1967) *Rendita e distribuzione in un modello economico plurisettoriale*, Milan: Giuffré.

(1986) 'Technological Scarcity: An Essay on Production and Structural Change', in M. Baranzini and R. Scazzieri (eds.) *Foundations of Economics. Structures of Inquiry and Economic Theory*, Oxford and New York: B. Blackwell, pp. 311–38.

Quadrio Curzio, A., and Antonelli, G. (eds.) (1998) *The Agro-technological System Towards 2000*, Amsterdam: North Holland.

Quadrio Curzio, A., and Pellizzari, F. (1999) *Rent, Resources, Technologies*, Berlin: Springer.

Rosenberg, N. (1976) *Perspectives on Technology*, Cambridge: Cambridge University Press.

(1982) *Inside the Black Box, Technology and Economics*, Cambridge: Cambridge University Press.

(1994) 'Energy Efficient Technologies: Past and Future Perspectives', in A. Quadrio Curzio, M. Fortis and R. Zoboli (eds.) *Innovation, Resources and Economic Growth*, Berlin: Springer, pp. 63–82.

(1996) 'The Impact of Technological Change on Resources for Growing Population', in B. Colombo, P. G. Demeny and M. F. Perutz (eds.) *Resources and Population: Natural, Institutional and Demographic Dimensions of Development*, Oxford: Clarendon Press, pp. 113–25.

Ruttan, V. W., and Binswanger, H. (1978) *Induced Innovation: Technology, Institutions, and Development*, Baltimore: Johns Hopkins University Press.

Scitovsky, T. (1954) 'Two Concepts of External Economies', *Journal of Political Economy*. 62.2, pp. 143–51.

Scott, A. (1962) 'The Development of the Extractive Industries', *Canadian Journal of Economics and Political Science*, 28.1, pp. 70–87.

Singer, H. W. (1950) 'The Distribution of Gains between Investing and Borrowing Countries', *American Economic Review*, 40.2, pp. 473–85.

Spaventa, L. (1959) 'Dualism in Economic Growth', *BNL Quarterly Review*, 12.51, pp. 386–434.

UNIDO (2011) *Promoting Industrial Diversification in Resource Intensive Economies*, Vienna: UNIDO.

(2013) *The Industrial Competitiveness of Nations*, Vienna: UNIDO.

Wright, G. (1990) 'The Origins of the American Industrial Success, 1879–1940', *American Economic Review*, 80.4, pp. 651–68.

Wright, G., and Czelusta, J. (2004) 'The Myth of the Resource Course', *Challenge*, 47.2, pp. 6–38.

Part V

Towards a political economy of resources and structural change

23 Resources, scarcities and rents: technological interdependence and the dynamics of socio-economic structures

Roberto Scazzieri, Mauro L. Baranzini and Claudia Rotondi

1. Foreword

This volume has addressed from multiple perspectives the relationship between resources and production in a dynamic framework. This plurality of perspectives goes hand in hand with the commitment of all contributors to a common view of political economy in which structural dynamics plays a central role. The aim of this concluding chapter is to draw together the manifold lines of investigations pursued in the volume, to discuss their common core, and to suggest further lines of research. Three principal fields of inquiry are central in the investigative strategy of the volume:

1 The first is the economic theory of *structural scarcities*. Structural scarcities may derive from different sources. There are structural scarcities associated with natural resources of different types, and those deriving from the use of techniques and technologies (combinations of interdependent techniques) that constrain the processes of capital accumulation along specific trajectories. Structural scarcities have important consequences on income distribution and emphasize the fundamental role of rents and non-proportional dynamics.

2 The second is the analysis of *macroeconomic distribution and growth* when social and institutional factors introduce conditions external to the production sphere and influence resource utilization at the aggregate level. Economic systems may switch from one dynamic trajectory to another depending on the initial configuration of those conditions and its transformation over time.

The three authors – Roberto Scazzieri, Mauro L. Baranzini, and Claudia Rotondi – are primarily responsible, respectively, for the treatment of structural dynamics and structural rents, macroeconomic distribution and growth, and stylized economic history. They are jointly responsible for the overall argument of the chapter, while Roberto Scazzieri is mainly responsible for the conceptual organization of the whole final draft. Roberto Scazzieri is grateful to Alberto Quadrio Curzio for long discussions and stimulating suggestions on the structural analysis of resources and economic dynamics over the span of many years and during the preparation of this chapter. These discussions are part of an ongoing research programme.

3 The third is the *historical evolution of resource utilization patterns*. Economic and technological history shows a great variety of resource types and modes of resource utilization, and often structural change is associated with the switch from one resource base to another. The stylized history of resource utilization emphasizes the mutual influence of scarcities and producibility as economic systems move from one configuration to another in the growth process.

The relationship between scarcities and producibility calls attention to the relationship between resources and socio-economic structures, as alternative configurations of interests in society may lead to different patterns of resource utilization and different dynamic trajectories. In this way, the structural analysis of resources leads to the political economy of resources and structural change.

2.   Resources, structural dynamics and structural rents

2.1   Rents in structural economic theory

The formation of structural rents is associated with changes in the cost-effectiveness of individual techniques (and/or of technologies as collections of interdependent techniques) due to utilization of non-produced resources (these may be considered as a prototype for scarce resources in general). In the structural approach, the determination of the unit wage and of the rate of profit can be explained according to different criteria, which however reflect a common mechanism. This is that productive factors are associated with different degrees of producibility, ranging from the means of production that can be augmented 'almost without any assignable limit, if we are disposed to bestow the labour necessary to obtain them' (Ricardo, 1951 [1817], p. 12) to those means of production, such as natural resources, whose availability cannot be increased from the point of view of economic system as a whole.

In the former case (complete producibility of means of production) it is *structurally possible* to increase the quantity of the given input, while assigning a uniform rate of return (which is often called *uniform rate of net product*) to the different units of that input, as long as the same production technique is in use.[1]

In the latter case (means of production that cannot be produced, or can only be produced within limits), it is *structurally necessary* to envisage that different techniques would be in use above a given scale of production. In this case,

---

[1] This structural condition may lead to a uniform rate of profit in the case of commodities 'on the production of which competition operates without restraint' (Ricardo, [1817] 1951, p. 12).

the price of the commodity produced with multiple techniques must cover the costs of the most expensive technique in use. Therefore the least expensive techniques would generate structural rents over and above the rate of return of the most expensive technique.

Starting from these well-known classical propositions Alberto Quadrio Curzio outlined a theory of 'structural scarcity' and a corresponding theory of 'structural rent' (Quadrio Curzio, 1967, 1975, 1980, 1986, 1987a, 1987b, 1990, 1996), which was completed and systematized in Quadrio Curzio and Pellizzari (1999). According to this theory, a positive rate of profit must be earned on the most costly technique *and* a uniform rate of profit must hold for all techniques in operation. The same is true for the unitary wage. Both the uniform rate of profit and the uniform unit wage can be easily explained by assuming perfect competition. However, it is important bearing in mind that perfect competition is a sufficient but not a necessary condition for a uniform rate of profit and a uniform unit wage. The structural point of view explains why this is so. For the rate of profit accrues to reproducible capital of the same quality in all processes. The same is true for labour if labour is taken to be similarly homogeneous and reproducible.[2]

This means that, if techniques with different rates of return are in operation, the rate of return will be equal to the rate of profit on the most expensive technique, while it will be higher than the rate of profit on all other techniques. This difference between the rates of return of different techniques is a necessary condition for the emergence of structural rents on all 'most efficient' techniques (that is, on all techniques except the most expensive one). However, alternative institutional set-ups may generate alternative constellations of

---

[2] The consideration of reproducibility conditions for a stationary or an expanding economy is central to structural economic analysis. This type of investigation is generally carried out on the basis of simplifying assumptions concerning the length of the reproduction period for the economic system as a whole. As Leontief points out, this approach rests upon the conventional (or pragmatic) choice of the fundamental time unit considered to be relevant for the analysis of reproducibility conditions. In fact, any given economic system would normally include reproduction periods of different lengths, and structured either 'in an integrated fashion, so that in the final analysis the reproduction of each individual element is directly or indirectly dependent on the simultaneous existence of all the other elements', or 'it may be seen as a composite structure in which the whole consists of several independently reproducible groups' (Leontief, [1928] 1991, p. 185). The differences in the reproduction periods of different elements of a production economy (for example, differences in the reproduction periods of different types of capital goods) are at the root of the distinction between stocks and flows and are at the origin of the distinction between the analytical representation of the economy as a scheme of inter-sectoral flows (Leontief, 1941), and the analytical representation of the economy as a collection of stocks connected with one another along the time dimension (von Neumann, 1937). Nicholas Georgescu-Roegen highlighted this distinction while calling attention to the need of a representation capable of combining the consideration of inter-sectoral flows with recognition that reproduction periods are normally different for different components of the economy (Georgescu-Roegen, 1971, 1990).

rates of profit and rates of rent depending on market conditions, property and taxation regimes, and limitations upon the use of scarce resources. In short, technical or 'structural' income categories should be distinguished from 'institutional' income categories.[3] This distinction is at the root of the distinction between (structural) order of efficiency and (institutional) order of rentability originally introduced by Quadrio Curzio (1977, 1980).

The analytical framework outlined here has been developed by considering a single commodity (raw material) obtained by using a given non-produced resource and examining the income distribution between wages, profits and rents on a dynamic path. The final stage is reached when the unit product associated with the less efficient method of production using the non-produced resource under consideration just covers the unit wage and nothing is left on it for either profits or rents. In a multi-sectoral economic system, the implications of this point of view are far-reaching. In particular, a change of the rate of profit or of the unit wage may affect the price system in two different ways: (i) without inducing any change in the order by which techniques are activated one after the other; (ii) by inducing changes in the activation order, and therefore also changes in the relative rentability ranking of the processes producing a given commodity. The number of these last processes can also change according to the scale limits associated with the available quantity of each non-produced means of production.

The structural theory of variable returns and rents, as first conjectured by Sraffa (1960), was developed by Quadrio Curzio into a new theory of structural scarcities and rents both under single-period and dynamic conditions (Quadrio Curzio 1980, 1986, 1987a, 1990, 1996, 1998). This theory was systematized in Quadrio Curzio and Pellizzari (1999) by also highlighting a number of lines of investigation for further research. The starting point of the theory is a structural system of $k + m$ equations. The first k equations ($h = 1,\ldots,k$) concern the same commodity ('corn') produced by a different natural resource ('land') t_h ($h = 1,\ldots,k$), and generating a rent (r_h) that will be greater the higher the degree of utilization of resource t_h. On the last plot of land ($t_h = t_k$) there is no rent (rent being of a differential nature). The k equations are augmented by the m equations, each one expressing the input–output relation for the other m commodities produced in the economy. This structural system allows the determination of the $m+1$ prices, the rate of profit and the unitary wage (one of the two must be exogenously given in Sraffa's approach), the k rates of rent per unit of land. The price of the commodity directly produced with a non-produced resource is chosen as *numéraire* and rent on the less

[3] The consequences of this distinction are far-reaching. For example, structural rents *may* or *may not* generate actual distributional rents depending on a variety of institutional conditions, such as specific property rights, tax arrangements, and so on.

efficient process utilizing land is set equal to zero. Variations of the unit wage (w) and/or of the profit rate (π) will have a direct influence on rents also by changing the orders of efficiency and 'rentability' of the processes using the same non-produced resource. As a consequence, changes in the process that yields zero rent come to complicate the w/π relationship and the overall price system.

The above point of view is central to the structural theory of distribution and growth if non-produced resources are explicitly considered. It must be emphasized that in a structural approach non-produced resources are not necessarily associated with decreasing returns to the scale of productive activity. Non-produced resources and structural rents lead to the activation of production techniques according to a given sequence. If this sequence is determined by the order of rentability of the different techniques, it does not necessarily follow that techniques will be activated from the most to the least efficient one since the reverse sequence of activation is also possible.

Indeed, activating techniques according to the order of rentability does not always presuppose a tendency to decreasing returns, as rents may accrue to the techniques (the 'lands') that have been made more productive through the introduction of improvements (see, on this point, the analysis by James Anderson, 1777). However, what came to be known as the classical formulation of rent theory made rents to depend on the assumption of decreasing returns from land and other non-produced inputs such as mines (Malthus, 1815a and 1815b; Ricardo, 1815). This may explain why the structural analysis of non-produced resources and rents is mostly undertaken in historical periods in which the scarcity of resources is acutely felt, and decreasing returns from land or other non-produced resources are emphasized (such as the age of Napoleonic Wars, the coal scarcity fear of the 1860s, the 1970s oil-shock). However, structural theory in its most recent formulations provides a comprehensive analysis of the relationships between scale and productive efficiency both for the decreasing and increasing efficiency cases as activity levels are varied (Quadrio Curzio, 1980, 1986, 1990; Scazzieri, 1993a; 2014).

2.2   *Resources, technology and structural rents*

The contemporary reappraisal of the concept of 'rent' in economic theory is to a large extent a contribution of structural economic analysis. As a matter of fact, with the exception of Sraffa's *Production of Commodities by Means of Commodities* (Sraffa, 1960): '[t]he attention given by theoretical models to natural resources, their scarcity, rent, non-produced and scarce means of production, and their quasi-rent was negligible. Basically, almost all post-war economic theory considered these problems irrelevant, or at least secondary' (Quadrio Curzio and Pellizzari, 1999, p. 31). Quadrio Curzio's contribution was the first to provide a systematic development and generalization of the structural analysis of non–produced resources (considered as a prototype for scarce resources that are fully utilized and cannot be increased in a predictable way). The analysis of the structural conditions for the emergence of rents, and of the dynamics of rents over time, has been central to this research programme since its very beginning. Quadrio Curzio has investigated the structural relationships between non-produced resources, rents and technical changes emphasizing the inherently 'open' (and to a large extent context-dependent) character of structural change due to the influence of appropriable resources available in limited amounts. This analysis is based on two fundamental premises: (i) the introduction of primary productive factors (different from labour), or more generally of non-reproducible or non-produced productive factors, in a structural model of production interdependencies; (ii) the consideration of rents as special incomes associated with the availability of different techniques of production for any given commodity whose production requires the utilization of non-produced, scarce and essential inputs. Quadrio Curzio's contribution focuses on the interrelations between the price-distribution system and the quantity system of different produced commodities in so far as both systems depend on the existence of interdependent techniques and technologies. In this analytical framework, full account of structural interdependencies under conditions of limited availability of non-produced resources requires building upon the contributions of Wassily Leontief, Jan von Neumann and Piero Sraffa along new and to a large extent unexplored lines of inquiry. Leontief's emphasis is on the physical interdependence of productive sectors (Leontief, [1928] 1991, 1941; Leontief, Chenery et al., 1953), Sraffa's attention is mainly for the analysis between values, prices and income distribution in single-period situations (Sraffa, 1960), and von Neumann's contribution relates to the mathematical conditions for economic growth at the maximum rate (von Neumann, 1937). The central features of the structural theory of scarcity as developed by Quadrio Curzio are set out below:

1 Rent becomes the critical factor in determining income distribution, so that the order of priority between rents, profits and wages is significantly changed relative to the classical (mainly Ricardian) scheme in which total wages (based on the 'natural' wage rate) are determined first, then total rents and total profits are determined residually from a net product whose splitting (between rents and profits) is determined by a variety of factors associated both with the structure of production and institutional conditions. The approach of structural analysis to income distribution also differs from that of the post-Keynesian theory, according to which the rate of profit allowing full-employment investment is determined first, while wages are a kind of residual (with upper and lower bounds to its range of variation). Here, instead, structural rent is fundamentally

determined by technological conditions through the efficiency ranking of techniques, the scale of production, and the structure of production. This means that, given the rate of profit, it is possible to determine the order of efficiency and the order of rentability of production processes using non-produced resources (NPR), but also that the order of rentability and the rents on each process can change as the scale of production is varied.

2 The concepts of 'global technologies' and of 'splitting technical coefficients' are introduced. This is done by dropping the one-to-one correspondence between production techniques and produced commodities and introducing a special category of technical coefficients that allows for the 'splitting' of the productive contribution of each resource-using process according to the different techniques in use for that process (corn inputs delivered by technique I would thus be treated as different inputs from corn delivered by technique II). This way of representing production technology allows for the analysis of continuous variations of the scale, structure and efficiency of production when production activity is carried out by any number of processes using non-produced resources as inputs (Quadrio Curzio, 1987a, 1990, 1996; Quadrio Curzio and Pellizzari, 1999).

3 The concept of 'compound (or composite) technologies' is introduced. This is done by defining 'compound (or composite) technology' as a combination of multiple fixed-coefficient techniques, each of which is limited in scale by the need of using a non-produced resource (NPR). This means that any given technique, after reaching its own maximum scale of production (as a result of the accumulation of internally generated net products), enters a stationary state. However, its vector of net products provides the initial inputs to other techniques that may in turn be introduced to overcome the upper bounds upon the scale of the technique that had first been in use. This process is repeated as the scale of production expands, which leads to compound (or composite) technologies consisting of an increasing number of techniques (Quadrio Curzio 1986, 1990, Quadrio Curzio and Pellizzari, 1999).

4 Different types of rent are discussed pointing out that, while surplus rent and structural rent depend on the different fertility of lands on which two simultaneous processes produce the same commodity,

> 'technological rent' . . . takes into consideration broader dynamic aspects of technology. These latter aspects emerge as effect of some scarcities generated by either increased levels of production or changes in income distribution or movements in the order of efficiency between processes that make use of scarce resources. (Quadrio Curzio and Pellizzari, 1999, p. 32; see also Quadrio Curzio, 1990)

The concept of 'technological rent' is central from the point of view of structural theory in so far as it calls attention to the conditions for the emergence of rents in the interdependencies among productive sectors (or processes) rather than in the relative scarcities of different resources.[4]

2.3   Natural scarcities, technological scarcities and uneven dynamics

The structural analysis of non-produced resources (NPRs) and rents suggests a fresh look at the dynamics of economic systems under natural or technological scarcities. The task is that of solving the *dilemma* of choosing among means of production and commodities that are reproducible without limits and those that are not. This is done within a long-term time horizon, or even in terms of an infinite-time horizon. This duality may generate a path of uneven dynamics, in which periods of sustained growth are followed by periods of slowdown or stationary state. As a matter of fact,

One of the cornerstones of the production schemes *à la* von Neumann, *à la* Leontief, or *à la* Sraffa is that, with the accumulation of the entire surplus, the rate of growth of production and surplus coincide and remain constant ... One of the cornerstones of the economic dynamics with non-produced means of production is ... the absence of the above identities, and the change over time of the rates of growth. (Quadrio Curzio and Pellizzari, 1999, p. 33; see also Quadrio Curzio, 1986, 1990.)

The uneven dynamics of economic systems using non-produced means of production is due to technological complementarities within compound technologies; that is, among fixed-coefficient techniques that are kept disconnected one from the other, though they remain linked over time in so far as the activation of any new technique takes place by using means of production that are generated as net products by already active techniques that cannot grow any further after having reached full utilization of their NPR. There will therefore be techniques under conditions of stationary state whose net products are accumulated into new techniques that make use of NPRs for which the scarcity threshold has not been attained yet (Quadrio Curzio, 1986, 1990; Quadrio Curzio and Pellizzari, 1999).

Under these conditions, economic growth takes place at rates that may be different for different produced commodities and different time periods. This raises the issue of structural compatibility among different subsystems of techniques within any given economic system.[5] In particular, the dynamic

---

[4] The concept of 'technological rent' had partially been anticipated by the analysis of 'quasi rents' originating within manufacturing production when certain produced inputs (such as machines) are temporarily in short supply, so that processes of different unit costs may be carried out side by side within the same productive establishment or the same industry (see Marshall, 1961 [1890]; Sraffa, 1960; see also Mangoldt, 1863, and Nazzani, 1872).

[5] The identification of production subsystems from a single-period point of view is discussed in Sraffa (1960; Appendix 'On Subsystems'). The utilization of subsystems as tools for dynamic analysis is often associated with consideration of the way in which 'local' changes generate

process generates residuals, that is, net products that cannot be used in the accumulation process. This point of view calls attention to the role of 'technological scarcity', which may derive both by the limited availability of NPRs and by the limited availability of 'new techniques' in which the net product of techniques in stationary state can be invested without leaving non-accumulated residuals (Quadrio Curzio, 1986, 1990; Quadrio Curzio and Pellizzari, 1999).

The structural analysis of non-produced resources and economic dynamics leads to the identification of complex patterns of interdependence among wages, profits and rents, and shows that manifold combinations of interests across different groups of income earners are possible depending on specific conditions of economic dynamics and production technology. In particular, the emergence of residuals due to the mismatching of techniques within a given production technology rules out 'the possibility of determining in advance the evolution of the distributive shares' and brings about 'a great variety of antagonisms between the different categories of income earners' (Quadrio Curzio and Pellizzari, 1999, p. 202).

The complexity of the distributional outcomes associated with the consideration of non-produced resources and rents deeply modifies the traditional approach to income distribution between profits and wages. In particular, the reconstruction of any given historical context is necessary if one has to determine, by means of structural economic theory, the existence of conflict or compatibility among different categories of income and/or social groups.

Finally, the analysis of structural dynamics centred on the interdependence between productive sectors or processes when non-produced resources are used calls attention to the distinction between *technical progress*, defined as efficiency improvement within specific production processes, and *technological progress*, defined as efficiency improvement for a compound production technology as a whole (Quadrio Curzio, 1986, 1990; Quadrio Curzio and Pellizzari, 1999).[6] Technical progress is possible even if the efficiency of production technology is unchanged. However, this case could

---

macroeconomic outcomes, and *vice versa* (Simon and Ando, 1961; Simon, 1962; Ando and Fisher, 1963; Goodwin and Punzo, 1987; Goodwin and Landesmann, 1996; Landesmann and Scazzieri, 1996c). The way in which 'single-period' representations of production interdependencies may capture the transformation of those interdependencies under technical progress is discussed in Pasinetti (1962b, 1965, 1973); Gossling (1972); Hicks (1985); Landesmann and Scazzieri (1993); see also Hagemann, Landesmann and Scazzieri (2003). The system-subsystem dynamics that may be generated under scarcity conditions and through the interdependencies between partially incompatible subsystems was identified by Quadrio Curzio (1975, 1986, 1990) and is discussed in this chapter.

[6] The distinction between *technical progress* and *technological progress* was introduced by Quadrio Curzio in a number of essays published at various dates and collected in Quadrio Curzio (1990), and it was given final shape in Quadrio Curzio and Pellizzari (1999). According to this distinction, technical progress is the set of 'changes that bring about an increase in the physical efficiency of a single technique', whereas technological progress is the set of changes

make it impossible to accumulate a greater net product into the new technique due to the weaker structural compatibility among techniques activated over time. On the other hand increased structural compatibility (*technological progress*) among techniques is possible independently of technical progress for any specific technique. As a result, increased net product accumulation and higher growth rates are possible even if the effectiveness of individual techniques does not vary.

The distinction between technical progress and technological progress has far-reaching consequences for what concerns the structural dynamics of economic systems, in so far as the accumulation and growth potential of any given system is significantly affected by the specific combination of technical progress and technological progress that prevails at any given stage of its history.[7] The same distinction also influences the dynamics of structural income distribution among the different categories of income earners, and determines to a significant extent the attitude of those groups to different forms of technical or technological progress.

3.   Social distribution and rents in the macro-economy

3.1   Saving propensities and macroeconomic growth

The analysis of income distribution and economic dynamics can be carried out by following two distinct yet complementary paths. On the one hand, it is possible to concentrate on the structural interdependencies between productive sectors or processes in order to identify the technological conditions for the expansion of any given economic system and to assess which types of income distribution are compatible with those conditions and their consequences. On the other hand, it is possible to directly concentrate on the relationship between income distribution and macroeconomic growth.

These two approaches are complementary yet should be kept distinguished. Macroeconomic schemes are fundamental both for examining the aggregate behaviour of social classes and the institutional decisions and policy measures that in turn affect economic variables. Structural schemes are fundamental to explain the dynamics of the interdependent productive, technical and price-distribution variables that affect macroeconomic variables while also being affected by them.

'that bring about an increase in the physical efficiency of a compound technology' (Quadrio Curzio and Pellizzari, 1999, p. 208).

[7] It may be argued that not only technological progress but also technical progress (as defined above), and the technical learning at its root, may reflect structural compatibilities (or lack thereof) within existing production arrangements (Rosenberg, 1969; Andreoni, 2014).

In particular, the formation of rent as a result of specific property rights is central in the macroeconomic theory of distribution and growth. This point of view emphasizes the relationship between saving formation and the distribution of income, highlights the link between saving propensities and wealth accumulation, and addresses the issue of alternative saving and bequest patterns leading to the formation or disappearance of socio-economic classes. The origins of this approach are to be found in the literature on dynamic macroeconomic theory. When in the late 1930s and in the 1940s the first macroeconomic models of economic growth were developed, the theory of income distribution was caught in an impasse, represented by the well-known Harrod-Domar equilibrium condition $s=n(K/Y)$, where s is the aggregate saving ratio, n the natural rate of growth, and K/Y the capital/output ratio. If these three variables were all constant, then it is unlikely that the Harrod-Domar condition could be satisfied. Hence, in order to have a model in which the possibility of steady growth is assured, it is necessary to relax one or another of the assumptions. The equality between s and $n(K/Y)$ may be obtained by (a) flexibility in K/Y, the technology assumption that was primarily adopted by the marginalist or neoclassical school; (b) flexibility in s, the saving assumption, which was originally put forward by Nicholas Kaldor (1955–6), and later taken up by Luigi L. Pasinetti (1962a); and (c) flexibility in n, which was initially labelled as the labour-market and/or labour-supply assumption, and later taken up by neoclassical economists, giving rise to the so-called endogenous growth models developed from the 1980s onwards. We now know for sure (see Mari, 2010) that Nicholas Kaldor presented his Keynesian theory of income distribution at a meeting of the Secret Seminar that took place in Ruth Cohen's rooms in Newnham College on Monday 31 October 1955. Assuming that there exist in the economic system two constant and different saving rates, one for the workers' class and one for the capitalists' (or entrepreneurs') class, Kaldor was able to formulate the equilibrium rate of profits of the system keeping in equilibrium the *ex ante*–determined full-employment investment with *ex post* total savings of the system. But in order to obtain the so-called Cambridge equation $P/K=n/s_c$, Kaldor had to assume, along classical lines, that the propensity to save of the workers' class is equal to zero. His analysis drew a lot of attention; but it was hampered by his very restrictive assumption of zero saving out of wages.

In 1962 Luigi Pasinetti generalized this outcome, and showed that even if *both* saving rates were positive, the equilibrium rate of profits is totally independent of the saving behaviour of the working class. It is in fact determined only by the saving rate of the pure capitalists (s_c) and by the rate of growth of the system (n). The solution for the rate of profits $P/K=n/s_c$ was soon labelled as the *Kaldor-Pasinetti's Theorem* or (*New*) *Cambridge Equation*. (By the same token the share of profits in national income comes to be equal to

$P/Y = (n/s_c)K/Y$. Such a rate of profits is, however, independent of the production function and of the capital/output ratio. In this way the Cambridge (or Post-Keynesian) School was in a position to:[8]

a) Provide a solution to the Harrod-Domar dilemma by specifying an aggregate saving ratio determined by the exogenously given rate of growth of population, the capital/output ratio and capitalists' propensity to save.
b) Determine the long-period equilibrium value of the rate of profits, the distribution of income between profits and wages, and the distribution of disposable income between the classes.
c) Allow for the existence of an income residual (very much in line with classical and neo-Ricardian models) namely the wages, consistent with the assumption of a relationship between the savings of that class of individuals (the capitalists or entrepreneurs) who determine the process of production and the patterns of capital accumulation.
d) Provide valuable insights into the process of accumulation of capital by specifying the equilibrium capital shares of the socio-economic classes.

The decisions relative to investment and growth of the productive system then comes to be taken by a sort of 'entrepreneurial *élite*'. The case of our modern and post-industrial societies is quite illuminating: public authorities, *via* their fiscal and monetary policies, try to reach a predetermined 'required' rate of growth for the system that will allow them both to check public expenditure and to reach other economic policy goals. Wages are hence an 'endogenous' residual; full employment investment determines profits, not *vice versa*. The model has been extended to include numerous sub-lines of research, as has been pointed out in Quadrio Curzio (1972, 1993b), Baranzini and Mari (2011) and Baranzini and Mirante (2013).

3.2   Rent, income distribution and the dynamics of socio-economic classes

The macroeconomic approach to rent formation considers rent incomes a result of saving behaviour and specific property rights. This approach concentrates attention upon the different ways in which savings from disposable income can be used and introduces a distinction between income from productive investment (profit) and income from ownership of wealth (rent). This point of view emphasizes the relationship between saving formation and the distribution of income, highlights the link between saving propensities and wealth accumulation, and addresses the issue of alternative saving and bequest patterns leading

---

[8] Mauro Baranzini is indebted to Sir James Alexander Mirrlees, who was his thesis supervisor in Oxford, on this point.

to the formation or disappearance of socio-economic classes. The line of research that introduces rent in a macro-economic model has been followed by various authors, starting with analytical hints in Keynes, Robinson, Kaldor and Pasinetti. In particular, these developments have considered the relationship between the accumulation of savings giving rise to wealth assets and the generation of rent as a share of national income. Pasinetti (1977b, p. 58) suggested a model with two classes of savers (workers and capitalists-rentiers) and three categories of income (wages, profits and rents). He argues that in this case the equilibrium rate of profits, provided that the Samuelson and Modigliani's Dual Theorem does not apply, is determined by the formula $P/K=n/[(1+\beta)s_c]$ where P/K and n are the rate of profits and the natural rate of growth respectively, s_c is the saving propensity of the capitalists-rentiers and β is the 'long-run ratio of total rent to capitalists' profits'.

The long-run income distribution along the steady state, full employment path of an economy that starts the accumulation process with three categories of income (wages, profits and rents) and three classes of savers (workers, capitalists and rentiers) yields to the discovery of interesting features of economic dynamics. Consider a model with three distinct classes of savers, in which equilibrium growth with full employment is determined by the natural rate of growth and by the rentiers' propensity to save (see Baranzini and Scazzieri, 1997). The solution of this model yields one degree of freedom with regard to the determination of the interest rate and of the ratio of total rents to rentiers' profits. In other words the conditions for equilibrium growth determine the ratio of rentiers' total income to the rentiers' capital stock, but leaves undetermined the composition of their income between rent and interest on accumulated savings. This investigation leads to the discovery of an important dichotomy inherent to an economic system with three different classes of savers. On the one hand we find that the capitalists' propensity to save remains the central feature as long as the capital share of the rentiers is irrelevant. As soon as the system allows for the rise of a rentiers' class, with a positive capital share, in the very long run the capitalists' capital share tends asymptotically to zero: this leads to a socio-economic structure characterized by the presence of workers and rentiers only. It is worth examining this situation in more detail.

Let us consider an economic system in which total net income, Y, is divided into wages, profits and rent; and total net savings are divided into three categories: workers' savings (S_w), capitalists' savings (S_c) and rentiers' savings (S_r). Workers receive wage and profit payments, the latter in the form of interest on their accumulated savings. Capitalists are pure profit-earners. Rentiers receive interest on their accumulated savings and, at the same time, receive a rent. The term 'rent' refers, in the present framework, to a range of incomes that may include, among others, Ricardian rents and monopolists' extra-profits. Such a general formulation may be justified by the fact that the purpose of these kinds of analyses is that of studying those characteristics of steady-state growth that do not depend on the differences among all such incomes. In addition, we focus on the long-run distribution compatible with steady growth, so that this definition of rent is independent of any particular assumption about production technology. For instance, the long-term steady-state conditions have to be satisfied in the cases both of decreasing and of constant-returns technology. Social classes, as usual, are supposed to be intergenerationally stable, with s_w, s_c and s_r denoting, respectively, the saving propensies oif the workers, capitalists and rentiers (where $0 \leq s_w < s_c$, $s_r \leq 1$) By denoting P_w, P_c and P_r, the amount of profits received respectively by workers, capitalists and *rentiers*, and K_w, K_c and K_r, the capital stock owned by the same classes, it is possible to write the savings equation as follows: $S = S_c + S_w + S_r = s_c r K_c + s_w (r K_w + W) + s_r (r K_r + r K_r \delta)$, where the variables r and δ are the rate of profits and the long-run ratio of total rent to *rentiers'* profits (R/P_r) respectively.[9] The last term may be rewritten as $s_r \phi K_r$; in this way, $\phi = r(1+\delta)$ becomes the long-run ratio of *rentiers'* income to their capital stock. Solving the model by setting *ex-ante* investment equal to the *ex-post* determined savings, in long-run equilibrium one obtains the following solutions (or combinations of them) for the rate of profits (r), the income/capital ratio (Y/K), and the long-run ratio of rentiers' income to their capital stock (ϕ) respectively: $r = n/s_c$, $Y/K = n/s_w$, $\phi = n/s_r$.

The first solution is the well-known Cambridge Equation, as originally formulated by Kaldor (1955–56) and extended by Pasinetti (1962a) to the case of a positive workers' propensity to save. The second solution corresponds to Meade-Samuelson-Modigliani's Dual Theorem, which applies only under very restrictive conditions of an extremely high workers' propensity to save. The third solution may be defined as the rentiers' long-run equilibrium. In this case, the long-run ratio of rentiers' income to their capital stock, ϕ, is equal to the long-run equilibrium rate of growth divided by the propensity to save of the rentiers' class. This result is therefore independent of production technology and of the saving propensities of the other two socio-economic classes. In this case the capitalists' share of the capital stock falls to zero, so that only the workers and the rentiers end up owning a positive share of capital. Table 23.1 shows the long-run capital shares of the three classes of savers in the case of long-run equilibrium.

---

[9] This relation might seem at odds with the established view that rent does not derive from the ownership of a capital stock; however it is important to stress that it is simply an *ex-post* analytical relation that does not represent the process of rent determination; it refers instead to the link that exists between rent and *rentiers'* capital stock (both life-cycle and intergenerational) when *rentiers* contribute a positive share of overall savings.

Table 23.1 *Long-run capital share of the three classes*

Long-run equilibrium condition	K_w/K (workers' share)	K_c/K (capitalists' share)	K_r/K (*rentiers'* share)
$r=n/s_c$	$s_w \dfrac{s_c Y/K - n}{n(s_c - s_w)}$	$s_c \dfrac{n - s_w Y/K}{n(s_c - s_w)}$	0
$Y/K = n/s_w$	1	0	0
$\phi = n/s_r$	$s_w \dfrac{s_r Y/K - n}{n(s_r - s_w)}$	0	$s_r \dfrac{n - s_w Y/K}{n(s_r - s_w)}$

The implications of the results obtained within this three-class framework are worth discussing in some detail. It seems to us that our analysis brings to the fore a number of noteworthy features of the dynamic path that may be followed by a capitalist economy that is subject to intense structural dynamics. This is bound to show a pattern of differentiation among diverse flows of income and wealth, with the emergence of rent as a category of income characteristically associated with technological disequilibria and market asymmetries. This investigation shows the inherent instability of the three-class configuration (workers, capitalists and rentiers) and the existence of alternative long-run equilibria corresponding to different socio-economic structures. One case (which sees the coexistence of entrepreneurs and workers) corresponds to the classical situation of a capitalist economy. Another case (workers only) corresponds to a worker-owned economy in which pure capitalists and rentiers have disappeared. The latter socio-economic structure points to the possibility of some kind of 'capitalists' euthanasia' along an expanding path, a situation to be compared and constrasted with Keynes's '*rentiers'* euthanasia' within the framework of a mature economic system (see Keynes, 1936, Chapter 24).

3.3   *The macroeconomic and the structural approaches to rent formation*

The macroeconomic and the structural approaches to rent formation call attention to different features of rents relative to the economic system as a whole. In particular, the macroeconomic approach emphasizes the connection between the formation of rents and the existence of a rentiers' class whereas the structural approach emphasizes the relationship between formation of rents and technological interdependencies among productive sectors. The two approaches are complementary in so far as dynamics affecting inter-sectoral relationships influence macroeconomic conditions (for instance through changes in the growth potential of the economy), while changes in macroeconomic variables (such as changes in the overall scale of the economy) may require necessary transformations in the relative proportions of productive sectors and in their pattern of interdependence.

The inter-sectoral approach examines structural relationships of the techno-logical type that are to a large extent independent of behavioural or insti-tutional conditions (for example, technological rents can arise from productive interdependencies independently of which individuals or groups are able to appropriate them). On the other hand, the macroeconomic approach is based on relationships of the behavioural or institutional type such as saving propensities, or attitudes and institutions influencing the intergenerational transfer of wealth. These relationships are independent of specific techno-logical conditions (for example, financial rents can arise from wealth assets either of the physical or immaterial type). The inter-sectoral and macroeco-nomic theories call attention to features of rent formation that are often combined in any given historical context. For example, the opportunities and constraints generated by natural or technological scarcities are structural fea-tures that may or may not be realized depending on behavioural or institutional conditions. Likewise, macroeconomic rents may or may not be sustainable depending on whether long-run total rent (and therefore also the long-run ratio of total rent to *rentiers'* profits R/P_r) is compatible with the overall income (net product) produced in the economic system.

4.   Accumulation, multi sectoral linkages and variable returns to activity levels

Economic systems subject to successively binding resource constraints are bound to follow one or another among the feasible trajectories compatible with those constraints. It is important to realize that this point of view is completely different from the one usually associated with the study of resource allocation among alternative objectives. For in the latter case resources become more costly as they become scarcer, so that the direct impact of physical constraints can be avoided. On the other hand, the consideration of binding physical constraints makes visible complementarities and bottlenecks that would otherwise be overlooked. Structural theory is to this day the most comprehensive attempt to investigate the impact of scarcities upon production economies without assuming that economic behaviour guided by the substitu-tion principle would allow the circumvention of those physical bottlenecks. That theory is thus an important heuristic device when trying to assess the influence of unfolding constraints upon the dynamics of economic systems.

Natural and technological scarcities may or may not have a direct impact on the actual dynamics of economic systems, depending on the existing social structures and institutional arrangements. However, structural analysis allows the identification of the trajectories of structural change that would make existing natural or technological scarcities compatible (or incompatible) with desired levels of employment and rates of economic growth. From this point of view, structural analysis can provide an analytical benchmark useful to assess the feasibility and effectiveness of specific policy measures under given social and institutional constraints. A given availability of non-produced resources may or may not have a direct impact on income distribution depending on the characteristics of the production structure. Similarly, the existence of constraints upon the availability of non-produced resources may have different consequences depending on which institutional set-up is considered. For example, an institutional set-up giving priority to a long time horizon is likely to generate a configuration of diminishing returns different from the one associated with an institutional set-up giving priority to a short time horizon.

We may conjecture that short and long time horizons would be associated with different ways of ranking production structures, and thus with different trajectories of growth and variable returns. The consideration of a sequence of binding constraints on the availability of non-produced resources makes it possible to identify a *range* of feasible paths of structural change compatible with the historically given availability of non-produced resources. Any such path would reflect both resources availability under given conditions and the specific ranking of production structures under those conditions.[10]

As we have seen in Sections 2.1 and 2.2, natural or technological scarcities may lead to trajectories of diminishing or increasing efficiency depending upon whether the dominant role of scarcities is in bringing about less efficient (more costly) techniques or technologies, or (alternatively) in inducing the switch to (a) more efficient techniques (*technical progress*), or (b) to more efficient technologies resulting from better structural compatibility between the subsystems of any given compound (or composite) technology (*technological progress*). In either case, it is the scaling up of the economic system that brings about the closing down (*scale-technology contraction*) or opening up (*scale-technology expansion*) of technical and technological opportunities (Scazzieri, 1993a, 1999, 2014).

Structural analysis allows the reconstruction of scale-dependent trajectories of structural change by following three steps: (i) identification of the resource constraints relevant to the economic system under consideration; (ii) recognition of the alternative ranking criteria (of techniques and technologies) that may be followed in that system; (iii) identification of the alternative trajectories of structural change that the economic system may follow depending on which

---

[10] The distinction between the trajectories that are structurally feasible and those that are actually followed by any given economic system is central to the analysis of Adolph Lowe (Lowe, 1954, 1965, 1969, 1976; see also Gehrke and Hagemann, 1996; Scazzieri, 1998). Lowe devotes special attention to the fact that structural analysis points to the existence both of feasibility constraints *and* of degrees of freedom for economic policy once the full range of the structurally feasible options is acknowledged (see also Sylos Labini, 1984; Scazzieri, 2007).

specific ranking criterion is considered. Economic systems may switch from one trajectory to another by substituting one ranking criterion for another. This change of ranking criterion would often be associated with the substitution of one institutional and industrial set-up for another as the different ways in which technological alternatives are ranked may reflect alternative time horizons for policy making.

The aforementioned relationships between different types of scale-dependent structural change has been emphasized by Alberto Quadrio Curzio, who noted that production systems using non-produced essential resources are likely to generate a complex structural dynamics in which periods of decline in the maximum growth rate that the economic system may achieve may be interrupted by periods of an *increasing* maximum growth rate due to a better fit between the different subsystems within the production system under consideration (Quadrio Curzio, 1975, 1980, 1986, 1990; Quadrio Curzio and Pellizzari, 1999). An important result of this type of structural analysis that the formation of rent does not presuppose diminishing returns. For the formation and dynamics of rents on a growth trajectory mainly depend on the order of efficiency of production techniques, their order of rentability, the size and structure of net products available for accumulation but not necessarily immediately accumulated because of their structure vis-à-vis that of the different techniques in use.

The analytical representation of productive structures by means of compound (or composite) technologies brings to the fore the way in which natural or technological scarcities may determine structural conditions of scale-technology contraction or expansion. This can be seen as follows. Let $\mathbf{q}$ $(\mathbf{I})$ be the vector of the quantities of commodities produced by operating the production processes represented by technology matrix $\mathbf{A(I)}$. If matrix $\mathbf{A(I)}$ is subject to the availability constraint $T_i (I) \leq T_i*(I)$ on non-produced resource i $(i= 1,...,k)$, an economic system using only technology matrix $\mathbf{A(I)}$ and following its maximum expansion trajectory will reach its upper activation bound at $T_i (I) = T_i*(I)$. This may happen under two different conditions regarding the maximum feasible accumulation of the net products delivered by $\mathbf{A(I)}$:

a. All net products delivered by $\mathbf{A(I)}$ can be accumulated (invested) within $\mathbf{A(I)}$ itself until the production subsystem using $\mathbf{A(I)}$ (in short, subsystem $\mathbf{A}$ $(\mathbf{I})$) enters a stationary state (no further accumulation is possible within that subsystem due to its upper activation bound at $T_i (I) = T_i*(I)$). From this point onwards, the net products of subsystem $\mathbf{A(I)}$ are accumulated (invested) within subsystem $\mathbf{A(II)}$, while the net products of subsystem $\mathbf{A}$ $(\mathbf{II})$ can be accumulated (invested) within $\mathbf{A(II)}$ itself until $\mathbf{A(II)}$'s upper activation bound is eventually reached (that is, until $T_i (II) = T_i*(II)$).

b. The net products delivered by **A(I)** can be only partially accumulated (invested) within **A(I)** itself. These non-accumulable net products would become part of the net products flowing from subsystem **A(I)** to subsystem **A(II)** once technology **A(II)** gets started. From this point onwards, the net products of both subsystems **A(I)** and **A(II)** can be accumulated (invested) within subsystem **A(II)** until **A(II)**'s upper activation bound is reached (that is, until $T_i \, (II) = T_i^*(II)$).

As to the partial or full accumulation within subsystem **A(II)** of the net products delivered by subsystem **A(I)**, the two following cases are possible:

1 Subsystems **A(I)** and **A(II)** have matching structures of requirements regarding the utilization of produced commodities as inputs for the production of other commodities. In this case, the complete accumulation (investment) of net products delivered by **A(I)** is possible within **A(II)**, and no residuals are generated.
2 Subsystems **A(I)** and **A(II)** have different structures of requirements regarding the utilization of produced inputs. In this case, the net products delivered by **A(I)** cannot be fully accumulated (invested) within **A(II)** and the formation of non-accumulable **A(I)**'s residuals is unavoidable. These residuals may be stored, consumed or transferred outside the system (for instance, exported).[11]
3 As time goes on, the residual net products delivered by **A(I)** may eventually be used for the introduction of *additional* production subsystems different from **A(II)** (say, **A(III)**, **A(IV)**, and so on). This may raise the overall growth potential of the economic system as the system moves across trajectories characterized by different technological conditions and natural resource requirements.

The aforestated set of conditions highlights the dynamic possibilities of an economic system in which natural scarcities interact with technical and technological progress, and in which the relationship between scarcity and producibility is the major trigger of structural change. In particular, our analysis calls attention to structural compatibility (or lack thereof) between production subsystems as a fundamental characteristic of structural economic dynamics. Technical or technological progress may give rise to residuals that cannot be accumulated within the economy (*structural mismatch*). But it is precisely this lack of compatibility between different (partially coordinated) subsystems that

---

[11] The possibility of stocking or exporting residuals may indirectly increase productive capacity. This would require either the transfer of commodity stocks to some date further away in the future, or the immediate export of residuals in order to import the commodities needed in the accumulation process.

may allow the introduction of new techniques or technologies and eventually take the economic system on a higher-growth trajectory (see, in particular, Quadrio Curzio, 1975, 1986, 1990; Quadrio Curzio and Pellizzari, 1999).

To sum up, successively binding scarcity constraints induce a structural dynamics within production systems due to *technology contraction* (the disappearance of certain technical possibilities from the range of technical options available to producers). In turn, technology contraction is generally associated with the introduction of 'inferior' technical arrangements previously feasible but inactive. Finally, those 'inferior' arrangements may eventually bring technological complementarities about and thus trigger a process of *technology expansion*, whereby it becomes possible to activate technical opportunities previously known but not feasible (see Scazzieri, 1993a, 2014). Clearly, technology contractions and expansions generated by successively binding constraints may or may not trigger specific structural change trajectories depending on which sequence is followed in activating production techniques. Different sequences of activation are likely to be associated with different sequences of binding constraints. They are also likely to be associated with differences in the way in which binding constraints may bring new opportunities about through the discovery of technological complementarities and technology expansion. For example, a diminishing returns trajectory associated with successively binding constraints on land resources is likely to be different from a diminishing returns trajectory generated by successively binding constraints on one or more types of mineral ore. However, in either case the structural dynamics of the production system shows similar principles at work. Initially resource constraints bring technology contraction about; subsequently technology contraction may either proceed unchecked or trigger a reverse process of technology expansion (see previous argument in this section). It is important to realize that technology contraction and expansion do not produce symmetrical effects. The former is necessarily associated with the activation of certain 'inferior' technical structures (due to the need to activate superior and inferior techniques side by side along the dynamic path that is being followed). The latter may or may not be associated with the activation of a 'superior' technical structure depending on whether the opportunities associated with technology expansion are actually taken.

5.   **Scarcities in stylized economic history and in the history of economic analysis**

5.1   Scarcity, production and economic dynamics

Both the structural and the macroeconomic approaches to scarcities and rents highlight the role of economic and technological history in making visible constraints and opportunities arising from the changing relationship between natural or technological scarcities and the producibility of resources and goods. Different historical contexts also had an important influence in drifting the economists' attention from scarcity to producibility, or the other way round, and in shaping the economic theory of resources accordingly (Quadrio Curzio and Scazzieri, 1986).

The dynamic relationship between scarcity and producibility provides a useful heuristic for assessing the economists' changing concentration of attention for the allocation of given resources or for the overcoming of resource bottlenecks through the transformation of production structures. The two approaches emerge from different historical contexts and lead to different treatments of scarcities. In the former case, scarcities call attention to what may be called the *transformation apparatus*, delivering finished consumer goods from non-produced resources, and the economic problem becomes that of finding the 'best' allocation of limited resources among competing uses. In the latter case, scarcities call attention to what may be called the *structural apparatus*, delivering consumer goods through increased utilization of reproducible capital goods, and the economic problem becomes that of reducing scarcities by enhancing the self-replacing and accumulation capacities of the economic system (see, in particular, Quadrio Curzio and Scazzieri, 1986, 1990; see also Quadrio Curzio, 1999a, 1999b; Quadrio Curzio, 2011a, 2011b; Quadrio Curzio, Pellizzari and Zoboli, 2011).

Stylized economic history and the history of economic analysis have shown a shifting degree of attention for scarcity issues, particularly for what concerns the specific role of natural resources. Nowadays, as in other periods of economic history, natural scarcities have emerged as fundamental in determining the dynamic path followed by most economic systems. The world economy again feels the constraints due to the availability of natural resources and raw materials, partly as a consequence of the accelerated growth of a number of developing and heavily populated countries.

The problem of natural resource bottlenecks was recognized as a central issue at least since the mid seventeenth century (Wrigley, 1962, 1987, 1988, 1991, 1994, 2006, 2010). In particular, the economists' attention for scarcity issues has been shaped by the duality between the *scarcity* of natural resources and the *producibility* of commodities. This duality has been partially overcome through economic history by scientific and technological progress in so far as the latter has been effective in reducing the mismatch between resource availability and resource utilization. The history of economic analysis provides a vantage point from which to investigate the way economists have addressed the aforementioned duality and dealt with scarcity issues. The following main approaches may be distinguished: (i) the classical approach with its emphasis upon the dynamic relationship between producibility and specific natural scarcities (for instance, the scarcity of land); (ii) the neoclassical approach with its emphasis upon a generalized concept of scarcity; (iii) the macro-dynamic approach with its concentration of attention upon consistency conditions for aggregate magnitudes and relative neglect for natural scarcities; (iv) the structural approach; (v) the empirical approach with its emphasis on resource utilization and conservation, and on measurement of the relationship between resource-use efficiency and economic growth (Quadrio Curzio, 1999a, 1999b, 2011).

The analysis of scarcity from a historical perspective raises a number of questions. In fact, we may ask for how long can the distinction between exhaustible and renewable natural resources be maintained, given that most resources have been renewed and augmented through substitution processes. We may also ask whether the remaining scarcities will continue to be 'relative' rather than 'absolute' (see previous discussion). And, finally, we may ask to what extent natural scarcities will exert an influence upon economic dynamics. History of economic analysis highlights both the rich set of conceptual tools economists developed in order to deal with the aforementioned issues and the difficulties met in assessing the role of natural resources on a long-run dynamic trajectory. However, in many cases difficulties met in the past resurface today. For this reason, the history of economic analysis is an invaluable tool in detecting the specific context of scarcity and in identifying which assessment and policy measures would be most adequate in each case.

5.2   Absolute scarcity and relative scarcity in classical economic theory

The limited availability of natural resources has traditionally been at the origin of the treatment of natural scarcities in economics. There is, however, a fundamental difference between the analysis of natural scarcities from the allocation point of view and the analysis of natural scarcities from the structural point of view. In the former case, natural scarcities are considered a particular case of limited supply, and attention is focused on the influence of limited supply on price determination under market conditions. In the latter case, the central problem is how to overcome the limited availability of resources by means of structural changes that modify the mix of production techniques in operation at any given time. The switch from the allocation to the structural point of view is associated with the change from a conception of national wealth as a *stock* of given resources to be allocated among individuals and/or social groups to a conception of national wealth as a *flow* of goods produced and reproduced within the economic system. The latter point of view is clearly expressed in François Quesnay ([1758] 1958, [1759] 1972) and Adam Smith ([1776] 1976) and is at the root of their analysis of the *net product* as a fundamental prerequisite for the growth of national wealth. In fact, according to the structural point of view, national wealth may be considered to be growing only if the flow of produced goods is – directly or indirectly – able to reproduce the material conditions for its own production. The economic system is represented as a circular flow of goods entering as inputs in the production of themselves or of other goods (see also Leontief, [1928] 1991), and natural scarcities intervene in so far as they may influence the internal structure of the circular flow.

Natural scarcities in Malthus and Ricardo are first of all triggers of structural change (Andreoni and Scazzieri, 2014). In his *Essay on the Principle of Population* (Malthus, [1798] 1993) Malthus had introduced the idea of an *absolute scarcity* of natural agricultural resources, envisaging the stationary state as the long-term condition for the evolution of economic systems. A few years later, Malthus focused on the structural changes induced in the production system by population pressure and examined the relationship between diminishing returns on non-produced natural resources (land) and the formation of rents (Malthus, 1815a, 1815b). A structural approach to natural scarcities is also central in David Ricardo (1951 [1817]), but in his case the distinction between *absolute scarcity* and *relative scarcity* is emphasized. For according to Ricardo decreasing returns from land utilization would set in *unless* technical progress could offset the tendency towards the introduction of more costly techniques once the less costly techniques are no longer feasible. In Ricardo's theory, the price of the product generated by this natural resource (i.e. the price of corn produced on land) would vary depending on the degree of land scarcity, which would in turn increase as a result of economic growth and increased land utilization. Ultimately, Ricardo too emphasizes that stationary state is unavoidable, since in his view technical progress can only delay the onset of absolute scarcity (Ricardo, 1951 [1821]). John Stuart Mill ([1848] 1965) also acknowledged the likelihood of the stationary state but emphasized that it should not necessarily be seen in negative terms, as it could be a condition enhancing moral and social progress. Considering the potential impact of an increase in available land, Mill thought that capitalists could even choose a stationary state before population growth induces the full utilization of natural resources:

Nor is there much satisfaction in contemplating the world with nothing left to the spontaneous activity of nature; with every rood of land brought into cultivation, which is capable of growing food for human beings; every flowery waste or natural pasture ploughed up, all quadrupeds or birds which are not domesticated for man's use exterminated as his rivals for food, every hedgerow or superfluous tree rooted out, and scarcely a place left where a wild shrub or flower could grow without being eradicated as a weed in the name of improved agriculture. If the earth must lose that great portion of its pleasantness which it owes to things that the unlimited increase of wealth and population would extirpate from it, for the mere purpose of enabling it to support a larger, but not a better or a happier population, I sincerely hope, for the sake of posterity, that they will be content to be stationary, long before necessity compels them to it. (Mill [1848] 1965, Book IV, ch. VI, p. 756)

In short, Ricardo distanced himself both from Smith's optimism and Malthus's pessimism by focusing on the 'antagonism-coexistence' between producibility and scarcity, that is, by acknowledging both the constraints introduced by natural scarcities and the opportunities arising from technical progress. Ricardo saw the relationship between producibility and scarcity as the central causal mechanism in explaining the dynamics of the wealth of nations. He also committed himself to the view that, due to the combined pressure of population dynamics and natural scarcities, a stationary state is ultimately unavoidable. As a result, he interpreted the antagonism-coexistence of producibility and scarcity as a temporary condition rather than as a set of opportunities open to uncertain outcomes. In this way, he was unable to fully exploit the principle of relative scarcity that his theory had introduced. For he acknowledged that technical progress might turn the absolute scarcities of non-produced resources into relative scarcities, while also expressing the view that in the long-term a stationary state would be unavoidable (Quadrio Curzio, Pellizzari, and Zoboli, 2011).

5.3   General scarcity in the marginalist or neoclassical view

The specific role assigned to non-produced resources in the structural theory of production, distribution and economic dynamics (and of which Ricardo's treatment of land and mines is a prominent example) was gradually lost as economists switched to a theory of rational resource allocation under conditions of generalized scarcity (Bharadwaj, 1978; Hennings, 1986). The assumption of generalized scarcity went hand in hand with the adoption of a theory of generalized diminishing returns based on the law of variable proportions. According to this theory, diminishing returns were seen as a possibility inherent to any change in the proportions between productive inputs in any process of production, under the assumption that the quantity of a single input (or collection of inputs) is varied while the quantities of all other inputs are fixed (Turgot, 1808 [1768]); Edgeworth, 1911–13; Scazzieri, 1981, 1982, 1993a). The allocation point of view also suggests approaching natural scarcities independently of the utilization of non-produced resources within a specific structure of production by considering alternative utilization paths across time for resources that are not only limited in availability at any given time but also exhaustible over sufficiently long periods of time (Jevons, 1865; Hotelling, 1931; Dasgupta and Heal, 1974; Solow, 1974b). The issue of resource exhaustion is central in Harold Hotelling's (1931) classic contribution to the analysis of the optimal rate of depletion for any given resource on the assumption that the owner of the exhaustible resource is a profit maximizer. In Hotelling's view, given a limited resource stock, an increase in current depletion rate entails a reduction in future utilization. Under conditions of perfect competition, it would thus be possible to increase profits by changing the rate of depletion in different periods. If extraction costs are negligible, resources must be depleted so as to allow prices to increase in line with interest rates. An interesting implication of this result, which is known as *Hotelling's rule*, is that ownership of an exhaustible resource is equivalent to ownership of any financial activity. Hotelling also proved competitive depletion to be socially optimal by defining social well-being in terms of resource consumption and discounting the benefits derived from future consumption. Subsequent research has addressed Hotelling's rule by discussing in particular the discounting criterion presupposed by the rule and assessing the conditions under which a given level of *per capita* consumption may be maintained over time (Stiglitz, 1974).

An important bridge between the structural and the optimization approaches to natural scarcities is provided by William Stanley Jevons in his essay *The Coal Question* (Jevons, 1865). In that work, Jevons foresaw the end of British industrial leadership due to the rapid exploitation and progressive depletion of coal mines. According to him, an increase in the efficient use of coal (due to technical progress) could not prevent the onset of economic stagnation in the long term, since it would not be associated with greater preservation of coal reserves, but to further increases in the scale of production and thus to increased exploitation of mines. There is thus a clear link between Jevons' approach and the view of the classical economists in so far as technical progress (via greater efficiency in coal utilization and discovery of alternative sources of energy) is considered to be unable to check the ultimate prospect of stagnation. Jevons contributed to highlighting a problem that is still important nowadays; i.e. that of identifying an upper bound to economic growth due to the limited availability of natural resources (see Quadrio Curzio, Pellizzari, and Zoboli, 2011).

5.4   'With' and 'without' natural scarcities: the structural and the macroeconomic views

The reappraisal of classical economic theory in the twentieth century led to a reformulation of the structural theory of non-produced resources and scarcity. This process was carried out through a sequence of steps (Quadrio Curzio, 2011). First, producibility was again assigned a central role in explaining the structure and dynamics of any given economic system. Second, scarcity as non-producibility was introduced as both a constraint and a motive force for any economic system using non-produced resources available in limited amounts. The emphasis on producibility is common to both the structural and the macroeconomic approaches developed since the 1930s starting, respectively, with the contributions of Wassily Leontief ([1928] 1991, 1941) and Jan von Neumann (1937) for the structural approach, and with the contributions of John Maynard Keynes (1936) and Roy Harrod (1939, 1948) for the macroeconomic approach. Contributions to the structural line of research were initially more 'Smithian' than 'Ricardian' in character, due to the almost exclusive attention for producibility and the initial neglect of non-produced resources and the associated scarcities. This standpoint is manifest in the contributions of Leontief and von Neumann, in which no scale constraints arising from the scarcities of non-produced resources are considered. Leontief's analysis of the 'circular flow' of a production economy is rooted in the idea of interdependence among the flows of products in any economic system in which commodities are produced by means of labour and other produced commodities (Leontief, [1928] 1991). This point of view led Leontief to empirically investigate the interindustry structure of the economy of the United States over the period 1919–29, and to outline on that basis what he called the *Tableau* of the American economy (Leontief, 1941). He subsequently made use of the interindustry framework in exploring the features of an economic system evolving though time (Leontief, Chenery *et al.*, 1953). Jan von Neumann investigated other properties of a circular and multi-sectoral economy by identifying the conditions for this economy to expand at the maximum growth rate allowed by the available technology and by the structural interdependencies among productive sectors (von Neumann, 1937; see also Champernowne, 1945/46).[12] Neither Leontief nor von Neumann considers constraints due to the non-producibility of some essential inputs. However, Leontief also noted the 'invisible' but important contribution of natural resources to the inter-sectoral product flows described in his tables:

'Invisible in all these tables, but ever present . . . are the natural resources . . . Absence of systematic quantitative information, similar to that which has been collected . . . with

---

[12] Von Neumann's contribution has been seminal in providing analytical foundations to a structural approach to multisectoral dynamics in which the 'standard formulation of the economic problem' centred 'around "scarcity" of given resources in relation to the multiplicity of consumers' wants' is avoided (Chakravarty, 1989, p. 71), and in which the possibility of a 'double description procedure of growth, a causal and an optimizing one' is highlighted (Chakravarty, 1989, p. 75). According to Chakravarty, the latter feature of von Neumann's model makes it conducive to a type of structural analysis in which it is possible to discuss the coherence between specific policy objectives and systemic goals (such as growth rate maximization), and the effectiveness of the policy instruments that may be correspondingly adopted. In this light, Chakravarty emphasizes the similarities between von Neumann's approach and Adolph Lowe's 'instrumental analysis' of 'political economics' issues (Lowe, 1976, pp. 11-16).

respect to capital and labour, prevents us as yet from introducing this important element explicitly into this preliminary analysis' (Leontief, 1953; reprinted 1986, p.91).

Keynes's and Harrod's macroeconomic contributions are close to the structural contributions in their emphasis on producibility rather than on the scarcity issues associated with utilization of non-produced resources (Keynes, 1936; Harrod, 1948). Harrod, in particular, explains the long-run evolution of an economic system in terms of the accumulation of capital, the dynamics of the labour force and technical progress, while the dynamics of diminishing returns from land is considered to be quantitatively negligible.

Recent contributions to the structural and macroeconomic research lines have also privileged the producibility standpoint, even as the role of non-produced resources has attracted increasing attention. Piero Sraffa (1960) investigated the relationships between sectoral interdependencies and the distribution income by also considering the role of land and land–rent. However, Sraffa's contribution does not deal with dynamic issues and is thus not directly concerned with the way in which changes of scale may bring about changes in the technology in use and in the relative prices of commodities (Sraffa, 1960, Chapter XI). Luigi Pasinetti's contribution to a theory of structural economic dynamics also privileged the producibility point of view in his construction of a theory of structural economic dynamics. For such a theory is developed by considering

a theoretical model for an industrial economic system ... of pure production [in which] all considered commodities are produced, and can be made in practically whatever quantity may be wanted, provided that they are devoted that amount of effort they technically require. To avoid unnecessary complications, scarce resources will not be considered. This does not imply any disregard of the problems of rationality ... [furthermore] the procedure does not mean that natural resources are assumed to be homogeneous and non-scarce ... [but only that] the basic theory will be developed *independently* of the optimum allocation of scarce resources. (Pasinetti, 1981, pp. 23–4, emphasis in original)[13]

There is, however, one important respect in which these later contributions to structural analysis differ from those of the early Leontief and of von Neumann, as both Sraffa and Pasinetti acknowledge the role of non-produced resources in a production economy, even if they do not assign a central analytical position to the scarcities generated by the limited availability of those resources. Alberto Quadrio Curzio (1967, 1975, 1977, 1980, 1986, 1990, 2005, 2011; with Pellizzari, 1996a, 1999) was the first economist to develop a

---

[13] Pasinetti had already expressed this point of view when introducing the distinction between goods 'of the production type' and goods 'of the scarcity type' (Pasinetti, 1965), and maintained it in later formulations of his theory of structural economic dynamics (Pasinetti, 1993, 2007).

comprehensive structural and multi-sectoral theory in which non-produced resources and rent are assigned a central position in the economic analysis of production, distribution and structural dynamics. His contribution has emphasized the interdependencies between activity levels and structural dynamics, the structural determination of scarcities and rents, and the complex interplay of increasing and decreasing returns characterizing the dynamic paths of economic systems subject to limited availability of non-produced resources (see also Antonelli and Quadrio Curzio, 1988; Quadrio Curzio and Fortis, 2005a and 2005b; Quadrio Curzio, Prosperetti and Zoboli, 1994; Quadrio Curzio and Zoboli, 1995a, 1995b, 1998).

5.5   Historical-quantitative research and empirical indicators

Empirical research on the long-term patterns of resource utilization have broadly confirmed the view of relative (rather than absolute) scarcity (see Kuznets, 1955a, 1955b, 1971, 1973). Kuznets also addressed the environmental impact of innovation, and maintained that technological change may eventually be able to find adaptation mechanisms, overcoming possible negative effects on the environment. A different but complementary line of empirical research is worth mentioning. This is the work by Wassily Leontief, Anne Carter and Peter Petri (1977) on the dynamics prospects of the world economy under constraints of limited availability of natural resources. In their contribution they consider a number of interconnected input–output sub-models for different parts of the world economy, and analyse the interrelationships between the production/consumption of goods and services, and the availability/utilization of natural resources. Their results are in broad agreement with those of Kuznets, considering that, according to them, the principal checks upon economic growth are likely to arise from socio-economic and institutional factors, rather than from physical bottlenecks. More recently, there has been a renewed interest in global modelling, which has developed partly as a response to climate-change anxiety. Global ecological models and climate models, as well as multidisciplinary models of the large-scale interactions between ecological and social systems have been proposed, together with revised formulations of models in the tradition of the global modelling of the 1970s (Meadows *et al.*, 1972). In more recent years, research in climate change and other perceived environmental emergencies has led to renewed interest in global modelling (Mokyr, 1995; Zoboli, 1996; Jaffe, Newell and Stavins, 2003; OECD, 2002). A key feature of these models is the role played by innovation, and its function in overcoming global constraints. Once again the relationship between relative and absolute scarcity appears to be central in assessing the long-run prospects of the world economy. The main difference between the global modelling analyses (of which a classic instance is provided in Meadows *et al.*, 1972) and the interindustry contributions *à la* Leontief (see also Duchin and Lange, 1994) concerns the distinction between absolute scarcity (privileged by the former approach) and relative scarcity (privileged by the latter approach). The different assessment of technical change and its impact is at the root of the differences between the two points of view, a difference that in the most recent contributions extends to the evaluation of scarce environmental resources (Quadrio Curzio, 2011).

In the last two decades, empirical indicators of intensity and efficiency of resource use in relation to population and GDP dynamics have been an important focus of research. The historical evolution of these indicators underlines a decoupling process, that is, a decrease in the energy/emissions intensity of economic activity, and/or an increase in the efficiency/productivity of resource use (Zhang, 2000; OECD, 2002). Whatever economic efficiency indicator is used, the economic interpretation of the underlying innovation mechanisms is difficult. Due to increasing demand for additional advances in resource-use efficiency, indicators of energy intensity/efficiency have been monitored for years by international and national institutions.[14] A generally shared view is that the decline in energy intensity from primary sources at first involved industrialized countries and, more recently, a number of developing countries still in the initial stages of industrialization.[15]

Since the 1970s the increasing efficiency of energy utilization has significantly intensified, partly as a result of increasing energy prices and of the resulting perception of energy scarcity. This led to the adoption of technological policies aimed at encouraging energy conservation (Martin, 1990; Rosenberg, 1994, 1996).[16] Overall, changes in relative input prices generated technological innovation reducing the use of the relatively more expensive factors.[17] For example, increases in energy and raw material prices in the

---

[14] See, for example, the IEA (International Energy Agency) and national agencies such as the DOE (US Department of Energy).

[15] The consumption of primary energy per unit of GDP was already decreasing by the late nineteenth century in the United Kingdom and by the 1920s and 1930s in the United States, Germany and France. According to Zhang (2000), in China, despite a sizable increase in the demand for energy, the institutional changes of the late 1970s, aimed at raising energy prices, led the energy intensity of national income to decrease by 50% between 1980 and the late 1990s.

[16] This evidence suggests the relevance of the hypothesis of 'induced invention', which was originally formulated in a macro-dynamic framework by John Hicks in his *Theory of Wages* (Hicks, 1932, ch. VI 'Distribution and Economic Progress'), and was subsequently applied to the analysis of the impact of markets and prices upon innovative choices (see, for example, Hicks, 1985; Quadrio Curzio and Zoboli, 1995a, 1995b, 1998).

[17] The Hicksian induced-invention (or 'induced-innovation') hypothesis has had numerous theoretical and applied developments in the recent past (Kemp, 1997; Ruttan, 2002; Mazzanti and Zoboli, 2005), and has been re-proposed by numerous models of 'endogenous innovation' applied to energy and climate policies (Carraro, Gerlagh and van der Zwaan, 2003).

1970s resulted in specifically induced innovations aimed at conserving the resources that global markets indicated as in relatively short supply (Quadrio Curzio, 1983; Sylos Labini, 1984; Quadrio Curzio, Fortis and Zoboli, 1994; Quadrio Curzio, Prosperetti and Zoboli, 1994; Mokyr, 1995; Rosenberg, 1996; Popp, 2002). However, relative energy prices cannot be considered as the only (and not even as the primary) driving force towards energy-related innovations (Quadrio Curzio, Pellizzari, and Zoboli, 2011).[18]

5.6   Technological scarcity

Several features of the recent dynamics of developed economies point to a state of relative rather than absolute scarcity. This may be due to the fact that technological progress, together with structural changes, has reduced the utilization coefficients of certain material inputs. Yet the overall picture is still one of increasing overall consumption of resources and energy. Economic history has highlighted the uniqueness of the experience regarding the relationship between scarce resources and innovation that characterized the development process in eighteenth- and nineteenth-century England. The Industrial Revolution started a transition based on natural resources and technology with no precedents in history (Landes, 1969). As E. A. Wrigley pointed out, this development was associated with the transition from organic to fossil fuels (Wrigley, 1962, 1988, 2006, 2010). A question thus naturally arises: how is it possible to maintain continuously high economic development without massive recourse to fossil resources? Answering this question brings to the fore the idea that the prospects of modern economic growth depend on technological transition and on the capacity to work out 'useful knowledge' (Mokyr, 2002).

Within this framework, as we have already seen, the central role of 'technological scarcity' – which may be defined, following Quadrio Curzio, as *scarcity related to our knowledge* – comes to the foreground.[19] Natural and technological scarcities have dynamically complementary roles. Unless technical and /or technological progress are effective and persistent, natural

---

[18] This is especially due to the fact that resources and the environment are subject to public policies influencing the prices themselves, the quantities supplied and demanded, investments in research and development. In particular, taxation and regulation policies have traditionally played an important role in filtering changes in energy prices (Jaffe, Newell and Stavins, 2003; Baranzini, Benjuino and Teixeira, 2003; Popp, 2004).

[19] Quadrio Curzio and his research associates have investigated also, in several empirical and applied works, the structural interdependence of natural scarcities and technological change, and have devoted attention to the influence of changes in the utilization of raw materials upon the growth potential and actual dynamics of economic systems (Quadrio Curzio, 1983; Quadrio Curzio and Antonelli, 1988; Quadrio Curzio, Fortis and Zoboli, 1994; Quadrio Curzio, Prosperetti and Zoboli, 1994; Quadrio Curzio and Zoboli, 1995a, 1995b; Quadrio Curzio and Fortis, 1996).

scarcities could bring economic growth to a halt. Technological scarcity is sometimes due to institutional rather than structural reasons. For example, technical progress may drastically reduce the non-producibility of *hydrocarbures* (Carrà, 2008). However, bottlenecks may arise due to social and historical conditions, or to lack of structural compatibility within the given production system and this can make structural changes difficult or altogether impossible. This brings to the fore the relationship between resources and structural policies, which will be examined in the following section.

6.   Resources, institutions and social structures: the political economy approach

6.1   Preliminary remarks

The structural analysis of non-produced resources calls attention to the interdependence between resource appropriation and utilization, formation of structural rents, and appropriation of those rents by a variety of social groups. It is therefore a privileged field of investigation for political economy, in so far as the latter examines the interdependence between social groups and the implications of that interdependence for the dynamics of the whole economic system. This section will consider in turn: (i) the relationship between changes in the utilization pattern of non-produced resources and changes in the relative position of relevant social groups; (ii) the role of a primary commodity such as gold (that is, of a commodity produced by means of a non-produced input, such as gold mines) as a possible unit of account (*numéraire*) for the price system; (iii) the emergence of environmental rents as an instance of rent formation due to specific institutional conditions (in this case, environmental taxes).

6.2   Social groups and structural-technological systems

Structural interdependencies call attention to the role of resource bottlenecks in generating mutually related *constraints and opportunities* in the dynamics of social groups within economic systems. Evolving structural conditions in resource-constrained economic systems may also influence the *relative positions* of social groups as those systems evolve over time. This may significantly affect the actions that are possible in any given social and institutional context. In particular, dynamic trajectories associated with decreasing *or* increasing returns may be possible under the same conditions concerning the availability of non-produced resources.

Due to the formation and evolution of rents, actions aimed at changing the structural interdependence between natural resources, technology and economic dynamics (*structural policies*) exert an influence upon the distribution of income and wealth among social groups.

As a result, certain structural policies may or may not be feasible depending on the way in which they are likely to change the social distribution of income and wealth, and thus the relative positions of relevant social groups. The structural approach to variable returns highlights the relevance of different configurations of interests for what concerns the character of scarcities (absolute or relative), the relationship between scarcities and producibility, and the possibility to overcome bottlenecks under specific social and institutional conditions.

Any given resource endowment may or may not be associated with binding constraints upon production structures depending on the level of analytical aggregation and the assignment of functions to productive tasks. For example, a lower level of aggregation calls attention to the fact that a decreasing returns trajectory may be avoided depending on whether non-produced resources can be shifted from one unit of production to another. Decreasing returns can materialize within any set of production activities if the quantity of essential non-produced resources cannot be increased for that set of activities *taken as a whole* (Sraffa, [1925] 1998, pp. 342–3, 357–8; Scazzieri, 1993a, pp. 195–9). In general, low levels of aggregation highlight the institutional bottlenecks and opportunities associated with any given distribution of a particular non-produced resource across different units of production: decreasing returns may be avoided or not for any particular unit of production depending on whether that unit is able to obtain a larger share of the overall endowment of the given resource (Andreoni and Scazzieri, 2014). Correspondingly, a higher level of aggregation highlights two alternative possibilities: decreasing returns may be avoided if the larger set of productive activities under consideration can secure a larger quantity of the non-produced resource, but decreasing returns may be unavoidable if the larger set of productive activities hits the availability upper bound for that resource.

Alternative assignments of functions to productive tasks may significantly alter the way in which any given collection and distribution of non-produced resources may or may not be conducive to decreasing returns. For example, the switch from specific to versatile tasks may reduce the requirements of certain non-produced resources in the production process thereby delaying the onset of decreasing returns. On the other hand, the switch from versatile to specific tasks may bring about a greater modularization of productive functions thereby making it possible to avoid the waste of limited resources in the performance of functions for which they may be only discontinuosly needed (Cardinale and Scazzieri, 2013). Both task versatility and task specialization have an impact on the pattern of resource utilization but their respective modes of operation are different. An increasing degree of task versatility may reduce the utilization requirements for certain non-produced resources in so far as the same resources can be used for a variety of simultaneous or partially overlapping processes; on the other hand, an increasing degree of task specialization allows modular functions to be introduced thereby 'freeing' resources from redundant uses into which they might have been previously locked. A change in the assignment of tasks to productive functions may alternatively delay or expedite the onset of decreasing returns. For increasing versatility makes decreasing returns less likely under conditions of low product differentiation and a generally low scale of productive activity; on the other hand, increasing specialization may delay decreasing returns when the overall scale of product-ive activity is expanding (this is due to the introduction of a greater range of intermediate functions and/or products and the associated reduction of waste).

The need to use non-produced resources in the production process may also activate increasing returns trajectories. In this case, different levels of analyt-ical aggregation of production processes and different degrees of task versatil-ity or specialization within each process call attention to distinct routes along which the activation of increasing returns is possible. For example, switching to a *lower* level of aggregation may bring to light complementarities among production processes that could otherwise remain unnoticed, whereas switch-ing to a *higher* level of aggregation may reveal economies of scale due to the working together of separate processes using the same indivisible fund of non-produced resources. Correspondingly, switching from task versatility to task specialization opens up a route to increasing returns when an increasing overall scale of production makes it possible to introduce specialized functions and intermediate products thereby reducing unused capacities in the utilization of indivisible funds of non-produced resources.

To sum up, different levels of process aggregation and task specialization are associated with different sources of decreasing and/or increasing returns from the utilization of non-produced resources. This calls attention to the role of institutional factors in determining the actual shape of the decreasing and increasing returns trajectories that are possible under given structural condi-tions. In particular, the distribution of non-produced resources among individ-uals and/or social groups is a major factor in determining at which level of aggregation decreasing returns are most likely, and at which level of aggrega-tion a countervailing tendency to increasing returns can arise. This has note-worthy implications for the relative positions of social groups in the economic system. For differential rents (that is, rents associated with the utilization of different production techniques for any given productive sector) may or may not arise, depending on which level of aggregation is considered. Indeed, we may conjecture that different levels of aggregation will be associated with the possibility of different types of differential rents since the characteristics of production techniques will be different when moving across those levels of aggregation. This situation may have far-reaching consequences for the analysis of socio-economic dynamics. For a conflict of interests may arise between groups in control of different resources and/or of different types of technological know-how. For example, a group associated with the ownership of resources for which a certain rent may be received may find itself in conflict with a group associated with resources and/or technologies that can for a time reduce the rents accruing to the former group. This suggests a close relationship between the sectoral decomposition of the productive structure, the social decomposition of the economy into competing or co-operating groups, and the dynamics of decreasing and increasing returns, both at the national level and at the level of the world economy (see, for example, Nurkse, 1953; Hirschman, 1958, 1968; Prebisch, 1971; Kaldor [1981] 1989)[20].

The political economy of non-produced resources is a privileged field of investigation when examining the intertwined dynamics of production systems and socio-economic structures. The aim of this volume is to explore the structural approach to the political economy of non-produced resources. This is done by addressing the relationship between non-produced resources and the distribution of income and wealth among social groups, by investigating the influence of non-produced resources on the sectoral and social composition of the economy, and by assessing the institutional and policy issues arising from this interdependence of sectoral and social dynamics.

6.3   The role of a primary commodity (gold) as a physical numéraire

The utilization of a primary commodity as a physical unit of account (numéraire) for the price system is important and very complex for both theoretical and institutional reasons. A physical unit of account makes the price system not only independent of short-run demand-and-supply fluctuations but also from the quantity of money. This is because a physical numéraire makes the price system depend upon a standard of value that is itself invariable as long as the production process delivering that numéraire remains unchanged. The use of gold as numéraire is an interesting case in point (Quadrio Curzio 1981, 1982b, 1985). David Ricardo considered gold to be the perfect numéraire provided it was itself produced by a constant quantity of labour 'from the mine which paid no rent' (Ricardo, 1951 [1817], p. 87). In structural analysis, gold is a commodity produced under scarcity conditions, so that there will normally

---

[20] Different ways of decomposing any given economic and political system (or of constructing an aggregate system from more elementary components) may be associated with different representations of sectoral versus aggregate interests, and with different approaches to policy (Rae and Taylor, 1970; Rogowski, 1987; and, in particular, Cardinale, 2012; Cardinale and Coffman, 2014).

be a variety of production processes delivering gold from different mines. The best and inframarginal processes (mines) will deliver structural rents, whereas the least effective (most expensive) process will determine the value of the *numéraire*. This means that the value of the *numéraire* will be given as long as the more expensive gold-producing process remains the same. As soon as this process changes, there will also be a change (an increase) in the value of the *numéraire*, so that the prices of all other commodities relative to the *numéraire* will decrease (this issue is examined in Quadrio Curzio, 1999b).

Different physical units of account have different properties for what concerns the analytical requirement of expressing the price system in terms of a relatively invariable standard. Gold has historically performed the role of physical unit of account, store of value and *medium* of exchange for reasons that are partly external to the sphere of market transactions in so far as gold was often taken to be the expression of personal or social worth (Grierson, 1977). This analysis points to the possibility of 'fixing' the price of gold in terms of its unit cost of production with the most expensive technique. This makes the value of the *numéraire* constant as long as this cost is unchanged, but brings about a change in the system of relative prices whenever the unit cost of producing gold with the most expensive technique is itself changed. Indeed, changes of this cost are increasingly likely the more the cost of producing gold is affected by changes in the production methods (and costs of production) of other commodities entering gold production as inputs. As a result, gold is only an imperfect physical unit of account in so far as it is itself subject to a variety of influences that may determine a change of its value. On the other hand, it has the advantage of calling attention to the conditions affecting the changes in value of the given *numéraire*, and in particular to the interdependence between technological and socio-institutional changes that may bring about significant *but relatively predictable* changes in the value of the *numéraire* itself (see also Quadrio Curzio and Pellizzari, 1999, pp. 237–8; Quadrio Curzio, 1981, 1982b; 1985; Oppenheimer, 1982, Sylos Labini, 1982).[21] Furthermore, the value of gold can be affected by technical progress only in a limited way, in so far as gold continues to be an important store of value. In this case, decreasing gold production cost may be offset by the demand for gold as store of value; so that changes in the relative prices of produced commodities in terms of a gold *numéraire* would be a measure of structural effectiveness for the production system as a whole.

---

[21] The property of *relative invariance* of gold as standard of value is central to the importance of gold in Central Banks' official reserves, as well as to recent proposals to introduce gold as collateral for EuroUnionBond issues, especially for those involving the financing of infrastructural investment (Prodi and Quadrio Curzio, 2012).

6.4   *Environmental scarcities, rents and socio-institutional dynamics*

Environmental resources draw attention to analytical issues that are partly similar and partly different from those associated with non-produced resources such as land or mines. The main difference is due to the fact that most environmental resources, once consumed as a result of pollution, cannot be controlled or reproduced by technical progress[22] (Quadrio Curzio, 1999a, 1999b; Quadrio Curzio and Zoboli, 1995a,b). It is also important to note that environmental resources are seldom appropriated in a conventional way (either by private or collective agents). On the other hand, they may introduce scale constraints upon the activation of certain production techniques and thus become important triggers of structural change. The structural analysis of non-produced resources provides conceptual tools that can also be used in the structural analysis of environmental resources, provided attention is paid to the specific features of environmental scarcities. Appropriation criteria are central in determining whether environmental scarcities give rise to structural rents accruing to owners of resources or to owners of technology. For example, the emergence of environmental scarcities in the absence of appropriation or appropriability is likely to increase extraction costs (such as the cost of searching for clean fisheries, or the cost of searching for clean air) with technological rents accruing to processes capable of accessing best quality resources. In the same vein, positional advantage may give access to the best fishery, or the best offshore drilling opportunity, even if traditional property rights cannot be enforced. In this case, the environmental resource (or fractions of it) cannot be appropriated in a permanent way but different 'appropriation techniques' can be used in order to achieve temporary access to it (see Poni and Scazzieri, 2007, pp. 84–7).

Under these conditions, environmental scarcities may give rise to structural rents of the technological type, even if in this case rents are likely to accrue to owners of the best appropriation technique rather than to owners of specific fractions of any given resource fund. Taxation and the regulatory framework may also exert an important influence upon whether a scale expansion leads to lower prices offered by the most efficient producers (thereby driving out the least efficient ones), or to a higher common price compatible both with survival of least efficient producers and with formation of rents accruing to owners of the most efficient processes (see Quadrio Curzio and Pellizzari, 1999). In this case too, the structural analysis of non-produced resources points to the relationship between material, technological and institutional interdependencies, as well as to the role of political economy in identifying the specific positions and interests of different socio-economic groups.

---

[22] The greenhouse effect is a case in point.

7.   Epilogue

The principal objective of this volume has been to examine the specific role of non-produced resources in the analysis of structural economic dynamics. This analysis is undertaken by initially focusing on the relationship between non-produced resources and the distribution of income and wealth in society. The volume then moves to considering the role exerted by non-produced resources in the medium- and long-term dynamics of economic systems. Finally, the volume addresses policy issues associated with the governance of a resource-constrained economy, and considers ways in which an economy of that type may be able to redefine the relationship between scarcities and the 'common interest'. Taken in their unity, the chapters in this volume suggest a core set of issues to be addressed when investigating the economy of a resource-constrained system, such as the intertwining of sectoral interests and aggregate performance, the scale dependence of production structures, and the scale dependence of income distribution among social groups. A general lesson to be drawn from the volume is that utilization of any given endowment of non-produced resources is compatible with multiple feasible dynamic paths, which may or may not be realized depending on context. Structural economic analysis allows for identification of those paths. It additionally draws attention upon the interdependence of material and institutional conditions in determining the historical evolution of the economic system. This approach allows economic analysis to endogenize features that are often taken as given. For example, the aggregate propensities to save and accumulate can be determined through the composition of multiple sectoral effects, and the relative position of socio-economic classes can be shown to reflect the interdependence between sectoral wealth formation, bequest motives and demographic patterns. The political economy of a resource-constrained system points to a surprisingly large field of application; additionally it calls attention to the fact that conditions usually taken as given may become the object of action and change.

REFERENCE BIBLIOGRAPHY[23]

Adelman, I., and Taft Morris, C. (1988a) *Comparative Patterns of Economic Development 1850–1914*, Baltimore: Johns Hopkins University Press.
  (1988b) 'Interactions between Agriculture and Industry during the Nineteenth Century', in G. Antonelli and A. Quadrio Curzio (eds.), *The Agro-Technological System Towards 2000. A European Perspective*, Amsterdam, New York, Oxford and Tokyo: North-Holland, pp. 24–31.

---

[23] The reference bibliography includes all references to the works mentioned in this chapter and a number of additional references used in drafting the chapter even if not explicitly mentioned in the text.

Alchian, A. (1987) 'Rent' in J. Eatwell, M. Milgate and P. Newman (eds.) *The New Palgrave Dictionary of Economics*, London: Macmillan, vol. 3, pp. 141–3.

Anderson, J. (1777) *Observations on the Means of Exciting a Spirit of National Industry*, Edinburgh: Cadell and Elliot.

Ando, A., and Fisher, F. M. (1963) 'Near Decomposability, Partition and Aggregation, and the Relevance of Stability Discussions', *International Economic Review*, 4.1, pp. 53–67.

Ando, A., and Modigliani, F. (1963) 'The Life-Cycle Hypothesis of Saving: Aggregate Implications and Tests', *American Economic Review*, 53.1, pp. 55–84.

Andreatta, N. (1958) *Distribuzione del reddito e accumulazione del capitale*, Milan: Giuffrè.

Andreoni, A. (2011) 'Manufacturing Agrarian Change: Inter-Sectoral Learning, Agricultural Production and Technological Capabilities', DRUID Working Paper series no. 11–13.

(2014) 'Structural Learning: Embedding Discoveries and the Dynamics of Production', *Structural Change and Economic Dynamics*, 29.2, pp. 58–74.

Andreoni, A., and Scazzieri, R. (2014) 'Triggers of Change: Structural Trajectories and Production Dynamics', *Cambridge Journal of Economics*, 38.6, pp. 1391–1408.

Antonelli, G., and Quadrio Curzio, A. (eds.) (1988) *The Agro-Technological System Towards 2000. A European Perspective*, Amsterdam and New York: North Holland.

Araujo, J. T. (1992) 'The Government Sector in Kaldor-Pasinetti Models of Growth and Income Distribution', *Journal of Post Keynesian Economics*, 15.2, pp. 211–28.

(1995) 'Kaldor's Neo-Pasinetti Theorem and the Cambridge Theory of Distribution', *Manchester School of Economic and Social Studies*, 63.3, pp. 311–17.

Araujo, J. T., and Harcourt, G. C. (1993) 'Maurice Dobb, Joan Robinson and Gerald Shove on Accumulation and the Rate of Profits', *Journal of the History of Economic Thought*, 15.1, pp. 1–30.

Araujo, R. A., and Teixeira, J. R. (2002) 'Structural Change and Decisions on Investment Allocation', *Structural Change and Economic Dynamics*, 13.2, pp. 249–58.

(2004) 'Structural Economic Dynamics: An Alternative Approach to North-South Models', *Cambridge Journal of Economics*, 28.5, pp. 705–17.

Arena, R. (1982) 'Réflexions sur la compatibilité des approches ricardiennes et keynésiennes du fonctionnement de l'activité économique', *Économie Appliquée*, 35.3, pp. 405–48.

(1992) 'Une synthèse entre post-keynésiens et néo-ricardiens est-elle encore possible?', *L'Actualité économique*, 68.4, pp. 587–606.

Arena, R., and Porta, P. L. (eds.) (2012a) *Structural Dynamics and Economic Growth*, Cambridge: Cambridge University Press.

(2012b) 'Introduction: Structural Dynamics and Contemporary Growth Theory', in R. Arena and P. L. Porta (eds.) *Structural Dynamics and Economic Growth*, Cambridge: Cambridge University Press, pp. 1–33.

Atkinson, A. B. (1971) 'The Distribution of Wealth and the Individual Life-Cycle', *Oxford Economic Papers*, 23.2, pp. 239–54.

(1974) 'A Model of the Distribution of Wealth', University of Essex and MIT, mimeo.

Baldone, S. (1996) 'Vertical Integration, the Temporal Structure of Production Processes and Transition between Techniques', in M. Landesmann and R. Scazzieri (eds.) *Production and Economic Dynamics*, Cambridge: Cambridge University Press, pp. 81–104.

Baranzini, A., Goldemberg J., and Speck S. (2000) 'A Future for Carbon Taxes', *Ecological Economics*, 32, pp. 395–412.

Baranzini, M. (1979) 'Review of *Protagonisti del pensiero economico*, Vol. I: *Nascita e affermazione del marginalismo (1871–1890)*; Vol. II: *Tradizione e rivoluzione in economia politica (1890–1936)*', ed. by A. Quadrio Curzio and R. Scazzieri, *The Economic Journal*, 89.3, pp. 480–2.

(1987) 'Distribution Theories: Keynesian', in *The New Palgrave Dictionary of Economics*, vol. I, London: Macmillan, pp. 876–8.

(1991) *A Theory of Wealth, Distribution and Accumulation*, Oxford: Clarendon Press.

(1995) 'Distribution, Accumulation and Institutions', in A. Heertje (ed.) *The Makers of Modern Economics*, vol. II, Aldershot, UK and Brookfield, Vt.: E. Elgar, pp. 1–28.

(2001) 'The Foundations of the Cambridge School of Income Distribution and Structural Change', in J. R. Teixeira and F. G. Carneiro (eds.) *Growth, Redistribution and Structural Change*, Brasilia: Universa Editora, pp. 11–45.

(2005) 'Modigliani's Life-Cycle Theory of Savings Fifty Years Later', *Banca Nazionale del Lavoro Quarterly Review*, 58.233–4, pp. 109–72.

(2008) 'Flexible Saving and Economic Growth', in R. Scazzieri, A. Sen, and S. Zamagni (eds.) *Markets, Money and Capital. Hicksian Economics for the Twenty-First Century*, Cambridge: Cambridge University Press, pp. 287–308.

Baranzini, M., Benjuino, S. O., and Teixeira, J. R. (2003) 'Taxation on Intergenerational Bequest and Redistribution of Wealth in a Class-Setting', Discussion Paper no. 279, Dept. of Economics, University of Brasilia.

Baranzini, M., and Harcourt, G. C. (eds.) (1993) *The Dynamics of the Wealth of Nations: Growth, Distribution and Structural Change: Essays in Honour of Luigi Pasinetti*, Basingstoke: Macmillan; New York: St. Martin's Press.

Baranzini, M., and Mari, C. (2011) 'The Cantabrigensis-Italian School of Income and Wealth Distribution', in *Gli economisti post-keynesiani di Cambridge e l'Italia*, Rome: Accademia Nazionale dei Lincei, Atti dei Convegni Lincei, no. 261, pp. 235–340.

Baranzini, M., and Mirante, A. (2013) 'The Cambridge Post-Keynesian School of Income and Wealth Distribution', in G. C. Harcourt and P. Kriesler (eds.) *The Oxford Handbook of Post-Keynesian Economics*, vol. 1, Oxford: Oxford University Press, pp. 288–361.

Baranzini, M., and Quadrio Curzio, A. (2012) 'From Adam Smith to Structural Dynamics: Luigi Pasinetti's Life-Long Contribution', paper presented at the Conference 'The Economics of Structural Change: Theory, Institutions and Policies', in honour of Luigi L. Pasinetti, Gonville and Caius College, Cambridge, 12–13 September 2012.

Baranzini, M. and Scazzieri, R. (eds.) (1986a) *Foundations of Economics. Structures of Inquiry and Economic Theory*, Oxford and New York: B. Blackwell.

(1986b) 'Knowledge in Economics: A Framework', in M. Baranzini and R. Scazzieri, (eds.), *Foundations of Economics. Structures of Inquiry and Economic Theory*, Oxford and New York: B. Blackwell, pp. 1–87.

(1990a) *The Economic Theory of Structure and Change*, Cambridge: Cambridge University Press.

(1990b) 'Introduction', in M. Baranzini and R. Scazzieri (eds.), *The Economic Theory of Structure and Change*, Cambridge: Cambridge University Press, pp. 1–20.

(1990c) 'Economic Structure. Analytical Perspectives', in M. Baranzini and R. Scazzieri (eds.) *The Economic Theory of Structure and Change*, Cambridge: Cambridge University Press, pp. 227–333.

(1997) 'Profit and Rent in a Model of Capital Accumulation and Structural Dynamics', in P. Arestis, G. Palma and M. Sawyer (eds.) *Essays in Honour of Geoff Harcourt*, vol. I, London and New York: Routledge, pp. 121–32.

Bharadwaj, K. (1978) *Classical Political Economy and Rise to Dominance of Supply and Demand Theories*, New Delhi: Orient Longman.

Blaug, M. (1968) *Economic Theory in Retrospect*, 2nd edn, London: Heinemann (1st edn 1964).

Bliss, C. J. (1975) *Capital Theory and the Distribution of Income*, Amsterdam and Oxford: North-Holland.

(1997) *Institutions, Behaviour and Economic Theory. A Contribution to Classical-Keynesian Political Economy*, Cambridge: Cambridge University Press.

Britto, R. (1968) 'A Study in Equilibrium Dynamics in Two Types of Growing Economies', *Economic Journal*, 78.311, pp. 624–40.

(1972) 'On Differential Savings Propensies in Two-Class Growth Models', *Review of Economic Studies*, 39.4, pp. 491–4.

Byé, M. (1928) *Les lois des rendements non proportionnels*, Paris: Sirey.

Cardinale, I. (2012) 'The Political Economy of Circular Interdependencies and Vertical Integration: Opening the Black Box of "National Interest"', SSRN Scholarly Paper ID 2357981. Rochester, NY: Social Science Research Network. http://papers.ssrn.com/abstract=2357981.

Cardinale, I., and Coffman, D. (2014) 'Economic Interdependencies and Political Conflict: Towards a Structural and Historical Approach to Taxation', *Economia Politica. Journal of Analytical and Institutional Economics*, 31.3, pp. 277–300.

Cardinale, I., Coffman, D., and Scazzieri, R. (2015) 'Towards a Political Economy of Industrial Fluctuations', in A. Aftalion, *Periodic Overproduction Crises*, London: Anthem Press (1st French edn: Paris, 1913).

(eds.) (2015) *The Political Economy of the Eurozone*, (Cambridge, Cambridge University Press, forthcoming), forthcoming.

Cardinale, I., and Scazzieri, R. (2013) 'Technology and Production: The Economic Analysis of Tasks, Functions, and Material Structures', paper presented at the *Interdisciplinary Workshop on Techniques and Technology*, 25–7 October 2013, University College London.

Carrà, S. (ed.) (2008) *Le fonti di energia*, Bologna: Il Mulino.

Carraro, C., Gerlagh, R., and van der Zwaan, B. (2003) 'Endogenous Technical Change in Environmental Macroeconomics', *Resource and Energy Economics*, 25, pp. 1–10.

Champernowne, D. G. (1945/46) 'A Note on J. v. Neumann's Article on "A Model of Economic Equilibrium"', *Review of Economic Studies*, 13.1, pp. 10–18.

Chakravarty, S. (1989) 'John von Neumann's Model of an Expanding Economy: An Essay in Interpretation', in M. Dore, S. Chakravarty and R. Goodwin (eds.) *John von Neumann and Modern Economics*, Oxford: Clarendon Press, pp. 69–81.

Chenery, H. B. (1960) 'Patterns of Industrial Growth', *The American Economic Review*, 50.4, pp. 624–54.

(1975) 'A Structuralist Approach to Development Policy', *The American Economic Review*, 65.2, Papers and Proceedings of the Eighty-seventh Annual Meeting of the American Economic Association, pp. 310–16.

Chenery, H. B., and Syrquin, M. (1975) *Patterns of Development, 1950–1970*, Oxford: Oxford University Press for the World Bank.

Clark, J. B. (1891) 'Distribution as Determined by a Law of Rent', *Quarterly Journal of Economics*, 5.3, pp. 289–318.

Costabile, L., and Scazzieri, R. (2012) 'Tendenze recenti del pensiero economico italiano', in P. L. Porta and V. Zamagni (eds.) *Il contributo italiano alla storia del pensiero. Economia*, Rome: Istituto dell'Enciclopedia Italiana, pp. 739–65.

Dasgupta, P. S., and Heal, G. (1971) *Economic Theory and Exhaustible Resources*, Cambridge: Cambridge University Press.

(1974) 'The Optimal Depletion of Exhaustible Resources', *Review of Economic Studies*, 41, pp. 3–28.

Denicolò, V., and Matteuzzi, M. (1990) 'Public Debt and the Pasinetti Paradox', *Cambridge Journal of Economics*, 14.3, pp. 339–44.

Dixit, A. (1977) 'The Accumulation of Capital Theory', *Oxford Economic Papers*, 29.1, pp. 1–29.

Dore, M., Chakravarty, S., and Goodwin, R. (eds.) (1989) *John von Neumann and Modern Economics*, Oxford: Clarendon Press.

Duesenberry, J. (1952) *Income, Savings and the Theory of Consumer Behavior*, Cambridge, Mass.: Harvard University Press.

Duchin, F., and Lange, G.-M. (1994) *The Future of the Environment. Ecological Economics and Technological Change*, Oxford and New York: Oxford University Press.

Eatwell, J. (1977) 'The Irrelevance of Returns to Scale in Sraffa's Analysis', *Journal of Economic Literature*, 15.1, pp. 61–8.

(1980) 'On the Theoretical Consistency of Theories of Surplus Value', *Capital and Class*, 10, pp. 155–8.

(1991) 'Institutions, Efficiency, and the Theory of Economic Policy', *Social Research*, 61.1, pp. 35–53.

(2012) 'The Theory of Value and the Foundations of Economic Policy, *In Memoriam Pierangelo Garegnani*', *Contributions to Political Economy*, 31.2, pp. 1–18.

Eatwell, J., and Milgate, M. (2011) *The Fall and Rise of Keynesian Economics*, Oxford: Oxford University Press.

Eatwell, J., Milgate, M., and Newman, P. (eds.) (1987) *The New Palgrave: A Dictionary of Economics*, London: Macmillan.

Edgeworth, F. Y. (1911–1913) 'Contributions to the Theory of Railway Rates', *Economic Journal*, 21.83, pp. 346–70; 21.84, pp. 551–71; 22.86, pp. 198–218; 23.90, pp. 206–26.

Ferguson, C. E. (1969) *The Neoclassical Theory of Production and Distribution*, Cambridge: Cambridge University Press.

Furtado, C. (1965) 'Development and Stagnation in Latin America: a Structuralist Approach', *Studies in Comparative International Development*, 1.11, pp, 159–75.

(1967) *Teoria e política do desenvolvimento económico*, São Paulo: Companhia Editora Nacional.

Furtado, C., and Maneschi, A. (1968) 'Un modelo simulado de desenvolvimento e estagnação na America Latina, *Revista brasileira de economia*, 12 (September), pp. 5–32.

Garegnani, P. (1960) *Il capitale nelle teorie della distribuzione*, Milan: Giuffrè.

(1984) 'Value and Distribution in the Classical Economists and Marx', *Oxford Economic Papers*, 36.2, pp. 291–325.

(1987) 'Surplus Approach to Value and Distribution', in J. Eatwell, M. Milgate and P. Newman (eds.) *The New Palgrave: A Dictionary of Economics*, London: Macmillan, vol. IV, pp. 560–74.

(1989) 'Some Notes on Capital, Expectations and the Analysis of Changes', in G. R. Feiwel (ed.) *Joan Robinson and Modern Economic Theory*, London: Macmillan, pp. 344–67.

(1990) 'Sraffa: Classical *versus* Marginalist Analysis', in K. Bharadwaj and B. Schefold (eds.) *Essays on Piero Sraffa: Critical Perspectives on the Revival of Classical Theory*, London: Unwin Hyman, pp. 112–58.

Gehrke, C., and Hagemann, H. (1996) 'Efficient Traverses and Bottlenecks: a Structural Approach', in M. Landesmann and R. Scazzieri (eds.) *Production and Economic Dynamics*, Cambridge: Cambridge University Press, pp. 140–66.

Georgescu-Roegen, N. (1971) *The Entropy Law and the Economic Process*, Cambridge, Mass.: Harvard University Press, Chapter IX ('The Analytical Representation of Process and the Economics of Production'), pp. 211–75.

(1990) 'Production Process and Dynamic Economics', in M. Baranzini and R. Scazzieri (eds.) *The Economic Theory of Structure and Change*, Cambridge: Cambridge University. Press, pp. 198–226.

Goodwin, R. M., and Landesmann, M. A. (1996) 'Structural Change and Macroeconomic Stability in Disaggregated Models', in M. A. Landesmann and R. Scazzieri (eds.) *Production and Economic Dynamics*, Cambridge: Cambridge University Press, pp. 167–87.

Goodwin, R. M., and Punzo, L. (1987) *The Dynamics of a Capitalist Economy: A Multi-Sectoral Approach*, Cambridge: Polity Press and B. Blackwell.

Gossling, W. F. (1972) *Productivity Trends in a Sectoral Macro-economic Model: A Study of American Agriculture and Supporting Industries, 1919–1964*, London: Cass for Input-Output Publishing Company.

Grierson, P. (1977) *The Origins of Money*, London: Athlone Press.

Grilli, E. (2005) *Crescita e sviluppo delle nazioni. Teorie, strategie e risultati*, Turin: UTET.

Gualerzi, D. (2002) *Consumption and Growth: Recovery and Structural Change in the US Economy*, Cheltenham: E. Elgar.

Hagemann, H. (2012) 'Luigi Pasinetti's Structural Economic Dynamics and the Employment Consequences of New Technologies', in R. Arena and P. L. Porta (eds.) *Structural Dynamics and Economic Growth*, *op. cit.*, pp. 204–17.

(2009) 'Hicks's Traverse Analysis. From *Capital and Growth* to *Capital and Time*', in H. Hagemann and R. Scazzieri (eds.) *Capital, Time and Transitional Dynamics*, Abingdon and New York: Routledge, pp. 133–49.

Hagemann, H., Landesmann, M. A., and Scazzieri, R. (eds.) (2003a) *The Economics of Structural Change*, Cheltenham, UK and Northampton, Mass.: E. Elgar.

(2003b) 'Introduction', in H. Hagemann, M.A. Landesmann and R. Scazzieri (eds.), *The Economics of Structural Change*, Cheltenham, UK and Northampton, Mass.: E. Elgar, vol. I, pp. xi–xlii.

Hagemann, H., and Scazzieri, R. (eds.) (2009a) *Capital, Time and Transitional Dynamics*, Abingdon and New York: Routledge.

(2009b) 'Capital Structure and Economic Transitions: An Introductory Essay', in H. Hagemann and R. Scazzieri (eds.) *Capital, Time and Transitional Dynamics*, Abingdon and New York: Routledge, pp. 1–39.

Harcourt, G. C. (2006) *The Structure of Post-Keynesian Economics: The Core Contributions of the Pioneers*, Cambridge: Cambridge University Press.

(2012) 'Luigi Pasinetti: the Senior Living Heir of the Cambridge School of Economics and the Last of the Great System-Builders', in R. Arena and P. L. Porta (eds.) *Structural Dynamics and Economic Growth*, Cambridge: Cambridge University Press, pp.137–44.

Harcourt, G. C., and Kenyon, P. (1976) 'Pricing and the Investment Decision', *Kyklos*, 29, pp. 449–77.

Harcourt, G. C., and Kerr, P. (2009) *Joan Robinson*, London and New York: Palgrave Macmillan.

Harcourt, G. C., and Riach, P. A. (eds.) (1997) *A 'Second Edition' of The General Theory*, 2 Vol., London and New York: Routledge.

Harcourt, G. C., and Roncaglia, A. (eds.) (1995) *Income and Employment in Theory and Practice: Essays in Memory of Athanasios Asimakopulos*, Basingstoke: Macmillan.

Harrod, R.F. (1939) 'An Essay in Dynamic Theory', *Economic Journal*, 49.193, pp. 14–33.

(1948), *Towards a Dynamic Economics*, London: Macmillan.

Hennings, K. (1986) 'The Exchange Paradigm and the Theory of Production and Distribution', in M. Baranzini and R. Scazzieri (eds.) *Foundations of Economics. Structures of Inquiry and Economic Theory*, Oxford and New York: B. Blackwell, pp. 221–43.

Hicks, J.R. (1932) *The Theory of Wages*, London: Macmillan.

(1969) *A Theory of Economic History*, Oxford: Clarendon Press.

(1976) '"Revolutions" in Economics', in S. J. Latsis (ed.) *Method and Appraisal in Economics*, Cambridge: Cambridge University Press, pp. 207–18.

(1977) 'The Mainspring of Economic Growth', in J. Hicks, *Economic Perspectives. Further Essays on Money and Growth*, Oxford: Clarendon Press, pp. 1–19. (Nobel lecture reprinted from Swedish Journal of Economics, 1973, 75.4, pp. 336–48.)

(1979) 'The Ricardian System: A Comment', *Oxford Economic Papers*, 31.1, pp. 133–4.

(1985), *Methods of Dynamic Economics*, Oxford: Clarendon Press.

Hill, G. (2001) 'The Immiseration of the Landlords: Rent in a Kaldorian Theory of Income Distribution', *Cambridge Journal of Economics*, 25.4, pp. 481–92.

Hirschman, A. (1958) *The Strategy of Economic Development*, New Haven and London: Yale University Press.

(1968) 'The Political Economy of Import-Substituting Industrialization in Latin America', *The Quarterly Journal of Economics*, 82.1, pp. 1–32.

Hotelling, H. (1931) 'The Economics of Exhaustible Resources', *Journal of Political Economy*, 39, pp. 137–75.

Jaffe, A. B., Newell, R.G., and Stavins, R.N. (2003) 'Technological Change and the Environment', in K. G. Mäler and J. R. Vincent (eds.) *Handbook of Environmental Economics*. Amsterdam: Elsevier, vol. I: Environmental Degradation and Institutional Response, pp. 462–516.

Jevons, W. S. (1865) *The Coal Question: An Inquiry Concerning the Progress of the Nation, and the Probable Exhaustion of Our Coal-Mines*, London: Macmillan.

Kahn, R. F. (1959) 'Exercises in the Analysis of Growth', *Oxford Economic Papers*, 11.2, pp. 143–56.

Kaldor, N. (1955–56) 'Alternative Theories of Distribution', *Review of Economic Studies*, 23.2, pp. 83–100.

(1960) *Essays on Value and Distribution*, London: Duckworth.

(1966) 'Marginal Productivity and the Macro-Economic Theories of Distribution. Comment on Samuelson and Modigliani', *Review of Economic Studies*, 33.4, pp. 309–19.

([1981] 1989) 'The Role of Increasing Returns, Technical Progress and Cumulative Causation in the Theory of International Trade and Economic Growth', *Economie Appliquée*, 4. Reprinted in F. Targetti and A. P. Thirlwall (eds.) (1989) *Further Essays on Economic Theory and Policy*, London: Duckworth, pp. 201–23.

Kemp, R. (1997) *Environmental Policy and Technical Change: a Comparison of the Technological Impact of Policy Instruments*, Cheltenham: E. Elgar.

Kerr, P., and Scazzieri, R. (2013) 'Structural Economic Dynamics and the Cambridge Tradition' in G. C. Harcourt and P. Kriesler (eds.) *The Oxford Handbook of Post-Keynesian Economics*, Oxford and New York: Oxford University Press, vol. I, pp. 257–87.

Kessler, D., and Masson, A. (eds.) (1988) *Modelling the Accumulation and Distribution of Wealth*, Oxford: Oxford University Press.

Keynes, J. M. (1936) *The General Theory of Employment, Interest and Money*, London: Macmillan.

(1973–) *The Collected Writings of John Maynard Keynes*, eds. E. A. G. Robinson and D. E. Moggridge, London: Macmillan; Cambridge: Cambridge University Press.

Kotlikoff, L. J., and Summers, L. H. (1981) 'The Role of Intergenerational Transfers in Aggregate Capital Accumulation', *Journal of Political Economy*, 89.4, pp. 706–32.

(1988) 'The Contribution of Intergenerational Transfers to Total Wealth: A Reply', in D. Kessler and A. Masson (eds.), *Modelling the Accumulation and Distribution of Wealth*, Oxford: Oxford University Press, pp. 53–67.

Kregel, J. A. (1971) *Rate of Profit, Distribution and Growth: Two Views*, London: Macmillan.

(1973) *The Reconstruction of Political Economy: An Introduction to Post-Keynesian Economics*, London: Macmillan.

(1980) 'Economic Dynamics and the Theory of Steady Growth: A Historical Essay on Harrod's "Knife-Edge"', *History of Political Economy*, 12.1, pp. 97–123.

Kurz, H. D. (1978) 'Rent Theory in a Multisectoral Model', *Oxford Economic Papers*, 30.1, pp. 16–37.

(ed.) (2000) *Critical Essays on Piero Sraffa's Legacy in Economics*, Cambridge: Cambridge University Press.

Kurz, H. D., Pasinetti, L. L., and Salvadori, N. (eds.) (2008) *Piero Sraffa: The Man and the Scholar, Exploring His Unpublished Papers*, London and New York: Routledge.

Kurz, H. D., and Salvadori, N. (2001) 'Classical Economics and the Problem of Exhaustible Resources', *Metroeconomica*, 52.3, pp. 282–96.

(eds.) (2003) *The Legacy of Piero Sraffa*, Volumes I and II, Cheltenham, UK and Northampton, Mass.: E. Elgar.

Kuznets, S. (1955a) 'Toward a Theory of Economic Growth', in R. Lekachman (ed.), *National Policy for Economic Welfare at Home and Abroad*, New York: Doubleday, pp. 12–85.

(1955b) 'Economic Growth and Income Inequality', *American Economic Review*, 45.1, pp. 1–28.

(1966) *Modern Economic Growth: Rate, Structure, and Spread*, New Haven; London: Yale University Press.

(1971) *Economic Growth of Nations: Total Output and Production Structure*, Cambridge, Mass.: Harvard University Press.

(1973) *Population, Capital and Growth*, New York: Norton.

Landes, D. S. (1969) *The Unbound Prometheus: Technical Change and Industrial Development in Western Europe from 1750 to the Present*, Cambridge: Cambridge University Press.

Landesmann, M.A. (1990) 'Specification of Structure and Economic Dynamics', in M. Baranzini and R. Scazzieri (eds.) *The Economic Theory of Structure and Change*, Cambridge: Cambridge University Press, pp. 95–121.

Landesmann, M.A. and Scazzieri, R. (1993) 'Commodity Flows and Productive Subsystems: An Essay in the Analysis of Structural Change', in M. Baranzini and R. Scazzieri (eds.) *The Dynamics of the Wealth of Nations. Growth, Distribution and Structural Change*, Houndmills and London: Macmillan; New York: St. Martin's Press, pp. 209–45.

(eds.) (1996a, 2009) *Production and Economic Dynamics*, Cambridge: Cambridge University Press.

(1996b) 'Introduction' in M. A. Landesmann and R. Scazzieri (eds.) *Production and Economic Dynamics*, Cambridge: Cambridge University Press, pp. 1–30.

(1996c) 'Coordination of Production Processes, Subsystem Dynamics and Structural Change', in M. A. Landesmann and R. Scazzieri (eds.) *Production and Economic Dynamics*, Cambridge: Cambridge University Press, pp. 304–43.

Leon, P. (1967) *Structural Change and Growth in Capitalism*, Baltimore: Johns Hopkins University Press.

Leontief, W. W. (1941) *The Structure of the American Economy, 1919–1929*, Cambridge, Mass.: Harvard University Press.

(1947) 'Introduction to a Theory of the Internal Structure of Functional Relationships', *Econometrica*, 15 (October), pp. 361–73.

(1953) 'Domestic Production and Foreign Trade. The American Capital Position Re-examined', *Proceedings of the American Philosophical Society*, 97, pp. 332–9. Reprinted in Leontief (1986) *Input-Output Economics*, 2nd edn, Oxford: Oxford University Press, pp. 65–93.

(1966) *Essays in Economics. Theories and Theorizing*, New York: Oxford University Press.

(ed.) (1977) *Structure, System and Economic Policy*, Proceedings of Section F of the British Association for the Advancement of Science held at the University of Lancaster 1–8 September 1976, Cambridge: Cambridge University Press.

Leontief, W. W. ([1928] 1991) 'The Economy as a Circular Flow', *Structural Change and Economics Dynamics*, 2.1, 1991, pp. 181–212. (English translation of the 1928 German original 'Die Wirtschaft als Kreislauf'.)

Leontief, W. W., Carter, A. P., and Petri, P. A. (1977) *The Future of the World Economy. A United Nations Study*, New York: Oxford University Press.

Leontief, W. W., Chenery, H. B. *et al..* (1953) *Studies in the Structure of the American Economy: Theoretical and Empirical Explorations in Input-Output Analysis*, White Plains, NY: International Arts and Sciences Press.

Leontief, W. W., and Duchin, F. (1986) *The Future Impact of Automation on Workers*, New York and Oxford: Oxford University Press.

Lima, G. T. (2003) 'Whose Saving Behaviour Really Matters in the Long Run? The Pasinetti (Irrelevance) Theorem Revisited', *Nova Economia*, 13.2, pp. 11–35.

Lombardini, S. (1993) 'Rationality and Economic Behaviour', in M. Baranzini and G. C. Harcourt (eds.) *The Dynamics of the Wealth of Nations: Growth, Distribution and Structural Change: Essays in Honour of Luigi Pasinetti*, Basingstoke: Macmillan; New York: St. Martin's Press, pp. 384–402.

(1996) 'Joan Robinson's Contribution to Economic Development', in M. C. Marcuzzo, L. L. Pasinetti and A. Roncaglia (eds.) *The Economics of Joan Robinson, op. cit.*, pp. 135–47.

Lombardini, S., and Quadrio Curzio, A. (eds.) (1972) *La distribuzione del reddito nella teoria economica*, Milan: Franco Angeli.

Lopez, R. A. (2008) *Progress in Sustainable Development Research*, New York: Nova Publisher.

Lowe, A. (1954) 'The Classical Theory of Economic Growth', *Social Research*, 21.2, pp. 127–58.

(1965) *On Economic Knowledge. Toward a Science of Political Economics*, New York/Evanston: Harper and Row.

(1969) 'Toward a Science of Political Economics', in R. L. Heilbroner (ed.) *Economic Means and Social Ends. Essays in Political Economics*, Englewood Cliffs, NJ: Prentice-Hall, pp. 1–36.

(1976) *The Path of Economic Growth*, Cambridge: Cambridge University Press.

Lydall, H. (1979) *A Theory of Income Distribution*, Oxford: Clarendon Press.

Malthus, T. R. (1815a) *The Grounds of an Opinion on the Policy of Restricting the Importation of Foreign Corn*, London: John Murray.

(1815b) *An Inquiry into the Nature and Progress of Rent and the Principles by Which it is Regulated*, London: John Murray.

([1798] 1993) *An Essay on the Principle of Population*, edited with an introduction by G. Gilbert, Oxford: Oxford University Press.

Maneschi, A. (1974) 'The Existence of a Two-Class Economy in the Kaldor and Pasinetti Models of Growth and Distribution', *Review of Economic Studies*, 41.1, pp. 149–50.

(1993) 'Ricardian Comparative Advantage and the Perils of the Stationary State', in M. Baranzini and G. C. Harcourt (eds.) *The Dynamics of the Wealth of Nations: Growth, Distribution and Structural Change: Essays in Honour of Luigi Pasinetti*, Basingstoke: Macmillan; New York: St. Martin's Press, pp. 124–46.

Mangoldt, H. von (1863) *Grundriss der Volkswirthschaftslehre*, Stuttgart: Engelhorn.

Marcuzzo, M. C., Pasinetti, L. L., and Roncaglia, A. (eds.) (1996) *The Economics of Joan Robinson*, London and New York: Routledge.

Marengo, L., and Scazzieri, R. (2014) 'Embedding Production: Structural Dynamics and Organizational Change', *Structural Change and Economic Dynamics*, 29.1, pp. 1–4.

Marglin, S. A. (1984) *Growth, Distribution and Prices*, Cambridge, Mass.: Harvard University Press.

Mari, C. (2010) *Kaldor, Cambridge and the Keynesian Theory of Income Distribution*, PhD thesis, Lugano, Switzerland: USI.

Marrelli, M., and Salvadori, N. (1979) 'The Rate of Profit in an Expanding Economy: Some Existence, Uniqueness and Stability Conditions', *Australian Economic Papers*, 18.33, pp. 283–92.

Marshall, A. (1961 [1890]) *Principles of Economics*, 9th (variorum) edn with annotations by C. W. Guillebaud, London: Macmillan for the Royal Economic Society.

Martin, J. M. (1990) 'Energy and Technological Change. Lessons from the Last Fifteen Years', *Science, Technology and Industry Review*, July, Paris: OECD.

Matuszewski, T. I. (1965) *Un système rectangulaire d'échanges inter-industries à rendements non proportionnels*, paper presented at the 1st World Congress of the Econometric Society, Rome.

Mazzanti, M., and Zoboli, R. (2005) 'Delinking and Environmental Kuznets Curves for Waste Indicators in Europe', *Environmental Sciences*, 2.4, pp. 409–25.

Meade, J. E. (1963) 'The Rate of Profits in a Growing Economy', *Economic Journal*, 73.292, pp. 665–74.

(1966a) 'The Outcome of the Pasinetti Process: A Note', *Economic Journal*, 76.301 pp. 161–5.

(1966b) 'Life-Cycle Savings, Inheritance and Economic Growth', *Review of Economic Studies*, 33.1, pp. 61–78.

(1968) *The Growing Economy*, London: Allen & Unwin.

(1973) 'The Inheritance of Inequalities: Some Biological, Demographic, Social and Economic Factors', *The Proceedings of the British Academy*, 59, pp. 355–81.

Meade, J. E. and Hahn, F. H. (1965) 'The Rate of Profit in a Growing Economy', *Economic Journal*, 75.298, pp. 445–8.

Meadows, D.H. *et al.* (1972) *The Limits to Growth. The First Report to the Club of Rome*, New York: Universe Book.

Mill, J. S. ([1848] 1965) *Principles of Political Economy with Some of Their Applications to Social Philosophy*, ed. by J. M. Robson, with an Introduction by V. W. Braden, Toronto: University of Toronto Press; London: Routledge and Kegan Paul.

Modigliani, F. (1986) 'Life Cycle, Individual Thrift, and the Wealth of Nations', *American Economic Review*, 76.3, pp. 297–313.

(1988) 'Measuring the Contribution of Intergenerational Transfers to Total Wealth: Conceptual Issues and Empirical Findings', in D. Kessler and A. Masson (eds.) *Modelling the Accumulation and Distribution of Wealth*, Oxford: Oxford University Press, pp. 21–52.

Modigliani, F., and Brumberg, R. (1954) 'Utility Analysis and the Consumption Function: An Interpretation of Cross-Section Data', in K. K. Kurihara (ed.) *Post-Keynesian Economics*, New Brunswick, NJ: Rutgers University Press, pp. 388–436.

Mokyr, J. (1995) 'Environmental Crises and Technological Change', in A. Quadrio Curzio and R. Zoboli (eds.) *Science, Economics and Technology for the Environment*, Milan: Cariplo Foundation for Scientific Research, pp. 223–43.

(2002) *The Gifts of Athena. Historical Origins of the Knowledge Economy*, Princeton: Princeton University Press.

Mongiovi, G. (2001) 'The Cambridge Tradition in Economics: An Interview With G. C. Harcourt', *Review of Political Economy*, 13.4, pp. 503–21.

Mongiovi, G., and Petri, F. (eds.) (1999) *Value, Distribution and Capital: Essays in Honour of P. Garegnani*, London and New York: Routledge.

Muldrew, C. (2011) *Food, Energy and the Creation of Industriousness. Work and Material Culture in Agrarian England, 1550–1780*, Cambridge: Cambridge University Press.

Myrdal, G. (1953) *The Political Element in the Development of Economic Theory*, London: Routledge and Kegan Paul (1st edn 1930).

Nazzani, E. (1872) *Sulla rendita fondiaria*, Forlì: Tipografia Sociale Democratica.

Nell, E. J. (1998) *The General Theory of Transformational Growth*, Cambridge: Cambridge University Press.

Neumann, J. von (1937) 'Über ein ökonomisches Gleichungssystem und eine Verallgemeinerung des Brouwerschen Fixpunktsatzes', in *Ergebnisse eines Mathematischen Kolloquiums*, vol. VIII, Vienna, pp. 73–83. (English translation as 'A Model of General Economic Equilibrium', *Review of Economic Studies*, 1945/6, 13.1, pp. 1–9.)

Nicola, P. C. (2012) *Efficiency and Equity in Welfare Economics*, Berlin: Springer.

Nicola, P. C., Quadrio Curzio, A., and Rotondi, C. (2010) 'Distribution and Growth, Technology and Development. Reflections on Nino Andreatta's Theoretical Analysis', *Rivista Internazionale di Scienze sociali*, 118.2, pp. 155–97.

Nurkse, R. (1953) *Problems of Capital Formation in Underdeveloped Countries*, Oxford: B. Blackwell.

OECD (2002) *Indicators to Measure Decoupling of Environmental Pressure from Economic Growth*, Paris: OECD.

Oppenheimer, P. M. (1982) 'Possible and Desirable Roles for Gold in the International Monetary System: Reconsideration and Proposals', in A. Quadrio Curzio (ed.) *The Gold Problem. Economic Perspectives*, Oxford: Oxford University Press, pp. 187–203.

Panico, C. (1985) 'Market Forces and the Relationship between the Rate of Interest and the Rate of Profits', *Contributions to Political Economy*, 4.1, pp. 37–60.

Panico, C., and Salvadori, N. (eds.) (1993) *Post Keynesian Theory of Growth and Distribution*, Aldershot: E. Elgar.

Parisi, D., and Rotondi, C. (1999) 'Keynesian Elements in a Long-Term Analysis: Two Views of Two Influencial Pre- and Postwar Italian Economists', in L. L. Pasinetti and B. Schefold (eds.) *The Impact of Keynes on Economics in the 20th Century*, Cheltenham, UK and Northampton, Mass.: E. Elgar, pp. 153–9.

Park, M. S. (1994) 'Long Period', in P. Arestis and M. Sawyer (eds.) *The Elgar Companion to Radical Political Economy*, Aldershot and Hants: E. Elgar, pp. 249–55.

    (1997) 'Accumulation, Capacity Utilisation and Distribution', *Contributions to Political Economy*, 16.1, pp. 87–101.

Pasinetti, L. L. (1959) 'On Concepts and Measures of Changes in Productivity', *The Review of Economics and Statistics*, 41.3, pp. 270–82.

    (1960) 'A Mathematical Formulation of the Ricardian System', *Review of Economic Studies*, 27.2, pp. 78–98.

    (1962a) 'Rate of Profit and Income Distribution in Relation to the Rate of Economic Growth', *Review of Economic Studies*, 29.4, pp. 267–79.

    (1962b) 'A Multi-Sector Model of Economic Growth', a PhD dissertation submitted to the Faculty of Economics and Politics of the University of Cambridge, September.

    (1964/5) 'Causalità e interdipendenza nell'analisi econometrica e nella teoria economica', in *Annali dell'Università Cattolica del Sacro Cuore 1964–65*, Milan: Vita e Pensiero, pp. 231–50.

    (1965) *A New Theoretical Approach to the Problems of Economic Growth*, Vatican City: Pontificiae Academiae Scientiarum Scripta Varia.

    (1966a) 'The Rate of Profit in a Growing Economy: A Reply', *Economic Journal*, 76.301, pp. 158–60.

    (1966b) 'New Results in an Old Framework: Comment on Samuelson and Modigliani', *Review of Economic Studies*, 33.4, pp. 303–6.

    (1973) 'The Notion of Vertical Integration in Economic Analysis', *Metroeconomica*, pp. 1–29. Reprinted in L. L. Pasinetti (ed.) (1980) *Essays on the Theory of Joint Production*, London: Macmillan, pp. 16–43.

    (1974a) *Growth and Income Distribution. Essays in Economic Theory*, Cambridge: Cambridge University Press.

    (1974b) 'The Rate of Profit in an Expanding Economy', in L. L. Pasinetti, *Growth and Income Distribution. Essays in Economic Theory, op. cit.*, pp. 121–46.

    (1977a) *Lectures on the Theory of Production*, London: Macmillan; New York: Columbia University Press.

    (1977b) 'Reply to Professor Stiglitz', in M. Morishima, 'Pasinetti's Growth and Distribution Revisited', *Journal of Economic Literature*, 15.1, pp. 57–8.

    (ed.) (1980) *Essays on the Theory of Joint Production*, London: Macmillan.

(1981) *Structural Change and Economic Growth: A Theoretical Essay on the Dynamics of the Wealth of Nations*, Cambridge: Cambridge University Press.

(1983) 'The Accumulation of Capital', *Cambridge Journal of Economics*, 7.3–4, pp. 405–11.

(1986a) 'Theory of Value – A Source of Alternative Paradigms in Economic Analysis', in M. Baranzini and R. Scazzieri (eds.), *Foundations of Economics, Structures of Inquiry and Economic Theory*, Oxford and New York: B. Blackwell, pp. 409–31.

(1986b) 'Sraffa's Circular Process and the Concept of Vertical Integration', *Political Economy: Studies in the Surplus Approach*, 2, pp. 3–16.

(1988) 'Growing Sub-Systems, Vertically Hyper-Integrated Sectors and the Labour Theory of Value', *Cambridge Journal of Economics*, 12, pp. 125–34.

(1993) *Structural Economic Dynamics. A Theory of the Economic Consequences of Human Learning*, Cambridge: Cambridge University Press.

(1999) 'Economic Theory and Technical Progress', *Economic Issues*, 4.2, pp. 1–18.

(2007) *Keynes and the Cambridge Keynesians. A 'Revolution in Economics' to be Accomplished*, Cambridge: Cambridge University Press.

(2011a) 'La "rivoluzione in economia" di Keynes e i post-Keynesiani', in *Gli economisti postkeynesiani di Cambridge e l'Italia*, Rome: Accademia Nazionale dei Lincei, Atti dei Convegni Lincei, no. 261, pp. 13–29.

(2011b) 'Considerazioni conclusive con alcune ipotesi contro-fattuali sulla presente crisi', in *Gli economisti postkeynesiani di Cambridge e l'Italia*, Rome: Accademia Nazionale dei Lincei, Atti dei Convegni Lincei, no. 261, pp. 433–57.

(2012a) 'Growth and Structural Change: Perspectives for the Future', in R. Arena and P. L. Porta (eds.) *Structural Dynamics and Economic Growth*, Cambridge: Cambridge University Press, pp. 276–82.

(2012b) 'Second Afterword: the Significance of Structural Economic Dynamics', in R. Arena and P. L. Porta (eds.) *Structural Dynamics and Economic Growth*, Cambridge: Cambridge University Press, pp. 283–7.

Pasinetti, L. L., and Scazzieri, R. (1987) 'Structural Economic Dynamics', in J. Eatwell, M. Milgate and P. Newman (eds.) *The New Palgrave: A Dictionary of Economics*, London: Macmillan, vol. IV, pp. 525–8.

Pasinetti, L. L., and Solow, R. M. (eds.) (1994) *Economic Growth and the Structure of Long Term Development*, London: Macmillan.

Pellizzari, F. (1985) *La teoria economica delle risorse naturali*, Milan: Angeli.

Perrings, C. (1987) *Economy and Environment: A Theoretical Essay on the Interdependence of Economic and Environmental Systems*, Cambridge: Cambridge University Press.

Perroux, F. (1939) *Cours d'économie politique*, 2nd edn, Paris: Domat Montchrétien.

Poni, C., and Scazzieri, R. (2007) 'Environmental Crisis and Property Rights: Historical Contexts and Theoretical Frameworks', in A. Prinz, A. E. Steenge and J. Schmidt (eds.) *The Rules of the Game: Institutions, Law and Economics*, Berlin: LINT Verlag, pp. 81–101.

Popp, D. (2002) 'Induced Innovation and Energy Prices', *American Economic Review*, 92.1, pp. 160–80.

(2004), *R&D Subsidies and Climate Policy: is There a "Free Lunch"?*, National Bureau of Economic Research, Working Paper 10880.

Prebisch, R. (1971) *Change and Development – Latin America's Great Task; Report Submitted to the Inter-American Development Bank*, New York: Praeger.

Prodi, R., and Quadrio Curzio, A. (2012) 'Gold in the Past and EuroUnionBond for the Future', *Economia Politica. Journal of Analytical and Institutional Economics*, 29.3, pp. 295–303.

Quadrio Curzio, A. (1965) 'Reddito e saggio di interesse nelle decisioni di consumo e risparmio nell'ipotesi di comportamento razionale', in F. Forte and S. Lombardini (eds.) *Saggi di economia*, Milan: Giuffrè, pp. 3–52.

(1967) *Rendita e distribuzione in un modello economico plurisettoriale* [Rent and Distribution in a Multi-sectoral Economic Model], Milan: Giuffrè.

(1972) 'La distribuzione del reddito nella teoria economica: un commento', in S. Lombardini and A. Quadrio Curzio (eds.) *La distribuzione del reddito nella teoria economica*, Milan: Franco Angeli, pp. 13–49.

(1975) *Accumulazione del capitale e rendita* [Accumulation of Capital and Rent], Bologna: Il Mulino.

(1977) 'Rendita, distribuzione del reddito, ordine di efficienza e di redditività', in L. L. Pasinetti (ed.) *Contributi alla teoria della produzione congiunta*, Bologna: Il Mulino, pp. 301–27.

(1980) 'Rent, Income Distribution and Orders of Efficiency and Rentability', in L. L. Pasinetti (ed.) *Essays on the Theory of Joint Production*, London: Macmillan, pp. 219–40. Reprinted in H. D. Kurz and N. Salvadori (eds.) (2003) *The Legacy of Piero Sraffa*, Cheltenham: E. Elgar, vol. II, pp. 311–41.

(1981) 'Un diagramma dell'oro tra demonetizzazione e rimonetizzazione', *Rivista internazionale di scienze economiche e commerciali*, 10–11, pp. 915–40.

(1982a) 'Materie prime: identità di un problema e finalità di un rapporto', *Materie Prime*, 1, pp. 9–12.

(1982b) *The Gold Problem. Economic Perspectives*, Oxford: Oxford University Press.

(1983) 'Primary Commodity Prices, Exhaustible Resources and International Monetary Relations: Alternative Explanations', in J. A. Kregel (ed.) *Distribution, Effective Demand and International Economic Relations, op. cit.*, London: Macmillan, pp. 142–52.

(1985) 'Dal rifiuto del numerario aureo ai prezzi quasi ufficiali dell'oro', *Rivista internazionale di scienze economiche e commerciali*, October–November, pp. 965–87.

(1986) 'Technological Scarcity: An Essay on Production and Structural Change', in M. Baranzini and R. Scazzieri (eds.) *Foundations of Economics. Structures of Inquiry and Economic Theory*, Oxford and New York: B. Blackwell, pp. 311–38.

(1987a) 'Produzione ed efficienza con tecnologie globali. Parte I', *Economia Politica*, 4 (1), pp. 11–32.

(1987b) 'Land Rent', in J. Eatwell, M. Milgate and P. Newman (eds.) *The New Palgrave: A Dictionary of Economics*, London: Macmillan, vol. III, pp. 118–21.

(1988) 'Le «scarsità relative» nella storia della teoria economica e rilevanza attuale', in C.M. Guerci and G. Zanetti (a cura di), *Sviluppo economico e vincolo energetico*, Bologna: Il Mulino, pp. 39–53.

(1990) 'Rent, Distribution and Economic Structure: a Collection of Essays', *Quaderni IDSE*, 1, Milan: Consiglio Nazionale delle Ricerche-CNR (this volume includes Quadrio Curzio 1980, 1986, 1987a, 1987b).

(1991) 'Technology and Natural Resources in the Growth of Economies', *Innovazione e Materie Prime*, special issue, pp. 1–16.

(1993a) 'On Economic Science, Its Tools and Economic Reality', in M. Baranzini and G. C. Harcourt (eds.) *The Dynamics of the Wealth of Nations: Growth, Distribution and Structural Change: Essays in Honour of Luigi Pasinetti, op. cit.*, pp. 246–71.

(1993b) 'Distribuzione della ricchezza e del reddito', *Enciclopedia delle Scienze Sociali*, Rome: Istituto della Enciclopedia italiana Treccani, pp. 194–207.

(1993c) 'Innovation, Primary Commodities and the World Economy: A Survey on Twelve Years of Contributions through Two Journals', *Innovazione e Materie Prime*, II, 2–3, pp. 5–20.

(1996) 'Production and Efficiency with Global Technologies', in M. A. Landesmann and R. Scazzieri (eds.) *Production and Economic Dynamics*, Cambridge: Cambridge University Press, pp. 105–26.

(1997) 'Rendita', in *Enciclopedia delle scienze sociali*, Istituto della Enciclopedia italiana, Treccani, vol. VII, Rome: Istituto dell'Enciclopedia Italiana, pp. 395–407.

(1998) 'Rent', in H. Kurz and N. Salvadori (eds.) *The Elgar Companion to Classical Economics*, vol. L-Z, Cheltenham, UK and Northampton, Mass.: E. Elgar, pp. 289–93.

(1999a) 'Historical and Theoretical Introduction to Rent, Resources, and Technologies' in A. Quadrio Curzio and F. Pellizzari (eds.) *Rent, Resources, Technologies*, Berlin: Springer, pp. 1–35.

(1999b) 'Conclusions and Further Lines of Research', in A. Quadrio Curzio and F. Pellizzari (eds.) *Rent, Resources, Technologies*, Berlin: Springer, pp. 233–43.

(2005) 'Risorse scarse e tecnologia', in *Pragmatica*, special issue, August, pp. i–viii.

(2007) *Economisti ed economia. Per un'Italia europea: paradigmi tra il XVIII e il XX secolo*, Bologna: Il Mulino.

(2011a) 'Risorse e dinamica economica, tecnologia e rendite', in *Gli economisti postkeynesiani di Cambridge e l'Italia*, Rome: Accademia Nazionale dei Lincei, Atti dei Convegni Lincei, no. 261, pp. 409–32.

(2011b) 'Resources and Economic Dynamics, Technology and Rents', *Quaderni Cranec*, Milan: Vita e Pensiero.

Quadrio Curzio, A., and Antonelli, G. (eds.) (1988) *The Agro-Technological System Towards 2000*, Amsterdam: Elsevier.

Quadrio-Curzio, A., and Fortis, M. (1996) 'Growth and Productive Structure: A Medium-Term Perspective', in B. Colombo, P. Demeny and M. F. Perutz (eds.), *Resources and Population: Natural, Institutional and Demographic Dimensions of Development*, Oxford: Clarendon Press-Pontificia Academia Scientiarum, pp. 137–56.

(eds.) (2002) *Complexity and Industrial Clusters. Dynamics and Models in Theory and Pratice*, Heidelberg: Physica-Verlag.

(2005a) 'Introduction – Research, Technology, Innovation: Analysis and Cases' in A. Quadrio Curzio and M. Fortis (eds.) *Research and Technological Innovation: The Challenge for a New Europe*, Heidelberg: Physica-Verlag, pp. 1–13.

(2005b) *Research and Technological Innovation: the Challenge for a New Europe*, Heidelberg: Physica-Verlag.

Quadrio Curzio, A., Fortis, M., and Zoboli, R. (1994) 'Innovation, Resources and Economic Growth. Changing Interactions in the World Economy', in A. Quadrio Curzio, M. Fortis and R. Zoboli (eds.) *Innovation, Resources and Economic Growth*, Berlin-Heidelberg, Springer Verlag.

Quadrio Curzio, A., and Pellizzari F. (1981) 'La teoria economica delle risorse naturali', *Energia*, 2, pp. 14–29.

(1991) 'Structural Rigidities and Dynamic Choice of Technologies', *Rivista internazionale di scienze economiche e commerciali*, 38.6–7, pp. 481–517.

(1996a) *Risorse, tecnologie, rendita*, Bologna: Il Mulino.

(1996b) 'Distribuzione dinamica del reddito e risorse scarse', in T. Cozzi, A. Quadrio Curzio, P. C. Nicola and L. L. Pasinetti (eds.) *Benessere, equilibrio e sviluppo. Studi in onore di Siro Lombardini*, vol. III, Milan: Vita e Pensiero, pp. 203–54.

(1998) 'Extensive and Intensive Rent', in H. D. Kurz and N. Salvadori (eds.) *The Elgar Companion to Classical Economics (ECCE)*, Cheltenham: E. Elgar, pp. 279–83.

(1999) *Rent, Resources, Technologies*, Berlin: Springer.

(2004) 'Rent, Technology, and the Environment', in R. Arena and N. Salvadori (eds.) *Money, Credit and the Role of the State. Essays in Honour of Augusto Graziani*, Burlington: Ashgate, pp. 335–48.

Quadrio Curzio, A., Pellizzari, F., and Zoboli, R. (2008) 'Technological Innovation, Relative Scarcity, Investments', *Encyclopaedia of Hydrocarbons*, Rome: ENI and Istituto per l'Enciclopedia Italiana Treccani, IV, pp. 11–22.

(2011) *Natural Resources and Technologies*, Cranec Working Paper, Milan: Vita e Pensiero.

Quadrio Curzio A., Prosperetti, L., and Zoboli R. (eds.) (1994) *The Management of Municipal Solid Waste in Europe: Economic, Technological and Environmental Perspectives*, Amsterdam: Elsevier.

Quadrio Curzio, A., and Rotondi, C. (eds.) (2013) *Un economista eclettico. Distribuzione, tecnologie e sviluppo nel pensiero di Nino Andreatta*, Bologna: Il Mulino.

(2015) 'Ricardo on Gold', in Kurz, H. D. and Salvadori, N. (eds.) *The Elgar Companion to David Ricardo*, Cheltenham, UK and Northampton, Mass.USA: E. Elgar, forthcoming.

Quadrio Curzio, A., and Scazzieri, R. (eds.) (1977–1982) *Protagonisti del pensiero economico*, 4 vols., Bologna: Il Mulino.

(1983) *Sui momenti costitutivi dell'economia politica*, vol. II of *Protagonisti del pensiero economico*, Bologna: Il Mulino.

(1986) 'The Exchange-Production Duality and the Dynamics of Economic Knowledge', in M. Baranzini and R. Scazzieri (eds.) *Foundations of Economics. Structures of Inquiry and Economiuc Theory*, Oxford and New York: B. Blackwell, pp. 377–407.

(1990) 'Profili di dinamica economica strutturale: introduzione', in A. Quadrio Curzio and R. Scazzieri (eds.) *Dinamica economica strutturale*, Bologna: Il Mulino, pp. 11–51.

(2008) 'Historical Stylizations and Monetary Theory', in R. Scazzieri, A. Sen and S. Zamagni (eds.), *Markets, Money and Capital: Hicksian Economics for the Twenty-First Century, op. cit.*, pp. 185–203.

Quadrio Curzio, A., and Zoboli, R. (eds.) (1995a) *Ambiente e dinamica globale. Scienza, tecnologia ed economia a confronto*, Il Mulino: Bologna.

(1995b) *Science, Economics and Technology for the Environment*, Milan: Fondazione Cariplo per la Ricerca Scientifica.

(1998) 'The Costs of Sustainability', in M. Giampietro *et al.* (eds.) *Il contributo italiano alla realizzazione della "Carta della terra" nel cinquantesino anniversario delle Nazioni Unite*, Proceedings of the International Conference, Rome: Accademia Nazionale delle Scienze detta dei XL, pp. 97–110.

Quesnay, F. ([1758] 1958) 'Maximes générales de gouvernement economique d'un royaume agricole', in *François Quesnay et la Physiocratie*, Paris: Institut National d'Études Démographiques, pp. 949–76.

([1759] 1972) *Quesnay's Tableau Economique*, edited with new material, translations and notes by M. Kuczynski and R. L. Meek, London: Macmillan; New York: A. M. Kelley, for the *Royal Economic Society* and the *American Economic Association*.

Rae, D.W. and Taylor, M. (1970) *The Analysis of Political Cleavages*, New Haven: Yale University Press.

Ricardo, D. (1815) *An Essay on Profits*, London: John Murray.

(1951) *On the Principles of Political Economy and Taxation,* vol. I of *The Works and Correspondence of David Ricardo*, P. Sraffa ed. with the collaboration of M. H. Dobb, Cambridge: Cambridge University Press (1st edn 1817; 2nd edn 1819, 3rd edn 1821).

(1951–73) *The Works and Correspondence of David Ricardo*, 11 vols., P. Sraffa ed. with the collaboration of M. H. Dobb, Cambridge: Cambridge University Press.

Robbins, L. (1932) *An Essay on the Nature and Significance of Economic Science*, London: Macmillan.

Robinson, J. V. (1956) *The Accumulation of Capital*, London: Macmillan.

(1962) *Essays in the Theory of Economic Growth*, London: Macmillan.

Rogowski, R. (1987) 'Political Cleavages and Changing Exposure to Trade', *The American Political Science Review*, 81.4, pp. 1121–37.

Roncaglia, A. (1977) 'The Sraffian Revolution', in S. Weintraub (ed.) *Modern Economic Thought*, Oxford: B. Blackwell, pp. 163–77.

(1978) *Sraffa and the Theory of Prices*, New York: John Wiley and Sons.

(2005) *The Wealth of Ideas: A History of Economic Thought*, Cambridge and New York: Cambridge University Press.

Rosenberg, N. (1969) 'The Direction of Technological Change: Inducement Mechanisms and Focusing Devices', *Economic Development and Cultural Change*, 18.1, pp. 1–24.

(1994) 'Energy Efficient Technologies, Past and Future Perspectives', in A. Quadrio Curzio, M. Fortis and M. Zoboli (eds.) *Innovation, Resources and Economic Growth*, Berlin-Heidelberg: Springer, pp. 63–82.

(1996) 'The Impact of Technological Change on Resources for Growing Population', in B. Colombo *et al.* (eds.) *Resources and Population*, Oxford: Clarendon Press, pp. 113–25.

Ruttan, V. W. (2002), 'Sources of Technical Change: Induced Innovation, Evolutionary Theory and Path Dependence', in A. Gruebler *et al.* (eds.) *Technological Change and the Environment*, Washington, DC: Resources for the Future, pp. 9–39.

Salvadori, N. (1996) '"Productivity Curves" in the Accumulation of Capital', in M. C. Marcuzzo, L. L. Pasinetti and A. Roncaglia (eds.) *The Economics of Joan Robinson*, London and New York: Routledge, pp. 232–48.

Samuelson, P. A., and Modigliani, F. (1966a) 'The Pasinetti Paradox in Neoclassical and More General Models', *Review of Economic Studies*, 33.4, pp. 269–301.

(1966b) 'Reply to Pasinetti and Robinson', *Review of Economic Studies*, 33.4, pp. 321–30.

Sardoni, C., and Kriesler, P. (eds.) (1999) *Keynes, Post-Keynesianism and Political Economy: Essays in Honour of Geoff Harcourt*, London: Routledge.

Scazzieri, R. (1981) *Efficienza produttiva e livelli di attivita'*, Bologna: Il Mulino.

(1982) 'Scale and Efficiency in Models of Production', in M. Baranzini (ed.) *Advances in Economic Theory*, Oxford: B. Blackwell, pp.19–42.

(1983) 'Economic Dynamics and Structural Change: A Comment on Pasinetti', *Rivista Internazionale di Scienze Economiche e Commerciali*, 30.1, pp. 73–90.

(1990) 'Vertical Integration in Economic Theory', *Journal of Post-Keynesian Economics*, 13.1, pp. 20–46.

(1993a) *A Theory of Production: Tasks, Processes and Technical Practices*, Oxford: Clarendon Press.

(1993b) 'Action, Processes and Economic Theory', in A. Heertje (ed.) *The Makers of Modern Economics*, vol. I, Aldershot, UK and Brookfield, Vt.: E. Elgar, pp. 84–114.

(1994) 'Models of Long-Term Development: Comment', in L. L. Pasinetti and R. M. Solow (eds.) *Economic Growth and the Structure of Long Term Development*, London: Macmillan, pp. 171–5.

(1996a) 'Introduction to Pasinetti's Structural Economic Dynamics: A Symposium', *Structural Change and Economic Dynamics*, 7.2, pp. 123–5.

(1996b) 'The Accumulation of Capital and Structural Economic Dynamics', in M. C. Marcuzzo, L. L. Pasinetti and A. Roncaglia (eds.) *The Economics of Joan Robinson, op. cit.*, pp. 174–87.

(1998) 'Hierarchy of Production Activities and Decomposition of Structural Change: An Essay in the Theory of Economic History', in H. Hagemann and H. D. Kurz (eds.) *Political Economics in Retrospect. Essays in Memory of Adolph Lowe*, Cheltenham, UK and Northampton, Mass.: E. Elgar, pp. 195–207.

(1999) 'A Theory of Resilient Flow–Fund Linkages', in K. Mayumi and J. Gowdy (eds.) *Bioeconomics and Sustainability*, Cheltenham, UK and Northampton, Mass.: E. Elgar, pp. 229–56.

(2007) 'Paolo Sylos Labini: A Memoir', *Structural Change and Economic Dynamics*, 18.2, pp. 279–81.

(2009) 'Traverse Analysis and Methods of Economic Dynamics', in H. Hagemann and R. Scazzieri (eds.) *Capital, Time and Transitional Dynamics*, Abingdon, UK and New York: Routledge, pp. 96–132.

(2010) 'Douglass C. North's Understanding the Process of Economic Change: Analytical Principles and Historical Narratives', *Structural Change and Economic Dynamics*, 21.2, pp. 135–8.

(2011) 'Structural Economic Dynamics: Looking Back and Forging Ahead', in *Gli economisti postkeynesiani di Cambridge e l'Italia*, Rome: Accademia Nazionale dei Lincei, Atti dei Convegni Lincei, no. 261, pp. 205–33.

(2012a) 'The Concept of "Natural Economic System": A Tool for Structural Analysis and an Instrument for Policy Design', in R. Arena and P. L. Porta (eds.) *Structural Dynamics and Economic Growth, op. cit.*, pp. 218–40.

(2012b) 'Structural Economic Dynamics: Methods, Theories and Decisions', in H. M. Krämer, H. Kurz and H.-M. Trautwein (eds.) *Macroeconomics and the History of Economic Thought: Essays in Honour of Harald Hagemann*, Abingdon, UK and New York: Routledge, pp. 314–28.

(2014) 'A Structural Theory of Increasing Returns', *Structural Change and Economic Dynamics*, 29.2, pp. 75–88.

Scazzieri, R., Sen, A., and Zamagni, S. (eds.) (2008) *Markets, Money and Capital: Hicksian Economics for the Twenty-First Century*, Cambridge: Cambridge University Press.

Scazzieri, R., and Zamagni, S. (2008) 'Between Theory and History: on the Identity of Hicks's Economics', in R. Scazzieri, A. Sen and S. Zamagni (eds.), *Markets, Money and Capital. Hicksian Economics for the Twenty-First Century, op. cit.*, pp. 1–37.

Schumpeter J.A. (1949) *The Theory of Economic Development*, Cambridge, Mass.: Harvard University Press.

Simon, H. A. (1962) 'The Architecture of Complexity', *Proceedings of the American Philosophical Society* 106.6, pp. 467–82. doi:10.2307/985254.

Simon, H.A., and Ando, A. (1961) 'Aggregation of Variables in Dynamic Systems', *Econometrica*, 29.2, pp. 111–38.

Skott, P. (1989) *Conflict and Effective Demand in Economic Growth*, Cambridge: Cambridge University Press.

(1995) 'Cumulative Causation and the "New" Theories of Economic Growth', *Journal of Post Keynesian Economics*, 17.3, pp. 381–402.

Silva, E. G., and Teixeira, A. A. C., (2008) 'Surveying Structural Change: Seminal Contributions and a Bibliometric Account', *Structural Change and Economic Dynamics*, 19.4, pp. 273–300.

Smith, A. ([1776] 1976) *An Inquiry into the Nature and Causes of the Wealth of Nations*, General Editors R. H. Campbell and A. S. Skinner, Textual Editor W. B. Todd, Oxford: Clarendon Press.

Solow, R. M. (1956) 'A Contribution to the Theory of Economic Growth', *Quarterly Journal of Economics*, 70.1, pp. 65–94.

(1974a) 'Laws of Production and Laws of Algebra: the Humbug Production Function: A Comment', *Review of Economics and Statistics*, 56, p. 121.

(1974b) 'Intergenerational Equity and Exhaustible Resources', *Review of Economic Studies*, 41.1, pp. 29–45.

Sraffa, P. (1926) 'The Laws of Returns under Competitive Conditions', *Economic Journal*, 36.144, pp. 535–50.

(1951) 'Introduction' to *The Works and Correspondence of David Ricardo*, ed. P. Sraffa with the collaboration of M. H. Dobb, Cambridge: Cambridge University Press, vol. I, pp. xiii–lxii.

(1960) *Production of Commodities by Means of Commodities: Prelude to a Critique of Economic Theory*, Cambridge: Cambridge University Press.

([1925] 1998) 'On the Relations between Cost and Quantity Produced', in L.L. Pasinetti (ed.) *Italian Economic Papers*, Bologna: Il Mulino; Oxford: Oxford University Press, pp. 323–63.

Steenge, A. E., and van Den Berg, R. (2007) 'Transcribing the *Tableau Économique*: Input-Output Analysis *à la* Quesnay, *Journal of the History of Economic Thought*, 29.3, pp. 331–58.

Stigler, G. J. (1941) *Production and Distribution Theories*, New York: Macmillan.

Stiglitz, J. E. (1974) 'Growth with Exhaustible Natural Resources: Efficient and Optimal Growth Paths', *Review of Economic Studies*, 41, pp. 123–37.

Sylos Labini, P. (1979) 'Prices and Income Distribution in Manufacturing Industry', *Journal of Post Keynesian Economics*, 2.1, pp. 3–25.

    (1982) 'On the Instability of Raw Materials Prices and the Problem of Gold', in A. Quadrio Curzio (ed.) *The Gold Problem. Economic Perspectives*, Oxford: Oxford University Press, pp.163–70.

    (1984) *The Forces of Economic Growth and Decline*, Cambridge, Mass: MIT Press.

    (1993) 'Long-Run Changes in the Wage and Price Mechanisms of the Processes of Growth', in M. Baranzini and G. C. Harcourt (eds.), *The Dynamics of the Wealth of Nations: Growth, Distribution and Structural Change: Essays in Honour of Luigi Pasinetti, op. cit.*, pp. 311–47.

    (1994) 'Wages, Profits and Theories of Growth: Comment', in L. L. Pasinetti and R. M. Solow (eds.) *Economic Growth and the Structure of Long Term Development, op. cit.*, pp. 112–15.

Syrquin, M. (1988) 'Patterns of Structural Change', in H. Chenery and T. N. Srinivasan (eds.) *Handbook of Development Economics*, Amsterdam: Elsevier, vol. 1, pp. 203–73.

Syrquin, M., and Chenery, H. B. (1989a) *Patterns of Development, 1950 to 1983*, Washington, DC: The World Bank.

    (1989b) 'Three Decades of Industrialization', *The World Bank Economic Review*, 3, pp. 145–81.

Targetti, F., and Thirlwall, A. P. (eds.) (1983) *Further Essays on Economic Theory and Policy*, London: Duckworth.

Teixeira, J. R. (1996) 'Structural Economic Dynamics: Review Article', *Revue Tiers-Monde*, 36, pp. 461–2.

Teixeira, J. R., and Sarquis, S. (1996) 'Evaluating Gains from International Relations According to Structural Dynamics – A Pasinettian Approach', *Texte de recherche*, 32, IEDES, Panthéon-Sorbonne, Paris.

    (1998) 'On Micro-Foundations for the Kaldor-Pasinetti Growth Model with Taxation and Bequest', *Anais do XXVI Encontro Nacional de Economia*, 1, pp. 505–18. Reprinted (2002) in the *Brazilian Journal of Business Economics*, 2.1, pp. 9–23.

Tobin, J. (1960) 'Towards a *General* Kaldorian Theory of Distribution', *Review of Economic Studies*, 27.2, pp. 119–20.

Tugan Baranovsky, M. I. ([1894, 1900] 1913) *Les crises industrielles en Angleterre*, translated from the second Russian edition by J. Schapiro, Paris: Giard et Brière.

Turgot, A. R. J. ([1768] 1808) 'Observations sur le mémoire de M. de Saint-Péravy en faveur de l'impôt indirect', in *Oeuvres de Turgot*, Paris: Imprimerie De Delance, IV, pp. 312–43.

Walsh, V., and Gram, H. (1980) *Classical and Neoclassical Theories of General Equilibrium*, New York: Oxford University Press.

West, E. (1815) *Essay on the Application of Capital to Land*, London: T. Underwood.

Wicksell, K. (1893) *Über Wert, Kapital und Rente nach den neueren nationalökonomischen Theorien*, Jena: Fischer. (English translation as *Value, Capital and Rent*, London: Allen & Unwin, 1954.)

Wicksteed, P. H. (1894) *An Essay on the Coordination of the Laws of Distribution*, London: Macmillan. Reprinted 1932, London: The London School of Economics.

(1933) *The Common Sense of Political Economy*, London: G. Routledge & Sons (1st edn 1910).

Williamson, O. (1985) *The Economic Institutions of Capitalism: Firms, Markets, Relational Contracting*, New York: Free Press.

Wood, A. (1975) *A Theory of Profits*, Cambridge: Cambridge University Press.

(1978) *A Theory of Pay*, Cambridge: Cambridge University Press.

Woodfield, A., and McDonald, J. (1979) 'On Relative Income Shares in the Pasinetti and Samuelson-Modigliani Systems', *Economic Journal*, 89.354, pp. 329–35.

Wrigley, E. A. (1962) 'The Supply of Raw Materials in the Industrial Revolution'. *Economic History Review*, 15.1, pp. 1–16.

(1987) 'The Classical Economists and the Industrial Revolution', in E.A. Wrigley, *People, Cities and Wealth: the Transformation of Traditional Society*, Oxford: Basil Blackwell, pp. 21–45.

(1988) *Continuity, Chance and Change: the Character of the Industrial Revolution in England*, Cambridge: Cambridge University Press.

(1991) 'Energy Availability and Agricultural Productivity', in B. M. S. Campbell and M. Overeton (eds.) *Land, Labour and Lifestock: Historical Studies in European Agricultural Productivity*, Manchester: Manchester University Press, pp. 323–39.

(1994) 'The Classical Economists, the Stationary State, and the Industrial Revolution', in G.D. Snooks (ed.), *Was the Industrial Revolution Necessary?* , London: Routledge, pp. 27–42.

(2006) 'The Transition to an Advanced Organic Economy: Half a Millenium of English Agriculture', *Economic History Review*, 59, pp. 435–80.

(2010) *Energy and the English Industrial Revolution*, Cambridge: Cambridge University Press.

Zamagni, S. (1984) 'On Ricardo and Hayek Effects in a Fixwage Model of Traverse', *Oxford Economic Papers*, 36 (Supplement), pp. 135–51.

Zhang, Z. (2000) 'Decoupling China's Carbon Emissions Increase from Economic Growth: An Economic Analysis and Policy Implications', *World Development*, 28.4, pp. 739–52.

Zoboli, R. (1996) 'Technology and Changing Population Structure: Environmental Implications for the Advanced Countries', *Dynamis-Quaderni*, 6, Milan: IDSE-CNR.

Name Index

Subject Index

For EU product safety concerns, contact us at Calle de José Abascal, 56–1°,
28003 Madrid, Spain or eugpsr@cambridge.org.

www.ingramcontent.com/pod-product-compliance
Ingram Content Group UK Ltd.
Pitfield, Milton Keynes, MK11 3LW, UK
UKHW012155180425
457623UK00007B/48